HANDBOOK OF ORGANIZATIONAL COMMUNICATION

COMMUNICATION AND INFORMATION SCIENCE

Edited by
BRENDA DERVIN
The Ohio State University

Recent Titles:

HANDBOOK OF ORGANIZATIONAL COMMUNICATION

edited by

Gerald M. Goldhaber

George A. Barnett

Department of Communication
State University of New York at Buffalo
Buffalo, New York

ABLEX PUBLISHING CORPORATION
NORWOOD, NEW JERSEY

Printed in the United States of America

Library of Congress Cataloging-in-Publication Data

Handbook of organizational communication.

    (Communication and information science)
    Bibliography: p.
    Includes index.
    1. Communication in organizations.   I. Goldhaber,
Gerald M.   II. Barnett, George A.   III. Series.
HD30.3.H357   1988   658.4'5   87-19380
ISBN 0-89391-446-0

Ablex Publishing Corporation
355 Chestnut Street
Norwood, New Jersey 07648

TABLE OF CONTENTS

Chapter 1
Foreword

Gerald M. Goldhaber
and
George Barnett

Most recent published surveys have indicated that the field of organizational communication is one of the fastest growing fields within the communication discipline, if not within most academic disciplines. Certainly, if we use traditional academic metrics to measure growth — number of departments offering organizational communication as a major, number of organizational communication courses taught, number of students enrolled in these courses or programs, number of books, papers and monographs authored, etc. — we would confirm this conclusion. Further evidence of growth comes from professional surveys such as the recent International Association of Business Communicators' survey that documented an average budgetary increase of 50% in revenues spent by business communication executives as their own commitments to organizational communication expand.

But has the growth in academic and professional demand for the discipline been matched by intellectual growth and scholarly commitments? Over the past decade has new theoretical ground been broken to define our discipline? Have scholars in the field provided academic leadership that offers research directions and challenges to our colleagues? In 1972, W. Charles Redding of Purdue University, whom many have called the "father of organizational communication", labeled the state of scholarship in the field as reminiscent of a "toe-path", clearly referring to the many gaps in our knowledge. As we review the last 15 years, have we paved the road? If so, how many lanes does it have? Is it a super highway or a simple country road? Or, is it still filled with large and dangerous pot-holes waiting to be filled?

The main purpose of the *Handbook of Organizational Communication* is to provide some answers to the above questions. What is the current intellectual state of our discipline? How do we define the parameters of organizational communication? What paradigms and philosophical approaches define our field? What theoretical propositions have evolved from the past two decades of research in organizational communication? What research trends and themes have been supported and discounted? Where is the agreement among scholars and where is there differentiation among viewpoints? What direction is current and future research taking in the field of organizational communication? In short, what do we currently know and what don't we know about this discipline?

Were George and I to do this book either together or alone, we would probably have produced a "handbook" which reflected our common academic heritage grounded in our empirical logical positivist tradition. Our functionalist viewpoint, probably shared by most

1

traditional scholars of organizational communication, regards organizational life as mechanistic and uses systems theory to suggest that communication is the means by which organizations control and coordinate their human, capital and other resources. According to Putnam and Cheney (1983), this functionalist paradigm's assumptions include:

1. Work as purposeful-rational action dominates social existence.
2. Social reality is objective, materialistic, and subject to prediction and technical control.
3. The goals of research are understanding and prediction for the purpose of exerting technical control.

While the functionalist relies upon an empirical tradition and orientation, a perspective which relies more upon an anecdotalist's mode of thinking is growing in popularity among some organizational communication scholars and researchers. This paradigm, called "interpretive", presumes that social reality is intersubjectively created (Sotirin, 1984) and that organizing and communicating are interdependent processes of organizational life (Putnam, 1982). Further, if organizational life is identified as culture, then, according to Sotirin, organizing and communicating become the focal activities of organizational culture. In fact, Pacanowsky and O'Donnell-Trujillo (1982) have stated that organization culture is "not just another piece of the puzzle, it *is* the puzzle." Those who subscribe to the interpretive approach tend to conduct naturalistic research using participant-observation techniques to collect the "talking and writing", the primary data that reflects the social reality of the organization's participants (Hawes, 1976).

It should be apparent that approaches to and definitions and perceptions of organizational communication differ widely and, depending upon one's philosophical heritage and viewpoint, research questions asked and methodologies employed will also differ. As editors of the *Handbook of Organizational Communication,* it is not our role to pass judgement on the merits and limitations of each approach. It is our goal to present to the scholarly world a compilation of the writings and thinking of the leading scholars in organizational communication so that the reader can make his or her own judgements about where this field has been, where it is now and where it is likely to be in the coming decades.

We have assembled 32 authors who, we believe, reflect the best scholarship in our field today. We have organized the *Handbook* into three sections to present the theoretical and methodological directions of this field, along with some insights into the future growth in the information age of the new communication technologies and their effects on our public and private-sector organizations. As you read the chapters in the *Handbook*, we hope you will feel the excitement that we as editors felt as we realized the quality of the scholarship and the diversity of viewpoints we were confronting. Naturally, as editors, we assume complete responsibility for the content of the book and with gratitude offer thanks to the authors of the chapters for their significant contribution to both our *Handbook* and our discipline. Finally, we are indeed grateful to Patti Rackl for her able assistance in the preparation of the manuscript; to Mary Beth Eckert for her insightful comments as she helped us read the chapters; to our patient editors at Ablex as they awaited our logistical efforts in coordinating the work of 32 different authors separated by thousands of miles; and to our wives and families for their love and understanding throughout this very tedious, but ultimately rewarding process.

REFERENCES

Hawes, L. (1976). How writing is used in talk: a study of communicative logic-in use. *Quarterly Journal of Speech, 62,* 350–360.

Pacanowsky, M. & O'Donnell-Trujillo, N. (1983). Organizational communication as cultural performance. *Communication Monographs, 50,* 126–147.

Putnam, L. (1982). Paradigms for organizational communication research: an overview and synthesis. *Western Journal of Speech Communication, 46,* 192–206.

Putnam, L. & Cheney, G. (1983). A critical review of research traditions in organizational communication. Paper presented at a meeting of the International Communication Association, Dallas.

Redding, W. C. (1972). *Communication Within the Organization.* New York: Industrial Communication Council, and Lafayette, Ind.: Purdue Research Foundation.

Sotirin, P. (1984). Organizational culture – a focus on contemporary theory/research in organizational communication. Paper presented at a meeting of the Speech Communication Association, Chicago.

REFERENCES

...

Chapter 2

Organizational Communication – Past and Present Tenses

W. Charles Redding and Phillip K. Tompkins

ABSTRACT

This chapter presents a long-range perspective from which to view the historical evolution of the field. After recalling selected antecedents going back to antiquity, the chapter proposes two frames of reference: the first, applicable to the period 1900–1970; the second, 1970 to the present. Organizational communication concepts and proto-theories are shown to be derivatives of three primary sources: (a) traditional rhetorical doctrine, (b) the older version of "human relations" theory, and (c) various components of management-organization theory. Two themes are identified as broad categories of "conceptual foundations" up through the 1960s: the individual-behavioral, and the systemic-operational. These became translated, during the 1940s and 1950s, into three conceptual frames of reference (roughly parallel to three chronological phases): (a) the formulary-prescriptive, (b) the empirical-prescriptive, and (c) the applied-scientific.

For the more recent years (beginning around 1970), three other orientations—analogous to, but different from, the frames of reference for 1900–1970—are suggested as fruitful ways to understand modern theory and research in the field: (a) the "modernist," (b) the "naturalistic," and (c) the "critical." Each of these is explicated in terms of 11 dimensions, or "defining characteristics," differentiated across all three categories. The eleven dimensions are discussed under the following labels: (a) goals, (b) ontology, (c) epistemology, (d) form of knowledge claim, (e) perspective, (f) rationality, (g) causality, (h) levels/boundaries, (i) root metaphor, (j) organizations, and (k) communication. The chapter concludes with recommendations for researchers of the future.

As an academic field of study, organizational communication is obviously a relative newcomer upon the scene. Indeed, in the 1980s disputants are still wrestling with such fundamental questions as: (a) Can the field even be identified? and (b) Assuming that it can be identified, where does it belong? For example, should the study of organizational communication be assigned to departments of (a) speech communication? (b) communication(s)? (c) English? (d) business communication (in business schools)? (e) organizational behavior (also in business schools)? Leipzig and More (1982), for instance, attempt to delineate boundaries among organizational communication, organizational behavior, and business communication. They suggest that organizational communication deals primarily with "communication theory as applied to organizations" and only "secondarily (through Business and Professional Speaking) with the development of oral skills"; organizational behavior, with "the theoretical foundations of how individuals behave within and between organizations"; and business communication, with "the development of written skills for business" (p. 78).

Three writers have gone so far as to conclude that something called "managerial communication" is an "emerging" new discipline (Smeltzer, Glab, & Golen, 1983, p. 77). However, they find themselves unable to provide an answer to the question: "Should the course and faculty be housed in management, business communication, or the speech/communication department?" This is not surprising, since:

> Managerial Communication is a hybrid . . . Knowledge of rhetoric, linguistics, small-group dynamics, grammar, business administration, psychology, and sociology should hypothetically be required. . . . Few such faculty individuals exist. (Smeltzer et al., 1983, p. 76)

We can agree with Leipzig and More (1982) that, to date, "no systematic integration" of subject matter in our field has yet emerged:

> Consequently, while we have multiple bodies of knowledge about similar phenomena, the conceptual boundaries of organizational communication remain unresolved. (p. 78)

It should be remembered that the label "organizational communication" is itself of recent vintage, not having replaced "business and industrial communication" until the late 1960s or early 1970s (Redding, 1985) — although it had appeared sporadically in the 1950s (Bavelas & Barrett, 1951; Argyris, 1957; Zelko & O'Brien, 1957). In view of the eclectic and ill-defined character of the field — a situation existing as these words are being written — we find it virtually impossible to single out certain dates or events permitting us to declare, with an air of confident finality, "Here is where it all started." Indeed, in a disturbingly large number of instances, it has been difficult to decide whether or not a specifc publication "really belongs" to organizational communication. Despite these perplexities, we nevertheless have devised a Schema (see Exhibit 1) to identify what we perceive as the major themes characterizing the field — up to about 1970. For the years after 1970, we propose a different set of categories (see Exhibit 3).

We suggest that the modern study of organizational communication — although not under that label — dates from 1942, the year that Alexander R. Heron's book *Sharing Information With Employees* appeared. This is the first book-length publication addressed explicitly and exclusively to management–employee communication. However, beginning around 1900, writers and teachers had been dealing with "business English" and "business speech" instruction (the Era of Preparation). These pioneers were obviously focusing almost exclusively on narrow subdivisions of the field as we recognize it today. To be sure, there were those with a broader perspective, especially the ones who made major contributions in 1938 and 1939. We have in mind those few business managers and social scientists who perceived communication as a subsidiary — albeit important — topic within the fields of management theory, industrial sociology, or social psychology; for example, Barnard (1968), Lewin, Lippitt, and White (1939) and Roethlisberger & Dickson (1939).

In their perceptive, although brief, review of the literature in organizational communication, Sincoff, Pacilio, Blatt, Hunt, and Anton (1975) believed that they could discern three "eras": the Prescriptive, the Descriptive, and the Predictive. The basis of partition was apparently methodological, although the authors were rather vague on this point. Events, they said, could be "categorized both by their nature and the chronological sequence in which they occurred" (p. 4); but the word "nature" tells us little. Hay (1974), addressing himself to the history of organizational communication "through the 1940s," also used the term "era." He proposed just two: the Pre-Behavioral and the Human Relations (mentioning, in a footnote, that a third—"The Behavioral Science Era—would include that period of time from 1955 to the present" [p. 10]).

We view the evolution of the field, since the turn of the century, in terms of three major periods:

1. *The Era of Preparation: About 1900 to About 1940* (Transition Years: 1938–1942)
2. *The Era of Identification and Consolidation: About 1940 to About 1970* (Transition Years: 1967–1973)
3. *The Era of Maturity and Innovation: Since About 1970*

During the Era of Preparation the groundwork was laid, in both academe and the business world, for singling out communication processes and skills—especially skills—as organizational phenomena worthy of special study. During the Era of Identification and Consolidation, both practitioners and academics began to shape the contours of a new subject-matter area, generally called "business and industrial communication." During the Era of Maturity and Innovation, there has occurred a proliferation of empirical research, accompanied by innovative efforts to develop concepts, theoretical premises, and philosophical critiques.

Historical Perspective: The Illusion of Novelty

As the mathematician Kline (1980) has suggested, "The origins of any important idea can always be traced back decades and even hundreds of years" (p. 127). We know that organizations resembling modern bureaucracies flourished in ancient times, in such empires as the Egyptian, the Babylonian, the Persian, and the Roman (George, 1972, pp. 1–27). Without attempting the absurdity of recapitulating thousands of years of history, we can still profit from examining a few illustrations of historical continuity.

The illusion of novelty is a perceptual impairment associated with historical innocence. It can induce, for example, the supposition that the concepts studied by contemporary researchers—empathic listening, accuracy of serial transmission, superior-subordinate relations, and the like—are inventions of the twentieth century. It is chastening, therefore, to reflect upon such passages as those that follow. They are from a self-help manual addressed to a young man expecting to assume an official position in a governmental bureaucracy (many centuries before Christ):

> If thou art one to whom petition is made, be calm as thou listenest to what the petitioner has to say. Do not rebuff him before he has swept out his body or before he has said that for which he came. It is not [necessary] that everything about which he has petitioned should come to pass, [but] a good hearing is soothing to the heart. (George, 1972, p. 6)

> If you are the guest of a superior, speak only when he addresses you, for you do not know what will offend him.

> If you carry a message from one noble to another, be exact in the repetition.

> Avoid stirring up enmities by the perversion of truth; nor should you violate confi-
> dences — [something which] is abhorrent to the soul.

> If you speak in the presence of an expert, you may be deeply embarrassed. But if you
> know what you are talking about, speak with authority, and avoid false modesty.

> If you have done someone a favor, do not hasten to remind him of it the next time you
> meet him. (Gray, 1946, p. 452)

These are only a few of the recommendations to be found in what has been called "the oldest book in the world," the *Precepts* of Ptah-hotep, Vizier to one of the Egyptian Pharaohs of the Old Kingdom. The original manuscript — from which innumerable copies were produced over a span of centuries — may have been composed as early as 2700 or 2600 B.C. (Gray, 1946). It happens to be the earliest extant text in a long series of similar manuals, all of them intended for the guidance of aspiring bureaucrats (Gray, 1946; Garraty & Gay, 1972, pp. 77-78). A persuasive argument can be made that the world's first bureaucracies — staffed as they were by armies of scribes generating untold thousands of written records — were the administrative organizations established under the pharaohs of ancient Egypt (Gray, 1946; Garraty & Gay, 1972, pp. 77-78; George, 1972, pp. 4-9).

Especially noteworthy is the fact that the oldest surviving literary work should be a book on communication and human relations in the organizational context: the *Precepts* of Ptah-hotep. Indeed, we shall be so bold as to nominate Ptah-hotep as the "Dale Carnegie of ancient Egypt." After all, given (a) the antiquity of organizationial structures, and (b) the fact that, as Barfield (1977, p. 63) has remarked, "There is not much that is more important for human beings than their relations with each other," one should hardly be surprised to learn that writings on communication and human relations in the organization are almost as old as civilization itself.

The truth, notwithstanding illusions of novelty, is that a *very* large proportion of "modern" concepts and principles associated with organizational communication have long histories. Thayer was right when he observed, "The record of our understanding of the processes of communication has been one of constantly reinventing the wheel" (1968, p. 307). A worthy enterprise awaits the scholar who would document in explicit detail the historical sources of theoretical principles promulgated by twentieth-century researchers. For example, it was a social scientist, James G. March, who arrived at the conclusion that:

> In many respects, Dale Carnegie appears to have been rediscovering the truths of
> Machiavelli. And if one reads a treatise on management by a modern-day successful
> manager, one is frequently struck by the extent to which Aristotle probably said it better
> and apparently understood it more. (March, 1965, p. xiii)

No claim is being made, of course, that the early writings constitute neatly systematized sets of formally stated, experimentally validated propositions. With the outstanding exception of Aristotle's *Rhetoric* (fourth century B.C.), the literature relevant to our field, at least until the end of the nineteenth century, consisted primarily of rules-of-thumb, derived in turn from everyday experience and observation. And, as Kline reminds us, "labelling [a] rule of thumb a principle does not improve its logical structure" (1980, p. 160).

In the brief compass of the present chapter, it would be inappropriate to devote more space to writers of antiquity. We shall not, therefore, labor the profound influence of Aristotle's masterwork, the *Rhetoric*. We find social scientists of the 1980s declaring that "it seems fair to assert that much of the conceptual and substantive fabric for contemporary study of persuasion was woven by Aristotle" (Miller, Burgoon, & Burgoon, 1984, p. 401). Nor is it feasible to explore the insights of Machiavelli, who may, for example, have been the first to articulate advice on utilizing upward communication—see *The Prince,* Chapter XXIII. What Machiavelli produced, according to Kenneth Burke (1950, pp. 158–159), was an "administrative rhetoric." And, not too long ago, Antony Jay's *Management and Machiavelli* (1967) was a popular item on the reading lists of executive development programs.

Only historical innocence could induce one to suppose that more "sophisticated" or "scientific" methods of supervision are exclusively twentieth-century inventions. Such communication concepts, for example, as treating subordinates with "consideration" (see Fleishman, Harris, & Burtt, 1955) or providing them with "feedback" about their job performance (see Cusella, 1980) were parts of the managerial repertoire long before social scientists examined them in the years following World War II.

An early—albeit harsh—version of "Zero Defects" strategy is exemplified in the methods used to accomplish quality control in the famous "cloth factories" of seventeenth-century France. Jean Baptiste Colbert (1619–1693), the celebrated Controller General of Finance to Louis XIV, is regarded by some historians as the founder of "modern" bureaucratic methods. To assure excellence in the quality of cloth, Colbert created elaborate sets of rules and regulations, among which were the following:

> Each piece had to bear the name of the workman who made it; defective pieces were to be seized by government inspectors and exposed on a post with the name of the responsible workman in full view. In the case of a second offense, the careless workman was to be publicly censured by the members of his guild; for a third offense, he himself was to be tied to the post with a sample of his defective workmanship attached to his neck. (Garrett, 1940, p. 296)

A more humane application of the same techniques was instituted by the famous industrialist and social reformer Robert Owen (1771–1858), as early as the first decade of the nineteenth century. In his highly profitable factory at New Lanark, Scotland, the practice was that:

> a little cube of wood was hung over each employee, with a color painted on each side denoting, according to shade from light to dark, the different grades of deportment: white for excellent; yellow, good; blue, indifferent; black, bad. (George, 1972, p. 62)

Moreover, Owen adopted an "open door" policy, whereby "anyone could complain to him about any rule or regulation" and "could inspect the deportment book and . . . appeal if he felt he had been unjustly rated" (George, 1972, p. 62). Frequently called "the father of personnel management," Owen devoted many years to a vigorous advocacy of an employer-employee relationship that "reached the threshold of much modern thinking"—especially that of Elton Mayo more than a hundred years later (Merrill, 1970, p. 10). The remarkably profitable "success of his labor policies attracted wide attention," says Merrill, "but little imitation" (1970, p. 10).

In an essay written in 1813, Owen stressed two major themes: (a) that the entire workforce, combined with the physical plant and equipment, shold be regarded "as a system composed of many parts"; and (b) that it would be both morally right and financially advantageous if factory owners would pay as much careful attention to "the more delicate, complex living mechanism" as they customarily bestowed upon their "inanimate machines." A central premise was that workers should be treated "with kindness," and an important corollary, that employers could "prevent an accumulation of human misery, of which it is now difficult to form an adequate conception" (from "An Address to the Superintendents of Manufactories," excerpted in Merrill, 1970, pp. 11–13). Owen carried his crusades to the United States, where he became famous (or notorious) for attempting to establish a communal mode of living at New Harmony, Indiana (1824).

It is interesting to observe that the official statement of purpose, announced by the American Management Association (AMA) when it adopted that name in 1923, included the following passage:

> The day when American management can afford to treat the human factor as "taken for granted" has gone by and today emphasis must be laid on the human factor in commerce and industry and we must apply to it the same careful study that has been given during the last few decades to materials and machinery. (Quoted in Bendix, 1956, p. 288, Footnote 61)

Then, more than a quarter of a century later, came the manifesto *Human Relations in Modern Business,* issued in 1949 by a consortium of leaders in business, industry, religion, labor, and academe. (This document is sometimes called the Magna Carta of Human Relations.) Thus, echoes of Robert Owen's argument, first propounded in the early 1800s, kept reverberating in books, articles, and public lectures of the 1920s, 1930s, and 1940s.

Since, of course, most of the methods for supervising people and managing organizations have long ago been tried and — depending upon circumstances — found to be successful or unsuccessful, we should not be surprised to discover that the "human relations" component of modern organizational communication contains a large proportion of rule-of-thumb principles originating in past centuries. This fact holds whether we are referring to the academic versions of human relations — such as those identified with the Harvard Business School and the Institute for Social Research at Michigan — or to the popular expositions associated with such names as Dale Carnegie.

The conceptual linkages between traditional rhetorical theory and modern human relations doctrine are numerous and powerful. Admittedly, it is difficult to discern boundaries between these two intellectual domains. However, primarily since World War I, what are designated as Areas A and B in Exhibit 1 have developed identifiably separate literatures — even though the enormously influential popularizer Dale Carnegie (whose first important book came out in 1926, ten years before *How to Win Friends and Influence People*) exemplified an amorphous mixture of ideas from both rhetoric and human relations.

It seems safe to assert that the first "prototheory" to emerge as a systematic articulation of abstract principles was rhetoric. And, in fact, virtually all the textbooks in "business English," "business speaking," and "persuasion," published up through the 1930s, were watered-down derivatives of classical rhetoric. In the present context, "rhetoric" denotes the study of formal, structured public discourse — either written or oral — with special emphasis upon persuasion.

This is intentionally a narrower conception of rhetoric than such modern definitions as "the art of symbolic inducement" (Ehninger, 1972, p. 10), or "the rationale of informative and suasory discourse" (Bryant, 1953, p. 404). Not that we quarrel with the broader definitions; in fact, quite the contrary. We incline toward agreeing with Conrad's (1985) sweeping assertion that, "in essence, communication in organizations is rhetorical communication" (p. 172). However, viewed historically, the textbooks and treatises commonly labeled "rhetoric" — almost without exception those published before World War II — dealt with a narrower domain than "symbolic inducement" or even "informative and suasory discourse." They dealt, in fact, with the principles governing effective speeches and their written counterparts (the Aristotelian triad of forensic, deliberative, and epideictic, later supplemented by sermons). Hence, Area A in Exhibit 1 is designated: "Structured discourse (oral or written), emphasizing a speaker or writer addressing an audience." It is associated with "traditional rhetorical theory."

Area B in Exhibit 1 refers to "informal, interpersonal interaction, in dyads and small-group situations (primarily oral)," typically identified with "human relations." Naturally, these two areas overlap; and modern views of rhetorical theory would no doubt make the claim that all kinds of human symbolic interaction are rhetorical:

> Today . . . [the assumption is] that rhetoric not only is inherent in all human communication, but that it also informs and conditions every aspect of thought and behavior; that man is inevitably and inescapably a rhetorical animal. (Ehninger, 1972, p. 9)

Conrad, in his recent college-level textbook, exemplifies this position when he declares that organizational communication always has "an *instrumental* purpose" and that "it is *rhetorical communication* which allows organizations and their members to succeed and which helps them to fail"—hence, "Effective organizational communication depends on the rhetorical skills of employees" (1985, p. 172; emphasis in the original).

In our view, then, the academic field of organizational communication can trace most (but not all) of its conceptual roots to three sources: (a) *traditional rhetorical theory* (as modified and truncated in business writing and business speaking texts), (b) *human relations models* (actually, mini-theories and prototheories rather than full-blown theories), and (c) *early versions of management-organization theories* (again, prototheories would be a more accurate designation). What finally emerged in the 1940s and 1950s—typically under such labels as "business and industrial communication"—was a vaguely defined amalgam of subject matter drawn from these three bodies of knowledge. But all three had in common a firm allegiance to a pragmatic, utilitarian philosophy. More specifically, the overriding concern was with understanding the means whereby *effectiveness* (of the individual, of the organization) could be achieved. A frequently recurring synonym for "effectiveness" was "success"—there was even an inspirational, self-help magazine, published from 1897 to 1924, under the name *Success* (Huber, 1971).

Starting primarily in the late 1960s and early 1970s, when "organizational" was replacing "business and industrial" as the accepted modifier of "communication" (see Redding, 1985), specialists in the field made significant paradigm shifts, utilizing a much broader range of concepts drawn from contemporary rhetorical theory, the social sciences, and philosophy of science; hence, the Era of Maturity and Innovation. However, the bright glow of sophisticated research during the 1970s and 1980s should not blind us to this important fact: The dominant impulse behind the study of organizational communication has always been pragmatic—attempting to discover how individuals or organizations, or both, can be made to function more effectively. With some exceptions in recent years, this impulse has characterized our "scientific" research as well as the massive body of literature providing readers with prescriptions on how to get "results." One thinks, for example, of the "scientific" studies on "overcoming resistance to change" (Coch & French, 1948), on "measuring the effectiveness of industrial communications" (Funk & Becker, 1952), on "how to choose a leadership pattern" (Tannenbaum & Schmidt, 1958), on "quantifying the frame of reference in labor-management communication" (Weaver, 1958).

A PANORAMIC VIEW: CONCEPTUAL FOUNDATIONS (1900–1970)

The two main headings in Exhibit 1 represent themes postulated to underlie the main corpus of teaching and research in organizational communication through the late 1960s or early 1970s. (The year 1970 is, of course, no more than a convenient and arbitrary marker, actually symbolizing a span of several years, roughly 1967–1973.) Theme-I we have designated the "individual-behavioral"; Theme-II, the "systemic-operational." Brief definitions are provided in Exhibit 1.

The distinction between Themes I and II is an important one. Teaching and research carried out in the individual-behavioral spirit of Theme-I positions the individual as figure and the organization as ground. The systemic-operational approach of Theme-II reverses this, regarding the organization as figure and the individual member as ground.

Historically, publications (especially textbooks) governed by Theme-I thinking have sometimes gone so far as to ignore the organizational context altogether; at the same time, many titles associated with Theme-II thinking have treated the organization as an impersonal, disembodied entity, populated by faceless blobs. Admittedly, these are the extremes. But they exist. Examples of the first are to be found especially in those early "business and professional speaking" texts, where the only acknowledgment of an organization consisted of an uncritical acceptance of the overarching "business culture." Examples of the second type are to be found in some of the mathematically-based investigations of communication networks, whose "nodes" are mere points on a geometric plane.

More commonly, teaching and research dominated by Theme-I have been concerned with skills and attitudes believed to make the individual organizational member a more effective communicator on the job (especially when the communicator occupies a supervisory or managerial position). Thus, attention has been focused upon such topics as persuasion (in both speaking and writing); gaining credibility; participating in decision-making groups; giving orders or instructions; writing letters and reports; building "cooperation," "loyalty," and "teamwork" among subordinates; making sales presentations; conducting interviews; and, in general, creating "good human relations" in the work place. In contrast, teaching and research reflecting Theme-II thinking have been concerned with the organization qua organization (the term "organization" includes sub-organizational units such as departments and work groups). Hence, attention has been focused upon topics like these: reporting and feedback methods; communication aspects of reward systems; communication networks; readability of in-house publications; the differential uses and effects of upward-directed, downward-directed, and horizontal channels; the dimensions and effects of "communication climate," especially "managerial-communication climate"; relationships between information diffusion and employee morale; correlates of "communication satisfaction"; and the communication dimensions of various managerial "styles."

Obviously, any single publication may—and frequently does—include elements of both thematic orientations. However, regardless of overlaps and gray zones, concepts related to *Area A* (see Exhibit 1) have historically been derived from rhetorical theory; those related to *Area B,* from one or another version of human relations theory (itself an amalgam of clinical psychology, social psychology, sociology, antropology, etc.); and those related to *Area C,* from a mixed bag of management and organization theories. (We recognize the differences between theories of management and theories of organization. But the two share so many areas of communality—displayed, for example, in Barnard's classic *Functions of the Executive*—that we have chosen, for present purposes, to group them together.)

**Exhibit 1. Schema: Major Themes Underlying the Study of
Organizational Communication (With primary reference to the period 1900–1970)**

Over-all frame of reference for teaching, theory, and research:
Pragmatic and Utilitarian (Effectiveness)

THEME I — *The Individual-Behavioral:* Understanding the sources of effective communication performance on the part of individual organizational members—

All members in general, or (more often) managers in particular

With central concern for:

AREA A — Structured discourse (oral or written), emphasizing a speaker or writer addressing an audience (taken as a unitary group)

Salient body of knowledge providing concepts and principles: Traditional rhetorical theory

(Familiar derivatives: Business English, Business Speech, Business and Professional Speaking, Salesmanship, Persuasion)
[In part: Industrial Journalism[a]]

AREA B — Informal, interpersonal interaction, in dyads and small-group situations (primarily oral)

Salient body of knowledge providing concepts and principles: "Human relations"

1. Proto-human relations, antedating "scientific" research.
2. "Scientific" human relations: primarily associated with Harvard Business School (Mayo, Roethlisberger); and Institute for Social Research, University of Michigan (Likert)

(Familiar derivatives: Group Dynamics, Small-group Communication, Sensititivity Training, T-groups, Encounter, Interpersonal Communication, Interviewing, Superior–Subordinate Communication, Conference Leadership)

THEME II — *The Systemic-Operational:* Understanding the sources of over-all organizational effectiveness, without reference to individuals per se, as such effectiveness seems to be related to communication phenomena; hence, involves such topics as media, modalities, channels, networks, policies, corporate planning, etc.

With central concern for:

AREA C — Internal communication; i.e., those communication events and policies having to do with operations occurring inside the (arbitrarily defined) boundaries of the organization.

Salient body of knowledge providing concepts and principles: Management-Organization Theory
(supplemented by *Journalism,* both print and electronic)[a]

(Familiar derivatives: Administrative Communication, Corporate Communication, Communication Management, Managerial Communication, Industrial and Labor Relations, Employee Publications, Industrial Journalism.)

AREA D — External communication; i.e., those communication events and policies having to do with two-way interaction between the organization and its environment (especially, however, messages directed from the organization to "outsiders")[b]

Salient body of knowledge providing concepts and principles: Public Relations; Advertising[b]

(Familiar derivatives: Salesmanship, Employment Interviewing)

NOTES

[a] At the level of the individual reporter or editor, the principles of journalistic writing are essentially adaptations of rhetorical doctrine; but such matters as layout, headline writing, typography, etc., are specialized topics commonly taught in schools or departments of journalism.

[b] Until very recently — perhaps ten years ago — external communication received no more than cursory attention from specialists in organizational communication. Theoretically, external phenomena cannot be divorced from internal. Indeed, communication staff personnel (including industrial editors) are frequently housed in corporate departments of public relations. On the other hand, public relations and advertising are usually assigned to separate units. The fact remains that, before the early 1970s, Area D could not, realistically, be considered a significant subdivision of organizational communication. (However, courses in business English and business speech typically included exercises focused upon public relations situations.)

Area D—External Communication—requires special comment. As the broken line in Exhibit 1 is intended to suggest, topics relating to boundary-spanning communication— with two exceptions—have generally received little attention from specialists in organizational communication. The two exceptions are (a) salesmanship, and (b) employment interviewing. But even these topics, as everyone knows, have long been the object of study in fields other than communication (see, for example, Jablin & McComb, 1984, on research in employment interviewing). If we look at some of the earliest textbooks in business speech (Phillips, 1908; Hoffman, 1923; Sandford & Yeager, 1929), we find that sales presentations were among the most prominent topics. However, dating from the 1920s, industrial psychologists and other social scientists have produced a large body of empirical studies—as well as "practical" textbooks—dealing with both sales and interviewing techniques.

As the study of organizational communication became more "scientific" in the 1950s and 1960s, researchers became preoccupied with "internal" communication phenomena, relegating the study of "external" communication to the periphery of attention. Meanwhile, starting around the time of World War I, two new fields rapidly evolved into major specialties: public relations and advertising. These are the fields that have dealt explicitly with communication between organizations and their environments—that is, with external communication. Thus, specialsts trained in public relations or advertising almost never identified themselves with organizational communication. Over the years, administrative arrangements (and campus politics) have contributed to the separation of organizational communication from journalism, public relations, and advertising.

Especially after the close of World War II, organizational communication became progressively dichotomized along two dimensions: (a) the academic vs. the nonacademic, and (b) the internal vs. the external. Thus, relatively autonomous bodies of literature came into being, with an especially wide gulf separating the academic from the nonacademic. For instance, *Communication World* (published by the International Association of Business Communicators) and the *Public Relations Journal* (published by the Public Relations Society of America) have little in common with such academic journals as *Communication Monographs, Human Communication Research,* or *Administrative Science Quarterly.*

The Special Case of Journalism. From the 1920s to the 1970s, the overwhelming majority of practitioners in the field of organizational communication have been journalists. Two facts account for this. In the first place, journalists (understandably) are generally the ones hired to edit in-house publications ("house organs"). Until the widespread adoption of closed-channel television—a fairly recent development—virtually all formal, structured management–employee communication depended upon print media. As early as 1921, one survey reported a total of 334 employee magazines being published (National Industrial Conference Board, 1925, p. 3). In the second place, journalists also formed the backbone of the new profession called "public relations," which emerged primarily during the period 1915–1925. Thus, journalists became entrenched in work related to both internal and external communication. Moreover, with the rapid expansion of journalism schools and departments (the first professional school of journalism was established at the University of Missouri in 1908), journalism graduates have typically been products of a specialized education bearing little resemblance to course work in organizational communication. It is true, of course, that most of the basic principles of journalistic writing can be regarded as derivatives of traditional rhetorical doctrine. But, in all other respects, journalism education—until relatively recent times—represented no substantial overlap with curricula in other communication-related fields. It is also undeniable that, by its very nature, journalism has always encouraged a one-way, downward-oriented approach to corporate communication practicles; and this fact, we believe, has had a profound impact upon the way in which most managers view employee communication.

It is still true, in the late 1980s, that the most appropriate "entry jobs" for organizational communication graduates are likely to be in the area of employee publications, an area where journalists occupy a majority of the positions (according to annual surveys conducted by the International Association of Business Communicators). In the light of all these circumstances, one can readily understand some of the reasons why organizational communication has yet to solve its identity problem.

The Identity Problem: 1940s–1960s

From its beginnings, organizational communication has been an assemblage of data and concepts derived in large part (some critics would say entirely) from a variety of other academic fields. To be sure, the accidents and the politics of academic administration are partially responsible for this state of affairs. But more profound forces have been at work. The important point to be made here is that, until a recognizable cluster of concepts is identified — regardless of its location on an academic map — theoretical progress will be stunted.

Thus, it must never be forgotten that it was only as recently as the 1940s that "industrial" or "business" communication began to be seen as a potentially autonomous subject of inquiry, worthy of study in its own right. Even so, the area was viewed from a number of different perspectives, as investigators with different academic (and nonacademic) orientations carved up the subject matter in a variety of ways. In the 1940s, for example, industrial psychologists were evaluating the "readability" of corporate publications (Paterson & Jenkins, 1948; Colby & Tiffin, 1950); specialists in the Industrial Relations Section at Princeton were analyzing media and channels of information diffusion (Baker, Ballantine, & True, 1949); and corporate managers were conducting surveys to assess the effectiveness of a wide range of communication practices (Heron, 1942; Peters, 1949). Moreover, prior to the 1940s, as we have earlier noted, there were the crucial conceptual contributions of (a) the corporate executive, Chester Barnard (1938/1968); (b) the social psychologists working at Iowa with Kurt Lewin (Lewin et al., 1939); and (c) the human relations group at the Harvard Business School, assembled by Elton Mayo (Roethlisberger & Dickson, 1939).

Despite the recognition of industrial communication as a researchable entity, the overwhelming majority of investigators actually doing the empirical research typically treated communication either as a subtopic in an established discipline or as one variable — among many others — in a larger conceptual domain, such as social psychology, industrial psychology, business administration, or organization theory. Through a curious combination of circumstances, however, it was in departments of speech — rather than in any of the social sciences or in a business school — that *formally designated, sustained programs* of study were organized, at the Ph.D. level, dealing *explicitly* with "industrial communication." Reasons for this turn of events have been discussed in an earlier paper (Redding, 1985) and will not be recounted here.

It happens that the first Ph.D. dissertation specifically addressed to a topic in industrial communication was completed, in 1952, in personnel administration, a department of the business school at Ohio State University. The author was Keith Davis, and the title was "Channels of Personnel Communication Within the Management Setting." Davis became widely known for inventing (in his doctoral research) the "ECCO" technique for analyzing grapevine messages in an organization (see Davis, 1952, 1953). The Davis study remained a unique event. No sustained doctoral program in the business school materialized. However, in another department at Ohio State — the department of speech — a Ph.D. program in industrial communication, directed by Franklin H. Knower, was getting under way at about the same time that Davis was working on his research in the business school.

What happened is this: Shortly after World War II, on a handful of campuses, a few speech professors saw the possibility of undertaking doctoral-level research as an extension of undergraduate work in (a) "basic communication skills," a product of military and industrial training programs established during the war; and (b) "business speech." The result was the completion, in 1953 and 1954, of a small number of Ph.D. dissertations in "industrial communication" at four universities: Northwestern, Ohio State, Purdue, and Southern California. By the end of the fifties, a modest total of around 15 to 18 dissertations had been produced by speech departments. But it was not until after 1960 that any universities other than the original four began to account for significant additions to the list.

Meanwhile, from 1948 until the end of the 1950s, social scientists representing a variety of academic affiliations were publishing empirical studies dealing in one way or another with "industrial communication." Especially productive programs included those affiliated with the Harvard Business School, the Institute for Social Research (University of Michigan), the Industrial Relations Center at the University of Minnesota, and the Leadership Studies program at Ohio State. To the best of our knowledge, the sole example of a *formally organized* research entity *explicitly* designated as an "Industrial Communication Research Center" was the one established within the speech department at Purdue (in 1952) by Paul Emerson Lull. However, important annual conferences were sponsored by speech departments at Penn State (starting in 1950), Kent State (1952), and Ohio State (1952); the directors were, respectively, Harold P. Zelko, James N. Holm, and Franklin H. Knower.

Although not an annual event, the Centennial Conference on Communications at Northwestern, held in 1951, brought together Fritz Roethlisbergr of Harvard, the psychologist Carl R. Rogers, and Irving J. Lee (of the Northwestern School of Speech). This event made possible a significant linkage between two influential centers of theory and research in our field: one, under the direction of Lee, representing a speech/General Semantics orientation; the other, under the direction of Roethlisberger, a social science/human relations orientation. (For a more detailed account of the period discussed in this and the preceding paragraph, see Redding, 1985.)

It was probably not until 1958 or 1959 that the field — almost always referred to as "business" or "industrial" communication, it must be remembered — had crystallized to the point where at least those who were studying it could identify what they were studying. Redding (1985) has arbitrarily designated 1959 as the "Year of Crystallization." True, the Zelko and O'Brien text (mentioned earlier in the chapter) had appeared in 1957; but it was predominantly concerned with prescriptive advice for improving a manager's oral communication skills. In 1958 there appeared the revised edition of Redfield's *Communication in Management*. Although this book was also intended to help practicing managers meet their communication responsibilities, it contained many features of a comprehensive treatise, covering all aspects of the field as the field was then defined. And 1958 was also the year that saw the publication of the first anthology (albeit restricted in scope and tilted toward written communication skills), the *Business Communication Reader* (Janis, 1958).

Then, in 1959, two publications appeared upon the scene, symbolizing the fact that (at least in the eyes of a cadre of social scientists) industrial communication was finally being identifid as a recognizable entity: (a) a monograph published by the Foundation for Research on Human Behavior (loosely affiliated with the Institute for Social Research at the University of Michigan), *Communication in Organizations—Some New Research Findings;* and (b) the first literature review to appear in an academic journal, under the label "business communication" (Sexton & Staudt, 1959). A total of 178 entries appeared in the Sexton and Staudt review. Almost all of these—including the "scientific" studies—were utilitarian or prescriptive in basic orientation. By our estimate, no more than 60 (or about a third) of the 178 titles could have met accepted standards of scholarly work, whether conceptual/theoretical or empirical/scientific. The vast majority fell into the category of informal, anecdotal, or impressionistic essays, sometimes carrying such jazzy titles as "Management's Story—32 Million Times" or "Words Are Dynamite." We also estimate, however, that Sexton and Staudt omitted as many as 25 or 30 items that would easily have satisfied scholarly criteria; for example, studies authored by social scientists at such places as the Harvard Business School, Ohio State University, and the University of Michigan, in addition to a dozen or more doctoral dissertations completed in speech departments.

If "crystallization" had been achieved by 1959, general acceptance (in academe) of a field to be designated "organizational communication" did not arrive until at least 1967 or 1968. By 1965, Guetzkow had published his less-than-comprehensive, but perceptive, review of the theoretical and empirical literature, under the title "Communications in Organizations." Significantly, this appeared in the *Handbook of Organizations* (March, 1965), rather than in a volume devoted to communication. Guetzkow took occasion to deplore what he called the "dearth of studies about [communication in] organizations, either from the field or laboratory" (1965, p. 535). However, such an assertion can be challenged. In his bibliography of 134 items, Guetzkow included no mention whatever of studies associated with the Harvard human relations program, the Ohio State leadership group, the Industrial Relations section at Minnesota, or the dissertations completed in speech departments; and he cited only two or three publications from the Institute of Social Relations (Michigan). But there can be no quarrel with Guetzkow's hypothesis that communication research had "lagged behind studies concerning other features of organizational life, such as authority, division of work, and status" because of the "*contingent* nature of the findings" (1965, p. 569; emphasis added). He concluded his review by raising two provocative questions:

> Do we find in communications [*sic*] in organizations an area of study in which there is special richness in contingent, interactive effects? Or is it merely that a clarifying perspective . . . remains hidden? (1965, p. 569).

Although the field has yet to find—and probably never will find—a magic "clarifying perspective," the first book-length bibliography, published two years after Guetzkow's review had appeared, contained 315 entries—all categorized as "organizational communication" (Voos, 1967). Moreover, in 1967 the Marshall Space Flight Center (a branch of NASA) convened its "Conference on Organizational Communication" at Huntsville, Alabama (see Richetto, 1967). Featured at this meeting was a paper by Tompkins (1967) presenting the first "state-of-the-art" review of empirical research in the history of the field. The word "empirical" is important. The Tompkins paper was restricted to those studies that met two criteria: (a) they had to be "conducted in real-world [vs. laboratory] organizations," and (b) they had to utilize "controlled observation or quantification" in data collection. Despite these constraints, Tompkins was able to locate approximately 100 titles (Tompkins, 1967).

A quick review of the major headings under which Tompkins categorized the research literature will convey to modern readers a sense of what was meant by "organizational communication" in the late 1960s (see Tompkins, 1967, pp. 5–21):

Formal channels of communication
  Downward-directed communication (including hypothesized relationships between downward-directed communication and "morale")
  Relative effectiveness of different media
  Upward-directed communication (including feedback)
  Horizontal communication
Communication, supervision, and human relations (with an emphasis upon "interpersonal trust")
Measuring and data-gathering instruments
Informal channels of communication

Finally, there appeared in 1967 Lee Thayer's monograph, "Communication and Organization Theory," perhaps the first serious effort to formulate a theoretical frame of reference for the field (Thayer, 1967). The following year Thayer expanded his ideas into a book, *Communication and Communication Systems* (Thayer, 1968). (We also could mention, in passing, that in 1968 the Organizational Communication Division of the society now known as the International Communication Association was inaugurated.)

Considering all these events, we conclude that, by 1967 or 1968, "organizational communication" had finally achieved at least a moderate degree of success in two respects: (a) breaking out from its "business and industrial" shackles, and (b) gaining a reasonable measure of recognition as an entity worthy of serious academic study.

Development of Theory and Research, 1900–1970: Three Phases

Earlier in the chapter, we identified three "eras" to describe, in broad terms, the strictly chronological evolution of the academic field "organizational communication." To be placed alongside this triad of eras, we now offer another way of analyzing the evolution of our field. This time, the focus is more on the conceptual than on the chronological (although the latter does not disappear from view). Our concern is to characterize what we believe to be the dominant approaches—or orientations, if you will—that have governed the production of serious theory and research during the period roughly marked off by the years 1900 and 1970. Since these approaches seem to have appeared upon the scene in an identifiable chronological sequence, we have chosen the term *phase* as a label for each category.

The basis of partition is primarily methodological—but methodological taken in the broadest sense: *the means whereby evidentiary warrants are established* (or the bases upon which they are justified). By "evidentiary warrants," we refer to the kinds of data adduced, either explicitly or implicitly, to support findings, conclusions, principles, propositions, or recommendations. We emphasize that the term *phase* does not represent a rigid, time-bound compartment, with sharply defined beginning and ending. Although it is true that the three phases correspond to an approximate chronological ordering, more importantly they represent three frames of reference for doing scholarly work. Whatever chronological sequentiality can be attributed to our scheme applies only to the order in which each phase *got started*. None of the phases—including the first—has yet ended. Each, in varying degrees, is still with us in the 1980s. Exhibit 2 displays, in outline form, our view of these three phases.

Exhibit 2. The Three Phases of Organizational Communication: Approximately 1900–1970

Phase I. The Formulary-Prescriptive

Description: Predominant dependence upon "common sense" principles and/or traditional lore passed down through the years and incorporated in school rhetorics or their equivalents. The term "formulary" denotes a marked tendency to promulgate formulas—sets of rules; "how-to-do-it" recommendations, etc. The term "prescriptive" is probably self-explanatory, indicating that publications in this phase have as their central objective the giving of direct advice: Do this, don't do that, and you will be successful.

Approximate period of major influence: Turn of the century through the 1940s, but a continuing theme thereafter. ["the overwhelming bulk of activities in the field (even to date) are of the prescriptive variety . . ." Sincoff et al., 1975, p. 4.]

Examples of key ideas: The general ends of discourse—clearness, impressiveness, belief, action, entertainment (Phillips, 1908); the fundamental qualities of effective oral presentation—sense of communication, sincerity, animation, good health (Sandford & Yeager, 1929); formula for "winning people to your way of thinking"—"think always in terms of the other person's point of view" (Carnegie, 1936, pp. 162, 165); basic principles of good business writing—organized, simple, short, concrete, familiar, palatable (Zelko & O'Brien, 1957).

Representative contributors: Phillips (1908), Hotchkiss and Drew (1916), Saunders and Creek (1920). Sandford and Yeager (1929), Borden (1935), Monroe (1935), Carnegie (1936), Huston and Sandberg (1943), Whyte (1952), Zelko and O'Brien (1957).

Commentary: This first phase is most prominently represented in that massive body of literature designated as "self-help," more particularly under such labels as "business English," "business and professional speaking," "winning friends and influencing people," and the like. In a critical review, one of the authors several years ago identified the following major themes in the "business speech" textbooks of the period, roughly delineated by the decades of the 1920s, 1930s, 1940s, and 1950s (Redding, 1977):

- focus upon one-way communication and influence
- concern for message-sender's "success" (usually in the business sense)
- emphasis upon platform (public) speaking—but with increasing attention to dyads (especially interviewing) and small-group conferences
- application of traditional public speaking (rhetorical) doctrine to dyadic and small-group settings ("Whether the audience numbers two or two hundred, it's still public speaking . . ." [*Supervisional Training—Communications,* workshop syllabus, Goodyear Tire and Rubber Co., 1953])
- nearly complete omission of topics having to do with dissent, controversy, union activity or the like; stress on harmony, teamwork, cooperation
- assumption that managers—or those aspiring to become managers—rather than rank-and-file employees are the really important individuals
- virtually no recognition of such organizational realities as hierarchies of status and power, roles and role expectancies, functional division of labor, and the like; consequently (with a few exceptions), no recognition of concepts associated with General Systems thinking

Note: Business English. During the period roughly delineated by the years 1915–1935, the courses and textbooks in both "business speech" and "business writing" drew upon the same basic conceptual source: traditional rhetorical theory. Frequently, the course work in speaking and writing was taught by the same instructors, typically affiliated with departments of English or of business writing. Since the textbooks in business English, especially before World War II, were highly repetitious in thematic content, and since they remained almost exclusively prescriptive in their rationale, no attempt will be made here to include them among our documentary references—with the exception of the pioneering and highly influential books by Hotchkiss and Drew (1916) and Saunders and Creek (1920). For a concise account of the origins of curricula in business writing, see Weeks (1985).

Phase II. The Empirical-Prescriptive

Description: Predominant dependence upon anecdotal and case-study data, later supplemented by surveys (including polls and questionnaires); generally descriptive statistics, if any. Objectives remain primarily prescriptive, although a few rather neutral, descriptive studies crop up occasionally. (Readability studies occupy a kind of grey zone between Phases II and III, in that the data themselves are basically objective; however, the goals of the writers almost always are clearly prescriptive.)

Approximate period of major influence: Chiefly the decade of the 1950s, with a few studies having been completed in the late 1940s; a few more in the early 1960s; relatively infrequent today.

(Continued)

Exhibit 2 *(Continued)*

Examples of key ideas: Communication skills (speaking, listening, writing) important for supervisory or managerial effectiveness in "leading men"; concepts borrowed from General Semantics (and other versions of semantics), emphasizing barriers to "understanding," factors producing "distortion," etc.; "good" communication widely regarded as essential precondition for employee morale; early "network" concepts, based upon descriptive studies of relatively small populations in field settings (prescriptive component, although present, not greatly stressed), demonstrating that formal organization charts fall far short of depicting all the important communication channels and activities occurring in an organization.

Representative early contributors: Especially important here, Ph.D. dissertations, e.g.: Davis, 1952 (Ohio State); Angrist, 1953 (Ohio State); Nilsen, 1953 (Northwestern); Lewis, 1954 (Southern California); Ross, 1954 (Purdue); Freshley, 1955 (Ohio State); Piersol, 1955 (Purdue); Level, 1959 (Purdue); Sanborn, 1961 (Purdue). Also, the Harvard group of case studies, e.g.: Ronken and Lawrence, 1952; Lombard, 1955. Influential surveys, e.g.: Paterson and Jenkins (1948); Baker, Ballantine, and True (1949); Peters (1949); Jacobson and Seashore (1951).

Commentary: As the years went by, methodological sophistication increased. These studies provided, in most instances, unusually detailed "in-depth" information, much of which is still highly useful. A few even positioned the case study as a quasi-test of commonly accepted principles or hypotheses — especially those associated with the then popular "human relations" paradigm (derived especially from the Harvard-supervised studies in the Hawthorne plant of Western Electric). Although the emphasis in doctoral dissertations understandably downplayed prescriptive advice to practicing managers, there was always a strong current of prescription — at least in the conclusions. Two pioneer network studies, conducted in the field rather than in the laboratory, were those of Keith Davis (1952) — in which he developed the ECCO technique — and Jacobson and Seashore (1951). Although these were primarily descriptive, it is easy to detect evaluative and prescriptive implications in the published reports.

A considerable number of the studies classifiable under the next heading (Phase III, The Applied-Scientific), although featuring sophisticated experimental designs and statistical analyses, could also be listed here, since the prescriptive component was indisputable. As examples we may note some of the studies at Michigan supportive of Likert's "System 4" style of management: Morse and Reimer (1956); Indik, Georgopoulos, and Seashore (1961), and Bowers and Seashore (1966).

Phase III. The Applied-Scientific

Description: Predominant dependence upon "objective," "scientific" data, typically obtained in (a) experimental, or quasi-experimental, studies; (b) correlational and comparative-analytic studies; (c) psychometric, sociometric, and content-analytic studies (e.g., construction and validation of questionnaire instruments, network analyses using advanced mathematical methods, stylistic and readability analyses); and (d) "explanatory" (vs. descriptive) surveys.

Approximate period of major influence: Except for a few precursors in the 1930s (such as the famous Hawthorne studies), chiefly in the period 1948 through the early 1970s; still a dominant theme in the 1980s.

Representative—early, pioneering—studies: Lewin, Lippitt, and White (1939); Roethlisberger and Dickson (1939); Coch and French (1948); Katz, Maccoby, and Morse (1950); Katz, Maccoby, Gurin, and Floor (1951); Bavelas and Barrett (1951); Pelz (1952); Dahle (1954); Freshley (1955); Funk (1956); Morse and Reimer (1956); Lawrence (1958).

Commentary: This phase represents basically the widespread use of "traditional" scientific methods, those commonly associated with measurement theory, logical positivism, variable-analysis, and hypothetico-deductive designs. The Institute for Social Research at the University of Michigan, established in 1946 and directed for many years by Rensis Likert, was responsible for a preponderance of the pioneering work, especially during the period 1948–1956. In the early 1950s, speech (later Speech Communication) departments at Ohio State and Purdue began producing conventional-scientific investigations, almost always reported as Ph.D. dissertations. [*Note:* Likert (1955) has observed that the basic research design, utilized in many of the earlier studies of supervisory leadership and communication at Michigan, was simply "to measure and examine the kinds of leadership . . . being used by the best units in the organization in contrast to those being used by the poorest." This nonexperimental strategy was essentially the kind of communication research program proposed years before by the literary scholar I. A. Richards (1936, p. 3): we should be investigating, said he, "how much and in how many ways may good communication differ from bad?"]

Admittedly, the line between the "empirical-prescriptive" and the "applied-scientific" phases is a fuzzy one. Nevertheless, we believe that the difference is real and that it is crucial. In the former phase, investigators were

Exhibit 2 *(Continued)*

concerned primarily with solving organizational (especially managerial) problems, and with demonstrating that certain preferred solutions were supported by "scientific" findings. But in the third phase, although prescription was still a component of most of the research being done, the investigators clearly presented themselves (whether accurately or not) as neutral, "objective" scientists. The decade of the 1960s probably exemplifies the applied-scientific rationale in its heyday. Note, for instance, the numerous studies of superior–subordinate relations and "organizational-communication climates" (cast, to be sure, in an ideological frame of reference derived, in modified form, from earlier "human relations" doctrine): Indik, Georgopoulos, and Seashore (1961); Fleishman and Harris (1962); Read (1962); Tompkins (1962); Maier, Hoffman, and Read (1963); Pyron (1964); Bowers and Seashore (1966); Cook (1968); Lawler, Porter, and Tennenbaum (1968); Schwartz (1968); Sutton and Porter (1968); Allen and Cohen (1969); Minter (1969); Richetto (1969); Sincoff (1969).

We have identified, then, three phases in the evolution of the field—(a) the formulary-prescriptive; (b) the empirical-prescriptive; and (c) the applied-scienific—for the approximate period 1900–1970. We emphasize that the second and third phases never fully supplanted the first. Each phase is with us yet. We maintain our selection of 1970 as an arbitrary marker between the "older" and "newer" periods in the academic field of organizational communication. As will shortly become clear, however, the theory-and-research orientations of the 1970s and 1980s do not represent a complete break with the past.

ORIENTATIONS TO INQUIRY IN THE 1970s AND 1980s

Exhibit 3 is our attempt to display the important characteristics of three basic orientations to theory and research that became visible in the study of organizational communication during the 1970s and 80s. The three column headings—Modernist, Naturalistic, and Critical—were created in the interest of expanding somewhat Putnam's (1983) dichotomy of functionalist–interpretive approaches. Only in retrospect did we see the similarities between Habermas' (1971) three methods of inquiry—empirical-analytic, historical-hermeneutic, and critically-oriented—and Putnam and Cheney's (1983) use of Habermas' categories in a critical review of organizational communication. In defense of our categories, we believe they have the virtue (perhaps also the defect) of having emerged from *within* the study of organizational communication rather than from an externally-defined philosophical system. They should therefore be judged by how well they describe the former rather than the latter. The characteristics defined across the three approaches are of our own creation and are designed parsimoniously as a propaedeutic for enhancing critical reflection on theory and research.

The modernist or empirical orientation, as we have shown earlier in the chapter, is, of course, a very old one in organizational communication. We illustrate this tradition by subdividing it into several categories. One is the psychological, exemplified by the research on the superior–subordinate dyad summarized by Jablin (1979). Another is the sociological, exemplified by the network analytic research of Richards (e.g., 1985). Other examples, if not orientations, will be introduced below as we discuss the defining characteristics.

The naturalistic orientation has recently manifested itself in a "new" way by the cultural approach of Pacanowsky and O'Donnell-Trujillo (1982, 1983), although it is similar in some ways to the case studies directed at Purdue by Redding in the late 1950s and early 1960s. Tompkins' studies of NASA (1977, 1978) followed this case-study tradition (see also Yin, 1981), and can be fairly called theoretically-oriented naturalism. The "rhetorical" theories of organizational communication—Bormann (1983); Tompkins and Cheney (1985)—also belong in this category. We may note, in passing, that the earlier naturalistic case studies contained a strong prescriptive element, whereas the more recent ones make it a point to exclude any hint of evaluation.

As it is encountered in the work of Deetz and Kersten (1983) and Conrad and Ryan (1983), the critical orientation, like naturalism, appears to be a new development. But, again, one could establish a genealogy reaching back to Whyte's *Is Anybody Listening?* (1952). More recent exemplars are Scott and Hart's *Organizational America* (1979) and Redding's (1979) critique of ideological assumptions in communication research.

With this brief overview as a general introduction to the three orientations, we now propose (see Exhibit 3) the defining characteristics for each category.

1. The *goals* of the modernist empirical approach historically have been (and for some, still are) prediction and control. The linear model of inferential statistics is the traditional mode of prediction, if not control. The goal of control sounds a bit more ominous in 1985 than it did in the methods textbooks of the 1950s and 60s, perhaps in part because of intervening critiques of social scientific practice. In any case, the ambitious goal of prediction has not yet been achieved, and as time goes by it appears to be increasingly elusive. "Unexplained variance" has proved to be a stubborn foe. McCloskey (1985) has proposed what he calls the "Ten Commandments" of "modernism in economics and other sciences":

Exhibit 3. Three Orientations to Inquiry in Organizational Communication : 1970s and 1980s

	Modernist	Naturalistic	Critical
1. GOAL	Prediction and control	Understanding and anticipation	Consciousness-raising and emancipation
2. ONTOLOGY	Objective reality as given	Reality as socially constructed	Material interests as determinant
3. EPISTEMOLOGY	Logical positivism	Language and other forms of symbolic action	Dialectical Materialism
4. FORM OF KNOWLEDGE CLAIM	Nomothetic	Ideographic	Critique
5. PERSPECTIVE	Management	Pluralism	Workers
6. RATIONALITY	Privileged	Multiple	Dialectic of rationalities
7. CAUSALITY	Manipulative	Reciprocal	Coercive/Hegemonic
8. LEVELS/BOUNDARIES	Differentiated	Permeable	Dichotomous
9. ROOT METAPHOR	Machine	Organism	Conflict/struggle
10. ORGANIZATIONS	Purposive, goal-seeking	Cultures, language communities	Instruments of oppression
11. COMMUNICATION	Tool	Negotiated Order	Distortion

1. Prediction and control is the point of science.
2. Only the observable implications (or predictions) of a theory matter to its truth.
3. Observability entails objective, reproducible experiments; mere questionnaires interrogating human subjects are useless, because humans might lie.
4. If and only if an experimental implication of a theory proves false is the theory proved false.
5. Objectivity is to be treasured; subjective "observation" (introspection) is not scientific knowledge . . .
6. Kelvin's Dictum: "When you cannot express it in numbers, your knowledge is of a meager and unsatisfactory kind."
7. Introspection, metaphysical belief, aesthetics, and the like may well figure in the discovery of an hypothesis but cannot figure in its justification . . .
8. It is the business of methodology to demarcate scientific reasoning from nonscientific . . .
9. A scientific explanation of an event brings the event under a covering law.
10. Scientists . . . ought not to have anything to say as scientists about the oughts of value, whether of morality or art (McCloskey, 1985, pp. 7–8).

McCloskey, himself a distinguished econometrician, notes that the positivistic philosophy undergirding modernism has been abandoned by philosophers. He recommends Scott's (1967) rhetoric-as-epistemic as the postmodernist theory of knowledge for the field of economics.

The goals for the naturalistic tradition are a bit more modest: understanding and anticipation—or the *"anticipation* and *interpretation* of human communicative action" (Tompkins & Cheney, 1983, p. 142). These goals are closer to the aims of historical or anthropological inquiry than to those of quantitative empiricism. The much discussed "thick description" of Geertz's (1973) cultural approach is consistent with these goals.

The critical approach seeks a kind of consciousness-raising among, if not emancipation for, organizational members themselves. As with the empirical modernists, however, the critical theorists (and others of a similar stripe) still assume that there is a "truth" out there to be discovered. The critical theorists act as if their version of the truth will set workers free, while the positivists use another version of the truth to effect control. Both groups appear to be more interventionist in their objectives than do the naturalists.

2. *Ontologically,* the modernists tend to view the "substance" of organizations as objective reality, a reality that is given. Even when that reality is conceded to be subjective, it can be measured objectively by means of such psychometric techniques as questionnaires and rating scales. The naturalistic approach assumes that reality is largely a function of social construction, hence its emphasis on gaining an insider's subjective understanding (*Verstehen*) of the organization-as-lived-experience. The critical theorist would see organizational reality at least in part as the reflection of material interests and resources, the latter usually being distributed unequally among owners, managers, and workers.

3. The *epistemological* assumptions of the modernist approach have been more precisely and elaborately defined—in the rationale of logical positivism—than have those of the other positions, but the philosophical premises of positivism have also come under withering attack from all directions. After decades of unquestioned acceptance of positivism as *the* philosophy of science (social as well as physical), this may well be an overreaction. The naturalists would place language and other forms of symbolic action at their epis-

temological base, assuming that symbolism is more or less identical with "culture." Verbal reports, interviews, even "conversations" (see Kaufman, 1960) have been the essential research methods of naturalistic scholars, combined often with the researcher's role as participant-observer, a role that can only be played after one has acquired the "native" language of the organizational actors. The epistemological position of critical theorists is more difficult to label. Some scholars have been influenced by phenomenological thinking: an example is Weick's (1979) reliance on Schutz. Other scholars of this orientation follow some versions of Marxism (whether of the "early" or "late" Marx), sometimes indicated by the prefix *Neo-*.

A difficulty here is that Marx did not, either early or late, write a theory of knowledge or epistemology; at least, none is available to us. We can infer, however, that dialectical materialism does have profound epistemological implications. The material Marxist world, including organizations, is taken as *real,* without reservations. Dialectic adds to this the interconnectedness of things — often in the form of oppositions — which is not unlike some of the assumptions of "systems" theory. Dialectical materialism would also imply that organizations must be investigated historically, in order to understand (a) the current state of affairs and (b) the trends or directions of change produced by the inherent dialectics or contradictions within the current state of affairs. An exemplar is Edwards's *Contested Terrain: The Transformation of the Workplace in America* (1979). The title suggests historical changes in American organizations produced by the "contest" for control by the opposing forces of workers and owners (later joined by managers). As Tompkins and Cheney (1985) have pointed out, Edwards has couched his analysis of control in *essentially communicative terms.* To recapitulate, many critical theorists seem to operate (ironically) from a tacit epistemology of dialectical materialism which, aside from its emphasis on historical methods, is remarkably similar to the one espoused by positivists (in their insistence upon a "received" world).

4. The *forms of knowledge claims,* or research outcomes — admittdly clumsy phrases — attempt to describe the *idealized* types of knowledge claims each group of scholars aspires to produce. The modernists' aim is nomothetic or nomological, the production of law-like regularities. The goal of the naturalists appears to be ideographic, or Gestalt-like, knowledge of wholes, or a hermeneutic understanding of part-to-whole and vice versa. For example, the superior–subordinate research cited above sought to develop generalizations or laws concerning such dyadic interaction, while Kaufman's study (1960) — cited for its use of "conversation" as a research method — sought to describe the U.S. Forest Service as an entity, a system of communication (i.e., identification) responding to the centrifugal forces of fragmentation. A representative of the critical orientation would produce a research report or critique designed to convince its readers that either the basic theories (Zey-Farrell & Aiken, 1981) or the practices of organizations (Edwards, 1979) are oppressive; hence, people ought to be convinced of a need for change — or even for emancipation. We shall argue below that all three of these forms of knowledge claims, or research outcomes, are necessary to a mature social science of organizational communication.

5. In order to do organizational research, one must have a place to stand, a *perspective* from which to "see" organizational communication in action. The modernists have in general taken the managerial perspective, asking questions about communication "effectiveness" clearly derived from managerial concerns. Redding (1985) has shown how this biasing perspective has been present from the very beginning of the field of organizational communication. The naturalists have leaned toward a pluralistic perspective, wanting to hear from all organizational actors, regardless of hierarchical position. For example, in

their separate yet coordinated studies of NASA, Tompkins (1977, 1978) concentrated on top and middle management of the Marshall Space Flight Center, while Richetto (1969) studied the rest of the hierarchy reaching down to the level of laboratory workers. Critical theorists for the most part adopt the perspective of the worker. What is crucial here is not the taking of *a* perspective—intelligible research is impossible without one—but that perspectives (biases) *not be concealed*. In organizational communication, as with almost all social science, the modernism of the 1950s and '60s assumed that its perspective was neutral, objective—in short, scientific. But in fact its biases were obscured. Indeed, "consulting" with top managers about how to improve productivity among workers was probably seen by some as a logical extension of scientific inquiry.

6. Closely related to this hidden managerial bias are the assumptions of organizational *rationality*. To the extent that modernists have been in the grip of a managerial bias— and we believe this to have been widespread in the past and still prevalent today—they have tended to view organizations as purposive, goal-seeking—in short, rational—instruments. Managers, better than any other organizational actors, were assumed to possess this rationality just as naturally as they should possess the key to the executive washroom. Naturalists have been more willing to see rationality as a plural term. Managers, board members, clients, and even workers are seen as capable of rationality. These several rationalities are regarded as equally valid, differing only in regard to the premises undergirding the conclusions. The critical theorists, as might be expected, have tended to favor the workers' rationality, or in some cases they see history as a dialectic of opposing rationalities.

7. In considering the criterion of *causality,* we see some strong similarities between the polar positions in relation to the middle position. Modernists have assumed causality in the language of "dependent and independent variables" (despite the more reserved stance of technical terms like *correlation* and *function*), and much effort has been devoted to showing—unsuccessfully, alas—that high morale is correlated with (read: *causes*) high productivity. This determinism was perhaps an unavoidable assumption in the commitment to positivistic social science. The naturalists, on the other hand, tend to assume organizational actors to be capable of voluntarism, able to exercise the ancient concept of "free will" if you will, stressing human action (a result of choice or decision) over human motion (a result of causal forces or vectors). This is consistent with naturalism's closer proximity to the humanities and to the attendant assumptions about persons as human beings responsible for their choices by virtue of reason, bounded by emotion and values. This rationale can be illustrated by an entire issue of *Administrative Science Quarterly* (December, 1979) given over to qualitative research in organizations, including Manning's (1979) use of Kenneth Burke's "master tropes," a kit of humanistic tools, in his study of a police department. Like the modernists, the critical theorists also assume a determinism in the interconnected world of organizational life; indeed, they would see life in capitalist organizations as largely coerced (see Afanasyev, 1971).

8. The naturalist and critical theorists have in recent years raised a new criterion for evaluating organizational theory by questioning the validity of *levels and boundaries* of the organizational domain (see Zey-Ferrell & Aiken, 1981). That is, where the positivists have seen clear levels of differentiation in the hierarchy (Barnard thought nearly all organizations had eight or ten hierarchical levels) and clear boundaries marking domains internal and external to the organization, the naturalists have posited a set of more permeable membranes—or, to shift metaphors, organizations whose order, levels, and boundaries are negotiated in communication. The critical theorists would call these distinctions meaningless if not misleading, and would reduce society and organization to the dichotomy of

owner (manager) vs. worker, or to processes of hegemony and legitimation in which organizations participate.

9. If one accepts our claim that some perspective is necessary in order to do theory and research in organizational communication, one has already accepted the corollary that all theorizing about organizations is *metaphoric*. In any case, we find metaphors for organization lurking in the terms of all the schools and approaches. For the positivists, we see the machine, a metaphor consistent with the view of communication (to be developed below) as a tool. The machine is designed for a purpose, a rational purpose, and can be predicted with law-like regularity to perform as ordered. By contrast, the naturalists — favoring an organic metaphor — see truth as ideographic, perceiving the organization as an entity permeable in relation to its environment. The critical theorists would view the capitalist organization metaphorically as a field of warfare: *"contested terrain,"* the locus of class conflict.

10. As can easily be inferred from what has been developed above, the concept of the *organization qua organization* varies across orientations. The modernist view is of the organization as purposive, goal-seeking. Naturalists are more comfortable examining an organization as a culture, each one as exotic as if found on a remote Pacific atoll, or as a unique language community; this orientation would place more stress on the consummatory or social aspects than would modernism, less stress on its instrumentality. Critical theorists would again be, in their view of organization, closer (albeit ironically) to the modernist than to the naturalist position, granting the instrumentality of organization. Indeed, organization could well be labelled an "instrument" of oppression.

11. Although our analysis up to this point has assumed that communication (whether implicit or explicit) is the figure against the ground of organizational theory and research, we consider now the different conceptions of the communication process associated with the different orientations. Modernists have seen communication as a tool of considerable force, primarily when handled by management. Communication conceived as a tool promulgates rational organizational goals, gives orders or directions to achieve those goals, and disciplines workers on the basis of their compliance with them. Upward communication, only lately discovered, was viewed as a tool useful to management, for example, in such manifestations as suggestion systems. It may be that modernists, owing to their worldview, have accorded too much causal force to communication as a management tool. Such was the point of Whyte's question, posed in 1952 after adding up the millions of dollars spent on management-to-employee-publications (*Is Anybody Listening?*, 1952). This positivist view implies a linear and mechanical model of communication in which it is assumed that pressing the right buttons will set workers in the proper motions.

Naturalists see communication as constitutive of organization, and they see order as negotiated through communication. Barnard had advanced a "constitutive" view of organizational communication as early as 1938:

> An organization comes into being when (1) there are persons able to communicate with each other (2) who are willing to contribute action (3) to accomplish a common purpose. The elements of an organization are therefore (1) communication; (2) willingness to serve; and (3) common purpose. These elements are necessary and sufficient conditions initially, and they are found in all such organizations (Barnard, 1968, p. 82).

Barnard not only made communication the first among three prerequisites for organizations, but his analysis of the second element — willingness to serve — made clear that no organization could be activated without communication, more specifically persuasion, in some cases "propaganda" (Barnard, 1968, pp. 150–151, 152, 156). Barnard's third element, common purpose, must also be communicated, whether in verbal or nonverbal messages. One could argue, then, that Barnard was an early proponent of the position that communication constitutes organization; or, put another way, that communication is the necessary condition of organization and facilitates its two sufficient conditions. The naturalistic researches of the Tompkins (1977, 1978) case studies of NASA, and the Tompkins and Anderson (1971) case study of Kent State University during its crisis, were ideographic in nature, explicitly employing the "constitutive" view of organizational communication as first articulated by Barnard in his organic theory of organization in 1938.

The critical theorists tend to view communication as a method of "falsifying" the material realities of organization. That is, the owner/manager's interests are falsely joined with those of the worker in ideological communication which creates a "false consciousness." Notice the irony: in attributing the creation of false consciousness to communication, the critical theorists, like the positivists, have granted to communication a powerful, perhaps hyperbolic, causal status. This ability of organizational leaders to control employees' decisions by controlling the premises from which choices flow, has been featured in recent essays on organizational communication by Poole (1985), McPhee (1985), Tompkins and Cheney (1985) and Conrad and Ryan (1985) in McPhee and Tompkins (1985). In the "Introduction and Afterword" to the volume embracing those essays, Tompkins and McPhee (1985) call this process "microhegemony."

By explicating our matrix of approaches in terms of defining characteristics, we may have given the reader the impression that we entertain grave objections to the modernist approach, in favor of the other two. Some explanation of this unavoidable (and accurate) impression is called for. First, both of us were educated in the positivist tradition at a time of unquestioned acceptance—in academe—of its philosophic and methodological assumptions. But each of us, at different times and in different degrees, has come to question positivism's "received truth." Second, the long dominance of modernism has provided a convenient target for others to shoot at, and our essay in large part reflects the cumulative criticism mounted by others. We predict that criticism of the other approaches will rapidly accumulate, and that the result will be a healthier environment in which to do organizational communication—in a more reflective and philosophically self-conscious way than has been true in the past (see Tompkins, 1983).

We now wish to set aside our acknowledged bias and argue (from a more analytic perspective *outside* our matrix of categories) that *all forms of inquiry* are vital to continued progress in the study of organizational communication. Let us illustrate this by reference to one of our defining characteristics—knowledge claim or research outcome.

Although we have observed that the modernists have not yet produced the "laws" that were promised, even an incomplete attempt at nomothetic explanation is still useful. Indeed, the ideographic aim of explication of wholes cannot proceed without certain nomothetic assumptions. That is, before approaching the study of any organization in terms of communication, one must first assume that *all organizations engage systematically in communication.* Similarly, generalizations produced by the nomothetic approach will only be meaningful, will only come alive, for organizational actors when richer data are available as the result of naturalistic research and "thick description." In like manner, without the idealized models of organizational communication inherent in the critical approach, conventional organizational research can provide us only with *what-is,* but seldom (if ever) with *what-might-be.*

This coda to our essay should not, however, be read as a plea for unfettered relativism. Mindless replication of research—by whatever orientation or method—will not bring automatic progress; at best it will bring mere repetition. All orientations and methods must be grounded in rigorous conceptualizations and appropriate evidentiary warrants. We have noticed with alarm that some students appear to be attracted to "interpretive," "cultural," or "critical" approaches because they entertain the misguided notion that such approaches are somehow "easier" to implement than the modernist-empirical. A major aim of this chapter is to insist on the indispensability of rigor for *all* approaches — much in the spirit of Rychlak's (1977) plea for a "psychology of rigorous humanism." (We also concede the wisdom of Kline's [1980] warning: "There is no rigorous definition of rigor" [p. 315].) We suggest that a good way to promote research that meets the highest standards of rigor (however rigor may be defined) is to devote careful reflection to "defining characteristics," such as those shown in our matrix (Exhibit 3). This means identifying and analyzing the ontological and epistemological assumptions underlying one's theory and methodology.

And after each trip to the field, any researcher should evaluate his or her findings against a set of defining characteristics and criteria — either those proposed in our matrix or others derived from an analogous base. We will feel some small measure of satisfaction when all research reports in our field routinely identify the philosophic assumptions underlying their constructs and methods.

REFERENCES

Afanasyev, V. G. (1971). *The scientific management of society.* Moscow: Progress Publishers.

Allen, T. J., & Cohen, S. I. (1969). Information flow in research and development laboratories. *Administrative Science Quarterly, 14,* 12-19.

Angrist, A. W. (1953). A study of the communications of executives in business and industry. *Speech Monographs, 20,* 277-285.

Argyris, C. (1957). *Personality and Organization.* New York: Harper.

Baker, H., Ballantine, J., & True, J. (1949). *Transmitting information through management and union channels.* Princeton, NJ: Industrial Relations Section, Princeton University.

Barfield, O. (1977). *The rediscovery of meaning and other essays.* Middletown, CT: Wesleyan University Press.

Barnard, C. I. (1968). *The functions of the executive.* Cambridge, MA: Harvard University Press. (Originally published 1938.)

Bavelas, A., & Barrett, D. (1951). An experimental approach to organizational communication. *Personnel, 27,* 366-377.

Bendix, R. (1956). *Work and authority in industry.* New York: Wiley.

Borden, R. C. (1935). *Public speaking—As listeners like it!* New York: Harper.

Bormann, E. G. (1983). Symbolic convergence: Organizational communication and culture. In L. L. Putnam & M. E. Pacanowsky (Eds.), *Communication and organizations: An interpretive approach* (pp. 99-122). Beverly Hills, CA: Sage.

Bowers, D. G., & Seashore, S. E. (1966). Predicting organizational effectiveness with a four-factor theory of leadership. *Administrative Science Quarterly, 11,* 238-263.

Bryant, D. C. (1953). Rhetoric: Its functions and its scope. *Quarterly Journal of Speech, 39,* 401-424.

Burke, K. (1960). *A rhetoric of motives.* New York: Prentice-Hall.

Carnegie, D. (1936). *How to win friends and influence people.* New York: Simon and Schuster.

Coch, L., & French, J. R. P., Jr. (1948). Overcoming resistance to change. *Human Relations, 1,* 512-532.

Colby, A. N., & Tiffin, J. (1950). The reading ability of industrial supervisors. *Personnel, 27,* 156-159.

Conrad, C. (1985). *Strategic organizational communication.* New York: Holt, Rinehart and Winston.

Conrad, C., & Ryan, M. (1985). Power, praxis, and self in organizational communication theory. In R. D. McPhee & P. K. Tompkins (Eds.), *Organizational communication: Traditional themes and new directions* (pp. 235–257). Beverly Hills, CA: Sage.

Cook, D. M. (1968). The impact on managers of frequency of feedback. *Academy of Management Journal, 11,* 263–278.

Cusella, L. P. (1980). The effects of feedback on intrinsic motivation: A propositional extension of cognitive evaluation theory from an organizational communication perspective. In D. Nimmo (Ed.), *Communication yearbook 4* (pp. 367–387). New Brunswick, NJ: Transaction Press.

Dahle, T. L. (1954). An objective and comparative study of five methods of transmitting information to business and industrial employees. *Speech Monographs, 21,* 21–28.

Davis, K. (1952). *Channels of personnel communication within the management group.* Unpublished doctoral dissertation, Ohio State University, Columbus.

Davis, K. (1953). Studying communication patterns in organizations. *Personnel Psychology, 6,* 301–312.

Deetz, S. A., & Kersten, A. (1983). Critical models of interpretive research. In L. L. Putnam & M. E. Pacanowsky (Eds.), *Communication and organizations: An interpretive approach* (pp. 147–171). Beverly Hills, CA: Sage.

Edwards, R. (1979). *Contested terrain: The transformation of the workplace in the twentieth century.* New York: Basic Books.

Ehninger, D. (1972). Introduction. In D. Ehninger (Ed.), *Contemporary rhetoric* (pp. 1–14). Glenview, IL: Scott, Foresman.

Fleishman, E. A., & Harris, E. F. (1962). Patterns of leadership behavior related to employee grievances and turnover. *Personnel Psychology, 15,* 43–56.

Fleishman, E. A., Harris, E. F., & Burtt, H. E. (1955). *Leadership and supervision in industry.* Columbus, OH: Bureau of Educational Research, Ohio State University.

Foundation for Research on Human Behavior (1959). *Communication in organizations.* Ann Arbor, MI: University of Michigan.

Freshley, D. L. (1955). *A study of the attitudes of industrial management personnel toward communication.* Unpublished Ph.D. dissertation, Ohio State University, Columbus.

Funk, F. E. (1956). *Communication attitudes of industrial foremen as related to their rated productivity.* Unpublished Ph.D. dissertation, Purdue University, West Lafayette, IN.

Funk, H. B., & Becker, R. G. (1952). Measuring the effectiveness of industrial communications. *Personnel, 29,* 237–240.

Garraty, J. A., & Gay, P. (Eds.) (1972). *The Columbia history of the world.* New York: Harper and Row.

Garrett, M. B. (1940). *European history: 1500–1815.* New York: American Book.

Geertz, C. (1973). *The interpretation of cultures.* New York: Basic Books.

George, C. S., Jr. (1972). *The history of management thought.* Englewood Cliffs, NJ: Prentice-Hall.

Goodyear Tire and Rubber Co. (1953). *Goodyear supervisional training, 1952–53 sessions: Communications.* Akron, OH: Goodyear Tire and Rubber Co.

Gray, G. W. (1946). The "Precepts of Kagemni and Ptah-hotep." *Quarterly Journal of Speech, 32,* 446–454.

Guetzkow, H. (1965). Communication in organizations. In J. G. March (Ed.), *Handbook of organizations* (pp. 534–573). Chicago, IL: Rand McNally.

Habermas, J. (1971). *Knowledge and human interests.* Boston, MA: Beacon Press.

Hay, R. D. (1974). A brief history of internal organization communication through the 1940s. *Journal of Business Communication, 11,* 6–11.

Heron, A. R. (1942). *Sharing information with employees.* Palo Alto, CA: Stanford University Press.

Hoffman, W. G. (1923). *Public speaking for businessmen.* New York: McGraw-Hill.

Hotchkiss, G. B., & Drew, C. A. (1916). *Business English, principles and practice.* New York: American Book.

Huber, R. M. (1971). *The American idea of success.* New York: McGraw-Hill.

Human Relations in Modern Buiness—A guide for action by American business leaders. (1949). New

York: Prentice-Hall. (Also known as "The Robert Wood Johnson Report.")

Huston, A. D., & Sandberg, R. A. (1943). *Everyday business speech.* New York: Prentice-Hall.

Indik, B. P., Georgopoulos, B., & Seashore, S. (1961). Superior–subordinate relationships and performance. *Personnel Psychology, 14,* 357–374.

Jablin, F. M. (1979). Superior–subordinate communication: The state of the art. *Psychological Bulletin, 86,* 1201–1222.

Jablin, F. M., & McComb, K. B. (1984). The employment screening interview: An organizational assimilation and communication perspective. In R. Bostrom & B. Westley (Eds.), *Communication yearbook 8* (pp. 137–163). Beverly Hills, CA: Sage.

Jacobson, E., Seashore, S. E. (1951). Communication practices in complex organizations. *Journal of Social Issues, 7,* 28–40.

Janis, J. H. (1958). *Business communication reader.* New York: Harper.

Jay, A. (1967). *Management and Machiavelli: An inquiry into the politics of corporate life.* New York: Bantam Books.

Katz, D., Maccoby, N., Gurin, G., & Floor, L. G. (1951). *Productivity, supervision and morale among railroad workers.* Ann Arbor, MI: Institute for Social Research, University of Michigan.

Katz, D., Maccoby, N., & Morse, N. (1950). *Productivity, supervision and morale in an office situation: Part I.* Ann Arbor, MI: Institute for Social Research, University of Michigan.

Kaufman, H. (1960). *The forest ranger: A study in administrative behavior.* Baltimore, MD: Johns Hopkins Press.

Kline, M. (1980). *Mathematics — The loss of certainty.* New York: Oxford University Press.

Lawler, E. E., III, Porter, L. W., & Tennenbaum, A. (1968). Managers' attitudes toward interaction episodes. *Journal of Applied Psychology, 52,* 432.

Lawrence, P. R. (1958). *The changing of organizational behavior patterns: A case study of decentralization.* Boston, MA: Graduate School of Business Administration, Harvard University.

Leipzig, J. S., & More, E. (1982). Organizational communication: A review and analysis of three current approaches to the field. *Journal of Business Communication, 19,* 77–92.

Level, D. A., Jr. (1959). *A case study of human communications in an urban bank.* Unpublished Ph.D. dissertation, Purdue University, West Lafayette, IN.

Lewin, K., Lippitt, R., & White, R. K. (1939). Patterns of aggressive behavior in experimentally created "social climates." *Journal of Social Psychology, 10,* 271–299.

Lewis, I. G. (1954). *A survey of management's attitudes regarding oral communication needs and practices in large industries of Los Angeles County.* Unpublished Ph.D. dissertation, University of Southern California, Los Angeles.

Likert, R. (1955). *Developing patterns in management.* General Management Series, No. 178. New York: American Management Association. [Reprinted in E. A. Fleishman (Ed.). (1961). *Studies in personnel and industrial psychology* (pp. 338–355). Homewood, IL: Dorsey.]

Lombard, G. F. F. (1955). *Behavior in a selling group: A case study of interpersonal relations in a department store.* Boston, MA: Division of Research, Graduate School of Business Administration, Harvard University.

McCloskey, D. N. (1985). *The rhetoric of economics.* Madison, WI: University of Wisconsin Press.

McPhee, R. D. (1985). Formal structures and organizational communication. In R. D. McPhee & P. K. Tompkins (Eds.), *Organizational communication: Traditional themes and new directions* (pp. 149–177). Beverly Hills, CA: Sage.

McPhee, R. D., & Tompkins, P. K. (Eds.) (1985). *Organizational communication: Traditional themes and new directions.* Beverly Hills, CA: Sage.

Maier, N. R. F., Hoffman, L. R., & Read, W. H. (1963). Superior–subordinate communication: The relative effectiveness of managers who held their subordinates' positions. *Personnel Psychology, 16,* 1–11.

Manning, P. K. (1979). Metaphors of the field: Varieties of organizational discourse. *Administrative Science Quarterly, 24,* 602–611.

March, J. G. (1965). Introduction. In J. G. March (Ed.), *Handbook of organizations* (pp. ix–xvi). Chicago, IL: Rand McNally.

Merrill, H. F. (1970). Introduction. In H. Merrill (Ed.), *Classics in management* (pp. 1–8). New York: American Management Association.

Miller, G. R., Burgoon, M., & Burgoon, J. (1984). The functions of human communication in changing attitudes and gaining compliance. In C. Arnold & J. Bowers (Eds.), *Handbook of rhetorical and communication theory* (pp. 400–474). Boston, MA: Allyn and Bacon.

Minter, R. L. (1969). *A comparative analysis of managerial communication in two divisions of a large manufacturing company [4 vols.].* Unpublished Ph.D. dissertation, Purdue University, West Lafayette, IN.

Monroe, A. H. (1935). *Principles and types of speech.* Chicago, IL: Scott, Foresman.

Morse, N., & Reimer, E. (1956). The experimental change of a major organizational variable. *Journal of Abnormal and Social Psychology, 52,* 120–129.

National Industrial Conference Board. (1925). *Employee magazines in the United States.* New York: National Industrial Conference Board.

Nilsen, T. R. (1953). *The communication survey: A study of communication problems in three office and factory units.* Unpublished Ph.D. dissertation, Northwestern University, Evanston, IL.

Owen, R. (1970). An address to the superintendents of manufactories. In H. Merrill (Ed.), *Classics in management* (pp. 11–15). New York: American Management Association. (First published, 1813; republished, 1825; reprinted, 1970.)

Pacanowsky, M. E., & O'Donnell-Trujillo, N. (1982). Communication and organizational cultures. *Western Journal of Speech Communication, 46,* 115–130.

Pacanowsky, M. E., & O'Donnell-Trujillo, N. (1983). Organizational communication as cultural performance. *Communication Monographs, 50,* 126–147.

Paterson, D. G., & Jenkins, J. J. (1948). Communication between management and workers. *Journal of Applied Psychology, 32,* 71–80.

Pelz, D. C. (1952). Influence: A key to effective leadership in the first-line supervisor. *Personnel, 29,* 209–217.

Peters, R. W. (1949 and 1950). *Communication within industry.* New York: Harper.

Phillips, A. E. (1908). *Effective speaking.* Chicago, IL: Newton.

Piersol, D. T. (1955). *A case study of oral communication practices of foremen and assistant foremen in a mid-western corporation.* Unpublished Ph.D. dissertation, Purdue University, West Lafayette, IN.

Poole, M. S. (1985). Communication and organizational climates: Review, critique, and new perspectives. In R. D. McPhee & P. K. Tompkins (Eds.), *Organizational communication: Traditional themes and new directions* (pp. 79–108). Beverly Hills, CA: Sage.

Putnam, L. L. (1983). The interpretive perspective: An alternative to functionalism. In L. L. Putnam & M. E. Pacanowsky (Eds.), *Communication and organizations: An interpretive approach* (pp. 31–54). Beverly Hills, CA: Sage.

Putnam, L. L., & Cheney, G. E. (1983). A critical review of research traditions in organizational communication. In M. S. Mander (Ed.), *Communications in transition* (pp. 206–224). New York: Prager.

Pyron, H. C. (1964). *The construction and validation of a forced-choice scale for measuring oral communication attitudes of industrial foremen.* Unpublished Ph.D. dissertation, Purdue University, West Lafayette, IN.

Read, W. H. (1962). Upward communication in industrial hierarchies. *Human Relations, 15,* 3–15.

Redding, W. C. (1977). *Business and Professional Speaking: Corpse, ghost, or angel?* Paper presented at the annual meeting of the Speech Communication Association, Washington, DC (December).

Redding, W. C. (1979). Organizational communication theory and ideology: An overview: In D. Nimmo (Ed.), *Communication yearbook 3* (pp. 309–341). New Brunswick, NJ: Transaction Books.

Redding, W. C. (1985). Stumbling toward identity: The emergence of organizational communication as a field of study. In R. D. McPhee & P. K. Tompkins (Eds.), *Organizational communication: Traditional themes and new directions* (pp. 15–54). Beverly Hills, CA: Sage.

Redfield, C. E. (1958). Communication in Management (rev. ed.). Chicago, IL: University of Chicago Press.

Richards, I. A. (136). *The philosophy of rhetoric.* New York: Oxford University Press.

Richards, W. D., Jr. (1985). Data, models, and assumptions in network analysis. In R. D. McPhee & P. K. Tompkins (Eds.), *Organizational communication: Traditional themes and new directions* (pp. 109–128). Beverly Hills, CA: Sage.

Richetto, G. M. (Ed.) (1967). *Conference on organizational communication: August 8–11, 1967.* Huntsville, AL: George C. Marshall Space Flight Center, National Aeronautics and Space Administration.

Richetto, G. M. (1969). *Source credibility and personal influence in three contexts: A study of dyadic communication in a complex aero-space organization.* Unpublished Ph.D. dissertation, Purdue University, West Lafayette, IN.

Roethlisberger, F. J., & Dickson, W. J. (1939). *Management and the worker.* Cambridge, MA: Harvard University Press.

Ronken, H., & Lawrence, P. R. (1952). *Administrative change: A case study of human relations in a factory.* Boston, MA: Division of Research, Graduate School of Business Administration, Harvard University.

Ross, R. S. (1954). *A case study of communication breakdowns in the General Telephone Company of Indiana, Inc.* Unpublished Ph.D. dissertation. Purdue University, West Lafayette, IN.

Rychlak, J. F. (1977). *The psychology of rigorous humanism.* New York: Wiley.

Sanborn, G. A. (1961). *An analytical study of oral communication practices in a nationwide retail sales organization.* Purdue University, West Lafayette, IN.

Sandford, W. P., & Yeager, W. H. (1929). *Business and professional speaking.* New York: McGraw-Hill.

Saunders, A. G., & Creek, H. L. (1920). *The literature of business.* New York: Harper.

Schwartz, D. F. (1968). *Liaison communication roles in a formal organization.* Unpublished Ph.D. dissertation, Michigan State University, East Lansing.

Scott, R. L. (1967). On viewing rhetoric as epistemic. *Central States Speech Journal, 18,* 9–17.

Scott, W. G., & Hart, D. K. (1979). *Organizational America.* Boston, MA: Houghton Mifflin.

Sexton, R., & Staudt, V. (1959). Business communication: A survey of the literature. *Journal of Social Psychology, 50,* 101–118.

Sincoff, M. Z. (1969). *An experimental study of the effects of three "interviewing styles" upon judgments of interviewees and observer-judges.* Unpublished Ph.D. dissertation. Purdue University, West Lafayette, IN.

Sincoff, M. Z., Pacilio, J., Jr., Blatt, S. J., Hunt, G. T., & Anton, P. (1975). Organizational communication: Perspectives and prospects. *Ohio Speech Journal, 13,* 3–18.

Smeltzer, L. R., Glab, J., & Golen, S. (1983). Managerial communication: The merging of business communication, organizational communication, and management. *Journal of Business Communication, 20,* 71–78.

Sutton, H., & Porter, L. W. (1968). A study of the grapevine in a governmental organization. *Personnel Psychology, 21,* 223–230.

Tannenbaum, R., & Schmidt, W. H. (1958). How to choose a leadership pattern. *Harvard Business Review, 36* (March-April, No. 2), 95–101.

Thayer, L. (1967). Communication and organization theory. In F. Dance (Ed.), *Human communication theory* (pp. 70–115). New York: Holt, Rinehart and Winston.

Thayer, L. (1968). *Communication and communication systems.* Homewood, IL: Irwin.

Tompkins, P. K. (1962). *An analysis of communication between headquarters and selected units of a national labor union.* Unpublished Ph.D. dissertation, Purdue University, West Lafayette, IN.

Tompkins, P. K. (1967). Organizational communication: A state-of-the-art review. In G. M. Richetto (Ed.), *Conference on organizational communication: August 8–11, 1967* (pp. 4–26). Huntsville, AL: Marshall Space Flight Center, National Aeronautics and Space Administration.

Tompkins, P. K. (1977). Management *qua* communication in rocket research and development. *Communication Monographs, 44,* 1–26.

Tompkins, P. K. (1978). Organizational metamorphosis in space research and development. *Communication Monographs, 45,* 110–118.

Tompkins, P. K. (1983, November). *On the desirability of an interpretive science of organizational communication.* Paper presented at annual meeting of the Speech Communication Association, Washington, DC.

Tompkins, P. K., & Anderson, E. (1971). *Communication crisis at Kent State: A case study.* New York: Gordon and Breach.

Tompkins, P. K., & Cheney, G. E. (1983). Account analysis of organizations: Decision making and identification. In L. L. Putnam & M. E. Pacanowsky (Eds.), *Communication and organizations: An interpretive approach* (pp. 123–146). Beverly Hills, CA: Sage.

Tompkins, P. K., & Cheney, G. E. (1985). Communication and unobtrusive control in contemporary organizations. In R. D. McPhee & P. K. Tompkins (Eds.), *Organizational communication: Traditional themes and new directions* (pp. 179–210). Beverly Hills, CA: Sage.

Tompkins, P. K., & McPhee, R. D. (1985). Introduction and afterword. In R. D. McPhee & P. K. Tompkins (Eds.), *Organizational communication: Traditional themes and new directions* (pp. 7–13). Beverly Hills, CA: Sage.

Voos, H. (1967). *Organizational communication: A bibliography.* New Brunswick, NJ: Rutgers University Press.

Weaver, C. H. (1958). The quantification of the frame of reference in labor-management communication. *Journal of Applied Psychology, 42,* 1–9.

Weeks, F. W. (1985). The teaching of business writing at the collegiate level, 1900–1920. In G. Douglas & H. Hildebrandt (Eds.), *Studies in the history of business writing* (pp. 201–215). Urbana, IL: Association for Business Communication.

Weick, K. E. (1979). *The social psychology of organizing* (2nd ed.). Reading, MA: Addison-Wesley.

Whyte, W. H., Jr. [and the Editors of *Fortune*]. (1952). *Is anybody listening?* New York: Simon and Schuster.

Yin, R. K. (1981). The case study crisis: Some answers. *Administrative Science Quarterly, 26,* 58–65.

Zelko, H. P., & O'Brien, H. J. (1957). *Management–employee communication in action.* Cleveland, OH: Howard Allen.

Zey-Ferrell, M., & Aiken, M. (Eds.). (1981). *Complex organizations: Critical perspectives.* Glenview, IL: Scott, Foresman.

SECTION 1

THEORETICAL PERSPECTIVES AND CONCEPTUAL ADVANCES IN ORGANIZATIONAL COMMUNICATION

The first section of this volume describes the diversity of theoretical perspectives and recent conceptual advances in the field of organizational communication. This variance of opinion has resulted for many reasons. Communication scholars have come from many disciplines—speech, journalism, philosophy, education, information science, and the social sciences, including sociology, anthropology, management, political science, and psychology. As these scholars entered the new discipline of communication, they brought with them the particular paradigms and theoretical perspectives of their original fields. Another reason is the perceived inability of systems theory to capture certain aspects of the communication process deemed important by those who study organizational communication.

Scholars almost universally agree that organizations are social systems (Thayer, 1968; Rogers & Agarwala-Rogers, 1976; Farace, Monge, & Russell, 1977; Katz & Kahn, 1978; Goldhaber, Dennis, Richetto, & Wiio, 1984). A system is a set of interdependent components or parts. These components may be individuals, groups, or machines. Together, the sum of these parts produces a set of emergent properties which could not result if the components behaved independently. One emergent property of the components' interaction, and which is the focus of this book, is the organization itself. Organizations are goal-seeking systems. The components' interdependent (coordinated) behaviors make it possible for the organization to achieve goals such as the continued manufacturing of products or the performance of services. These products or services are also some of the emergent properties of organizations.

Another focus of this volume is the role communication plays in social systems. Indeed, it is communication which makes possible the interdependency and, thus, the achievement of system goals. Communication facilitates the coordination of the components' activities through mutual adjustment of the behavior of the individual parts. Further, in more complex social organizations (those with managerial heirarchies), communication is the control mechanism which regulates individual activities. By providing direct supervision, feedback to ongoing behavior, and socialization of new members, management can direct the system toward its goals (Hage, 1974; Mintzberg, 1983).

Despite the obvious relevance of systems theory to organizations, its abstract nature has made its application to communication processes difficult. General systems theory emerged as an attempt to unify the ever-increasing specialization which characterized the natural and social sciences (von Bertalanffy, 1956). Its goal was to identify those common elements which could be generalized across all scientific specialities. Communication among the disciplines was to be facilitated through the shared understanding of these common principles. This would result in further scientific advancements. The problem was that the underlying principles became very abstract, in order to accommodate the unique principles of each speciality.

General systems theory brought together two types of scientific explanation, teleology and positivism. Without attempting to provide an in-depth discussion of these types of explanations, let it suffice to describe teleology as primarily descriptive — things are the way they are because that is as they should be. In an organizational context, management consciously designs organizations. Over time, a system evolves to look like it does because that is how management wants it to be (Schein, 1983). Thus, it is important to describe the organization as it is and how it is understood by its members. By doing so, insights may be gained about how and why the organization operates as it does and the role communication plays in these activities.

Organizations are conscious goal-directed systems. This compels some organizational scholars to view communication as a human activity guided by individual intentions. (For example, see Cushman, King, & Smith, Chapter 4).

Others view organizations mechanistically or organically, with communication acting as the causal force which makes the interdependency possible (Burns & Stalker, 1961; Lawrence & Lorsch, 1967; Hage, 1974; Woelfel & Fink, 1980; Rogers & Kincaid, 1981). This second type of explanation, positivism, stresses the causal relations among components. By examining the influences of the components (including the environment) upon one another, and the time-ordered changes within the organization, insights may be gained about how to manipulate certain variables to help the organization more effectively and efficiently achieve its goals. Positivism has been the more frequent epistemic approach.

Communication scholars, however, have tended to examine organizational activities from either orientation rather than both. This has resulted in theories that reflect only one of the orientations.

Thus, what is seen in this volume is an abandonment of systems theory in favor of less general fields of knowledge. While the task is less ambitious, it may prove more fruitful in understanding social organizations and the role of communication in the activities of these human products. This is not to suggest that systems theory is dead, although certain chapters in this section may leave that impression. For example, network analysis (see Wigand, Chapter 14) is an outgrowth of the systems theory. This approach describes the structural aspects of organizational communication. What appears to be happening is the emergence of theories of the "middle range" (Merton, 1957) rather than "grand theories" that might be suggested by the systems paradigm. These theories are somewhat narrower and less abstract being based on empirical research. As a result, they are more managable. This may facilitate an understanding of communication's role in organizational activities, and may guide research and the management of social organizations. Indeed, in the future, the systems perspective may reemerge as a grand theory combining a number of the perspectives in this volume.

The first chapter in this section is a discussion among Leonard Hawes, Michael Pacanowsky, and Don Faules. It presents three different approaches to the study of organizations — "pluralism," "criticism," and "interpretivism." Pluralism is taken to be all methods from statistical modeling of management science (structural-functionalism) to ethnographies of cultural anthropologists. Interpretivism is a gloss for organizational research, ranging from ethnology and ethnography, through ethnomethology, hermeneutics, and phenomenology, to literature — fiction, in particular. Criticism is used in two ways: (a) the production of coherent readings of texts, and (b) the negative dialectic that underlies conventional meaning. This thought-provoking discussion is timely, and suggests that there is value in the investigation of communication activities from a variety of perspectives.

Donald Cushman, Sarah King, and Ted Smith explore the utility of studying organizational communication from the rules perspective. They discuss in detail the philosophical and theoretical development of the rules perspective, providing cogent arguments in support of a theoretical approach which accommodates human intentions. They review the research of communication scholars who have employed a rules perspective, and, finally, they present a case study of an organization using one approach to rules research.

The next three chapters in this section focus on the role of symbolic language and its place in organizational communication. Particular emphasis is placed on the relationship between language and organizational culture. In "Organizational Communication: Contingent Views," Osmo Wiio suggests that the best predictor of organizational communication is a contingency model. One factor in this model is the culture of the society in which the organization is embedded. Rather than using a rational statistical model, he suggests the examination of the values as they are manifest in the communication or language of the organization. He describes how an examination of Japanese values help one understand Japanese organizational communication. He concludes that communication scholars could gain insights from the use of semiotic/cultural models.

George Barnett discusses communication and organizational culture, and develops a model of the sort suggested by Wiio. He defines culture from the symbols-and-meaning perspective, i.e., as an emergent property of the members' communication activities which in turn acts to restrict future communication. The chapter then defines organizational culture, and discusses the role of communication in the process of formulating and changing organizational culture and the procedures for examining and altering organizational culture. The chapter concludes with a case study in which these procedures are applied to describe an organization's culture.

The chapter which follows, Eric Eisenberg and Patricia Riley's, "Organizational Symbols and Sense-Making," continues this focus on symbols and symbolic processes by organizational members. They suggest that it is through the use of symbols that organizations create, maintain, and change organizational realities. They describe the leading theoretical perspectives on organizational symbolism—negotiated order theory, dramatism, cultural approaches, structuration, and information theory. Next, the role symbols play in constituting organizational reality is explored, followed by symbolic approaches to organizational change. The chapter concludes with a discussion of the issues for future research on symbols and symbolization in the organizational context.

At this point, the emphasis of section one changes from its focus on theoretical perspectives to place greater stress upon conceptual advances based upon the knowledge gained from empirical resarch. The change is not clear-cut. The chapters that follow do not simply report research findings, but discuss them within conceptual frameworks. For example, Raymond Falcione and Charmaine Wilson discuss socialization processes in organizations. They describe various models and perspectives for examining organizational socialization, placing particular emphasis on communication sources and strategies for the socialization process. Next, they relate socialization to organizational outcomes, and present a model of the organizational socialization process. They conclude by offering recommendations for future research. This chapter provides an excellent transition between the discussion of language and organizational culture presented above and the chapter on organizational outcomes which follows.

Cal Downs, Phillip Clampitt, and Angela Laird Pfeiffer review the research of communication scholars in their attempt to specify the relationship between communication processes and outcomes of organizational activities. They conclude that communication impacts upon job satisfaction and productivity, but not in a uniform manner. These relations are not highly correlated. They are contingent upon many factors, including the communication strategies in which the organization is engaged.

Peter Monge and Katherine Miller discuss participative processes in organizations. They review the concept of participation and the diversity of participative systems that have been developed and implemented in Europe, Japan, China, and the United States. Next, they examine the behavioral theories and empirical research studies that incorporate participation and communication. Finally, they suggest future research to investigate the relationship between communication variables and their role in participative processes.

Along the line of Monge and Miller, Lee Thayer examines the concept of leadership from the perspective of a communication scholar. Thayer has been one of the most influential systems theorists in organizational communication. Thus, it is with special attention one should read "Leadership/Communication: A Critical Review and Modest Proposal." In this narrative essay, he challenges the prevailing notions about leadership, communication, and organization as held by positivist scholars. He suggests that both are abstracts that have meaning only in terms of the individual stakeholders: those who behave in reference to the organization which they enact. He reviews the current theories about leadership, and concludes that leaders and their followers create and maintain their relationship through communication.

The final chapter in Section 1 is by Roger D'Aprix, who grounds it in the observations of a communication manager. He considers the lack of trust as the major problem facing corporate management at the end of the twentieth century. Three major developments, international competition, deregulation, and a more highly educated work force, point to a change in employee communications. These changes necessitate an increase in trust. Foreshadowing Section 3, which discusses organizational communication in the information age, D'Aprix argues that designing new communication systems will facilitate organizational survival and employee communication. He suggests that three elements should be considered: communication strategy, accountability, and communication training. Combined with shared leadership, organizations should survive and prosper.

REFERENCES

Burns, T., & Stalker, G. M. (1961). *The management of innovations.* London: Tavistock.

Farace, R., Monge, P., & Russell, H. (1977). *Communicating and organizing.* Reading, MA: Addison-Wesley.

Goldhaber, G. M., Dennis, H. S., Richetto, G. M., & Wiio, O. A. (1984). *Information strategies: New pathways to corporate power* (rev. ed.). Norwood, NJ: Ablex Publishing Corporation.

Hage, J. (1974). *Communication and organizational control: Cybernetics in health and welfare settings.* New York: Wiley-Interscience.

Katz, D., & Kahn, R. L. (1978). *The social psychology of organizations.* New York: John Wiley & Sons, Inc.

Lawrence, P., & Lorsch, J. (1967). *Organization and environment: Managing differentiation and integration.* Cambridge, MA: Harvard University Press.

Merton, R. (1957). Patterns of influence: Local and cosmopolitan influentials. In R. Merton (Ed.), *Social theory and social structure.* New York: Free Press.

Mintzberg, H. (1983). *Structures in fives: Designing effective organizations.* Englewood Cliffs, NJ: Prentice Hall.

Rogers, E., & Agarwala-Rogers, R. (1976). *Communication in organizations.* New York: The Free Press.

Rogers, E. M., & Kincaid, D. L.. (1981). *Communication networks.* New York: Free Press.

Schein, E. H. (1983). The role of the founder in creating organizational culture. *Organizational Dynamics, 12,* 13-28.

Thayer, L. (1968). *Communication and communication systems.* Homewood, IL: Richard D. Irwin.

Von Bertalanffy, L. (1956). General systems theory. *General Systems, 1,* 1-10.

Woelfel, J., & Fink, E. L. (1980). *The Galileo system: A theory of social measurement and its application.* New York: Academic.

Chapter 3

Approaches to the Study of Organization: A Conversation Among Three Schools of Thought

Leonard Hawes, Michael Pacanowsky, and Don Faules

ABSTRACT

This "conversation" is a reconstruction of four conversations held between July and October of 1984. Each position is arguing from a school of thought on the most profitable way to theorize about, and inquire into, organizational behavior. The designation "school of thought" is more appropriate than "perspective" or "theory," because none of us fully develops his own point of view in the conversation. By arguing from those schools, we wanted to sharpen those points of view and draw them out in greater detail to more clearly comprehend their significance for organizational theory and practice.

"Pluralism" should be read very generously as glossing disciplinary biases ranging from the statistical modeling of management science, at one end of the continuum, to the ethnologies and ethnographies of cultural anthropology, at the other—and as being, apparently, supportive of "interpretivism" and "criticism." "Interpretivism" is a gloss for organizational work ranging from ethnology and ethnography through ethnomethodology, hermeneutics, and phenomenology to literature—fiction in particular. "Criticism," never defined in so many terms, is used in two not necessarily complementary ways: first, as the production of coherent readings of texts; and second, as the negative dialectic, that which undermines conventional understandings.

Interpretivist: Let's begin by characterizing the three perspectives of organizational research and analysis to be discussed. Interpretivism stands in opposition both to parts of pluralism and to criticism. Interpretivism begins with the premise that every way of seeing is also a way of not seeing. The managerial concerns of structural-functionalism get operationalized quantitatively; interpretivism is an attempt to open up that quantitized domain for other styles of investigation. Clifford Geertz (1973) would say we're expanding our universe of discourse.[1]

Pluralist: Pluralism represents here a number of theoretical positions: All inquiry rests on metaphors, and within each metaphor something is missing. There are strengths

---

[1] Interpretive approaches to organizational communication and organizational culture have been outlined in several recent volumes (Putnam & Pacanowsky, 1983; Frost, Moore, Louis, Lundberg, & Martin, 1985). Similarly, the issue of writing interpretive accounts of organizational communication has also been an item of concern (Strine & Pacanowsky, 1985). For an example of the kind of artistic ethnography advocated here, see Pacanowsky (1983).

and weaknesses within each position. The cultural metaphor suggests that organizational life is socially constructed, it continually evolves and changes; but there is also structure that both constrains and makes possible how people behave. Structural-functionalism is limiting in that it simplifies, but that simplification allows us to see. Interpretive approaches offer the advantages of richness and complexity. The two approaches start from different premises, but the contrast allows us to see how they elaborate one another.[2]

Critic: Critical discourse comprehends organizations/institutions as sets of materially organized practices for displacing, reformulating, or otherwise transforming their own generative contradictions. Potential sites for organizational/institutional criticism, then, are the spatio-temporal locations at which the ideology of organizations as formal cooperative systems glosses contradictions and hides privileged interests. Pluralism acknowledges a variety of sites for beginning theoretical work; its shortcoming is its inability or unwillingness to formulate itself dialectically. It isn't interested in locating contradictory practices and their material consequences, but in selecting one or more perspectives and applying them to managerial ends.[3]

Pluralist: The pluralist position recognizes ends other than managerial. However, is the purpose of organizational/institutional criticism, as you envision it, to generate theoretical structures and effects not contained by managerial bias?

Critic: Not at all; a privileged, unbiased, objective position is an illusion. But you have to admit that there isn't much American organizational or institutional analysis that is manifestly critical of the managerial bias. Consultants have to gain access to the organization, and so the referent group — the parties not to be offended, the parties whose interests are being served — are the managers who control formal accesses and alliances. Like a good journalist, a good consultant is not likely to report the negative side of the dialectics of managerial practices.

Interpretivist: I don't believe that one necessarily or ultimately represents only one interest. Going into an organization and getting permission to do interpretive work does not necessarily mean that management's interests alone, or even in tandem with other interests, are being served. I'm not sure we can say in advance whose interests are being served. There are a lot of audiences out there. Consider Fred Weissman's documentary, *The Store,* about Nieman-Marcus. It's filmic ethnography of an organization. I can imagine Nieman-Marcus management people approving that film even though it's critical of certain sales practices. The difficulty you have in the position you're taking is that you make anybody who walks into an organization suspect.

Critic: Critical discourse which is animated dialectically is, by its very nature, contradictory in structure and polemical in style. Let me give you a sample: much of the American organizational literature is ahistorical, apolitical, asocial and noneconomic — a dangerous

---

[2] For discussion and emergent issues that arise from pluralist positions, see Morgan (1983); Churchman (1971); Mason and Mitroff (1981); Mitroff and Kilmann (1978); Lincoln (1985); Faules (1982).

[3] What follows is an eclectic collection of references — ranging from Marx through Bell to Lyotard — serving as a makeshift introduction to the critical study of organizations and their institutional structures and dynamics. For the foundations of the Marxist critique, see (Marx, 1964, 1967, 1973). For a comprehensive introduction to the Frankfurt School, and the positions of negative dialectics in response to Marxism, see Buck-Morss (1977). See also Marcuse (1941, 1964). For a more recent idealist version of Germanic critical theory, see Habermas (1971, 1973). For a critical non-Marxist critique of the industrial revolution, see Rodgers (1978) and Jacoby (1976). For a more pluralist-American critical reading of organizational institutions, see Bell (1973, 1976) and Shorris (1981). For a French reading of postmodern institutional life, see Lyotard (1984).

state of affairs in the socioecological reality of advanced capitalism. The history of organizatioinal behavior — and, more broadly, institutional behavior — is largely ignored in favor of a synchronic, systemic, structural-functionalist characterization. Such characterizations are formal as opposed to dialectical, and have a two-dimensional flatness rather than a spatio-temporal texture. Stated differently, organizational contexts are not elaborated theoretically; they are simply presupposed. Concerns with morale, productivity, and discontinuity anchor an internal prooccupation which frequently excludes acknowledgement of internal/external (i.e., boundary) relations. Looking internally without looking externally distorts our understanding by denying the dialectics of organizational dynamics. The consequence is an empiricist literature which has little interest in economic and cultural history, and even less curiosity about whose interests such scholarship serves and who's profiting from the enterprise. What sorts of subjects and objects does such theoretical discourse construct? How are they animated and motivated? I'm arguing for the oppositional positioning of theoretical discourses. There aren't many Alinskyist, or Ghandiist, or Maoist, or Marxist theories of the dynamics of, say, how to produce value and power from alienation and desire.

Pluralist: Segments of the pluralist position certainly represent interests of the status quo. I do not believe that those interests are always opposed to the folks at the bottom. Change agents may gain access to organizations by being willing to win small battles rather than great wars. It is a way to modify and make changes even in a slight way. Rather than trying to reform the whole system, it might be better to take the position that this is the world with which we have to work. This means recognizing the power structure and making a difference, not by reforming everyone, but by modifying and making the best case for more equitable and humane activity.

Critic: But equitable for whom and humane by whose standards? I'm not arguing that consultants should stop doing managerially sanctioned change programs. I'm arguing your theory and practice, what we've been characterizing as pluralism, requires a thoroughgoing critique and reformulation. The theoretical concerns need overhauling. The discourse or organizational theory ought to speak for a variety of opposing interests in many opposing voices, rather than assuming theoretical power to be materialized through a single, unified, coherent voice of authority. The crucial voice in animating that pluralism of interests is the critical voice; the voice of the discursive consciousness. One now must account to an audience other than the managerial hosts for what's being done, whose interests one is fortifying, and what audience one is addressing. Critical discourse addresses the interstices of theory/practice. The critical voice provides criteria for valuing the practical significance of theory, and the theoretical significance of practice. The relative absence of such a critical reflexivity in organizational theory makes it second-rate management science.

Interpretivist: I hear a conflicting evaluation of pluralism and interpretivism. On the one hand, you say you need them, and on the other hand your characterization of them is negative. For you, interpretivism is a political travelogue; pluralism is the identification and elaboration of teleologies. You're being very intolerant in respecting all theoretical perspectives. Why do pluralism and interpretatism get characterized so negatively?

Critic: The short answer is because interpretivist, and to a much greater extent pluralist, discourses have been appropriated, and, as the State's theory (i.e., the consensus perspective of funding agencies and journal editorial boards), it legitimates the current relations and forces of production and reproduction — relations uneven in terms of power. The longer answer is that both pluralism and interpretivism ignore the power/desire dialectic.

Theorizing organizational behavior, or even making a meaningful description of organizational practices, one must come to theoretical terms with power. Organizing is the dialectical working through of contradictions which are both the products of, and the resources for, relations of power and desire. To ignore that is to attribute power to psychologized homonids or to the natural order of common sense. Power is a function of hierarchized structures of organizing processes; the objects of those processes are those very contradictions being elided.

Pluralist: The notion of pluralism certainly denies the idea of a single, unified, coherent voice of authority. In addition, there are a variety of positions that have nothing to do with accountability to managers. Nevertheless, there is nothing in pluralism or interpretivism that precludes the study of power. I grant that there hasn't been nearly enough study; but I think Tompkins and Cheney (1985), is a recent contribution.

Critic: But pluralism and interpretivism are both predicated ultimately on the assumption that formal logic, and its practical foundation — common sense — can be used to construct explanations of descriptions and accounts. Pluralism describes the workings of self-fulfilling prophesies syntactically animated by the tenets of formal logic. Interpretivism assumes that meaning is a product of the process of perpetual interpretation; such meaning is shared by means of conventional practices. But, as the argument goes, there are correct and unified meanings being produced in the interests of equilibrium and cooperation. Dialectical thinking presupposes opposition; the concern is with the play of those oppositions. For example, consider the opposition between students and professors; their interests are not the same, they do not share the same common sense, they are animated by very different interests. The hierarchized contradictions are those sites on the organizational surface that serve certain interests in the forms of power relations. Power, after all, is invested neither in someone's job description nor in someone's "personality." Rather, it's those material practices, policies, and procedures that limit and bind prevailing common sense. Rather than to define power as a psychological variable, it becomes instead a critical constant.

Interpretivist: Interpretivism focuses on phenomena which are possible to interpret more than one way. What you're identifying as an impossibility of interpretivism is, in fact, a weakness in the work that has been done in the name of interpretivism. Most characterizations of interpretivism stress that organizations are not monolithic, that organizational cultures are not uniform and not singular. You see, I don't understand what is unique about your version of criticism. What is inherently oppositional about what you're doing? What makes it critical? An enterprising interpretivist could go to the library and do background work on the big picture of what's going on. That doesn't seem to be at all oppositional.

Critic: I was intending "oppositional" in the sense of organizational problematics. What do you find worthy of attending to and writing about? A critic begins with the assumption that organizations are contradictory elaborations of paradoxical foundations. There are many interests at play. There's no final resolution or transcendence. What we share is the collusion of conventionalized practices produced temporarily for certain practical projects. There are a variety of interpretations, but, to a member of any one of those interpreted systems, each is internally coherent. Within its domain, it makes coherent, unified, unitary sense. Interpretivism is working to create ideological closure for understanding how it is that, say, banana time works. The produced understanding is a sort of narrative; it's a structure that closes itself. It's the coherency of any of those interpretations of which criticism is suspicious, but most of us don't have the perspicacity of a Joseph Heller to formulate irony from contradiction.

Interpretivist: I object to the way interpretivism is being characterized here. You're assuming that we see our task as, value free description which we all know is impossible. I will admit that many, if not most, interpretivists are naturalists — people who model social science on natural science. And they take interpretivism to be social science, so they report what they do as though they have no presence in the field, as though they have no political views, as though they have no subjectivity. The product reads like Carlos Castaneda's (1973) sociological version of his M.A. thesis — two dimensional discourse. Let me hold up as a model de Tocqueville (1945) and his writing on America. He visited this country, not as a social scientist, but as a tourist; not a wife-three-kids-plus-instamatic tourist, but a literate, intelligent perceptive observer and commentator. He had a point of view, a presence, and he produced a masterful account of American life in the early 1800s.

Pluralist: Pluralism — that entire range of organizational theories — recognizes that all of the positions, whether they're interior or exterior, have strengths and weaknesses. I'm dissatisfied with functionalism but I'm also dissatisfied with interpretivism. Each approach creates a different world, and you have to treat them accordingly, always appreciating that something is missing from each. Combinations of approaches don't necessarily reinforce one another; in fact, if the multiple methods are grounded in different theories, once the method is employed the phenomenon is no longer the same. Convergence is illusion; there's no independent point of measurement, no independent point of reality against which to measure. Structural-functionalism holds that there is objective reality and one is trying to discover it. Interpretivism holds that reality is socially constructed and created. The two approaches are diametrically opposed.

Critic: Who is pluralism's audience, then? What are its motivating interests? Who benefits from such work? Do you assume any responsibility as consultant to teach your clients?

Pluralist: My major interest is in the development of theoretical/conceptual knowledge, so the academic audience is primary. But that does not mean that the organization can not use pertinent material. My responsibility is to lay out the premises of the perspectives. I've used traditional techniques — questionnaires and statistical analyses. But I've also examined the language of how employees talk about their work. I make the best case I can for the positions I take, and leave the choice there; that's where decisions are made anyway. I have several perspectives that make sense in particular situations, and my reasons for using those perspectives might differ from an organization's, but primarily I use a perspective to gain insight into the perspective itself as well as into how the organization functions.

Critic: If we were to characterize these three positions politically, interpretivism would be independent, pluralism would be liberal, and criticism would be leftist. Interpretivism is independent insofar as its theoretical interests identify its objects of study but don't identify with them. Interpretivism doesn't have member interest to play out; its focus is the double opposition of the independence/alienation and spectator/tourist dialectics.

Interpretivist: As a spectator, I'm independent insofar as I can and do avail myself of literature and understandings from the political right and the left.

Critic: But your objective is not necessarily to produce a politicized interpretation; you wouldn't necessarily be interested in examining the power-haves and the power-have-nots, and how they are managing their contradictions.

Interpretivist: It wouldn't be excluded necessarily, but it would not be something I would include necessarily.

Critic: I'm stuck with the implications of both pluralism and interpretivism. On the one hand, they're committed to both practical and discursive understanding; on the other hand, they are both ahistorical. If I were a manager, I'd be impatient with your professional pluralism and your liberal model of nondirective social therapy thinly disguised as consultation.

Pluralist: If the organization doesn't like my work, it won't use it; if I tell managers what they don't want to hear, they won't do it anyway. Upon laying out what is a sensible position and several points of view, I've met my responsibility. But I'm more researcher than consultant; and in the classroom, I lay out alternatives. The one I dislike most sometimes is the one students embrace, which gives me great pain, but that's what they're going to do anyway.

Interpretivist: Let me elaborate some of the implications developing in our discussion of interpretivism to this point. I don't like the "tourist" to characterize such work, because I don't know that you can ever escape the spouse, three kids, instamatic, flowered shirts, 10 days and eighteen stops typification. "Spectator" isn't exactly it, either, although it displays the facets of distanced appreciation. "Voyeur" is partially fitting, although it has pornographic connotations of anonymity. Watching videotapes of a family interacting is not only voyeuristic and spectatorial; we are touring through a moment of someone's life. One of the interests being served in my interpretivist work is my quest for experience. Interpretivism is born of the realities of the modern world—a stratified, fractured, fragmented world. I don't know much about how other people live, and I wonder about those lives. But my wonder is not simply intellectual curiosity. What I want to admit about this position for myself is something that may be unseemly from a liberal, professional, point of view. I don't write necessarily so as to serve society's best interests. Deep down, interpretivist research does something *for me.* It refines me and my sensibilities and makes me feel like I am making human contact. Such humanist/sensualist motivations don't have a very direct expression in pluralism or criticism. If one doesn't know how to read criticism, one doesn't experience much joy or wonderment. So if the phrase "spectator of the American scene" can be used in a respectful way—describing someone who sees with clarity and intellect—then what I want to do is to be a spectator of organizational life. But back to aesthetics for a moment. The crucial nature of participation is aesthetic. The social science tradition makes a dubious distinction between nonparticipant and participant observation, and that's not even the distinction worth making. Your presence in any kind of social situation makes you a participant; the generative question is whether one's participation includes an asethetic sensibility or not.

Critic: What audience does such aesthetically sensitive interpretivism serve? Whose aesthetic interests does it privilege?

Interpretivist: My interest is in accumulating world experience, not necessarily with a theoretical interest in increasing disciplinary knowledge. The presumption that draws me to interpretivism (i.e., that we inhabit a stratified, fragmented world) is the same presumption I have about the audience for my work. My audience also lives in a fragmented, stratified world. They don't know what this particular organization is like, or that particular business. The voice of interpretivism is much the same as the voice of the travel writers of the 19th century who were writing about places they had visited but the folks back home had not.

Pluralist: But don't you want to produce more than travelogue?

Interpretivist: Of course. That's why de Tocqueville (1945) is such a good example, because, however popular his book was in France, it was equally popular in America. The people he wrote about also found what he had to say worthwhile. That would be one criterion of the success of such a project.

Pluralist: Let me overstate some of the dissatisfaction I have with that position. Interpretivism doesn't sound like systematic study; it's simply an artful embellishment of the curious and interesting. You're more of a writer, a literary person who picks out something interesting and displays it aesthetically.

Interpretivist: That depends on your concept of systematicity. Agee's (1939), de Tocqueville's (1945), and Goffman's (1959) works are the result of systematic, rigorous, and thorough practices. They were not the results of mere flights of fanciful imagination. But it most certainly is not systematic in the sense that anybody can produce it equally well if they follow the technical instructions. I'm clearly not in favor of a standardized methods approach to quality. The produced document is what is available to people, and that's where the truth needs to be. It doesn't reside in the fact that I've spent the requisite number of hours interviewing the requisite numbers of people.

Pluralist: But training in such procedures and techniques may be an essential step in the development of skills necessary to produce the quality of work you're advocating. And such training must be systematic. Do you expect a student/apprentice who simply sidesteps the technical training ever to produce creativity or theoretically valuable work? Systematic, procedural and technical training may not be sufficient, but it is necessary for the production of the best work. If there is no systematicity, how am I to evaluate and assess it critically? What are the evaluative criteria for interpretivist discourse? How do I know you weren't hallucinating, or that you didn't simply fabricate your observations?

Interpretivist: How do I know your organizational survey report isn't fraudulent? I don't. I trust that you did not fabricate the data. We don't know the exact context of the experiment, the conditions which influence those supposedly replicable findings. Critical evaluation is really about two questions: the first addresses the basis of that trust in the objective world, and the second question addresses the worth or the value of the interpretation.

Pluralist: It's easier to identify the technical correctness of a piece of work than its aesthetic sensibility, and that's what specifiable methods allows us to do.

Interpretivist: But it's precisely all the emphasis on technical and procedural rigor that should arouse our suspicion of the social sciences. Technical competence has overtaken and now presupposes moral and theoretical concerns. Progress, as the argument goes, is acting on technical, but not necessarily moral or theoretical, possibility. The social sciences's most ironic flaw may be that the methods and procedures are followed so compulsively. It's done with such preoccupation with technical precision as to miss the point.

Pluralist: I don't want to overstate the case for systematic, explicit methods, but I think it's an issue because it takes us back to our concerns about the audience for interpretivism. Your audience is yourself; the experience gained is yours. But, if I don't know your methods, I don't know how to read your texts. Making your evaluative criteria explicit would instruct me in how to read the significance of what you write. With nothing to go on, I have to question the scholarly merit of what you produce.

Interpretivist: Being systematic is neither necessary nor sufficient for the production of quality interpretivist work. If by systematic you mean internal coherence, then keeping journals of observations is being systematic. But being systematic need not entail codification. The discourses of interpretivism and criticism are their own evidence of their own systematicity. Both method and product are the codes of language, rather than, say, mathematics or music. Interpretivism and criticism show their systematicity in their respective discourses. Why is being systematic so salient to pluralism?

Pluralist: The concern is that the research is thorough and that the limitations are spelled out. Interpretive research ought to be systematic to the extent that contradictory as well as complementary evidence surfaces. A researcher may find some things that are terribly interesting and develop those without seeing the exceptions. If the world is so fragmentary, perhaps interpretivist discourse ought to reflect that. What's to keep you from wandering off on tangents? What guides your inquiry?

Interpretivist: What's wrong with happening onto things that are interesting? Karl Weick (1983) refers to such work as confirmatory rather than falsificatory. I presume there is something—e.g., loose-coupling—that exists in the world and I explicate those insights.

Critic: Michael Herr's (1984) treatment of Viet Nam in *Dispatches* is a good examplar of interpretivist discourse systematically displaying its fragmentary structure of modern experience. Fragmented, stratified worlds are not unitary or univocal; organizing activity doesn't begin and end. Anthropomorphizing modern organizations in the form of heroic narratives does not resolve the contradictions productive of the fragmentations normalized by those narratives—e.g., Iacocca/Chrysler and the American consumer.

Interpretivist: It may not be the responsibility of interpretivism to specify its own evaluative criteria; it's the task of the critic to read new forms of discourse. How is organizational ethnography to be read most productively? That is one of the tasks for organizational criticism. We can't know the criteria for an emergent genre in advance.

Pluralist: What kind of generalizations does interpretivism make? What knowledge does interpretivism lay claim to?

Interpretivist: The knowledge claims of pluralism are in large measure methodological and procedural; the competence with which a study is executed, and its relationship to some theoretical knowledge, are pluralism's epistemological concerns. Pluralism's knowledge is theoretical. But, from an interpretivist point of view, knowledge is moral; interpretivism is making, not simply theoretical claims, but moral claims as well. One of the problems with pluralism crediting fiction as legitimate social science discourse is that fiction doesn't produce explicitly theoretical knowledge. William Goldings's (1954) *Lord of the Flies,* which is often used in organizational classes, might be more profitably read morally than theoretically. As it is used theoretically, discussion usually centers on who was the better leader, Ralph or Jack—or which style of leadership is better, laissez-faire or autocratic? But these discussions end up entangled in the complexity of the "life" of the novel. Unless you get to more profound *moral* complexities, you can't begin to untangle these questions. (e.g., What is the nature of man? What is the nature of sin?)

Critic: But such questions cannot be extracted from questions of organizing. The moral issues demonstrate themselves both diachronically and synchronically; temporality and morality are interpenetrated.

Pluralist: How do such moral generalizations articulate with theoretical knowledge? A generalization is something that tells me something beyond a single instance, but that "something beyond" is not necessarily theoretical knowledge.

Interpretivist: There are interpretivist researchers who don't see themselves producing moral knowledge. They see themselves producing academically grounded, theoretical knowledge. Larry Browning's (1978) article on grounded theory is not trying to say anything about the morality of organizational life. He is devising variables that sound much like what's in the literature. Under those circumstances it is fair to ask how good one's collection procedures were, or how biased they were. When concern is with moral knowledge, one can say that empirical truth is spelled with a small "t" and I'm working on something with a capital "T," so if I need to I'll dismiss your methodological considerations.

Critic: Let's try another tack. Try juxtaposing narrative structures—stories—and serial structures — lists — as ways of knowing. Science supposedly produces theories; literature supposedly produces narratives. Lists lead to theory, and narratives lead to myth. Consequently, theory is superior to narrative as epistemology. That is the moral force, in part, of what's behind the suspicion of literary discourse and the deference to theoretical discourse. We're trained as social scientists to assume that serial, theoretical knowledge is superior to narrative, practical knowledge.

Pluralist: So where does that position the critic? What do critics write? Do they write lists or narratives?

Critic: Marshall Berman's (1983) *All That is Solid Melts Into Air* makes the argument that our experience of modernism is a recurring experience dating at least as far back as Goethe's (1970) *Faust.* Berman rereads *Faust* and he rereads Dostoevsky's (1981) *Notes from Underground.* He reads the development of St. Petersburgh and the deconstruction of Brooklyn — different historical moments and different cities. Now I can produce an outline of Berman's book, and I can give you lists that constitute his arguments. But what gives that critical work its power is that it is animated narratively. The strength of what Berman's doing is how he writes. His narrative subsumes the lists, which is also true of powerful theory. As such, theory as narrative constitutes the explanation and the understanding of observations as list. Criticism is another way of reading our experience. If you remove the narrative from the data, you deflate the project.

Interpretivist: How would you critique interpretivism?

Critic: Without the particular texts, I can't do much but give you broad thematics: interpretivism tends to be ahistorical, apolitical, but insightful and usually well written.

Interpretivist: That's fair. That's what Pacanowsky (1983) was trying to do in his short story about the cop and his wife. Organizational life doesn't end when a cop leaves work. So the struggle is about more than what happens while the cop's on duty. In fact, the story's about what happens to him while he's off duty. It's about him and her, him and his job, her and his job. It's about stresses and tensions that are there and are managed on the surface, better or not so well every day, by being close to one another, by griping at one another, by soothing one another. A critic might attend instead to the policeman's role as an authority figure and the legitimacy or nonlegitimacy of that role with a community which, ironically, produces those very situations that arise for any police officer's social life.

Pluralist: Much of structural-functionalism presumes a "best" way of operating organizations and of improving them; an ideal model is presupposed. Interpretivism, on the other hand, presupposes a modernist, fragmented, segmented world. Is there any value in reintergrating this fragmentation? If life is inevitably and inherently fragmented, then much of structural-functionalism reads like so much idealism. Structural-functionalism contends that there are ways of picking up the fragmented stitches of modern American experience. Teaching, researching, and consulting are aimed at doing just that.

Critic: One might presume that fragmentation is the flip side of the organization/ fragmentation dialectic. The opposing argument is that most people's only experience of community is as members of those very organizations and institutions supposedly responsible for the fragmentation in the first place. Here's the scenario. Even in my alienation from my work, I am with familiar, if not desirable, coworkers in familiar, if not desirable, settings. When I am fired, phased out, laid off, or retired, that positionality dissolves. The house I find myself in isn't home in the sense of being a center of experience and practical consciousness. My kids are older, and I no longer have much in common with my spouse. I miss the office, the action, the community — even if oppressive and degrading much of the time — and, in my own house, there's no community. That's not supposed to be the way it works, and that crisis of work ethic ideology is disorienting for many. You're not going to do away with contradictions and paradoxes, so why not learn from them and transform them, recontextualize them, and accelerate them? In splitting contradictions and materializing paradoxes, the contingencies are read for what must be done.

Pluralist: Interpretivism presupposes that people are not rational; structural-functionalism assumes rationality and conscious behavior, but we all suspect that's not the way reality works. There is tension between what should be and what is: this is not the way the world works, but we are trying to make it work better. When a critic criticizes what is happening, what is that better way? What is your ideal position that you're working from? What are you working toward?

Critic: There is no ideal, final position or resolution. Social reality is inherently contradictory. I am working with the aim of more adequately theorizing practical and discursive consciousness. Places to look for such practices are in the contradictions which constitute the moral, ethical, legal, and mundane issues of everyday life. Thus, one aim of criticism is to formulate theory to live life by.

Pluralist: Do you go beyond writing? Do you do anything that has material consequences?

Critic: Producing discourse is a material practice. Writing is real; theory is real, even if not valid at times. Criticism need not distinguish between theory and practice. To see theory and practice as independent of one another, and to argue that what we need to do to generate theory is get hands-on experience in the organization, is to make a serious mistake. Practice is senseless without theory. Theory interpenetrates practical consciousness, producing discursive consciousness. If the theory is ineffectual, the practices will be too.

Interpretivist: How can we identify a good piece of critical scholarship? How can we judge it? What do we look for?

Critic: Three criteria might be first, the extent to which a piece of criticism provides an alternative reading or interpretation—another way of seeing. The second is the extent to which a critical work elucidates our understanding about the animating contradictions of organizational dynamics. The third is the extent to which the critique achieves irony.

Interpretivist: If irony is what you are striving for, doesn't that undercut desire for change? Isn't irony merely a passive appreciation of contradiction?

Critic: The critical distance produced by irony is not synonymous with either acceptance or passivity. A certain amount of text (i.e., layered, sedimented practices) is required to get sufficient insight to enable an ironic response. The project is predicated on the inevitability of contradiction. The task is to locate that ironic position, whether as a theorist, critic, consultant, or therapist. Once the absurdity and irony of one's practices materialize, it is increasingly difficult—so goes the argument—to continue practicing them. The hidden contradictions of practical consciousness have become the objects of discursive consciousness. You now appropriate experience differently.

Interpretivist: But if the extreme rationality that Heller ridicules in *Catch-22* (1955) is exposed, wouldn't the powers-that-be maintain that insufficient rationality has been achieved; more is needed.

Critic: Change,given that it is inevitable, ought to be made a matter of discursive consciousness as much as possible. It's most difficult to see options when one is a true and unquestioning believer, a native, a member, when you're so in the middle of things that all you can see are particulars. Criticism is a set of discursive practices for producing perspective and difference from practical consciousness. Irony is one of its many forms. The more pervasive the bureaucratization, the more necessary it is to demonstrate its absurdity, structural cruelty, and lethal naivete. Contemporary organization theory is not a very interesting, engaging, or useful discourse. One commitment of criticism, then, is to produce dialectical discourse, discourse which continues to confront itself and examine itself, turning itself on its ear. Those are the sorts of objectives that might motivate organizational criticism.

Pluralist: You mentioned that, sometimes, people are so close to particularities they can't comprehend the structurations. How close does a critic get? Do you value getting into the organizational trenches?

Critic: Historically grounded criticism is necessary, which means that it has to be concrete and particular. The contradictions unearthed aren't concocted, independent of material practice. Members can see and recognize them for what they are; i.e., their own experience. Members might not like such criticism. It might make them uncomfortable, it might even "liberate" them, but it must be concrete and particular to even have such possibilities. If the concrete particulars of the contradictions aren't the objects of criticism, then it's just so much vacuous theorization.

Pluralist: If the world is fragmented and we have to cope with that fragmentation, then we have to cope with contradiction and incongruity. Reading Heller's *Catch-22* (1955), to continue with that example, one could drawn an overall conclusion that war's insane, but all of the contradictions aren't, in any sense, out of place because they constitute and sustain that very system. There are irrational behaviors we know to be irrational behaviors yet necessary in some sense. Irrational behaviors serve certain functions and sometimes they seem to be the best alternatives.

Critic: A critic might call those functions ideology or its quotidian corollary—common sense—which enables its subjects to not notice contradictions. A critic exposes contradictory practices demonstrating how ideology normalizes faults in the system. Those contradictions need explicating, and it's not necessarily in the best interests of members or consultants do do so.

Interpretivist: You said earlier that you can't expect members of a system to transform their consciousness; that change is initiated from the outside. If a member were to do it, the action would be treason or unpardonable naivete or schizophrenia, and such a subject would in some way be disempowered. I don't believe it. Organizations and organizational members are not so cut off from their reflexes.

Critic: When you're living life and doing work, it's difficult to be reflexive systematically. One of Bateson's (1972) metalogues is relevant here. It's his two levels of change involved in deutero-learning (i.e., learning to learn). First-order change is change within a system, and second-order change is a transformation of a system—shifting gears rather than increasing acceleration to go faster. One has an accelerator function and a transmission function, and one can't get from first to second gear by accelerating. An outside, foreign logic is necessary. The question is what's the nature of the intervention? A theory of practice and discursive consciousness are essential to informed answers.

Pluralist: In *Process Consultation,* Schein (1969) sets up several relationships between the outside person and the organization. One is the doctor/patient relationship, where the outsider offers a cure for organizational problems. Another relationship emphasizes the combined efforts of outsider and organization, so that the problem areas can be identified in a collaborative fashion. Solutions also become a negotiated effort. I would align my position with the collaborative relationship. My expertise should be in generating alternatives rather than offering cures. I ought to work myself out of a job if I'm successful. When the organization can't figure out what I'm doing there, because now they're doing it themselves, there's no reason for me to be there and the members reappropriate their world. That's part of the desired change, to have them pay attention to what they are doing, appropriate those practices, change, and get on with things.

Interpretivist: None of these discourses stand alone and apart from the others, so the important question is whether a pluralist or a critic or an interpretivist can read the other accounts. Probably a critic is most able to read and generate productive discourse from an interpretivist account. Most interpretivists, just by the nature of what they're doing, aren't going to work off somebody else's work as substance; they may work off somebody else's work as style or form, in the way that very few fiction writers ever reference any other fiction explicitly.

Critic: For a critic, discourse is method; for a pluralism, method is likely to be a technique or procedure for evaluating what counts as data. The writing is simply reportage. If you want your work in the professional journals, you know how to write and what the limits are. Interpretivists—Castaneda (1973), for example—destroy their work by following conventional academic criteria. The structuration of Castaneda's discourse is, in fact, his method. It's through reading of his writing that one comes to comprehend the culture he's displaying. This is a similar argument I made earlier for systematicity: writing has a very different status in the three schools of thought we're characterizing here. What counts as theory is also different for the three schools of thought.

Interpretivist: All of our positions, in reality, can and do inform one another, and can and do undermine one another, but for very different reasons.

REFERENCES

Agee, J. (1939). *Let us now praise famous men.* New York: Ballantine.

Bateson, G. (1972). *Steps to an ecology of mind.* New York: Ballantine.

Bell, D. (1973). *The coming of post-industrial society.* New York: Basic Books.

Bell, D. (1976). *The cultural contradictions of capitalism.* New York: Basic Books.

Berman, M. (1983). *All that is solid melts into air.* New York: Simon & Schuster, 1982.

Browning, L. (1978). A grounded organizational communication theory derived from qualitative data. *Communication Monographs, 45,* 93–109.

Buck-Morss, S. (1977). *The origin of negative dialectics.* New York: The Tree Press.

Castaneda, C. (1973). *Journey to Ixtlan.* New York: Touchstone.

Churchman, C. W. (1971). *The design of inquiring systems.* New York: Basic Books.

Dostoevsky, F. (1981). *Notes from underground.* New York: Bantam.

Faules, D. F. (1982). The use of multi-methods in the organizational setting. *Western Journal of Speech Communication, 46,* 150–161.

Frost, P. J., Moore, L. F., Louis, M. R., Lundberg, C. C., & Martin, J. (1985). *Organizational culture.* Beverly Hills, CA: Sage.

Geertz, C. (1973). *The interpretation of cultures.* New York: Basic Books.

Goethe, J. (1970). *Faust.* Toronto, Canada: University of Toronto Press.

Goffman, E. (1959). *The presentation of self in everyday life.* Garden City, New York: Doubleday Anchor.

Golding, W. (1954). *Lord of the flies.* New York: Putnam.

Habermas, J. (1971). *Knowledge and human interests* (J. Shapiro, Trans.). Boston, MA: Beacon Press.

Habermas, J. (1973). *Theory and practice* (J. Viertel, Trans.). Boston, MA: Beacon Press.

Heller, J. (1955). *Catch-22.* New York: Dell.

Herr, M. (1984). *Dispatches.* New York: Avon.

Jacoby, H. (1976). *The bureaucratization of the world* (E. Kanes, Trans.). Berkeley, CA: University of California Press.

Lincoln, Y. S. (Ed.). (1985). *Organizational theory and inquiry: The paradigm revolution.* Beverly Hills, CA: Sage.

Lyotard, J. T. (1984). *The postmodern condition: A report on knowledge* G. B. Bennington & B. Massumi (Trans.).

Marcuse, H. (1941). *Reason and revolution: Hegel and the rise of social theory.* New York: Oxford University Press.

Marx, K. (1964). *Economic and philosophic manuscripts of 1844* (D. J. Struik, Ed., M. Milligan, Trans.). New York: International Publishers.

Marx, K. (1967). *Capital* (S. Moore & E. Aveling, Trans.). New York: International Publishers.

Marx, K. (1973). *Grundrisse: Foundations of the critique of political economy* (M. Nicolaus, Trans.). New York: Vintage Books.

Mason, R. O., & Mitroff, I. I. (1981). *Challenging strategic planning assumptions.* New York: John Wiley.

Mitroff, I. I., & Kilmann, R. H. (1978). *Methodological approaches to social science.* San Francisco, CA: Jossey-Bass.

Morgan, G. (Ed.). (1983). *Beyond method: Strategies for social research.* Beverly Hills, CA: Sage.

Pacanowsky, M. (1983). A small town cop. In L. L. Putnam & M. E. Pacanowsky (Eds.), *Communication and organizations: An interpretive approach* (pp. 261–282). Beverly Hills, CA: Sage.

Putnam, L. L., & Pacanowsky, M. E. (Eds.). (1983). *Communication and organizations: An interpretive approach.* Beverly Hills, CA: Sage.

Rodgers, D. T. (1978). *The work ethic in industrial America.* Chicago, IL: University of Chicago Press.

Schein, E. (1969). *Process consultation.* Reading, MA: Addison-Wesley.

Shorris, E. (1981). *Scenes from corporate life.* New York: Penguin.

Strine, M. S., & Pacanowsky, M. E. (1985). How to read interpretive accounts of organizational life: Narrative bases of textual authority. *Southern Speech Communication Journal, 50,* 283–297.

Tocqueville, A. de. (1945). *Democracy in America.* New York: Vintage.

Tompkins, P., & Cheney, G. (1985). Communication and unobtrusive control in contemporary organizations. In R. D. McPhee & P. K. Tompkins (Eds.), *Organizational communication: Traditional themes and new directions* (pp. 179–210). Beverly Hills, CA: Sage.

Weick, K. (1983). Organizational communication: Toward a research agenda. In L. L. Putnam & M. E. Pacanowsky (Eds.), *Communication and organizations* (pp. 13–29). Beverly Hills, CA: Sage.

Chapter 4

The Rules Perspective on Organizational Communication Research

Dr. Donald P. Cushman

SUNY-Albany
Albany, NY

Dr. Sarah S. King

Central Connecticut State University
New Britain, CT

Dr. Ted Smith III

University of Virginia
Charlottesville, VA

ABSTRACT

Rules theories of organizational communication are explored in four stages. First, a review is undertaken of various philosophical, theoretic, and operational rules perspectives on human communication processes. Second, a review is conducted of the various applications and extensions of these rules theories into the organizational communication arena. Third, an evaluation of the strengths and limitations of these applications and extensions is provided. Finally, a case study is provided of the rules employed by IBM in dealing with investors, workers and consumers in an attempt to respond to the critiques provided of rules research in organizational communication.

Any attempt to discriminate communication from other human activities is confronted with at least two significant issues. *First,* there must be some agreement regarding what will constitute the basic unit of analysis in discussing human communication processes. *Second,* such a unit of analysis should suggest basic distinctions which will provide a method for explaining, predicting and controlling a wide range of communication phenomena. In the September 1972 issue of the *Journal of Communication,* Donald P. Cushman and Gordon C. Whiting argued that a concerted effort to make communication rules an explicit focus of study will be fruitful for developing communication theory: The fruitfulness will take the form of pointing out distinctions to be employed in research, and the means whereby past research can be integrated into a more comprehensive whole. (Cushman & Whiting, 1972, p. 218)

It will be the purpose of this essay to explore in some detail the nature of this claim and its utility for studying organizational communication. In so doing, we will (a) examine the rationale for such a claim, (b) explore the philosophic and theoretic development of the rules perspective, (c) review the research contributions of organizational communication scholars employing a rules perspective, and (d) present an original case study of the IBM Corporation employing one approach to rules research.

THE RATIONALE FOR A RULES PERSPECTIVE ON ORGANIZATIONAL COMMUNICATION

In order to establish the claim that human communication can fruitfully be viewed as a class of human activity whose significance is largely dependent upon the existence of certain consensually shared rules, four propositions have been argued. *First,* coordinated behavior is characteristic of a wide variety of human activity. *Second,* the transfer of symbolic information facilitates coordinated behavior. *Third,* the transfer of symbolic information requires the interaction of sources, messages, and receivers guided and governed by rules. *Fourth,* communication rules form general and specific patterns which provide grounding for the scientific explanation and prediction of communication behavior (Cushman & Whiting, 1972). While the first two propositions are fairly obvious, the latter two require elaboration.

A.　The Transfer of Symbolic Information Requires the Interaction of Sources, Messages, and Receivers Guided and Governed by Rules

Coordination tasks are a class of behaviors where two or more actors engage in the joint determination of outcomes. In such situations, each actor has to select from a group of alternative behaviors by considering the expectations of other actors. Only in fitting together their joint action can they perform their coordination task. The most common manner of coordination is for two actors to employ a language to set up common expectations. However, language can serve the function of coordinating human behavior only if its meanings are patterned in some common manner. Norms or rules are thus established which function as criteria for choice among alternative meanings and uses of symbolic patterns. Communication is said to have taken place when information has successfully been transmitted from one participant to another. Successful communication thus of necessity requires rules or criteria for choice in establishing common expectations.

The basic unit of analysis in such a conceptualization of communication is not a rule, rather it is a system of rules or a "standardized usage." Our point is that

> there exist systems of rule governed meaning associations which are relatively persistent because the participants engaged in some task have found that system particularly useful for coordinating their activities in regard to that task. We shall term such a system of appropriate choice among alternative interpersonal meanings as standardized usage. (Cushman & Whiting, 1972, p. 224)

The decision to take a standardized usage as our basic unit of analysis requires that we determine: (a) the functions, purposes, or goals which are recurrently employed to coordinate human behavior; and (b) the systems of standardized content and procedural rules which develop to coordinate behavior in regard to these goals.

Several implications are drawn from this analysis. *Communication is viewed as the transfer of symbolic information. The function of human communication is the regulation of consensus in order to coordinate human behavior. The structure of human communication is comprised of the code and network rules involved in regulating consensus. The process of human communication is the functioning and adaptation of the rules involved in regulating consensus.* The basic unit of analysis in such a conceptualization of the communication process is a standardized usage.

Cushman and Florence (1974) and again Cushman and Craig (1976) attempted to delineate, at their most general level, the function which all individuals must perform and for which there must of necessity be a standardized usage. *Mass communication* serves to coordinate human activity in regard to social and cultural institutions. The standardized usage involved is employed by all persons participating in society. The content and procedural rules employed provide information about social institutions and prescribe the communication patterns for social roles. The structural characteristics of statements within a mass communication message are of the form: "You (in the generic sense of all individuals within a culture) may vote for president on the 4th day of November," or "You may obtain gasoline at 5th and Oak." In each case, information which all members of a culture must have to perform their normal functions is provided. The subject or object of such a statement is the generic "you," and the remainder is information about cultural institutions or roles.

Organizational communication has as its principal function the coordination of human activity in regard to production. The standardized usage is employed by all persons who contribute to the production in an organization. The content and procedural rules employed provide information about objects of production and prescribe the communication patterns for organizational roles. The structural characteristics of statements within an organizational communication message are of the form: "X is a necessary component in the production of Y," or "Mr. Mitchell will be supervising this operation." In each case, information necessary to organizational productivity is provided. The subject or object of such a statement is a particular production element or organizational role, and the remainder is information about the prescribed course of action with regard to that object or role.

Interpersonal communication has as its principal goal the coordination of human activity in regard to the development, presentation, and validation of individual self-concepts. If an individual's self-concept is viewed as the information he or she has regarding his or her relationship to objects or others, then the development, presentation, and validation of an individual's self-concept will take the form of descriptions, assertions, and denials regarding an individual's relationship to objects or others. The standardized usage employed is person specific. The content and procedural rules employed provide information regarding an individual relationship to objects or persons, and prescribe the communication patterns about interpersonal rules. The structural characteristics of a statement within an interpersonal communication message are of the form: "I am a teacher," or "You are a good student." In each case, the subject or object of such a statement is the personal form of "you," and the remainder of the statement describes, asserts, or denies the relationship between that person and some particular physical or social object or person.

The stratification of communication by systems levels has several important implications. To begin with, each systems level has its own mechanism for generating communication regularities. Such regularities or standardized usages consist of the dynamic networks of partial and complete consensus which organize and direct behavior. A standardized usage is learned through a process of role-taking. If role-taking is the central mechanism for the learning of content and procedural rules at each systems level, then it ought to be possible to measure an individual's mastery of a standardized usage either by asking the individual what he or she is expected to do or by reports of individuals who observe his or her use of the standardized usage. Such a measure, along with knowledge of the generative mechanism, should allow us to develop a theory of communication for that level. A theory at one systems level will not be in competition with a theory at another level, because they will presuppose different generative mechanisms and different levels of complexity. While researchers may for a given purpose of inquiry wish to develop a theory at one or more of the systems levels, any complete theory of communication must be rich enough to account for all the systems levels without blurring the difference between each level.

B.   Communication Rules Form Patterns Which Provide a Basis for Explanation

Explanation in the physical and behavioral sciences alike functions to relate a phenomenon to a more general pattern of relationships whose intelligibility can be presumed. Explaining a given unit of communicative behavior as undertaken to reduce dissonance, or as appropriate to a forensic occasion, resembles explaining the roll of a ball down an inclined plane by reference to gravity. In each case, a coherent pattern of activity is explained by placing it within a general set of relationships whose intelligibility can be presumed. However, in the explanation of behavior where information is symbolically coded, a fundamental distinction must be respected, namely the distinction between rule-conforming and law-governed phenomena. As Toulmin writes:

> The essential mark of rule-conforming behavior lies in the normative force of relevant rules. An agent who recognizes that he is deviating from a rule acknowledges (at any rate prima facie) a claim on him to correct his behavior. . . . By contrast, if we consider natural phenomena of a purely law-governed kind, no such distinction makes sense. (Toulmin, 1974, p. 191).

Thus, the resemblance between physical and communication explanations is limited. The explanation of human action and its significance will not be in terms of law-like idealizations, but rather in terms of patterns of cultural choice discovered in existential settings. When a physical phenomenon is explained, we do so in terms of patterns of understanding which we have created, not discovered, to account for the natural, physical course of events. How we construct our theories involves an arbitrary decision on our part.

> This is the force of characterizing the physicist's "paradigms" or "self-explanatory patterns," as ideals of natural order, and it reflects the Platonist element in the ancestry of mathematical physics. (Toulmin, 1974, p. 211).

On the other hand, explanation of communication behavior functions in an Aristotelian manner.

> We do not impose patterns or ideal forms on human behavior, as instruments within an intellectual analysis. Rather we recognize such general patterns as operative factors in human behavior as "intelligible" in an infant, an adolescent, a normal adult, or a moron, be-

cause we find them manifested generally, as expressions of different drives or ambitions, cultural habits or intellectual skills; and then explain particular actions by relating them to such recognized modes of behavior. (Toulmin, 1974, p. 212).

In explanations of communication behavior, our general self-explanatory behavioral patterns (e.g., dissonance theory, forensic rhetoric) are neither as universal nor as deterministic as the paradigms in the physical sciences. When we explain communication behaviors, patterns of action that are "natural and intelligible" in our cultural milieu or context may be unnatural and incomprehensible in another. In communication explanations, the modes of natural intelligible behavior to which we appeal are to a significant extent relative to particular standardized usages. The predictive power of such explanations in a given situation depends on our skill in discovering and stating the standardized usage, and upon the degree of consensus that communicating participants in the situation have regarding the appropriate communication rules, i.e., the degree to which usage is indeed standardized.

In examining the rationale for a rules approach in the study of human communication, we have tried to explicate two propositions: (a) that the interchange of information involves a transaction among symbol-using participants with the understanding which results being guided and governed by communication rules; and (b) that communication rules form general and specific patterns which provide the basis for a scientific explanation and prediction of communication behavior. In this partial discussion of these two propositions, we have attempted to indicate that rules researchers believe that communication rules should become a controlling and fundamental concern for developing Communication Theory.

THE PHILOSOPHIC AND THEORETIC DEVELOPMENT OF A RULES PERSPECTIVE

The philosophic and theoretic roots of a rules perspective on human communication processes can be found in the action theory tradition of human behavior. The action theory tradition centers on a conception of the human being as a generative force in nature, as an agent capable of intentionally transferring meaning to another through a rule-governed symbol system in order to achieve coordination in regard to some goal. In the next few pages we shall examine: (a) the conceptual antecedents of this tradition, (b) the diversity of philosophic positions on human action, (c) explanations and justifications of human action, and (d) the diversity of theoretic positions linking human action to communication rules.

A. Conceptual Antecedents to the Action Theory Tradition

The conceptual antecedents of this tradition are found in the works of Immanuel Kant and Max Weber. Following in a Kantian tradition, action theorists argue for a fundamental epistemological and metaphysical distinction between two types of causation: *motions* and *actions*. Motions can be considered to exhibit lawful uniformity, the laws being universal, invariant and not spatio-temporally bound. Actions, or the initiation of events by an agent, are intentional, situational, and involve an agent attempting to bring about some end in view. In order to understand Kant's analysis of actions or agent causation, we must examine his view that human perception and thought must be seen as activities human beings perform, things they do in accordance with a rule. To view human experience as the passive reception of stimuli is, for Kant, to misunderstand perception. To perceive something is to construct a spatio-temporal object from incoming stimuli on the basis of rules. Similarly, to view thought as the passive recording of sequences of objects is to misunderstand human thought. Thinking is the ordering of ideas on the basis of rules. Since experience is not given to us but is prescribed by us in accordance with the rules we apply to it, what we as agents know are things as they appear to us, never things in themselves. If we are to understand how and why agents respond to their environment as they do, we must explore the rules for organizing stimuli which an agent employs.

Kant's views on agent causality are closely associated with the exercise of will, or the process of practical reasoning. Human beings have interests which can be captured by rules. Human beings guide their perceptions, thoughts, and behavior in accordance with such rules. When human perception, thought, and behavior proceed in this manner, the agent acts from the mere conception of a rule, human interest, rather than being blindly pushed by the forces in his or her environment. Agent causality on this account is mediated by meanings, by considerations arising from an agent's understanding of the divergent interests which can pattern perception, thought, and behavior. Reason is considered practical in a sense different from Aristotle (Modrack, 1976); when an agent decides what should be done in light of the situation confronting him or her and his or her interests in that situation. Practical reasoning is thus willed, or undertaken intentionally with some end in view, some knowledge of what an agent is aiming at and why (Kant, 1929).

In summary, Kant's analysis has four important implications for action theory: (a) two types of causality are distinguished: that which governs *motions,* the uniform concomitance in nature, and that which governs *actions,* with agents as initiators of regularities in nature; (b) human perception, thought, and behavior are activities or things done in accordance with rules; (c) rules thus function as criteria for choice among alternative intentional constructions of experience; and (d) human actions are an exercise in practical reasoning, with behavior willed through the application of rules to situations with some knowledge of what an agent is aming at and why.

Following in the tradition of Weber, action theorists argue that at least one class of human actions, interactive behaviors, fall within the purview of social actions or things human beings do in accordance with consensually shared or public rules. Weber is consistent with Kant in maintaining that the term "action" refers to that class of human behaviors which is based on an agent's subjective meanings or intentions. According to Weber, actions are to be considered *"social"* insofar as the "subjective meanings attached to a situation by an agent attempt to take account of the behaviors of other agents" (Weber, 1968, p. 119). The term *"social relations"* is employed to denote the activities of plurality of agents, insofar as "in its meaningful content, the actions of each take account of others and is oriented in these terms" (Weber, 1968, p. 118). Social action, in this definition, involves action conditioned by an agent's attempt to attach significance to other agents' intentional behaviors. A social relationship invokes a reciprocal subjective awareness on the part of each agent as a basis for interpersonal orientation. *Verstehen* is the term Weber employs to designate an agent's subjective awareness or interpretive understanding.

Weber distinguishes between two types of understanding. *Aktuelles Verstehen* is translated as "direct observational understanding," or the sense of identity of an act, such as chopping wood, speaking in public, or driving a car. *Erklarendes Verstehen* is translated as "explanatory understanding," or the intention of an act, such as chopping wood to earn money, public speaking in order to get elected to Congress, or driving a car to work. Observational understanding allows us to grasp the conventional meaning of an act and is required in order to locate and perceive patterns of like action. Explanatory understanding allows us to grasp culturally typical motivational contexts within which such activities occur. It follows that, in order to identify an action as social, an observer must not only interpret the discernable patterns of behavior manifested by an agent, but must also discover the culturally typical purpose or intentions of an agent. That an agent has such a set of conceptions implies that he or she understands a set of conventions shared by a social group, by virtue of which meanings are attached to the activities of other agents. One common manner in which such a set of conventions is shared depends on an agent belonging to a community whose language includes the appropriate conventions or concepts. Language is one social institution for shared conventional interpretations of an agent's subjective meanings (Weber, 1968).

In summary, Weber's analysis has three important implications for action theory — (a) human actions are divided into two classes: *personal actions,* which involve person specific patterns of intentions, and *social actions,* which are conventional, shared and culturally typical; (b) culturally typical conventions are of two types: *Aktuelles Verstehen,* or a direct observational understanding of the identity of an act, and *Klarendes Verstehen,* or an explanatory understanding of the cultural intentions which motivate an act; and (c) language is one social institution for sharing conventional interpretations of agent's meanings.

B. The Diversity of Philosophic Positions on Human Action

The development of philosophic positions in action theory center on the work of various scholars in analytic philosophy, linguistics, sociology, and communication. Such theorists grant prima facie the distinction between actions and motions, and set about analyzing the nature of human action, and the manner in which explanations and justifications of human actions function and the task of locating adequate conceptualizations of these concepts and processes has occupied the attention of various scholars for over five decades (Fay & Moon, 1977). The positions advanced, analyses provided, and refutations undertaken would fill many volumes, and cannot be reproduced here in their full richness. However, it is possible in this brief survey to sample the flavor of the central controversies while arraying the appropriate references.

Brian Fay and Donald Moon begin our analysis by providing a more detailed distinction between actions and motions:

> According to this distinction, actions differ from mere movements in that they are intentional and rule-governed: they are performed in order to achieve a particular purpose, and in conformity to some rules. These purposes and rules constitute what we shall call the "semantic dimension" of human behaviouùr — its symbolic or expressive aspect. An action, then, is not simply a physical occurrence, but has a certain intentional content which specifies what sort of an action it is, and which can be grasped only in terms of the system of meanings in which the action is performed. A given movement counts as a vote, a signal, a salute or an attempt to reach something, only against the background of a set of applicable rules and conventions, and the purposes of the actor involved. (Fay & Moon, 1977, p. 210)

Next, we shall indicate the features of this conceptualization which are common to all theories of action, and those which are in dispute. A consensus seems to exist that to attribute or ascribe the quality of action to a human behavior is to claim that some agent is the author, or cause, of what is brought about (MacMurray, 1938; Meldon, 1956; MacIntyre, 1962; Anscombe, 1957; Hampshire, 1965; Grice, 1957; R. Taylor, 1960; Davidson, 1963; C. Taylor, 1964; Chisholm, 1964; Yolton, 1966; Sellars, 1966; Stoutland, 1976; Toulmin, 1969; Von Wright, 1971). Beyond this claim, little consensus remains. Let us sample the breadth of this diversity.

(1) **Philosophy of Agency.** Agency theorists argue that many objects have certain powers. Acid has the power to dissolve metal, magnets to attract iron, and agents to do things or attempt to bring about things. When we try to explicate the notion of my bringing something about, we may conclude, as do R. Taylor and Chisholm, that, if an agent brings about the neural events which in turn cause the muscular activity of his or her body, and these neural events were not caused by events other than those initiated by the agent, then and only then do we have an action. Agent causation is thus explained in terms of (a) direct causation by an agent, plus (b) ordinary causation by events. If "producing" or "bringing about" is the basic sense of cause employed in action, then there is no possible way of further explicating these terms. Reference to the purposes, intentions, wants, and beliefs of an agent are inappropriate. (R. Taylor, 1966; Chisholm, 1970).

Several attacks have been lodged against the theory of agency. Goldman attacks this position by asking, "How are we to distinguish the absence of causation from causation by an agent?" (Goldman, 1970, p. 84). Goldman's point is that a chain of events may occur following upon an agent's actions where we find no event which caused the chain. In such cases, agency theory provides no way of separating accidental concurrence from agent causation. Advocates of agency theory respond by suggesting that agents are directly aware of when they cause something to happen (Anscombe, 1957, p. 68). However, we may well wonder about the veracity of the direct awareness of agent causation, given the number and range of events claimed to have been brought about which later have been found to have other causes. Stephen Toulmin and George H. Von Wright extend Goldman's analysis by pointing out that, unlike the powers of zinc and magnets, human actions may be exercised on occasion automatically or habitually, on other occasions deliberately, and on still other occasions not be employed at all. In addition, human actions are acquired through some combination of maturation, learning, and opportunity to exercise the powers. The theory of agency is thus defective, in that it fails to provide an explanation of human powers in such a manner as to allow an understanding of these processes (Toulmin, 1969, p. 75–87; Von Wright, 1976, p. 419–430).

(2) **Mental Causation Philosophy.** Such theorists argue that having a reason is a necessary and sufficient condition for an agent causing the appropriate neural and muscular events involved in an action. The concept "reason" as employed by mental causation theorists has a technical meaning which is somewhat removed from its traditional signification in our discipline. Donald Davidson and Alvin Goldman explicate the concept "reason" in terms of an agent's want, desires, or "pro-attitudes" to obtain a given end, and an agent's beliefs that he or she has the requisite knowledge, skill, and opportunity to bring about the end in view. Reasons on this account are viewed as psychological states or motives for action. Mental causation theorists argue that the necessary and sufficient condition for an agent performing an intentional action are the agent's behavior which brought about the results of the act, that there is some end the agent *wanted* and which he or she *believes* his or her behavior will bring about, and that these wants and beliefs caused the behavior. Mental causation is thus explained in terms of (a) psychological causation and (b) the ordinary cau-

sation by events (Davidson, 1963; Goldman, 1970). There are several standard objects against such theories: (a) there are intentional actions not accompanied by such mental events; (b) there are intentional actions which are habitual and thus may, on one occasion, have such antecedents, and on others not have such antecedents; (c) there are agents who have such antecedents but who fail to act. Goldman responds to the first of these objections by pointing out that the concepts, wants, and beliefs are the defining characteristics of an intention in mental causation theory; therefore, without such mental states, you do not have an intention. However, Goldman admits that the concept of "wants" must be interpreted in a very broad sense to include 'fleeting wants — wants that rise to mind suddenly and fade away just as quickly" (Goldman, 1970, p. 49). Harre and Secord (1972) provide one answer to the claim that habitual actions at one time involve mental antecedents and at others do not. They suggest that even habitual actions are corrected by an agent when they fall in error, and that the monitoring of such an error presupposes the mental antecedent of an appropriate action (Harre & Secord, 1972, chapt. 1). Finally, Donald Gustafson (1975) replies to the claim that agents have such mental antecedents but fail to act by distinguishing the range of issues which must be resolved before "wants" or "pro-attitudes" and beliefs technically qualify as an intention, mental cause, or reason for acting. Such a reason must include that someone intended that he or she could intentionally do something in a particular manner, for a particular purpose, to a particular object at a particular time, and believes that he or she has the skill, knowledge, and opportunity to do so. Mental causation theorists maintain that, when an agent's wants, pro-attitudes, and beliefs meet this technical definition of intention, they necessitate an action. Those who claim agents have intentions accompanied by mental states, but fail to act, do not employ the terms "reason" or "mental acts" in this technical sense (Gustafson, 1975). It is important to distinguish this technical sense of "reason" (reason as cause) from those considerations which when accompanied by deliberation *incline* one to act (reason as inclination).

(3) **Intentional Philosophy.** Intentional theorists reacted against mental causation theory by arguing that decomposing intentional behavior into the basic elements of wants, pro-attitudes, beliefs, and causality is an attempt to explicate the concept of intentional action by eliminating it in favor of psychological states plus natural causation. Intentional theorists argue that it is intentionality that is basic to action, and it is the explication of this concept, not its elimination, which will yield a theory of action (Stoutland, 1976, p. 297).

Von Wright (1976) argues that an intention consists of an agent aiming at a result plus the agent's opinion of what is required for the intention to become effective. The relationship between an agent's intentions and behavior is neither causal nor logical; rather, it is practical. It is an agent's *understanding* of the aim, and the agent's *understanding* of what is required for the intention to become effective, which generate the behavioral sequence. This understanding creates the practical force which motivates the action. An agent's intentions or understanding of ends and means for obtaining them is influenced by four factors. First, factors *internal* to an agent, such as wants, attitudes, and beliefs, *may* influence intention formation. Such internal influences are neither causal nor logical in nature. They are conceptual. Second, factors *external* to an agent, such as duties and obligations, *may* exert an influence on intention formation. Such external influences are neither causal nor logical; rather, they exert normative pressure on an agent's intention formation. In addition, *abilities* and *opportunities* influence in a negative manner the domain or range of a human being's freedom to act (Von Wright, 1976).

Three significant attacks have been advanced against intentional theory: (a) the distinction between intentions and causes is circular, (b) the concept of practical force is obscure, and (c) the theory is so imprecise as to be untestable (Von Wright, 1976, p. 371–413). Von Wright responds to the first of these objections by arguing that intentions and causes are grounded in two different types of counter-factual conditionals and, as such, cannot be circular (Von Wright, 1976, p. 337). Intentional theorists respond to the second objection by aguing that practical force consists in an agent's intention to achieve a goal and the understanding of what an agent considers necessary for achieving a goal. Next they argue that an agent's intention to locate the presence of causal forces in nature is just such a goal, and that the understanding of how to construct an experimental manipulation allowing for proof of the existence of such causal forces is the result of practical force. Thus, practical force is not only not obscure, it is basic to knowledge of causal relationships (Von Wright, 1971, p. 72). Von Wright responds to the third attack by indicating that practical relationships, or the relationship between an intention and a behavior, are *predictive* without being *causal,* and that both of these claims are objectively verifiable (Von Wright, 1976, p. 475).

(4) **Contextual Philosophy.** Contextual theorists argue that there is nothing which constitutes an action as distinct from a motion, apart from its recognition as an appropriate social response to a context. A. I. Meldon argues that we are agents who participate in an ongoing social system, while pursuing our own goals. It is hopeless to attempt to explain the necessary and sufficient conditions for the infinite variety of such acts. However, as part of our socialization, we have all learned to recognize our own and others' behaviors as actions or behavior in accordance with customary patterns of behavior. This recognition makes possible interaction with others as well as moral assessments. There is nothing which constitutes an action as distinct from a motion apart from this context (Meldon, 1961). John Yolton argues that contextual theory is not a theory at all, rather it merely describes behavioral regularities in culturally relevant terms (Yolton, 1966, p. 17).

What then, has our rather brief analysis regarding the nature of human action revealed? Several conclusions suggest themselves. First, a consensus seems to exist that to attribute or ascribe action to a human behavior is to claim that some agent is the author or cause of what was brought about. Second, attempts to further explicate actions leads to a variety of claims: (a) that further explication is impossible; (b) that an agent's intentions can be explicated in terms of wants, pro-attitudes, beliefs, and causes; (c) that an agent's intention can be explicated in terms of an agent's aiming at some end in view, what is considered necessary to bring about the end, and practical force; and (d) that actions are too complex to analyze, but may be viewed as a socially appropriate response to a given context.

C. Explanations and Justifications of Human Actions

Given the preceding controversy regarding the nature of human action, it is not surprising that only those analytic philosophers in the mental causation and intentional theory tradition have pursued systematically the processes of explanation and justification from within an action theory perspective. It is only within the assumptions of these two traditions that such processes are unique, investigatable, and merit further analysis. Both mental causation and intentional philosophics take as their point of departure for the explanation of human action the concept of intention. Charles Taylor indicates the link both of these theories see between perception, thought, and intentions when he argues:

> Explanation in terms of purpose therefore involves taking into account the conceptual
> forms through which agents understand and come to grips with their world. That people

> think of their environment in certain concepts, that is, use certain modes of classification as an element in accounting for what they do. Indeed, it can be said to define what they do. For if we think of actions as defined by the purposes or intentions which inform them, then we cannot understand man's action without knowing the concepts in which they frame their intentions. (C. Taylor, 1970, p. 60)

While both mental causation and intentional theorists agree that an action theory explanation of behavior must go beyond the description of mere behavioral regularities to include a specification of what the behavior is to the actor, they disagree on the concepts and type of relationships involved in such an explanation.

Davidson's version of the process of explanation from within a mental causation perspective is both subtle and suggestive. Stoutland (1976) models that analysis as follows:

> A has a pro-attitude towards act B.
> A believes that behavior which eventuates in result C is necessary for B.
> This pro-attitude and belief cause A's behavior. (Stoutland, 1976, p. 282)

Davidson argues that the conclusion is entailed by the premises, and that the premises constitute both a causal explanation for the behavior involved in the conclusion and analysis of intentional action. When the premises are true, it follows that A performed C intentionally, and that he or she did it for the reasons cited in the first two premises (Davidson, 1969).

Von Wright (1971) provides an analysis of the process of explanation from within an intentional theory perspective when he argues that intentional explanations of human action have two parts. The first consists of an inner part, or intention. The second consists of an outer part which has two aspects: the exercise of a *muscular* activity which interferes with a cause in nature, and the *consequences* which follow from that interference. For exmple, A intends to elect B chairman. In order to elect B chairman, A exercises his vocal cords and utters the expression "aye." This exercise of muscular activity leadiing to the consequences which follow, such as someone counting the number of "aye" and "nay" votes, *can only be understood* or explained in terms of their subsumption under a specific intention, namely, intending to elect B chairman. The mere citation of a regularity between the utterance of the word "aye" and the counting of "aye" and "nay" utterances is insufficient to explain the behavioral regularities.

Explanations of human actions are formally modeled by an intentional pattern of reasoning termed the practical syllogism:

> A intends to bring about B.
> A *considers* that he cannot bring about B unless he does C.
> A *sets* himself to do C.

Intentional reasoning, when cast in this mood, is termed a first person practical syllogism. Its distinctive feature is that it is formulated from an actor's point of view and explains what an actor *considered practically necessary* for the fulfillment of his or her intention, and indicates that an actor *sets* himself or herself to fulfill the intention. Note that, even if an actor's perceptions of what must be done to fulfill intentions are in error, the first person practical syllogism is still a valid explanation of *why* he or she set to do what was done. According to Von Wright, the intentional or practical syllogism provides the humanities and social sciences with "something long missing from their methodology: an explanatory model in its own right which is a definite alternative to the subsumptive-theoretic covering law model" (Von Wright, 1971, p. 27).

The formal structure of the practical syllogism is unique in that it provides a basis for assessing the generality and necessity of propositions which are to serve as the basis for scientific *explanations* of comunication phenomena, and for the *justification* of an effective persuasive appeal. The same structure can account for theories of communication and persuasion. David Gauthier provides an analysis of when and how practical reasoning serves these two functions. Central to Gauthier's analysis is the distinction between *an agent's personal reasons* (or motivation for acting), *an agent's public reasons* (or explanations for actions), and *an audience's socially prescribed reason* (or social expectation for undertaking an appropriate action). A piece of practical reasoning offers a scientific explanation of behavior when an agent's *personal reasons* or motivation for acting are the *public reasons* an agent gives for action. Practical reasoning explains action only in those cases in which the reasons which motivate an agent's actions are public reasons or explanations for actions. A piece of practical reasoning *offers a justification* or effective persuasive appeal when an agent's *public reason* or explanation for actions are an audience's *socially prescribed* reasons or social expectation for undertaking an appropriate action. Practical reasoning justifies action only in those cases in which the public reasons an agent gives to explain his or her actions are the prescribed reasons for acting in such a situation.

What then has our rather brief analysis of explanation and justification revealed? First, that the explanation and justification of human action is only possible within a mental causation and intentional theory approach to action. Second, that these two theories hold in common the view that behavioral sequences which are to count as action must be understood through an agent's intentions, and are a form of practical reasoning which is capable under the appropriate conditions of explaining and justifying human action. Finally, these two theories differ in regard to the manner in which one explicates intentions and the type of relationship which exists between intentions and behavior.

D.   The Diversity of Theoretic Positions on the Relationship of Human Action to Communication Rules

Whereas the philosophical positions regarding the nature of human actions were the center of heated intellectual controversy from the mid 1960s to the mid 1970s, the theoretic positions regarding the link between human actions and communication rules have been the center of heated intellectual controversy from the mid 1970s to the mid 1980s. However, after a decade of research and controversy, three rather substantial theoretic positions and lines of research have emerged.

(1)   The Functionalist Rules Theory as Evidenced in the Work of Cushman and His Associates. Cushman and his associates (Cushman & Whiting, 1972; Cushman & Pearce, 1977; Cushman, 1977; Cushman, Dietrich, & Valentinsen, 1982; Cushman & Sanders, 1982; Cushman & Cahn, 1985; Cushman & King, 1986, 1987; Cushman, 1986) argue that communication rules are cultural-specific prescriptions which indicate what and when to communicate in order to achieve a socially specified end. Cushman and his associates have delineated the standardized communication rules in the United States, Japan, and Korea for coherently initiating such interpersonal relationships as friend and mate. The explanatory force for these rules is enforced by the cultural-specific expectations of actions, and is modeled by the practical syllogism. Three objections have been brought against this functional approach to rules theory and research: (a) that it is essentially correct but incomplete (Pearce, 1972; Cronen & Davis, 1978); (b) that meanings are for the most part not conventional (Pearce, 1976); and that communication is more than its conventional use (Philipsen,

1981). All of these critiques serve to limit the domain of the functionalist rules theory to sit-uations in which there is a strong generative mechanism for communication rules which monitors and sanctions appropriate communication behavior (Adler, 1980).

In addition, considerable controversy surrounds the verification procedure appropri-ate for establishing the geneerality and necessity of the practical syllogism. Charles Taylor (1971) claims that the verification of such an explanation is an interpretive or hermeneutic process. He denies that practical reason can be tested employing positivistic verification procedures. He argues that an agent's intentions and nonstandard use of symbols has inter-pretive, not positivistic, antecedents. Thus a hermeneutic science is regarded for verifica-tion, not a positivistic one. (Eglin, 1975)

Terry Pinkard's disagrees with Taylor, claiming that, while human actions do have an unmistakable hermeneutic component, that does not deny the applicability of positivistic verification procedures. Pinkard argues that the verification of an agent's interpretation of intentional acts requires an interpretive procedure. However, determining what elements are involved in an interaction, the agent's symbols and observable relations between them involves positivistic verification procedures.

Ted Smith indicates the exact conditions under which hermeneutic and positivistic verification procedures will each be applicable. First-person practical reasoning seeks to ex-plain why an agent uttered what he or she did, not whether that utterance was successful in transferring personal meaning. Once a researcher locates what an agent intended to do and hears the utterance, regardless of its effect, he or she can explain the agent's actions. Thus, only hermeneutic verification procedures are involved in first-person practical reasoning. Third-person practical syllogisms explain what an agent must utter to successfully transfer meaning. Once a researcher locates what must be said to count as coherent message for some audience, he or she will know if the utterance will be successful. Thus, positivistic pro-cedures can be employed to verify these propositions. However, on occasions, first- and third-person practical reasoning corresponds — what an agent *intentionally says* is what *must be said* for the transfer of meaning — and, in those cases, both verification procedures can be employed, although they will each validate different explanations. Hermeneutics ex-plains *why an agent acted,* positivistic procedures explain *what an agent must do to be suc-cessful* in communicating (Smith, 1978).

Cushman and Pearce have developed and tested at least one positivistic procedure for verifying the generality and necessity of the practical reasoning involved a standardized us-age. They argue that a communication study which makes claims regarding the practical force of rules must address the epistemic claims that there are normative rules which apply to a particular domain, including the instances being studied, that such rules have force, and that the communication which occurred was governed by these rules. Such claims can be established by (a) locating the coordination task which serves as a generative mechanism for a standardized usage; (b) describing the episodic sequences which constitute the stand-ardized usage, and assessing its generality and practical force; and (c) indicating which structure of the practical syllogism must be employed given the generality and necessity in-volved (Cushman & Pearce, 1977).

However, Peter Eglin claims that any attempt to verify communicative behaviors must make interpretive assumptions which can only be redeemed hermeneutically. He then argues that enthnomethodology can be employed as one such interpretive verification pro-cedure (Eglin, 1975).

James Heap (1977) agrees with Eglin's claims that communicative behavior can only be verified hermeneutically, but denies that enthomethodological research can perform that function. Heap argues that enthomethodological research suffers from the same weakness as positivistic research, namely, that it seeks the unequivocal identification of communicative acts. Heap suggests that all one can locate is the ordinary language interpretations employed by interactants, and that such interpretations admit of a number of equally legitimate alternative meanings.

When we analyze the verification controversy in light of the distinctions between personal, interactive, and standardized meaning or communication patterns, we find that the controversy dissolves when one specifies precisely which type of meaning one is attempting to verify. When one seeks to *verify personal meanings* as modeled by the *first-person practical syllogism,* one must determine what a given agent intended to communicate and what nonstandard pattern of symbols would lead his or her auditor to grasp his or her intentions. Taylor and Heap demonstrate that *only* a hermeneutic method will suffice for verification in such instances. Since the meaning is personal to the agent, an outside observer can only attempt through interpretation to approximate the agent's meanings. Such a process is hermeneutic, and allows *the agent to determine* when an outside observer has drawn the proper implications from the nonstandard symbol pattern. It *does not allow* the observer to verify meaning independent of an agent's interpretations.

When one seeks to *verify interactive meaning* as modeled by *the convergence of first- and third-person practical syllogism,* one must determine both what a given agent intends to communicate by a nonstandard pattern of symbols and how that pattern overlaps with another agent's nonstandard pattern to form a standard pattern of agreements on meanings. Pinkard (1976) and Smith (1980) demonstrate that, in such cases, both hermeneutic and positivistic procedures are required. Interpretive procedures are required for each participant to verify the accurate transfer of personal meanings. Positivistic procedures are required to verify the negotiated overlap in personal meanings, which then become the vocabulary of interactive meanings which are intersubjectively verifiable by each agent, independently of the other.

Finally, when one seeks to verify a standardized usage as modeled by the third-person practical syllogism, one must determine if an agent is fulfilling the system role or intention in the prescribed manner. Cushman and Pearce (1977) demonstrate that a positivistic verification procedure will allow an outside observer to determine if the system intention is being fulfilled in the prescribed manner. It does appear that Heap (1977) is correct in arguing that enthnomethodological procedures are applicable only to the verification of standardized meaning or third-person practical reasoning (Adler, 1980).

(2) The Structural and Functional Theoretic Position as Evidenced in the Research Program of Pearce, Cronen and Associates. Pearce and Cronen (Pearce, 1976, 1977; Pearce, Cronen, & Conklin, 1977; Pearce, Harris, & Cronen, 1982; Pearce, Cronen, Johnson, Jones, & Raymond, 1980; Cronen, Pearce, & Snavely, 1979; Pearce & Cronen, 1980; Cronen & Pearce, 1981; Pearce, 1980) argue that communication rules may be either structural (flowing from the logic of previously established communication patterns), or functional (aimed at goal attainment). In the former case, they have logical force, while, in the latter case, practical force. They then develop a calculus for including both types for foci as influencing behavioral outcomes. One of the unique features of this approach is a hierarchical analysis of the sources of logical force, consisting of cultural patterns, life scripts, relationships, episodes, speech acts, and content. This hierarchy of systems serves as the explanatory mechanism for logical force, while the practical syllogism serves that same function for practical force. Pearce and Cronen then go on to indicate how conflicts between these systems levels in interaction with others destroys standardized and interactive meanings, and leads to perceived enmeshment in enigmatic episodes, unwanted repetitive episodes, value expressive rituals, positive spirals, alienating sequences, and profunctory rituals. They then delineate the difference between communications in minimal, satisfactory, and optimal communication competency based on system level coordination between interactants. Three objections have been brought against this position: (a) that personal communication rules cannot be varied (Cushman & Larkin, 1981); (b) that their theory's lack of predictive and control power limits its explanatory power (Cushman & Larkin, 1981; Harris, 1980); and that the varification procedure employed is expost-act-tu (Cushman & Larkin, 1981). Pearce and Cronen respond to these claims by arguing their theory is not meant to be predictive and is explanatory, and that its verification procedure can thus be expost-act-tu.

(3) **The Contingency Rules Theory as Explicated by Mary Smith (1984), Which Draws Upon the Research of Numerous Scholars.** The contingency rules theory (Miller & Burgoon, 1978; Cody, Woelfel, & Jordan, 1983; McLaughlin, Cody, & O'Hair, 1983a; McLaughlin, Cody, & Rosenstein, 1983b; Smith, 1982d; Schanck-Hamlin, Wiseman, & Georgecarakos, 1982; Cody & McLaughlin, 1980) assumes that communication activities are governed antecedently by four varieties of self-evaluative and adaptive contingency rules, and that the actual contexts where communication takes places determine the configuration of rules governing the interactants' communication behavior. Thus, the actual context is a function of volitional behavior within fixed potential rules boundaries. This approach to rules theory assumes that communication behaviors, defined as message strategy selection and strategic responses to messages, are purposive actions that are governed antecedently by their anticipated consequences. *Self-identity rules* link behavior to personal values that constitute one's conception of the private self; *image-maintenance rules* link communication behavior to impressive management concerns; *environmental contingency rules* link communication behavior to concerns for physical well being of the self and important others; *interpersonal relationship rules* link communication behaviors to general, social, and, cultural norms. Given an interaction context, some subset of these rules comes into play to constrain and channel communication behavior. Smith has attempted to delineate the rules involved in compliance-gaining and compliance-resisting behavior, based on the contingency rules theory. While contingency rules theory is sufficiently new that it has not as yet attracted criticism, several problems appear to suggest themselves: (a) that the four sources of rules are not structurally or functionally necessary and, as such, lack the power of explanation, prediction, and control; (b) that the four sources for rules appear to be dynamic and, as such, represent unstable measurement domains over time; and (c) that the theory does not allow for the explanation, prediction, and control of human communication behavior, because individuals can select which rule sets to pay attention to, and which to ignore, in a given context.

While functional, structural and functional, and contingency rules theories each have theoretic limitations, each has in turn provided us with substantial theories of friendship and mateship formation, varying episodic types and compliance gaining and avoiding behavior, as well as persistent, focused, and theoretically motivated research programs.

A REVIEW OF ORGANIZATIONAL COMMUNICATION RESEARCH EMPLOYING A RULES PERSPECTIVE

A careful review of the organizational communication research reveals a small but significant body of literature contributing to the development of rules theory in this area. These contributions include important extensions of each of the existing rules theories, and the proposal of a new rules theory. Let us examine each in turn.

Functional rules theory has been extended into the organizational communication area by Farace, Monge, and Russell (1977), McPhee (1978), Donohue, Cushman, and Nofsinger (1980), Donohue, Dietz, and Hamilton (1984), and Cushman and King (1985), with important implications. Farace, Monge, and Russell, in their 1977 book *Communicating and Organizing,* provide a chapter on communication rules in organizational hierarchy. In so doing, they explore the functional communication rules which govern and guide hierarchical communication within an organization. They explore content and procedural rules or role specific communication, its power influence (i.e., one up, one down, one across), its coorientation accuracy (i.e., pluralist ignorance, monolithic consensus, false consensus and dissensus), and their groupings into functional rule sets (i.e. innovation, maintenance, sequencing, and initiation).

McPhee (1978) attempted to formulate a rules theory of organizational communication. Following Cushman and Florence (1974), McPhee defined organizational communication as the process of coordinating interaction in regard to production. McPhee then isolated two classes of variables: task variables and coordination rule-variables. Three task variables were examined: patterning of interdependence, intensity of interdependence, and direction of interdependence. Six coordination rule-variables were examined: understanding, agreement, realization, normative force, rule differentiation, and rule integration. Sixteen propositions were developed linking these variables. Finally, McPhee examined the relationship of his task and coordination variables in creating the dominance of one of three organizational control mechanisms: task control structures, hierarchial control structures, and associative (or friendship) control structures.

Donohue and associates (1980, 1981, 1984) provide a model of rule use for negotiation interaction. This is the result of an effort to (a) translate research in the field into practical bargaining strategies that address both "content and relational dimensions" of communication, and (b) construct interconnected utterance matrices to measure how winners and losers use rules differently. They focus on the most highly competitive negotiation situation namely, "distributive," which is described as a zero-sum game. Dononhue terms the negotiations a "mixed motive" situation in which agents have different goals which are not mutually exclusive. Donohue's model makes three basic assumptions.

(1) Because of the competitive setting, "each utterance represents some tactic designed to gain advantage."
(2) Both negotiators will formulate strategies based on their discovery of the other's "expectations."
(3) Each utterance is taken at face value in the present.

Dononhue suggests that the manner in which negotiators structure their interaction in relation to the other party will influence outcome. Donohue seeks the generative mechanism of this structure. Dononhue argues with Cushman that rules will guide the structure and outcome of the conflict. He cites Searles. "Constitutive rules" govern how to interpret a sequence of utterances, and "regulative rules" govern when and how the actor performs based upon normative expectations. Therefore, those who know the constitutive and regulative rules can theoretically dominate their adversary through manipulating these rules.

Donohue derived his rules from research. The locus of Dononhue's rule validation procedure is "in talk" whose application has some effective impact on negotiation outcome, as opposed to a cognitive approach. At the level of the agents, Donohue states that whether a rule exists consciously or unconsciously is not as important as how it is used to win, and that winners and losers will use rules differently. Donohue uses an interactional perspective; i.e., agents respond reciprocally to each other. He organizes negotiation tactics into three groups: attacking—taking ground; defending—holding ground; regressive—giving ground. Donohue builds on Cushman and Craig's (1976) negotiation skills needed to employ his tactics, i.e., cueing and responding rules. He then constructs a code whereby the negotiation rules serve as the categories for analysis (ergo, 14 negotiation rules results in 14 categories).

Donohue's interactional perspective of analysis is also reflected in his coding scheme, which codes each utterance twice: (a) as a "response to the prior utterance"; (b) as a "cue to the subsequent utterance." This theory is therefore theoretically contingent and sequential, as the rule used and the order in which it is used will determine results. (His results, however, did not indicate information about the sequential structure, and he calls for a rethinking of the structure.) The variance in patterns of interaction of winners vs. losers is used to predict the degree to which rules structure negotiation interaction. Donohue employs a negotiation game developed by Stephen Williams regarding a mock civil suit. This suit was conducted by 48 undergraduate students from the University of Minnesota. The agents were taped and their interactions analyzed according to Donohue's model. The results indicated that winners and losers use cueing and responding rules differently. Basically, winners make more offers and reject more loser concessions. Contrary to the old negotiation adage—cooperation breeds cooperation—the losers give more conditional support and winners more outright rejection, which indicates, according to Donohue, that a hard line is more effective.

Cushman and King (1985) analyze the intersection of national and organizational cultures in specifying the appropriate rules to be employed in resolving organizational conflicts in Japan, the United States, and Yugoslavia. They map the intersection of cultural and organizational values in each country and explicate the preferred conflict resolution model in each society, with the following results (see Table 1).

Cushman and King then detail the rule-governed rituals, myths, and social dramas involved in each culture's preferred means of conflict resolution. *In Japan,* this involves the myth of *nemawashi;* the rituals of one-on-one consultation, *ringi* and go-betweens; and the social drama of cultural isolation. *In the United States,* this involves the myth of rugged individualism; the rituals of conciliation, mediation, fact-finding, and arbitration; and the social drama of appeal. *In Yugoslavia* this involves the myth of self management; the rituals of socio-political community, the worker's council and the joint committee; and the social drama of the sociopolitical community.

Structural and functional rules theory was extended into the organizational communication arena by Harris and Cronen (1979), with important implications. Harris and Cronen studied the social reality of the faculty in a social science department in a state university. They interviewed 10 persons, half of the faculty, as members of an organization. The analysis led to the discovery of many convoluted logics which allowed each to explain observed forms of behavior, and to predict forms of the episodes that were desired by members but would not occur. The members were examined with respect to the organization's master contract or culture. The organizational culture is shared, but only imperfectly. At the level of "image," the culture includes constructs for self-definition as well as beliefs and goal states. The cultured rules include constitutive rules through which organizational meanings are established, and regulative rules through which members coordinate their everyday interaction.

Table 1. National Cultural Values

	Japan	United States	Yugoslavia
POLITICAL AND ECONOMIC VALUES	1. Minority gives in to majority	Majority rule with minority rights.	Direct democracy.
	2. Private ownership of property.	Private ownership of property.	Direct democracy.
	3. Competition based on government monopolies.	Open competition regulated by the government.	Collective development of competitive advantage.
TRADITIONAL VALUES	1. A strong sense of hierarchy.	Individual freedom.	A respect for ethnic diversity.
	2. Homogenous collective values.	Equality of opportunities.	Homogenous ethnic values.
	3. A strong commitment to the firm.	A strong sense of competition.	A commitment to equality.
	4. Pride in work.	A desire for individual acceptance.	A commitment to equality of economic reasons.
	5. Maintain public face.	A commitment to the accumulation of personal wealth.	A commitment to compromise when values conflict.
ORGANIZATIONAL VALUES	1. Life-long employment	1. Short-term employment	1. Life-long employment
	2. Slow evaluation and promotion	2. Rapid evaluation and promotion	2. No evaluation and limited promotion
	3. Nonspecific job assignment	3. Specialized career path	3. Shifting job path
	4. Implicit control	4. Explicit control	4. Negotiated control
	5. Consensual decision making	5. Individual decision making	5. Intergroup decision making
	6. Collective responsibility	6. Individual responsibility	6. Diverse collective concern
	7. Collective concern	7. Individual concern	7. Diverse collective concern
PREFERRED CONFLICT RESOLUTION STRATEGY	1. Collaboration	1. Competition	1. Compromise

In an organization, constitutive rules may function to organize meaning in light of the organizational image showing how certain actions and beliefs "count" in light of the constructs which define the collectivity. To construct regulative rules, organizational members must engage in role-taking. They must reconstruct how speech acts or episodes are related to meaningful constructions of organization members. In an organization, there is practical necessity and logical necessity. With respect to practical necessity, in an organization the culture specifies the important goals and how to accomplish these goals. These goals, if consensually shared, can lead to a common organizational image. If individuals are oriented to different master contracts, attempts to coordinate in order to accomplish a goal together are unsuccessful. When practical force is high, coordinated task accomplishments are facilitated by high consensus on goals and ways to achieve them. If there is no agreement, or if rules describe all behavior as legitimate or irrelevant, practical force is low: a person cannot expect others to follow his or her lead and cannot anticipate how they will interpret his or her actions.

With respect to logical force, two individuals may begin conjoint activity, oriented toward the same goal, but the unique logic created by their regulative rules could generate a force that is more powerful than their practical goal orientation. The question emerges: how much consensus is minimally necessary for effective organization functioning?

Three levels of competence were distinguished for both coorientation and coordination: minimal, satisfactory, and optimal. In this study, Harris further distinguished between two general types of competence: *strategic,* where one can know what is wrong with an organization; and *tactical,* where one knows how to repair it. The organizational image was determined by identifying the degree of consensuality in the constructs used by the faculty. In a second phase, subjects completed questionnaires which elicited four types of information: their own belief, and their perception of the other faculty members beliefs in the actual and ideal condition of the department. Finally, subjects were asked to indicate on the nine-interval bipolar adjective scales all of the intervals they perceived as legitimate positions about the state of the department, and all of those they perceived as rejected.

On the "scientific-historical–critical" scale there were significant differences between what members thought their coworkers perceived as the actual and ideal status of the organization, and a significant difference between what members said was the ideal state and what they thought their coworkers would say is the ideal state. The same results were found for the "community of scholars — backbiting" scale. With respect to the "power–powerless" scale, three significant differences emerged between: What members thought coworkers perceived as the actual state of the organization; what members themselves reported were ideal and actual states of the organization; what members report is the actual state; and what they think coworkers perceive as the actual state.

On the last scale, "service–substance," only one significant difference emerged between what members report as the actual state of the organization and what they think their coworkers hold as the ideal.

Two important conclusions can be drawn. First, on the scientific-historical–critical construct, the members believe that the department is where it should be ideally, but they (erroneously) think they disagree about the actual and ideal state of the department. These different conceptions of a social reality produce regulative rules that lead to self-perpetrating misconceptions. For example, a faculty member may in accordance with what he or she thinks the organization believes in, be rewarded for it, because each member wants to act in accordance with what the group believes.

Second, on the service-theoretical–substance construct, members agree that the ideal position is near the midpoint, and that it is where the department actually is, but each feels he or she is a minority and that the others prefer an extreme emphasis on substance. Hence, members think it is inappropriate to ask others to join them in service projects.

The contingency rules theory was extended into the arena of organizational communication by Schall (1983), with important implications. Schall argues that organizations, cultures, and cultural rules can be synthesized as communication phenomena within the contingency rules perspective. The author then selects two units within the same organization to study — an information systems group (consisting of 23 people, 5 managers, and 18 computer programmers) and an investment group (consisting of 17 people, 3 managers, 2 professional staff and 12 clerks). She explored the formal and informal communication rules within the organization for dealing with power and influence, and each group's image of the corporate culture. *Formal rules* were gathered from the organization's documents and corrected by the CEO. *Informal rules* were gathered by participant observation and corrected by the workers. Five person-specific characterizations of the organizational culture were formulated. Both rule sets, and all five characteristics of the culture, were evaluated by all participants in the study. The results suggested that each department was a subculture which emphasized different informal rules and conceptions of the organizational culture. Both departments ranked the formal rules for the culture the least important for behavior, and their preferred informal rule set the most important. Diversity existed regarding which characterization of the organization's culture was most accurate. This study suggests an organization may not have a single culture, but may consist of several separate subcultures.

Structurational rules theory is a new theory of rules advocated by Poole and McPhee (1983), and Poole, Seibold, and McPhee (1985), in relation to their work on organizational decision making and organizational climate. Poole and McPhee argue:

> The theory of structuration is based on a distinction between system and structure. Structures are the rules and resources people use in interaction. Systems are the observable results of the application of structures, "regularized relations of interdependence between individuals and groups." Structuration refers to the production and reproduction of social systems via the application of generative rules and resources in interaction. For example, the status hierarchy in a work group is an observable system. The structure underlying this system consists of rules, such as norms about who takes problems to the boss, and resources such as a special friendship with the boss or seniority. The status system exists because of the constant process of structuration in which rules and resources are both the medium and outcome of interaction. Members use rules and resources to maintain their places or to attempt to rise in the hierarchy; the structure of rules and resources thus produces the status system. At the same time, by invoking rules and using resources, as well as by socializing new members, members are also reproducing and perpetuating the system. (Poole & McPhee, 1983, p. 210)

Poole and McPhee then apply this analysis to the construct of organizational climate by distinguishing four layers of social practices or organizational rules.

(1) System patterns are the observable relationships and regularities that constitutes the social system for a particular practice.
(2) Practical structures are the rules and resources that directly govern interaction in the social system.
(3) Background structures are rules and resources that give meaning to the practice and provide grounds for interaction.
(4) Collective attitudes are members' generalized conceptions about the social system. (Poole & McPhee, 1983, pp. 211–212)

Next, they measure the degree of coorientation on each level of rules, and the degree of influence between levels, in an attempt to explore structuration dynamically. A case study of climate production is then provided as an exemplar of this rules approach. This dynamic view of organizational communication, as both structured and influenced by each level of system structuring, places rules theory in a process of mutual influence between the rules, the people employing them, and the system level goals.

What, then, has our brief review of organizational commmunication research from a rules perspective revealed? *First,* from a *functional rules theory perspective,* we have seen a general methodology for rules research proposed by Farace, Monge, and Russell (1977) and McPhee (1978). *Second,* Dononhue and his associates (1980, 1981, 1984), and Cushman and King (1985), have begun to map the negotiation strategies, rituals, myths, and social dramas governing conflict resolution in the United States, Japan, and Korea. *Third,* from the *structural and functional rules theory perspective,* Harris and Cronen (1979) have begun to analyze organizational cultures, and how diverse interpretations of the state of that culture's real and ideal goals can lead to destructive communication patterns in terms of goal attainment. *Fourth,* from *the contingency rules theory perspective* (Schall, 1983), we find that organizational cultures may best be viewed as various subcultures, with diverse if normal rule sets and images rather than a single formal culture espoused by the organizational and its CEO. *Finally,* we witnessed the emergence of a *structurational rules theory perspective.* Poole and McPhee (1983), Poole, Seibold, and McPhee (1985), and Poole and McPhee (1985) aimed at accounting for the dynamic qualities of organizational climates which view communication rules as both an influence on behavior and as being influenced by employees' conceptions of appropriate behavior.

While rules theory as a research perspective is fairly new, and its extensions into the organizational communication arena even more recent, several broad and important criticisms can now be made of this body of research. *First,* almost all the research is descriptive, when the unique quality of a rules perspective is its prescriptive approach. More specifically, studies need to be undertaken of the best organizations and the commuication rules they employ, rather than just any available organization. Then we will learn how to improve organizational performance by contrasting the best with other organizations. *Second,* almost all the research seeks to extend existing rules theories into the organizational arena, without first providing a unique analysis of the most salient features of that environment for a rules analysis. More specifically, what is it about communication within the organizational communication arena that rules theory can shed the most light upon? *Third,* almost all the research is limited to exploring one aspect of communication rules, such as negotiation, culture, or climate, without linking these processes with a more general conception of communication rule. In an attempt to be responsive to these criticisms and advance our understanding of communication rules theories of organizations, we offer the following case study.

A CASE STUDY OF COMMUNICATION RULES IN A HIGH SPEED MANAGEMENT CONTEXT

Our case study will proceed in three stages: (a) a justification of the study, (b) an analysis of IBM's organizational communication rules, and (c) the drawing of some conclusions regarding the implications of the study for rules theory development.

A. Justification

This case study of communication rules theories in the organization context aims at (a) locating and evaluating the communication rules of one of our nation's best run corporations, (b) providing a unique analysis of the most salient features of the organizational environment in which the corporation functions, and (c) creating a general framework for analyzing communication rules theory which can guide systematic and comprehensive rules perspective development.

Why Select IBM As An Exemplar of the Best Run Corporation in the United States? In four successive studies by *Fortune* magazine, each a year apart, which evaluated the management teams of the 200 largest corporations in the United States, a high-technology firm, IBM, was ranked in first place as the most admired corporation in American (Makin, 1983; Perry, 1984; Sellers, 1985; Hutton, 1986). Of the 43 firms which Peters and Waterman (1983) judged to be "excellent" in their study *In Search of Excellence,* almost half were high-technology firms, and the list was headed by IBM. Of the five U.S. corporations which Ouchi (1980) described as having management teams capable of meeting the Japanese economic challenge, three (IBM, Hewlett Packard, and Kodak) were high-technology corporations, and again IBM headed the list. In 1986, IBM was the most profitable company on the Fortune 500 list, with revenues of $50 billion and a net income of 6 billion (Hutton, 1986). The *New York Times* (1986) reports that, in the fall quarter of 1985, sales of IBM's 3090 Sierra mainframe computer were sufficient to raise the United States GNP 1%, accounting for more than one third of the nations 2.3% growth rate in that quarter. We have selected the IBM corporation for our case study because it is considered one of the nation's best managed, most competitive, most profitable, and thus most important, companies.

What Are the Most Salient Features of the Communication Environment Within Which IBM Functions? Regardless of which nation ends up number one in high-technology development, the world high-technology environment warrants careful analysis, because it has given rise to a new important system of management.

Rapidly changing technology, quick market saturation, unexpected competition—these all make succeeding in business, particularly a high-technology business, harder than ever today. Managing in the classic sense is not enough. You have to manage differently. The skills that make up this new technique—called high-speed management—are not easy to master. Business schools don't teach them. But learning them is becoming increasingly imperative, even in industries not commonly regarded as high-tech (Fraker, 1984). This high-speed management system is a set of tools for coming up with new products, making sure they are what the consumer wants, and getting them to market quickly in order to realize large profits.

At the very core of the high-speed management system are creative uses of human and machine communication processes aimed at developing and maintaining recurrent and focused innovation, product quality, and customer satisfaction through rapid decision making, increased productivity, and greater employee commitment to an organization. The principles or rules which govern and guide these communication processes have only recently become the focus of careful study and the subject of management training programs.

Rapidly changing technologies, quick market saturation, and unexpected competition, as previously indicated, are characteristic of high-technology environments. Most of these characteristics arise from a single source—namely, the fact that firms in high-technology environments are confronted by shrinking product life cycles. The product life cycle is the period of time available from the inception of an idea until the market for that idea is saturated or disappears due to new product development. A product life cycle normally involves several stages—product conceptualization, design, testing, refinement, mass production, marketing, shipping, selling, and servicing. Dominique Hanssens, a professor in UCLA's Graduate School of Management, has studied the product life cycle in electrical applicances for years. He reports (Fraker, 1984) that, years ago, the product life cycle for refrigerators took over 30 years to mature, providing considerable time for each phase of the product life cycle to develop. However, all of this has changed. The market for microwave ovens has taken 10 years to mature; CB radios, 4 years; computer games, 3 years; etc.

Perhaps the most dramatic example of shrinking product life cycle as a result of rapidly changing technology, quick market saturation, and unexpected competition can be found in the microcomputer industry. The first commercially successful machine, an 8-bit micro, came to market in 1977; 4 years later, in 1981, the 16-bit micro appeared. Then, 2 years later, in 1983, came the 32-bit micro, followed 1 year later in 1984 by the 64-bit micro computer and one year later in 1985 by the 1000-bit micro. The industrial shakedown from such rapid changes has taken its toll on Commodore, Atari, Digital, and Texas Instruments, and is threatening one of the industry's corporate legends in innovation, Apple Computers. Large companies once dominant in their respective markets were unable to respond effectively to the end of one product life cycle and the beginning of a new one. There are new techniques and skills which companies and managers must master to respond to this challenge.

* * * *First, companies must stay close to both their customers and their competitors.* Successful companies always know what the customer needs and attempt to provide it. When products and manufacturing processes change rapidly, it is crucial to keep up with the investment strategies and product costs of rival companies. In order to accomplish this, companies must develop and maintain a rapid and accurate intelligence system capable of preventing surprises.

* * * *Second, companies must think constantly about new products and then back that thinking with investment, fast.* A good new product strategy requires a large, active, and focused research and development team with ready access to, and the prudent use of, large amounts of capital.

* * * *Third, rapid, and effective delivery requires close cooperation between design, manufacturing, testing, marketing, delivery, and servicing systems.* The interdependence of these systems, combined with the short lead time in product delivery, makes certain that any error within or between systems will delay product delivery, endangering market penetration. Close cooperation between these systems requires strong, quick, and responsive coordination and control systems.

* * * *Fourth, product quality, user friendliness, ease of service, and competitive pricing are essential for market penetration.* In an environment where consumer and investor representatives compare, rate, and effectively communicate product differences, market penetration depends on quality, useful, and readily serviceable products. This in turn requires the active monitoring, testing, and checking the servicing of one's own and one's competition's products.

* * * *Fifth, companies which introduce new products must consider the processes and costs required to cannablize their own products and to retrench the divisions and workers involved.* Companies faced with rapidly changing technology, quick market saturation, and unexpected competition must be prepared to change or withdraw their own products rather than let their reputation and market shares be eroded by a competitor. Corporate planning for new products must include contingencies for shifting, retraining, or retrenching large product sectors rapidly.

* * * *Sixth, corporate cultures must be developed which emphasize change, allow for the inclusion of whole units with alternative values, and encourage members to learn from mistakes without reprisal.* Corporate cultures which cannot change rapidly will impede market adaptation. Corporations faced with still competition will often acquire other corporations with alternative values which will have to be integrated without delay into their corporate culture. Finally, a certain number of new initiatives are doomed to failure for all the reasons previously cited. Talented members of an organization must learn quickly from their failures and press on to new projects. A corporate culture's responsiveness to these issues will involve close cooperation between labor and management, group and individual needs, and the interests of cnsumers, investors, and the corporation.

IBM's corporate management will have as its goal the creation of new products which meet the customers needs, and the delivery of that product to market before its competitors in an effort to achieve market penetration and large profits. The success of this goal will rest upon the previously cited six environmental rules and the development of management tools for operationally applying these principles in a rapidly changing environment.

What Type of General Theoretic Framework is Best Suited to the Analysis of Communication Rules Theories in Such An Organizational Context? At the heart of an organization's rules system is its culture. A culture, according to Richard Weaver (1964), is a complex of values polarized by an image which contains a vision of its own excellence. Ideally, a culture provides its members with a coherent world of shared meanings, a set of values which differentiate cultural roles and guide appropriate behavior. A culture in this sense is an orientational system from which its most powerful and humble members can borrow to give dignity, direction, and a sense of belonging to their lives. From within a culture's vision, this ideal of its own excellence, comes the culture's power to inspire and to motivate significant collective effort. Every culture relies upon this power to deal with the inevitable tensions which arise between the impulse of individuals to be free and the constraints placed upon individual freedom by the community in order to attain collective goals.

The term "culture" thus denotes two very different but interrelated things. On the one hand, culture refers to a *conceptual reality,* to specific ways of thinking, and to core values for orienting one perceptually to the world. Participation in this conceptual reality provides one with a world view and a sense of group belonging. On the other hand, culture refers to a *phenomenal reality,* to culturally specific patterns of behavior. Participation in this phenomenal reality provides one's life with a sense of direction, a sense of what is appropriate and inappropriate behavior.

Organizational cultures, according to Gutknecht (1982), serve at least three functions: legitimation, motivation, and integration. *First,* a culture provides its members with socially legitimate patterns of interpretation and behavior for dealing with culturally relevant problems. *Second,* a culture provides its members with a hierarchical motivation structure which links their identity to culturally relevant roles and values. *Third,* a culture provides its members with a symbolically integrated framework which regulates social interaction and goal attainment through the creation of cultural meanings.

A culture's scope or domain of activity is made operational, according to Philipsen (1981), through the use of myth, ritual, and social drama. A *myth* is a symbolic narrative which captures a culture's core values, specifies culturally legitimate ways of coping with cultural problems, and holds a grip on the communal imagination by manifesting culturally relevant ideals. Myths give cultural life meaning and coherence. A *ritual* is a patterned sequence of symbolic action, the correct performance of which constitutes participation in the culture by paying homage to the culture's sacred values. Such rituals are based on socially shared rules, the adherence to which gives meaning and coherence to human action and provides for social alignment. A *social drama* is a dramatic presentation of a breach in cultural values, the crises it causes, the redress of the offender, and the reintegration of the offender into the community or the community's recognition of a moral dissensus. According to Philipsen —

> Social dramas play an important function in communal life. Whereas rituals have as their dominant function the celebration of a code, and myths have as theirs the using of the code to make sense of the communal conversations, social dramas serve as occasions for defining the boundaries of the group and for reintegrating into the group those individuals whose acts have tested the community's moral boundaries. Whereas ritual is a way to affirm it, and myth is a way to articulate and apply it, a social drama is a way to remake and negotiate a particular peoples sense of community life. (Philipsen, 1981, p. 9).

Peters and Waterman (1983) argue that "every excellent company we studied is clear on what it stands for and takes the process of value shaping seriously." In fact, we wonder if it is possible to be an excellent company without clarity of values. Posner, Koyzes, and Schmidt (1985) conducted a study of 1500 managers from across the U.S., representing all types of organizations and levels of management, aimed at discovering the role of shared values between a corporate culture and a manager's personal values. They found that shared values related to

1. Feelings of personal success
2. Organizational commitment
3. Self confidence in understanding superiors, colleagues, and subordinates
4. Ethical behavior
5. Lower levels of job and personal stress
6. Organizational goal attainment
7. Positive orientations towards organizational stockholders

Shared value thus appears to be at the core of successful corporate performance.

However, as Harris and Cronen (1979) and Schall (1983) remind us, the formal values espoused by an organization as the basis for its culture, and the actual rituals, myths, and social dramas employed by each work unit, *may be* two quite different cultural systems or even several quite different subcultural systems. When this happens, the power of the culture to legitimate, motivate, and integrate corporate activities is impaired. To understand when and if such impairment has arisen, one must explore carefully the operational link between an organization's formal values, its employee selection, socialization, and monitoring procedures, and its processes for correcting violations of its values, rituals, myths, and social dramas. Only then can we begin to understand the appropriate or inappropriate diffusion of the culture throughout the organization, and the culture's real power to legitimate, motivate, and integrate the members of the culture.

As Philipsen (1981), Harris and Cronen (1979), Smith (1984), and Schall (1983) point out, individuals who interact within an organization's domain have interests and values of their own which may or may not intersect with the organization's culture in a productive way. Understanding this intersection is important in analyzing a corporate culture's ability to motivate significant and successful efforts. Three audiences appear significant in respect to an organization's functioning: the investors, the workers, and the consumers. The fit between these three audiences' interests and values, and a corporate culture's interests and values, we shall term *a corporate climate*. Corporate climate is thus variable, based on the goodness of fit between the organization's values and interests and the values and interests of those individuals necessary for the appropriate functioning of the organization. The degrees of positive or negative fits significantly affect corporate climate. Corporate climate can thus be decomposed into investment climate, work climate, and sales climate, with the fit of each ranging from good to bad. Third, and equally obvious, a corporate culture, as manifest in its values, rituals, myths, and social dramas, may or may not productively intersect with the demands of a high technology environment. The degree of positive fit significantly influences the competitiveness of an organization. *Finally,* it is important to recognize that the communication of a corporation's values, rituals, myths, and social dramas is the major focus of a rules theory approach to organizational communication. They require communication patterns of a particular sort for their use; they are standardized usages upon which an organization's productive capabilities depend for success. However, their successful use is conditioned by the interests and values manifested by investors, workers, consumers, and the organization's competitive environment.

Attention is now directed towards demonstrating the utility of this analytic framework for evaluating rules theories. In so doing, we shall develop a case study of the IBM corporate culture by analyzing: (a) IBM's values, socialization, and monitoring process for the implementation and maintenance of its corporate culture, and (b) the interests and values of IBM's investors, workers, and consumers, and the positive or negative corporate climate they create when intersecting IBM's corporate culture.

A. IBM's Corporate Culture – Its Values, Socialization, and Monitoring Systems

Forbes magazine reports that, in 1957, "young Tom Watson's IBM . . . became an impressive business statistic. . . . when it joined the exclusive fraternity of U.S. companies grossing $1 billion or more." In 1983, it estimated that "IBM passed $1 billion revenues the second week in January" (*Think,* 1983, p. 3). What accounts for this phenomenal growth rate? How was it achieved? Who is responsible for guiding such a meteoric growth rate? An adequate answer to each of these questions begins with an understanding of IBM's basic corporate beliefs, its corporate goals, its managerial duties, and how these are sustained by a rigid socialization process for all employees, with an impeccable and encompassing monitoring system which sets as a gyrocompass, giving warning if the individual strays too far from the company's purposes and methods and indicating the punishment for doing so or the rewards for staying on course.

Values

> . . . I firmly believe that any organization, or order to survive and achieve success, must have a second set of beliefs on which it premises all its policies and actions.
>
> Next, I believe that the most important single factor in corporate success is faithful adherence to those beliefs.
>
> And finally, I believe that if an organization is to meet the challenges of a changing world, it must be prepared to change everything about itself except those beliefs as it moves through corporate life. (Watson, 1963)

Thus did Thomas Watson, Jr., a moving figure in the early history of IBM, begin his lecture series at Columbia University discussing the ideas and beliefs which built and sustained IBM. To him, it was not the technological advancements of the company, nor the marketing of its products, but the power of IBM's beliefs, and the reflection of the character, experiences, and convictions of his father, T. J. Watson, Sr., which had led to the success of IBM.

The basic beliefs that guide IBM activities are expressed as principles of action. The first three were formulated by Tom Watson, Sr., the last four being added as time went on.

1. Respect for the Individual. This principle manifests itself in a number of ways based on the rights and dignity of the individual, and specifies that IBM should —

Help each employee to develop his or her potential, and make the best use of his or her abilities.
Pay and promote on merit.
Maintain two-way communication between manager and employee, with opportunity for a fair hearing and equitable settlement of disaagreements. (IBM, 1985b)

As a management principle, this results in an emphasis on job security (which has been part of the company policy since 1914), an "open door" policy and maintenance of good human relations, continual opportunity for advancement, and a respect for individual achievement (Watson, 1963; IBM, 1985b).

2. Service to the Customer. IBM has earned the rank of American's most admired corporation for the fourth year in a row in *Fortune's* annual survey of corporate reputations (Hutton, 1986), and with good cause. Their dedication to the best possible service includes that they

Know customer needs and help them anticipate future needs.
Help customers use products and services in the best possible way.
Provide superior equipment maintenance and supporting services. (IBM, 1985b)

This service to the customer depends on the team of employees who are committed to the IBM principles. IBM begins with the highest standards for the selection of all personnel. Among these standards is a compatibility with the principles and beliefs of IBM which brings about the commitment to service which will allow for long nights and weekends of work when necessary to complete a job.

3. Superior Accomplishment of All Tasks. IBM's demands and expectations for a superior performance from all of its employees in whatever they do sets a tone for dealing with all their publics — managers, employees, stockholders, suppliers, customers. Nothing is left to change. Managers are admonished to —

Lead in new developments.
Be aware of advances made by others, better them where possible, or be willing to adopt them to fit the needs of the corporation.
Produce quality products of the most advanced design and at the lowest possible cost.

These three beliefs were the ones by which Thomas Watson, Sr. operated his management of IBM, and were picked up by Watson, Jr. when he assumed the position of head of the corporation. As time went by, other beliefs or principles were included in the management literature which furthered the value structure set forth by the three basic beliefs. These included "managers must lead effectively," "obligations to stockholders," "fair deal for the supplier," and "IBM should be a good corporate citizen."

4. Managers Must Lead Effectively. Sensitivity, intelligence, and aggressive management are demanded to make every individual in the corporation an enthusiastic partner in IBM. In order to achieve this, managers have to follow certain procedures.

Provide the kind of leadership that will motivate employees to do their jobs in a superior way.
Meet frequently with all their people.
Have the courage to question decisioons and policies.
Have the vision to see the needs of the company, as well as of the division or department.
Plan for the future by keeping an open mind to new ideas, whatever the source.

5. Obligations to Stockholders. Stockholders are viewed as the persons having the capital which created the jobs in IBM, and, because of this, IBM has obligations to them. These obligations require IBM employees to —

Take care of the property the stockholders have entrusted to the company.
Provide an attractive return on invested capital.
Exploit opportunities for continuing profitable growth.

6. Fair Deal for the Supplier. Even the often overlooked supplier of goods and services should be treated fairly and impartially, by —

Selecting suppliers according to the quality of their products or services, their general reliability, and competitiveness of price.
Recognizing the legitimate interests of both supplier and IBM when negotiating a contract.
Avoiding suppliers becominng unduly dependent on IBM.

7. IBM Should Be a Good Corporate Citizen. Competition is essential for protecting the immediate and long-term public interest, but the competition should be vigorous and in a spirit of fair play, with respect for competitors and with respect for the law. Improve the quality of society, create an environment in which people want to work and live, and make the world a better place (IBM, 1985b). In addition to these general beliefs or values, IBM's corporate culture consists of several well articulated role-specific and decision-specific duties. For example, the five basic duties of a manager are to employ, to teach, to supervise, to promote people who deserve it, and to discharge, when necessary. Specific rituals are then set up for the discharge of each duty, such as interviewing, personnel reports, and employee counseling (IBM, 1985b).

While these general beliefs, specific duties, and rituals for performing these duties are meant to be at a sufficient level of generality to be timeless, IBM management periodically issues general corporate goals and specific departmental and individual goals which are meant to be time bound and well monitored. In 1983, IBM issued the following for general goals for the 1980s: (a) to grow with the industry; (b) to exhibit product leadership across the entire product line by excelling in technology, values, and quality; (c) to be the most efficient in everything; to be a low cost producer, seller, and administrator; and (d) to sustain profitability which funds growth. Specific division, department, and individual performance plans are set up and monitored on a yearly basis for meeting these goals (*Think,* December 1983).

T. J. Watson used to tell his employees, "It is better to aim at perfection and miss than it is to aim at imperfection and hit it" (Watson, 1963).

Prior to 1946, it was not difficult for employees of IBM to be aware of the values and beliefs of the company of which they were a part, and of the traditions under which they were expected to live and work. But the socialization process became more difficult as the company grew, and because persons assuming management roles might have been with the company for a shorter time than previous managers. Early in the process, it was found that "an ingrained understanding of the beliefs of IBM, far more than technical skill, has made it possible for our people to make the company successful" (Watson, 1963). The five lessons which grew out of his for IBM were—

1. There is simply no substitute for good human relations and for the high morale they bring.
2. There are two things an organization must increase far out of proportion to its growth rate . . . communication, upward and downward and education, and retraining.
3. Complacency is the most natural and insidious disease of large corporations.
4. Everyone must place company interest above that of a division or department.
5. Beliefs must always come before politics, practices, and goals. (Watson, 1963)

Socialization

Socialization of employees to the IBM culture had always been important. In the early years, it was accomplished informally by one-on-one interaction. However, as time went on and the company grew to current multinational size, informality gave way to a highly structural system. Richard Pascale in 1985 published a rather detailed report on several large corporation socialization systems. This report was supplemented by IBM reports which detailed the goals and operations of the various processes involved.

Step One in the Socialization Process Involves the Careful Selection of Entry Level Candidates. IBM in a given year interviews over 200,000 prospective employees, selecting less than 1% as employees. Trained recruiters use standardized procedures in employee selection. Trainers never attempt to oversell the company, and use an extensive filtering process of deselection. Recruiters conduct multiple interviews aimed at locating individuals whose personal values already conform to IBM's corporate beliefs. They are particularly careful to select employees who are motivated to learn, can handle change, are group achievement oriented, have college degrees, graduated in the top of their class, have demonstrated social leadership, present themselves well, and score high on IBM-administered aptitude tests in their respective areas of expertise. Such a careful screening process increases receptivity for the second stage (Lewis, 1985; Pascale, 1985).

Step Two Involves a Humility, Inducing Experience. In the first month of on-the-job training, new employees are placed in difficult situations and frequently work long hours on problems that cannot be solved without help. Early training sessions at IBM frequently cause employees to work from 8:00 a.m. to 2:00 p.m. for several days in a row. Lunches are confined to the work room. Humility tends to flourish under certain conditions, particularly long hours and intense work that pushes one to the limit.

Step Three Involves "In-the-Trenches Training." This leads to a mastery of one's core discipline under the rules and values established by the organization. For example, let's take a close look at the training program for an IBM marketing representative.

IBM marketing representatives do sell IBM products, but they are hardly salesmen or saleswomen in the conventional sense of those words. Many of the products they sell have to do with computer systems: central processing units, terminals, input/output devices, printers, storage units, controllers, and other elements that make up an information processing configuration. The marketing representatives are well acquainted with almost any kind of equipment or system needed to solve almost any kind of business problem. Their orientation is the customer, not a particular set of products or systems. To sell a full range of systems and products, many calling for substantial capital investment, marketing representatives must know two things. First, they must know IBM's business — that is, they must know in depth the capabilities of the products and systems they recommend. Second, they must know their customer's business, and the kinds of problems their customers face in daily operations.

The training program, called "The Core Curriculum," for marketing representatives is 22 weeks. The entire program focuses on what a marketing representative actually does in performing his or her job at IBM. People in these positions are assigned to an IBM branch office where they spend 3 to 5 weeks becoming knowledgeable about IBM's policies, practices, and its full line of products. In addition, they study the needs of IBM customers and, in particular, the ways in which IBM's processing products and systems can help solve problems they encounter in the marketplace. After this session, they are sent to Dallas, Texas, for 3 weeks to be trained in what is called "computer concept and marketing." The next move is to be returned to the branch office for 5 to 9 weeks to test how well this information can be applied in a real work situation. Application Design and Marketing is the next move, with a segment of training taking place again in Dallas, Texas, on design applications, problem identification, and problem solving, following by a stint back at the branch applying what has been learned. This last segment of training lasts for 5 to 7 weeks.

An intensive period of training follows again in Texas for 3 weeks of Systems and Account Marketing training in various operating systems, including processing applications. Trainees go back to the branch office again for 6 to 8 weeks before returning to Dallas for 1 week of industry application, during which the concentration is on learning one particular industry. After learning one area well, the employee returns to the branch office to search out clients and become familiar with the territory.

Once the marketing representatives have completed all of this training and began to settle into their areas, they are sent to marketing school for 2 weeks, either in Dallas or in Poughkeepsie, New York, to polish their marketing skills. The training program which has been outlined has been utilized for approximately 5 years. The program is carefully monitored by IBM, and is subject to change when there is reason to believe that any part of it does not achieve what it was set up to do (IBM, 1985a).

Pascale (1985) summarizes the culmination of this socialization process:

> The first phase of socialization aims to attract the right trainees predisposed toward the firm's culture. The second instills enough humility to evoke self-examination; this facilitates "buying in" to the firm's values. Increasingly, the organizational culture becomes the relevant universe of experience . . . the task is how to cement this new orientation. While IBM hires some MBAs and a few older professionals with prior work experience, almost all go through the same training and start at the same level. It takes six years to grow an IBM marketing representative, twelve years for a controller. . . . The gains from such an approach are cumulative. When all trainees understand there is one step by step career path, it reduces politics. There is no quick way to jump ranks and reach the top. Because the evaluation process has a long time horizon, short term behavior is

counterproductive. Cutting corners catches up with you. Relationships, staying power and a consistent proven track record are the inescapable requirements of advancement. Those advancing, having been grown from within, understand the business not as financial abstraction but as a hands on reality. Senior managers can communicate with those at the lowest ranks in the "short hand" of shared experience (Pascale, 1985:30–31).

Step Four Involves a Training and Retraining Program. Each year, all IBM employees are required to undergo at least 4 weeks of training focusing on implementing IBM's corporate culture in their respective jobs. In addition, each promotion is followed by at least 2 weeks' worth of additional training on the application of IBM's culture to their new job. Finally, remedial training sessions are held for those employees having difficulty in applying IBM's values to the job at hand. In all, IBM schedules over 1½ million hours of training for its employees each year (IBM, 1983).

Monitoring

Meticulous attention is given at IBM to tracking division, department, and individual performance in order to reward those who excel and correct the behavior of those who err. The evaluation systems employed are comprehensive, consistent, and interlocking, focused on determing adherence to corporate values and effectiveness in meeting corporate goals. Pascale illustrates:

> One example of comprehensive, consistent, and interlocking systems are those used at IBM to track adherence to its value of "respecting the decency of the individual." This is monitored via climate surveys; "Speak up!" (a confidential suggestion box); open door procedures; skip level interviews; and numerous informal contacts between senior-level managers and employees. The Personnel Department moves quickly when any downward changes are noted in the above indices. In addition, managers are monitored for percent of performance appraisals completed on time and percent of employees missing the required one week a year of training. All first-level managers receive an intensive two-week course in people management and each managerial promotion results in another week-long refresher. These systems provide a near "fail-safe" network of checks and double checks to ensure adherence to IBM's core value of respecting individual dignity. (Pascale, 1985, p. 32)

At IBM, deviations from cultural expectations are dealt with face-to-face in (a) counseling and corrective action sessions, (b) discussions of performance appraisal reports, and (c) by a device known as the "penalty box." Pascale explains:

> Included in IBM's mechanisms for respecting the individual is a device known as the "Penalty Box." Often a person sent to the "penalty box" has committed a crime against the culture—for example, harsh handling of a subordinate, overzealousness against the competition, gaming the reporting system. Most penalty box assignments involve a lateral move to a less desirable location—a branch manager in Chicago might be moved to a nebulous staff position at headquarters. For an outsider, penalty box assignments look like normal assignments, but insiders know they are off the track. Penalty boxes provide a place for people while the mistakes they've made or the hard feelings they've created are gradually forgotten—and while the company looks for a new useful position. The mechanism is one among numerous things IBM does that lend credence to employees' beliefs that the firm won't act capriciously and end a career. In the career of strong, effective

managers, there are times when one steps on toes. The penalty box is IBM's "half-way house" enabling miscreants to contemplate their errors and play another day. (Don Estridge, maverick pioneer of IBM's success in personal computers and currently head of that division, came from the penalty box.) (Pascale, 1985, pp. 31–32)

When counseling and corrective action sessions, discussions of performance appraisal reports, and the penalty box fail to bring corrective action, the result is separation from the organization. However, it is noteworthy that IBM has one of the lowest turnover rates for employees of any major company in the United States (IBM, 1984 Annual Report).

B.   The Interests and Values of IBM's Investors, Workers and Consumers and the Corporate Climate they create.

There are several groups upon whom IBM depends for corporate success, and with whom its culture must interact successfully for these relationships to be mutually rewarding. Attention is now directed to exploring the interests and values of each group, and their positive or negative intersection with IBM's corporate culture in creating IBM's corporate climate and attracting investors.

Investors' confidence in an organization substancially influences the company's net worth and the stability of its management team. In an attempt to locate standard investor interests and values in determining whether to put money into or withdraw it from a stock, *Fortune* magazine in 1982 pulled a random sample of financial analysts in order to determine the dimensions along which investors evaluate corporate performance. From this sample, eight key attributes of corporate reputation emerged as central to investor confidance. These were (a) innovativeness; (b) ability to attract, develop, and keep talented people; (c) quality of management; (d) long-term investment value; (e) community and environmental responsibility; (f) quality of products or services; (g) financial soundness; and (h) use of corporate assets. These eight attributes represent the values and interests of investors in evaluating corporate performance. It is obvious that several of these values directly intersect IBM's corporate culture: in particular, service to the customer, superior accomplishment of all tasks, effective management, obligations to stockholders, and corporate citizenship. In addition, IBM's goals for the 1980s – to grow with the industry, exhibit leadership across product lines, to be efficient, and to sustain profits – intersect investor values. If IBM's socialization and monitoring systems are effective and can operationalize these values and deliver on these goals, we would expect investors to be very pleased with or invest in IBM stock.

Once each year for the past 4 years, *Fortune Magazine* has polled 8,000 executives, outside directors, and financial analysts regarding their evaluation of the most admired corporations in America, employing as criteria for evaluation the eight values listed by investors as important. Each year for the last 4 years, IBM was ranked in first place. In 1986, 3M and Dow Jones came out second and third. In 1986, IBM ranked first on five of the eight attributes: (a) ability to attract; (b) develop and keep talented people; (c) quality of management, (d) long-term investment value (financial soundness), and (e) use of corporate assets. IBM did not rank in the top three in regard to (a) innovativeness, (b) community and environmental responsibility, and (c) quality of product, despite the fact that the last two are explicitly stated corporate values and that IBM ranks first in the United States in regard to money spent and research and development. This may suggest the need for additional socialization and monitoring in these areas. In April of 1986, *Business week* evaluted the top 1,000 U.S. corporations in regard to *investment value,* as determined by price of the companies stock multiplied by the number of shares sold. IBM headed the list as the most prized stock in America by Investors (*USA Today,* 1986).

Thus, regardless of whether one employs the eight key attributes of investment analysts or actual stock market sales as criteria for evaluation corporate performance, IBM's corporate performance as guided by its values and goals clearly create *a very positive investment climate.*

Workers

Worker commitment to a corporation, motivation, and quality of work significantly influence a corporation's performance. We have already indicated that IBM hires workers whose values are consistent with that of the corporation, and socializes and monitors worker performance aimed at enhancing and operationalizing those values in pursuit of specific goals. First, each year, over 200,000 workers seek employment with IBM, with only 1% being hired. This suggests a strong worker interest in IBM as an employer. Workers who find employment at IBM like their company so much that fewer than 1% leave by choice each year. "IBM knows how to pick the people it needs," said Victor Heckler, a Chicago consultant, "develop them and motivate them. So they stay, grow in their jobs and become more valuable" (Luciana, 1985). Promotions are made on merit only, recognition is frequent and tangible, equality is a goal, training and retraining programs are available, and participation is valued. Job security has always been a policy at IBM, and the no-layoff policy encourages commitment and going that extra mile for the company (*Forbes,* 1985; Moskowitz, 1985; Luciana, 1985). Since 1963, IBM has provided for what Watson called their "wild ducks" by instituting the IBM Fellows, who are given 5 years of freedom and the money to pursue any project they wish as research fellows for IBM. One of the first of these units developed IBM's highly successful personal computer. There are, at present 10 of these semi-autonomous units operating with employees throughout the world recognized as research fellows. Empirical evidence from a nationwide survey of American managers lends credence to the claim that, when employees and the corporation share values, there is benefit to both.

> The strength of this relationship affects both the quality and character of managerial commitment, and the direction of energy and effort on behalf of the organization. Strong shared values provide individuals with a sense of success and fulfillment, a healthy (less cynical) assessment of the values and ethics of their colleagues, subordinates, and bosses, and a greater regard for organizational objectives and significant organizational constraints. (Posner et al., 1985)

Thus, whether one employs the criteria of worker interest in being employed, or employee satisfaction with IBM as an employer, IBM's corporate performance as guided by its values and goals *appears to create a very positive work climate.*

Consumers

Consumer interest in a corporation's products is in many ways the ultimate test of a corporation's reliability, profitability, and influence upon the market place. In an attempt to locate consumer values, we turn to consumer advocate Ralph Nader (1985), who argues that, at bottom, consumers want quality, service, performance, and value from a product. Again, IBM's corporate values intersect these consumer interests or values in several areas—respect for the individual, service to the customer, superior accomplishment of all tasks, effective leadership, and good corporate citizenship. Also, IBM's corporate goals of industry growth, product leadership, and efficiency seem to intersect consumer values and interests. IBM's Information Systems Division attempts to monitor consumer needs through an extensive program of consumer feedback which includes focused group evaluation during product development, pretesting new equipment, monitoring service calls, monitoring customer evaluation of IBM products in competition with other products, and sales reports. These evaluations include equipment users and equipment purchase decision makers. In addition, IBM's advertising and marketing consultants and programs are aimed at developing brand name recognition and unique feature recognition in all IBM products, in order to develop clear expectations regarding what a product can and cannot do. *Business Marketing* (1985) reports that IBM spends more money in advertising and marketing ($650 million on print, radio/TV, and direct mail advertising) than any company in America.

IBM's product lines are divided into 19 groups. Byron Quann, Director of Communication for IBM's Information Systems Division, reported in January of 1985 that IBM products were the top choice of both users and decision makers in 11 of these 19 areas, and in the top three of both users and decision makers in seven more areas, indicating broad-based consumer preference for IBM's product line. IBM's market shares ranged from 75% of the main frame market to a low of 35%, and was the nation's leader for sales in the microcomputer market. The most frequently cited reasons for consumer preference were service, performance, and cost (Quann, 1985, pp. 107–108).

Thus, whether one employs market dominance or market shares as criteria for evaluating consumer performance for IBM products, IBM's corporate performance as guided by its values and goals appears to create *a very positive consumer climate.*

In conclusion, IBM's investor, worker, and consumer climates appear strongly positive, and are a direct indication that IBM is effectively communicating its corporate values and goals to all these individuals. While it is clear that IBM has, on the whole, been effective in implementing its corporate culture, several gaps in the socialization and monitoring processes have revealed themselves. *First,* in regard to corporate values, additional work is required implementing the values of innovateness, product quality, and corporate citizenship. *Second,* the value of product quality and the goal of product leadership in 8 of its 19 product groups requires additional effort. *Third,* these values and objectives are particularly important, given the competitive nature of the high-technology environment and its tendency toward rapid market saturation and unexpected change, if IBM is to advance its current market position.

IMPLICATIONS OF THE IBM CASE STUDY FOR RULES THEORIES OF ORGANIZATIONAL COMMUNICATION

We began the final section of this essay by critiquing previous rules theory research in organizational communication and attempting an initial response to those criticisms by (a) evaluating the prescriptive values employed by one of our nation's best run companies, (b) testing a new conceptualization of organizational communication which focused on the construct corporate climate, and (c) exploring the possibility of this new construct providing a basis for evaluation of the diverse conceptualizations of rules theories within an organizational communication context. Let us now explore the implications of our case study for each of these issues.

Evaluating Prescriptive Rules

What has our IBM case study taught us about the prescriptive character of communication rules? *First,* effective values of communication rules, suggesting how one appropriately obtains a given goal, must be general and aimed specifically at intersecting the values and goals of those with whom one must interact in order to successfully obtain those goals. Mutual entailment of one's values and goals substantially increases the practical force of the rules involved. *Second,* effective corporate cultures require extensive socialization and monitoring processes in order to gain and maintain high conformity to the rules, even when those rules are mutually shared and beneficial to all involved. Included must be some creative processes for dealing positively with rules violations. *Third,* effective corporate cultures must be adapted to the general environment in which an organization functions, and change when that environment changes. This suggests that corporate values must be general and capable of adaptive interpretations.

Corporate Climate as an Integrating Construct

What has our use of corporate climate as an integrating construct taught us about organizational communication rules? *First,* at the heart of all communication rules analysis is the recognition that coordination is essential for significant group efforts, and that one must have some set of shared values or communication rules to guide such activities. The construct "corporate climate" focuses research inquiry on the ideal interests and values of the corporation and those who interact in goal attainment, and on the convergence of those interests, values, and goals as a direct measure of the practical force. *Second,* by dividing the organizational communication climate into the three central groups required for effective coordination—investers, workers, and consumers—this construct seeks generalizability to all organizational environments while revealing the interdependence of groups involved. *Third,* corporate climate has the capacity to reveal both positive and negative intersections of values and goals, thus allowing for an evaluation of the communication rules being employed from the point of view of each group.

Evaluating Multiple Rules Theoretic Approaches. What does this case study tell us about various approaches to the perspectives on rules theories? *First,* while this case study undertakes a functional approach to organizational communication rules (i.e., what values guide behavior in goal attainment), the general approach involved of analyzing corporate climate admits of structural and functional, contingency and structural, rules analysis. *Second,* corporate climate as a construct can be refined and developed through the unique insights of each of these theoretic approaches. *Third,* values, socialization and monitoring can all be explored productively and uniquely from each of these approaches. The theoretic perspectives thus appear to be complementary, not mutually exclusive.

REFERENCES

Adler, K. (1980). On the falsification of rules theories. *Quarterly Journal of Speech, 64,* 427–438.
Anscombe, G. E. M. (1957). *Intention.* Oxford, England: Blackwell.
Business Marketing (1985, May). 100 leading advertisers' ad spending, pp. 61–72.
Chisholm, R. M. (1964). The descriptive elements in the concept of action. *Journal of Philosophy, 41,* 613–624.

Chisholm, R. (1970). The structure of intentions. *Journal of Philosophy, 47,* 633–647.

Cody, M. J., & McLaughlin, M. L. (1980). Perceptions of compliance-gaining situations: A dimensional analysis. *Communication Monographs, 47,* 132–148.

Cody, M. J., McLaughlin, M. L., Jordan, W. J., & Schneider, M. J. (1979). A multidimensional scaling of three sets of compliance-gaining strategies. *Communication Quarterly, 28,* 34–46.

Cody, M. J., McLaughlin, M. L., Jordan, W. J., & Schneider, M. J. (1983). *A proposed working typology of compliance-gaining message strategies.* Unpublished manuscript, Department of Speech Communication, Texas Tech University.

Cody, M. J., Woelfel, M. L., & Jordan, W. J. (1983). Dimensions of compliance-gaining situations. *Human Communication Research, 9,* 99–113.

Cronen, V. E., & Davis, K. (1978). Alternative approaches for the Communication theorist: Problems in the laws, rules, systems trichotomy. *Human Communication Research, 4,* 120–128.

Cronen, V. E., Pearce, W. B., & Harris, L. (1982). The coordinated management of meaning: A theory of communication. In F. E. X. Dance (Ed.), *Comparative communication theory.* New York: Harper and Row.

Cronen, V. E., Pearce, W. B., & Snavely, L. (1979). A theory of rule structure and forms of episodes, and a study of unwanted repetitive patterns (URP). In D. Nimmo (Ed.), *Communication yearbook 2.* New Brunswick, NJ: Transaction Press.

Curran, J. J. (1986, February). Computer makers on the mend. *Fortune,* pp. 31–45.

Cushman, D. P. (1977). The rules perspective as a theoretical basis for the study of human communication. *Communication Quarterly,* Winter, *23,* 19–30.

Cushman, D. P. (1987). The rules approach to communication theory: A philosophical and operational perspective. In L. Kincaid (Ed.), *Communication theory from an Eastern and Western perspective.* New York: Academic Press.

Cushman, D. P., & Cahn, D. (1985). *Communication in interpersonal relationships.* Albany, NY: State University of New York Press.

Cushman, D. P., & Cahn, D. (1986). Cross-cultural communication and interpersonal relationships. In J. Stewart (Ed.), *Bridges not walls.* New York: Random House, pp. 324–335.

Cushman, D. P., & Craig, R. T. (1976). Communication systems: Interpersonal implications. In G. Miller (Ed.), *Explorations in interpersonal communication* (pp. 37–58). Beverly Hills, CA: Sage.

Cushman, D. P., Dietrich, D., & Valentinsen, B. (1982). A rules theory of interpersonal relationships. In F. Dance (Ed.), *Comparative theories of human communication* (pp. 90–107). New York: Harper and Row.

Cushman, D. P., Donohue, W., & Nofsinger, R. (1980). Creating and confronting social order: A comparison of rules perspectives. *Western Speech, 44,* 5–19.

Cushman, D. P., & Florence, B. T. (1974, Fall). The development of interpersonal communication theory. *Today's Speech,* pp. 11–15.

Cushman, D. P., & King, S. S. (in press). The impact of high technology on international management. In R. Shuter & S. Chatterjee (Eds.), *International management and comparative management systems.* Wawatosa, WI: Cultural Press.

Cushman, D. P., & King, S. S. (1985). National and organizational cultures in conflict resolution: Japan, the United States, and Yugoslavia. *Informatologia Yugoslavia, 17,* 127–136. (Reprinted in W. Gudykunst, L. Stewart, & S. Ting-Toomey (Eds.), *Communication, culture, and organizational processes, international and intercultural handbook* (vol. 9) (pp. 114–133). Beverly Hills, CA: Sage.

Cushman, D. P., & King, S. S. (1986). The role of communication rules in explaining intergroup interaction. In W. Gudykunst (Ed.), *Intergroup communication* (pp. 39–51). London: Edward Arnold Publishers.

Cushman, D. P., & Larkin, T. J. (1981). The location of rules in the explanation of human communication. *Communication, 6,* 117–133.

Cushman, D. P., & Pearce, W. B. (1977). Generality and necessity in three types of theory about human communication, with special attention to rules theory. *Human Communication Research, 3,* 344–352.

Cushman, D. P., & Sanders, R. (1982). Rules theories of human communication process: A structural and functional perspective. In B. Dervin & M. Voight (Eds.), *Progress in communication sciences: An annual review* (pp. 49–83). Norwood, NJ: Ablex Publishing Corp.

Cushman, D. P., & Sanders, R. (1984). Rules, constraints, and strategies in human communication. In C. Arnold & J. Bowers (Eds.), *Handbook of rhetoric and communication* (pp. 230–269). Rockleigh, NJ: Allyn & Bacon.

Cushman, D., & Whiting, G. C. (1972). An approach to communication theory: Toward consensus on rules. *Journal of Communication, 22,* 219–238.

Davidson, D. (1963). Action, reasons and causes. *Journal of Philosophy, 60,* 685–700.

Davidson, D. (1971). Agency. In R. Binkley, R. Bronaugh, & A. Marras (Eds.), *In Agents, action and reason.* Toronto, Canada: U. of Toronto Press.

Davidson, D. (1969). The logical form of action sentences. In N. Rescher (Ed.), *The Logic of Decision and Action.* Pittsburgh: University of Pittsburgh Press.

Donohue, W. A. (1981). Development of a model of role use in negotiation interaction. *Communication Monographs, 48,* 106–121.

Donohue, W. A., Cushman, D. P., & Nofsinger, R. E. (1980). Creating and confronting social order: A comparison of rules perspectives. *Western Journal of Speech Communication, 44,* 5–19.

Donohue, W. A., Dietz, M., & Hamilton, A. (1984). Coding naturalistic negotiation interaction, *Human Communication Research, 10,* 3.

Eglin, P. (1975). What should sociology explain: regularities, rules, or interpretations? *Philosophy of the Social Sciences, 5,* 377–391.

Farace, R., Monge, P. R., & Russell, H. (1977). *Communicating and organizing* (pp. 127–154). Reading, MA: Addison Wesley.

Fay, B., & Moon, D. (1977). What should an adequate philosophy of social science look like? *Philosophy of the Social Sciences, 7,* 208–277.

Fraker, S. (1984, March). High-speed management for the high-tech age. *Fortune,* pp. 4–6, 64, 66–68.

Gauthier, D. (1963). *Practical reasoning.* Oxford, England: Clarendon Press.

Goldman, A. I. (1970). *A theory of human action.* Englewood Cliffs, NJ: Prentice-Hall.

Grice, H. P. (1957). Meaning. *The Philosophical Review, 66,* 377–388.

Gustafson, D. (1975). The range of intentions. *Inquiry, 181,* 83–95.

Gutknecht, D. (1982). Conceptualizing cultures in organizational theory. *California Sociologist, 72,* 22–47.

Hampshire, S. (1965). *Thought and action.* London: Chatto and Windus.

Harre, R., & Secord, P. F. (1972). *The explanation of social behavior.* Totowa, NJ: Rowman and Littlefield.

Harris, L. M. (1980). The maintenance of social reality: A family case study. *Family Process, 19,* 19–33.

Harris, L., & Cronen, V. (1979). A rules based model of the analysis and evaluation of organizational communication. *Communication Quarterly, 27,* 12–28.

Heap, J. L. (1977). Verstehen, language and warrants. *The Sociological Quarterly,* Spring, *18,* 177–181.

Hutton, C. (1986, January). America's most admired corporations. *Fortune,* 16–27.

IBM (1983, December). IBM's goals for the 1980's. *Think,* 11–23.

IBM (1985a). *IBM Management Development Center.* Armonk, NY: IBM.

IBM (1985b). *On managing: A selection of management briefing letters from IBM's chief executives.* Armonk, NY: ISG Business Systems.

IBM (1985c). *Marketing and systems engineering careers.* Armonk, NY: International Business Machines Corp.

IBM (1985d). *National Accounts Division Entry Marketing Education Program.* White Plains, NY: International Business Machines Corp.

Kant, I. (1929). *Critique of pure reason* (N. Kemp Smith, Trans.). London: MacMillian. (Original work published 1781.)

Lewis, D. (1985, May). Interview with Dick Lewis, Account Executive in National Accounts Division, IBM, Atlanta, Georgia. Quoted by Scott Blaney, Training Program for IBM Marketing Department (unpublished paper).

Luciana, L. (1985, November). Seeing the future work at IBM, *Fortune,* p. 165.

MacIntyre, A. (1962). A mistake about causality in social sciences. In Laslett, R. & Runamen, A., *Philosophy, politics and society* (pp. 48–70). Oxford: Blackwell.

MacMurray, J. (1938). What is action? *Proceedings of Aristotlian Society,* (Suppl.), *17,* 69–85.

Makin, J. (1983, January). America's most admired corporations. *Fortune,* pp. 34–44.

McLaughlin, M. L., Cody, M. J., & O'Hair, H. D. (1983a). The managemen41.

Some contextual determinants of accounting behavior. *Human Communication Research, 9,* 208–224.

McLaughlin, M. L., Cody, M. J., & Robey, C. S. (1980). Situational influences on the selection of strategies to resist compliance-gaining attempts. *Human Communication Research, 7,* 14–36.

McLaughlin, M. L., Cody, M. J., & Rosenstein, N. E. (1983b). Account sequences in conversations between strangers. *Communication Monographs, 50,* 102–125.

tion, Michigan State University.

Makin, J. (1983, January). America's most admired corporations. *Fortune,* pp. 34–44.

Meldon, A. I. (1956). Action. *The Philosophical Review, 45,* 523–541.

Meldon, A. I. (1961). *Free action.* London, England: Routledge and Kegal Paul.

Meldon, A. I. (1956). Action. *The Philosophical Review, 45,* 523–541.

Miller, G. R., & Burgoon, M. (1978). Persuasion research: Review and commentary. In B. Ruben (Ed.), *Communication yearbook 2* (pp. 29–47). New Brunswick, NJ: Transaction Books.

Modrak, D. K. (1976). Aisthesis in the practical syllogism. *Philosophical Studies, 30,* 379–391.

Moskowitz, M. (1985). Lessons from the best companies to work for. *California Management Review, 27,* 42–47.

Nader, R., & Kelley, G. (1985). *More action for a change: Students serving the public institution.* New York: Dembner Books.

New York Times (1986 February 12). The I.B.M. in G.N.P., p. E61.

Ouchi, W. (1980). *Theory Z: How American management can meet the Japanese challenge.* New York: John Wiley and Sons.

Pascale, R. (1985). The paradox of "corporate culture"; Reconciling ourselves to socialization. *California Management Review, 27,* 26–41.

Pearce, W. B. (1980). *Communication rules: Some structuralist approaches.* A paper presented at the Eastern Communication Association Conference, Ocean City, Maryland.

Pearce, W. B. (1972). Consensual rules in interpersonal communication: A reply to Cushman and Whiting. *Journal of Communication, 23,* 16–168.

Pearce, W. B. (1976). The coordinated management of meaning: A rules based theory of interpersonal communication. In G. R. Miller (Ed.), *Explorations in interpersonal communication.* Beverly Hills, CA: Sage.

Pearce, W. B. (1979). The logics of coordinated management of meaning: A substantive approach to communication education. *Communication Education, 28,* 22–38.

Pearce, W. B. (1977). Naturalistic study of communication: Its function and form. *Communication Quarterly, 25,* 51–56.

Pearce, W. B., & Cronen, V. C. (1980). *Communication, action, and meaning: Creating social realities.* New York: Praeger.

Pearce, W. B., Cronen, V. C., & Conklin, F. (1979). On what to look at when studying communication: A hierarchial model of actor's meanings. *Communication, 4,* 195–220.

Pearce, W. B., Cronen, V. C., Johnson, K., Jones, G., & Raymond, R. (1980). The structure of communication roles and the forms of conversation:: An experimental stimulation. *Western Journal of Speech Communication, 44,* 20–34.

Pearce, W. B., Harris, L., & Cronen, V. C. (1982). The coordinated management of meaning: Human communication in a new key. In C. Wilder and J. Weakland (Eds.), *Communication from an interactional view*. New York: Praeger.

Pearce, W. B., & Wiseman, R. (1983). Rules theories: Varieties, limitations, and potentials. In W. Gudykunst (Ed.), *Intercultural communication theory*. Beverly Hills, CA: Sage.

Perry, E. (1984 January). America's most admired corporations. *Fortune*, pp. 50–66.

Peters, T. J., & Waterman, R. H., Jr. (1983). *In search of excellence: Lessons from America's best run companies*. New York: Free Press.

Philipsen, G. (1981). *The prospect for cultural communication*. Paper presented at the Seminar on Communication Theory from Eastern and Western Perspectives, East-West Communication Institute, East-West Center, Honolulu, Hawaii.

Pinkard, T. (1976). Interpretation and verification in the human sciences: A note on Taylor. *Philosophy of Social Science, 6,* 165–173.

Poole, M. S. (1985). *A structurational theory of organization climate*. Paper presented at the International Communication Association Conference, Honolulu, HI.

Poole, M. S., & McPhee, R. D. (1983). A structural analysis of organizational climate. In L. Putnam & M. Pacanowski (Eds.), *Communication and organizations: An interpretive approach* (pp. 195–219). Beverly Hills, CA: Sage.

Poole, M. S., Seibold, D. R., & McPhee, R. D. (1985). Group decision-making as a structurational process. *Quarterly Journal of Speech, 71,* 74–102.

Poole, M. S., Seibold, D. R., & McPhee, R. D. (1985). A structurational approach to theory-building in group decision-making research. In R. Y. Hirokawa & M. S. Poole (Eds.), *Group decision making and communication*. Beverly Hills, CA: Sage.

Posner, B. Z., Kouzes, J. M., & Schmidt, W. H. (1985). Shared values make a difference: An empirical test of corporate culture. *Human Resource Management, 24,* 293–309.

Quann, B. G. (1985, January). How IBM assesses its business-to-business advertising, *Business Marketing*, pp. 106, 108–111, 112.

Schall, M. S. (1983). A communication rules approach to organizational culture. *Administrative Science Quarterly, 28,* 557–582.

Schenck-Hamlin, W. J., Wiseman, R. L., & Georgeacarakos, G. N. (1982). A model of properties of compliance-gaining strategies. *Communication Quarterly, 30,* 92–100.

Sellars, W. (1966). Thoughtland action. In Keith Lehren (Ed.), *Freedom and determinism*. New York: Random House.

Sellers, P. (1985, January). America's most admired corporations. *Fortune*, pp. 17–29.

Sherman, S. (1984, October). Eight masters of innovation. *Fortune*, pp. 66–94.

Shimanoff, S. B. (1980). *Communication rules: Theory and research*. Beverly Hills, CA: Sage.

Smith, M. J. (1982a). *Persuasion and human action: A review and critique of social influence theories*. Belmont, CA: Wadsworth.

Smith, M. J. (1982b). Cognitive schemata and persuasive communication: Toward a contingency rules theory. In M. Burgoon (Ed.), *Communication yearbook 6* (pp. 330–362). Beverly Hills, CA: Sage.

Smith, M. J. (1982c). The contingency rules theory of persuasion: An empirical test. *Communication Quarterly, 30,* 359–367.

Smith, M. J. (1984). Contingency rules theory, context, and compliance behaviors. *Human Communication Research, 10,* 489–513.

Smith, T. (1977). *Practical inference and its implications for communication theory*. Preliminary examination paper, Michigan State University.

Smith, T. (1978). *The development of self through interaction: A test of a communication paradigm*. Unpublished Ph.D. dissertation, Michigan State University.

Smith, T. (1980). On the nature and sources of practical necessity. *Philosophy of the Social Sciences, 10,* 279–296.

Stanback, M., & Pearce, W. B. (1981). "Talking to the Man"; some communication strategies used by subordinants and their implications for intergroup relations. *Quarterly Journal of Speech, 67,* 21–30.

Stoutland, F. (1976). The causal theory of action. In Mannien, R. & Thomela, T. (Eds.), *Essays on Explanation and Understanding* (pp. 271–304). Amsterdam, Holland: D. Riedell.

Strawson, P. F. (1964). Intention and convention in speech acts. *The Philosophical Review, 73,* 439–460.

Taylor, C. (1964). *The explanation of behavior.* London: Rutledge.

Taylor, C. (1970). The explanation of purposive behavior. In R. Borger & F. Cloffi (Eds.), *Explanation in the behavioral sciences* (pp. 49–80). Cambridge, England: Cambridge University Press.

Taylor, C. (1971). Interpretation and the sciences of man. *Review of Metaphysics, 25,* 13–48.

Taylor, R. (1960). I can. *The Philosophical Review, 49,* 78–89.

Taylor, R. (1966). *Action and purpose.* Englewood Cliffs, NJ: Prentice-Hall.

Think (1983), p. 3.

Toulmin, S. (1969). Concepts and the explanation of human behavior. In T. Mischel (Ed.), *Human action* (pp. 71–104). New York: Academic Press.

Toulmin, S. (1970). Reasons and causes. In R. Borger & F. Cioffi (Eds.), *Explanation in the behavioral sciences* (pp. 1–27). Cambridge, England: Cambridge University Press.

Toulmin, S. (974). Rules and their relevance for understanding human behavior. In T. Mischel (Ed.), *Understanding other persons.* Oxford, England: University Press.

U.S.A. Today (1986, April 11). IBM leads pack on most valuable list.

Uttal, B. (1984, December). Is IBM playing too tough? *Fortune,* pp. 34–37.

Von Wright, G. H. (1971). *Explanation and understanding,* Ithaca, NY: Cornell University Press.

Von Wright, G. H. (1972). On so-called practical inference. *Acts Sociologica, 15,* 39–53.

Von Wright, G H. (1976). Replies. In Mannien, R. & Thomela, T. (Eds.), *Essays on explanation and understanding* (pp. 371–413). Amsterdam, Holland: D. Riedel.

Watson, T. J., Jr. (1963). *A business and its beliefs: The ideas that helped build IBM.* New York: McGraw-Hill.

Weaver, R. (1964). *Visions of order: The cultural crises of our time.* Baton Rouge, LA: LSU Press.

Weber, M. (1968). *Economy and society.* New York: Bedminister Press.

Yolton, J. W. (1966, January). Agent causality. *American Philosophical Quarterly,* pp. 14–26.

Yolton, J. (1973, April). Action in metaphysic and modality. *American Philosophical Quarterly,* pp. 71–85.

Chapter 5

Organizational Communication: Contingent Views

Osmo A. Wiio

This is not a usual "state-of-the-art" article. This is, perhaps, a "state-of-the-artless" article. There is so little we know and so much we don't know. Rather than listing again old and new research results I prefer explorations into less known areas of organizational communication.

THE NATURE OF ORGANIZATIONAL COMMUNICATION

It is still difficult for communication scholars to make a distinction between two dimensions of communication in organizations: (a) communication as an intervening variable and (b) communication as an organizational tool.

Organizational communication can be defined (Wiio, 1978) as such an interchange of information between systems which interfaces organizational systems in different situations so that they are able to function in a compatible and coordinated fashion to achieve organizational and individual goals.

Organizational communication is primarily a tool, an interfacing variable instead of an intervening variable. It makes everything else possible in an organization. Without communication there can be no organization, no management, no cooperation, no motivation, no sales, no demand nor supply, no marketing and no coordinated work processes.

Methodologically speaking communication "pollutes" all other organizational variables. Or, if you will, there is a permanent "Hawthorne effect" by communication in any organizational research situation.

However, communication seldom EXPLAINS the functions of an organization, just as little as a paint brush would explain da Vinci's Mona Lisa. (I am only slightly exaggerating.) Here lies the fundamental error in much of the organizational research.

Much of the research has been a search for a "communicational explanation" for organizational functions. Would it not be more fruitful to try to explan COMMUNICATION by organizational functions? For different tasks we need different tools.

To confuse the matter even more I have to admit that SOMETIMES communication can be an intervening variable, per se.

If there is too little communication the functions of the organization may suffer (or job satisfaction). Too much communication — overload — may be as bad. In fact a human organization is simply a communication network: if communication fails a part of the organizational structure fails.

It is sometimes difficult to make a distinction between the tool function and the intervening variable function. This is especially true when considering the contents of organizational messages. Thus the confusion in organizational communications research is understandable.

The confusion would be an academic matter if not its practical consequences were so severe. Research results may be interpreted as problems in communication processes when the problems may be somewhere else. Communication may be only an overt indication of underlying factors. It does not help to improve organizational problems if one changes only communication processes.

CONTINGENCY APPROACH: SITUATIONAL BEHAVIOR

It seems that the best predictor of organizational communication behavior is a contingent or situational approach. (Wiio, 1978; Goldhaber, Dennis, Richetto, & Wiio, 1979). It even explains some of the earlier conflicting results.

The contingency model is complicated: it includes internal and external organizational and communication contingencies. There are at least five main components in the organizational communication:

1.   structure, quality and size of the communication system,
2.   quantity of information exchange in the system,
3.   content of the messages,
4.   timing of the communication process, and
5.   system constraints of the communication situation.

Because of the complexity of the contingency model it would seem that it is not a predictive model: there are so many intervening factors that the net effect is difficult to see.

Human behavior is complicated, all simple models are poor predictors anyway. Organizational communication research has been able to collect information about different organizational situations. Consequently it is possible to use the model in a predictive capacity when the major system constraints are known in different situations. However, much more information is needed. (See e.g. Wiio, Goldhaber, & Yates, 1980 or Goldhaber, Dennis, Richetto, & Wiio, 1979).

THE MYTH OF RATIONALITY

The underlying hypothesis of much of the organizational communication research and consulting is the idea of "rational man." "A member of an organization will behave rationally when he or she has the relevant information through proper communication forms." Rational behavior is functional, non-rational behavior is dysfunctional!

Based on this academically biased idea we (researchers) pose rational questions to members of the organizations, treat the answer in a most rational way (statistics) and draw rational conclusions about problems and solutions.

Please understand that I am not saying that this is necessarily wrong. On the contrary, it has been a necessary phase in communication research and my personal preference is empirical research. What I AM saying is that we have tended to forget the irrational, emotional side of human behavior in our studies of organizational communication behavior.

This omission is rather strange when we consider that communication scholars have been interested in the irrational aspects of communication at least since Lasswell's early propaganda studies.

THE SEMIOTIC APPROACH

Recent studies of the functions of the brain hemispheres have indicated that we have two parallel information processing systems. The left hemisphere is our "serial processor," the logical, rational processor of language. The right hemisphere is our "parallel processor," the holistic professor of space and relations as well as emotions.

This model is not as new as it seems; it only confirms some of the thoughts expressed by the European school of linguistics called "formalists" early this century. Its modern forms are called "semiotics" or "structuralism."

Formalism was started by de Saussure from Switzerland at the turn of the century. It was popular in pre-revolutionary Russia and some of the scholars moved first to Prague and then to other countries, Roman Jakobson to the U.S.A. More recent names of the school are Levi-Strauss and Greimas in France, Eco in Italy.

The formalists suggested early that there are two kinds of human information processing: a logic-linear processing and a mythic-poetic processing. Various names have been suggested for these two types of thinking: diachronic and synchronic or syntagmatic and paradigmatic thinking.

Syntagmatic thinking is the logical "left side" thinking and paradigmatic thinking is the "irrational" thinking of the right side of the brain.

The formalists and the semiotic scholars have shown the existence of these two kinds of thinking in folklore, myths and plays. They suggested that we inherit certain patterns of thinking which is reflected in the way we describe the world. A typical inherited paradigmatic pattern is the "good guy — bad guy" dichotomy of the plays and films. A Swedish researcher found the pattern even in television news shows.

MANAGEMENT AND MYTHOLOGY

More recently there has been much international interest in semiotic studies of management processes. It seems that organizational decisions are not as rational as the textbooks seem to make them.

Greimas (1979) studied decision making in French organizations and developed a business actant model based on early formalist thinking. His actants are:

1. subject
2. object
3. sender
4. receiver
5. helper
6. adversary

According to Greimas these actants describe any cultural value set — also business values. When values have visual forms we may speak of "myths" (Broms & Gahmberg, 1982).

Broms and Gahmberg (1982) studied the "Chrysler Crisis" using content analysis of 20 articles from *Fortune* and *Business Week*. They found the American business discussion about the Chrysler case strongly mythical. They write (1982, p. 23):

"The Chrysler crisis may be seen as an actant system where the most obvious actants would be:

1. subject: Chrysler
2. object: welfare of Chrysler
3. helper: Federal funds, loans, U.A.W.
4. adversary: GM & Ford, foreign automakers
5. sender: American economy in late 70's
6. receiver: Chrysler"

"The subject of the spectacle is Chrysler in the first analysis. But the spectacle moves to a higher, national level because of the metaphorical importance of the auto industry at the center of the American value set. The real subject of the discussion is the American value set. We notice too that the subject is also an all-important part of that which ought to be the sender: the 'Great American Economy' " (1982, p. 25).

"Some media other than the prudent BW and F are even more sure of the relation between Chrysler and the American Myth. In some cases, it is stated with utmost clarity. Commenting on the Chrysler crisis in a Voice of America broadcast on Feb. 22, 1980, Charles May said: 'The American Dream is over' " (1982, p. 28).

ORGANIZATIONAL VALUE SYSTEMS

Peters and Waterman discussed the concept of "value systems" in their book, *In Search for Excellence* (1982), about some of the most successful U.S. companies. They write:

"The second feature of the stability pillar is the value system, which encompasses the missionary 'form.' It may seem strange to talk about values under the heading of organizational structure, but remember, structure, most broadly defined, is communication patterns" (1982, p. 315).

The semiotic literature often compares Western and Eastern thinking in terms of the syntagm and paradigm model: Western thinking is linear, logical and syntagmatic; Eastern thinking is mythical, paradigmatic.

There have been many explanations for the "Japanese economic miracle" and the efficiency of the Japanese business enterprise. At closer look it would rather seem (to a Western observer) that the Japanese organization MUST be ineffective: the decision processes are extremely slow and there are more people for each task in Japan than in Western companies. But the Japanese are winning hands down in almost any field of enterprise. Why?

I think that the core of the matter is the value system or "shared values" of the Japanese business enterprise, its mythology, if you will. A Western businessman in Tokyo asked me to compare the value systems of a Japanese businessman and a Western businessman. He said that the value hierarchy of the Japanese is: the welfare of Japan, of his company, his family and himself. The value system in Western countries is likely to be just the reverse.

A Japanese exists for his social system – his ultimate aim is to benefit the society. The Western cultures are more or less based on individualism.

Human cooperation is a mighty tool if used for common purposes or "shared values." Remember that Germany was a bankrupt, chaotic country in 1930–33 when Hitler came to power. A few years later Germany was ready to challenge all the superpowers of the day.

INTENTIONAL OBSCURITY

A part of the "myth of rationality" – and I use the word myth here in a semiotic sense – is the idea that the purpose of the organizational communication process is to make the receiver understand the exact meaning of the sender. The closer the two meanings are the better.

Such is not necessarily the case with the Japanese organizational communication at all. In fact it may not be an exaggeration to claim that the purpose is often "intentional obscurity." Accurate and timely information has another meaning in Japan than in Western cultures.

The Japanese abhor the Western habit of organizational announcements. When you announce "officially" something then its final and you cannot back out. If you fail, you loose face. This does not mean that the Japanese organizational communication cannot be straight to the point if needed. When human values are concerned, the dialogue is usually circular; paradigmatic, not syntagmatic. It is typical that the Japanese have nineteen ways of saying NO.

I think that the Western organizations could learn something from this although one must always be careful in the application of cultural values to other cultures. I have voiced my doubts about the benefits of the "openness" in communication voiced by the American literature on therapeutic uses of communication. Instead of one disturbed person you may have several more after an "honest discussion."

Western thinking tends to look at the bottom line: what is the benefit of this and that. I challenge anybody who doubts my analysis above to compare the relative number of people in psychiatric care in the U.S. and Japan or compare the relative number of strikes and other open job related conflicts in any Western country to that of Japan. "It is the bottom line that counts."

SOME OF US ARE MORE SOCIAL THAN OTHERS

Christie (1981) studied the application of modern communication technology at the Commission of European Communities office in Brussels. Christie suggests that there are two main types of organizational communication: Type A and Type B.

Type A is an interpersonal communication situation and Type B is an information usage communication situation: reading, writing and watching television or using a data terminal.

The interesting finding is that there were Type A persons and Type B persons. Type A persons prefer interpersonal relations, they are usually unhappy in B situations. Type B persons are comfortable in B situations – such as using a data terminal.

Christie's findings may have important practical consequences for the application of modern office automation and advanced communication technology. Personality factors should be taken into account in job situations.

Freud's friend and student Carl Jung suggested long ago two personality types: extrovert and introvert personalities. Christie's Type A looks much like Jung's extrovert and Type B looks like Jung's introvert.

There may be large cultural differences in our social behavior: some cultures are more social than others. Or some cultures are more Type A and others are more Type B. Japanese are very much Type A and Finns are very much Type B.

In organizational communication research we tend to view things statistically and "on the average" basis. There can be, however, fundamental personal and cultural differences which should be taken into account.

REFERENCES

Broms, H., & Gahmberg, H. (1982). *Mythology in management culture.* The Helsinki School of Economics and Business Administration, D-58.

Christie, B. (1981). *Face to file communication: a psychological approach to information studies.* Wiley.

Goldhaber, G., Dennis, H., Richetto, G., & Wiio, O. (1979). Information strategies: new pathways to corporate power. Prentice-Hall.

Greimas, A., & Courtes, J. (1979). *Semiotique, dictionnaire raisonne de le theorie du langage.*

Pascale, R. T., & Athos, A. G. (1981). *The art of Japanese management.* Warner Books.

Peters, T. J., & Waterman, R. H. (1984). *In search for excellence.* Harper & Row.

Wiio, O. A. (1978). Contingencies of organizational communication. Helsinki.

Wiio, O. A., Goldhaber, G., & Yates, M. (1980). Organizational communication research; time for reflection? *Communication Yearbook 4.* Transaction books.

Chapter 6

Communication and Organizational Culture*

George A. Barnett

Department of Communication
State University of New York at Buffalo

ABSTRACT

This chapter focuses upon communication and organizational culture. It defines culture from the symbols-and-meaning perspective, i.e., as an emergent property of the members' communication activities which, in turn, acts to restrict future communication. The chapter then specifically defines organizational culture, differentiates it from climate, and discusses the role of communication in the process of formulating and changing organizational culture and the procedures for measuring and altering organizational culture. The procedures include interviewing organizational informants and content analysis, as well as the use of the Galileo System to precisely measure the cultural meaning system. The chapter concludes with an example in which these procedures were used to describe an organization's culture.

INTRODUCTION

Recently, there has been growing interest in organizational cultures and their impact upon the processes in which formal organizations engage (Barnett, 1979; Pettigrew, 1979; Deal & Kennedy, 1982; Pacanowsky & O'Donnell-Trujillo, 1982, 1983). This chapter focuses upon communication and organizational culture. It defines organizational culture, differentiates it from climate, and discusses the role of communication in the process of formulating and changing organizational culture and the procedures for measuring and changing organizational culture. These procedures include interview techniques and content analysis, as well as the Galileo System for metric multidimensional scaling. Galileo allows for the precise measurement of organizational culture and the design of communication strategies. When applied, they have the potential to alter the culture as desired by management to effectively achieve the organization's goals. The chapter concludes with an example in which these procedures were used to describe an organization's culture.

* The author would like to thank J. David Johnson and Mary Beth Eckert for their insightful comments on earlier drafts of this manuscript, and Charles Munro for his creative use of Macintosh's graphics.

This chapter does not take a cultural studies or interpretive approach to the study of organizational communication. Rather than viewing organizations as cultures and using only naturalistic research methods, it takes what may best be described as a symbols-and-meaning approach to culture (Shweder & LeVine, 1984). This approach makes explicit the role of communication in the transmission of cultural meanings through systematic codes, such as language. Cultural meanings are shared by the members of social systems (formal organizations), and are an emergent property of the interactions of the group's members.

DEFINITIONS OF CULTURE

Sociologists and anthropologists have offered many definitions of culture. Some center upon extrinsic factors, such as the artifacts that are representative of a social system (clothing, food, or technology). Others stress behavioral patterns. Still others focus upon intrinsic factors such as the attitudes, values, and beliefs of the members of a group (Barnett & Kincaid, 1983). Kluckhohn (1951) identifies eight aspects of culture. They are:

1. Culture is learned.
2. Culture derives from the biological, environmental, psychological, and historical components of human existence.
3. Culture is structured.
4. Culture is divided into aspects (social, psychological, technological).
5. Culture is dynamic.
6. Culture is variable.
7. Culture exhibits regularities that permit its analysis by the methods of science.
8. Culture is the instrument whereby the individual adjusts to his or her total setting, and gains the means for creative expression.

Simply, culture can be described as a "historically created system of explicit and implicit designs for living, which tends to be shared by all or specially designated members of a group at a specific point in time" (Kluckhohn & Kelly, 1945, p. 98).

Culture consists of the habits and tendencies to act in certain ways, but not the actions themselves. It is the language patterns, values, attitudes, beliefs, customs, and thought patterning. This notion of thought patterning has become central in most recent definitions of culture. Goodenough (1964, p. 36) defines culture, not as things or behavior, but rather as "the forms of things that people have in mind, their models for perceiving, relating, and otherwise interpreting them." Triandis, Vassiliou, Vassiliou, Tanaka, and Shanmugan (1972) label the values, feelings and meanings as they are expressed in a society's language as subjective culture. Geertz (1973) treats culture as an ordered system of meanings and of symbols, in which social interaction takes place and develops. He writes (1973, p. 89),

> [Culture is] an historically transmitted pattern of meaning embodied in symbols, a system of inherited conceptions expressed in symbolic form by means of which men communicate, perpetuate and develop their knowledge about and attitudes toward life.

Nieberg (1973) defines cultures as socially shared activities, and therefore, the property of groups rather than individuals. Culture is normative and may be best represented by the average or other measure of central tendency of the group mind (Durkheim, 1938). It does not derive from the internal conditions of the individual mind, but rather, from society's social conventions. Durkheim (1953, pp. 25–26) calls these shared cognitions "collective representations."

> collective representations are exterior to individual minds, it means that they do not derive from them as such, but from association of minds, which is a very different thing. No doubt in the making of the whole each contributes his part, but private sentiments do not become social except by combination under the action of the sui generis forces developed in association. In such a combination with the mutual alterations involved they become something else. . . . The resultant surpasses the individual as the whole part. It is in the whole as it is by the whole. In this sense it is exterior to the individual. No doubt each individual contains a part, but the whole is found in no one. In order to understand it as it is one must take the aggregate in its totality into consideration.

These collective representations are formed during the process of social interaction. As the members of social groups communicate, they negotiate the shared meanings of symbols. As such, culture is an emergent property of the communication of society's members. Communication as a shared symbolic process, creates, gives rise, and sustains the collective group consciousness (Bormann, 1983). On the other hand, culture determines how group members communicate. The meanings that are attributed to verbal symbols and nonverbal behaviors are determined by the society as a whole. They represent cultural knowledge (D'Andrade, 1984). Culture may be taken to be a consensus about the meanings of symbols, verbal and nonverbal, held by the members of a community. This consensus is necessary for encoding and decoding messages (LeVine, 1984). Without general agreement about the meaning of symbols and other communication rules, social interaction would be impossible.

As new members are socialized into groups, they acquire its culture (Ochs & Schieffelin, 1984). This process is made possible by individuals exchanging symbols—stimuli which are culturally defined with generally recognized conventions of meaning. Individuals are transformed into group members as a result of their interactions with other members of the group. It is through common social activities that the new members learn the meanings of the group's symbols and the generalized set of attitudes, values, and beliefs common to members of a social organization. These make it possible to coordinate their activities.

The circular causal relationship between communication and culture has led scholars to define culture as a communication phenomenon. Gudykunst and Kim (1984, p. 11), for example, define culture as, "that relatively unified set of shared symbolic ideas associated with societal patterns of cultural ordering." One type of cultural ordering is society's formal organizations. Pacanowsky & O'Donnell-Trujillo (1982) define organizational culture in terms of the communication activities of social groups.

DEFINITIONS OF ORGANIZATIONAL CULTURE

In their book *Corporate Cultures,* Deal and Kennedy (1982) do not provide a formal definition of organizational culture. Instead, they offer an informal one (attributed to Marvin Bower, former managing director of McKinsey & Company): "the way we do things around here." Other scholars, however, do offer more formal definitions. Pettigrew (1979, p. 574). defines organizational culture as "the system of such publicly and collectively accepted meanings operating for a given group at a given time." He includes the amalgam of beliefs, ideology, language, ritual, and myth under the label "organizational culture." Schwartz and Davis (1981, p. 32) take an organization's culture to be its members' attitudes and values, the management style, and the problem-solving behavior of its people. But, as Schein (1983, p. 14) points out, culture is not overt behavior or artifacts of a company. "Rather, it is the assumptions that underlie the values and determine not only behavior patterns, but also such visible artifacts as architecture, office layout, dress codes, and so on."

According to Bormann (1983), the important components of organizational culture include the shared norms, reminiscences, stories, rites, and rituals that provide the members with unique symbolic common ground. An organization's culture includes its self-definition, consisting of the unique constraints for identifying the collectivity, as well as the members' particular beliefs and goals which make up the self-image (Harris & Cronen, 1979). Organizational culture is influenced by the culture of the environment (Horan, 1981), society as a whole, but it is more narrowly defined. There is less variance in range of acceptable attitudes, values, and behaviors, and less tolerance for deviance. In part, it is this restricted range which sets an organization's culture apart from society's.

In summary, organizational culture from the symbols-and-meaning perspective may be defined as

> consisting of learned systems of meaning, communicated by means of natural language and other symbol systems, having representational, directive [task] and affective [socio-emotional] functions, and capable of creating cultural entities and particular senses of reality. Through these systems of meaning, groups of people adapt to their environment and structure interpersonal activities. Cultural meaning systems affect and are affected by the various systems of material flow of goods and services, and an interpersonal network of commands and requests. . . . Various aspects of cultural meaning systems are differentially distributed across persons and statuses, creating institutions such as family, market, nation and so on, which constitute social structure. (D'Andrade, 1984, p. 116)

Communicating Organizational Culture

An organization's culture is communicated in many ways. The most important of these is through the organization's informal interpersonal networks (Rogers & Agarwala-Rogers, 1976; Goldhaber, 1983). As mentioned earlier, the specific culture of an organization may be considered an emergent property of these interpersonal interactions. It is through interactions with long-time members that new recruits are enculturated. This is how they learn the language and appropriate behaviors of the group, hear its stories and legends, and observe the rites and rituals in which its members engage. These interactions make possible nonverbal communication. Members must determine what is appropriate dress, how to arrange one's office, and how much leeway they have in being on time for appointments and in meeting deadlines.

An organization's culture is also communicated through a variety of other channels. Internally, cultural information reaches members through formal or informal written communication, in the form of memos, house-organs, annual reports, statements of corporate philosophy, and official policy. It may also be displayed on bulletin boards or in posters which present policy messages.

The culture of an organization may be communicated by sources external to the organization. Advertisements in the mass media, both print and electronic, provide cultural information. As an organization communicates to the environment, it reveals its values and style to those outside the organization, as well as, to its members. How it conducts its public relations, announcements of new products, or services and speeches by its officers tell the public what it would be like to be part of the organization. For example, IBM's commercials present a sophisticated company concerned about the intellectual well-being of its public. Mobil's "Observations" presents a hard-driving company willing to fight for its interests. Finally, interpersonal interactions of the organization's members with individuals in the environment communicates its culture. The way in which sales people and buyers interact with customers and suppliers reinforces the cultural image of the organization to its members. In other words, the external communication feeds back to impact upon its internal culture.

The more frequently these channels communicate these messages, the more the organization acts to reinforce its culture. One result of organizational communication will be less variance in members' perceptions of the organization. There will be greater integration of members' meaning systems, particularly concerning the domain of symbols related to the organization (Shweder, 1984). Over time, the culture will become more consistant with similar messages about the organization coming from a variety of different sources.

Organizational Subcultures

Subcultures may occur within organizations that are larger than simple structures (Mintzberg, 1983). Organizations with simple structures are characterized by a loose division of labor, minimal differentiation among its units, few support staff, and a small managerial hierarchy. They tend to be small organizations with centralized decision making. Entreprenurial firms and ad hocracies generally have simple structures. Everyone is able to communicate with one another, producing a restricted organizational culture.

As organizations grow, they tend to develop subcultures. This is a result of well-defined communication networks in which individuals communicate with a restricted group of people within the organization. This may be due to organizational hierarchy, division of labor, geographical dispersion of work units, differential professional socialization, or environmental demands (Falcione & Kaplan, 1984). Organizations with elaborated structures or technical support staffs would tend to have well-defined subcultures, groups whose meaning systems are significantly different.

Organizational structure may be viewed as an emergent property of cultural understandings (D'Andrade, 1984). Roberts (1984) has pointed out that division of labor, social organization, is a result of differential cultural knowledge. Organizations differ in "who knows what." The distribution of cultural understandings creates social roles in which those who occupy certain positions share certain understandings (subcultures) about what other positions are likely to know (Swartz & Jordan, 1976; Goldhaber, Barnett, Mitchell, & Bales, 1983). Thus, organizational structure may be taken to be an aspect of its culture — the achievement of systematicity across persons through shared meanings.

Organizational Culture and Climate

This chapter is concerned with organizational culture, as opposed to organization climate. In the past, writers have failed to distinguish among the two terms, and often have defined climate similarly to the way in which culture has been in this chapter (Tagiuri & Litwin, 1968; James & Jones, 1974; Falcione & Kaplan, 1984). How do culture and climate differ?

Schwartz and Davis (1981) distinguish the terms as follows. Climate concerns whether people's expectations about what it should be like to work in an organization are being met. In other words, climate refers to how satisfied they are about certain organizational activities. Climate is only one aspect of organizational culture—the patterns of beliefs and expectations shared by the organization's members. While climate refers to whether or not expectations are being met, culture is concerned with the nature of the expectations themselves.

In organizational communication research, climate is generally considered to be an index of an individual's psychological state in the context of the organization (Falcione & Kaplan, 1984). This index is multidimensional focusing on the members' perceptions of such factors as the supportiveness of superior–subordinate relations, quality and accuracy of downward communication, relational openness, opportunities and efficacy of upward communication, reliability of information from subordinates and coworkers, communication satisfaction, and organizational commitment (Redding, 1972; Dennis, 1975; Falcione, 1978).

Organizational climate may be investigated using the ICA Organizational Communication Audit (Goldhaber et al., 1978; Goldhaber & Rogers, 1979). This research is concerned with how satisfied organizational members are with the various aspects of organizational life as specified above. Implicit is the notion that individuals' levels of satisfaction may be taken to be the extent to which their organizational expectations are being met. Thus, while culture is an emergent property of group interaction, climate may be taken to be individuals' psychological perceptions of the characteristics of an organization's practices and procedures.

This chapter discusses organizational culture because of the growing interest within management and communication, and because it is a better label than "climate" to describe organizational (rather than individual) processes. The term "culture" is consistent in meaning with its definition as expressed by the other social sciences—sociology, anthropology, and geography. Adopting this term will facilitate our understanding of organizational processes. The knowledge gained in the other social sciences about the cultures of social systems may be generalized to formal organizations. The operationalizations of culture used in these fields may be applied, facilitating future research and greater understanding of culture's role in organizational life.

Another reason for the use of the term "culture" rather than "climate" is that the later is an inappropriate metaphor to describe organizational processes. Climates are, by definition, very stable. They change very slowly. When climatic change does occur, it is often traumatic. For example, the climate change of the onset of the first ice age brought about the death of dinosaurs. Organizations' cultures do change. Its members' attitudes, values, beliefs, and expectations are dynamic. They may not change overnight, like the weather. But they do change, as members leave the organization and are replaced by new members with different past experiences. Organizations generally survive changes in culture. Other sources of cultural change are changes in the environment from increased competition, technological innovations, government intervention, and war. Cultural change may be internally induced. In fact, much of this chapter describes how communication research may be used to design message strategies which, when introduced into an organization's information environment, act to alter its culture.

It should be noted that Falcione and Kaplan (1984) take the opposite point of view when discussing the relationship between culture and climate. They suggest that culture may be viewed as an organization's system of values, norms, beliefs, and structures that persist over time. It is a set of organizational traits. They take climate, on the other hand, to represent the state of these elements at a given point in time.

Recently, AT&T has begun the process of changing its organizational culture. Traditionally, it was a government-regulated monopoly providing service without competition. Its culture reflected these environmental conditions. Ma Bell was old and slow. She was not very responsive to the individual needs of its customers. Today, AT&T exists in a market-driven environment, in competition with many vendors to supply equipment and services. It is adapting to these conditions. To do so, its culture must change. Its service representatives must become account representatives, tailor-making telecommunications systems for individual organizations. This was unthought of only a few years ago. As a result, its employees' shared attitudes toward doing business (its culture) is changing. Despite the extent of these changes, there may be little change in whether or not one's expectations about organizational life (its climate) are being met. Thus, climate seems less appropriate than culture in describing a major organizational change.

THE ELEMENTS OF ORGANIZATIONAL CULTURE

While organizational culture has been defined above, it is important to describe the phenomenon in greater detail. Analytically, what are the elements which make up organizational culture? The goal of this discussion is to identify and describe those components which must be measured when studying an organization's culture. This section examines the following elements: language, values, behaviors, including organizational rites and rituals, stories, or organizational myths, and legends which often describe an organization's heroes and villains and extrinsic aspects of culture—the organization's artifacts. Deal and Kennedy (1982) include two additional components of organizational culture—the business environment and the organization's communication network. Since these two components are covered in detail elsewhere in the book, they will not be discussed in this chapter.

Language

Language is the most central aspect of organizational culture. This includes the symbols, jargon, or specialized vocabulary (vernacular or argot) which are used by an organization's members (Hirsch & Andrews, 1983). Meaning may only be attributed to a word or sign in the context of the organization and its history (Pacanowsky & O'Donnell-Trujillo, 1983). It is through its shared symbol system that an organization communicates its values, behavioral expectations, common experiences, and self-image among its members. (See Eisenberg & Riely in this volume.) Included in this category would be organizational metaphors (Pacanowsky & O'Donnell-Trujillo, 1982). These are indicative of how an organization structures its members' experiences. Examples would be the idioms team (Team Xerox), family, or military (the chain-of-command), with code names for certain operations or product developments (General Motors' X or J cars).

Values

Values are enduring beliefs that specify a mode of conduct or end-state of existence that is personally or socially preferable to its opposite (Rokeach, 1973). They provide people with general standards of competence and morality which guide or determine attitudes, behaviors, judgements and comparisons of self and others (Rokeach, 1979). Within an organizational context, they are the basic conceptualizations and beliefs of an organization (Deal & Kennedy, 1982). As such, they are indicators of the instrinsic or subjective aspects of its culture. Values provide the assumptions upon which organizational activities are based. They define its goals, and the criterion by which it is determined whether the goals have been successfully achieved. They are often thought of as the organizational or corporate ideology (Mills, 1951; Pettigrew, 1979). Values mobilize the collective consciousness and its members' actions by connecting social obligations with general ethical principles (LeVine, 1984). The result is a commitment by organizational members to perform everday activities according to some grand scheme (Pettigrew, 1979). Values are shared by all the group's members, and deviance from these shared standards is not tolerated.

IBM provides an example of how an organization's values effect its activities (Peters & Waterman, 1982). As an organization, IBM values customer service. Behaviorally, this means keeping in touch with the customers, answering every customer complaint within 24 hours, providing the customer with the least expensive product that will get the job done, and servicing the customer after the sale has been completed. Customer satisfaction is measured monthly, and employee attitudes are measured quarterly. This value is shared. From top management to the lowest salesman, all agree that "IBM means service." This message is consistently communicated both within the company and externally to its customers. Further, there are strong sanctions for violating this norm. Salaries are docked for losing current customers.

Behaviors

Another component of culture is the behavior of the organization's members (Benedict, 1934). These are the programmatic and routinized activities of everyday life that enable the organization to accomplish its goals, both task and socio-emotional. This is how things are done around here. As with organizational values, knowledge of these behaviors and the norms and rules for appropriate behavior is shared (Harris & Cronen, 1979). These activities are directed by the cultural meaning system, and are therefore part of the collective consciousness. While the activities are normative, the directive force, the symbolic meaning system, is consensual (D'Andrade, 1984). There are expectations regarding their performance. These expectations, and the task interdependencies that develop out of division of labor, necessitate sanctions for the violation of these behavioral norms. It is important to point out that the behaviors, per se, are not cultural; rather, the understanding of these activities is what makes up an organization's culture.

Included in the behavior category are organizational rituals, rites, and ceremonies (Gusfield & Michalowicz, 1984; Trice & Beyer, 1984). These practices provide examples of the organization's culture, the perception of which helps to structure the social reality. Participation in these activities reinforces the individual's membership in the organization by providing him or her with shared experiences, and, therefore, incorporating the culture's value system.

Pacanowsky and O'Donnell-Trujillo (1983) describe four types of organizational rituals. They are (a) Personal rituals, the behavior of specific organizational members. (b) Task rituals, the practices for getting the job done. These may be specified in manuals or learned during the socialization process. (c) Social rituals, such as Tandem Computer's Friday beer blasts. (d) Organizational rituals, such as shareholders' meetings.

Trice and Beyer (1984) differentiate organizational rites and ceremonies by their manifest, expressive, and social consequences. They suggest six types:

1) Rites of passage, which facilitate the transition of organizational members into new roles or statuses. Management training programs serve as rites of passage.
2) Rites of degradation, in which social identities and their power are dissolved. For example, firing and replacing a top executive often takes on a ceremonial forum, with a board of directors voting to remove an officer from his or her position.
3) Rites of enhancement, which enhance social identities and their powers. Mary Kay Seminars and IBM's One-hundred Per Cent Club spread good news and public recognition of individual accomplishments within the organization.
4) Rites of renewal, such as organizational development activities, serve to refurbish social structures and improve their training functioning by reassuring members that organizational problems are being resolved.
5) Rites of conflict resolution, such as collective bargaining, which function to reduce conflict.
6) Rites of integration, which encourage and revive common feelings that bind members together and commit them to the organization. The office Christmas party is a ceremony of integration.

Stories and Legends

One component of culture includes an organization's stories, legends, folk-tales, and myths (Martin, Feldman, Hatch, & Sitkin, 1983; Korpowski, 1983). Every organization has stories which are exchanged among its members and taught to all new members as part of the socialization process. It is through hearing these stories that new members learn the cultural meanings of symbols used in the stories. They describe the organizational experience and provide one method of communicating an organization's culture to its members. From the telling of these stories, organizational myths and legends develop. A shared social reality or "group fantasy" develops (Bormann, 1983) which serves as organizational "facts" or history. This is what group members come to view as "social knowledge" (Pacanowsky & O'Donnell-Trujillo, 1982). It is through these stories that individuals learn about the organization's heroes and villains.

Bormann (1983) labels this aspect of culture "organizational sagas." These are detailed narratives about the achievements and events in the life of a person (hero or villain), group, or community (an organization) which include shared fantasies, rhetorical vision, and the narrative of achievements, events, goals, and ideal states of the entire organization. These narratives provide answers to such questions as, What kind of organization is this? What kind of people are members of the organization? What are our goals and purpose? What past events are we proud of? And, What will we do in the future?

These are stories about organizational heroes and villains, individuals that personify the culture's values and provide role models for group members to follow (or not, in the case of villains) (Deal & Kennedy, 1982). By studying these individuals, one can learn a culture's values, desired behaviors, and the symbols of success and failure for an organization. Within a few months of joining an organization, the new recruit learns the stories and legends of the heroes and villains. Often, they concern the founder of the company (Schein, 1983). At IBM, one hears about the Watsons. At HP, there are stories about David Packard and Robert Hewlett.

Founders bring many of the underlying organization's cultural assumptions with them when they establish the company (Schein, 1983). They often start with a theory or cultural paradigm in their heads. They deliberately choose to build organizations which reflect their personal philosophies. This is communicated to the organization's members initially through direct interpersonal communication, organizational policy, or modeling, and later through the stories of these individuals' activities which are embedded on the organization's culture.

Organizational stories need not be so detailed or serious. The culture of an organization may also be revealed by the jokes that are told inside the organization and through its songs. The seven dwarfs sang, "Hi Ho, Hi Ho. It's off to work we go." The song was indicative of their hard working culture. As a group they dug and hacked for gold in the mountains and did not come home until it was completely dark, leaving Snow White home alone to contend with her evil step-mother.

Pacanowsky and O'Donnell-Trujillo (1983) identify four types of organizational stories. They are: (a) Personal stories about individuals. (b) Collegial stories which are shared about other members of the organization. (c) Corporate stories which are representative of organizational ideology. And (d) stories about organizational "facts" or history. This is what organizational members come to view as "social knowledge" (Pacanowsky and O'Donnell-Trujillo, 1982).

Extrinsic Aspects of Organizational Culture

The extrinsic aspects of an organization's culture must also be examined. This would include the artifacts that are produced by its members. A company's products tell a great deal about an organization. As symbols, they have meaning for the organization's members. For example, HP has a reputation of producing upscale technological products for the sophisticated user (usually a scientist or engineer). Atari or Commodore produce computers for every home. The organization's physical environment is also indicative of its culture. Control Data Corporation builds its facilities in the inner city, while IBM is known for its corporate country clubs. The symbolic value of these settings is not lost on its members.

THE PRECISE MEASUREMENT OF ORGANIZATIONAL CULTURE

Introduction to the Galileo System

The organized patterns of thought of a cultural group, its cultural meaning system, can be precisely measured following Woelfel and Barnett's (1974, pp. 6-7) procedures for measuring collective consciousness:

> That aggregate psychological configuration which constitutes the culture of a society and toward which individual beliefs may seem to tend, may be represented accurately as the average matrix S, where any entry s_{ij} is the arithmetic mean conception of the distance or dissimilarity between objects i and j as seen by all members of a culture.

These objects may be abstract symbols — aspects of belief, attitudes, ritual, and patterned activity, including such things as an organization's language, its products, competition, or public relations and advertisements. Typically, they are defined in relation to the self, the individual members of the social system. It is this representation of culture that will be used as the theoretical basis for the measurement of organizational culture. Known as the Galileo System, the measurement procedures which operationalize this theoretical perspective entails two steps: (a) the determination of the critical concepts or symbols which make up an organization's culture, and (b) pair-comparisons to precisely measure the relations between these concepts. These procedures are described below.

The process of measuring an organization's culture begins by determining the domain of concepts (words or phrases) its members use when describing the organization. Generally, the labels for the components of organizational culture are determined through content analysis of direct observations of organizational activities, its documents and media, and in-depth interviews with its members, although theory may guide the selection of concepts. For example, a concept of self (me, myself, you, yourself), the organization's name, and a concept such as "my job" should be included. This makes it possible to measure attitudes toward the organization and members' organizational roles, as well as the organization's self-image.

Geertz (1984) suggests that the concept of person—what selfhood is—varies among groups. By analyzing the symbolic forms which people actually use to represent themselves, one can determine the nature, function, and mode of operation of the self and its role in social systems, such as formal organizations.

These concepts may be determined through the direct observation of performances and the physical organizational space (Pacanowsky & O'Donnell-Trujillo, 1982). Also, an organization's documents and media, both internal and external, may be examined. This would include the following internal documents: house organs and public memos—newsletters, annual reports, statements of corporate philosophy, and official policy. The following external communication should be examined: advertisements (print and electroinic), speeches by officers, press releases, and other public relations and product announcements.

In-depth interviews with a representative sample of the members of the organization may be conducted to determine a culture's significant concepts. The members who are interviewed act as informants. This has been the most widely used procedure to determine the concepts which make up public opinion (Barnett, 1981). The reason is that reality is socially constructed through the words, symbols, and behaviors of group members (Berger & Luckmann, 1967). Interviews attempt to get at the symbols that people use when evaluating the organization. They attempt to get "inside" members' day-to-day interpretations of the organization's culture. The procedure is inductive, free of a priori categories. The goal of the interviews is for the researcher to become intimately familiar with organizational life, so that he or she can understand the symbols which make up its subjective culture.

It is important to interview a representative sample of the organization to guarantee a pluralistic perspective (Weick, 1979). The goal of the interviewing process is to identify the shared symbols which make up the culture. Also, it is important to avoid managerial bias, and insure multiple prspectives (Putnam, 1983; Silverman, 1970). A bias description of organizational culture can be avoided by interviewing a random sample of its members and entering the process without a predetermined list of the concepts which constitute its culture. However, since culture represents a consensus of a community, interviewing a few group members will reveal the important organizational symbols. However variable the members' attitudes and behaviors, the common symbols will emerge from the interviews because there is general agreement about organizational life and the symbols which express it. In other words, the social life of the organization produces redundancy across informants. This results from the counsensual or shared meanings for the symbols.

There is no set number of interviews which should be conducted. The interviews should continue until the point where additional interviews do not yield new symbols, or very few words that were not mentioned in previous interviews.

The symbols which define an organization's culture may be also determined through focus group discussions rather than personal interviews. While group discussions generally should be avoided in organizational measurement to guarantee respondent anonymity, they may be acceptable for cultural analysis under certain conditions. In situations with little subcultural differentiation, where there is substantial agreement on the cultural definitions of the critical symbols, it may be appropriate to have groups discuss the organization's values, language, rites and rituals, heroes and villians, and folk history. These groups should be composed of diagonal slices of the organization to insure a representative cross-section of its members. The investigator should limit his or her participation to an initial stimulus question, such as, "What is it like to work here at _____?" Afterward, his or her role should be simply one of recording the symbols which the group uses and which are representative of the culture.

This procedure has a number of advantages. One, it is less expensive to use groups than to conduct personal interviews. Two, the symbols will be discussed in the context of their natural language. Three, the collection of idiosyncratic data may be avoided, because perceptions which are unique to individuals will not be substantiated by the other participants in the discussion.

The disadvantage of the method is that the deviant perceptions will not be brought to the surface. In organizations with diverse cultures or with taboos, the use of focus groups would be inappropriate. When the researcher is interested in cultural variation, the standard interview procedures should be employed. Further, since one does not know the degree of variation in culture before the data collection process, the use of focus groups when auditing organizational culture is not recommended.

Content Analysis

The next step in examining organizational culture is a content analysis of the direct observations, documents, and interviews (or group discussions), to identify the critical shared symbols. The goal of this process is to determine those symbols whose meaning is consensual and socially constructed apart from the individual. The extent of consensus may be determined through a frequency count of occurrence of each unique symbol (words or phrases). He or she should also consider synonyms (Barnett, 1980), antonyms, and those instances in which the same word is used as more than one part of speech, or there are other grammatical differences which render words with equivalent meaning different.

Traditionally, this process has been conducted by hand. The researcher simply collected the interviewers' notes and counted the various words and phrases the respondents used. Recently, however, word frequency programs for micro-computers have been developed. They may be used to count the occurrences of the various words or phrases in the interviews. One such program is the *Sensible Speller* (Hartley, 1983), which operates on Apple and CP/M computers. Danowski and Edison-Swift (1985) used Oasis's *Wordfreq* to determine the frequency of various words in a year long study of the use of electronic mail in a service organization. The results indicated that, while the frequency of word use remained stable, the language of the organization changed dramatically during a crisis.

Problems with these procedures are that these routines are not designed to deal with multiple word utterances, and that the time necessary for data entry can also be lengthy.

However, cultural analysis is often part of a larger organizational research which uses verbatim quotes to help in interpretation. Also, they may be reported to the client. As a result, it may be more efficient to type the data into a word processing system which allows one the luxury of automated content analysis.

A more sophisticated approach to the selection of the concepts has been developed by Joseph Woelfel and Richard Holmes (1982). It is known as CATPAC. The procedure operates as follows. The interviews or other content are entered into a computer. The CATPAC program reads the words, which may be in any order or format (single words, phrases, sentences, or paragraphs). Groups of words may be delimited by commas, to guarantee their analysis as phrases rather than as single words. The program then reads the words and deletes any of a list of 107 articles, prepositions, and conjunctions which in the past have proved problematic. At this point, the program counts the occurrences of the remaining words. The infrequently occurring words are deleted, such that the remaining are the 100 or fewer most frequent. From this pool, a words-by-episodes matrix of frequencies is created. These episodes may be the interview questions or subjects. This matrix is then post multiplied by its transpose, resulting in a words-by-words matrix of coocurrences. A heirarchical cluster analysis is performed on the coocurrence matrix (Johnson, 1967). The results of CATPAC are a diameter cluster analysis and the frequencies for each unique symbol. In this way, the categories which make up culture can be determined.

James Danowski (Danowski, Andrews, & Edison-Swift, 1985) has suggested that network analysis may be used for online content analysis, the results of which may be used to describe the culture of a group. He demonstrated this process with an example from the message content of an electronic mail system. Messages were first parsed by a window five words wide. If two words cooccurred in this window, they were assigned a link. This process was repeated for all message content for a 1-month period. This period of time allowed different strengths of the links among words to emerge. These data were then entered into NEGOPY (see chapter 14). This network analysis procedure identified groups of words, words which linked groups of words, and others which were structurally isolated. Thus, groups may be used in the same way as in the cluster from CATPAC, to guide the selection of symbols for the second phase of cultural analysis.

These procedures provide the researcher with a great deal of information upon which to select the symbols for the pair-comparison stage. Redundant symbols may be avoided. While two symbols may occur very frequently, they may cooccur and be part of the same cluster or group. Their measured relation would provide little new information when the other concepts are considered. This is important because the pair-comparison stage is limited by the number of stimuli that can be included. Concepts may be selected as representatives of clusters rather than simply based upon their frequency alone. In this way, one might choose a supraordinate concept to represent a group of frequently occurring symbols, or a single representative from the center of a cluster or group of symbols.

Pair-Comparisons

The next step in examining organizational culture is to precisely measure the relationships among the symbols selected above as most representative of the culture. This is done using the method of pair-comparisons (Thurstone, 1927; Woelfel & Fink, 1980). Randomly selected subjects from the organization complete a series of direct pair-comparisons among all possible pairs of symbols. They estimate the dissimilarity, distance, or differences between $n(n-1)/2$ pairs of symbols (n = the number of cultural symbols). The researcher provides a criterion pair or metric standard for the subjects to use as a unit measure when making the comparisons. Subjects make direct magnitude estimates of the differences among the symbols as ratios to the criterion metric. Typically, the question is worded using the form:

If X and Y are U units apart, how far apart are concepts A and B?

This format allows the respondent to report any positive number, rather than being forced to choose a point on a fixed choice scale, as is the case with Likert or Osgood's Semantic Differential scales. The direct magnitude scale has a number of advantages (Danes & Woelfel, 1975; Wigand & Barnett, 1976; Woelfel, Holmes, Kincaid, & Barnett, 1980b; Barnett, Hamlin, & Danowski, 1981). They do not build error into the measurement process. The fixed choice scales build in 14% to 20% error, because they discriminate only five or seven differences. This error, coupled with unreliability, often renders the results of the measures useless. Further, because the crude scales only make gross discriminations, they are incapable of precisely measuring cultural change over time, especially when the rate of change is nonlinear (Barnett, 1981; Barnett & Kincaid, 1983; Rice & Barnett, 1985). The traditional scales are bounded. This truncates extreme opinions and distorts the change of strongly held opinions.

The procedures advocated here have none of these problems. They do not build error into the measurement process. They are capable of fine discriminations and are ideal to describe nonlinear rates of change. In addition, because they are more precise, fewer cases are needed to obtain the same information about organizational culture.

Subjects perform direct magnitude estimates of the distances among concepts reliably. Barnett (1972) and Danes and Woelfel (1975) report reliability coefficients for the method of .85–.90 when measuring public opinion. Gordon (1976) reports reliabilities ranging from .93 to .99, with approximately 100 subjects in controlled situations. Because there is less variation in organizations than in the general population, the later levels of reliability should be expected.

The Results of a Galileo Analysis

The completion of the data collection process results in a concepts-by-concepts-by-subjects matrix (S) which has the following properties. It is square and symmetrical, and it is of order n (n = the number of scaled concepts). Each cell in the matrix (s_{ij}) represents the distance between concepts i and j. The diagonal contains zeros, because s_{ii} represents the dissimilarity of concept i from itself, by definition.

To determine an organization's culture, S is typically averaged across subjects to form an n-by-n concepts matrix, $\overline{S}$, where any entry $\overline{s}_{ij}$ is the mean distance between concepts i and j, as seen by the average member of the group (Barnett et al., 1981). Alternative measures of central tendency may be applied in those instances where the distribution of opinion is not normal but highly skewed due to a few individuals holding extreme views — deviant cultural opinions. For example, Barnett and McPhail (1980) used medians rather than means in their investigation of the impact of American television on Canadian national culture. Neuendorf, Kaplowitz, Fink, and Armstrong (1984) used a logrithmic transformation to control for extreme opinions.

The variances about the means should also be examined. This is a measure of the extent of agreement within a culture. Peters and Waterman (1982) argue that consistency in culture, one with little variance, is desirable because people's expectations will be met. Successful organizations have little variance in their cultures. Variance represents another indicator of organizational climate, the extent to which member expectations are met. Where the variances are great, the expectations may be too diffuse to be met, resulting in a weak culture.

Harris and Cronen (1979) indicate that it is important to examine the variance, latitude, range, or extent of consensus in an organization's cultural image. A wide range of organizationally legitimate behaviors allows for a greater probability that the individual can find behaviors which are legitimate for both the self and the organization. This variance allows for creativity.

Matrix S may be converted to a multidimensional space, with each concept located on a series of reference axes or dimensions. Mathematically, the process is analogous to converting a matrix of intercity distances to a Cartesian coordinate system where latitude, longitude, and altitude are the reference axes and the cities locations on each of these dimensions given. From these coordinates, a graphic representation such as a map may be drawn. In that special case, an n-by-n matrix of cities is reduced to a three-dimensional configuration with no loss of information. This process is known as multidimensional scaling (Torgerson, 1958). D'Andrade (1984) suggests that multidimensional scaling is an appropriate technique to describe a group's cultural meaning system.

The algorithms are described by Serota (1974) and Woelfel (1974), and are part of the Galileo computer program (Woelfel, et al., 1976a). Technically, Galileo operates as follows. A constant is added to the mean distance matrix to establish the origin at the centroid of the distribution. The grand mean of the matrix is set equal to zero. This transformed matrix is premultiplied by its transpose to create a scalar products matrix (Torgerson, 1958) which is, subsequently, orthogonally decomposed to obtain a coordinate matrix whose columns are orthogonal axes and whose rows are the projections of the concepts' locations on each of the axes. These are the continua through which members share and describe the organizational image (Harris & Cronen, 1979). This process also results in a vector of eigenroots which indicates the proportion of variance attributable to each dimension.

While physical space has only three dimensions, organizational culture may be more complex. Typically, the variance in culture is accounted for by n-1 dimensions, although is some cases it may be less (Barnett & Woelfel, 1979). Further, some of the dimensins may have negative eigenroots. Thus, the cultural space is not Euclidean but Riemannian (Woelfel & Barnett, 1982). Woelfel and Barnett (1982) have shown that these imaginary dimensions (those with negative roots) are reliable, and that they may be explained by the inconsistencies in public attitudes. Further, Barnett (1984) and Barnett and Rice (1985) have examined organizations' communication networks with this methodology. They found that, in cases in which one node (an individual or group) is more central than the rest, the organizational structure must be described by a Riemannian space. A statistic, wrap, indicates the degree of inconsistency. It is expressed as a ratio of the total (real and imaginary) variance to the real variance. A value of 1.0 indicates a consistant attitude structure (an Euclidean space). The sources of the inconsistancies may be determined by examining the concepts' locations of the imaginary dimensions.

The spatial coordinates describe organizational culture and provide a number of advantages for management. (a) A graphic representation of the organization's cultural meaning system is created. The symbols are arrayed in a space of limited dimensionality. This makes it easy to "see" the culture as it is held by the average member of the group. The positive and negative aspects are clearly and precisely arrayed in relation to each other and the other elements of the culture. This facilitates its understanding and future intervention. (b) The warp indicates the degree of inconsistency within the culture, and the locations on the imaginary dimensions make it possible to identify the sources of these inconsistencies. With this information, management can remove the problem areas in the culture. (c) The spatial coordinates provide the information necessary to change organizational culture in a desired and predictable manner.

Subcultures may be determined by simply performing the procedures separately for each predefined group. For example, management might be interested in the differences in culture between union and nonunion, exempt and nonexempt, hour and salaried, or full- and part-time employees. Or they might be interested in cultural differences between various function units or geographical sites in the organization (Goldhaber et al., 1983).

Changing Organizational Culture

The manipulation of organizational culture is made possible with Galileo. Messages generated from the cultural meaning system may be implemented through formal organizational channels. By providing messages which present different relations among the symbols in the information environment, the organization's culture may be changed. The source of these initial messages is formal, from management. However, they may act to set the agenda for interpersonal discussions. The result is that new perceptions of the relationships among the cultural symbols will emerge.

The spatial coordinates allow for the generation of message strategies which will rearrange the arrangement among the concepts in the cultural meaning system as desired (Woelfel et al., 1976b; Serota, Cody, Barnett, & Taylor, 1977). Vector analysis may be applied to determine the optimal message strategy for the measured concepts. First, a target vector is described between the concept whose position management wishes to alter and its desired location. Typically, the desired location is the position of the average self. This is because empirical research has shown that, the more frequently one performs a behavior or the more positive one's attitudes toward a concept, the closer that concept is to a measured self-concept (Barnett, Serota, & Taylor, 1976; Barnett & McPhail, 1979; Woelfel, Cody, Gillham, & Holmes, 1980a). For example, when applied to market research, the product label closest to the self-concept is purchased with the greatest frequency. In political polling, candidates receive the number of votes in proportion to their distance from the self-concept.

Second, the Galileo program searches all possible combinations of concepts' locations whose resultant vector will move the concept toward its desired location. Only one-, two-, three-, and four-concept messages are analyzed, because the computations rapidly become uneconomical and messages with more than four concepts are generally too complex to be effective (Deal & Kennedy, 1982). Third, the best message is determined by comparing the resultant vectors of the various message combinations with the target vector. The optimal message is that one which produces the smallest angle (greatest cosine or correlation) between the target and resultant vector, and whose position (in the vector analysis) is closest to the desired location.

Practically, this procedure will help an organization's management change the direction of, and the variance within, its culture. Directionally, focus may be changed away from the dysfunctional aspects of culture and toward the goals as defined by management in statement of corporate philosophy. For example, Albrecht (1979) found that people varied in their identification with their job based on their position in the organization's communication structure. Consistent with corporate philosophy, management would have wanted all employees to identify more closely with the company and their job. This technique could have been applied to develop message strategies to reduce the distance between the self-concept and the concepts "my job" and "the company."

Since successful organizations have consistent cultures, management may wish to eliminate the variance in organizational culture. Over time, the variance in organizational culture would become smaller if its members receive consistent messages (Woelfel & Saltiel, 1978). This technique provides a message strategy which, when applied consistently, would reduce cultural variation.

Change in organizational culture may be examined by repeating the pair-comparison phase and transforming the data for each point in time into a multidimensional space. This allows management to observe and predict cultural change and effectiveness of the intervention. To compare several points in time, the spaces are first adjusted to a common origin. Typically, the time one space serves as the criterion. They they are rotated to a least squares best fit which minimizes the departure from congruence among the spaces. More complex algorithms exist for those situations in which the cultural concepts vary in their relative stability or importance (Woelfel et al., 1975; Woelfel, Holmes, & Kincaid, 1979). Change in the position of the concepts may be calculated by subtracting the coordinate values across time. From these change scores, one can fit trajectories of motion to describe the relative changes in culture. With these measured velocities (the rate of change over time) and the accelerations, which may be determined through differentiation, the future culture can be accurately predicted (Barnett, 1978).

Differences among subcultures may be examined in the same way as over-time differences. A separate coordinate system may be generated for each group. Then they are compared as if they were the same group at different points in time.

When interventions take place, it is expected that the culture of the organization should converge with management goals. For example, if management places a priority on service such that it is reflected in its formal communication by language, like "IBM means service," then, over time, the distance between the concepts "IBM" and "service" should become smaller. The equations for predicting cultural convergence are described in detail by M. Woelfel (1978), Barnett and Kincaid (1983), and Kincaid, Yum, Woelfel, and Barnett (1983). In those situations where there is great departure from the predicted equations, the culture is not converging with managements goals, then it is necessary to change the communication (message strategy) and human resources programs to put the culture back on track. In this way, the process of cultural change may be treated as a cybernetic process.

Prior Research with Galileo to Measure Organizational Culture

Galileo has been frequently applied to measure organizational or professional culture. Albrecht (1979) used Galileo to measure organizational culture (she labelled it "climate") and subcultures, based on individuals' positions in communciation structure as determined through network analysis. She found that key communicators (bridge links or liaisons) placed themselves ("me") closer to "my job" and "management." "My job" was more central in their cultural meaning system, and they were better able to relate the concepts than non-key communicators (group members or isolates). Non-key communicators generally had less identification with their jobs and managers, and tended to have more disparate and variable perceptions about the organization's culture.

In a follow-up study Albrecht (1984) examined how the perceptions of managers changed over time as a function of their position in the communication structure of an electronics firm. Using these procedures, she found that key communicators (which she labelled "linkers") identified more closely with their jobs than nonlinkers. Over time, the distance between the self and job became smaller for linkers but remained stable for nonlinkers. Linkers associated their jobs with teamwork, effectiveness, their salaries, and problems and pressures to a greater degree than nonlinkers. Also, they perceived themselves to be more knowledgable and less frustrated than did nonlinkers. Over time, these relations tended to remain stable. These two groups did not differ in their perceptions of their bosses and coworkers. However, over time, the linkers identified more closely with their bosses than with their coworkers.

Siegel (1980) examined the professional socialization of public accountants, because a larger number of individuals leave the profession for other careers. He found that students placed "public accountants" near "honest," "competent," "hard working," "intelligent," "independent," "respected," "creative," and "wealthy," and far from "boring." Thus, it was not the profession per se which caused the high turnover. One solution that has been proposed is the establishment of professional schools of accounting (PSA), like medical or law schools. They might significantly alter the professional culture by increasing the commitment of individuals to accounting. Siegel found that students attending PSAs saw themselves closer to the "Big 8 Firms" and "Sole Practitioner" than majors in accounting departments. These results may help decide further recruitment policies of several large accounting firms, as well as the educational policy of the profession.

Another study by Siegel (1981), for the American Institute of Certified Public Accountants, measured the professional culture of accountants. Based on a national random sample of CPAs, he found that the self-concept was close to "professional," "practice development," and "competition," which indicated that these concepts were central to accountants' professional culture. The self was far from "unprofessional." The concepts "advertising" and "solicitation" were far from the self-concept, and closer to the negative concepts "unprofessional" and "unethical." Given these results, it seems unlikely that accounting firms will use advertising or direct solicitation as methods to develop their practices until the culture of their profession changes.

Woelfel (1980) used these procedures to measure a major industrial firm's reputation as an employer of high technology computer personnel. The perceptions of individuals both inside and outside the company who were already working with computers were examined. The study was conducted in two phases. In the first, in-depth interviews were conducted in which people described themselves, the company, and its competition, IBM, Bell Labs, and Hewlett Packard. CATPAC analysis revealed over 1,000 unique words, underlain by 15 general clusters. In the second phase, subjects both internal and external to the company perform direct pair-comparisons on 15 concepts derived from these clusters. The study revealed significant differences in the perceptions held by the employees and the external sample. Specifically, the internal individuals saw the company as more financially rewarding, more interesting, and closer to management positions, computing, and engineering than did the external sample. The external sample saw itself closer to financial rewards, management positions, technology, and engineering than did their internal counterparts. In addition, Woelfel provided the company with message strategies for the recruitment of external computer professionals and for the retention of its own computer personnel. The message indicated that the company was an interesting place to work, that it dealt with computers, and that one could advance in the company.

Barnett and Carson (1983) studied the professional socialization of technical communicators using Galileo. They began by asking 100 professional technical writers to describe their field, what its requisite skills were, and the academic disciplines a technical communicator should study. A content analysis of these questions resulted in 15 concepts. Next, two different groups of professionals and teachers completed the pair-comparison stage. Their cultural spaces served as the criterion or goal of the training program. Students completed the pair-comparisons at three points during a graduate program in technical writing; the beginning, the middle, and upon completion of the program. The results indicated that the variance in culture among the students became smaller, and that they more closely identified with the profession and the material presented in the courses. When compared to both teachers of technical communication and the professionals, there was an initial increase in cultural discrepancy, but, by the completion of the program, the students' attitudes became highly congruent with both the professionals and teachers.

These results indicated that Galileo techniques may be used for the identification of problem areas in training programs. The graphics course did not provide the impetus to reposition the concept "graphics" in a location more congruent with the culture of practicing professionals. It had little impact upon the students. The expected cultural convergence did not occur. This suggested that the course curriculum should be changed to achieve its desired outcome.

These studies indicate how the Galileo system can be used to examine organizational or professional culture. The section that follows describes a specific example in which these procedures were applied to describe an organization's culture and to develop communication strategies to change the perceptions of the organization's members.

AN EMPIRICAL EXAMPLE

This study was undertaken at the author's initiative to demonstrate how the procedures discussed in this chapter may be used to describe an organization's culture. Specifically, the culture of an MIS unit of a large multinational computer company (Company X) Office Products Group located in upstate New York (Eastern City) was examined. Based upon the description, communication strategies were developed which would change the culture by emphasizing the positive or functional aspects, and minimizing the impact of the negative or dysfunctional aspects.

The Case

The examined organization was the MIS division of the Office Products Group of a worldwide company in the electronics-based information systems industry. The parent company was found during the late 19th century by an inventor-entrepreneur. Its initial product was an adding-listing machine. By the mid 1920s, its office products were sold in some 60 countries. From its headquarters in the mid-West, it had established major operations in South America, Europe, Africa, and Australia. Beginning in the late 1940s, the company grew in four principal areas: electronics, computer systems, defense and space, and diverse products which supported banking and business applications. Through the early 1960s, its computers were regarded as the most advanced for business and scientific applications.

Over the next decade, its earnings were exceptional. However, it was losing market share of its major products, adding and bookkeeping machines, and calculators. At the same time, it was having difficulty entering the computer business, concentrating on two main markets, banks and the federal government. These activities were conducted at the expense of its main business. In order to sustain its high levels of growth from the 1960s, it failed to invest in the future. There were other management problems, including marketing, pressures of product and personnel costs, and a lack of corporate leadership.

By the late 1970s, management had to address problems in the areas of lack of senior management talent, weak spots in their product line, such as computer software and product delivery, and a lack of research in distributed processing and office automation. These problems set the stage for a new CEO, a dynamic former cabinet member who took over in 1980. He was a visible leader, well known to bankers, who made up 35% of the company's business. His reputation and expertise would turn the sagging company around. While he has made tremendous strides, the company has what might be described as a culture of failure. They advertise little. There is little talk about its products relative to IBM, HP, or Apple. While few analysts expect the company to fail, it still has a second-rate image, perhaps living off its size. It is not one of the computer companies that readily comes to mind.

The Office Products Group (OPG) is located in upstate New York. Its main products are printed forms to be used with the parent company's hardware. It was acquired in the 1950s, and many employees still remember the days before the change in ownership. It also has a culture of failure. OPG has been a consistant money-losing venture. There have been rumors about the parent selling the operations. In fact, since this research was conducted, OPG has been sold. Further, there are perceptions that OPG is an anachronism. Electronic storage of information and high speed printers will soon replace the traditional practice of using printing forms.

Within this context is the MIS group. Its members are independent, highly-trained computer programmers who write software for the parent company's customers. This group is housed at the same site as OPG, and there is communication among them. The culture of this group was examined.

Methods

The research was conducted in two phases and completed during June, 1984.

Phase 1. The purpose of the first phase was to determine the concepts (words or phrases) most frequently used by MIS personnel to describe their job, the MIS unit, the Office Products Division, and Company X. From these concepts, a symbolic description of the organizational culture would be precisely determined in Phase 2.

These concepts were determined through confidential personal interviews with 23 MIS management and staff members. Subjects for the interviews were selected at random, with the provision that an adequate number of managers and staff would be selected and that they would come from all functional units. The actual sample included 9 managers and 14 staff, 6 of whom were women and 17 were men. The interviews were conducted at Company X's Eastern City site by graduate students studying organizational communication, at the State University of New York at Buffalo, under the author's direction.

Subjects were asked eight general questions about Company X/Eastern City, the goals of MIS, its heroes, special language, stories and legends, rituals and ceremonies, status symbols, what they might talk about if asked to give a public speech about Company X, and how they receive news about the company. A copy of the interview protocol can be found below. It was developed based upon the theory presented in this chapter, conversations with the Human Resources Manager, internal documents which he provided, and a case study conducted by a university professor which described the history and current conditions of Company X.

As you know, I'm with the State University of New York at Buffalo research team. We're here at our initiative in order to conduct a study of OPG's communication structure and organizational culture. In a few weeks we will be giving everyone in the MIS department a short questionnaire. We have randomly selected you to participate in these interviews as part of our research. It will be conducted in strict confidence—only the members of the research team will have access to your interview. No one at Company X, OPG, or MIS will be able to trace anything you say directly back to you. Are you ready to begin?

1. TELL ME A LITTLE BIT ABOUT COMPANY X/EASTERN CITY. What kind of business are you in? Who do you compete with? What is your job here?

2. WHAT IS THE MISSION OF OPG? (What are you in the business to do?) IS OPG ACCOMPLISHING ITS MISSION? (Why or why not?)

   WHAT WOULD YOU SAY ARE THE GOALS AND OBJECTIVES OF MIS? HAVE YOU BEEN ACHIEVING THEM? (Why or why not?)

   When I came into the building, I noticed signs in the halls that refer to the word "excellence." WHAT DOES THIS MEAN (in the context of Company X/Eastern City)? HOW DO YOU FEEL ABOUT THAT? HOW DO OTHERS FEEL?

3. ARE THERE ANY PEOPLE IN COMPANY X WHO ARE NOTED FOR THEIR OUTSTANDING CONTRIBUTIONS? (heroes) What have they done?

   ARE THERE ANY PEOPLE WHO ARE THOUGHT OF AS HAVING HAD A NEGATIVE INFLUENCE ON COMPANY X? (villains) What did they do that was so bad?

4. A few minutes ago we were talking about excellence; WHEN NEW PEOPLE JOIN COMPANY X, ARE THERE ANY OTHER WORDS OR PHRASES OR SPECIALIZED VOCABULARY THAT THEY WOULD BECOME FAMILIAR WITH?

5. (If applicable) Earlier you mentioned _____. CAN YOU TELL ME A GOOD OR REPRESENTATIVE STORY OR FOLK-TALE ABOUT _____ THAT MIGHT HELP ME BETTER UNDERSTAND WHY HE IS DESCRIBED AS _____?

   IF YOU WERE TO GIVE A SPEECH ABOUT OPG (to the Rotary Club, for example), WHAT STORIES OR FOLK-TALES MIGHT YOU USE TO BEGIN YOUR SPEECH?

6. IS THERE ANYTHING DIFFERENT OR UNIQUE ABOUT THE WAY THINGS ARE DONE AT OPG—such as the way work is organized and accomplished? IS THERE ANYTHING DIFFERENT HERE AT MIS? Are the way decisions are made unique?

   IF I WANTED TO BE SUCCESSFUL AT OPG, WHAT WOULD I DO? WHAT WOULD I NOT DO?

   ARE THRE ANY RITUALS OR CEREMONIES OR SPECIAL EVENTS THAT YOU SEE OR PARTICIPATE IN AT OPG? What does _____ mean to you and others?

   WHAT ABOUT STATUS SYMBOLS? Are there any? What do they mean? What impact do they have?

   By the way, on the way in I noticed on the bulletin board a statement about Company X's Human Resources Philosophy—did you happen to read it? (If so) HOW DO PEOPLE REACT TO IT? ARE THE PHILOSOPHIES FOLLOWED? (Why or why not?) HOW DO YOU FEEL ABOUT THEM?

7. If the "Democratic and Chronicle" or the "Times Union" were to run a story on Company X/OPG, WHAT KINDS OF THINGS WOULD THEY SAY? IF YOU WERE TO WRITE THE STORY, WOULD YOU SAY ANYTHING DIFFERENTLY? What?

8. IF YOU WERE TO HEAR GOOD NEWS ABOUT THE COMPANY X CORPORATION HOW AND FROM WHOM WOULD YOU RECEIVE IT? NOW THAT YOU'VE HEARD IT WHO WOULD YOU FIRST TELL IT TO? HOW? WHAT WOULD BE THE GOOD NEWS?

THANK YOU FOR YOUR COOPERATION

Eastern City Company X Interview Protocol
June, 1984

The responses to these questions were content analyzed in two ways. First, they were entered into an Apple IIe microcomputer, and the frequency of use by MIS personnel for each symbol (word or phrase) determined with the use of Sensible Speller IV (Hartley, 1983). In this way, the organizational culture could be described using the same symbols (words or phrases) that are used by the members of the cultural group (MIS personnel). Over 2,400 words (excluding articles, prepositions, and conjunctions) were used — an average of 300 unique words per question. This suggested that the culture of MIS is diverse.

Second, the interview team discussed the responses to determine the common themes in the interviews. In this way, the subjective impressions of the interviewers also could be taken into account in the analysis, and greater confidence placed in the selection of the concepts for the second phase. This would include such aspects of culture as the physical environment and the dress of the organization's members.

Based upon these analyses, 14 words or phrases were chosen as the core set which defines the organizational culture of MIS at Eastern City. The concepts selected for the second phase were those words or phrases which occurred most frequently and were deemed as most representative of the culture by the research staff. The concepts were:

1. People-oriented
2. Support-services
3. Private offices
4. Eastern City/OPG
5. Excellence
6. The Human Resources Philosophy
7. Me
8. MIS
9. Company X/WHQ
10. Marketing
11. Failure
12. Reserved Parking Spaces
13. Independence
14. Products and Supplies

Concept 7, Me, was selected because it provides the means for evaluating each respondent's own perception relative to the other concepts which make up organizational culture. In this study, it turned out to be one of the most frequently mentioned concepts. It is worth noting that the MIS personnel view their organization in structural terms. Four of the key cultural concepts, MIS, Eastern City/OPG, Company X/WHQ, and Marketing, may be viewed as describing Company X's organizational structure.

Phase 2. The purpose of the second phase of research was to measure precisely the relations among the symbols generated in Phase 1. Based upon these measurements, the culture of the MIS organization was accurately described, and communication strategies developed which, when implemented, would be effective in improving the culture.

Each of the words or phrases from Phase 1 was included in a paired-comparison questionnaire. The questionnaire asks respondents to report the difference in meaning between all possible pairs of concepts on a numerical scale which set Products and Services as 50 units different. If a respondent felt that two concepts were more similar than products and services, he or she would write a number less than 50. If he or she felt that they were less similar, he or she would write a larger number; if they were identical, zero for no difference. Past research has shown that measurements of this type are extremely accurate with populations similar to Company X's MIS staff.

During the week of June 18, 1984, questionnaires were distributed to all 80 MIS personnel. They were instructed to complete the questionnaire and, to insure confidentiality, seal it in the accompanying envelope. Of the 70 questionnaires returned, 68 were partially or totally completed. Two were returned blank.

Results. The mean distances reported and the standard deviations about these values are reported in Table 1. On the average, the completion rate was 88% (59.6 of 68). It ranged from 100% to 71% depending on the specific pair. Respondents were instructed to leave a space blank if they could not estimate the difference between the concepts. Of the estimates, 1.3% were removed due to their extreme value. The average percent relative error was less than 10.2%.

The mean reported value was 55.1, somewhat further than the distance between Products and Services. The concepts which the respondents viewed as most dissimilar were Excellence and Failure. They were 120.3 units apart. MIS personnel viewed themselves as People-oriented (20.9), near to Support-services (25.8) and Excellence (23.7). MIS and Independence were moderately close, 37.4 and 42.0 units, respectively. Eastern City/OPG was somewhat further away (47.4). All other concepts were viewed as distant from the self, including Company X/WHQ (90.4), Reserved parking (96.0), and Failure (94.4).

MIS personnel viewed MIS and Eastern City/OPG as equally excellent, 47.9 and 49.1 units. Company X/WHQ was somewhat further from Excellence (57.0). But they perceived MIS and Company X about equally distant from Failure, 57.0 and 54.5 units. Eastern City/OPG was placed relatively close to Failure, 39.5 units, despite being perceived as excellent as MIS. Thus, Excellence was not viewed as a requirement for success. This was the most significant discrepancy in the organization's culture.

Table 1. Means and Standard Deviations of Distances Among Pairs of Concepts

	1	2	3	4	5	6	7	8	9	10	11	12	13	14
People-oriented		29.6	57.7	62.6	33.2	34.5	20.9	53.7	74.9	43.8	58.7	78.2	38.3	53.7
Support Services	23.8		58.5	49.5	37.8	50.9	25.8	40.4	64.1	47.8	58.1	93.5	56.1	43.7
Private Offices	38.9	41.9		55.2	56.6	65.6	83.2	65.2	44.6	38.5	67.4	30.0	36.5	60.2
Eastern City OPG	47.2	40.9	45.8		49.1	59.7	47.2	38.2	68.4	48.0	39.5	50.0	39.1	27.9
Excellence	30.2	30.4	44.9	34.9		40.6	23.7	47.9	57.0	68.5	120.3	77.1	45.6	46.1
Human Res. Philosophy	33.2	33.4	51.2	59.8	32.3		48.2	56.4	55.8	56.4	61.2	70.5	56.0	51.5
Me	23.3	27.2	71.2	40.2	20.0	39.4		37.4	90.4	78.0	94.4	96.0	42.0	54.8
MIS	36.4	31.6	45.8	28.2	34.8	41.4	39.4		59.5	61.4	57.0	87.9	54.9	51.4
Company X/WHQ	47.7	40.9	42.3	40.7	34.6	48.8	72.8	43.4		54.4	54.5	63.7	49.9	44.5
Marketing	35.1	35.0	39.0	39.3	40.3	41.6	62.8	43.0	42.7		42.9	39.0	36.1	32.7
Failure	45.0	47.4	52.2	29.4	67.3	47.1	62.8	48.8	37.7	36.7		73.9	81.1	68.9
Reserved Parking	46.1	48.9	43.5	44.6	53.7	60.1	53.0	57.6	49.6	45.1	57.9		58.1	73.1
Independence	26.7	35.0	34.0	30.5	42.5	38.3	39.5	38.4	36.4	31.0	52.8	39.8		61.4
Products & Supplies	42.3	32.7	38.9	24.4	34.3	30.7	41.2	39.8	30.7	29.5	52.2	53.7	35.3	
GRAND MEAN	55.1													
N = 68														
ERROR < 10.2%														

The means are presented in the upper triangle and the standard deviations are presented in the lower triangle of the matrix.

There was considerable variance in the culture. This was reflected in the large number of words and phrases elicited in the Phase 1 interviews, and in Phase 2, where the average standard deviation was 40.9. This was 74% of the overall mean and 82% of the distance between Products and Services. This diversity of opinion may be problematic, because there was no clear set of expectations about the meaning of cultural symbols.

The mean values were next converted to Caretsian coordinates. From the resulting coordinates, a cultural "map" was drawn. It is presented as Figure 1. While physical distance can be described accurately in two (or three) dimensions, psychological distance is both multidimensional and non-Euclidean. The two dimensions in Figure 1 account for only 61% of the total differentiation among the concepts. The remaining 39% is distributed among 11 additional axes. As a result, any conclusions drawn from Figure 1 should be viewed with caution.

An examination of Figure 1 reveals the functional (positive) and disfunctional (negative) aspects of MIS's culture. To the left of the vertical axes are the concepts which are viewed somewhat negatively; Failure, Reserved Parking, and Private Offices, as well as the structural terms Marketing, Company X/WHQ, and Eastern City/OPG. Viewed relatively more positively are the self (Me), Excellence, MIS, Support Services, Independence, The Human Resource Philosophy, and Products and Supplies. Communication strategies should be implemented to make the perceptions of Company X/WHQ and Eastern City/OPG more positive.

One dimension that is not plotted describes the inconsistencies in the culture. It differentiates Excellence, Failure, and Eastern City/OPG. This dimension exists in the non-Euclidean portion of the space. The reason is that, while Eastern City/OPG is perceived as close to both Failure and Excellence, these two concepts are viewed as very discrepant. As a result, the sum of angles of a triangle composed of the distances among the three concepts exceeds 180 degrees. This inconsistency was addressed when attempts are made to alter the organization's culture.

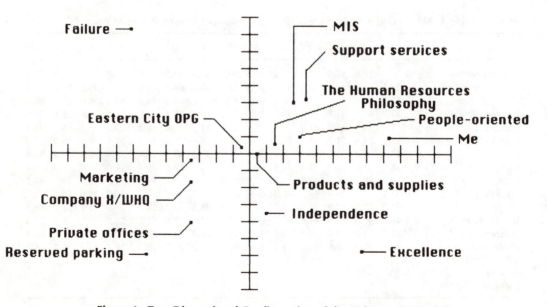

Figure 1. Two Dimensional Configuration of the Culture of MIS Unit

The Cartesian coordinates made it possible to develop communication strategies which, when implemented, would reposition the concepts as desired. Vector analyses were performed by considering the concepts' positions. The resultant vectors, based upon the concepts' locations, reposition the concepts, to be changed as close to the desired locations as possible. From this group of concepts, communication strategies were developed. The explanation of the procedure is as follows: Messages act as forces which alter the position of concepts in cultural space. When two words are associated in the same message, they approach each other in the space. When any number of concepts are associated in the same message, all concepts in the message approach the common center of the concepts in the message. Since the distances among the points in the space represent the relationships among these concepts in the minds of MIS personnel, these movements represent changes in cultural beliefs. Thus, when trying to "move" OPG closer to the self (Me), one is in effect trying to bring OPG closer to the kind of organization with which the respondents would identify.

Three communication strategies were developed. The first was developed to reposition Eastern City/OPG closer to the self. This would increase MIS personnel's identification with OPG. Research has shown that increased identification with a concept (a shorter distance between the self and a concept) increases behaviors involving that concept and improves attitudes toward the object. In effect, this would address one of the negative aspects of the culture, the perception of OPG as a failure. A second communication strategy was developed to reposition Company X/WHQ closer to the self. A third analysis was performed to reposition Eastern City/OPG away from Failure and closer to Excellence. This was done to resolve the major inconsistency in the culture, that OPG, while excellent, was still viewed as a failure.

To reposition Eastern City/OPG closer to the self, 281 positive messages were examined. All 1, 2, 3 and 4 concept combination messages which would move OPG in the desired direction were examined. Each message was evaluated to the extent to which it has the potential to move Eastern City/OPG closer to the position held by the average of the respondents' self. Four particularly good messages were identified. They were:

Message Concepts	Distance from Self (%)	Angle
1. People-oriented, Excellence, MIS	21.4	11.9
2. People-oriented, Support services Excellence, MIS	23.8	13.5
3. People-oriented, Support services Excellence	28.1	15.1
4. People-oriented, MIS	29.7	17.2

There were 488 messages that, if applied, would reposition Company X/WHQ closer to the self. By far the single best message for this purpose was simply that Company X is People-oriented. Its final distance from the self was only 23.1% of the initial distance, and the departure of this message vector from the ideal was only 9.8 degrees. The next best message final distance was 36.4%, with an angle of 14.5 degrees.

To reposition Eastern City/OPG closer to Excellence, 488 positive messages were also evaluated. Again, there was one clearly exceptionally effective messages strategy. It involves People-oriented, Company X/WHQ, and Me. Its final position was only 15.5% of the initial distance between the two concepts. The angle was only 7.9 degrees off the ideal message vector. The next best message final distance was 35.2%, with an angle of 17.6 degrees.

Communication strategies should be implemented using the concepts from these three messages. This may be done using various forms of the media (bulletin boards, letters, and memos) and interpersonal communication. When employed, they will have the effect of reducing the negative impact upon MIS's organizational culture. The inconsistency in the culture, the perception that Eastern City/OPG can be both excellent and a failure at the same time, will be resolved. Further, the application of a consistant set of messages, over time, will reduce the considerable variance in the culture.

Future research should be conducted in a number of areas. One, if implemented, these communication strategies should be reevaluated in the future. Because of the interdependent nature of the cultural space, change at any location may alter the effectiveness of any given message. Using a communication strategy over too long a period of time without evaluation runs the risk of having a negative effect on the culture. The author had planned to go back and gather follow-up data to examine the changes in organizational culture. With the sale of OPG, there are tentative plans to examine the changes in organizational culture as the group becomes incorporated into a different organizational culture. Two, the study may be expanded to evaluate the culture of Company X's entire operation at Eastern City. Of concern are the perceptions of failure in the culture of MIS about OPG. If these perceptions are shared by OPG, it may impact on their productivity to such a degree that it may lead to the eventual failure of the division, irrespective of the corporate strategic plan. Finally, an analysis of this type may be conducted corporate-wide to develop communication strategies which would create a culture of excellence at Company X. This would make its culture competitive for the future.

SUMMARY

This chapter has described the phenomenon of organizational culture from the symbols-and-meaning perspective. It has defined organizational culture and discussed the role of communication in the process of formulating and changing organizational culture. Considerable attention was paid to the process of examining organizational culture. These procedures include interviewing and other naturalistic research methods, content analysis, and the Galileo System of multidimensional scaling. These procedures go beyond the mainstream naturalistic approaches used to study organizational culture (Putnam, 1983). They include cultural descriptions based upon a set of emergent symbols in the actual language of the organization's members. In addition, they include the precise measurement of organizational culture, using the actual symbols from the qualitative research. This makes possible the ability to alter culture as desired to achieve organizational objectives. Finally, this chapter concluded with an empirical example which applied these procedures.

REFERENCES

Albrecht, T. L. (1979). The role of communication in perceptions of organization climate. In D. Nimmo (Ed.), *Communication yearbook 3*. New Brunswick, NJ: Transaction Books.
Albrecht, T. L. (1984). Managerial communication and work perception. In R. Bostrom (Ed.), *Communication yearbook 8*. Beverly Hills, CA: Sage.

Barnett, G.A. (1972). *Reliability and metric multidimensional scaling.* Unpublished manuscript. Department of Communication, Michigan State University, East Lansing.

Barnett, G. A. (1978, April)). *An associational model for the diffusion of complex innovations.* Paper presented at the International Communication Association convention, Chicago. Abstracted in *Resources in Education,* December, 1978.

Barnett, G. A. (1979). The measurement of organizational culture. In G. M. Goldhaber & O. Wiio (Eds.), *Proceedings of organizational communication conference.* Buffalo, NY: State University of New York.

Barnett, G. A. (1980, May). *Frequency of occurance as an estimate for inertial mass: Pigs in space.* Paper presented at the International Communication Association convention, Acapulco, Mexico.

Barnett, G. A. (1981). A multidimensional analysis of the 1976 presidential campaign. *Communication Quarterly, 28,* 156–164.

Barnett, G. A. (1984, February). *Precise procedures for longitudinal network analysis.* Paper presented at the Sunbelt Social Networks Conference, Phoenix.

Barnett, G. A., & Carson, D. L. (1983, May). *The role of communication in the professional socalization process.* Paper presented at the International Communication Association convention, Dallas. Abstracted in *Resources in Communication,* March, 1984.

Barnett, G. A., Hamlin, D. M., & Danowski, J. A. (1981). The use of fractionation scales in communication audits. In M. Burgoon (Ed.), *Communication yearbook 5.* New Brunswick, NJ: Transaction.

Barnett, G. A., & Kincaid, D. L. (1983). A mathematical theory of cultural convergence. In W. B. Gudykunst (Ed.), *Intercultural communication theory: Current perspectives.* Beverly Hills, CA: Sage.

Barnett, G. A., & McPhail, T. L. (1980). An examination of the relationship of U.S. television to Canadian identity. *International Journal of Intercultural Relations, 4,* 219–232.

Barnett, G. A., & Rice, R. E. (1985). Network analysis in riemann space: applications of the galileo system to social networks. *Social Networks, 7,* 287–322.

Barnett, G.A., Serota, K. B., & Taylor, J. A. (1976). Campaign communication and attitude change: A multidimensional analysis. *Human Communication Research, 2,* 227–244.

Barnett, G. A., & Woelfel, J. (1979). On the dimensionality of psychological professes. *Quality and Quantity, 13,* 215–232.

Benedict, R. (1934). *Patterns of culture.* Boston, MA: Houghton Mifflin.

Berger, P. L., & Luckmann, T. (1967). *The social construction of reality.* Garden City, NY: Anchor Books.

Bormann, E. G. (1983). Symbolic convergence: Organizational communication and culture. In L. Putnam & M. Pacanowsky (Eds.), *Communication and organizations: An interpretive approach.* Beverly Hills, CA: Sage.

D'Andrade, R. G. (1984). Cultural meaning systems. In R. A. Shweder & R. A. LeVine (Eds.), *Cultural theory: Essays on mind, self, and emotion.* Cambridge, England: Cambridge University Press.

Danes, J. E., & Woelfel, J. (1975, April). *An alternative to the "traditional" scaling paradigm in mass communication research: multidimensional reduction of ratio judgements of separation.* Paper presented at the International Communication Association convention, Chicago.

Danowski, J. A., Andrews, J. R., & Edison-Swift, P. (1985, February). *A network analysis method for representing social concepts: An illustration with words cooccuring across electronic mail.* Paper presented at the Sunbelt Social Networks Conference, Palm Beach, FL.

Danowski, J.A., & Edison-Swift, P. (1985). Crisis effects on intra-organizational computer-based communication. *Communication Research, 12,* 251–270.

Deal, T. E., & Kennedy, A. A. (1982). *Corporate cultures: The rites and rituals of corporate life.* Reading, MA: Addison-Wesley.

Dennis, H. S. (1975, April). *The construction of a managerial communication climate inventory for use in complex organizations.* Paper presented at the International Communication Association convention, Chicago.

Durkheim, E. (1938). *The rites of sociological method* (2nd ed.) (S. A. Sulovay &J. H. Mueller, Trans.) G. C. Catlin, Ed.). Glencoe, IL: Free Press.

Durkheim, E. (1953). *Sociology of philosophy* (D. F. Pocock, Trans.). Glencoe, IL: Free Press.

Falcione, R. L. (1978, May). *Subordinate satisfaction as a function of communication climate and perceptions of immediate supervision.* Paper presented at the Eastern Communication Association convention, Boston.

Falcione, R. L., & Kaplan, E. A. (1984). Organizational climate, communication, and culture. In R. Bostrum (Ed.), *Communication yearbook 8.* Beverly Hills, CA: Sage.

Geertz, C. (1973). *The interpretation of cultures.* New York: Basic Books.

Geertz, C. (1984). From the native's point of view. In R. A. Shweder & R. A. LeVine (Eds.), *Culture theory: Essays on mind, self, and emotion.* Cambridge, England: Cambridge University Press.

Goldhaber, G. M. (1983). *Organzational communication* (3rd ed.). Dubuque, IA: Wm. C. Brown.

Goldhaber, G. M., Barnett, G. A., Mitchell, J. J., & Bales, R. W. (1983, May). *Network analysis from a functional perspective.* Paper presented at the International Communication Association convention, Dallas.

Goldhaber, G. M., & Rogers, D. P. (1979). *Auditing Organizational Communication Systems: The ICA Communication Audit.* Dubuque, IA: Kendall/Hunt Publishing Company.

Goldhaber, G. M., Yates, M., Porters, T., & Lesnick, R. (1978). Organizational Communication: 1978. *Human Communication Research, 5,* 76–96.

Goodenough, W. H. (1964). Cultural anthropology and linguistics. In D. Hymes (Ed.), *Language in culture and society.* New York: Harper & Row.

Gordon, T. F. (1976, August). *Subject abilities to use MDS: effects of varying the criterion pair.* Paper presented at the Association for Education in Journalism convention, College Park, MD.

Gudykunst, W. B., & Kim, Y. Y. (1984). *Communicating with strangers: An approach to intercultural communication.* Reading, MA: Addison-Wesley.

Gusfield, J. R., & Michalowicz, J. (1984). Secular symbolism: studies of ritual, ceremony, and symbolic order in modern life. *Annual Review of Sociology, 10,* 417–435.

Harris, L., & Cronen, V. E. (1979). A rules-based model for the analysis and evaluation of organizational communication. *Communication Quarterly, 27,* 12–28.

Hartley, C. A. (1983). *Sensible speller IV.* Southfield, MI: Sensible Software, Inc.

Hirsch, P., & Andrews, J. (1983). Ambushes, shootouts, and knights of the round table: The language of corporate takeovers. In L. R. Pondy, P. J. Frost, G. Morgan, & T. C. Dandridge, (Eds.), *Organizational symbolism.* Greenwich, CT: JAI Press.

Horan, H. (1981). *Contingencies of perceived organizational communication effectiveness: A comparison of American and European organizations.* Unpublished doctoral dissertation, State University of New York at Buffalo.

James, L. R., & Jones, A. P. (1974). Organizational climate: A review of theory and research. *Psychological Bulletin, 81,* 1096–1112.

Johnson, S. C. (1967). Hiearchal clustering schemes. *Psychemetrika, 32,* 241–254.

Kincaid, D. L., Yum, J. O., Woelfel, J., & Barnett, G. A. (1983). The cultural convergence of Korean immigrants in Hawaii: An empirical test of a mathematical theory. *Quality and Quantity, 18,* 59–78.

Kluckhohn, C. (1951). The study of culture. In D. Lerner & H. D. Lasswell (Eds.), *The policy sciences.* Stanford, CA: Stanford University.

Kluckhohn, C., & Kelly, W. H. (1945). The concept of culture. In R. Linton (Ed.), *The science of man in the world crisis.* New York: Columbia University Press.

Korpowski, E. J. (1983). Cultural myths: clues to effective management. *Organizational dynamics, 12,* 39–51.

LeVine, R. A. (1984). Properties of culture: An ethnographic view. In R. A. Shweder & R. A. LeVine

(Eds.), *Culture theory: Essays on mind, self, and emotion.* Cambridge, England: Cambridge University Press.

Martin, J., Feldman, M., Hatch, M., & Sitkin, S. (1983). The uniqueness paradox in organizational stories. *Administrative Science Quarterly, 28,* 438–453.

Mills, C. W. (1951). *White collar, the American middle classes.* New York: Oxford University Press.

Mintzberg, H. (1983). *Structures in fives: Designing effective organizations.* Englewood Cliffs, NJ: Prentice Hall.

Neuendorf, K. A., Kaplowitz, S., Fink, E. L., & Armstrong, B. (1984, May). *Assessment of meaning of self-referent concepts in multidimensional scaling.* Paper presented at the International Communication Association conference, San Francisco.

Nieberg, H. L. (1973). *Cultural storm: Politics and the ritual order.* New York: St. Martins Press.

Ochs, E., & Schieffelin, B. B. (1984). Language acquisition and socialization: three developmental stories and their implications. In R. A. Shweder & R. A. LeVine (Eds.), *Cultural theory: Essays on mind, self, and emotion.* Cambridge, England: Cambridge University Press.

Pacanowsky, M. E., & O'Donnell-Trujillo, N. (1982). Communication and organizational cultures. *Western Journal of Speech Communication, 46,* 115–130.

Pacanowsky, M. E., & O'Donnell-Trujillo, N. (1983). Organizational communication as cultural performances. *Communication Monographs, 50,* 26–147.

Peters, T. J., & Waterman, R. H. (1982). *In search of excellence: Lessons from America's best run companies.* New York: Warner Books.

Pettigrew, P. M. (1979). On studying organizational culture. *Administrative Science Quarterly, 24,* 570–581.

Putnam, L. (1983). The interpretive perspective: an alternative to functionalism. In L. Putnam & M. Pacanowsky (Eds.), *Communication and organizations: An interpretive approach.* Beverly Hills, CA: Sage.

Redding, W. C. (1972). *Communication within the organization: an interpretive review of theory and research.* New York: Industrial Communication Council.

Rice, R. E., & Barnett, G. A. (1985). Group communication networking in an information environment: applying metric multidimensional scaling. In M. McLaughlin (Ed.), *Communication yearbook 9.* Beverly Hills, CA: Sage.

Roberts, J. M. (1984). The self management of cultures. In W. Goodenough (Ed.), *Explorations in cultural anthropology: Essays in honor of George Peter Murdock.* New York: McGraw-Hill.

Rogers, E., & Agarwala-Rogers, R. (1976). *Communication in organizations.* New York: Free Press.

Rokeach, M. (1973). *The nature of human values.* New York: Free Press.

Rokeach, M. (1979). Value theory and communication research: review and commentary. In D. Nimmo (Ed.), *Communication yearbook 3.* New Brunswick, NJ: Transaction Books.

Schein, E. H. (1983). The role of the founder in creating organizational culture. *Organizational dynamics, 12,* 13–28.

Schwartz, H., & Davis, S. M. (1981). Matching corporate culture and business strategy. *Organizational dynamics, 10,* 30–48.

Serota, K. B. (1974). *Metric multidimensional scaling and communication: Theory and implementation.* Unpublished masters thesis, Department of Communication, Michigan State University, East Lansing.

Serota, K. B., Cody, M. J., Barnett, G. A., & Taylor, J. A. (1977). Precise procedures for optimizing campaign communication. In B. Ruben (Ed.), *Communication yearbook 1.* New Brunswick, NJ: Transaction Books.

Shweder, R. A. (1984). Preview: A colloquey of culture theorists. In R. A. Shweder & R. A. LeVine (Eds.), *Culture theory: Essays on mind, self and emotion.* Cambridge: Cambridge University Press.

Shweder, R. A., & LeVine, R. A. (1984). *Culture theory: essays on mind, self and emotion.* Cambridge, England: Cambridge University Press.

Siegel, G. (1980, April). *Benchmark measures of professionalization: Results of the pilot study phase of the national study on professional accounting education.* Unpublished research report, Department of Accounting, University of Illinois, Chicago.

Siegel, G. (1981). *The attitudinal survey on direct, uninvited solicitation.* New York: American Institute of Certified Public Accounting.

Silverman, D. (1970). *Theory of organizations.* London: Heinemann.

Swartz, M., & Jordon, D. K. (1976). *Anthropology: Perspectives on humanity.* New York: Wiley.

Tagiuri, R., & Litwin, G. (1968). *Organizational climate.* Boston, MA: Harvard University Press.

Thurstone, L. L. (1972). Method of paired-comparisons for social values. *Journal of Abnormal Social Psychology, 21,* 384–400.

Torgerson, W. (1958). *Theory and methods of scaling.* New York: Wiley.

Triandis, H. C., Vassiliou, V., Vassiliou, G., Tanaka, Y., & Shanmugan, A. V. (1972). *The analysis of subjective culture.* New York: Wiley.

Trice, H. M., & Beyer, J. M. (1984). Studying organizational cultures through rites and ceremonials. *Academy of Management Review, 9,* 653–669.

Weick, K. E. (1979). *The social psychology of organizing* (2nd ed.). Reading, MA: Addison-Wesley.

Wigand, R. T., & Barnett, G. A. (1976). Multidimensional scaling of cultural processes: The case of Mexico, South Africa and the United States. *International-Intercultural Annual, 3,* 139–172.

Woelfel, J. (1974, December). *Metric measurement of cultural processes.* Paper presented at the Speech Communication Association meeting, Chicago.

Woelfel, J., & Barnett, G. A. (1974, April). *A paradigm for mass communication research.* Paper presented at the International Communication Association convention, New Orleans.

Woelfel, J., & Barnett, G. A. (1982). Multidimensional scaling in riemann space. *Quality and Quantity, 16,* 469–491.

Woelfel, J., Cody, M., Taylor, J., & Fink, E. L. (1976b, April). *A mathematical procedure for optimizing political campaign strategy.* Paper presented at the International Communication Association convention, Portland, Oregon.

Woelfel, J., Cody, M., Gillham, J., & Holmes, R. (1980a). Basic premises of attitude change theory. *Human Communication Research, 6,* 153–168.

Woelfel, J., & Fink, E. L. (1980). *The Galileo system: A theory of social measurement and its application.* New York: Academic.

Woelfel, J., Fink, E. L., Serota, K. B., Barnett, G. A., Holmes, R., Cody, M., Saltiel, J., Marlier, J. & Gillham, J. R. (1976a). Galileo — A Program for Multidimensional Scaling. Honolulu: East-West Communication Institute.

Woelfel, J., & Holmes, R. (1982, May). *CATPAK demonstration.* Paper presented at the International Communication Association convention, Boston.

Woelfel, J., Holmes, R., & Kincaid, D. L. (1979, May). *Rotation to congruence for general Riemann surfaces under theoretical constraints.* Paper presented at the International Communication Association convention, Philadelphia.

Woelfel, J., Holmes, R., Kincaid, D. L., & Barnett, G. A. (1980b). *How to do a galileo study.* Troy, NY: Good Books.

Woelfel, J., & Saltiel, J. (1978). Cognitive processes as motions in a multidimensional space. In F. Casmir (Ed.), *International and intercultural communication.* New York: University Press.

Woelfel, J., Saltiel, J., McPhail, R., Danes, J. E., Cody, M. J., Barnett, G. A., & Serota, K. B. (1975, August). *Orthogonal rotation to theoretical criteria: Comparison of multidimensional spaces.* Paper presented at the Mathematical Psychology Association meeting, West Lafayette, IN.

Woelfel, M. (1978). *An experimental analysis of the effects of variance in influence, level of influence and attitudinal change on stress.* Unpublished M.A. thesis, Michigan State University, East Lansing.

Chapter 7

Organizational Symbols and Sense-Making

Eric M. Eisenberg and Patricia Riley

Department of Communication Arts and Sciences
University of Southern California

ABSTRACT

The primary goal of this chapter is to review research on symbols and symbolic processes in organizations. As the study of organizational communication has broadened to include the view that communication is the means by which organizing occurs, this sense-making process and the symbols which are its substance become focal points for research.

First, the leading theoretical perspectives on organizational symbolism — negotiated order theory, dramatism, cultural approaches to organization theory, structuration, and information theory — are discussed. Second, the role symbols play in constituting organizational reality is explored through research on: socialization; corporate image and social legitimacy; and communication, dominance, and power. Third, symbolic approaches to organizational change are investigated through studies of leadership and organizational development. Finally, four key issues in the development of future research on symbols and symbolization — shared meanings, conscious and unconscious use of symbols, socially constructed reality, and methods of study — are analyzed and suggestions are given.

I. INTRODUCTION

Human organizing is a complex undertaking, an alchemy wherein individuals become socialized, develop interpersonal relationships, systematize their activities, and make sense of their surroundings. Fundamental to this process is the creation of meanings for actions and events that shape work environments and personal identities within a system. Such interactions are inherently symbolic, for it is only in symbols that meaning can be observed (Duncan, 1968).

Symbols appear in organizations in a myriad of forms, including words, acts, objects, and events (Morgan, Frost, & Pondy, 1983). Specific examples include organizational stories, myths, and metaphors; organizational charts, paperwork, and records; corporate rites and rituals; and the architecture of office buildings. In a more practical vein, numerous authors have concluded that the manipulation of symbols is the primary goal of managers (e.g., Pascale & Athos, 1981; Peters & Waterman, 1982; Weick, 1980).

The nature of symbols and the appropriate methods for their study have been the subjects of numerous scholarly treatises and disputes (e.g., Boulding, 1956; Cassirer, 1944; Langer, 1963; Ogden & Richards, 1936). While the importance of symbols has been long accepted in the sacred, ritualized arenas of human existence, the secular world has traditionally paid less attention to the expressive and aesthetic aspects of their experience (Morgan et al., 1983). Only recently have the study of human organizing, and the deeply embedded social practices that create institutions, been examined systematically in this light. From this perspective, symbols are not merely the "carriers of events"; they are the very substance of bestowing meaning and codifying experience (Burke, 1965). Communication, seen in this way, is not a process that takes place in organizations, it is the constitutive means by which organizing occurs (Putnam, 1983).

The earliest sustained research into organizational symbols came from sociologists, primarily symbolic interactionists (e.g., Denzin, 1978; Duncan, 1968). Fueled by several special conferences and issues of journals,[1] communication and management theorists have promoted a variety of theoretical perspectives on organizational symbolism, not all of which give communication the primacy we believe is appropriate. This chapter focuses on studies in which communication is the central process in organizing, and where emphasis is placed on the use of symbols by organizational members in the creation, maintenance, and transformation of organizational realities. First, we briefly describe leading theoretical perspectives on organizational symbolism. Second, we explain how world views emerge in organizations, how certain perspectives are maintained and come to dominate over time, and how symbols and symbolic processes are involved in changing these views. Third, we propose four emerging themes which should become central concerns in future research and theory-building.

II. THEORETICAL PERSPECTIVES ON ORGANIZATIONAL SYMBOLISM

A variety of approaches are available for the study of organizational symbolism. This chapter will discuss five of the most fundamental viewpoints: negotiated order theory, dramatism, cultural approaches to organizations, structuration theory, and information theory.

A. Negotiated Orders

Early research on symbols and sense-making was dominated by symbolic interactionists. They employed the concept of negotiated order, popularized by Strauss, Schatzman, Erlich, Bucher, and Sabshin (1963) and prevalent in the work of Mead, Hughes, Long, Dalton, and Goffman (Fine, 1984). As with other interactionist approaches, the fundamen-

---

[1] Three recent conferences have addressed topics related to organizational symbolism—the first in Alta, Utah (Putnam & Pacanowsky, 1983), the second in Urbana, Illinois (Pondy et al., 1983) and the third in Vancouver, British Columbia (Frost, Moore, Louis, Lundberg, & Martin, 1985). A related book on information processing in organizations was based on a conference held at Carnegie Mellon University (Sproull & Larkey, 1984). Finally, a recent issue of the Journal of Management (1985) was devoted entirely to the subject of organizational symbolism.

tal assumption of negotiated order is that communication, and hence meaning, is the central feature of social life. Thus negotiated order theory sees organizational structures and practices as emergent through ongoing transactions and negotiation.

Four assumptions underlie Strauss's approach: (a) organization is not possible without negotiation, hence all social order is negotiated order; (b) specific negotiations are contingent on the structural conditions of the organization, and negotiations are patterned via lines of communication; (c) negotiations are constituted in time — renewed, revised, and reconstituted; and (d) structural changes in organizations entail revisions in negotiated order (Fine, 1984).

Research from the negotiated order perspective focuses on two levels of symbolic transactions, interpersonal and organizational. The interpersonal level presumes that people operate *within* structures, and that these structures influence world views. Examples of research guided by this presumption include studies of employees who informally negotiate their increased status, as well as investigations of how individuals operate strategically within the power constraints of social structures (Crozier, 1971; Ditton, 1979; Johnson, 1974).

On the organizational level, research focuses on collective negotiation. Although individuals do the actual negotiating, it is the relationships among groups and organizations that are of interest (Strauss, 1982). Examples of such research include studies of the role of communication in bargaining (Putnam & Jones, 1982). This research has illuminated the process through which structures are created. As Fine (1984) noted:

> In observing organizations from a distance, we may believe we see a stable, unchanging system of relationships. Yet, the negotiated order approach has sensitized researchers to the fact that these relations are ultimately dependent upon the agreement of their parties and that they are constructed through a social, rather than entirely policy driven, process. (p. 243)

Negotiation is continuous, leading to inevitable changes as individuals and groups react to their institutional circumstances and perceived structural constraints. According to Fine (1984), research on negotiated orders is related conceptually to dramatistic studies that focus on social action and symbolic communication (e.g., Manning, 1982). Both research traditions contend that people are aware of their situations, and will act to control others' perceptions of them. Thus the overarching concern for researchers is the interplay between social structures and the meanings that constitute these structures.

B. Dramatism

Dramatism is the theory of symbolic action developed by such theorists as Kenneth Burke and Talcott Parsons. Broadly conceived, dramatism distinguishes between action and sheer motion, and focuses on the structure and function of symbols in the achievement of human action. Writers such as Erving Goffman and Murray Edelman invoke dramatism in the organizational context, incorporating concepts like scene, role, and actor into their research. While there are many different approaches within dramatism, some typical examples include Goffman's (1959) field work on the ritual elements in human interaction, Thompson's (1967) description of superior/subordinate dramaturgy, Bormann's (1983) research on symbolic convergence, and Tompkins, Fisher, Infante, and Tompkins's (1975) Burkean analysis of organizational characteristics.

While dramatistic researchers have applied relatively similar concepts in their analysis of organizations, cultural research has been far more diffuse. The next section describes the more prominent views in the study of organizational culture.

C. Culture

One of the most popular concepts in the organizational literature today is culture. Although the notion of organizational culture has been met with much enthusiasm in both the academic and popular presses, there is a good deal of confusion surrounding the term.[2] This confusion may be traced to anthropological conceptions of culture, which are themselves unclear. "Culture" has been alternatively defined as a system of shared ideas, knowledge, and meanings; as socially transmitted patterns of behavior that relate communities to their settings; and as systems of social networks (cf. Kroeber & Kluckhorn, 1952).

These differing conceptualizations of culture in anthropology are mirrored, and to some extent expanded, in the organizational literature. Smircich (1983a) delineates five major themes in the study of organizational culture — cross-cultural, corporate culture, organizational cognition, organizational symbolism, and unconscious processes and organization. Each perspective is described below.

Traditionally, cross-cultural research and research on corporate culture do not view organizations as fundamentally symbolic; instead, culture is conceptualized as one of many variables that merit investigation in organizations. *Cross-cultural approaches* take culture to be synonymous with country, and explore issues such as nationality differences in organizational practices and employee attitudes (Everett, Stening, & Longton, 1982; Ouchi, 1981; Pascale & Athos, 1981). *Corporate culture research* examines the symbolic dimension as it is manifested in cultural artifacts, including ceremonies (Trice & Beyer, 1984), rituals (Gusfield & Michalowicz, 1984), stories (Martin, Feldman, Hatch, & Sitkin, 1983; Martin & Powers, 1983; Mitroff & Killman, 1976), myths (Boje, Fedor, & Rowland, 1982; Koprowski, 1983), and specialized language (Hirsch & Andrews, 1983). "Culture," from this perspective, is generally defined as the social or normative glue that holds an organization together (Tichy, 1983), or the set of important assumptions, often unstated, that members share (Sathe, 1985). In this manner, organizational culture is another key by which managers can direct the course of their organizations (Sathe, 1983; Wilkins, 1983).

Researchers who use culture as a root metaphor for conceptualizing organizations visualize culture as something an organization *is*, not something an organization *has* (Smircich, 1983a). The *organizational cognition* perspective examines networks of shared meanings that function in a rule-like manner. Examples include Harris and Cronen's (1979) master contract representation of an organization's self-image, Argyris and Schon's (1978) cognitive maps, and Schall's (1983) normative communication rules. A common thread through this research is the belief that thought is linked to action — one reason many of the studies have an interventionist component.

The *organizational symbolism* perspective also perceives culture to be a root metaphor for organization, and views culture primarily as patterns of symbolic discourse that need to be interpreted or deciphered to be understood (Manning, 1979; Van Maanen, 1977).

---

[2] For a more comprehensive treatment of organizational culture, see Barnett (in this volume) and Frost et al. (1985).

Examples of this type of research include studies of the discourse of police (Pacanowsky & Anderson, 1981) and the sense-making processes of executives (Smircich, 1983b).

The fifth view defines culture as the expression of *unconscious psychological processes*. Rooted in the work of anthropologist Levi-Strauss, this notion presumes that humans possess built-in psychological constraints that structure thought and physical action. Examples include investigations of organizational conflicts (Turner, 1983) and of Jungian archetypes in organizational stories (Mitroff, 1982). Other theorists are developing a transformational organization theory that includes a belief in deep underlying structures in the mind that must be theoretically integrated with more obvious surface processes (White & McSwain, 1983).

Each perspective on organizational culture has distinct concerns, despite the fact that similar phenomena are investigated. The culture-as-variable approach (e.g., cross-cultural and corporate culture research) and the culture-as-root-metaphor approach (e.g., research on organizational cognition, organizational symbolism, and unconscious psychological processes) both focus attention on language, myths, stories, and other symbolic phenomena. In the former perspective, these symbols are seen as artifacts, while in the latter approach they are viewed as generative processes that produce meaning and, in so doing, accomplish organization.

D. Structuration

Structuration theory posits that communication contributes both to the formation of individual personality and to the development of larger institutions through the production and reproduction of structures (Giddens, 1979). These structures can best be understood as the rules and resources people use in everyday interaction. Individuals consciously draw upon interpretive schemes (standardized stocks of knowledge) in the production of meaning. These interpretive schemes have a strong obligating quality—their chronic reproduction legitimizes the social actions they constitute. Interviews, business meetings, reports, and even incidental conversations can all be analyzed through the interpretive schemes people use in making sense of transactions.

Social systems that are "chronically reproduced" in day-to-day activity can be analyzed as institutions. These regularized practices are sustained by systems of meaning, role prescriptions, and socialization. Examples of this research include Poole and McPhee's (1983) work on organizational climate, and Riley's (1983) investigation of organizational culture.

While structuration is concerned with a wide range of behaviors that contribute to organizational structures, information theory concentrates specifically on the symbolic aspects of information use in organizations.

E. Information Theory

Information theory encompasses a diverse array of theoretical concepts, some of which are relevant to the study of organizational symbolism. Based on Herbert Simon's (1976) notion of bounded rationality, certain information processing theorists (e.g., Feldman & March, 1981; Sproull & Larkey, 1984) postulate that information in organizations (actual messages, documents, and organizational data) may be used in a "symbolic" manner. According to Larkey and Sproull (1984), "the symbolic value of information arises in part from its cultural imperative as a status or reassurance symbol. Thus it is easy to discover organizations buying or trading more information or different information than economic analysis would suggest they need" (p. 3). People in organizations gather, store, and disseminate information, not simply because they are trying to facilitate openness and efficiency, but because the process of handling information itself has important symbolic implications, many of which concern the appearance of legitimacy on the part of information handlers (Meyer & Rowan, 1977).

The approaches to organizational symbolism we have reviewed have one thing in common — they view communication as a central feature of organizational life. Underlying this assumption is the belief that it is through symbolic transactions that individuals make sense of their environments, and thus create, maintain, and transform definitions of organizational reality. In the next two sections, our focus shifts from specific theoretical perspectives on symbolism to a more general discussion of the role of symbols in constituting organizational realities.

III. CONSTITUTING ORGANIZATIONAL REALITY

Organizational reality can be viewed both as a generative process (how organization is accomplished) and as an outcome (what organizations accomplish). The primary areas of research concerning the constitution of organizational reality are: socialization; corporate image and social legitimacy; and communication, dominance, and power.

A. Socialization

Perhaps the most important context in which definitions of organizational reality are created and shaped is in the socialization of new members. For example, new employees receive messages designed to show them how their interests overlap with those of the organization, and hence are attempts to foster identification and commitment (Tompkins & Cheney, 1983). Rites and rituals of initiation are sometimes conducted to communicate a heightened sense of membership in the organization (Trice & Beyer, 1984). Through socialization, rules, norms, roles, and tacit assumptions about organizational life interactively emerge (Louis, 1980; Wentworth, 1980).

Whether formally, through orientation of training sessions, or informally, through storytelling, organizational communication is "the primary means used to socialize members into an organization's culture" (Kreps, 1983, p. 244). Such communication can involve familiarizing employees with a whole new vocabulary of symbols. Professional socialization, for instance, accrues over time as individuals learn jargon, ideology, and attitudes, values, and beliefs unique to the professional group (cf. Barnett & Carson, 1983). Caplow (1964), in his study of the "Inner Club" of the U.S. Senate, concludes that socialization primarily involves developing commitments to prominent organizational symbols. Evered (1983), in his study of the language of the Navy, describes in detail the vocabulary which must be learned before someone can be considered a member of the organization. In their study of the socialization of new machinists, Boland and Hoffman (1983) argue that physical tricks and humor are used to teach the "pecking order" in the shop as well as to convey the ethos of the skilled machinist.

One result of socialization is that over time, in-groups may develop through the use of private jokes and restricted vocabularies (Bormann, 1983). This can occur both within an organization, and between the members of an organization and outsiders. Shared fantasies, myths, and stories may indicate symbolic membership in an organization or sub-group (Kidder, 1981). The more inaccessible these jokes or other symbols are to outsiders, the more they serve to build in-group solidarity and produce feelings of alienation in organizational members who are left out.

The constitution of particular interpretations is not, of course, restricted to new members. Employees often are called upon to participate in activities designed to reinforce organizational values or practices. Research on maintaining existing organizational interpretations and preserving the status quo focuses on legitimacy as a key concept.

B. Corporate Image-Making and Social Legitimacy

The idea that an organization's legitimacy in society is tied to its procedures and practices is best reflected in Meyer and Rowan's (1977) theory of institutional organizations. In response to the traditional view, wherein organizations seek increased efficiency and productivity above all, the institutional model holds that certain types of organizations adopt and perpetuate policies, procedures, and structures because of their symbolic value to society. Because of their perceived value, these structures (e.g., certification of health professionals, or hiring individuals with doctorates at research universities) lend a sense of legitimacy to the organization and hence increase its likelihood of survival. In attempting to present a favorable image, institutional organizations may avoid evaluating their core activities (e.g., in schools, this means teaching; in hospitals, medical care) for fear that stringent evaluation would reveal inconsistencies that might cast the organization in an unfavorable light. Particularly in organizations populated by professionals, a "logic of confidence" (Meyer & Rowan, 1977) operates — since evaluation is avoided, it is taken on "good faith" that qualified professionals will do their jobs well.

Not everyone in an organization has an equal role in shaping its societal image. Individuals directly engaged in customer relations or marketing may have a disproportionately large influence; so too can people occupying "boundary roles" (Adams, 1980). Boundary role personnel, such as bank tellers and salespeople, as well as certain higher level executives (e.g., people who serve on more than one board of directors), help shape the image of the organization in the community (cf. Eisenberg, Farace, Monge, Bettinghaus, Kurchner-Hawkins, Miller, & Rothman, 1985). Other attempts to shape or create organizational images are less obvious, such as the sponsorship of sports events or concerts, or the use of product advertising that doubles as corporate image making.

As part of their maintenance activity, organizations sometimes perpetuate myths to their publics, and have been accused of spreading bureaucratic propaganda (Altheide & Johnson, 1980). For example, Larkey and Smith (1984) report that high level managers in a city government consistently attributed financial problems to uncontrollable, external factors, while Salancik and Meindl (1984) found that the managements of unstable firms with little environmental control would claim credit for both positive *and* negative outcomes to foster the illusion of control.

C. Communication, Dominance, and Power

Other key forces in the maintenance of organizational reality are the power relationships and the rules and resources that generate the power structures. Conrad and Ryan (1985) reject the notion of power as a static, overt phenomenon in organizations, and propose instead that communication processes are the substance of power relationships. This perspective holds that power inheres in language-in-use, and is similar to the perspectives of other theorists who maintain that a "deep structure" of power exists which is taken for granted and pre-conscious (e.g., Foucault, 1972; Giddens, 1979). In this formulation, power can be revealed through an analysis of the myths, metaphors, and stories organizational members tell. An exploration of the deep structure of power illuminates the underlying rules of behavior, the informal authority structure, and the obligating forces in the organization (Clegg, 1981).

Research from this perspective includes Conrad's (1983) work on power symbols in religious organizations, Riley's (1983) study of political symbols in professional organizations, Poole, Seibold, and McPhee's analysis of symbolic argument (1985), and Smith and Eisenberg's (in press) analysis of root-metaphors at Disneyland.

The political aspect of power is important because political language operates largely in the realm of symbolic outcomes and sentiments (Pfeffer, 1981). Edelman (1971) believes politics involves two sets of actors—one in a dominant position with a clearly defined self-interest, and the other more removed from the centers of authority and control. Strategic communication is key to maintaining this hierarchical relationship. For example, powerful executives may protect their privileged positions through deliberate vagueness and equivocation (Williams & Goss, 1975).

Although many scholars argue that the strategic manipulation of symbols is necessary for effective management (e.g., Pfeffer, 1981; Pondy, 1978; Weick, 1980), others in the critical school, following in the tradition of Habermas (1977), emphasize the ways in which the study of symbols can be used to uncover inequities and bring about social change. Critical research "seeks to contribute to the establishment of free and open communication situations in which societal, organizational, and individual interests can be mutually accomplished" (Deetz & Kersten, 1983, p. 148).

Walter's (1983) critique of the "symbolism of narcissism" is an example of the critical approach to the study of organizational symbolism. Recalling Argyris' early work, Walter argues that modern organizations keep members from attaining full personhood, and that "symbols play a major role in this influence process." Walter contends that the "symbolism of success"—the well-known markers of status such as expensive company cars, corner offices, etc.—in fact constitutes a "symbolism of narcissism." This narcissism places a heavy emphasis on performance, spectacle, and image management, dehumanizes people, and decreases the chances for genuine immersion and involvement for employees caught up in the game.

Evidence of symbolic domination also can be found in the language used by organizational members. O'Barr (1984) claims that power is often reflected in the choice of address terms and pronouns that indicate status (e.g., the female secretary is addressed by her first name, and her male boss is "Mr."). Communicator style can influence and reflect patterns of domination—managers wishing to assert their status can resort to "administrative talk" or other techniques to preserve their privileged positions (e.g., Varenne, 1978). In addition, the language of rules and regulations in organizations may be stated in ways that discourage individual or group responsibility (Fowler, Hodge, Kress, & Trew, 1979). For example, the common form of stating a rule (e.g., "No smoking in this area") renders the agent of the regulation virtually unchallengeable. Also, as different types of literacy become increasingly important in organizations (e.g., computer literacy), language differences may play a role in "reinforcing social and political inferiority and superiority, and in helping distribute political resources and rewards in society" (O'Barr, 1984, p. 279). The language of grant applications, contracts, and tax returns often acts to restrict an individual's access to valued resources.

The issue of "dominant" or official languages can also be important. The dominant language carries with it access to jobs and other activities as well as aspects of the cultural hierarchy. Research into nonstandard language in the workplace has found that access to resources, promotion, and other types of advancement are denied to speakers of non-dominant languages (cf. Banks, 1985).

The relationship between language and discrimination against women in the workplace has also been investigated. Traditionally, women have not spoken the "male language" of the business world and thus have had difficulty understanding the politics and being accepted as managers (Harragan, 1978, Henley, 1975).

Organizations and groups of professionals often develop a sophisticated jargon to deal routinely with specific issues and complex problems. Rounds' (1984) account of decision-making in a mental health services agency describes a situation where the language differences between groups (health professionals, and relatives of the patients and other concerned individuals) were so dramatic that many participants were consistently "talking past each other." In academe, such problems can exist within disciplines. For example, areas like particle physics or neuropsychology develop such highly specialized vocabularies that meaningful dialogue within the discipline is exceedingly difficult (Koch, 1976).

On a more macroscopic level of analysis, power relationships in organizations can be analyzed by viewing familiar organizational events as rites and ceremonies. Trice and Beyer (1984) delineate six major types of rites according to their expressive social consequences: (a) passage (e.g., military basic training or management training); (b) degradation (e.g., demotion, or publicly reprimanding an employee); (c) enhancement (e.g., sales clubs, employee of the month); (d) renewal (e.g., often found in organizational development projects and team-building); (e) conflict resolution (e.g., "false fights," and "tough stands" in collective bargaining); and (f) integration (e.g., holiday parties). Rites and rituals serve a basically conservative function in organizations—they preserve the status quo (Trice, 1984).

Another legitimating device is story-telling. Stories are similar to rites and ceremonies in that they usually serve to reinforce existing practices and values. Stories are emotionally compelling and draw our attention to actors and the consequences of what they do (McLaughlin, 1984). Thus stories may articulate a common vision and provide warrants for behavior (McGee, 1980) or guidelines for action (Kirkwood, 1983; Smith, McLaughlin, & Smith-Altendorf, 1985). Stories can promote unity among diverse groups (Eisenberg, 1984), and commitment to a particular group (Wilkins, 1983).

Research by Martin and Powers (1983) indicates that hearing a story often has greater influence on organizational members' attitudinal commitment than other types of evidence. They report that stories were in fact more persuasive than statistics, but *only* when the story was confirming of existing attitudes and beliefs. Perrow (1972) argues that stories constrain the assumptions and premises of organizational members. Several theorists posit that narrative (as opposed to other forms of argument) shields assumptions and claims from debate (Wilkins, 1983; Witten, 1986). According to Wilkins, stories facilitate recall of values and information, generate belief, and encourage commitment to key organizational values. In a similar vein, Witten argues that stories maintain the status quo in organizations through guiding problem definition, serving as exemplars for appropriate behavior, and embodying anticipated reactions to controversial events. Stories, then, can prevent challenges to existing practices and beliefs by articulating claims in a form that is not easily challenged, and hence may defuse (for better or for worse) potentially explosive issues.

Highly institutionalized stories are known as organizational sagas (Bormann, 1983). In his study of university founders, Clark (1970, 1972) examines the sagas which were passed down from generation to generation. Clark concludes that, in addition to providing a living history of the university, sagas helped to maintain morale among members during hard times.

Over time, some stories and sagas take on mythic proportions. Myths perform the dual function of preserving continuity and promoting change (Pondy, 1983). Westerlund and Sjostrand (1979) note the potential usefulness of myths and fairy tales often found in organizational "success formulas"—in addition to providing guidelines for action, myths serve to protect their adherents from becoming aware of the uncertainty that surrounds them. This process is described in more detail in the next section.

Other means of maintaining specific definitions of organizational reality are even less obtrusive; for example, making novel events seem routine (Pondy & Huff, 1985), and the sense-making process inherent in ordinary conversation. Gronn (1983) examines how informal talk reflects and affects patterns of administrative control in a school. He concludes that talk serves to "cloak" power relationships, and that, in organizations where information is the primary product, talk *is* the work. Together with the findings presented in the previous section, it seems clear that an analysis of conversation in organizations can both reveal existing power relationships and the strategies members use to protect and conceal their power bases.

Communication in organizations does not merely reinforce existing conceptions of reality. Much symbol usage in organizations is intended to bring about change. In the next section, the role of symbols in facilitating organizational transformation and change is explored.

IV. TRANSFORMING ORGANIZATIONAL REALITY: SYMBOLS OF CHANGE

Early views of organizations maintained that change comes about primarily for technical or environmental reasons, through rational decision-making. Recent work indicates that this view is over-simplified and that transformation is inherent in all transactions (Giddens, 1979). Understanding the role of symbols in the change process is critical to an appreciation of how organizational reality is transformed.

A. Leadership

In organizational research, a concept often linked with transformation is leadership. Although leadership was originally thought to be a quality possessed by "great men," in organizational writings it came to be defined as a series of behaviors that could be identified and taught. Researchers of organizational behavior focused on such issues as managerial style and the optimal mix between leaders, tasks, and situations (Blake & Mouton, 1964; Fiedler, 1964). Recently, an appreciation for the symbolic dimension of leadership has arisen in the literature. Peters (1978) notes that the most successful executives provide leadership through the use of a single, overarching symbol like "the system is the solution" (AT&T). Bennis (1982) and Kanter (1983) focus on the "vision" necessary for competent leadership, and Bennis marks the distinction between managers and leaders—"Managers do things right, leaders do the right things" (1982, p. 3). From this perspective, leaders are the purveyors of myths, the tellers of stories, and the empowerers of employees (Kanter, 1983; Martin, 1984). They do not merely exhibit desired behaviors, they create realities to legitimate their activities and to manage their employees and environments into the future.

Leadership can be thought of as "paradigm creation," a human activity that explains events and creates meaning for organizational members (Davis, 1982; Gadalla & Cooper, 1978; Pfeffer, 1981; Pondy, 1978; Smircich, 1983c). Taking this view of the executive, not just as a decision and policy maker, but also as a maker of meaning (Barnard, 1938; Selznick, 1957), some researchers see management as symbolic action and effective leadership skills as more akin to those of an evangelist than of an accountant (Weick, 1980).

The purposeful transformation of organizational reality is rarely easy. Leaders must retain a certain degree of stability, while at the same time create a climate for innovation (Kanter, 1983) and provide a vision for the future (Peters & Waterman, 1982). If future plans deny some important aspects of current practices, they may be undermined by feelings of inadequacy and illegitimacy. The effective use of symbols can be helpful in navigating this tension. Thus many leaders will choose to use less obvious tactics in attempting to bring about change, including slogans, myths, stories, and metaphors. Pondy (1983) argues that equivocal forms of discourse are effective both in legitimating the status quo and in bridging the gap between present practices and future possibilities. Speaking specifically about metaphor, Pondy (1983) argues: "Metaphor facilitates change by making the strange familiar, but in the very process it deepens the meaning of values in the organization by giving them expression in novel situations. . . . Because of its inherent ambivalence of meaning, metaphor can fulfill the dual function of enabling change and preserving continuity" (p. 164).

Just as the development of a restricted vocabulary helps to maintain in- and out-groups, changes in language may also significantly influence organizational change. Evered (1983), for example, insists that for an organization to change in any fundamental way, there must be a corresponding language change because change requires the development of new concepts. Hirsch and Andrews (1983) describe how the choice of specific metaphors in the context of corporate takeovers constrains future action; a takeover described as a "war" or "bloody battle" has different connotations than one seen as a "happy marriage." The point is that symbols are equivocal, and this characteristic can either be an asset or a hindrance in planned organizational change.

B. Organizational Development

From a symbolic perspective, organizational development interventions may focus on changing an organization's sense-making activities (Riley, 1985); on the stories that are told (Deal & Kennedy, 1982); or on symbolic strategies for innovation (Kanter, 1983). For example, Boje et al. (1982) discuss the role of myth-making in organizational development. Beginning with the idea that myths are both pervasive and can affect behavior in organizations, they recommend that organizational development consultants work with existing myths, and, in some cases, create new myths as part of their interventions.

In thinking about the role of symbolism in organizational change, it is important to remember that most symbolic processes in organizations act to maintain the status quo. When attempting to bring about change, the symbols currently in use in the organization can prove a formidable barrier. Interventions must take into account language, rites, rituals, stories, and myths which perpetuate existing structures and practices, because lasting change is unlikely in most cases without symbolic change. The symbolic approach to organizational development demands a consideration of how existing symbols perpetuate current conceptions of reality as well as how changing symbols or introducing new symbols can transform that reality.

So far, our discussion has focused on the specific role played by symbols in the creation, maintenance, and transformation of organizational reality. In the final section, four fundamental issues deserving of future attention are explored: (a) the nature of shared meaning and values in organizations, (b) the conscious and unconscious aspects of symbol use, (c) the relationship between organizations and socially constructed reality, and (d) the research methods most appropriate for the study of organizational symbolism.

V. KEY ISSUES

A. Shared Meanings

Most research and theory on organizational symbolism and sense-making presupposes shared meaning and, to some extent, values (e.g., Deetz & Kersten, 1983; Pfeffer, 1981; Smircich, 1983c). Considerable evidence indicates that such sharing can never be complete, and that the consequences of greater sharing may not be uniformly positive (cf. Bochner, 1984; Krippendorf, 1985; Parks, 1982). Furthermore, sharing an understanding of rules or contexts is not synonymous with agreement or consensus on specific issues (Wentworth, 1980). Quite often in organizations, coordination of action is more important than the coordination of attitudes and beliefs, and attempts at sharing can lead to dysfunctional conflicts (Weick, 1979). Some researchers even believe that ignorance can serve an important social function (e.g., Moore & Tumin, 1948). Poole and McPhee (1983) argue that the degree of sharing varies across organizations, and that each setting should be seen as having the *potential* to develop common world views; i.e., they are "culture-*bearing* milieu" (Louis, 1983). And Gregory's (1983) research indicates that organizations have multiple subcultures, or "native" views, and that organizational culture has both cohesive and divisive functions.

One approach to the study of shared meaning holds that individuals and, particularly, groups of individuals have differing world views based on self-interest or the negotiated realities of subcultures in organizations. From this political perspective, "stability" in organizations is produced not by shared overarching values that consensually guide employee actions, but by coordinating and negotiating dominant sectional interests that may have differing value structures (Riley, 1983). As a result, disparate conceptions of the organization can coexist along task, hierarchical, or more informal groupings (see Gregory, 1983).

Consequently, arguments extolling the virtues of "strong cultures" characterized by shared, deeply-held values and beliefs (e.g., Peters & Waterman, 1982) should be studied carefully. The contention that pervasive overarching values and beliefs actually exist is more likely myth than reality, and is probably related to the erroneous depiction of organizations as monoliths (Morgan, 1980). Further, the research on symbol use indicates that people can share allegiance to an abstract symbol without a great deal of commonality in their specific interpretation of the symbol. Becher (1981) suggests that agreement on common expressions, on feelings of solidarity and a "sense of oneness" at some grouping or level of the organization is more important than agreement on deeply held values and beliefs. Thus Carbaugh's (1985) definition of communication in organizations is particularly salient: "Communication can be understood as an intersubjective symbolic activity constituting a degree of shared meaning and a sense of community" (p. 37). Symbolic investigations of organizations should explore the potential for multiple or competing meaning systems, and the degree to which they are shared across time and space, in order to better understand the maintenance and transformation of organizational reality.

B. Conscious and Unconscious Use of Symbols

In many studies of symbols and sense-making in organizations it is important to understand the extent to which symbols are used strategically by individuals, particularly if the goal is organizational development.

While the literature focuses on the conscious or strategic use of symbols, obviously not all communication is produced in this manner (Langer, 1978; Morgan et al., 1983). Individuals may say things that are intended to be taken literally, but are seen by others as having greater significance, or vice versa (Morgan et al., 1983). Also, any communication (whether oral, written, or nonverbal) can fulfill multiple functions (Dandridge, 1983; Trujillo, 1983). Complicating this further, organizational actors sometimes use covert strategies to appear nonstrategic (Larkey & Smith, 1984). Research on organizational politics has shown that it is advantageous to appear nonstrategic and avoid the implication that proposed arguments or actions are in the individual's, and not the organization's, best interest (Moberg, 1978).

As specific symbols become commonplace in an organization (deeply embedded in the institutional fabric), their use can be viewed more as the chronic reproduction of organizational systems and less as individual strategies. For example, stories may be constructed by managers to exert control over subordinates (e.g., Martin & Powers, 1983; Wilkins, 1983), but they are elaborated by repetition and are no longer the intentional construction of one individual. Similarly, organizational systems that evolve over time (e.g., reward systems) can take on a life of their own, independent of any individual's intention (Putnam, in press).

One task of critical organizational theorists is to expose latent symbols of domination in these organizational systems. In order to effect change, or to give organizational members the insights necessary for emancipation, the relationship between institutionalized symbols and individual actions needs further exploration (Deetz & Kersten, 1983; Rosen, 1985; Stablein & Nord, 1985).

C. Organizations and Socially Constructed Reality

One task facing the symbolic approach to organizing is to articulate the relationship between symbolic processes and important, macro-organizational issues. Not enough research focuses on the link between talk and action (Weick, 1983). As Weick (1983) argues: "Until the linkage between talk and action is more clearly understood . . . conventional organizational wisdom will direct attention at conventional organizational variables – and not talk – to account for what goes on in organizations" (p. 17).

In defining social situations, symbols play one of their most important roles. As social reality is constructed in interaction (Berger & Luckman, 1967; Giddens, 1979), the concepts and procedures used provide the lens through which people in organizations conceive of their problems, solutions, and environment. The most interesting characteristic of these social typifications is that they become reified, or taken for granted, as if they were beyond social construction and in the realm of the material world. Bordieu (in Rounds, 1984, p. 113) named this process "genesis amnesia" – the means by which fundamentals of the system become unconscious in practice.

It is in this sense that the development of routines and taken-for-granted procedures become linked through ordinary interactions and conversation to embedded practices and long-term actions. Conversations which may appear trivial or "idle" at first (March &

Sevon, 1984) form patterns of contact and convention when repeated often enough, and can evolve into frames of reference and habits of thought that are difficult to break. Large changes in social systems often have "small beginnings" which have amplified over time, and one good strategy for effecting change is through the pursuit of "small wins" (Weick, 1979, 1984).

Lasting organizational change is rarely easy to accomplish. Many actions, events, and behaviors are part of a first-order, material reality that is difficult to bend to interpretations (Schein, 1985). While symbolic changes may shape technological ones, a more complete picture acknowledges the importance of a manager's ability to operate simultaneously at the symbolic and practical or technical level (e.g., the implementation of new technologies in the workplace; Bormann, 1983). Thus organizations differ in their resistance to change, as some can have a higher ratio of socially constructed to material realities. News organizations, from this perspective, exist more in the symbolic realm than do hospital emergency rooms or construction sites (Weick, 1983).

D.   Methods for Studying Organizational Symbolism

Just as the three issues discussed above are but a subset of potential areas of inquiry, so too are the methods used in prior research only a small sample of the potential means of investigation. Many researchers have rejected traditional quantitative methods in favor of ethnographic, qualitative methods. While these approaches are to be commended, researchers need to investigate organizational symbolic phenomena through a variety of methods. Putnam's (1983) pluralistic view of methodology in interpretive research seems advisable: be open to all types of evidence (e.g., statistical, historical, anecdotal) that provide useful answers to important questions about symbols and their interpretation.

The organizational symbolism literature has thusfar distinguished itself more for its theoretical vision than for its empirical rigor. This is to be expected; as Geertz (1983) notes, researchers choosing to study interpretive processes are "exchanging a set of well-charted difficulties for a set of largely uncharted ones" (p. 6). These efforts should be met with a mixture of criticism and support—not to be parochial about method but to identify good questions and pursue them systematically.

Conducting research is itself an organizing process, and a highly symbolic process at that. Each research perspective embodies a set of goals, values, and ideologies that become manifest during investigation and application. The call for pluralism is an example of just such a bias. Scholars must retain a jaundiced eye—findings from divergent paradigms may be incommensurable—but, in many cases, researchers can benefit from different approaches to similar phenomena. In this spirit, this chapter reviews multiple perspectives on organizational symbolism, but also proposes parameters for the study of sense-making in organizations.

REFERENCES

Adams, J. S. (1980). Interorganizational processes and organization boundary activities. In B. Staw and L. Cummings (Eds.), *Research in organizational behavior, Vol. II* (pp. 321–355). Greenwich, CT: JAI Press.

Altheide, D., & Johnson, D. (1980). *Bureaucratic propaganda*. Newton, MA: Allen.

Argyris, C., & Schon, D. (1978). *Organizational learning*. Reading, MA: Addison-Wesley.

Banks, S. (1985). *Toward viewing organizational cultures as semiotic texts.* Unpublished paper, University of Southern California.

Barnard, C. I. (1938). *The functions of the executive.* Cambridge, MA: Harvard University Press.

Barnett, G. A., & Carson, D. L. (1983). *The role of communication in the professional socialization process.* Paper presented at the annual meeting of the International Communication Association, Dallas, TX.

Becher, T. (1981). Towards a definition of disciplinary cultures. *Studies in Higher Education, 6,* 109–122.

Bennis, W. (1982). *Transformative power.* Unpublished paper, University of Southern California.

Berger, P. L., & Luckman, T. (1967). *The social construction of reality.* Garden City, NY: Doubleday.

Blake, R., & Mouton, J. (1964). *The managerial grid.* Houston, TX: Gulf Publishing.

Bochner, A. P. (1984). The functions of human communication in interpersonal bonding. In C. Arnold & J. W. Bowers (Eds.), *Handbook of rhetoric and communication theory* (pp. 544–621. Newton, MA: Allyn-Bacon.

Boje, D. M., Fedor, D. B., & Rowland, K. M. (1982). Myth-making: A qualitative step in OD interventions. *Journal of Applied Behavioral Science, 18,* 17–28.

Boland, R. J., & Hoffman, R. (1983). Humor in a machine shop: An interpretation of symbolic action. In L. Pondy, P. Frost, G. Morgan, & T. Dandridge (Eds.), *Organizational symbolism* (pp. 187–198). Greenwich, CT: JAI Press.

Bormann, E. (1983). Symbolic convergence: Organizational communication and culture. In L. Putnam & M. Pacanowsky (Eds.), *Communication and organizations* (pp. 99–122). Beverly Hills, CA: Sage Publications.

Boulding, K. (1956). *The image.* Ann Arbor, MI: University of Michigan Press.

Burke, K. (1965). *Permanence and change* (2nd ed.). Indianapolis, IN: Bobbs Merrill Co., Inc.

Caplow, T. (1964). *Principles of organization.* New York: Harcourt.

Carbaugh, D. (1985). Cultural communication and organizing. In W. Gudykunst, L. Stewart, & S. Ting-Toomey (Eds.), *Communication, culture, and organization processes* (pp. 30–47). Beverly Hills, CA: Sage Publications.

Cassirer, E. (1944). *An essay on man.* New Haven, CT: Yale University Press.

Clark, B. (1970). *The distinctive college.* Chicago, IL: Aldine.

Clark, B. (1972). The organizational saga in higher education. *Administrative Science Quarterly, 17,* 178–184.

Clegg, S. (1981). Organizations and control. *Administrative Science Quarterly, 26,* 545–562.

Conrad, C. (1983). Organizational power: Faces and symbolic forms. In L. Putnam & M. Pacanowsky (Eds.), *Communication and organizations* (pp. 173–194). Beverly Hills, CA: Sage Publications.

Conrad, C., & Ryan, M. (1985). Power, praxis, and person in social and organization theory. In P. Tompkins & R. McPhee (Eds.), *Organizational communication research and theory.* Beverly Hills, CA: Sage Publications.

Crozier, M. (1971). *The world of the office worker.* Chicago, IL: University of Chicago Press.

Dandridge, T. C. (1983). Symbols' functions and use. In L. R. Pondy, P. Frost, G. Morgan, & T. Dandridge (Eds.), *Organizational symbolism* (pp. 69–80). Greenwich, CT: JAI Press.

Davis, S. M. (1982). Tranforming organizations: The key to strategy in context. *Organizational Dynamics, 10,* 64–80.

Deal, T. E., & Kennedy, A. A. (1982). *Corporate cultures.* Reading, MA: Addison-Wesley.

Deetz, S. A., & Kersten, A. (1983). Critical models of interpretive research. In L. Putnam & M. Pacanowsky (Eds.), *Communication and organizations* (pp. 147–172). Beverly Hills, CA: Sage Publications.

Denzin, N. K. (1978). *The research act* (2nd ed.). New York: McGraw Hill.

Ditton, J. (1979). Baking time. *Sociological Review, 27,* 157–167.

Duncan, H. (1968). *Symbols in society*. New York: Oxford University Press.

Edelman, M. (1971). *Politics as symbolic action*. Chicago, IL: Markham Press.

Eisenberg, E. M. (1984). Ambiguity as strategy in organizational communication. *Communication Monographs, 51,* 227–242.

Eisenberg, E. M., Farace, R. V., Monge, P. R., Bettinghaus, E. P., Kurchner-Hawkins, R., Miller, K. I., & Rothman, L. (1985). Communication linkages in interorganization systems. In M. Voigt & B. Dervin (Eds.), *Progress in communication science, 6*. Norwood, NJ: Ablex.

Evered, R. (1983). The language of organizations: The case of the Navy. In L. Pondy, P. Frost, G. Morgan, & T. Dandridge (Eds.), *Organizational symbolism* (pp. 125–144). Greenwich, CT: JAI Press.

Everett, J. E., Stening, B. W., & Longton, P. A. (1982). Some evidence for an international management culture. *Journal of Management Studies, 19,* 153–162.

Feldman, M. S., & March, J. G. (1981). Information in organizations as signal and symbol. *Administrative Science Quarterly, 26,* 171–186.

Fiedler, F. (1964). A contingency model of leadership effectiveness. In L. Berkowitz (Ed.), *Advances in experimental and social psychology*. New York: Academic Press.

Fine, G. (1984). Negotiated orders and organizational cultures. *Annual Review of Sociology, 10,* 239–262.

Foucault, M. (1972). *Power/knowledge: Selected interviews and other writings*. New York: Pantheon Books.

Fowler, R., Hodge, B., Kress, G., & Trew, D. (1979). *Language and control*. London: Routledge & Kegan Paul.

Frost, P. J., Moore, L. F., Louis, M., Lundberg, C. C., & Martin, J. (Eds.). (1985). *Organizational culture*. Beverly Hills, CA: Sage Publications.

Gadalla, I. E., & Cooper, R. (1978). Towards an epistemology of management. *Social Science Information, 17,* 349–383.

Geertz, C. (1983). *Local knowledge*. New York: Basic Books.

Giddens, A. (1979). *Central problems in social theory*. Berkeley, CA: University of California Press.

Goffman, E. (1959). *The presentation of self in everyday life*. Garden City, NY: Doubleday.

Gregory, K. (1983). Native-view paradigms: Multiple cultures and culture conflicts in organizations. *Administrative Science Quarterly, 28,* 359–376.

Gronn, P. (1983). Talk as the work: The accomplishment of school administration. *Administrative Science Quarterly, 28,* 1–21.

Gusfield, J. R., & Michalowicz, J. (1984). Secular symbolism: Studies of ritual, ceremony, and symbolic order in modern life. *Annual Review of Sociology, 10,* 417–435.

Habermas, J. (1977). Hanna Arendt's communications concept of power. *Social Research, 44,* 3–24.

Harragan, B. L. (1978). *Games mother never taught you: Corporate gamesmanship for women*. New York: Warner Books.

Harris, L., & Cronen, V. (1979). A rules-based model for the evaluation of organizational communication. *Communication Quarterly, 27,* 12–28.

Henley, N. M. (1975). Power, sex, and non-verbal communication. In B. Thorne & N. Henley (Eds.), *Language and sex: Difference and dominance* (pp. 184–202). New York: Newbury House.

Hirsch, P., & Andrews, J. (1983). Ambushes, shootouts, and knights of the round table: The language of corporate takeovers. In L. Pondy, P. Frost, G. Morgan, & T. Dandridge (Eds.), *Organizational symbolism* (pp. 145–156). Greenwich, CT: JAI Press.

Johnson, D. (1974). Social organization of an industrial work group. *Sociology Quarterly, 15,* 109–126.

Journal of Management (1985). Special issue on organizational symbolism (Volume 11).

Kanter, R. M. (1983). *The change masters: Innovation for productivity in the American mode*. New York: Simon & Schuster.

Kidder, T. (1981). *The soul of a new machine*. Boston, MA: Little-Brown.

Kirkwood, W. (1983). Storytelling and self-confrontation: Parables as communication strategies. *Quarterly Journal of Speech, 69,* 58–74.

Koch, S. (1976). Language communities, search cells, and the psychological studies. In W. J. Arnold (Ed.), *Nebraska symposium on motivation 1975* (pp. 477–560). Lincoln, NE: University of Nebraska Press.

Korprowski, E. J. (1983). Cultural myths: Clues to effective management. *Organizational Dynamics, 12,* 39–51.

Kreps, G. L. (1983). Using interpretive research: The development of a socialization program at RCA. In L. Putnam & M. Pacanowsky (Eds.), *Communication and organizations* (pp. 243–256). Beverly Hills, CA: Sage Publications.

Krippendorff, K. (1985). *On the ethics of constructing communication.* Presidential Address, International Communication Association, Honolulu, Hawaii.

Kroeber, A. L., & Kluckhohn, C. (1952). *Culture: A review of concepts and definitions.* New York: Vintage Books.

Langer, E. J. (1978). Rethinking the role of thought in social interaction. In J. Harvey, W. Ickes, & R. Kidd (Eds.), *New directions in attribution research 2.* Potomac, MD: Erlbaum.

Langer, S. (1963). *Philosophy in a new key: A study in the symbolism of reason, rite and art.* Cambridge, MA: Harvard University Press.

Larkey, P. D., & Smith, R. A. (1984). The misrepresentation of information in governmental budgeting. In L. Sproull & P. Larkey (Eds.), *Advances in information processing in organizations, Vol. I* (pp. 63–92). Greenwich, CT: JAI Press.

Larkey, P. D., & Sproull, L. S. (1984). Introduction. In L. Sproull & P. Larkey (Eds.), *Advances in Information Processing in Organizations, Vol. I* (pp. 1–8). Greenwich, CT: JAI Press.

Louis, M. L. (1980). Surprise and sense making: What newcomers experience in entering unfamiliar organizational settings. *Administrative Science Quarterly, 25,* 226–248.

Louis, M. L. (1983). Organizations as culture-bearing milieux. In L. R. Pondy, P. Frost, G. Morgan, and T. Dandridge (Eds.), *Organizational symbolism* (pp. 39–54). Greenwich, CT: JAI Press.

Manning, P. K. (1979). Metaphors of the field: Varieties of organizational discourse. *Administrative Science Quarterly, 24,* 660–671.

Manning, P. K. (1982). Producing drama: Symbolic communication and the police. *Symbolic Interaction, 5,* 223–241.

March, J. G., & Sevon, G. (1984). Gossip, information, and decision-making. In L. Sproull & P. Larkey (Eds.), *Advances in information processing in organizations, Vol. I* (pp. 95–108). Greenwich, CT: JAI Press.

Martin, J. (1984). Stories and scripts in organizational settings. In A. Hastorf & A. Isen (Eds.), *Cognitive social psychology.* New York: Elsevier-North Holland.

Martin, J., Feldman, M., Hatch, M., & Sitkin, S. (1983). The uniqueness paradox in organizational stories. *Administrative Science Quarterly, 28,* 438–453.

Martin, J., & Powers, M. (1983). Truth or corporate propaganda: The value of a good war story. In L. Pondy, P. Frost, G. Morgan, & T. Dandridge (Eds.), *Organizational symbolism* (p. 93–108). Greenwich, CT: JAI Press.

McGee, M. (1980). The "ideograph:" A link between rhetoric and ideology. *Quarterly Journal of Speech, 55,* 1–16.

McLaughlin, M. L. (1984). *Conversation.* Beverly Hills, CA: Sage.

Meyer, J., & Rowan, B. (1977). Institutionalized organizations. *American Journal of Sociology, 83,* 340–363.

Mitroff, I. (1982). *Stakeholders of the organizational mind.* San Francisco: Jossey-Bass.

Mitroff, I., & Killman, R. H. (1976). On organizational stories: An approach to the design and analysis of organizations through myths and stories. In L. Pondy & D. Slevin (Eds.), *The management of organizational design, Vol. I* (pp. 189–207). New York: Elsevier-North Holland.

Moberg, D. J. (1978). *Factors which determine perception and use of organizational politics.* Paper presented at the annual Meeting of the Academy of Management.

Moore, W., & Tumin, N. (1948). Some social functions of ignorance. *American Sociological Review, 14,* 787–795.

Morgan, G. (1980). Paradigms, metaphors, and puzzle-solving in organizational theory. *Administrative Science Quarterly, 25,* 605–622.

Morgan, G., Frost, P., & Pondy, L. (1983). Organizational symbolism. In L. Pondy, P. Frost, G. Morgan, & T. Dandridge (Eds.), *Organizational symbolism* (pp. 3–37). Greenwich, CT: JAI Press.

O'Barr, W. M. (1984). Asking the right questions about language and power. In C. Kramarae, M. Schulz, & W. M. O'Barr (Eds.), *Language and power* (pp. 260–280). Beverly Hills, CA: Sage.

Ogden, C. K., & Richards, I. A. (1936). *The meaning of meaning.* London: Kegan, Paul, Trench, Trubner and Co.

Ouchi, W. G. (1981). *Theory Z.* Reading, MA: Addison-Wesley.

Pacanowsky, M., & Anderson, J. A. (1981). *Cop talk and media use.* Paper presented at the International Communication Association Annual Meeting, Minneapolis, MN.

Parks, M. (1982). Ideology in interpersonal communication: Off the couch and into the world. In M. Burgoon (Ed.), *Communication yearbook 5* (pp. 79–108). New Brunswick, NJ: Transaction Books.

Pascale, R. T., & Athos, A. G. (1981). *The art of Japanese management.* New York: Simon & Schuster.

Perrow, C. (1972). *Complex organizations.* Glenview, IL: Scott, Foresman.

Peters, T. (1978). Symbols, patterns, and settings: An optimistic case for getting things done. *Organizational Dynamics, 7,* 3–23.

Peters, T. J., & Waterman, R. H. (1982). *In search of excellence.* New York: Harper & Row.

Pfeffer, J. (1981). *Power in organizations.* Boston, MA: Pitman.

Pondy, L. (1978). Leadership is a language game. In M. M. Lombardo & M. W. McCall, Jr. (Eds.), *Leadership: Where else can we go?* (pp. 87–99). Durham, NC: Duke University Press.

Pondy, L. (1983). The role of metaphors and myths in organization and in the facilitation of change. In L. Pondy, P. Frost, G. Morgan, & T. Dandridge, (Eds.), *Organizational symbolism* (pp. 157–166). Greenwich, CT: JAI Press.

Pondy, L., Frost, P., Morgan, G., & Dandridge, T. (1983). *Organizational symbolism.* Greenwich, CT: JAI Press.

Pondy, L., & Huff, A. S. (1985). Achieving routine in organizational change. *Journal of Management, 11,* 103–116.

Poole, M. S., & McPhee, R. D. (1983). A structurational analysis of organizational climate. In L. Putnam & M. Pacanowsky (Eds.), *Communication and organizations* (pp. 195–220). Beverly Hills, CA: Sage Publications.

Poole, M. S., Seibold, D., & McPhee, R. (1985). Group decision-making as structurational process. *Quarterly Journal of Speech, 71,* 74–102.

Putnam, L. (1983). The interpretive perspective: An alternative to functionalism. In L. Putnam & M. Pacanowsky (Eds.), *Communication and organizations* (pp. 31–54). Beverly Hills, CA: Sage Publications.

Putnam, L. (in press). Contradictions and paradoxes in organizations. In L. Thayer & O. Wiio (Eds.), *Explaining organizations.* Norwood, NJ: Ablex.

Putnam, L., & Jones, T. (1982). The role of communication in bargaining. *Human Communication Research, 8,* 262–280.

Putnam, L., & Pacanowsky, M. (1983). *Communication and organizations: An interpretive approach.* Beverly Hills, CA: Sage.

Riley, P. (1983). A structurationist account of political cultures. *Administrative Science Quarterly, 28,* 414–438.

Riley, P. (1985). *Culture clash.* Paper presented at the annual meeting of the International Communication Association, Honolulu.

Rosen, M. (1985). Breakfast at Spiro's: Dramaturgy and dominance. *Journal of Management, 11,* 31–48.

Rounds, J. (1984). Information and ambiguity in organizational change. In L. Sproull & P. Larkey

(Eds.), *Advances in information processing in organizations, Vol. I* (pp. 11–142). Greenwich, CT: JAI Press.

Salancik, G., & Meindl, J. (1984). Corporate attributions as strategic illusions of management control. *Administrative Science Quarterly, 29,* 238–254.

Sathe, V. (1983). Some action implications of corporate culture: A manager's guide to action. *Organizational Dynamics* (Winter), 4–23.

Sathe, V. (1985). *Culture and related corporate realities.* Homewood, IL: Richard D. Irwin, Inc.

Schall, M. (1983). A communication-rules approach to organizational culture. *Administrative Science Quarterly, 28,* 557–581.

Schein, E. H. (1985). *Organizational culture and leadership.* San Francisco, CA: Jossey-Bass.

Selznick, P. (1957). *Leadership in administration.* New York: Harper & Row.

Simon, H. (1976). *Administrative behavior, 3rd edition.* New York: Free Press.

Smircich, L. (1983a). Concepts of culture and organizational analysis. *Administrative Science Quarterly, 28,* 339–358.

Smircich, L. (1983b). Implications for management theory. In L. Putnam & M. Pacanowsky (Eds.), *Communication and organizations* (pp. 221–242). Beverly Hills, CA: Sage.

Smircich, L. (1983c). Organizations as shared meanings. In L. Pondy, P. Frost, G. Morgan, & T. Dandridge (Eds.), *Organizational symbolism* (pp. 55–68). Greenwich, CT: JAI Press.

Smith, R., & Eisenberg, E. M. (in press). *Conflict and co-optation of root-metaphors at Disneyland. Communication Monographs.*

Smith, S., McLaughlin, M., & Smith-Altendorf, D. (1985). *A cultural themes perspective: Approaches to the use of stories in the study of the organizational socialization process.* Paper presented at the Annual Meeting of the Interational Communication Association, Honolulu, Hawaii.

Sproull, L., & Larkey, P. (1984). *Advances in information processing in organizations, Vol. I.* Greenwich, CT: JAI Press.

Stablein, R., & Nord, W. (1985). Practical and emancipatory interests in organizational symbolism: A review and evaluation. *Journal of Management, 11,* 13–28.

Strauss, A., Schatzman, L., Erlich, D., Bucher, R., & Sabshin, M. (1963). The hospital and its negotiated order. In E. Friedson (Ed.), *The hospital in modern society* (pp. 147–169). New York: Free Press.

Strauss, A. (1982). Interorganizational negotiation. *Urban Life, 11,* 350–367.

Thompson, J. (1967). *Organization in action.* New York: McGraw Hill.

Tichy, N. M. (1983). *Managing strategic change.* New York: John Wiley & Sons.

Tompkins, P. K., Fisher, J. Y., Infante, D. A., & Tompkins, E. L. (1975). Kenneth Burke and the inherent characteristics of formal organizations. *Speech Monographs, 42,* 135–142.

Tompkins, P. K., & Cheney, G. E. (1983). Account analysis of organizations: Decision-making and identification. In L. Putnam & M. Pacanowsky (Eds.), *Communication and organizations* (pp. 123–146). Beverly Hills, CA: Sage.

Trice, H. M. (1984). Rites and ceremonials in organizational culture. In S. Bacharach & S. Mitchell (Eds.), *Perspectives on organizational sociology, Vol. 4.* Greenwich, CT: JAI Press.

Trice, H. M., & Beyer, J. M. (1984). Studying organizational cultures through rites and ceremonials. *Academy of Management Review, 9,* 653–669.

Trujillo, N. (1983). "Performing" Mintzberg's roles: The nature of managerial communication. In L. Putnam & M. Pacanowsky (Eds.), *Communication and organizations* (pp. 73–98). Beverly Hills, CA: Sage Publications.

Turner, S. P. (1983). Studying organization through Levi-Strauss' structuralism. In G. Morgan (Ed.), *Beyond method: Social research strategies.* Beverly Hills, CA: Sage Publications.

Van Maanan, J. (1977). Experiencing organization. In J. Van Maanan (Ed.), *Organizational careers: Some new perspectives* (pp. 15–45). New York: Wiley.

Varenne, H. (1978). Culture as rhetoric: Patterning in the verbal interaction between teachers and administrators in an American high school. *American Ethnologist, 5,* 635–650.

Walter, G. A. (1983). Psyche and symbol. In L. Pondy, P. Frost, G. Morgan, & T. Dandridge (Eds.), *Organizational symbolism* (pp. 257–272). Greenwich, CT: JAI Press.

Weick, K. E. (1979). *The social psychology of organizing* (2nd ed.). Reading, MA: Addison-Wesley.

Weick, K. E. (1980). The management of eloquence. *Executive, 6,* 18–21.

Weick, K. E. (1983). Organizational communication: Toward a research agenda. In L. Putnam & M. Pacanowsky (Eds.), *Communication and organizations* (pp. 13–30). Beverly Hills, CA: Sage.

Weick, K. E. (1984). Small wins. *American Psychologist, 39,* 40–49.

Wentworth, W. M. (1980). *Context and understanding: An inquiry into socialization theory.* New York: Elsevier.

Westerlund, G., & Sjostrand, S. (1979). *Organizational myths.* New York: Harper & Row.

White, O. F, & McSwain, C. J. (1983). Transformational theory and organizational analysis. In G. Morgan (Ed.), *Beyond method: Social science research strategies.* Beverly Hills, CA: Sage Publications.

Wilkins, A. (1983). Organizational stories as symbols that control the organization. In L. Pondy, P. Frost, G. Morgan, & T. Dandridge (Eds.), *Organizational symbolism* (pp. 81–92). Greenwich, CT: JAI Press.

Williams, M. L., & Goss, B. (1975). Equivocation: Character insurance. *Human Communication Research, 1,* 265–270.

Witten, M. (1986). *The role of stories in maintaining the status quo in organizations.* Paper presented at the annual meeting of the International Communication Association, Chicago, IL.

Chapter 8

Socialization Processes in Organizations

Raymond L. Falcione and Charmaine E. Wilson
University of Maryland, College Park

ABSTRACT

Socialization processes in organizations are discussed in this chapter. Socialization is defined, and a number of models and perspectives of socialization are described. Communication is identified as a key element in the organizational socialization process, and communication sources of, and strategies for, organizational socialization are described. It is argued that the strategies employed by organizations influence the newcomer's view of, and activities in, the organization. Accordingly, outcomes of the socialization process, including organizational commitment, job satisfaction, and organizational climate, are identified and discussed. Finally, a descriptive model of the socialization process is presented, and directions for future research are offered.

Socialization is critically important to organizational effectiveness. Socialization processes, including helping the newcomer clarify expectations, acquire new values, modify old values, and learn the behaviors necessary for assuming an organizational role (Brim, 1966; Louis, 1980; Van Maanen, 1976; Van Maanen & Schein, 1979), have a major impact on a person's decisions concerning role behavior and career choice, particularly for the newcomer (Kotter, 1973). In addition, ineffective entry procedures are related to voluntary turnover (Wanous, 1980). Therefore, it is important to better understand organizational socialization, to conduct more effective research in this area, and to help organizations increase the effectiveness of their socialization programs.

Toward gaining a better understanding of organizational socialization, the purpose of this chapter is to (a) define organizational socialization; (b) describe various models and perspectives of the socialization process; (c) describe communication sources of, and strategies for, organizational socialization; (d) relate socialization to organizational outcomes; and (e) present a revised model of the organizational socialization process, and offer recommendations for future research.

DEFINITION OF ORGANIZATIONAL SOCIALIZATION

As Feldman (1981) suggests, research in the area of organizational soc hindered by definitional problems: socialization has been defined differently by nearly every researcher who has examined the construct. For example, Feldman (1976) defined organizational socialization simply as the process by which employees are transformed from organizational outsiders to participating and effective members. Wanous (1980) defined socialization as those changes that take place in the newcomer which are caused by the organization. Taking still different directions, Schein (1968) emphasized the learning of organizational rules, while Caplow (1964) focused on the development of new self images and involvements.

More recently, researchers have come to discuss socialization as the process by which an individual learns the norms, values, expected behaviors, and social knowledge necessary for adopting a particular role and participating as an organizational member (Brim, 1966; Louis, 1980; Van Maanen, 1976; Van Maanen & Schein, 1979), Feldman (1981) presents this integrated view of socialization more precisely by defining socialization as: (a) the acquisition of a set of appropriate role behaviors, (b) the development of work skills and abilities, and (c) the adjustment to the work group's norms and values. We agree with Feldman's definition, but seek to extend it by arguing that acquisition, development, and adjustment are brought about by response to *ambient* and *discretionary* cues, such that the notions of *intersubjectivity* and *structuration* must be stressed.

Ambient and discretionary cues (Hackman, 1976) are those stimuli which provide the developmental and perceptual cues associated with organizational socialization. Ambient cues constantly impinge on perceivers, and tend to operate unconsciously or subliminally. They are likely to function symbolically or indirectly. Discretionary cues are consciously perceived and/or manipulated. They are more direct and intentional. Together, these cues convey messages of, and about, the organization to the newcomer, and vice versa. They are an inherent part of the whole socialization process.

Members of organizations attend consciously and unconsciously to the cues around them. Newcomers seek to make sense of the new environment (Louis, 1980), and are particularly likely to be aware of their interactions with others and to adjust to cues and messages as they attend to them. The socialization process is intersubjective (Field & Abelson, 1982), in that newcomers assess the environment and attend to cues obtained through interactions with others in order to interpret the environment. Socialization is a reciprocal and transactional process where ambient and discretionary cues and intersubjectivity provide the foundation for structuration. Structuration is the development and establishment of rules and expectations which are used in the production and reproduction of organizational systems (Poole, 1985).

The process of socialization then becomes a process of self-development and self-maintenance through organizational interactions. These interactions are structured and mediated by the cognitive maps of the organizational members (Guion, 1973; Schneider, 1973). The cognitive map serves as the interpretive schema for both ambient and discretionary cues, and is a mediating link between the cues and structuration. For example, when an organizational policy change is implemented, the change is mediated by employee perceptions of such things as rewards, autonomy, resources, values, and relationships. Our cognitive maps provide the standards against which our expectations and assumptions are developed through organizational socialization.

By viewing socialization as an intersubjective process which relies on discretionary and ambient cues, and results in ongoing organizational structuration, we wish to emphasize the transactional and reciprocal nature of the entry process. Organizations influence and shape the new member, and new members influence and shape the organization (a process called "individualization" by Jablin, 1982a, 1984). Whereas the influence of a larger system on one individual may be more powerful and easier to observe, new members can and do succeed at changing organizations to better suit their needs. Individual and organizational influences interact to create those cues by which all organizational members structure rules, expectations, and resources necessary for developing and defining the organizational system.

In sum, organizational socialization is the acquisition, development, and adjustment of role behaviors, work skills, required abilities, norms, and values brought about through continuous intersubjectives structuration of cues and mediated by organizational members' cognitive maps.

THE PROCESS OF ORGANIZATIONAL SOCIALIZATION[1]

Hughes (1959) characterized the newcomer's socialization experience as "reality shock." The individual is typically overloaded with information, experiences a great deal of uncertainty and stress, and finds understanding the organizational mission and one's role in that mission difficult. The stressful and uncertain nature of entry motivates the newcomer to reduce the stress (Berlew & Hall, 1966) and, in response, the individual engages in a process of "sense-making" to cope with the new situation (Louis, 1980).

As time goes on, the newcomer gains some understanding of the new environment. Newcomers and veterans adapt to one another, learn common norms and expectations, and develop perspectives of one another as organizational members. The organization's culture becomes more apparent to members as they relate to one another informally (Rogers & Agarwala-Rogers, 1976). The perceived culture of an organization emerges as a property of these interpersonal transactions. As newcomers and veterans interact with one another through the sharing of the organization's stories and legends, and through the observation of the organization's rites and rituals, a perceived culture evolves (Deal & Kennedy, 1982; Pacanowsky & O'Donnell-Trujillo, 1983). As members communicate, they negotiate and share meanings of organizational symbols, stories, rites, and rituals, etc. This communication activity is a shared symbolic process which forms a collective group consciousness (Bormann, 1983). As new members become socialized, they exchange symbols which are culturally defined, which, in turn, affect the organization's culture and are affected by it (Barnett, this volume). Socialization is a process which is continuous throughout one's career, because both individuals and organizations experience ongoing change and reconstruction such that continuous learning, adjusting, and development is appropriate.

Generally, organizational socialization is viewed as a stage or phase process (e.g., Feldman, 1976; Gabarro, 1979; Jablin, 1982a; Schein, 1971; Van Maanen, 1976; Wilson, 1984). According to the most general model, the process consists of three phases: anticipatory socialization, encounter, and metamorphosis.

Organizational socialization begins before an individual enters an organization, in a stage entitled "anticipatory socialization" (Merton, 1957). Individuals are prepared for organizational positions through interaction with family and friends, involvement with educational institutions, and influence by the culture (Van Maanen, 1976). Information is gained and perceptions are further shaped through pre-entry contact with the organization (information-gathering interviews, annual reports, pamphlets). Prior to entry, newcomers anticipate their experiences as organizational members (Louis, 1980) and develop expectations of organizational life. These expectations are often unrealistic and inflated, and make assimilation a difficult process, even inhibiting successful integration (Jablin, 1982a, 1984; Wanous, 1977, 1980).

Feldman (1976, 1981) argues that individuals who gain and evaluate information during the anticipatory socialization phase will have a more accurate and realistic picture of both the job and the organization. These individuals will then be more able to match their skills, abilities, needs, and values to the organization's requirements and resources.

The second stage of organizational socialization is the "encounter" stage, when the individual enters the organization. During this stage, the newcomer gains a still clearer picture of the organization, his or her beliefs and expectations may be challenged, and the newcomer must "make sense" of the setting or "normalize" it (Louis, 1980); Van Maanen, 1976). Newcomers are involved with learning tasks, developing new relationships with coworkers, assessing their performance and progress, and resolving role ambiguity during this stage (Feldman, 1976).

To assess an individual's progress through the encounter phase, Feldman (1981) suggests examining the individual's ability to successfully manage five activities or "process variables." Specifically, the newcomers should show progress in dealing with those conflicts which arise between personal life and work (e.g., scheduling or work demands which require the employee's personal time or resources). The newcomer should also begin successfully managing intergroup role conflicts; that is, he or she should begin to be able to negotiate and handle conflicts between the demands of his or her own work group and other work groups in the organization. In addition, Feldman (1981) argues that the newcomer must define and sort out his or her role, gaining a better understanding of and ability to perform required tasks. Finally, the newcomer should show an awareness of group norms and should be establishing new friendships and good working relationships with others in the group.

The final socialization stage, "metamorphosis," represents the adaptation phase, where the newcomer continues to engage in new learning, shows mastery of required skills, and adjusts to the new environment (Van Maanen, 1976). In essence, the newcomer "settles in" to the new job and organization. Again, Feldman (1981) defines activities which are associated with successful progress through the stage. Specifically, during metamorphosis the newcomer not only performs work tasks successfully, but does so consistently and with greater self confidence. The newcomer has successfully developed interpersonal relationships such that feelings of mutual liking and trust exist. Finally, the newcomer who is successfully passing through the third stage of socialization should have adjusted, and be adhering, to the work group's norms and values.

The three-phase model of the socialization process just described is useful in providing a description of the essential phases of socialization, but the model does not adequately account for the interaction between individual and organizational influences. Moreover, the model does not account for individual differences which may moderate the socialization process.

Jones (1983) contends that two mediating factors—individual differences and attribution processes—must be considered if we are to sufficiently explain socialization. Jones argues that individuals have different life experiences, different degrees of self esteem, and different responses to the same situations, or, in short, different "psychological orientations." These individual differences influence how newcomers respond to socialization strategies, and how they interpret and react to the ambient and discretionary cues in the new environment. Further, Jones contends that attributions made by veterans and newcomers may be in conflict. Such inconsistent attributions may inhibit the sharing of cultural knowledge and may slow the sense-making process for the newcomer.

To emphasize the impact of individual differences and attribution processes on personal and organizational outcomes, Jones presents a model of the socialization process (shown in Figure 1) which is based on symbolic interaction theory (Mead, 1934; Silverman, 1970), social learning theory (Bandura, 1977, 1978), and attribution theory (Bem, 1967, 1972).

Each of the top circles (A, B, C) represents one possible relationship between an organization and a new hire. The relationship, according to Jones, is a function of the interac-

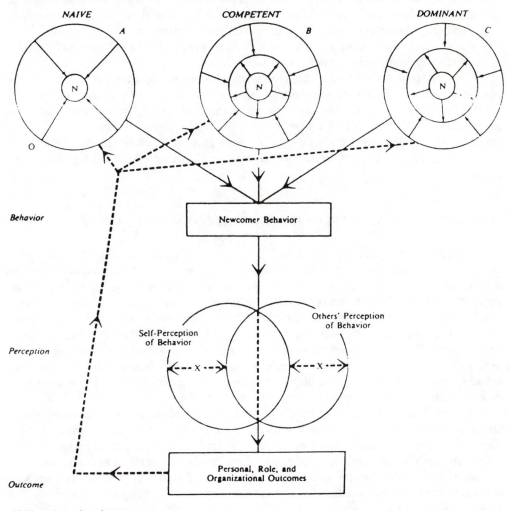

N--Newcomer orientation.
O--Organizational socialization practices.
X--Distance X may increase or decrease.

Note. From G. R. Jones, "Psychological orientation and the process of organizational socialization: An interactionist perspective", 1983, *Academy of Management Review, 8,* 464-474.

Figure 1. Initial Orientation and the Socialization Process

tion between: (a) the individual's psychological orientation (represented by the arrows directed outward, with the length of the arrows representing the intensity of the newcomer's psychological orientation); and (b) the potency of the organization's socialization strategies and the impact of the information transmitted to the employee (signified by the length of the arrows directed inwards). The interaction between individual orientation and organizational practices affects the neophyte's ongoing behavior in the organization.

The overlapping circles in the model represent the "sense-making" process, based on the newcomer's perceptions of his or her own behavior, and the interaction between self perceptions and member perceptions which allow for situations and appropriate behaviors to be negotiated. The distance in "X" represents the degree of divergence and convergence of these perceptions. Individual differences and attributions then influence the personal, role, and organizational outcomes associated with the socialization process. Finally, Jones includes a feedback loop to emphasize how socialization experiences link back to affect the newcomer's psychological orientation and future behavior.

The model presented by Jones is consistent with our notion of socialization. Its emphasis on individual differences and attributional processes is similar to our emphasis on the transactional nature of socialization based on intersubjectivity and structuration. The model does not, however, identify or discuss the specific communication activities and strategies which might occur during the socialization process. The next section of this chapter examines the nature and sources of communication employed in the socialization process.

COMMUNICATION SOURCES OF ORGANIZATIONAL SOCIALIZATION

Uncertainty reduction theory (Berger, 1979; Berger & Calabrese, 1975) can be useful for explaining organizational socialization (Lester, 1986; Wilson, 1986). According to the theory, communication provides information, cues, and knowledge which allow an individual to make predictions and reduce uncertainty about other individuals. While uncertainty theory was originally applied to initial interactions, it has been shown to apply to ongoing relationships (e.g., Parks & Adelman, 1983) and has implications for organizational socialization. The theory suggests that the new employee gains knowledge about the organization, the job, expected behaviors, rules, norms, and so forth through various communication channels. The information and knowledge are necessary for reducing uncertainty, making predictions, and gaining control in the new environment.

In the original explication of the theory, Berger and Calabrese (1975) assumed uncertainty was a function of the overall amount of communication. We take the position that, while amount of information is important, content and source of communication are also important. Both content and source of communication may affect the newcomer's interpretations of cues and messages and the newcomer's attributions regarding the cues and messages. The following sections describe the communication content dimensions and the various sources of communication which affect the socialization process.

Communication Content Dimensions

Wilson (1984) suggests that two dimensions of communication content — formal/informal and generalized/personalized — influence the reduction of uncertainty in organizational socialization. Further, the two dimensions have an intimacy component such that content on either dimension can range from nonintimate to highly intimate.

The formal/informal dimension reflects the degree to which information is formalized, prescribed, and fixed. Typically, this type of information is presented in organizational documents such as job descriptions, salary schedules, and so on. In contrast, informal information is not prescribed or fixed, and is exemplified by informal work group norms, individualized modes of conduct, and personal preferences. While both formal and informal information can help reduce uncertainty, formal information may be less helpful, in that formal information tends to be normative (what should be) while informal information tends to be descriptive (what actually is). Wilson further suggests that, when formal and informal information are contradictory, the informal information tends to be more effective for reducing uncertainty.

The second dimension—generalized/personalized—reflects the degree to which information applies to all members of the organization, a few members, or to the focal individual. Generalized information applies to most members of the organizational culture, such as information concerning vacation policy. Personalized information, on the other hand, applies to the individual in a particular way, such as individualized job descriptions, personal concerns, or idiosyncrasies. Personalized information facilitates prediction making because it is individualized.

In addition, uncertainty reduction theory would predict that the level of intimacy people are willing to convey to others regarding information on either dimension is directly related to the level of uncertainty. Employees tend to avoid sharing information which might be considered disruptive or risky. As uncertainty decreases, the exchange of more intimate information would be expected to increase.

A new employee will receive both formal/informal and personalized/generalized information during the socialization process. This information may come from official, downward-directed media sources, from immediate superiors, or from the individual's own work group. Cutlip and Center (1971) found that members receive organizational and role-related information from official, internal media such as house organs, handbooks, manuals, memos, and bulletin boards. Specific job information, such as instructions, performance feedback, and job rationale, typically comes from one's immediate supervisor (Jablin, 1979). Information which helps the newcomer overcome job-related problems, and understand and meet normative expectations regarding acceptable and reinforced behaviors, often is provided by the newcomer's work group. In fact, a considerable body of research suggests that, for both new and continuing organizational members, transactions between coworkers and work group members provide the greatest amount of information for understanding the organization (Jablin, 1985b).

Superior/Subordinate Socialization

The communication transactions which take place between superiors and subordinates are critical to organizational socialization (Graen, 1976). First, the supervisor may be considered a key communicator, in that he or she is in a position to receive formal organizational information, and so has access to a wide variety of information. Frequent and open communication with the supervisor can provide the newcomer with more opportunities to clarify concerns, ask questions, check perceptions, and become better acquainted with the organizational culture.

In addition, the supervisor typically assigns tasks and delegates responsibility, so is in a position to make expectations of the newcomer clear (Porter, Lawler, & Hackman, 1975). As the formal authority, the supervisor is in a position to resolve task ambiguity for the newcomer by clarifying, or negotiating and redefining, the role with the newcomer. The supervisor is also charged with conducting the formal performance evaluation and assigning organizational rewards. Individuals are especially likely to learn from interactions with those who can reward or punish behaviors (Brim, 1966), and, in fact, feedback from superiors is related to the subordinate's job performance (Jablin, 1985b).

The supervisor is in a position to interact frequently with the subordinate, and thus may function as a mentor or role model for the subordinate (Jablin, 1982b; Weiss, 1977). Role models and mentors are especially good socialization agents (Manz & Sims, 1981; Weiss, 1978), in that they can model appropriate behaviors which newcomers learn through observation (Bandura, 1977). For example, a newcomer who observes his or her superior consistently work late may gather that working extra hours is appropriate or expected.

Finally, Jablin (1982a) notes that the supervisor frequently has a personal relationship with the subordinate, beyond the formal relationship. Such friendships may help build trust and openness between the superior and the subordinate, and may facilitate information exchange. Subordinates may be less likely to distort upward information to a trusted superior (Jablin, 1985b), and supervisors may feel more comfortable sharing information and perceptions with a trusted subordinate. Open exchanges can facilitate interpersonal and cultural understanding.

While supervisors clearly affect their subordinates, it is important to note that subordinates may also influence their supervisors. Jablin notes that the subordinate's upward communication may provide feedback to the supervisor about work issues or organizational policy. Newcomers may suggest new work patterns, or offer innovations which their supervisors adopt or implement. Newcomers and supervisors also tend to negotiate comfortable modes of interaction (Dansereau, Graen, & Haga, 1975). In addition, the subordinate's level of performance affects the nature and tone of the feedback given by the supervisor (Jablin, 1979).

Finally, Jablin (1982a) argues that superiors and subordinates make attributions about one another's behaviors. The newcomer's behaviors, and intentional and unintentional messages, are likely to affect the superior's attributions, just as the superior's behaviors will affect the newcomer's attributions. In sum, the exchanges between supervisors and newcomers can significantly influence the development of perceptions, expectations, rules, and appropriate behaviors within the organization.

Work Group/Coworker Socialization

The new member's work group consists of employees at a similar organizational process. In a recent review of organizational group communication literature, Jablin and Sussman (1983) specified the formal organizational and individual functions served by communication within and between groups. First,

> *individual-oriented* organizational group communication functions to: (a) provide members with feedback about their self-concepts, (b) gratify needs for affiliation, (c) share and test perspectives about social reality, (d) reduce organization-related uncertainty and concomitant individual feelings of anxiety, insecurity, and powerlessness, or (e) accomplish employee-related (versus organization-related) tasks and resolve individual or group-related problems. (Jablin & Sussman, 1983, p. 13)

Clearly, to the extent the work group accomplishes these various functions, the work group will facilitate the socialization process. Work group members can help the newcomer define and adapt to organizational expectations and norms. By offering feedback, veterans can help clarify role expectations and reduce role ambiguity. Work group members can aid the newcomer in interpretation and understanding of confusing or unclear situations. Veteran members can serve as "sounding boards" for the newcomer, by listening to and clarifying the new hire's perceptions of the new system (Louis, 1980). Veteran work group members are in a position to possess informal and private cultural knowledge which may not be accessible from organizational documents or the supervisor. Finally, the work group may provide a forum for the newcomer to express and clarify his or her own needs and expectations and to negotiate his or her own role.

Jablin and Sussman (1983) also identify five organizational functions fulfilled by work groups in organizations. Groups operate to:

(a) generate information, (b) process information, (c) share information necessary for the coordination of interdependent organizational tasks, (d) disseminate decisions, or (e) reinforce a group's perspective/consensus. (Jablin & Sussman, 1983, p. 13)

Like the individual functions, these organizational functions can facilitate the socialization process. The newcomer gains a great deal of information related to both the job and the organization. The newcomer also has the opportunity to provide information and influence the processing of information. Further, the newcomer can gain an understanding of organizational priorities, norms, and values by observing both what kinds of decisions are made and how the decisions are made (Wilson, 1983).

The Jablin and Sussman (1983) review also examined a number of organizational group communication areas which may have a bearing on socialization. For example, task characteristics may affect the interaction patterns of group members. Specifically, as task certainty increases, the use of impersonal communication activities (rules, policies, procedures) increases (Van de Ven, Delbecq, & Koenig, 1976). The nature of the task also influences interaction patterns (Hackman & Vidmar, 1970). Some tasks may require very little discussion, while other tasks may call for open and relaxed discussion. In addition, work groups may differ in terms of their decision-making behaviors and their degrees of interpersonal trust. The group process, and the nature of group relationships and discussions, may influence the socialization process for the newcomer by influencing the extent to which the work group fulfills the individual and organizational functions discussed previously.

Summary. The ambient (unintentional) and discretionary (intentional) messages communicated between superiors and subordinates and among coworkers help construct the social reality for new employees. The newcomer uses these messages to make sense of the environment, and it is evident that the messages exchanged have an impact on employee attitudes and behaviors. In addition, trust is of particular importance for effective superior/subordinate relationships and work group development, and the nature and characteristics of the group's task may affect the interpersonal communication patterns exhibited (Jablin, 1985b).

STRATEGIES OF ORGANIZATIONAL SOCIALIZATION

Van Maanen (1978) suggests that the socialization process is characterized by certain strategies or tactics. The tactics may be used alone or in tandem, and by design or by accident

(Van Maanen & Schein, 1979). Van Maanen and Schein (1979) argue that the strategies are commonly used and that they do influence the newcomer's ongoing organizational experience.

Socialization strategies may be sequential or nonsequential. Sequential socialization strategies consist of a series of discrete stages through which a new employee must pass before a particular role or status is achieved. Militaristic and quasi-militaristic organizations, such as police and fire departments, use sequential strategies such that recruits are run through a series of physical and mental tests before they achieve a level of peer and organizational acceptance. Nonsequential strategies are less mechanistic, in that stages do not necessarily build on one another. For example, an employee who is promoted to department manager without having to progress through various training programs and stages has experienced nonsequential socialization.

Another socialization strategy is labeled fixed/variable socialization (Van Maanen, 1978). Fixed socialization is a strategy designed to follow a specific timetable and to give the newcomer specific information concerning the time needed to complete a career stage. This strategy standardizes a well-established process. Probationary periods, such as those commonly given to tenure-track assistant professors, provide classic examples of fixed socialization. In contrast, variable socialization is socialization which does not follow a specific timetable. Career stages, in this strategy, do not normally follow a clearly articulated timetable. Apprenticeship programs, internships, and university promotional practices for full professors are examples. Timetables for advancement are not always clear or under the control of the employee.

Tournament/contest socialization processes are also discussed by Van Maanen (1978). Tournament socialization consists of separating newcomers into clusters or tracks on the basis of abilities, educational background, career objectives, and so forth. This strategy may involve identifying "fast trackers" and providing different opportunities for them than for others. Alternatively, in contest socialization, distinctions among people at the same level are avoided. Progress is a function of one's ability to perform, and is not based on predetermined criteria. Career information and counseling are often provided to help reduce the individual's uncertainty and enhance career decision making.

Serial/disjunctive socialization strategies (Van Maanen, 1978) are frequently found in organizations. Serial socialization is characterized by the use of mentors or role models. Newcomers are trained and encouraged by more experienced employees to prepare them to take on their new roles. Serial socialization reduces uncertainty in a fairly systematic way, and tends to perpetuate stability. It may, however, stifle creativity and innovation. Contrastingly, disjunctive socialization allows the newcomer to learn the new role of his or her own. This usually occurs when the newcomer is not assuming a role previously held by a more experienced employee. Disjunctive socialization makes it more difficult for the newcomer to reduce uncertainty in a systematic manner because there is a greater reliance on information sources which may be inaccurate or inappropriate. While it may allow for more innovation and risk taking, it may also encourage chaos and confusion.

Investiture/divestiture is the last socialization strategy described by Van Maanen (1978). Investiture socialization assumes that the newcomer's qualities and qualifications are the necessary ingredients for job success, so these qualities and qualifications are nurtured and supported by the organization. Divestiture socialization involves the opposite process of trying to strip away certain characteristics of the newcomer. Divestiture socialization often relies on an unfreezing process which forces the newcomer to "pay his dues" before there is peer acceptance. For example, fraternity and sorority "pledges" must go through divestiture socialization before being accepted by their peers.

Another perspective of socialization strategies comes from the organizational culture literature which considers the use of rituals and stories as strategies for socializing organization members. Pacanowsky and O'Donnell-Trujillo (1983) describe four types of organizational rituals. *Personal rituals* are those behaviors performed by specific organizational members as a function of their position, role, or unique characteristics. *Task rituals* consist of what must be performed in order to get the job done. These rituals may take the form of training programs, instructional materials, or certain structured phases one goes through to learn job functions. *Social rituals* often take the form of office parties or "TGIF" social events, and other social gatherings held by organizational members. Lastly, *organizational rituals* are those meetings or activities formally sponsored by the organization such as shareholders meetings, staff meetings, or committees formed in order to conduct organizational business or activity.

Organizational stories exchanged by members describe the organization's culture and what it's like to experience that culture. These stories convey the organization's myths and legends. They help members learn about the organization's heroes and villians, as well as develop perceptions concerning the nature of the organization, the nature of the members, past events, and future considerations. Organizational stories personify the organization's values for the member. Pacanowsky and O'Donnell-Trujillo (1983) also identify four types of organizational stories. *Personal stories* describe individual members. *Collegial stories* are shared stories describing other members of the organization. *Corporate stories* describe the organization's ideology, values, and culture. Lastly, stories about *organizational history* describe factual information such as a chronology of historical events, as in the growth of product lines, mergers, etc.

In summary, the above socialization strategies are useful in providing insight into the nature of organizational socialization processes. The strategies employed by organizations communicate various messages to the newcomer, and they likely affect the newcomer's view of the organization. The strategies also reflect the extent to which the organization attempts to change the individual or is willing to be influenced by the individual.

OUTCOMES OF ORGANIZATIONAL SOCIALIZATION

Outcomes of the socialization process are of interest to both researchers and practitioners. Outcomes frequently discussed include organizational commitment (Buchanan, 1974; Feldman, 1981; Lodahl & Kejner, 1965), organizational climate (James & Jones, 1974), job satisfaction (Hackman & Oldham, 1976; Jablin, 1979; Wanous, 1977), decision making (Jablin, 1982a; Wilson, 1983), and longevity or turnover (Feldman, 1981; Jablin, 1984). In this section, we will examine the research findings which address the above outcomes.

Organizational Commitment

Socialization appears to play an influential role in the degree to which the employee is committed to the job and the organization. Two aspects of work which seem to significantly affect commitment are working with others rather than alone, and working interdependently within a team environment (Lodahl & Kejner, 1965). Integration into communication networks within the organization appears to have an influence on employee attitudes and perceptions of the job and organization. Network integration has been shown to be positively related to morale and commitment (Danowski, 1980; Eisenberg, Monge, & Miller, 1983). Newcomers tend to attach themselves to significant others, particularly in the early stages of socialization. This attachment exerts a lasting influence on the employee's later attitudes and commitment to the organization (Buchanan, 1974). Through interactions with and observations of veteran members, newcomers develop perceptions of the organization which are correlated with feelings of organizational commitment (Mowday, Porter, & Steers, 1982). Also, a positive relationship exists between task proficiency and commitment (Rabinowitz & Hall, 1977): as employees become more competent and successful in their jobs, their levels of commitment tend to increase (Bass, 1965; Vroom, 1962). Further Berlew and Hall (1966) claim that commitment increases for newcomers when reasonably high expectations are placed on them.

Organizational Climate

There is little doubt that socialization has an influence on employee perceptions of the organization's climate (Jablin, 1980; Roberts & O'Reilly, 1974). The ambient and discretionary messages received by employees as they become socialized in the organization help create their "psychological climate" (James & Jones, 1974). In an important longitudinal study (Jablin, 1984), it was found that newcomers' perceptions and expectations of the organization's communication climate were significantly reduced from their initial expectations within 6 weeks of work. Jablin (1984) also found that these deflated expectations remained relatively stable over time. Jablin concluded that the newcomers' communication climate perceptions were strongly influenced by their initial encounters in the organization, lending support to Buchanan's (1974) contention that the newcomer's early experiences in the organization exert a lasting influence over later perceptions.

Job Satisfaction

As we noted earlier, an employee's attitudes and perceptions about the work environment are a function of intersubjective structuration of messages. Expectations and perceptions are influenced by the ambient and discretionary messages communicated to the employee by others in the organization, and, to a large degree, the newcomer's job satisfaction is affected by those messages. Salancik and Pfeffer (1978) support this notion when the suggest that job satisfaction is a function of three things: (a) the employee's perceptions of the affective components of the organizational environment, (b) the messages provided to the employee by the social context about what is appropriate and what is not, and (c) the employee's self perception as influenced by individual history, past behaviors, and causal attributions. For example, as an individual begins to structure and restructure the organizational environment by reducing uncertainty through network integration and communication transactions, relational and task related expectations are clarified and roles become better defined. When uncertainty is reduced, expectations are negotiated, and role demands are clarified, the newcomer's job satisfaction is expected to be greater (Dansereau et al., 1975; Feldman, 1976).

Decision Making

Decision making is certainly a central process in organizations, and decisions made in organizations can serve as symbolic processes. The decision making process communicates a variety of things to organizational members (Edelman, 1964, 1971), and can be central to the socialization process (Wilson, 1983). For example, the decision to deny tenure to an assistant professor with excellent teaching and service records, but a mediocre publication record, conveys a symbolic message to other members about the organization's beliefs regarding the value of service and teaching compared to the value of research. Hence, decisions made can convey norms, values, and beliefs held by those in the organization.

Decision making can symbolically convey managerial attitudes toward upward communication, conflict, employee participation, and power. Additionally, the decision making process employed in organizations may instill feelings of confidence (or lack of) in the entire system. As Feldman and March (1981) suggest:

> decisions are orchestrated so as to ensure that decision makers and observers come to believe that the decisions are reasonable — or even intelligent . . . that the process is legitimate, that we are good decision makers, and that our organizations are well managed. (p. 178)

The decision making process can also influence individual attitudes and perceptions. Decisions and decision making can help to clarify organizational and personal goals for individuals (Christensen, 1979). Further, White and Ruh (1973) found a relationship between participation in decision making and job involvement, while Dansereau and his colleagues (1975) found that opportunity and latitude in negotiating roles and role expectations had a positive relationship with satisfaction.

Perhaps more importantly, the newcomer will come to understand and assimilate the decision making strategies used in the organization. Through observation and modeling, newcomers learn the strategies for decision making and apply those strategies in their own work (Jablin, 1982a).

In summary, it appears clear that various organizational outcomes, such as climate perceptions, job satisfaction, commitment, and decision making, are influenced by and may affect an employee's early work experiences during the socialization process.

ORGANIZATIONAL SOCIALIZATION: A DESCRIPTIVE MODEL

In the previous sections, we defined organizational socialization, highlighted representative models and perspectives of socialization, discussed communication and socialization, and identified outcomes associated with organizational socialization. In this section of the chapter, we present a descriptive model of organizational socialization (see Figure 2) which is designed to clarify and explain our conceptualization of the socialization process.

As suggested previously, individual influences and organizational influences interact to create the developmental and perceptual cues associated with organizational socialization. Based on the dichotomy proposed by Hackman (1976), these cues may be classifed as ambient and discretionary. Ambient cues are those cues in the environment which constantly impinge on perceivers and tend to operate unconsciously or subliminally. Discretionary cues, on the other hand, are those which are consciously perceived and/or manipulated. The ambient and discretionary cues are intersubjective in nature, and provide the foundation for structuration such that rules and expectations are developed and established and are used in the production and reproduction of organizational systems (Poole, 1985).

Communication is identified as an essential part of the socialization process. Communication between newcomers and veteran system members aids in uncertainty reduction by providing the information and cultural knowledge necessary for making predictions and

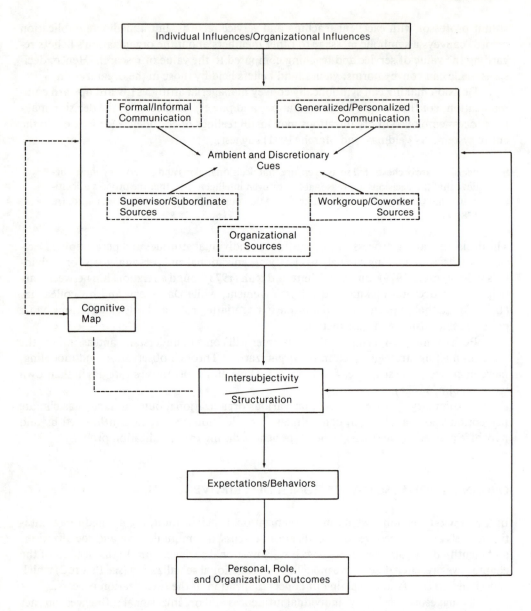

Figure 2. Organizational Socialization

maintaining control of the environment. Communication content is viewed as being formal/informal, and personalized/generalized, and may vary from highly intimate to nonintimate. Sources of communication in the work place include organizational sources, supervisor/subordinate sources, and coworker/work group sources. The communication sources interact to create messages of and about the organization.

Socialization then becomes a process of self-definition and maintenance through interaction and uncertainty reduction. Interactions are structured and mediated by the cognitive maps of the organizational members (Guion, 1973; Schneider, 1973). The cognitive maps can be viewed as the interpretive schema for both ambient and discretionary cues. The model depicts this cognitive map as a mediating link between the cues and structuration. The map is continually evolving, and provides the standards against which future cues are assessed. These cognitive maps provide a basis for the employees' expectations and behaviors concerning personal, role, and organizational outcomes.

FUTURE DIRECTIONS

The model of organizational socialization presented in this chapter suggests a number of future directions for both the research and practice of socialization. The current perspective of socialization emphasizes the intersubjective and individualized nature of socializing a newcomer. We noted that individuals have differing psychological orientations and may interpret cues and make sense of the environment in varying ways. As researchers, then, we may want to assess certain individual differences as we study socialization. For example, self esteem, dogmatism, and communication apprehension are individual difference variables which may affect a newcomer's socialization experience. Certainly, age, training, prior work experience, and familiarity with the job and organization could affect the newcomer's interpretation process. At Louis (1980) suggests, we may need to consider how "leavetaking and the letting go of old roles" affects the taking of new roles (p. 231).

Consideration of individual differences is also important for organizational members concerned with the socialization of employees. Those individuals new to the organization and the occupation may need more attention and more information than those who are familiar with the occupation. Further, role models, mentors, supervisors, and coworkers might do well to bear in mind that different individuals may respond differently to the same tactic, so that they develop a variety of approaches to socializing newcomers.

Communication and its role for reducing uncertainty and influencing socialization was also stressed. The need for a closer examination of the role of communication in socialization is great. The relationship between social network integration and socialization should thus be examined. Communication networks provide a means for information to pass from member to member, and integration into networks should facilitate socialization. Granovetter's (1974) research suggests individuals who acquire jobs through internal contacts become integrated into the system more easily. Hence, having a contact inside the organization prior to entry (a pre-established network link) should also facilitate socialization. An existing relationship would seemingly provide access to more information for the newcomer. In addition, notions of balance and transitivity would suggest that an existing relationship with an integrated veteran would lead to the development of other relationships with veteran members, wherein information of a more intimate and personalized nature may be shared more readily.

The current perspective also emphasizes the processual and interactional nature of socialization. Clearly, to better understand entry and assimilation, we would be well advised to conduct more longitudinal research where newcomers can be observed as they progress through the socialization process. While over-time research can be difficult and costly to conduct, the potential benefits are many. First, over-time analysis will allow for verification and refinement of the various theoretical models of the socialization process. Second, over-time analysis will allow us to assess the importance of communication channels and sources for the newcomer at various points in time. Third, over-time analysis will provide the opportunity to observe changes in the newcomer's attitudes and perceptions as they occur, allowing for a more precise understanding of the socialization process.

Finally, a more thorough analysis of the tactics and strategies for socialization are needed. Van Maanen (1978) has identified a variety of tactics, but the specific communication activities associated with the tactics are not specified. Further, the efficacy of the tactics for various organizations and individuals is not clear. We could benefit from a better understanding of the means by which newcomers make sense of their new roles, and the means by which newcomers negotiate and define their roles.

In sum, socialization is a critical process for organizations, but is not yet adequately understood. As researchers, as practitioners, and as system members, we can benefit from a better understanding of the process. It is our hope that an emphasis on communication, and a sensitivity for the reciprocal and transactional nature of socialization, combined with continued analysis, discussion, and research, will lead to a greater appreciation of this complex process.

REFERENCES

Bandura, A. (1977). *Social learning theory*. Englewood Cliffs, NJ: Prentice Hall.

Bandura, A. (1978). The self system in reciprocal determination. *American Psychologist, 33,* 344–358.

Bass, B. M. (1965). *Organizational psychology*. Boston, MA: Allyn & Bacon.

Bem, D. J. (1967). Self perception: An alternative interpretation of cognitive dissonance phenomena. *Psychological Review, 74,* 183–200.

Bem, D. J. (1972). Self perception theory. In L. Berkowitz (Ed.), *Advances in experimental social psychology* (Vol. 6, pp. 1–62). New York: Academic Press.

Berger, C. R. (1979). Beyond initial interaction: Uncertainty, understanding, and the development of interpersonal relationships. In H. Giles & R. N. St. Clair (Eds.), *Language and social psychology,* (pp. 122–144). Baltimore, MD: University Park.

Berger, C. R., & Calabrese, R. J. (1975). Some explorations in initial interaction and beyond: Toward a developmental theory of interpersonal communication. *Human Communication Research, 1,* 99–112.

Berlew, D. E., & Hall, D. T. (1966). The socialization of managers: Effects of expectations on performance. *Administrative Science Quarterly, 11,* 207–223.

Bormann, E. G. (1983). Symbolic convergence: Organizational communication and culture. In L. Putnam & M. Pacanowsky (Eds.), *Communication and organizations: An interpretive approach,* (pp. 99–122). Beverly Hills, CA: Sage.

Brim, O. E., Jr. (1966). Socialization through the life cycle. In O. E. Brim, Jr. & S. Wheeler (Eds.), *Socialization after childhood: Two essays* (pp. 1–49). New York: Wiley & Sons.

Buchanan, B. (1974). Building organizational commitment: The socialization of managers in work organizations. *Administrative Science Quarterly, 19,* 533–546.

Caplow, T. (1964). *Principles of organization*. New York: Harcourt, Brace and World.

Christensen, S. (1979). Decision making and socialization. In J. G. March and J. P. Olsen (Eds.), *Ambiguity and choice in organizations* (2nd ed.). Bergen, Norway: Universitetsforlaget.

Cutlip, S. M., & Center, A. H. (1971). *Effective public relations* (4th ed.). Englewood Cliffs, NJ: Prentice-Hall.

Danowski, J. A. (1980). Group attitude-belief uniformity and connectivity of organizational communication networks for production, innovation, and maintenance content. *Human Communication Research, 6,* 299–308.

Dansereau, F., Graen, G., & Haga, W. J. (1975). A vertical dyad linkage approach to leadership within formal organizations. *Organizational Behavior and Human Performances, 13,* 46–78.

Deal, T. E., & Kennedy, A. A. (1982). *Corporate cultures: The rites and rituals of corporate life*. Reading, MA: Addison-Wesley.

Edelman, M. (1964). *The symbolic uses of politics.* Urbana, IL: University of Illinois Press.

Edelman, M. (1971). *Politics as symbolic action.* New York: Academic Press.

Eisenberg, E. M., Monge, P. R., & Miller, K. I. (1983). Involvement in communication networks as a predictor of organizational commitment. *Human Communication Research, 10,* 179–201.

Feldman, D. C. (1976). A contingency theory of socialization. *Administrative Science Quarterly, 21,* 433–452.

Feldman, D. C. (1981). The multiple socialization of organization members. *Academy of Management Review, 6,* 309–318.

Feldman, M. S., & March, J. C. (1981). Information in organizations as a signal and symbol. *Administrative Science Quarterly, 26,* 171–186.

Field, R., & Abelson, M. (1982). Climate: A reconceptualization and proposed model. *Human Relations, 3,* 181–201.

Gabarro, J. (1979). Socialization at the top: How CEOs and subordinates evolve interpersonal contracts. *Organizational Dynamics, 7,* 3–23.

Graen, G. (1976). Role making processes within complex organizations. In M. D. Dunnette (Ed.), *Handbook of industrial and organizational psychology* (pp. 1201–1245). Chicago: Rand-McNally.

Granovetter, M. S. (1974). *Getting a job: A study of contacts and careers.* Cambridge, MA: Harvard University Press.

Guion, R. N. (1973). A note on organizational climate. *Organizational Behavior and Human Performance, 9,* 120–125.

Hackman, J. R. (1976). Group influences on individuals. In M. Dunnette (Ed.), *Handbook of industrial and organizational psychology* (pp. 1455–1525). Chicago: Rand-McNally.

Hackman, J. R., & Oldham, G. R. (1976). Motivation through the design of work: Test of a theory. *Organizational Behavior and Human Performance, 16,* 250–279.

Hackman, J. R., & Vidmar, N. (1970). Effects of size and task type on group performance and member reactions. *Sociometry, 33,* 37–54.

Hughes, E. C. (1959). The study of occupations. In R. K. Merton, L. Brown, & L. S. Cottrell (Eds.), *Sociology today: Problems and prospects.* New York: Basic Books.

Jablin, F. M. (1979). Superior-subordinate communication: The state of the art. *Psychological Bulletin, 86,* 1201–1222.

Jablin, F. M. (1980). Organizational communication theory and research: An overview of communication climate and network research. In D. Nimmo (Ed.), *Communication yearbook 4* (pp. 327–347). New Brunswick, NJ: Transaction.

Jablin, F. M. (1982a). Organizational communication: An assimilation approach. In M. E. Roloff & C. R. Berger (Eds.), *Social cognition and communication* (pp. 255–286). Beverly Hills, CA: Sage.

Jablin, F. M. (1982b). Formal structural characteristics of organizations and superior-subordinate communication. *Human Communication Research, 8,* 338–347.

Jablin, F. M. (1984). Assimilating new members into organizations. In R. N. Bostrom (Ed.), *Communication yearbook 8,* (pp. 594–626). Beverly Hills, CA: Sage.

Jablin, F. M. (1985a). An exploratory study of vocational organization communication socialization. *Southern Speech Communication Journal, 50,* 261–282.

Jablin, F. M. (1985b). Task/work relationships: A life-span perspective. In M. L. Knapp & G. R. Miller (Eds.), *Handbook of interpersonal communication* (pp. 615–654). Beverly Hills, CA: Sage.

Jablin, F. M. & Sussman, L. (1983). Organizational group communication: A review of the literature and model of the process. In H. H. Greenbaum, R. L. Falcione, & S. A. Hellweg (Eds.), *Organizational communication: Abstracts, analysis and overview* (Vol. 8, pp. 11–50). Beverly Hills, CA: Sage.

James, L. R., & Jones, A. P. (1974). Organizational climate: A review of theory and research. *Psychological Bulletin, 16,* 74–113.

Jones, G. R. (1983). Psychological orientation and the process of organizational socialization: An interactionist perspective. *Academy of Management Review, 8,* 464–474.

Kotter, J. P. (1973). The psychological contract: Managing the joining up process. *California Management Review, 15,* 91–99.

Lester, R. E. (1986). Organizational culture, uncertainty reduction, and socialization of new organizational members. In S. Thomas (Ed.), *Culture and communication: Methodology, behavior, artifacts, and institutions* (pp. 105–113). Norwood, NJ: Ablex Publishing Corp.

Lodahl, T. M., & Kejner, M. (1965). The definition and measurement of job involvement. *Journal of Applied Psychology, 49,* 24–33.

Louis, M. (1980). Surprise and sense-making: What newcomers experience in entering unfamiliar organizational settings. *Administrative Science Quarterly, 25,* 226–251.

Manz, C. C., & Sims, H. P., Jr. (1981). Vicarious learning: The influence of modeling on organizational behavior. *Academy of Management Review, 6,* 105–113.

Mead, G. H. (1934). *Mind, self and society.* Chicago, IL: University of Chicago Press.

Merton, R. K. (1957). The role set: Problems in sociological theory. *British Journal of Sociology, 8,* 106–120.

Mowday, R. T., Porter, L. W., & Steers, R. M. (1982). *Employee-organization linkages: The psychology of commitment, absenteeism, and turnover.* New York: Academic Press.

Pacanowsky, M. E., & O'Donnell-Trujillo, N. (1983). Communication and organizational culture. *Western Journal of Speech Communication, 46,* 115–130.

Parks, M. R., & Adelman, M. B. (1983). Communication networks and the development of romantic relationships: An expansion of uncertainty reduction theory. *Human Communication Research, 10,* 55–79.

Poole, M. S. (1985). Communication and organizational climates: Review, critique, and a new perspective. In P. Tompkins & R. D. McPhee (Eds.), *Organizational communication: Traditional themes and new directions* (pp. 79–108). Beverly Hills, CA: Sage.

Porter, L. W., Lawler, E. E., & Hackman, J. R. (1975). *Behavior in organizations.* New York: McGraw-Hill.

Rabinowitz, S., & Hall, D. T. (1977). Organizational research on job involvement. *Psychological Bulletin, 84,* 265–288.

Roberts, K. H., & O'Reilly, C. A. (1974). Measuring organizational communication. *Journal of Applied Psychology, 59,* 321–326.

Rogers, E., & Agarwala-Rogers, R. (1976). *Communication in organizations.* New York: Free Press.

Salancik, G. R., & Pfeffer, J. (1978). A social information processing approach to job attitudes and task design. *Administrative Science Quarterly, 23,* 224–253.

Schein, E. H. (1968). Organizational socialization and the profession of management. *Industrial Management Review, 9,* 1–16.

Schein, E. H. (1971). The individual, the organization, and the career: A conceptual scheme. *Journal of Applied Behavioral Science, 7,* 401–426.

Schneider, B. (1973). The perception of organizational climate: The customer's view. *Journal of Applied Psychology, 57,* 248–256.

Silverman, D. (1970). *The theory of organizations.* London: Heinemann.

Van de Ven, A. H., Delbecq, A. L., & Koenig, R. (1976). Determinants of coordination modes within organizations. *American Sociological Review, 41,* 332–338.

Van Maanen, J. (1976). Breaking in: A consideration of organizational socialization. In R. Dubin (Ed.), *Handbook of work, organization, and society* (pp. 67–130). Chicago, IL: Rand-McNally.

Van Maanen, J. (1978). People processing: Strategies of organizational socialization. *Organizational Dynamics, 7,* 18–36.

Van Maanen, J., & Schein, E. H. (1979). Toward a theory of organizational socialization. *Research in Organizational Behavior, 1,* 209–264.

Vroom, V. H. (1962). Ego-involvement, job satisfaction, and job performance. *Personnel Psychology, 15,* 159–177.

Wanous, J. P. (1977). Organizational entry: Newcomers moving from outside to inside. *Psychological Bulletin, 84,* 601–618.

Wanous, J. P. (1980). *Organizational entry: Recruitment, selection, and socialization of newcomers.* Reading, MA: Addison-Wesley.

Weiss, H. M. (1977). Subordinate imitation of supervisor behavior: The role of modeling in organizational socialization. *Organizational Behavior and Human Performance, 27,* 345–366.

Weiss, H. M. (1978). Social learning of work values in organizations. *Journal of Applied Psychology, 63,* 711–718.

White, J. K., & Ruh, R. A. (1973). Effects of personal values on the relationships between participation and job attitudes. *Administrative Science Quarterly, 18,* 506–514.

Wilson, C. E. (1983). *Organizational decision making: A tactic for socialization.* Paper presented at the annual meeting of the Speech Communication Association, Washington, DC.

Wilson, C. E. (1984). *A communication perspective on socialization in organizations.* Paper presented at the annual meeting of the International Communication Association, San Francisco.

Wilson, C.E. (1986). *The influence of communication network involvement on socialization in organizations.* Unpublished doctoral dissertation, University of Washington, Seattle.

Chapter 9

Communication and Organizational Outcomes

Cal W. Downs, Phillip G. Clampitt, and Angela Laird Pfeiffer

Organizations exist to accomplish definite outcomes. As one of the most important organizational processes, communication hopefully facilitates the accomplishment of desired outcomes. Yet the exact contribution of the communication processes toward the outcomes is often hard to assess, and the connection is more intuitive than demonstrated or empirically proven. Therefore, the objectives of this chapter are to review the work of communication scholars in their quest to define the link between communication and organizational outcomes.

Communication in Organizations

The first problem encountered in understanding this link is the complex nature of communication. Frequently called a "dynamic process," it actually comprises many processes. In other words, it is multi-dimensional, and even at its simplest level problems can occur at any of the following aspects.

Encoding messages
Decoding messages
Structuring the content of messages
Emphasis of ideas
Choosing which messages to send and which to omit
Choosing appropriate channels for messages
Choosing appropriate recipients of messages
Providing feedback

As these processes are duplicated over and over with different people functioning as receivers and senders, assessing the adequacy of communication becomes difficult.

A second problem is that communication can be studied at many levels in the organization: individual, interpersonal, group, system-wide, and inter-organizational. Furthermore, the variables at each level are so complex that it is never possible to assess all dimensions of communication in the organization.

A third and related problem is that several different communication subsystems exist in any organization, and they are designed to accomplish different purposes. The traditional divisions are: (a) instruction, (b) information, (c) persuasion, (d) integration, and (e) innovation. One should notice two things about this list. First. they are not mutually exclusive. Performance reviews, for example, may overlap into them all. Second, these five functions identify the actual outcomes wanted from communication in the organization. Therefore, the immediate responses to the communication may or may not be related to ultimate organizational outcomes. For example, a suggestion by an employee would normally be classified as a part of the innovative system. And if the idea is communicated so that the company representatives understand it, then this is an effective completion of the communication process by some definition. Can it be directly related to organization end products? It may or may not. If the idea suggests a new work procedure, it can be related directly to productivity. On the other hand, suppose the idea is turned down because it has some deficiencies, so that it cannot be implemented economically. In this case, the innovative system is still working, but it is not going to affect productivity immediately. Participation may have affected job satisfaction though. Many employees react negatively when their ideas are rejected; to turndown ideas; others may still appreciate the opportunity to participate. The main point of this discussion is that communication can be successful, even when the impact on an organizational end product is minor or even non-existent.

A fourth problem is that the *role* of communication has been conceptualized in numerous ways. Johnson (1977) and Weick (1969) have presented the orientation that communication is the process by which organizing is done. And the exchange of messages is certainly the means by which decisions about how to organize take place. In this sense, communication is the process by which anything involving several people gets accomplished.

On the other hand, organization is more often accepted as a given, with communication being one of many processes operating within it. One of the best descriptions of this is Likert's (1967) Causal Sequence (see Figure 1).

Like other models, this one is controversial. Some researchers support it; others do not. In discussions with Dennis, for example, he objects to the placement of communication as an intervening variable because (a) some dimensions of communication actually fit Likert's description of a causal variable, and (b) the variables identified as causal have some implicit communication aspects in them. Leadership behavior, for example, may be determined in part by how one communicates. On the other hand, there can be communication dimensions of all the other intervening variables, too. This merely accents how difficult it is to isolate communication.

But regardless of whether communication is classified as a causal or intervening variable, this model is helpful in raising several issues. First, it identifies some generally acceptable end products, job satisfaction and productivity. Second, it suggests that communication has a direct bearing on each of these end products. Third, it forces one to think in terms of contingencies. The same form of communication, for example, may impinge on productivity differentially, depending on changes in the causal variable of organizational climate or in the intervening variable of people's motivation.

Causal	Intervening	End Result
Leadership	Communication	Job Satisfaction
Organizational Climate	Motivation	Productivity
Organizational Structure	Decision Making	Profit
	Control	Labor–Management
	Coordination	Relations

Figure 1. Likert's Causal Sequence

While the Likert schematic was an attempt to represent how the main factors operated within an organizational system, systems theory would teach us that he left out a major element: the environment in which the system operates. Mackenzie (1980), for example, has focused attention on the role of the environment on organizational processes. The same processes successful for an organization in Kansas may not work at all in Kenya. Or what worked in the economic and social milieu of the '60s may not work in the '80s. And a new federal regulation may actually impede productivity, regardless of how well the organization communicates.

Like Likert, most managers and most communication scholars intuitively assume both that communication is one of the most important factors in any organization, and that it has a very direct bearing on organizational outcomes. But neither the managers nor the scholars can fully document the nature of this relationship. The remainder of the chapter investigates their attempts to document how it works.

COMMUNICATION AND PRODUCTIVITY

Productivity is simultaneously one of the most important and most difficult variables for communication researchers to study. For many years, they were more preoccupied with job satisfaction than with productivity. However, interest in productivity and what factors contribute to it intensified in the United States during the 1970s and 1980s. Currently, it is vital for communication professionals to grapple with the relationship between communication and productivity for two reasons: (a) improving productivity is of paramount concern to business and service organization, and (b) communication professionals need to be able to make realistic claims for their interventions and to document those results.

THE PRODUCTIVITY PROBLEM

From 1945 to 1967, productivity in the American private sector rose over 3% a year. From 1967 to 1978, the average was only 1.6%; and then it began to decline even further. (*Nation's Business,* October 1980, p. 6) Judson (1982) surveyed 236 top-level executives in 195 companies to explore what was happening in terms of productivity. He found that 52% of the companies reported annual gains in productivity of less than 5%; only 3% had gains over 10%; and 25% did not know what their productivity problem had been. Furthermore, Judson discovered that half the companies surveyed did not account for inflation, so his figures did not reflect that 32% actually experienced a decline in productivity. Economists, politicians, and business leaders have tried to dissect the problem, but its complexity evades any analysis. The reasons seemed to group into two areas: (a) Environmental, and (b) Utilization of Resources (Downs & Hain, 1981).

Environmental Factors

One of the major problems of assessing productivity is the influence of the environment on any work unit. Grayson described productivity at the national level as "the efficiency of our collective national effort," and "the effective use of all of our national resources, including, but not limited to, our human resources" (Cook & Jackson, 1980, p. 4). While one may want to examine only one organization, a systems perspective ought to draw attention to all the complex influences in the environment that affect the organization's productivity. Consultants may advocate internal stratgegies to affect productivity, but they should also be aware of the effects of government regulations, market trends, taxes, capital investments, technologies, inflation, and competitors. Keith Davis adds a different dimension to the environment by saying that "a major cause of low productivity is that society does not provide a rewarding environment outside of the company for motivation within the company" (Davis, 1980, p. 27). Finally, Mackenzie offers the best observation about the role of the environment.

> An improved organization design will not, by itself, produce better results. But a poorly designed one can prevent them. The environment is always impinging on the organization and will cause change. And if management understands its organization and has an active program of continual maintenance, it can be opportunistic in how it responds to change. (Mackenzie, 1980, p. 53)

Principal among the environmental factors affecting productivity are the following five.

1. Energy Costs. From 1948 to 1973, wages in the U.S. rose faster than the cost of energy. This condition prompted greater capital investment into productivity producing equipment. However, in the mid-'70s, OPEC began to raise oil prices dramatically so that the price of energy and capital rose faster than the wage index. Businesses then began to substitute labor for new machinery and equipment (*Wall Street Journal,* Oct. 28, 1980). In the mid-'80s, there was a glut of oil on the world market, so that energy costs went down, and the inhibition to productivity of energy costs was eased. As dramatic as the energy costs affect productivity levels, there are other variables.

2. Capital Investment. Another cause for the productivity slowdown was thought to be inadequate investment in new, productive facilities. The Council of Economic Advisors indicate that a drop in the rate of capital investment may be responsible for the loss of half a percentage point a year in productivity growth. Older equipment, facilities, and processes simply cannot be competitive with the newest technological developments. Again, the federal government in the '80s enacted tax laws to promote individual savings and corporate investment.

3. Federal Regulations. Many exports pointed to the impact the federal government's roles had on productivity. For example, General Motors reported that compliance with governmental regulations had created over 26,000 jobs—i.e., jobs that did not increase output. Cost is a factor in computing productivity, and some economists estimated that the extra costs for all businesses to comply with federal regulations exceeds $100 billion a year (*Wall Street Journal,* Oct. 28, 1980). The Carter Administration added some legitimacy to this complaint by ordering an economic impact report for any new regulation. In an even bolder but more controversial move, the Reagan administration attacked federal regulation on a number of fronts.

4. Shift to Services. The conventional wisdom is that the U.S. economy is shifting from a manufacturing economy to a service economy. Productivity is hard to measure for teachers, bureaucrats, and secretaries, making it harder to increase the productivity levels, too.

5. Changing Labor Force. In the '70s, there was a major change in the labor force. Actions to hire more youth, women, and minorities increased recruiting and training costs — over $217 million, according to a survey of 48 companies. Furthermore, the Council of Economic Advisors indicated that these changes cost productivity growth .3% annually from 1973 to 1979 (*New York Times,* May 4, 1979).

Internal Resources

Dr. Herbert Striner, Dean of Business Administration at American University, put it in a different perspective. "Productivity is certainly an economic problem, but it is also a behavior modification problem." Adding further that "we have not been willing to understand the nature of all the factors which affect productivity and the necessity to develop policies to deal with these factors," (p. 6) he listed twelve critical factors:

1. Research & Development
2. Promotion of Innovation
3. Institutional Relationships & Values
4. Business Saving & Investment
5. Personal Saving & Investment
6. Natural Resource Development
7. Government
8. Worker Quality & Skills
9. Production Techniques & Systems
10. Management Technique & Philosophy
11. Performance Information
12. Knowledge Transfer

These factors, taken together, certainly insist on a contingency approach to productivity. All factors would have to be melded.

As managers searched for answers, they undoubtedly realized that there were many factors over which they had no control. Therefore, they began to look at factors such as 2, 8, 10, 11, and 12 — which they could control. The result was a furious thrust for managerial innovation, and communication became a prime target.

One factor that stood out was the underutilization of human potential in most organizations. Foltz (1981) points out that the bulk of the increases that have occurred were related primarily to work methods and procedures, and little resulted from improvements in worker effectiveness. Managers and theorists (Roscow, 1979; Tubbs & Widgery, 1978; Davis, 1980; Glaser, 1980) have suggested that major increases in production must come from improvements in worker effectiveness, since most organizations spend 70%–80% of their budgets on personnel costs. This emphasis has led communication scholars to become increasingly interested in exploring ways in which communication contributes to enhancing worker effectiveness, thus contributing to overall productivity.

ISSUES IN LINKING COMMUNICATION TO PRODUCTIVITY

Of the many critical issues involved in relating communication to productivity, we have elected to focus on the following: (a) definition of productivity, (b) relating performance to productivity, (c) measurement problems, (d) cause–effect relations, (e) differences in organizations and their outputs, (f) multiple goals, (g) time frames, (h) research designs.

Definitions of Productivity

Accustomed to the complaints that definitions of communication vary too much for efficient coordination of research findings (Dance, 1970), communication scholars often are surprised that definitions of productivity are not both quantifiable and standardized. Actually, definitions vary widely. Sibson (1976) notes that conceptions of productivity vary greatly from company to company. Scott (1977), Cameron (1978), and Hall (1977) explain that this variance is inevitable, given the variance in goals and functions of organizations. Downs and Hain (1981) also point out that different definitions of productivity are used within the same company — one for an individual, another for the individual's unit, a different one for a different unit, and still another for the entire plant. Therefore, a primary issue to be faced is a consistent definition of productivity. Some different approaches are identified below.

1. The ratio between input and output is the traditional definition. Basically a measure of the efficient use of resources, output per man hour is the measure used in most of the governmental statistics. It is also the measure used by the American Productivity Center to plot trends in American productivity. Despite its widespread use, this definition is limited. For example, Sutermeister (1976) also adds that quality must be considered along with the output per man hour.

2. Mackenzie (1980, p. 35) has proposed a measure of relative productivity, which is the degree to which the organization adjusts its operation to its environment. He gauges an organization's relative production on the basis of how well it meets four conditions: (a) the selection of goals and strategies in the given environment is adapted to it, (b) the selection of the Organizational Technology is the given environment is adapted to it, (c) the Organizational Technology is consistent with the choice of goals and strategies, and (d) the results produced by the organization in interaction with its environment are consistent with its goals and strategies. Therefore, this definition seems to judge productivity as the ratio between goals and results, with the environment factored in. Similarly, Steers (1977) thought the attainment of organizational goals should be the universal definition.

3. Profitability is another measure of productivity. In this case, the ratio = \$output/ \$input. It is generally stipulated, however, that one needs to be aware of the long-term as well as the short-term economic ramifications of productivity. Crandall and Wooton (1978, p. 37), for example, claim that "the use of efficiency-oriented productivity criteria may be an inappropriate means for an organization's long term growth."

4. Paul Mali (1978, p. 6) links effectiveness and efficiency to obtain a productivity index: "Productivity is the measure of how well resources are brought together in organizations and utilized for accomplishing a set of results. Productivity is reaching the highest level of performance with the least expenditure of resources."

$$\text{Productivity index} = \frac{\text{output obtained}}{\text{input extended}} = \frac{\text{performance achieved}}{\text{resources consumed}} = \frac{\text{effectiveness}}{\text{efficiency}}$$

Mali also adds other ratios which can be used as productivity measures (Mali, p. 84):

> objective ratios — measures of achievements . . . related to the objectives that were
> planned.

cost ratios — measures of performance output related to corresponding costs.

work standards — measures of work units . . . achieved by individual work centers . . .
related to expected or normal standards.

time standard ratios — measures of performance output related to needed time.

total factor productivity = output/all inputs = output/labor + capital + resources + miscellaneous.

5. The variety in defining productivity can easily be demonstrated by examining the operational definitions used in several studies which have focused primarily on communication.

1. Efficiency (Tubbs & Hain, 1979)
2. Product quality (Tubbs & Hain, 1979)
3. Number of grievances (Tubbs & Hain, 1979)
4. Global individual performance rating by supervisor (Hatfield, 1981; Bednar, 1981; Clampitt, 1983; Lewis, Cummings, & Long, 1981).
5. Percent of standard (Hatfield et al., 1981)
6. Quality of work (Huseman, 1979)
7. Quantity of work (Huseman, 1979)
8. How well company meets customer needs (Day, 1981)
9. Self-perceptions of productivity (Downs, 1977; Laird, 1982; Clampitt, 1983)
10. Production of correct decision by groups (Downs & Pickett, 1977)
11. Global ratings of a work group's (Clampitt, 1983; Laird, 1982)
12. Productive action (Laird, 1982)
13. Employees' ratings of supervisor (Laird, 1982; Clampitt, 1983)
14. How well tasks are completed in light of unit costs, quality of output and quality control (Cohen, Fink, Gadon, & Willets, 1976)
15. Number of errors (Jenkins, 1983)
16. Project success (Ebadi & Utterback, 1984)
17. Turnover (Huseman, 1979)
18. Absenteeism (Tubbs & Hain, 1979)
19. Sum across three measure (Mott, 1972)

All of the definitions are quantifiable, but they are not all output in the structured organizational sense. Furthermore, having so many different definitions of productivity makes integration of the results of the studies difficult.

Relating Performance to Productivity

The fact that outputs are so hard to measure for some jobs has led to the use of performance as a measure of productivity. In a sense, this has become a new definition for productivity. In the strictest sense, performance is not output. It is a means to an end, not the end in itself. Nevertheless, people assume that improved organizational behavior brings better productivity. For example, Likert states, in a study of a governmental agency, that, "The improvement in the leadership and organization climate variables can therefore be expected to result in corresponding improvements in motivation, communication, team work, the functioning of the work groups" (Likert, 1979, p. 143). Whether or not the assumption is correct, linking performance with productivity has become standard practice; and indeed, it may be necessary, since it may be virtually impossible to assess a given individual's contribution to the ultimate productivity of a complex organization.

Performance, too, has measurement problems. There is a real question of what to evalute. Many people look for quantifiable indices. Huseman, Hatfield, Boulton, and Gatewood (1980, p. 182) used absenteeism and turnover along with quantity and quality of output as performance measures. Mali (1978, p. 99) advocates use of "productivity checklist indicators"; these are actions that experienced practitioners agree would lead to productivity. The actions for a motor maintenance worker would include such things as hecking voltage, noise, proper brush setting, etc. The actions for a mental health worker would be more abstract, such as setting an example of the behavior wanted, giving children choices, and helping children to try. Productivity is then measured as Indicators achieved/ Total indicators.

Frequently, however, the performance measures are still more general. Downs and Moscinski (1979, p. 6) surveyed large corporations and found the following factors to be most frequently evaluated (see Figure 2).

Measurement

Most of the definitions above refer to some form of input and output. These definitions are most suitable to industrial manufacturers, because the number of products coming off an assembly line can easily be counted. However, all work does not produce products. The U.S. is moving from a predominantly industrialized economy to one where service is rivaling industry, and the number of white-collar workers now outnumber blue collar workers (Mali, 1978, p. 168). Therefore, a measurement problem arises when one tries to measure the output of schools, hospitals, supervisors, postmen, or flight attendants. Grayson, head of the American Productivity Center, also claims that "it's hard to measure capital input, and it's also hard to measure the quality of labor" (Cook & Jackson, 1980, p. 5). Gregerman (1981) pinpoints an inherent problem of assessing the productivity of knowledge workers on the same scales intended for production workers. What is the "product" of

Factor	Number of Companies	Percentage
Quality of Work	55	93.2%
Quantity of Work	51	86.4%
Job Knowledge	43	72.9%
Interpersonal Communication Skills	37	62.7%
Organization and Planning	37	62.7%
Leadership Ability	36	61.0%
Goal Setting	33	55.9%
Judgment	33	55.9%
Potential for Development	31	52.5%
Teamwork	30	50.8%
Innovation	27	45.8%
Motivation	24	40.7%
Personality Characteristics	14	23.7%

The factors in this list are desirable behaviors, and people still *assume* that they will lead to productivity at both the individual and organizational levels.

Figure 2. Performance factors that are evaluated

a knowledge worker? The problems in measurement provide a tremendous conceptual challenge for communication scholars.

As organizations grow more complex, their productivity becomes multivariate. Productivity depends on contingencies of things like employee performance, technological development, availability of raw materials, and organizational design. Therefore, one cannot assume that a positive correlation always exists between any two items. Furthermore, locating the degree to which any new process or development in an organization leads to greater productivity is difficult; indeed, inputing cause at all is becoming more suspect. Yet, when one suggests a link between communication (input) and productivity (output), it is difficult to think in terms of causal relations.

One reason for this perhaps is that "communication has been operationalized in such diverse ways that making sense out of the overall relationship is impossible" (Huseman et al., 1979, p. 178). Messages, structure, relationships, skills, individual filtering processes, and media are all appropriate communication phenomena for study, but each is a piece of the overall process. Therefore our studies have necessarily been piecemeal attempts to undertstand productivity. Second, there is conflicting evidence. In some cases, studies seem to indicate that communication leads to improved productivity (see Hatfield et al., 1981). In other cases, high productivity seems to lead to better communication (see Benford, 1981). Third, most studies linking communication to productivity center on correlations as an indication of probable cause. Yet correlations do not prove causation, and high correlations may simply reflect that communication and productivity are both influenced by similar, other variables.

Differences in Organizations

Organizations have major differences; they do not operate exactly alike; they follow different communication rules (Laird, 1982); the job designs are different (Clampitt, 1983). These are reasons why studying productivity of organizations is difficult. This section will explore two major differences among organizations.

First, they differ in their focus, products, and goal. Service organizations, retail stores, volunteer agencies, and industrial organizations cannot be organized alike and cannot have their productivity gauged exactly alike. Recently, a number of studies have explored these differences in detail (Clampitt, 1983; Laird, 1982). Since the economy is becoming more service oriented, more attention is being paid to the fact that the output from the service to the client is far from undimensional, too.

Second, they differ in stages of development. Greiner (1972)) was one of the first to demonstrate that organizations go through predictable growth stages. As each stage develops, problems arise which must be corrected, and the correction leads to a new stage. Crandall and Wooton (1978, p. 43) suggest that different productivity problems, productivity measurement, and productivity strategies are appropriate at the different stages of growth. Therefore, the growth stage of the organization must be considered in any evaluation of its productivity. Insisting on the needs for new perspectives on productivity, they claim that "a developmental concept of productivity is an appropriate theory for organizations in a turbulent environment" (p. 46).

Multiple Goals

A list of performance criteria for jobs suggests that the productivity of individuals may need a multiplicity of performance goals or objectives by which they will be judged. Similarly, the organization's productivity is often evaluated in terms of a multiplicity of goals (Huseman et al., 1979). Some are contradictory, and others may be unstated. Nevertheless, the outputs can be evaluated in many ways. For example, Mackenzie (1980, p. 22) reports that there are 42 ratios used to judge savings and loan associations. Many are financial measures, such as profits, assets, and return on investments; others are performance measures, such as market price and growth rate; still others are indirect measures, like community respect and well being of its employees. The researcher now has the task of relating many organizational processes to any of several organizational outputs. Whether or not the organization is judged "productive" depends on which goal is used. It is difficult to accomplish all goals to be judged equally productive.

Time Frame

Another problem is analyzing the relation between communication and productivity centers in the limited time frame in which research is most often conducted. Research incentives contribute to this short-run perspective, as theses and dissertations must be completed in a limited time. Academic researchers are rewarded for number of publications, not always for quality, and thus there is great incentive to perform a larger number of short-term studies rather than to conduct longitudinal studies. This short-term orientation of much research creates special difficulties in studying the relationship of communication and productivity. Too often, studies of the effects of communication are measured only immediately following the intervention. Little data exists concerning the long-term effects of communication in producing change in productivity in organizations. In fact, there are real difficulties, since productivity is by definition a long-term process, whereas communication is a more instantaneous process.

Research Design

The design of the studies of the productivity–communication link are important, because differences in design yield different kinds of results. Much research is based on empirical case studies, experiments, and surveys. In general, most of the research has been based on functional-structural models of organizations which assume an independent existence of structures as forms. The actions of members of the organizations are then seen as enactments of those structures. Communication is defined by structural characteristics, such as networks and roles, and the functions that undergird them are then analyzed. Usually, no attempt is made to examine how each individual conceived of his or her role, nor to consider the synergistic relationship of role and actor. The structural functional approach makes sense for many research questions; on the other hand, it has certain limitations or blind spots: (a) it ignores the actor and individuality of meanings; (b) it looks at the amount of input and output, without considering the qualitative and individual nature of the relationship between communication and productivity; and (c) it cannot account for the role of context in meaning. For example, Laird (1982) reported that workers are determined "productive" in the context in which they are evaluated; and she found that manager's stopping by a subordinate's desk was judged productive and unproductive by the same employees, depending on whether they interpreted the context as a friendly greeting or as close supervision.

An alternative approach to investigating the productivity–communication link is a rules approach, such as the coordinated management of meaning. It considers how employees interpret meanings and appropriateness of actions through rules within a particular culture. It is an attempt to uncover the structuring processes that individuals use. For example, in finding out the constitution rules for productive action, the researcher could ask the employee to describe situations in which he or she has observed competent individuals, and then to describe the characteristics that made the person seem competent. Such an approach assumes that productivity is socially constructed, that this meaning of the term is contextually determined through communication. Laird (1982) and Barge (1984) used this approach with merit, to assess how employees themselves feel about productivity.

RESEARCH FINDINGS

Despite the fact that there has not been an exhaustive investigation of the impact of communication on productivity, there have been many studies to investigate aspects of the link. In this section, we give an overview of (a) Generally Perceived Links, (b) Organizational Links, (c) Work Unit Links, (d) Supervisor-Subordinate Links and (e) Individual Links.

GENERALLY PERCEIVED LINKS

There is a powerful intuitive link between communication and productivity. Since communication constitutes a major portion of the activities of managers, it is natural to assume that this activity influences the outcomes of the organization. Sutermeister (1969) highlights 33 "people factors" that can affect productivity, and many of these involve communication either explicitly or implicitly.

This intuitive link is reinforced by experience. Tavernier (1980) claims that International Paper Company made significant productivity gains after developing a new corporate communication program that emphasized open channels. After Tubbs and Widgery (1978) implemented a communication program for a manufacturing plant, efficiency increased by 7%, absenteeism decreased, and production cost increased by $7 million. Schulhof (1979) and Glaser (1980) also report dramatic productivity increases after implementing a program of upward communication and participative management. Even though it is difficult to say objectively that communication was the primary cause of this, it is hard to ignore such strong evidence.

The intuitive link is also made by managers and employees who believe that communication is vital to their organizational productivity. Jacobs and Jillson (1974) found that executives in Fortune 500 companies referred to a lack of communication as an important cause for lagging productivity. In a similar survey by Judson (1982), 35% of the responding executives said that effective communication was a significant means for improving productivity, and 32% said that poor communication was a cause for declining productivity. Laird (1982) surveyed employees in a service organization and a manufacturing plant. In both organizations, employees noted that how well they communicate makes a very strong impact on how productive they are. Clampitt (1983) also explored how employees viewed the relationship between productivity and communication in a manufacturing and service organization. Again, employees in both companies felt that communication had a significant impact on levels of productivity for individuals and for their departments. The president of the manufacturing organization expressed the link in strong terms: "That's all I have to get the job done."

One of the unique advances of Clampitt's study over what had been done was his design to get respondents to differentiate among a number of communication variables about how much each variable affected both personal and unit productivity. The variables were the eight factors of the Communication Satisfaction Questionnaire (Downs & Hazen, 1977), and the results of his study are presented in Figure 3. It is noteworthy that all eight factors were perceived as influencing productivity significantly. Not only did the respondents indicate this on questionnaire scales, but they also talked in interviews about *how* each factor influenced productivity. This is a powerful demonstration of the perceived linkage between communication factors and productivity. Furthermore, some insight was gained as to how communication elements affect it differently. First, Personal Feedback and Communication With Subordinates were perceived to affect it more than the others. Second, in Company S., Communication Climate was perceived to have a significantly greater impact on personal productivity than on unit productivity ($p = .00$). The reverse patterns were found for Communication with Subordinates ($p = .03$), Media Quality ($p = .03$), and Communication with Coworkers ($p = .00$).

ORGANIZATIONAL LINKS

Case Studies

The principal means of investigating the productivity–communication link at the system-wide level has been the case study of a particular communication program. A synthesis of case studies provide consistent evidence that introduction of an improved communication vehicle has a significant bearing on organizational productivity. The vehicles which have shown most gains are associates with job enrichment, participative management, open corporate channels, and quality circles. Several of these case studies are described below.

Participative Management

Glaser (1980) investigated the results of a program of increased worker participation and upward communication. In pre-post analysis, the two key corporate indicators of a volume of production and profitability showed dramatic productivity increases after introduction of the program. Rosenberg and Rosenstein (1980) also found that implementation of participative management in a firm led to sound profitability and production levels.

| | Company M | | Company S | |
Factor	Personal Productivity	Unit Productivity	Personal Productivity	Unit Productivity
Subordinate Communication	1	1	3	1
Personal Feedback	2	2	1	2
Communication Climate	3	3	2	3
Communication with Supervisor	4	6	4	5
Organizational Integration Messages	5	4	5	7
Communication with Coworkers	6	5	8	4
Media Quality	7	7	7	6
Corporate Information	8	8	6	8

Figure 3. Rank Order of Perceived Impact of Communication Factors on Productivity

Corporate Communication

After International Paper Company began a new program of corporate communication emphasizing open channels, the company recorded significant productivity gains (Tavernier, 1980). Tubbs and Widgery (1978) investigated the impact of a new communication program in divisions of General Motors. After the program was implemented, productivity increased .7%, absenteeism declined, and managerial relations with employees improved. It was estimated that these gains saved $7 million in production costs.

Job Enrichment

Orpen (1979) traced how a job enrichment program increased employee satisfaction, job motivation, and performance ratings by supervisor. Yamada, Kitajima, and Imaeda (1980) investigated the introduction of a fashion model of employee development. The program of job enrichment developed work procedures based on human and organizational needs. For example, employees were allowed to stop the production line when they noticed defects; formerly, they had been powerless in this situation. As a result, productivity increased.

Communication Effectiveness Scores

In one of the most comprehensive analyses of system-wide communication and productivity, Tubbs and Hain (1979) summarized eight field studies in which they had investigated the relationship between communication and organizational effectiveness. The departments which had the best ratings on grievances, absenteeism, and efficiency also had the highest scores for effective communication. In another study of 2,000 employees over a 5-year period, they concluded that "organizational performance is directly influenced by employee performance and . . . performance is directly influenced by management communication behaviors" (p. 4). Again, the more productive plants also had the highest ratings on communication effectiveness.

The case study approach is an interesting one that has promoted an understanding of the workings of communication somewhat. But since they have been focused on specific programs only, the results are a *perceived* understanding of how communication affects productivity in a larger sense. There is also the question of how generalizable the results are.

Networks

In the total organization, communication structure impacts productivity in significant ways of particular interest here on the analysis of (a) networks and (b) structural innovations in the organization (see Figure 4).

Communication Roles in Networks

During the 1940s–1950s, there was a proliferation of investigations of how individuals operated in different communication networks. Typically, these were small experimental groups of 4–5 members, and the design investigated the impact of the structured network on speed, number of mistakes, quality of decision making, and amount of distortion. All of these outcomes can be related productivity (Hawkins, 1980).

	SPEED OF DECISION	SATISFACTION	QUALITY OF DECISION	OVERLOAD	DISTORTION
 STAR	SLOW	HIGH	HIGH	MED	LOW
 WHEEL	FAST	Lo On Outside Hi On Inside	Dependent on Leader	HIGH	MED
 LINE	Slow in Making Fast in Implementation	Higher as you go up	Dependent on Leader	MED	HIGH
 COM-CON	Dependent on Situation	HIGH	HIGH	MED	MED-LO

Figure 4. Network Variables

The investigations were popular for a time, but then researchers graduated to actual organizations. A myriad of networks could be examined: the grapevine, informal communication networks, information networks, authority networks, expertise networks, task networks, and innovation networks; sophisticated macroanalytic procedures were developed to plot a matrix for any communication function. Farace, Monge, and Russell (1977) were among those to investigate the individual roles in the network, such as bridges, biases, and isolates. The communicative characteristics of the liaison individually were particularly important to productivity. In their investigations of networks and performance, Schuler and Blank (1976) and Roberts and O'Reilly (1979) found that individuals who participated in more central roles in communication networks were perceived as being more productive. More specifically, Roberts and O'Reilly concluded that (a) people who pass information more openly are more likely to be rated as high performers; (b) overload, redundancy, and gatekeeping are more characteristic of low performers; and (c) the level of activity in communication networks is greater for high performers than for isolates. In their study, isolates were those who withheld information and relied on telephone or written communication (Hellwig & Phillips, 1980). Lewis, Cummings, and Long (1982) discovered that organizational members who occupied more roles were perceived as being more productive.

The research at this time does not allow a prescription that one type of network or role will lead to productivity, and several of the studies still deal only with perceptions of productivity. Nevertheless, it is likely that one can use network and role analyses to discover communication blockages that can be assumed to inhibit productivity.

Structural Innovations

Two important structural innovations to be considered here are (a) team building and (b) quality circles. Both are forms of participative management which circumvent the normal hierarchy, and both have tremendous implications for changing communication in the organization.

Teams. There are many approaches to team-building which are essentially training devices that have no real structural component. T-groups, for example, were often designed to improve one's ability to work with others, but the structure did not change. However, one form of the team concept is structural in nature. Downs, Hummert, Russell, and Strippoli (1984) examined a plant that operates entirely on the team concept. All workers are divided into teams, based on the work they do and their geography. Unlike quality circles, where employees volunteer, working together as a team is a part of the job, and the responsibilities include hiring new employees for that team, disciplining deviant behavior, determining promotions on the basis of peer evaluation, training one another, deciding who to lay off in slowdowns, and solving whatever problems arise. In other words, the teams take over some of the typical supervisory functions. Over a 6-year period, production and profitability have been high, and the managers attribute their growth to the team implementation that draws ingenious, creative, and responsible contributions from employees. The design of these semi-autonomous teams has been instrumental in maximizing communication as well as productivity, and the workers see a direct connection between the two. Obviously, such teams have not been universally successful in all organizations that have tried them, but, in this case, the contingencies have worked just right.

Quality Circles. No discussion of the impact of communication on productivity would be complete without reference to quality circles. They, too, are a form of structural innovation. Originally called "quality control circles," they are designed specifically to solve productivity problems and refine productivity processes, and this focal differentiate them from other approaches to participative management, made up of small volunteer groups of employees, they have received greater attention in the 1980s than any other particular management device because they are popularly reported to be one of the reasons why Japanese industry has become so productive. As American productivity suffered, thousands of managers flocked to Japan to see how they operated. Today, a number of major American companies have reported great success using quality circles. IBM has used them in production for many years, and has even tried to introduce them into the white collar arena. The Continental Group, General Motors, Ingersoll-Rand, and Honeywell attributed some of their productivity gains to quality circles. Reports of savings range from $70,000 to $3,000,000 (Downs & Hain, 1981).

In addition to the company testimonials, a number of conceptual papers have linked quality circles to organizational effectiveness (Nishiyama, 1981; Ramsing & Blair, 1982; Word, Hall & Azvumi, 1982). The major justification of them, however, appears in William Ouchi's *Theory Z* (1981). For him, the circle is not just a communication device, but is a major factor in a management philosophy.

Despite the popularity of quality circles and the theoretical claims for them, Cole (1980) and others have warned that they are not a miracle cure. Furthermore, there have not been many empirical investigations of their relationship to organizational outcomes. In her New Zealand field study, Stohl (1984) found that participation in quality circles had positive consequences for workers' perceptions of the communication climate, organizational identification, corporate knowledge, and job satisfaction. The nature of the study, however, did not explain *how* the circle members communicate among themselves to produce desirable outcomes. This may be very important, since several companies have described how quality circles become ritualized and lose their effectiveness in affecting productivity. In other words, holding membership in the circle is not important within itself, but the participation of the members in particular activities may be the key to affecting productivity.

When Jenkins and Shimada (1983) conducted a controlled field experiment in an electronic company, they found quality circle training impacted job performance specifically. Workers were found to commit, not only fewer errors, but also errors of a less serious nature. Stinnett and Perrill (1982) found relationship between quality circles and job satisfaction and productivity in a circuit board factory.

On the basis of an exhaustive investigation of quality circles in Honeywell, Mohrman, Ledford, and Lawler (1984) found that "participative teams had a small but significant impact" on product quality, productivity, organizational communication, and employee participation. There was a group, however, in each location which felt that the participative process was actually affecting the organization detrimentally. Current participants felt that the groups were more instrumental than those who had formerly participated in groups and those who had never participated. This suggests a Hawthorne effect may be operating. It is useful to underscore this in order to avoid the inclination to tie quality circles to productivity in unrealistic ways.

WORK UNIT LINKS

Every organization is made up of many work units. The success of these units naturally affects the overall productivity of the organization. In this section, we will explore two primary units: (a) group relations and (b) supervisory and subordinate communication.

Group Relations

Communication among coworkers affects both the productivity of the unit and the organization. Not only does this conclusion make intuitive sense, but it has been demonstrated by research. First, Clampitt (1983) found that coworkers perceive that communication impacts their productivity in important ways, and they should know what affects them. Second, several studies explore how groups affect productivity more explicitly. Hewitt, O'Brien, and Hornik (1974) experimented with students to investigate the influence on work organization of productivity. Coaching and coordination groups were more productive than those requiring collaboration. Neither leadership style nor member compatibility accounted for very much of the variance. Using Schutz's FIRO-B scales to organize compatible and incompatible teams in an actual organization, Downs and Pickett (1977) found that compatibility and leadership variables affected productivity differentially, depending on the contingencies. For example, highly social compatible groups had the lowest levels of productivity. However, placing them under authoritarian leaders would enhance their productivity, but their satisfaction would go down.

Finally, there are the testimonials to how a lack of group communication blocks productivity. For example, we have worked with many managers who decry a lack of teamwork as one of the greatest inhibitors to productivity. One manager expressed his frustrations this way: "Management does not function as a team as well as we should. There is a desire, but little implementation. Production is against the Warehouse, which is against Maintenance. Our objectives and theirs are simply not the same, and we pay for it."

One aspect of style that seems to be tremendously important is receptivity to subordinate input. Part of the rationale for this stems from the general emphasis on involvement and participative management. More specifically, however, Downs and Conrad (1977) and Laird (1982) found that the best subordinates initiate communication. This will not happen if the supervisory style is not open to input.

SUPERVISOR–SUBORDINATE LINKS

The supervisor is structurally the most important communication link in the organization. Those people who have responsibility for directing the production process must necessarily be responsible for attaining organizational output goals. Therefore, supervisory communication has become one of the most important focal points for investigating productivity-communication linkages.

In this discussion, we shall review the research on (a) supervisory style and (b) communication behaviors of supervisors.

Supervisory Style

One would expect supervisory style to be related to productivity, because managerial styles are *defined* in part by the way they consider production. In Blake and Mouton's *Managerial Grid* (1962), for example, the ideal management style is one which has a high concern for both people considerations and production. Reddin (1967) uses the same people and production continuum, but suggests that the effectiveness of any particular managerial style depends on the situation. Peters and Waterman, in the best-selling book *In Search of Excellence* (1982), also suggest that there are certain aspects of style which excellent managers have in common. These various approaches have helped identify some critical issues for research, and some of the research findings are summarized below.

Bednar (1981) discovered a positive relationship between communication style and managerial performance. Subordinates rated their managers on Norton's Communication Style Measure, and these data were analyzed in terms of the performance ratings of the managers by their own managers. The most notable finding was that the style associated with productive performance varied in the two organizations Bednar studied. In one, "openness" was the significant factor. In the other, the most effective styles included being animated and less contentious. Both Laird (1982) and Clampitt (1983) report similar findings that productive style varies across organizations and may be idiosyncratic to organizational cultures. This has some rather profound implications for those who train supervisors how to communicate effectively.

Supervisory Communicative Behaviors

Communication style is a rather vague, fuzzy concept as operationalized so far. Therefore, it is perhaps easier to relate specific communication behaviors to productivity than style. On the other hand, it is difficult to pinpoint one class of behaviors as causing greater productivity. In the following studies, however, the researchers have identified several behaviors which seem to be productive.

1. Task Orientation. Lewis et al. (1982) analyzed several organizations to explore the relationships among communication, worker motivation, and worker productivity. Using supervisory ratings to judge productivity, and House's paper and pencil tests to judge motivation, they discovered major differences in the communication associated with the most productive individuals. If the organizational emphasis was an extrinsic motivation, then task communication activity was of primary importance. If the emphasis was on intrinsic motivation, then personal communication activity was of primary importance.

2. Consistency. Hawkins and Penley (1978) explored the effects of supervisory and managerial communication on performance in two organizations. They discovered that supervisory communication was more critical than managerial, but that the consistency of communication from the different levels was important. When there was agreement between the messages of top management and the supervisor, expectancy played a significant role in predicting employee performance. When they did not reinforce one another, prediction fell off drastically.

3. Frequency. Jenkins (1977) found a significant correlation between the frequency and amount of formal communication with supervisors and the quality and quantity of work performed. However, Clampitt (1983) found that the desirability of frequent communication with the supervisor depended on the job design, and Stettler (1976) found that it varies with role expectations. Some people do not need, nor do they wish, frequent supervisory communication. On the other hand, in studies of textile manufacturing plants, better performance was generally related to more communication (Hatfield et al. 1981). Cederblom (1982) proposed that the contingencies affecting frequency of communication are not well known and need to be researched. While he was addressing the frequency of feedback primarily, the idea applies to all kinds of communication.

Finding that examples of effective communication behavior varied widely across two organizations, Laird (1982) nevertheless identified some communication behaviors that were linked to perceived productivity in both companies. These included: listening, asking questions, settling disagreements directly without third parties, and offering suggestions. Supervisory communication that led to supervisors being seen as productive included swift feedback, prioritizing work assignments, and requesting input. However, it is important to note that the two companies also disagreed on the rules for productive communication both for superiors and subordinates. Differences for superiors revolved around the amount of information communicated to subordinates, motivation of subordinates by extra work, and the closeness of supervision. Differences for subordinates focused on the revelation to policies and the necessity of staying "busy."

Finally, the importance of communication behavior was identified by Clampitt (1983). Subordinators' perceptions of the productive level of their supervisors were positively related to their perceptions of the supervisor's communication behavior.

INDIVIDUAL LINKS

There are many things which affect the productivity level of any individual in an organization. However, generalizations across individual have not been very productive. Investigations of demographic differences have not given much information, even though education, age, sex, and tenure have been analyzed in depth. In certain audits, for example, motivation and productivity sometimes lag for people in their 50s, but the trend has not been consistent across audits. Career stage is another variable which has been investigated, but operationalizations of this concept are still weak. Rather than look for individual differences as the key to understanding productivity, we have elected to examine some systemic feature that affects the individual. Some of these, like supervisory communication, have already been discussed. Therefore, this section focuses on three aspects of information: (a) task information, (b) feedback about performance, and (c) motivation.

Task-Related Information

Task Information is necessary for work to be successful. The ICA audit (Goldhaber & Rogers, 1979) has typically asked people whether or not they get enough information to do their jobs. If the response is negative, specific instances are explored. In three audits, involving reservations agents for an airline, operators for a telephone company, and press operators in a printing plant, we have notable incidents of people not getting necessary information on time. The result in each case was increased errors and down-time, both of which affected productivity of the individual. There is no more pointed way of relating communication directly to productivity, and being well informed should not be overlooked as an important variable. Additionally, the adequacy of training for some jobs is tremendously important. If the training is inadequate, productivity suffers. Clampitt (1983) concluded that task communication impacted on individual productivity in two important ways: (a) as the most basic as well as the most direct link to the task processes, and (b) as a tool to motivate them to work harder.

Feedback

In recent years, no message system has been investigated in more depth than performance feedback to individuals and groups. Job performance reviews have become formalized in most organizations, and the principal reason for this is the expectancy that performance will improve (Downs & Moscinski, 1979). The degree to which it actually leads to greater productivity still needs investigating. For example, O'Reilly and Anderson (1980) explored the relationship of feedback to performance with 100 managers. Feedback was measured by an 11-item questionnaire, and performance was measured by supervisory ratings. They discovered a strong correlation between feedback and satisfaction, but weak relationships between feedback and performance. They concluded that feedback may be more beneficial in affecting attitudes than in affecting performance.

On the other hand, Clampitt (1983) discovered that personal feedback was perceived by employees to have the most significant impact on productivity of all communication factors studied in two companies. In investigating why it had such impact, respondents focused on two reasons. First, they talked in terms of its effect on morale. Second, there was a heavy emphasis on the *motivational* aspects of feedback. Finally, Clampitt concluded that feedback impacted productivity scores in different ways for each company. Supervisory ratings of employee productivity were related to their perceptions of the impact of feedback on productivity. In the service company, the higher the individuals were rated in their productivity by their supervisors, the less they tended to feel that personal feedback impacted on their productivity.

Messages

Downs, Johnson, and Barge (1984) have published an extensive review of the literature on feedback, and they concluded that feedback does indeed affect both individual and group task performance. However, they concluded, "we are only now beginning to understanding the complexity inherent in the process of communication feedback with organizations" (p. 41). Figures 3 and 4 depict some of the variables examined; a brief overview follows.

Supervisory feedback exists along with feedback from peers, subordinates, clients, and self. The degree to which supervisory feedback is effective depends on the source credibility associated with the supervisor (Greller, 1975, Ilgen & Knowlton, 1980). In information polls during management training seminars, Downs has found it rare when a majority of the managers will rate the feedback from their own managers as being the most important feedback they get.

There is also a legitimate question of how the nature of the feedback message affects the receiver. The research has focused on three dimensions: (a) evaluation content, (b) level of performance, and (c) goals.

Variations in evaluative content have been studied elaborately (Nadler, 1979; Cusella, 1982; DeNisi, Randolph, & Blencoe, 1982); yet the appropriate mix of negative and positive content remains unknown. Nevertheless, a number of studies have focused on the influence of praise. Kim and Hamner (1976) report that it affects performance positively. Alexander and Camden (1981) linked praise to increased job satisfaction and good superior-subordinate relations. They proposed that this would lead to greater productivity, but their conclusion is based on theoretical assumptions, not empirical data from the study. The importance of recognition, a form of praise, can also be documented from a number of communication audits, when people insist that they do not get enough recognition and are, therefore, not motivated to do more. It is unlikely that a formula can ever be developed because of individual differences. Nevertheless, we can conclude that, in general, there is a motivational aspect to positive feedback.

The other content variable messages focusing on goals and goal-setting has long been advocated as a means of increasing performance. Management by Objectives has become the most common approach to appraisals. And feedback, in combination with goals, has a significant effect upon performance (Locke et al., 1983; Kim & Hamner, 1976). Nemeroff and Cosentino (1979) found that goal-setting combined with feedback was superior to either no feedback or just feedback. The conclusion that can be drawn at this point is that goal-setting has a positive interaction with feedback in promoting performance, depending on (a) their origin, (b) their level, and (c) the possibility of attainment.

Whether or not feedback influences performance depends on the receiver, and the research points out that individual differences in motivation and self-esteem are particularly crucial. High achievers respond better to negative feedback than do low achievers, and Dossett, Latham, and Mitchell (1979) conducted one of the studies which showed that those high in self-esteem who received feedback after participating in goal setting out-produced those with low self-esteem under the same condition. In addition to motivation and self-esteem, several researchers have found significant influences among the other demographic data. Clampitt (1983) found that moderate performers in a manufacturing plant were less affected by feedback than either high or low performers. Hatfield et al. (1981) found that there was a stronger relationship between communication and performance for the younger, better educated employees. Schuler and Blank (1976) found that hierarchical level significantly moderated the relationship between communication and productivity. Penley and Hawkins (1979) found significant differences among Anglos and Mexican-Americans. While demographic differences are interesting, this data merely points out the necessity of being receiver oriented in communicating. On the other hand, none of these studies are inclusive enough to make real generalizations to entire populations. Finally, our society is so dynamic that things change rapidly. The moment a significant demographic difference is identified, the more exposure may activate forces to change it.

The relationship between communication and productivity may be mediated by other variables. A number of writers have argued that the relationship between communication is complex rather than a simple linear relation. Hawkins and Penley (1978) found that communication behaviors were related to perception of expectancy which were related to motivation, according to the Vroom model. Supervisors could affect subordinates' performance by motivating them though communication. They used their studies as a preliminary causal model, suggesting that motivation intervenes between communication and the outcomes.

$$\text{Superivision} \rightarrow \text{Communication} \rightarrow \text{Motivation} \rightarrow \text{Performance}$$

Huseman et al. (1980) hypothesized that the communication–performance linkage is moderated by individual characteristics, job characteristics, and organizational characteristics. An individual may be differentially affected by communication depending on his or her own personality and interpersonal needs, or by the nature of the job and interaction with others (see Figure 4). This was certainly demonstrated in the discussion of feedback.

ISSUES TO BE RESOLVED

As this survey of research has indicated, there are aspects of the communication productivity link to be investigated. In Figure 5, we have grouped some of the research in a general communication schematic. There are many categories which have little explanation.

1. General matrixes of the communication–productivity link will be helpful. The following were developed and tested by Huseman et al. (1980) (see Figures 6 and 7). They isolate message types, communication formats, and interaction participants as the communication components. Quantity of output is measured by a percent of standard. Since many of their samples were on the piece-rate system, this was an easy measure to obtain. Quality of output (as well as quantity) was measured by a global performance rating given by an individual's supervisor. Finally, absentee and turnover rates were easily obtainable and were used as measures of performance. This framework is in its early stages, and is "intended to enhance both research and theory development in organizational communication" (Huseman et al., 1980, p. 181). It might be criticized for its narrow view of communication; on the other hand, if it were to lead to a fuller understanding of the role of messages on productivity, it would make a major contribution.

Huseman et al. used this model as the basis for research on the hourly employee in five

A. Source Variables
    1. Type: Self, Boss, Subordinates, Peers, Friends, Clients
    2. Attributional influences by sources
    3. Source Credibility
B. Message Variables
    1. Evaluation Content
    2. Level of Performance
    3. Goals
C. Receiver Variables
    1. Level of motivation
    2. Self-esteem
D. Informational patterns
    1. Frequency and Timing
    2. Comparison of group and individual focus

Figure 5. Feedback

Communication Variables	Production Levels		
	Individual	Work Unit	Organization
Source	Style/Skills Training		Management Supervisors
Message	Task Information Praise Feedback Initiative of Subordinate	Feedback	Direction Innovative Suggestion
Channel	Oral vs. Written	Oral vs. Written	TEAMS Quality Circle
Receiver Characteristics	Motivation Receptivity to Feedback Interpersonal Compatibilities		
Content	Roles	Type of Group Interaction Interaction Group Compatibility Structure	Rules and Roles Structure/Network Job Design
Specific Communication Behavior	Task Orientation Consistency Frequency Two-Way Communication	Make suggestions	Make suggestions

Figure 6. Summary of Communication and Productivity Research

manufacturing plants. In their preliminary study of the first plant, they concluded that "a sizeable proportion of productivity variability can be accounted for by communication behaviors and to a larger extent by these than by some individual variables frequently identified as being related to productivity" (p. 14). However, after the full study gave mixed results, they concluded that "it is unlikely that a uniform set of message types would predict to performance across all tasks, organizations, and individual workers" (p. 181).

The technology now exists for a more comprehensive examination of productivity links to communication.

More than 100 instruments have been designed to audit some aspects of communication. Some of these could be used in combination to assess communication practices generally. The ICA Communication audit (Goldhaber & Rogers, 1979) procedure is a good example of how this could be done, since it was comprised of questionnaires, interviews, observations, critical incidents, and diaries. It was designed to give a comprehensive view of the organization's messages, media, relationships, structure, and outcomes. Much of the data from the audit is perceptual, and it should be pointed out that (a) the data is more likely to give a sense of satisfaction levels than productivity levels, and (b) no standards exist in the same sense as in a financial audit. One of the best attempts at compiling standards has been Goldhaber's keeping of a data bank across audits. Since the ICA audit limits itself to examining communication processes, it can be combined with other tools to study productivity.

One possibility is the productivity audit designed by Mali to monitor "whether functional units, programs, and the organization itself are utilizing their resources effectively and efficiently to accomplish objectives (1978, p. 132). Finances, personnel, equipment, space, time, and procedures are evaluated against standards of productivity. Some of these

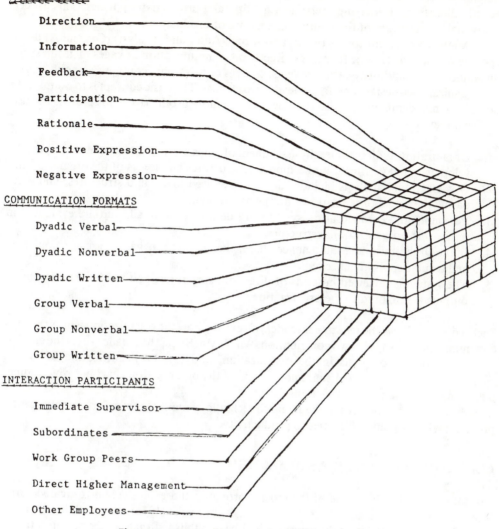

MESSAGE TYPES

    Direction

    Information

    Feedback

    Participation

    Rationale

    Positive Expression

    Negative Expression

COMMUNICATION FORMATS

    Dyadic Verbal

    Dyadic Nonverbal

    Dyadic Written

    Group Verbal

    Group Nonverbal

    Group Written

INTERACTION PARTICIPANTS

    Immediate Supervisor

    Subordinates

    Work Group Peers

    Direct Higher Management

    Other Employees

Figure 7. Matrix of Communication Components

| COMMUNICATION | MODERN VARIABLES | | | PERFORMANCE |
	Individual	Work Group	Organization	
Message types	Education	Task Characteristics	Organization Size	Quantity of Work
Communication Formats	Time in Job	Group Composition	Organization Structure	Quality of Output
Interaction	Time with Company	Group Size	Formal Reward Systems	Absences
	Age	Group Attraction	Rate of Internal	Turnover

Figure 8. The Communication–Performance Model

standards include productivity actions, resource accountability, performance standards, benefit allocations, leadership, personnel quality, and productivity policies. This list certainly makes one aware of the multivariate nature of productivity.

Another important tool is the organizational Audit and Analysis (OA and A) developed by MacKenzie (1980). It focuses directly on communication linkages in group structures, job design, authority-task problems, degrees of heirarchy, contiguity among processes, organizational design, and forces leading to change. The basic concept is to examine the organization in depth and then to re-design it to be more productive. This process consists of five phases.

1. Organization audit includes the assessment of goals and organizational design, the development and verification of a model of structures and logics of the organization.
2. Organizational analysis includes designing desired logics and structures, and comparing the actual organization with the new design.
3. Personnel and compensation systems are described in detail, and are evaluated in terms of the organizational structure.
4. In the Organizational Maintenance phase, changes in the organization are monitored and trouble spots are checked.
5. The system is reviewed in terms of direction, structures, and results. The results or outputs are tailored to the organization.

Such a process allows the researcher to identify exactly how the organization works through communication linkages. Two contributions which MacKenzie has made are (a) the emphasis on congruency of goals in the organization, and (b) the identification of virtual positions—i.e., positions which are not shown on the organization chart but which someone occupies because of the functions.

In summary, advances in the research technology make it easier for communication professionals to examine their ties to productivity.

COMMUNICATION AND JOB SATISFACTION

Job satisfaction has been one of the most thoroughly and extensively investigated variables in all the social sciences. Less than 10 years ago, Locke (1976) estimated that, at minimum, over 3,000 articles or dissertations had been published that related to job satisfaction. Prorating this average to present would indicate that, minimally, 5,000 articles have been published to date. Obviously, thoroughly reviewing all the literature of even the last 10 years would be overwhelming. Our purpose is less ambitious, although, hopefully, equally enlightening.

The object of this section is fourfold: (a) to describe the theoretical approaches to job satisfaction, (b) to examine the issues in linking communication to job satisfaction, (c) to examine the research findings, and (d) to discuss the implications of the job satisfaction—communication links.

THEORETICAL ORIENTATIONS

Any theoretical perspective implicitly or explicitly defines certain key terms, and these defintions necessarily alter both the conceptualization and measurement of the phenomena. The variable "job satisfaction" is no exception. Hence, the nuances of different theoretical perspectives are explained below.

Early theorists frequently conceived and measured job satisfaction as a single global factor. Employees were thought to react to the wide variety of work-related influences to form one general emotional response to "the job." Typically, job satisfaction was measured on a single scale in which employees rated their job on a continuum from "very dissatisfied" to "highly satisfied." Such approaches gave way to more precise conceptualizations and measurements.

Needs Theorists

Need theorists content that job satisfaction is the natural result of an employee's basic needs or motives being met (Maslow, 1943; Porter, 1962; Alderfer, 1972). Probably the most popular approach was introduced by Maslow (1943) and suggested five basic needs common to all people: physiological, security, social, ego, and self-actualization. These were arranged in a hierarchy which hypothetically implied that, as employees satisfied one level of needs on the job, new motivators were needed to induce job satisfaction. In short, job satisfaction became a multi-dimensional concept instead of a single unitary concept.

A related focal point of an extraordinary amount of research is Herzberg's (1966) two-factor theory. His basic contribution was the introduction of the notion that job satisfaction was a matter of two distinctly different types of factors: motivators and hygiene. Motivators included recognition, responsibility, and growth which could lead to job satisfaction, but not necessarily guarantee it. On the other hand, hygiene factors – like pay, benefits, and supervision – could guarantee job dissatisfaction if not properly maintained by the organization. Hence, there are two, not one, continua of measurement – one continuum dealing with satisfaction concerns the motivators, and one dealing with dissatisfaction concerns the hygiene factors.

Perceptual Theories

Another conceptualization of job satisfaction was introduced by a group of scholars that might be called the perceptual theorists (cf. Loucke, 1976). Their concern was not with universal motivators, or even demotivators. Rather they believed the key was how workers perceived or cognitively interpreted various aspects of the job. For instance, discrepancy theories argue that job satisfaction is the result of what employees *expect* to receive, versus what they actually do receive. What the employee "expects to receive" is ultimately determined by the employee.

In a related notion, Equity Theory (cf. Baron, 1983; Adams, 1965) with theoretical roots in Festinger's (1957) Dissonance Theory, maintains that, when employees perceive an inequity between inputs and outputs in organizational exchanges, the result is either satisfaction or dissatisfaction. While both these theories have some decidedly different viewpoints, they are similar in that the basis for the judgment of job satisfaction moves from the objective (i.e., universal), to the subjective (i.e., personal).

Work Satisfaction Theories

A more recent approach to job satisfaction is what might be called the "work satisfaction" school that proposes that job satisfaction is the result of doing useful, fulfilling, and meaningful work. Dissatisfaction obviously would result when the work does not achieve this objective. As a logical extension, emphasis is placed on "job enrichment."

Hackman and Oldman (1979) hypothesized that a job is motivating when the task involves skill variety, task identity, task significance, autonomy, and feedback. They suggest a method to calculate a "motivating potential score" (MPS) that should theoretically be related to both satisfaction and productivity:

$$MPS\ (\textit{skill variety}\ +\ \textit{task identity}\ +\ \textit{task significance})\ \times\ \text{Autonomy}\ \times\ \text{Feedback}$$

Pragmatic-Methodological Theories

Finally, there is what might be called the "pragmatic-methodological" school of thought on job satisfaction. It is pragmatic because they recognize the necessity of measuring job satisfaction in a multitude of organizations; it is methodological because the tools used to arrive at the dimensions of job satisfaction were primarily methodological instead of theoretical. Typically, the approach involves administering a large number of scales and then factor analyzing them into critical groups. These may or may not represent any real theoretical orientation, but do represent a set of items on scales that tend to be rated, not necessarily conceived of, similarly. One widely used instrument of this type is the Job Description Index (JDI), which consists of five critical factors of job satisfaction: supervision, work, pay, promotions, and coworkers (Smith, Kendall, & Hulin, 1969).

Observations

Some basic observations are in order. First, job satisfaction has a historical record of moving from a unitary to a multifactored phenomenon. However, the exact delineation of those factors varies from theorist to theorist. Hence, caution must be used in comparing results across studies.

Second, job satisfaction has been examined from two distinct theoretical perspectives. One perspective assumes a kind of universality in which researchers can assess the level of satisfaction on the basis of some comprehensive categories. Maslow's and Herzberg's theory obviously make these kind of assumptions. Yet, in effect, through a quest for interorganization comparisons, the pragmatic methodologists presume a type of universal set of categories around which employees can become satisfied or dissatisfied.

Another perspective on job satisfaction entails a more personal or subjective orientation, in which the emphasis is on how each individual uniquely determines what is satisfying and dissatisfying in the job. Such are the notions of equity theory and discrepancy theory. These two perspectives need not be at loggerheads, but the literature rarely reveals the difference or seeks to reconcile the positions. Communication scholars have dealt with such ideas before, and are in a unique position to make contributions to this debate. Finally, note how, within each approach to job satisfaction, communication is explicitly or implicitly an integral variable within the theory. To these issues we now turn.

"ISSUES" IN LINKING COMMUNICATION TO SATISFACTION

In order to understand the fundamental link between communication and job satisfaction, six basic issues need to be examined: (a) definition, (b) measurement, (c) conceptual purity, (d) cause versus correlation, (e) stability, and (f) influence of environment.

Definition

As a general rule, job satisfaction can be defined as "a pleasurable or positive emotional state resulting from the appraisal of one's job experiences" (Locke, 1976, p. 130). Yet, as the theoretical discussion above implies there are many variations on this general theme. For instance:

1. Is job satisfaction a simple global factor, or a multidimensional factor?
2. Is job satisfaction a product of some universal schemata, or is it a distinctly perceptual phenomena?
3. If job satisfaction is a multidimensional phenomena, then what are the key dimensions?

These are the kinds of questions for which scholars have a variety of answers. Consequently, there is no one precise definition of job satisfaction.

Nevertheless, there are some areas of agreement. First, job satisfaction deals primarily with affective or feeling states. The concern is with emotional reactions or evaluations to the job. Second, job satisfaction is exclusively used as an individualistic concept. That is, the major concern is with how an individual, as opposed to a group or company, reacts to the job. While the concept of productivity has been defined at both individual and group levels, job satisfaction has been defined at only the individual level. Third, the concept of job satisfaction has a central focal point. Evaluations must relate to some object or concern. In this case, the evaluation is related to the work, task, or job the employee does. The focal point of the concept of productivity is more ambiguous involving either individual productivity, group productivity, or company-wide productivity. Finally, job satisfaction is primarily an evaluation of the present or past feelings about the job (Locke, 1976).

Measurement

Inevitably, the definitional disagreements lead to differences in measurement techniques. The most common measurements of job satisfaction are paper and pencil tests, which include:

1. Job Description Index (Smith et al., 1969)
2. Single-Global Rating (Downs, 1977)
3. Need Satisfaction (Lofquist & Danis, 1969)
4. Difference scores between "what is" and "what should be" (Porter, 1961)
5. Motivating Potential Score (Hackman & Oldman, 1975)

Other major measures of job satisfaction include absenteeism levels, turnover, safety records, and health indices.

The problem with the wide variety of measures is that it is extremely difficult to synthesize results across studies when different measures are used. The different measures imply quite different notions of job satisfaction. Indeed, Wanous and Lawler (1972) tested nine different operational definitions of job satisfaction, and found that the measures were not empirically comparable. Hence, they conclude that "it appears quite likely that some of the conflicting results reported in studies of satisfaction are due to the different measures of job satisfaction that have been used" (p. 103).

Since a number of tributaries have led to different approaches to satisfaction, each of these approaches have ramifications for particular means of defining the concept. The nine different ways that job satisfaction has been operationalized are listed below.

1. Sum of job facet satisfaction $\quad$ JS = $\overset{\text{facets}}{\sum}$ JFS

2. Weighted sum of job facet satisfaction $\quad$ JS = $\overset{\text{facets}}{\sum}$ (Importance × JFS)

3. Sum of goal attainment or need fulfillment $\quad$ JS = $\overset{\text{facets}}{\sum}$ (Is Now)

4. Weighted sum of goal attainment $\quad$ JS = $\overset{\text{facets}}{\sum}$ (Importance × JFS)

5. Discrepancy between ideals and current characteristic $\quad$ JS = $\overset{\text{facets}}{\sum}$ (Should Be–Is Now)

6. Weighted discrepancy score $\quad$ JS = $\overset{\text{facets}}{\sum}$ [Importance × (Should Be–Is Now)]

7. Discrepancy between desire and current characteristics $\quad$ JS = $\overset{\text{facets}}{\sum}$ (Would Like–Is Now)

8. Weighted discrepancy scores $\quad$ JS = $\overset{\text{facets}}{\sum}$ [Importance × (Would Like–Is Now)]

9. Discrepancy between importance and current characteristics $\quad$ JS = $\overset{\text{facets}}{\sum}$ (Important–Is Now)

To these nine definitions can be added a tenth: a global measure in which people are merely asked to identify on a scale how satisfied they are.

Wanous and Lawler compared each definition empirically, and drew the following conclusions. First, there seems to be no best way to define it. But "this proliferation of different operational definitions . . . raises the very important construct validity questions . . . " (p. 95). In an unpublished study, Downs and Hazen, 1977, factor analyzed satisfaction items across the nine definitions and discovered that most factors were quite different across the definitions. Second, differences in the results of various research studies can probably be attributed to differences in definition. While we continue to write about satisfaction in a general way as if we know what is meant, the specific studies have vastly different orientations. Third, the definitions combine data from facet satisfaction in order to measure overall satisfaction. There are some problems in trying to add reactions to a number of work items in order to determine an ultimate satisfaction.

Conceptual Purity

Some controversy exists over whether the notions of job satisfaction and organizational climate can be distinguished. Johanesson (1973) and Guion (1973) have agreed that the concepts are redundant and overlapping. Muchinsky (1977) used three instruments to measure organizational communication, job satisfaction, and organizational climate. He found that some dimensions of organizational communication were strongly linked to both climate and satisfaction,. Yet others have conducted further research indicating that job satisfaction and organizational climate are, indeed, unique constructs that specify different variables of organizational effectiveness (Payne, 1973; Hellriegel and Slocum, 1974).

The critical distinction between the concepts is that climate is more descriptive while the satisfaction construct is more evaluative. Hence, climate is concerned with "what is" and satisfaction oriented to how employees "feel about what is." As Jablin (1980, p. 322) comments, "A major part of the problem in assessing the difference between satisfaction and climate is that researchers have combined evaluative and descriptive items in their questionnaires." Of course, the difficulty with clearly distinguishing between evaluative and descriptive items is that the subjects may not be able to make such fine distinctions. Nevertheless, the bulk of the research seems to suggest that, at least conceptually and to some extent operationally, the concepts of climate and satisfaction can be distinguished.

Cause Versus Correlation

Does effective communication cause job satisfaction? Or could job satisfaction induce effective communication? Clearly, these intriguing questions imply quite different relationships between the two variables. The difficulty is that most of the research cannot clearly determine the direction of the relationship, because of the use of correlational methods. For instance, Wheeless, Wheeless, and Howard (1984) found that communication satisfaction with the supervisor was related to job satisfaction. Yet this study, like others, cannot unequivocally state that one variable *causes* the other. Intuitively, it is appealing to communication scholars to say that communication causes job satisfaction, and that employees tend to perceive a similar direction in the relationship (Downs, 1977). Yet to make this argument with scientific certainty is still an elusive goal.

With so many variables affecting job satisfaction, it is difficult to say that certain forms of job communication cause job satisfaction. For example, one kind of information examined on ICA communication audits is "Pay and Benefits." It becomes readily apparent sometimes that, if one is not satisfied with one's pay, no amount of communication is likely to change that satisfaction level. In fact, the more communication about it, the more one is reminded how dissatisfied he or she really is. However, this is only one type of communication. Contrarily, Muchinsky (1977) discovered that people who have opportunties to initiate face-to-face interactions experience higher levels of job satisfaction. When one reads these conclusions, one is indeed tempted to say that communication *this way* did lead to satisfaction.

Stability

Typically, job satisfaction is measured only once during an individual research project. How much satisfaction fluctuates over a period of time? Does it stay relatively stable over the day, month, or year? Normally, the assumption is made that job satisfaction, while able to change, stays relatively stable over a period of time. Yet one critical event might alter satisfaction only temporarily, or could have lasting effects. In order to understand job satisfaction fully, researchers need to ascertain (a) if fluctuations do occur, and (b) if so, how significant the fluctuations actually are. Current methodologies based on "snap shots" really do not address this issue.

Influence of Environment

There is a viable question about the relationship between job satisfaction and general life satisfaction, family satisfaction, satisfaction with free time, and satisfaction with living conditions. It is readily apparent that one's work life cannot be entirely separated from the rest of one's life. In an interesting study of this connection, Near, Smith, Rice, and Hunt (1984) used regression analyses to determine how satisfactions with various areas of one's life are related. Among their findings was the "cross-domain spillover effect: working conditions influence nonwork satisfaction significantly, and living conditions are significantly related to job satisfaction" (p. 187). Such a finding makes it extremely difficult to discover exactly how job communication relates to job satisfaction.

Individual Differences

The form of output called satisfaction is quite different in kind from the output called productivity. Productivity generally is some measurable quantity of product that is the outcome of effort by an individual, work unit, or organization. Satisfaction, on the other hand, is purely an internal attribute of an individual. Therefore, individual differences abound which determine what does or does not satisfy. Furthermore, even unit or organizational satisfactions, labeled morale, are merely the aggregate data across individuals. And whatever communication strategies are based on such aggregations are also certain to miss many individuals.

LINKING COMMUNICATION TO JOB SATISFACTION

A number of specific studies have been conducted that explore the relationship between communication and job satisfaction. The four main focal points of the research have been (a) supervisory–subordinate relationship, (b) nonverbal settings, (c) communication satisfaction, and (d) auditing approaches. The finding of these studies are reviewed below.

Supervisory–Subordinate Relationship

Intuitively, the relationship between supervisor and subordinate would seem to be an extremely important factor in job satisfaction. Indeed, a number of studies have examined how communication impinges on that relationship. Richmond and McCroskey (1979) embarked on an intriguing series of studies that related managerial communication style (MCS) to job satisfaction. In one study involving public school teachers, they found that, as managers became more subordinate-centered and interactive, employee satisfaction was increased. Additionally, supervisory tolerance of disagreement and innovativeness was linked to job satisfaction. Replication of this study in other settings showed similar findings (Richmond, McCroskey, & Davis, 1982).

In another attempt to understand how supervisory–subordinate communication relates to job satisfaction, Hatfield and Huseman (1982) examined the congruencies between supervisors and subordinates. They found that, while *actual* congruence about the rules of communication between the supervisors and subordinates was an important predicator of job satisfaction, the *perception* of congruence may be more important. They assert "one implication is that, in terms of a subordinate's satisfaction, congruence between supervisor and subordinate may not be as important as the subordinate's own perception of factors affecting the superior-subordinate relationship" (p. 356). Hence the "myth" of congruence seems an extremely useful concept for further examination.

In a study with a different tack, Wheeless et al. (1984) explained a different kind of myth. Human relations theorists have often argued that allowing employees to get involved in the decision-making process should increase job satisfaction. Not so, according to this study of classified employees in an Eastern university. They did find that communication variables explained a substantial (.76) amount of the variance associated with job satisfaction. Yet "communication satisfaction with supervisor and supervisor receptivity in information were found to be more powerful predictors of job satisfaction than the decision participation variables" (p. 222).

Falcione, McCroskey, and Daly (1977) examined how job satisfaction related to communication apprehension, self-esteem, and perceptions of the immediate supervisor. Using a number of paper and pencil tests, the researchers determined that these variables did impact on job satisfaction. Based on their research, they speculate that "the supervisor's behaviors, particularly communication behaviors, might be expected to enhance or detract from subordinate satisfaction. However, it is also clear that certain employees—those with high oral communication apprehension and/or low self-esteem—are less likely to be satisfied with supervision regardless of the supervisor's behavior" (p. 373). Wippich (1983) used McCroskey's PRCA instrument to show a relationship between communication apprehension and job satisfaction. The implications of this research suggest a number of strategies for enhancing satisfaction, such as training supervisors to improve their communication skills or seeking to lower employee communication apprehension.

Nonverbal

Most studies have dealt with verbal communication instead of nonverbal aspects of the organization. This area of study, like some hidden orchard, has many potentially ripe and harvestable fruits. Sundstrom, Burt, and Kamp (1980) did venture into the garden, to discover that employees who had architectural and psychological privacy in their work spaces tended to be more satisfied. Much work still needs to be done.

Communication Satisfaction

The studies above have focused on specific communication variables. A series of studies have been done that deal with communication in much broader sense. The notion of communication satisfaction developed by Downs and Hazen (1976) involves eight dimensions of communication found in most organizations: Communication Climate; Supervisory Communication; Organizational Integration; Media Quality; Horizontal Communication; Corporate Perspective; Subordinate Communication; and Personal Feedback (Downs, 1977). An instrument has been developed that assesses employee satisfaction with these communication dimensions, as well as providing an alternative for employees to relate any other communicational concerns via open-ended questions.

The results of investigations using this instrument reveal a general trend in many organizations. Job satisfaction tends to correlate most with Communication Climate, Personal Feedback, and Supervisory Communication (Downs, 1977). One problem with the early studies using this instrument was that job satisfaction was measured as a single, unitary concept.

A number of theses and dissertations have employed the communication satisfaction instrument to analyze organizational communication. In general, these studies have been simple case studies. Avery's (1977) descriptive field study discovered a correlation between job satisfaction and communication satisfaction. More specifically, he found that job satisfaction was correlated with Horizontal Communication (.53), Subordinate Relations (.51), and Communication Climate (.51). In addition, he noted that the top level of the organizational hierarchy felt a higher degree of communication satisfaction. Thiry's (1977) examination of registered nurses in Kansas hospitals and clinics reveals that job satisfaction was most highly correlated with the Communication Climate, Personal Feedback, and the relationship with supervisors. She concluded that "in general, the more hierarchical and complex the organization, the less satisfied were the nurses" (p. 162).

A case study examination of five functional divisions of administration at a university revealed that most respondents were satisfied with Supervisory Communication and least satisfied with the Communication Climate (Gordon, 1979). Kio (1979) sought to describe Nigerian workers' attitudes about their jobs. The research revealed that job satisfaction was related most strongly to Supervisory Communication, Horizontal Communication, and Subordinate Communication.

Four researchers used the Communication Satisfaction Instrument as an investigative tool in the public school setting (Nicholson, 1980; Jones, 1981; Duke, 1981; Wippich, 1983). They all found significant relationships (at the .05 level) between job satisfaction and each of the communication factors. However, some factors were more strongly related than others. Specifically, Duke (1981) found job satisfaction most strongly correlated to the Communication Climate, Organizational Integration, and Horizontal Communication dimensions. Nicholson (1980) paralleled the Downs's (1977) findings, in that Communication Climate, Personal Feedback, and Supervisory Communication were most strongly correlated to job satisfaction. Both Jones (1981) and Wippich (1983) only highlighted two of these three factors as significant predictors of job satisfaction. For Jones, the important dimensions were Communication Climate and Feedback. In the Wippich (1983) research, the Supervisory Communication and Feedback dimensions were most significant.

Alum (1982) used the communication satisfaction instrument to investigate organizational communication practices in a Mexican social service company. He found that the current climate of economic uncertainty greatly affected the level of employee satisfaction and communication satisfaction. The crisis climate seemed to alter negatively communication practices at all levels of the organizations. In addition, he found that, with the exception of Subordinate Communication, all the factors correlated with job satisfaction. As in previous research, Personal Feedback, Supervisory Communication, and Communication Climate were most strongly related. Perhaps the most interesting finding was that the communication satisfaction factors were differentially related to job satisfaction and perceived productivity. Hence, communication that enhanced employee satisfaction would not necessarily increase perceived productivity.

A number of these researchers employed other instruments in conjunction with the Communication Satisfaction Questionnaire. Thiry (1977) also incorporated Porter's (1962) Need Fulfillment survey in her research, and found a highly significant interrelationship between the instruments. Gordon (1979) also used a portion of the ICA audit in her case study of university administrative staff. She notes how the two instruments could be used in tandem to develop organizational changes. A need satisfaction instrument and the Need Importance Index were the additional tools used in Kio's (1979) study. He found that the communication researchers have indicated that, in some ways, communication satisfaction is associated with need satisfaction or fulfillment, and communication apprehension. Yet little theoretical work has been done to detail the precise nature of that relationship.

The research uses of the Downs' Communication Satisfaction Survey to date have revealed the following basic findings: (a) Employees were most satisfied with Subordinate Communication and Supervisory Communication, while they were least satisfied with Personal Feedback. (b) Job satisfaction is related to a number of the communication satisfaction dimensions. The Communication Climate, Personal Feedback, and Supervisory Communication dimensions tend to be most strongly related to job satisfaction. (c) Communication satisfaction is related to the satisfaction and fulfillment of certain needs. (d) The communication satisfaction instrument is a useful tool in a wide variety of industries, cultures, and with various job classifications. Yet little theoretical work has been done to show if, how, and why there are differences between companies, cultures, and job types.

Auditing Approaches

Another broadly based approach involved examination of ICA data from the communication audit by Goldhaber, Yates, Porter, and Lesniak (1978). Using regression analyses, they concluded that "the best predictors of job satisfaction as an organization outcome are organizational communication relationships, amount of information received, and the age of the employee" (p. 91). A related analysis of Wiio's (1976, 1977) LTT data bank of 5,114 individuals revealed similar results, but it was also found that communication satisfaction tends to relate more to job satisfaction at higher levels of the organization.

Observations

Several observations appear to be in order. First, the evidence is fairly clear that communication is linked to job satisfaction. Every study outlined above found some sort of correlation between communication and job satisfaction. Thus, in a very basic way, organizational communication is related to job satisfaction.

Second, the communication between the supervisor and subordinate seems a particularly important predictor of job satisfaction. The Downs (1977), Thiry (1977), and Goldhaber et al. (1978) studies point to this in a general way. The Richmond and McCroskey (1979), Hatfield and Husemann (1982), and Wheeless, Wheeless, and Howard (1984) studies all point out more specific nuances of supervisory communication that are related to job satisfaction. For instance, improving supervisory communication skills by increasing tolerance for disagreement, encouraging innovation, and becoming more employee-centered could increase job satisfaction.

Third, most of the studies rely on correlational procedures to arrive at conclusions. Locke (1976) perceptively called this method "correlation with speculation." Yet the present studies do suggest some excellent starting points for further research using experimental designs. Perhaps didferent data gathering techniques like critical incidents, behavioral observations, and interviews could be useful as well.

Finally, even though the studies suggest correlational relationships, there is evidence that employees see communication as the causal agent. In particular, the Downs (1977) study revealed that employees believe that communication behaviors are causally linked to job satisfaction. Whether this perception can be verified is a matter of future research.

IMPLICATIONS

It is abundantly clear that communication does relate to job satisfaction. So what? There are really two ways to answer that question. First, it can be argued that job satisfaction is an important "end-product" of an organization. That is, it is one possible goal of an organization to produce satisfied employees. Hence, it is of importance to know how to induce satisfaction. A less altruistic way to answer the question is to assert that job satisfaction relates to other more critical, thus implicitly more useful, variables that relate to the "bottom line."

As indicated before, literally thousands of studies have been conducted on job satisfaction, and a great many have focused on these "bottom line" types of issues. Almost every literature review asserts that low levels of satisfaction results in higher absenteeism and turnover. These factors do effect the "bottom line." Additionally, job dissatisfaction has been shown to affect employee attitudes about life and family, physical health, and sometimes the length of life (Locke, 1976).

Nevertheless, job satisfaction may in and of itself be a legitimate end-goal. Clearly, much more could be done, particularly in the areas of nonverbal communication and comparisons across various organization settings.

In short, while some important steps have been made in understanding the relationship between communication and job satisfaction, many remain. As understanding grows about job satisfaction, so too must the communication research. Some of the other promising new areas include:

1. Recent research by Bateman and Organ (1983) has shown some relationship between job satisfaction and employee "citizenship" behaviors like helping coworkers, and keeping the work area clean. What role does communication play in this process?
2. Farrell (1983) suggested that, when employees are dissatisfied, they choose one of four responses: leave, talk to someone, loyally endure the situation, or become lazy and disruptive. What communication behaviors can managers use to encourage dissatisfied workers to invoke the more positive responses?
3. Recent work has been done that examines the relationship between job satisfaction and satisfaction with life in general (cf. Near et al., 1984). What role does the communication skill of an individual play in job satisfaction? Life satisfaction?

Study of these provocative issues can add to both a knowledge of satisfaction and communication.

Equally clear is the fact that job satisfaction cannot be shown to be linked to job performance or productivity. Schwab and Cummings (1970), in an extensive review of the literature on this subject, concluded that:

> We are frankly pessimistic about the value of additional satisfaction-performance theorizing at this time. The theoretically inclined might do better to work on a theory of satisfaction or a theory of performance. Such concepts are clearly complex enough to justify their own theories. Prematurely focusing on relationships between the two has probably helped obscure the fact that we know so little about the structures and determinants of each. (p. 429)

The implication for communication scholars is equally clear; it may be that communication strategies designed to increase satisfaction will not impact productivity, or may even lower it (Downs & Pickett, 1977). Increasingly, communication strategies may need to be designed to fulfill certain precise end-goals. Choices will need to be made that may not be all that pleasant. Instead of the objective being to "improve communication within the organization," practitioners will have to think in terms of "improving communication so that productivity will increase" *or* "improving communication in order to increase job satisfaction." Perhaps the opportunities are rare, and the choices few, when both objectives can be achieved through a single communication strategy.

One critical issue is the relationship among the end-products themselves. Intuitively, there may be some expected patterns that don't always work out empirically. One might assume, for example, that greater productivity will lead to greater profits; however, in fact, both farmers and OPEC have decreased production to drive the price up and increase profits. The relationship among satisfaction and productivity is a bit more complex. Perhaps as a holdover from the human relations movement, it is widely assumed that greater satisfaction leads to greater productivity. Some studies have even supported this

communication → satisfaction → productivity

relationship, but a general review of the literature challenges the credibility of that linkage. There have been some studies which discovered that people's productivity led to an increase in their satisfaction. Furthermore, an experiment by Downs and Pickett find that a strategy designed to increase satisfaction did in fact do so when reducing productivity, and, when strategies were developed to increase productivity, satisfaction ws lowered somewhat. On the other hand, there were certain contingencies which facilitated both satisfaction and production.

What can be concluded from this? Communication imparts the end-products of satisfaction and productivity in neither mutually exclusive nor highly correlated ways. The impact may be highly differentiated, depending on the particular communication strategy.

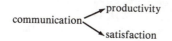

REFERENCES

Adams, J. S. (1965). Inequity in social exchange. In L. Berkowitz (Ed.), *Advances in experimental social psychology* (Vol. 2, pp. 267–299). New York: Academic Press.

Adkins, L. Getting a grip on white-collar productivity. *Dunn's Review, 114* (6), 120.

Alderfer, C. (1972). *Existence, relatedness, and growth: Human needs in organizational settings.* New York: The Free Press.

Alexander, A., & Camden, C. (1981, May). *Praise and organizational behavior.* Unpublished paper submitted to the International Communication Association.

Alum, C. V. (1982). *A case study of communication satisfaction in Nova Demonterrery.* Unpublished masters thesis, University of Kansas.

Avery, B. E. (1977). *The relationship between communication and job satisfaction in a government organization.* Unpublished masters thesis, University of Kansas.

Balmert, M. (1980). *Quality control circles.* Unpublished paper, Kansas University.

Barge, K. (1984). *Effective leadership and forms of conversation.* M.A. thesis, Kansas University.

Baron, R. A. (1983). *Behavior in organization: Understanding and managing the human side of work*. Boston, MA: Allyn & Bacon.

Bateman, T. S., & Organ, D. W. (1983). Job satisfaction and the good soldier: The relationship between affect and employee "citizenship." *Academy of Management Journal, 26,* (4), 587–595.

Baytos, L. M. (1979). Nine strategies for productivity improvement. *Personnel Journal, 58,* 450.

Bednar, D. A. (1981). *Relationships between communicator style and managerial performance in complex organizations.* Unpublished paper presented at the International Communication Association Convention.

Benford, R. J. (1981, May-June). Found: The key to excellent performance. *Personnel,* May-June, pp. 68–77.

Blake, R., & Mouton, J. (1962). *The managerial grid.* Houston, TX: Gulf Publishing Co.

Brower, B. (1980). *Productivity improvement: Alternative approaches.* Unpublished paper, Kansas University.

Burke, R., Weitzel, W., & Weir, T. (1978). Characteristics of effective employee performance review and development interviews. *Personnel Psychology, 31,* 903–919.

Cameron, K. (1978). Measuring organizational effectiveness in institutions of higher education. *Administrative Science Quarterly, 23,* 604–629.

Clampitt, P. (1983). *Communication and productivity.* Ph.D. dissertation, University of Kansas.

Cohen, A., Fink, S., Gadon, H., & Willets, R. (1976). *Effective behavior in organizations.* Homewood, IL: Richard D. Irwin, Inc.

Cole, R. (1980, August). Researcher cautions against seeing quality circles as a miracle cure. *Training,* p. 94.

Cook, M. C., & Jackson, G. (1980, September). On productivity improvement. *Training and Development Journal,* pp. 4–6.

Crandall, N. F., & Wooton, L. M. (1978). Developmental strategies of organizational productivity. *California Management Review, 21,* 37–46.

Crictiner, B. (1980). Productivity. *Nation's Business, 68(10),* 60–65.

Cummings, L. L. (1973). A field experimental study of the effects of two performance appraisal systems. *Personnel Psychology, 26,* 489–502.

Cusella, L. P. (1982). The effects of source expertise and feedback valence on intrinsic motivation. *Human Communication Research, 9(1),* 17–32.

Dance, F. E. X. (1970). The concept of communication. *Journal of Communication, 20,* 201–210.

Davis, K. (1980). Low productivity? Try improving the social environment. *Business Horizons, 23,* 27–28.

Day, C. R. (1981). Solving the mystery of productivity measurement. *Industry Week,* 61–66.

DeNisi, A. S., Randolph, W. A., & Blencoe, A. G. (1982). Level and source of feedback as determinants of feedback effectiveness. *Academy of Management Proceedings 1982,* 175–179.

Deutsch, C. (1980, June 9). Productivity: The difficulty of even defining the problem. *Business Week,* pp. 52–53.

Dossett, D. L., Latham, G. P., & Mitchell, T. R. (1979). Effects of assigned versus participatively set goals, knowledge of results, and individual differences on employee behavior when goal difficulty is held constant. *Journal of Applied Psychology, 64(3),* 291–298.

Downs, C. W. (1976, February). *Research methods.* Paper presented at the SCA/SWTSU Post Doctoral Program on Organizational Communication, San Marcos, Texas.

Downs, C., & Conrad, C. (1977). Effective subordinancy. *Journal of Business Communication, 18,* 28–37.

Downs, C. W., & Hain, T. (1981). Productivity and communication. In M. Burgoon (Ed.), *Communication yearbook 5.* International Communication Association. New Brunswick, NJ: Transaction Books.

Downs, C. W. (1977). The relationship between communication and job satisfaction in R. C. Huseman, C. M. Loque, & S. L. Freshley (Eds.), *Readings in interpersonal and organizational communication.* Boston, MA: Holbrook Press.

Downs, C. W., & Hazen, M. D. (1977). A factor analytic study of communication satisfaction. *Journal of Business Communication, 14* (3), 63–73.

Downs, C., Hummert, M. L., Russell, W., & Strippoli, G. (1984). *Case study of teams at TRW.* Unpublished manuscript, University of Kansas.

Downs, C., Johnson, K. M., & Barge, K. (1984). Communication feedback and task performance in organizations: A review of the literature. In H. Greenbaum et al. (Eds.), *Organizational Communication Abstracts, 9,* 13–47. Beverly Hills, CA: Sage Publications.

Downs, C. W., & Spohn, D. (1976, August). *A case study of an appraisal system in an airline.* Unpublished paper presented to the Academy of Management convention, Kansas City.

Downs, C. W., & Pickett, T. (1977). An analysis of the effect of nine leadership–group compatibility contingencies upon productivity and member satisfaction. *Communication Monographs, 44,* 220–230.

Downs, C. W., & Moscinski, P. (1979, August). *A survey of appraisal processes and training in large corporations.* Unpublished paper presented to the Academy of Management convention, Atlanta.

Duke, P. O. (1981). *Communication satisfaction of business education teachers in an urban school system.* Unpublished doctoral dissertation, Vanderbilt University.

Ebadi, Y. M., & Utterback, J. M. (1984). The effects of communication on echnological innovation. *Management Science, 30,* 572–585.

Falcione, R., McCroskey, J. L., & Daly, J. S. (1977). Job satisfaction as a function of employees' communication apprehension, self-esteem, and perceptions of their immediate supervisors. In B. Ruben (Ed.), *Communication yearbook 1,* New Brunswick, NJ: Transaction — International Communication Association.

Farace, R. V., Monge, P., & Russell, H. (1977). *Communicating and organizing.* Reading, MA: Addison-Wesley.

Farrell, D. (1983). Exit, voice, loyalty, and neglect as responses to job dissatisfaction: A multidimensional scaling study. *Academy of Management Journal, 26* (4), 596–607.

Festinger, L. (1957). *A theory of cognitive dissonance.* Evanston, IL: Row & Peterson.

Foltz, G., Jr. (1981, August). Productivity and communications. *Personnel Administrator,* p. 12.

Glaser, E. M. (1980, February). Productivity gains through worklife improvement. *Personnel,* pp. 71–77.

Goldhaber, G., & Rogers, D. P. (1979). *Auditing organizational communication systems: The ICA communication audit.* Dubuque, IA: Kendall/Hunt Publishing Company.

Goldhaber, G., Yates, M., Porter, T., & Lesniak, R. (1978). Organizational communication: 1978. *Human Communication Research, 5* (1), 76–96.

Goodnight, G. T., Crary, D. R., Balthrop, V. W., & Hazen, M. (1974, April). *The relationship between communication satisfaction and productivity, role discrepancy, and need level.* Paper presented at the International Communication Association convention, New Orleans.

Gordon, H. (1979). *Communication analysis of administrators in an academic organization.* Unpublished masters thesis, University of Kansas.

Gregerman, I. B. (1981). Knowledge worker productivity measurement through the nominal group technique. *Industrial Management, 23,* 5–8.

Greiner, L. E. (1972, July-August). Evolution and revolution as organizations grow. *Harvard Business Review,* pp. 37–46.

Greller, M. M. (1975). Subordinate participation and reaction to the appraisal interview. *Journal of Applied Psychology, 60,* 544–549.

Guion, R. M. (1973). A note on organizational climate. *Organizational Behavior and Behavior and Human Performance, 9,* 120–25.

Hackman, J. A., & Oldman, G. R. (1979). Development of the job diagnostic survey. *Journal of Applied Psychology, 55,* 259–286.

Hall, R. H. (1977). *Organizations: Structure and process.* Englewood Cliffs, NJ: Prentice-Hall.

Hatfield, J. D. et al. (1981, May). *Moderating effects of worker characteristics on the communi-*

cation–performance relationship. Paper presented at the annual meeting of the International Communication Association, Minneapolis, MN.

Hatfield, J. D., & Huseman, R. C. (1982). Perceptional congruence about communication as related to satisfaction. Moderating effects of individual characteristics. *Academy of Management Journal, 25* (2), 349–358.

Hawkins, B. (1980). *Managerial communication.* Santa Monica, CA: Goodyear Publishing.

Hawkins, B., & Penley, L. (1978, May). *The relationship of communication to performance and satisfaction.* San Francisco, CA: Academy of Management.

Hazen, M. D., & Balthrop, V. W. (1975, May). *A causal analysis of the relationship between communication satisfaction and productivity, role discrepancy, need level, and organizational position.* Paper presented at the annual meeting of the International Communication Association, Chicago, IL.

Hecht, M. L. (1978). Measures of communication satisfaction. *Human Communication Research, 4,* (14), 350–368.

Hellriegel, D., & Slocum, J. W. (1974). Organizational climate: measures, research, and contingencies. *Academy of Management Journal, 17,* 255–279.

Hellwig, S., & Phillips, S. (1980, August). *Communication and productivity in organizations.* Paper presented at the Academy of Management convention, Detroit, MI.

Herzberg, F. (1966). *Work and the nature of man.* Cleveland, OH: World Publishing.

Hewitt, T. T., O'Brien, G. E., & Hornik, J. (1974). Effects of worker organization, leadership style, and member compatibility upon the productivity of small groups working on a manipulative task. *Organizational Behavior and Human Performance, 11,* 283–301.

Hodgson, J. D. (1981, August). An impertinent suggestion for personnel practitioners. *Personnel Administrator,* pp. 23–28.

Huseman, R. C., Hatfield, J., & Gatewood, R. (1979). A conceptual framework for analyzing the communication-productivity relationship. *Academy of Management Proceedings 1979,* 178–182.

Huseman, R., Hatfield, J., Boulton, W., & Gatewood, R. (1979, August). Development of a conceptual framework analyzing the communication-performance relationship. *Proceedings of the Academy of Management,* Atlanta.

Ilgen, D. R., & Knowlton, W. A. (1980). Performance attributional effects on feedback from superiors. *Organizational Behavior and Human Performance, 25,* 441–456.

Jablin, F. (1980). Organizational communication theory and research: an overview of communication climate and network research. In D. Nimmo (Ed.), *Communication yearbook 4,* New Brunswick, NJ: Transaction — International Communication Association.

Jacobs, S., & Jillson, K. S. (1974). *Executive productivity.* New York: AMACOM.

Jain, H. C. (1973). Supervisory communication and performance in urban hospitals. *Journal of Communication, 23* 103–117.

Jenkins, K. M. (1977). *A study of the relationship between organizational communication and worker performance.* Unpublished doctoral dissertation, Arizona State University.

Johanesson, R. E. (1973). Same problems in measurement of organizational climate. *Organizational Behavior and Human Performance, 10,* 118–44.

Johnson, B. M. (1977). *Communication the process of organizing.* Boston, MA: Allyn and Bacon.

Jones, J. W. (1981). *Analysis of communication satisfaction in four rural school systems.* Unpublished doctoral dissertation, Vanderbilt University.

Judson, A. S. (1982, September-October). The awkward truth about productivity. *Harvard Business Review,* pp. 93–97.

Kim, J. S. (1975). *Effect of feedback on performance and job satisfaction in an organizational setting.* Unpublished doctoral dissertation, Michigan State University.

Kim, J. S., & Hamner, W. C. (1976). Effect of performance feedback and goal setting or productivity and satisfaction in an organizational setting. *Journal of Applied Psychology, 61,* 48–57.

Kio, J. B. A. (1979). *A descriptive study of communication satisfaction, need satisfaction, and need importance index among Nigerian workers.* Unpublished doctoral dissertation, University of Kansas.

Kirchner, W., & Reisberg, D. (1962). Differences between better and less effective supervisors in appraisal of subordinates. *Personnel Psychology, 15*, 295–302.

Laird, A. (1982). *Coordinated management of meaning: An empirical investigation of communication and productive action in two organizations.* Unpublished doctoral dissertation, University of Kansas.

Latham, G. P., & Yuke, G. A. (1976). Effects of assigned and participative goal setting on performance and job satisfaction. *Journal of Applied Psychology, 61*, 166–171.

Lewis, M. L., Cummings, H. W., & Long, L. W. (1982). Communication activity as a predictor of the fit between worker motivation and worker productivity. In M. Burgoon (Ed.), *Communication yearbook 6.* Beverly Hills, CA: Sage Publications.

Likert, R. (1967). *The human organization.* New York: McGraw-Hill.

Likert, R., & Araki, C. T. (1979). Improving the performance of a governmental agency. In S. J. Mushrin (Ed.), *Proposition 13 and its consequences for public management* (pp. 141–149). Cambridge, MA: Council for Applied Social Research.

Locke, E. A. (1962). What is job satisfaction? *Organization Behavior and Human Performance, 46*, 375–84.

Locke, E. A. (1976). The nature and causes of job satisfaction. In M. D. Dunnette (Ed.), *Handbook of industrial and organizational psychology* (pp. 1292–1350). Chicago, IL: Rand-McNally.

Locke, E. A., Frederick, E., Cousins, E., & Bobko, P. (1983). *The effect of previously assigned goals on self-set goals and performance.* Unpublished manuscript, University of Maryland.

Lofquist, L. H., & Danis, R. V. (1969). *Adjustment to Work.* New York: Appleton-Century-Crofts.

MacKenzie, K. D. (1980, February). *Concepts and measurement in organizational development.* Paper presented to the American Productivity Center, Houston, TX, February.

Mali, (1978). *Improving total productivity.* New York: John Wiley & Sons.

Maslow, A. H. (1943). A theory of human motivation. *Psychological Review, 53,* 370–96.

Meyer, H. H., Kay, E., & French, J. R. (1965). Split roles in performance appraisal. *Harvard Business Review, 43,* 123–129.

Migliore, R. H. (1970, Summer). Improving worker productivity through communication knowledge of work results. *Human Resource Management,* 101–109.

Milbourn, G., & Francis, G. S. (1981, August). All about job satisfaction. *Supervisory Management,* August, pp. 35–43.

Mohrman, S., Ledford, G., & Lawler, E. (1984). *Honeywell/USC Study of Participation Groups in Honeywell.* Unpublished report by the Center for Effective Organizations, University of Southern California.

Mott, P. (1972). *Characteristics of effective organization.* New York: Harper & Row.

Muchinsky, P. M. (1977). Organizational communication: relationships to organizational climate and job satisfaction. *Academy of Management Journal, 20,* 592–607.

Nadler, D. A. (1979). The effects of feedback on task group behavior: A review of experimental literature. *Organizational Behavior and Human Performance, 23,* 309–338.

Near, J. P., Smith, C. A., Rice, R. W., & Hunt, R. G. (1984). A comparison of work and non-work predictors of Life satisfaction. *Academy of Management Journal, 27* (1), 184–190.

Nemeroff, W. F., & Cosentino, J. (1979). Utilizing feedback and goal setting to increase performance appraisal interviewer skills of managers. *Academy of Management Journal, 22(3),* 566–576.

Nicholson, J. H. (1980). *Analysis of communication satisfaction in an urban school system.* Unpublished doctoral dissertation, Vanderbilt University.

Nishiyama, K. (1981, May). *Japanese Quality Control Circles.* Paper presented at the International Communication Association, Minneapolis, Minnesota.

O'Reilly, C. A. III, & Anderson, J. C. (1980). Trust and the communication of performance and job satisfaction. *Human Communication Research, 6,* 290–298.

Orpen, C. (1979). The effects of job enrichment on employee satisfaction, motivation, involvement, and performance: A field experience. *Human Relations, 32,* 189–217.

Ouchi, W. (1981). *Theory Z: How American business can meet the Japanese challenge.* Reading, MA: Addison-Wesley.

Payne, R. L. (1973). *Prospects for research on organizational climates.* Unpublished manuscript, Department of Psychology, The University of Sheffield.

Penley, L., & Hawkins, B. (1979). Communication Consistency as a factor in the prediction of motivation and performance, Southwest Academy of Management meetings.

Penley, L, & Hawkins, B. L. (1980). Organizational communication, performance, and job satisfaction as a function of ethnicity and sex. *Journal of Vocational Behavior, 16,* 368–384.

Peters, T. J., & Waterman, R. H. (1982). *In search of excellence.* New York: Harper & Row.

Porter, L. W. (1962). Job attitudes in management: Perceived deficiencies in need fulfillment as a function of job level. *Journal of Applied Psychology, 46,* 375–84.

Porter, L. W. (1961). A study of perceived need satisfaction in bottom and middle management jobs. *Journal of Applied Psychology, 45,* 1–10.

Porterfield, D. (1978, August). *Toward the integration of communication and management.* Paper presented at the annual meeting of the Academy of Management, San Francisco.

Richmond, V. P., & McCroskey, J. L. (1979). Management communication style, tolerance for disagreement, and innovativeness as predictors of employee satisfaction: A comparison of single-factor, two factor, and multiple-factor approaches. In D. Nimmo (Ed.), *Communication yearbook 3.* New Brunswick, NJ: Transaction-International Communication Association.

Richmond, V. P., McCroskey, J. L., & Davis, L. M. (1982). Individual differences among employees, management communication style, and employee satisfaction: Replication and extension. *Human Communication Research,* Winter *8* (2), 170–188.

Roberts, K. H., & O'Reilly, C. A., III. (1979). Some correlations of communication roles in organizations. *Academy of Management Journal, 22,* 42–57.

Rosenberg, R. D., & Rosenstein, E. (1980, April). Participation and productivity: an empirical study. *Industrial and Labor Relations Review,* pp. 355–367.

Rosow,, J. M. (1979, January-February). Human dignity in the public sector workplace. *Public Personnel Management,* pp. 197–214.

Rudolph, E. (1978, August). Why most employee communication programs do not work. *Paper presented at the annual meeting of the Academy of Management,* San Francisco.

Schuler, R. S. (1977). The effects of role perceptions on employee satisfaction and performance moderated by employee attributions. *Organizational Behavior and Human Performance, 23,* 98–107.

Schuler, R. S., & Blank, L. F. (1976). Relationships among types of communication, organizational level, and employee satisfaction and performance. *IEE Transactions on Engineering Management, 23,* 124–129.

Schulhof, R. J. (1979, June). Five years with Scanlon plan. *Personnel Administrator,* pp. 55ff.

Schwab, D. P., & Cummings, L. L. (1970). Theories of performance and satisfaction: A review. *Industrial Relations, 9*(4), 408–430.

Scott, R. (1977). Effectiveness of organizational effectiveness studies. In P. S. Goodman & J. M. Pennings (Eds.), *New perspective on organizational effectiveness* (pp. 63–95). San Francisco, CA: Jossey-Bass.

Sibson, R. E. (1976). *Increasing employee productivity.* New York: AMACOM.

Smith, P. C., Kendall, L. M., & Hulin, C. L. (1969). *The measurement of satisfaction in work and retirement.* Chicago, IL: Rand McNally.

Steers, R. M. (1977). *Organizational effectiveness: A behavioral view.* Santa Monica, CA: Goodyear Publishing.

Stettler, C. (1976). *An explanatory study of the area nurse role.* M.A. thesis, University of Kansas.

Striner, H. (1981). Regaining the lead in productivity and growth. *Combining the Best of American and Japanese Management, 2.*

Sundstrom, E., Burt, R. E., & Kamp, D. (1980). Privacy at work: Architectural correlates of job satisfaction and Job Performance. *Academy of Management Journal, 23* (11), 101–117.

Sutermeister, R. A. (1976). *People and productivity*. New York: McGraw-Hill Book Company.

Tavernier, G. (1980). Using employee communications to support corporate objectives. *Management Review, 69,* 8–130.

Thiry, R. V. (1977). *Relationship of communication satisfaction to need fulfillment among Kansas nurses*. Unpublished doctoral dissertation, University of Kansas.

Tubbs, S. L., & Widgery, R. N. (1978). When productivity lags, are key managers really communicating? *Management Review, 67,* 20–25.

Tubbs, S., & Hain, T. (1979, August). *Managerial communication and its relationship to total organizational effectiveness*. Paper presented at the Academy of Management convention, Kansas City, Kansas.

Wanous, J. P., & Lawler, E. E. (1972). Measurement and meaning of job satisfaction. *Journal of Applied Psychology, 56,* 95–105.

Weick, K. E. (1969). *The social psychology of organizing*. Reading, MA: Addison-Wesley Publishing Co.

Wheeless, L. A., Wheeless, V. E., & Howard, R. D. (1984). The relationship of communication with supervisor and decision-participation to employee job satisfaction. *Communication Quarterly, 32* (3), 222–232.

Wiio, O. A. (1976, April). *Organizational communication: Interfacing systems*. Paper presented at the annual meeting of the International Communication Association, Portland.

Wiio, O. A. (1977). Organizational communication: Interfacing systems. *Finnish Journal of Business Economics, 2,* 259–85.

Wiio, O. A., Goldhaber, G. M., & Yates, M. P. (1980). Organizational communication research: Time for reflection? In D. Nimmo (Ed.), *Communication yearbook 4*. New Brunswick, NJ: Transaction — International Communication Association.

Wippich, B. (1983). *An analysis of communication and job satisfaction in an educational setting*. Unpublished doctoral dissertation, University of Kansas.

Yamada, T., Kitajima, S., & Imaeda, K. (1980). Development of a new production management system for the co-elevation of humanity and productivity. *International Journal of Productivity Research, 18,* 427–439.

Yukl, G. A., & Latham, G. P. (1978, Summer). Interrelationships among employee participation, individual differences, goal difficulty, goal acceptance, goal instrumentality, and performance. *Personnel Psychology, 305–323.*

Chapter 10

Participative Processes in Organizations

Peter R. Monge

Annenberg School of Communications
University of Southern California

Katherine I. Miller

Department of Communication
Michigan State University

ABSTRACT

Communication is an integral part of participative processes in organizations. The first section of this chapter describes the major participative systems that are used throughout the world in terms of five major dimensions. The second section summarizes the research literature on the effects of participation. The third section presents cognitive, affective and contingency models of the relationship of the participative processes to organizational outcomes. The chapter concludes with a discussion of future directions for research on communication and participation.

It is a major anachronism of American society that democracy is defined as relevant only in the political sphere of life. The relative freedom of the political arena stands in sharp contrast to the authoritarian principles governing the American workplace. Clearly, a strong case can be made for bringing greater democracy into the workplace in order to create a citizenry that participates in all of the major areas affecting its daily circumstances and its future. (Gamson & Levin, 1985)

The participation of workers in organizational decision making has become "a major political, social, and economic issue throughout the world" (Strauss, 1982, p. 174). As we shall soon document, several different types of participative systems have been instituted in various countries around the globe. A critical dimension of the participative process is the role of communication. To date, however, little scholarly attention has been devoted to this process. In this chapter, we attempt to remedy this situation and examine the relationship between the participative and communicative processes.

The first section of this paper briefly reviews the concept of participation and the diversity of participative systems that have been developed and implemented around the world. The second section examines the behavioral theories that incorporate participative and communicative processes and provides an analysis of the research literature. The final section provides our desideratum for future research agendas, particularly for the investigation of communication variables in the participation process.

Dimensions of Participation

Like many high level abstractions, the concept of participation refers to a wide variety of actual human behaviors. Consequently, it is not surprising that organizational theorists have developed many different definitions of participation, some with multiple dimensions. Locke and Schweiger (1979) review the wide range of definitions of participation and note that the term is variously defined to include delegation, group involvement or group decision making, equalization of influence or power sharing, and worker ego involvement. Locke and Schweiger find that defining participation as "joint decision making" (p. 274) is the most useful. They note that this definition does not necessitate equal influence in the decision-making process, but simply states that two or more parties are involved in the decision process. In addition, this definition does not impose limits on which individuals are involved in the decision. Participation could include many combinations of employees at various organizational levels. It should also be noted that this definition specifically excludes delegation. Locke and Schweiger contend that delegation is not participatory as "the subordinate does not participate in the decision to delegate, nor does the supervisor participate in the decisions which are delegated" (p. 274).

Locke and Schweiger's definition of participation has great utility, but it is unlikely that any single definition of the concept would adequately represent the wide variety of participative systems in existence around the world. Thus, in considering global participative programs, it is useful to compare them in terms of dimensions of the participative process. Strauss (1982) developed a taxonomy of participation which provides a basis for classifying diverse participatory systems. It centers around four dimensions: (a) organizational level, (b) degree of control, (c) issues, and (d) ownership.

The first dimension of Strauss' taxonomy refers to the organizational level where the participation occurs. Within individual firms, this dimension varies from single individuals to work groups to plants or divisions and finally, to the entire company. At a more macro level, the concept of participation can be extended to entire industries and to participation on the level of national economic planning and policy.

Strauss' second dimension, degree of control, describes the extent to which the participation is advisory or determinative. In consultative systems, workers give advice and recommendations to management, but management is not required to abide by the consultation. In other applications of participative decision making, the views of all participants must be included in a final negotiated decision. In self-management, the determinative end of this continuum, there is little distinction between management and workers and everyone affected by the decision is included in the making of the decision.

The third dimension refers to the range of issues covered in the participatory system. Some systems are quite restricted in the number and kinds of issues that are considered legitimate topics for participation. For example, many organizations restrict participation to decisions which have a direct impact on the tasks of the participating workgroup. Other participative systems are quite broad, permitting worker participation in decisions involving everything from wages and personnel issues to major investment decisions.

The fourth dimension Strauss delineates addresses the issue of company ownership.

Most organizations have little or no worker ownership, since the firm is owned by investors, either the original entrepreneurs or public stockholders. A relatively new corporate form, called Employee Stock Ownership Plans, provides considerably more worker ownership. Finally, there are some organizations that are completely worker owned, the most typical of which are producer cooperatives.

A final dimension for classifying participative systems which was not included in Strauss' taxonomy is whether the participation is direct or representative. Though a great many participative systems involve representation, Strauss and Rosenstein (1970) suggest that this kind of participation may not reap all of the potential benefits:

> A major reason why formal participation schemes have had such limited success in rais-
> ing production is that they are focused on the wrong level and on the wrong subjects.
> There is reason to doubt whether vicarious participation, through representatives, in set-
> ting overall company or personnel policies will have the same impact as direct participa-
> tion in determining how to do ones own work. With representative participation active
> involvement is confined to only a few and the creative potential of the ordinary worker is
> ignored. Understandably, small changes in the formal structure at the top have not
> changed the meaning of the work at the bottom. (p. 213)

The next section of this chapter will consider a wide range of participative systems which have been instituted around the world. These systems will be discussed in terms of the dimensions of participation presented above.

Alternative Forms of Participation

The rise of industrialized societies over the past century has witnessed the parallel emergence of a large variety of complex organizational forms. Not surprisingly, both organizational leaders and social scientists throughout the world have devoted extensive thought and experimentation to understanding the alternative administrative techniques that lead to the effectiveness and efficiency of organizations and the well being of their members. The concept of participation has been a central issue in this theorizing and research. There are four major forms of participatory systems that will be discussed in this section: European industrial democracy, the American Scanlon Plan, Japanese Quality Control Circles, and Chinese "down-the-line" participation. A summary of these four systems, in terms of the dimensions of participation discussed above, is presented in Table 1.

European industrial democracy. European industrial democracy has its roots in legislation developed in Sweden in 1946. It was then that agreements were worked out between employers and employee organizations for the establishment of representative worker councils (Link, 1971). As Bass and Rosenstein (1978) indicate, this early legislation has led to a wide range of employee participation in Sweden, including:

> Job design, local councils of employees, profit sharing after one year's employment
> through loans to buy shares with full voting rights, production groups, changes to hourly
> pay from piece rates, job enrichment, job rotation, scrapping of the assembly line, in-
> creased employee autonomy, co-op organization, self-activation, suggestion systems,
> and information exchanges about investment decisions. (p. 2)

Elected representation on boards of directors and other committees at various organizational levels is the principle feature of European industrial democracy. This occurs

Table 1. Classification of Programs of Participation by Dimensions of Participation

	DIMENSIONS OF PARTICIPATION				
GLOBAL PROGRAMS OF PARTICIPATION	1. LEVEL OF ORGANIZATION	2. DEGREE OF CONTROL	3. RANGE OF ISSUES	4. EMPLOYEE OWNERSHIP	5. DIRECT OR REPRESENTATIVE
A. EUROPEAN INDUSTRIAL DEMOCRACY	ALL LEVELS, especially COMPANY-WIDE	HIGH	WIDE RANGE	SOMETIMES	REPRESENTATIVE
B. U.S. SCANLON SYSTEMS	WORK GROUP and ORGANIZATION	MODERATE (Consultative)	WIDE RANGE especially INNOVATIONS	PROFIT-SHARING	REPRESENTATIVE
C. JAPANESE QUALITY CIRCLES	WORK GROUP	RELATIVELY HIGH	INCREMENTAL WORK INNOVATIONS	RARELY	DIRECT
D. CHINESE DOWN-THE-LINE PROGRAM	ALL LEVELS	RELATIVELY HIGH	WIDE RANGE	NO	REPRESENTATIVE

in both capitalist countries like West Germany and in socialist countries like Yugoslavia. In some countries, representation has been legally institutionalized. For example, in 1976 West Germany passed a codetermination law requiring worker representation on boards of directors. Less formal arrangements exist in countries like Holland, where the "werkoverleg is a formal constituted consultative work group which carries no particular legal support" (Bass & Rosenstein, 1978, p. 2). Many of the forms of European industrial democracy also contain some form of employee financial benefits that accrue from their participation. These include profit sharing, ownership of the company as in Employee Stock Ownership Programs, or extra corporate contributions to employee pension plans.

To summarize in terms of the dimensions of participation discussed above, European industrial democracy typically takes place at all organizational levels, with a concentration on company-wide participation. The degree of control for participants varies from system to system, but is generally quite high, and usually workers participate on a wide gamut of organizational issues. Finally, European industrial democracy sometimes involves employee ownership, and is almost always representative in nature.

American Participation and The Scanlon System. The American emphasis on employee participation can be traced to the development of the human relations school management, most prominently supported by Argyris (1957), Likert (1967), and McGregor (1960). The human relations perspective emphasizes the importance of individual capabilities to contribute to the problems encountered in work, and to the necessity to make work a fulfilling and enjoyable experience for people. Human relations advocates argue that this approach maximizes both worker efficiency and satisfaction. A central concept in this school of thought is employee participation in decision making.

Although there have been several managerial systems developed to achieve human relations goals, the one that most centrally incorporates participation is the Scanlon system (Frost, Wakely, & Ruh, 1974). Developed in the 1940s by Joseph Scanlon, and endorsed and advocated by Douglas McGregor, the Scanlon system attempts to include workers in day-to-day work decisions and reward them with a periodic financial bonus that is tied to company productivity. Scanlon organizations usually institute a two-committee system for eliciting, evaluating, and implementing organizational innovations generated by the workforce. These committees are also responsible for providing feedback to individual contributors, for assessing the financial impact of each innovation, and for computing the monthly or quarterly bonus.

The Scanlon Plan, representative of American participative systems, is characterized by participation at the work group and organizational level. Representative participation is the norm. Participation is consultative in nature, as management reserves final decision-making power. Through the dual committee system, Scanlon employees participate on a wide range of issues, though concentration is placed on work system innovations. Finally, although the Scanlon system does not involve direct or indirect employee ownership, the Scanlon bonus provides for extensive profit sharing.

Japanese Quality Control Circles. The Japanese began to experiment with forms of worker participation in the middle 1960s. During this time, Juran (1967) and Deming (1970) combined the technological ideas of statistical quality control and the social technology of human relations (particularly McGregor, 1960, and Argyris, 1957) to develop the idea of quality control circles. Quality control circles were designed to foster the full participation of workers and to help them to "work smarter." The dramatic success of many Japanese businesses in the 1970s and 1980s has fostered an interest in quality circles in many countries, including the United States (see, for example, Thompson, 1982).

Quality control circles use several mechanisms to accomplish their objectives. First, as in many participative systems, organizations with quality circles treat workers as capable of highly productive, meaningful, responsible, and creative work. Second, they view the workers rather than outside "experts" as the ones who are best able to solve organizational problems. Third, they emphasize the need to focus on small, incremental innovations, in the belief that the accumulation of incremental innovations is more beneficial to the firm in the long run than the development of radical innovations. Fourth, they utilize peer group processes rather than traditional hierarchies for both assessing and implementing innovations. Finally, a strong emphasis is placed on employee education, particularly in the area of statistical control, to provide the tools to enable employees to work smarter.

In terms of our dimensions of participation, then, quality circles are characterized by direct participation at the work group level of the organization. The scope of decisions workers are involved in is relatively narrow, though workers have a fair amount of control over decisions within these constraints. Finally, quality circles rarely involve any form of employee ownership.

Participation in China. In recent years, the People's Republic of China has been conducting a large-scale social experiment with worker participation (see Laaksonen, 1985). These participative systems were initiated during the Cultural Revolution, and are designed to transform the country from a centralized, party-controlled industrial system to a system emphasizing worker participation and organizational independence.

The new participation system is based on workers' congresses elected by workers in each organization. The membership of each congress is designed to adequately represent all important features of the workforce, e.g., age, sex, and organizational function. These congresses have been constitutionally granted a large range of responsibilities, including: (a) the election of managers throughout all organizational levels, (b) individual performance appraisals, (c) the right to examine and approve management plans, (d) the right to review and approve all financial documents, and (e) the right to review and approve compensation, reward, and benefit systems.

An innovative feature of this experiment is what Laaksonen calls "down-the-line participation." Participation is often conceived of as involving subordinates in higher level decision making. Down-the-line participation reverses this notion of participation and attempts to involve higher level managers in the work of their subordinates. Laaksonen indicates that administrators, technicians, and other office workers currently spend approximately 1 day per week on the workshop floor. This is certainly a very different situation than most other participation systems that are in use in other parts of the world.

Thus, the Chinese system of participation consists primarily of representative participation at the organizational level. Workers participate in a wide gamut of decisions and have a fair amount of control in the decision-making process. The most innovative aspect of the Chinese system is the emphasis on "down-the-line" participation.

THEORIES OF PARTICIPATION

As demonstrated above, participative management has received a great deal of practical attention, and a wide range of applications of participative management is in place around the world. The role of participation in workplace decisions has also been the topic of considerable debate, philosophizing, theorizing and research in academia over the past 30 years. Since the advent of the human relations approach to management in the 1940s, the vast majority of theories of organizational behavior have either explicitly or implicitly addressed the issue of participation. Theorists have been concerned with both the *results* of participation in the workplace, and the *process* by which these results are obtained. Miller and Monge (1987), in a study of the Scanlon system of participation and allocation, developed a typology of the *effects* of participation in the workplace. The next section of this chapter will expand on this typology. Following this, we will present three models discussed by Miller and Monge (1986) which delineate various *processes* of participation which have been considered by theorists.

Effects of Participation

A wide range of effects of participation have been proposed in the research literature. This section will consider the most prevalent attitudinal, cognitive, and behavioral effects suggested by scholars in the fields of management, organizational behavior, industrial psychology, and communication.[1]

   Attitudinal Effects. The majority of research investigating participation in decision making has considered the effects of participation on the attitudes of workers. One of the most well-known early studies of participation considered an attitudinal effect, resistance to change. Coch and French (1948) proposed that, if workers were given the opportunity to participate in decisions about the implementation of work changes, the workers would identify with the changes and be less resistant to them. In a field experiment testing this hypothesis, Coch and French found that groups who had full or representative participation showed less resistance to changes in work procedures, and returned more quickly to high productivity levels, than workers who did not have an opportunity to participate. In recent years, Coch and French's work has come under some critical scrutiny (Bartlem & Locke, 1981). However, modern reinterpretations do not mitigate the influence of Coch and French's research on the area of participation. This influence has resulted in the consideration of a number of other attitudinal effects of participation.

   The attitudinal variable which has received the most attention as an effect of participation is job satisfaction. The link between the opportunity to participate in decisions and job satisfaction has been derived primarily from the human relations school of management (Argyris, 1964; McGregor, 1960). Human relations theorists advocate a management style which concentrates on satisfying the higher order ego needs of workers, including needs for achievement, affiliation, and independence. The link between participation and satisfaction suggests that (a) participation in decision making is one way to satisfy these higher order needs, and (b) the satisfaction of these needs will lead to greater satisfaction with work. A wide range of research has investigated this proposed link between participation in decision making and job satisfaction. Reviews of the literature (Locke & Schweiger, 1979; Miller & Monge, 1986) generally suggest that participation will, indeed, lead to higher levels of worker satisfaction in a great many organizational situations, though these effects vary in conjunction with the range of decisions workers participate in and the setting in which the research took place.

---

[1] The section on the effects of participation is based in large part on Miller and Monge (1987).

A third attitudinal variable which has been related to participation in decision making is job involvement (Lodahl & Kejner, 1965). Several researchers (Blood & Hulin, 1967; Ruh, White, & Wood, 1975; Siegel & Ruh, 1973) have suggested that participation in decision making will lead workers to see their jobs as a more central aspect of their lives. Like the link between participation and satisfaction, these researchers typically argue that workers will see a job with participation as more involving because of the satisfaction of higher order ego needs.

A final attitudinal variable which has been linked to participation in decision making is organizational commitment (Mowday, Steers, & Porter, 1979) This outcome has been most strongly advocated by researchers considering the Scanlon Plan of participative management (Frost et al., 1974). However, other theorists (e.g., Anthony, 1978) also propose that participation will strengthen the sense of team and organizational identity held by individual employees. The link between participation and commitment has usually been explained as a function of the development of more accurate and detailed cognitions about the organization (Frost et al., 1974). However, the link between participation and commitment could also be explained in terms of the "binding" behaviors that participation typically involves (Kiesler, 1971; Salancik, 1977).

Cognitive Effects. There have been two major cognitive effects of participation proposed in theory and research. First, it has been suggested that participation in decision making will lead to increased utilization of information from lower levels of the organizational hierarchy (Anthony, 1978, Vroom & Yetton, 1973). This line of reasoning assumes that the workers themselves have the most complete information about work that should actually be done in an organization. Thus, participative management should effectively utilize the knowledge and skills of all individuals in the organization.

A second proposed cognitive effect of participation is downward information dissemination. That is, theorists suggest that participation in decision making will result in the individual employee having increased knowledge about the organization and his or her part in the organization. Propositions regarding downward information dissemination have typically taken one of two forms. First, it has been proposed that participative workers will have more and better knowledge about particular decisions and thus will be better able to implement those decisions (Coch & French, 1948; Maier, 1963; Melcher, 1976; Strauss, 1963; Vroom & Yetton, 1973). It has also been proposed that participative employees will have a greater understanding of the entire organization, its standing in the marketplace, and the part that individual employees play in the greater scheme of things (Frost et al., 1974).

Third, some researchers have proposed that participation in decision making will lead individual employees to have a more accurate perception of reward contingencies in the organization. This cognitive effect has been proposed primarily by researchers using an expectancy approach to participation (e.g., Mitchell, 1973; Schuler, 1980). Specifically, these researchers have proposed that participation leads to more accurate knowledge of the effort–performance relationship and the performance–reward relationship. According to Mitchell (1973), "through participation, the individual should know fairly well which behaviors are likely to be rewarded and which are not" (p. 674).

Behavioral Effects. Perhaps the simplest behavioral effect of providing workers with the opportunity to participate in the workplace is that employees will, indeed, engage in more participative and communicative behaviors. At a level beyond this, however, two major behavioral effects of participation have been explored in the research literature.

First, Latham and his colleagues, working from Locke's (1966) theory of goal-setting (Latham & Marshall, 1982; Latham, Mitchell, & Dossett, 1978; Latham & Saari, 1979; Latham & Steele, 1983; Latham & Yukl, 1976) have investigated the hypothesis that participation in goal setting will lead to higher levels of worker productivity. For a review of this research, see Latham and Lee (1986). In general, this research has not borne out a strong relationship between participation in goal setting and individual performance, though such participation generally leads to the setting of higher goals.

In addition to the specific research on goal-setting, participation in general has also been linked to individual performance or productivity. The volume of research on this effect of participation has been second only to research on job satisfaction. In general, literature reviews (Locke & Schweiger, 1979; Miller & Monge, 1986) provide mixed conclusions about the effect of participation on productivity. In a meta-analytic review, Miller and Monge (1986) found a moderate relationship between participation and decision making and productivity in some field experiments, but no relationship (or a negative relationship) in other field studies and most laboratory studies. Despite these mixed conclusions, though, researchers and practitioners alike continue to assume its viability. For example, Mitchell (1980), after citing the inconclusive review of Locke and Schweiger (1979), states that "the results of the participation research, however, generally suggest that regardless of the nature of the moderating condition, the participation-attitude *and behavior* relationships are positive" (p. 332, emphasis added).

In sum, then, a variety of attitudinal, cognitive, and behavioral effects of participation have been proposed. Proposed attitudinal effects of participation include decreased resistance to change and increased job satisfaction, job involvement, and organizational commitment. Proposed cognitive effects of participation include increased upward sharing of information, increased knowledge about the organization and the individual's part in the organization, and more accurate perceptions of reward contingencies. Proposed behavioral effects of participation include increased communication and improved worker performance and productivity.

The next section of this chapter will consider the models of the process of participation which have been proposed in the literature. These models will concentrate primarily on the processes which have been proposed to link participation with improved worker satisfaction and productivity. However, the general form of these models could be extended to account for most of the other attitudinal, cognitive, and behavioral effects of participation discussed above. Three models of the participative process will be considered: the cognitive model, the affective model, and contingency models.[2]

The Process of Participation

Cognitive Models of the Participation Process. Cognitive models of participative effects suggest that participative management is a viable strategy because it enhances the flow and utilization of important information in an organization. Theorists supporting this model (e.g., Anthony, 1978; Frost et al., 1974) propose that workers typically have more complete knowledge of their work than management; hence, if workers participate in decision making, decisions will be made with a better pool of information. This is the "upward" information flow aspect of the participation process. In addition, the cognitive model sug-

---

[2] The section on the process of participation is based in large part on Miller and Monge (1986).

gests that if employees participate in decision making, they will have better knowledge for implementing work procedures after the decisions have been made (Maier, 1963; Melcher, 1976); that is, participation can improve the "downward" dissemination of information. Ritchie and Miles (1970; Miles & Ritchie, 1971) have called this reasoning the "human resources" theory of participation. They note that this model is "primarily concerned with the meaningful utilization of subordinates' capabilities and views satisfaction as a by-product of their participation in important organizational decisions" (Ritchie & Miles, 1970, p. 348). The process of participation as proposed by cognitive models is presented in Figure 1.

Affective Models of the Participation Process. Models which link participation to organizational outcomes through affective mechanisms are most adamantly espoused by human relations theorists (e.g., Likert, 1967; McGregor, 1960). As discussed in our section on attitudinal effects, these theorists propose that participation will lead to greater attainment of higher order ego needs such as self-expression, respect, independence, and equality. In turn, the attainment of these needs will lead to increased morale and satisfaction. In discussing this approach to participative management, Ritchie and Miles (1970) state that "managers who hold the Human Relations theory of participation believe simply in involvement for the sake of involvement, arguing that as long as subordinates feel they are participating and are being consulted, their ego needs will be satisfied and they will be more cooperative" (p. 348).

Affective models also propose increased productivity through participation, though the process through which this is achieved is less straightforward than in the cognitive models. Essentially, this school proposes that participation will lead to higher levels of productivity through intervening motivational processes. According to French, Israel, and As (1960):

> One effect of a high degree of participation by workers in decisions concerning their work will be to strengthen their motivation to carry out these decisions. This is the major rationale for expecting a relation between participation and production. When manage-

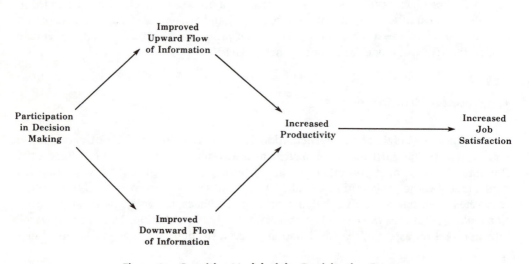

Figure 1.   Cognitive Model of the Participation Process

ment accords the workers participation in any important decision, it implies that workers are intelligent, competent, and valued partners. Thus, participation directly affects such aspects of worker-management relations as the perception of being valued, the perception of common goals, and coooperation. It satisfies such important social needs as the need for recognition and appreciation and the need for independence. These satisfactions and in addition the improvements in their jobs that are introduced through participation lead to higher job satisfaction. (p. 5)

The process of participation proposed by affective models is presented in Figure 2.

Contingency Models of the Participation Process. Several theorists suggest that it is not possible to develop models of participation which will hold across all individuals and situations. Scholars have offered a variety of contingency theories which center on personality, the decision situation, superior/subordinate relationships, job level, and values.

Vroom (1960) was the first to propose that personality might mediate the effects of participation on satisfaction and productivity. Specifically, he suggested that only employees who had a low authoritarian personality and a high need for independence would be positively influenced by participation. Vroom found some support for his hypotheses, and his work has stimulated other research. However, further studies have provided mixed support for his hypotheses (Abdel-Halim, 1983; Tosi, 1970).

Vroom was also involved in the major theoretical statement of situational influences on the participation process. Vroom and Yetton (1973), building on the work of Tannenbaum and Schmidt (1958), consider different decision situations and provide rules for deciding the optimal level of participation in the decision making process. They propose both rules to protect the quality of the decision and rules to protect the acceptance of the decision. Vroom and Yetton's work moves toward an integration of cognitive and affect models of participation. Their contingency rules for protecting the quality of decisions deals with the cognitive portion of the participation process, while their rules for protecting the acceptance of decisions addresses the affective components of participation.

Several other theorists have proposed additional intervening variables in the participation process. For example, some theorists suggest that the type of problems dealt with at various levels of an organization makes participation appropriate or inappropriate (Vroom & Deci, 1960). These investigators suggest that participation may be less applicable at lower levels of the organization where jobs are routine. The complex problems dealt with at higher levels of the organization are thought to be more appropriate for participation. Second, several scholars (e.g., Hulin, 1971; Singer, 1974) have suggested that it is values which mediate the participation–outcome relationship. Specifically, they suggest that many workers do not value participation to the extent that academicians do. Singer (1974) further criticizes, "While the necessity for determining a 'one best' leadership style for the 'composite worker' is understandable from a financial and expediency standpoint, to assume that all workers desire participation opportunities is to lack sensitivity to individual needs—the antithesis of the humanization that ardent proponents of participation advocate" (p. 359). Thus, these scholars predict that participation may only be effective for employees in cer-

| Participation in Decision Making | → | Satisfaction of Higher Order Ego Needs | → | Increased Job Satisfaction | → | Increased Worker Motivation | → | Increased Productivity |

Figure 2.   Affective Model of the Participation Process

tain types of organizations (for example, research or service organizations rather than manufacturing organizations), or only for middle or upper level employees.

FUTURE DIRECTIONS: COMMUNICATION AND PARTICIPATION

It should now be very clear that there has been a widespread practical interest in participation. Managers, seeing the possibility of increases in job morale, productivity, and profitability, have looked to participation in decision making as a means to increase worker involvement in organizational processes. Industrial interest in participation has been global, and has been manifested in a wide range of organizational forms. It should also be clear that a voluminous body of research has been conducted investigating the mechansims at work in participative systems and the effects of participation on individual workers. Although no definitive statements of the process and effects of participation have emerged, progress has been made in delineating the cognitive, affective, and contingency processes which lead to a variety of positively valued effects.

However, most of the research on participation in decision making has taken place in the fields of management, organizational behavior, and industrial/organizational psychology. As participation is at heart a communicative process, it is worthwhile to explore the ways in which communication theory and research could enhance our knowledge of participation in the workplace. We will suggest three particular directions for future research in this area.

Questioning Our Values About Participation

Clearly, the vast majority of organizational theorists and organizational practitioners positively value participation. Most feel that any kind of participation is better than no participation, and that direct participation is the best kind of participation of all. This view of participation is strongly rooted in a belief that equates clear and open communication with effectiveness (e.g., Bassett, 1974; Fisher, 1982; Frank, 1982; Sigband, 1976). Axley (1984) discusses a related view of communication in terms of the "conduit metaphor," which suggests that successful communication is easy and requires little effort. These views of optimal organizational communication as easy, clear, and open have permeated the literature on participative management, and, as Eisenberg (1984) points out, such views may be a counterproductive way to think about organizational communication:

> The overemphasis on clarity and openness in organizational teaching and research is both non-normative and not a sensible standard against which to gauge communicative competence or effectiveness. People in organizations confront multiple situational requirements, develop multiple and often conflicting goals, and respond with communicative strategies which do not always minimize ambiguity, but may nonetheless be effective. (p. 228)

Eisenberg's admonishments for organizational communication in general are particularly crucial for the area of participation. It is important that theorists, researchers, and practitioners resist the presumption that more participation is always better. Like theorists advocating contingency models of participation, we should look carefully at the situations and individuals for which participation is most appropriate. We should also remember that complex programs of participation may not be as effective as more personalized forms of decision-sharing. Miller (1985), in a study of firms using the Scanlon Plan of participative management, found that informal participation with the work group or supervisor was generally more effective in increasing employee morale than participation in formal power-sharing channels. Miller also found that individuals who participated directly in the committee structure seemed to reap no more benefits of participation than other employees. Thus, the notion that direct participation is always superior to representative participation may not have merit. Practitioners should also be wary of participative programs proposed as "easy fixes" for organizational problems; Axley suggests that such assumptions about communication can lead to complacency and overconfidence. Experiences of actual organizations with participative management (Zager & Rosow, 1982) clearly suggest that while such programs can indeed lead to many valued organizational outcomes, they should not be considered a panacea.

Investigating Participatory Interaction

A second way in which communication scholars can significantly add to our knowledge of participation is through the investigation of the actual interaction which takes place in participative decision making. Past studies of participation have typically performed simple comparisons of participative and nonparticipative groups and have considered the attitudes and behaviors of individuals in these groups. Research has rarely looked at the communicative content of the participation process itself. Research on what actually goes on in participatory management could take us a long way in explaining the disparate findings in the research literature.

Perhaps the initial and primary emphasis on actual participatory communication should be the interactional mechanisms through which power is shared in participation. A number of scholars conceptualize participation as power-sharing activity (e.g., Mulder, 1971). These theorists, though, concentrate on macro issues of information and resource distribution in the organization and do not look at the specific communicative behaviors through which power sharing is initiated. Recent work by Watson (1982) and Fairhurst, Rogers, and Sarr (1987) suggests that an interactional analysis of participative communication could be a fruitful avenue of future research. In addition to addressing the issue of power, such research could help pinpoint the mechanisms through which individual and organizational benefits of participation (e.g., job satisfaction, organizational commitment) are reaped.

Communication Theory and Participation

Finally, it seems crucial that we attempt to apply the theories which have been developed specifically in the field of communication to the research on participation in decision making. A number of theories from interpersonal communication, small group communication, and organizational communication could doubtless help us make sense of the processes and outcomes of participation. A few examples from these various communication "levels" will illustrate how such theories could be applied.

One of the most widely used theoretical statements in interpersonal communication is uncertainty reduction theory (Berger & Calabrese, 1975). These theorists suggest that one of the most important functions of interpersonal communication is the reduction of uncertainty about the situation and relational participants. Cognitive models of participation, presented above, are based on similar notions, as they suggest that participation will benefit organizational participants in part through the additional knowledge individuals gain about the organization and specific tasks. As these cognitive changes are serving to reduce the uncertainty of employees, the postulates of Berger and Calabrese could be used to examine the mechanisms through which participation influences an individual's attitudes and cognitions about the job and organization.

The small group communication literature also could provide some useful avenues for participation research. To take one small example, consider research on the polarity shift phenomenon (see, e.g., Meyers & Lamm, 1976; Boster & Mayer, 1984). Polarity shift research investigates decision making groups and the likelihood that these groups will make more polarized (both risky and cautious) decisions. Most of this research has taken place in laboratory settings. Thus, the polarity shift area could benefit from field research investigating decision making patterns in participatory organizational groups. The participation field could also benefit from this application, as it would lead to more consideration of the difference in decisions made individually and participatively. This comparison has received little attention in the research literature.

Finally, theory in organizational communication could fruitfully be applied to the area of participation. Again, to take one example, participation in decision making could be considered as an important portion of the organizational assimilation process (Jablin & Krone, 1986). Participation could be viewed as an important means through which the norms of the organization are communicated and through which an individual entering the organization can make sense of new experiences. Such a conceptualization would be especially useful in investigating the attitudinal and cognitive effects of participation and could lead to new hypotheses about the differential effects of participation on new and established organizational members.

These few examples only scratch the surface of the ways in which our knowledge of participative management could be enhanced through attention to theories of communication. Scholars in other areas have done well in delineating a host of variables which are, to a greater or lesser extent, related to participation in organizations. Perhaps the challenge for communication scholars is to specify the interactional mechanisms through which these attitudinal, cognitive, and behavioral effects are realized.

REFERENCES

Abdel-Halim, A. A. (1983). Effects of task and personality characteristics on subordinate responses to participative decision making. *Academy of Management Journal, 26,* 477–484.

Anthony, W. P. (1978). *Participative management.* Reading, MA: Addison-Wesley.

Argyris, C. (1957). *Personality and organization.* New York: Harper.

Axley, S. R. (1984). Managerial and organizational communication in terms of the conduit metaphor. *Academy of Management Review, 9,* 428–437.

Bartlem, C. S., & Locke, E. A. (1981). The Coch and French study: A critique and reinterpretation. *Human Relations, 34,* 555–566.

Bass, B. M., & Rosenstein, I. (1978). Integration of industrial democracy and participative management: U.S. and European perspectives. In B. King, S. Streufert, & F. E. Fiedler (Eds.), *Managerial control and organizational democracy.* Washington, DC: Winston.

Bassett, G. A. (1974, February). What is communication and how can I do it better? *Management Review,* 25–32.

Berger, C. R., & Calabrese, R. J. (1975). Some explorations in initial interaction and beyond: Toward a developmental theory of interpersonal communication. *Human Communication Research, 1*, 99–112.

Blood, M., & Hulin, C. (1967). Alienation, environmental characteristics, and worker responses. *Journal of Applied Psychology, 51*, 284–290.

Boster, F. J., & Mayer, M. E. (1984). Choice shifts: Argument qualities or social comparisons. In R. Bostrom (Ed.), *Communication yearbook 8* (pp. 393–410). Beverly Hills, CA: Sage Publications.

Coch, L., & French, J. R. P. (1948). Overcoming resistance to change. *Human Relations, 1*, 512–532.

Deming, W. (1969). Statistical control of quality in Japan. *Proceedings of the International Conference on Quality Control.* Tokyo: Union of Japanese Scientists and Engineers.

Eisenberg, E. M. (1984). Ambiguity as strategy in organizational communication. *Communication Monographs, 51*, 227–242.

Fairhurst, G. T., Rogers, L.E., & Sarr, R. A. (1987). Manager–subordinate control patterns and judgments about the relationship. In M. McLaughlin (Ed.), *Communication yearbook 10* (pp. 395–415). Beverly Hills: Sage Publications.

Fisher, D. W. (1982). A model for better communication. *Supervisory Management, 27*, 24–29.

Frank, A. D. (1982). *Communicating on the job.* Glenview, IL: Scott Foresman.

French, J. R. P., Israel, J., & As, D. (1960). An experiment in a Norwegian factory: Interpersonal dimensions in decision-making. *Human Relations, 13*, 3–19.

Frost, C. H., Wakely, J. H., & Ruh, R. A. (1974). *The Scanlon Plan for organization development: Identity, participation, and equity.* East Lansing, MI: Michigan State University Press.

Hulin, C. L. (1971). Individual differences and job enrichment: The case against general treatment. In J. R. Maher (Ed.), *New perspectives in job enrichment.* New York: Van Nostrant-Reinhold.

Jablin, F. M., & Krone, K. J. (1986, May). *Organizational communication and organizational assimilation: An intra- and inter-level analysis.* Paper presented at the Annual Meeting of the International Communication Association, Chicago, IL.

Juran, J. H. (1967). The QC circle phenomena. *Industrial Quality Control, 23*, 329–336.

Kiesler, C. A. (1971). *The psychology of commitment: Experiments linking behavior to belief.* New York: Academic Press.

Laaksonen, O. (1985). Participation down and up the line: Comparative industrial democracy trends in China and Europe. *International Journal of Social Science, 36*, 299–318.

Latham, G. P., & Lee, T. W. (1986). Goal setting. In E. A. Locke (Ed.), *Generalizing from laboratory to field settings: Findings from research in industrial/organizational psychology, organizational behavior and human resources management* (pp. 101–117). Boston, MA: Heath Lexington.

Latham, G. P., & Marshall, H. A. (1982). The effects of self-set, participatively set and assigned goals on the performance of government employees. *Personnel Psychology, 35*, 399–404.

Latham, G. P., Mitchell, T. R., & Dossett, D. L. (1978). Importance of participative goal setting and anticipated rewards on goal difficulty and job performance. *Journal of Applied Psychology, 63*, 163–171.

Latham, G. P., & Saari, L. M. (1979). The effects of holding goal difficulty constant on assigned and participatively set goals. *Academy of Management Journal, 22*, 163–168.

Latham, G. P., & Steele, T. P. (1983). The motivational effects of participation versus goal setting on performance. *Academy of Management Journal, 26*, 406–417.

Latham, G. P, & Yukl, G. A. (1976). Effects of assigned and participative goal setting on performance and job satisfaction. *Journal of Applied Psychology, 61*, 166–171.

Likert, R. L. (1967). *The human organization.* New York: McGraw-Hill.

Link, R. (1971, June). Alienation. *Sweden Now*, 36–40.

Locke, E. A. (1966). The relationship of incentives to level of performance. *Journal of Applied Psychology, 50*, 60–66.

Locke, E. A., & Schweiger, D. M. (1979). In B. M. Staw (Ed.), Participation in decision-making: One more look. *Research in Organizational Behavior, 1*, (pp. 265–339). Greenwich, CN: JAI Press.

Lodahl, T. M., & Kejner, M. (1965). The definition and measurement of job involvement. *Journal of Applied Psychology, 49,* 24–33.

Maier, N. R. F. (1963). *Problem solving discussion and conferences: Leadership methods and skills.* New York: McGraw-Hill.

McGregor, D. (1960). *The human side of enterprise.* New York: McGraw-Hill.

Melcher, A. J. (1976). Participation: A critical review of research findings. *Human Resource Management, 15,* 12–21.

Meyers, D. G., & Lamm, H. (1976). The group polarization phenomenon. *Psychological Bulletin, 83,* 602–627.

Miles, R. E., & Ritchie, J. B. (1971). Participative management: Quality vs. quantity. *California Management Review, 13,* 48–56.

Miller, K. I. (1985). *A system of participation and allocation preferences in organizations.* Unpublished doctoral dissertation, University of Southern California, Los Angeles.

Miller, K. I., & Monge, P. R. (1987). The development and test of a system of organizational participation and allocation. In M. McLaughlin (Ed.), *Communication yearbook 10* (pp. 431–455). Beverly Hills, CA: Sage Publications.

Miller, K. I., & Monge, P. R. (1986). Participation, satisfaction, and productivity: A meta-analytic review. *Academy of Management Journal, 29,* 727–753.

Mitchell, T. R. (1973). Motivation and participation: An integration. *Academy of Management Journal, 16,* 660–679.

Mowday, R. T., Steers, R. M., & Porter, L. W. (1979). The measurement of organizational commitment. *Journal of Vocational Behavior, 14,* 224–247.

Mulder, M. (1971). Power equalization through participation. *Administrative Science Quarterly, 16,* 31–38.

Ritchie, J. B., & Miles, R. E. (1970). An analysis of quantity and quality of participation as mediating variables in the participative decision making process. *Personnel Psychology, 23,* 347–359.

Ruh, R. A., White, J. K., & Wood, R. R. (1975). Job involvement, values, personal background, participation in decision making, and job attitudes. *Academy of Management Journal, 18,* 300–312.

Salancik, G. R. (1977). Commitment and control of organizational behavior and belief. In B. M. Staw & G. R. Salancik (Eds.), *New directions in organizational behavior* (pp. 1–54). Chicago, IL: St. Clair Press.

Schuler, R. S. (1980). A role and expectancy perception model of participation in decision making. *Academy of Management Journal, 23,* 331–340.

Siegel, A. L., & Ruh, R. A. (1973). Job involvement, participation in decision making, personal background, and job behavior. *Organizational Behavior and Human Performance, 9,* 318–327.

Sigband, N. B. (1976). *Communication for management and business* (2nd ed.). Glenview, IL: Scott Foresman.

Singer, J. N. (1974). Participative decision-making about work: An overdue look at variables which mediate its effects. *Sociology of Work and Occupations, 1,* 347–371.

Strauss, G. (1963). Some notes on power equalization. In H. J. Leavitt (Ed.), *The social science organizations: Four perspectives* (pp. 39–84). Englewood Cliffs, NJ: Prentice-Hall.

Strauss, G. (1982). Workers participation in management: An international perspective. In B. M. Staw & L. L. Cummings (Eds.), *Research in Organizational Behavior, 4,* (pp. 173–265). Greenwich, CN: JAI Press.

Strauss, G., & Rosenstein, E. (1970). Worker's participation: A critical point of view. *Industrial Relations, 9,* 197–214.

Tannenbaum, R., & Schmidt, W. (1958). How to choose a leadership pattern. *Harvard Business Review, 36,* 95–101.

Thompson, P. C. (1982). Quality circles at Martin Marietta Corporation, Denver Aerospace/Michoud Division. In R. Zager & M. P. Rosow (Eds.), *The innovative organization* (pp. 3–20). New York: Pergamon Press.

Tosi, H. (1970). A reexamination of personality as a determinant of the effect of participation. *Personnel Psychology, 23,* 91–99.

Vroom, V. H. (1960). *Some personality determinants of the effects of participation.* Englewood Cliffs, NJ: Prentice-Hall.

Vroom, V. H., & Deci, E. L. (Eds.). (1960). *Management and motivation.* Baltimore, MD: Penguin Books.

Vroom, V. H., & Yetton, P. W. (1973). *Leadership and decision-making.* Pittsburgh, PA: University of Pittsburgh Press.

Watson, K. M. (1982). An analysis of communication patterns: A method for discriminating leader and subordinate roles. *Academy of Management Journal, 25,* 107–120.

Zager, R., & Rosow, M. P. (Eds.). (1982). *The innovative organization: Productivity programs in action.* New York: Pergamon Press.

Chapter 11

Leadership/Communication:
A Critical Review and a Modest Proposal

Lee Thayer

ABSTRACT

About leadership, a condition which is increasingly on the cutting edge of our concerns about social and institutional life, communication scholars have been strangely silent. One reason may be that the dominant paradigm in communication study does not lend itself to the kinds of "free-form" social enterprises of which leadership may merely be the most complex exemplar.

This chapter examines, first, some consequences of the fact that our explanations of social happenings and of social agency in general are culture-bound: we see what we see because we understand the world the way we do, not the other way around. Thus, our approach to the study of leadership is conceptually impoverished at the outset because we do not begin with the posture that any theory of leadership must at the same time be a theory of followership, or that any theory of human or social behavior is at the same time a theory of "human nature." And since it is the problematics of communication that must ultimately inform the study of leadership, we can understand how it happened that inadequate and inappropriate concepts of human communication have led to a continuing impasse in the study of leadership.

Following a review of those scholars who have understood that leadership and followership are two aspects of the same thing, and that communication is not incidental but central to our thinking about leadership, the chapter concludes with a reassessment of leadership/followership as one special genre of communicative behavior.

Surprisingly, communication scholars have given little attention to leadership. And, by and large, leadership scholars have given even less attention to communication.

The most obvious reason for this seemingly mutual indifference, of course, is that the trivialization of the concept of communication into merely something that people *do* offers little that *should* interest those who are intrigued by something *else* that people do—lead or follow. The reigning concept of communication as merely the process of conveying ideas or information would hardly seem indispensable to those who wish to study leadership.

And because communication scholars have been burdened by such a trivialized concept of communication, there has apparently been little impetus to contemplate the possibility that communication might be the very life of leadership. Yet to attempt to explain organized social behavior of any sort without a grounded and heuristic concept of communication, of leadership, and of what the one has to do with the other is to build explanatory shortfall into the very attempt.

The aim of this chapter is to examine, first, the adequacy of our thinking in general about how things human and social happen, and then to suggest certain more advantageous and grounded ways of thinking about leadership.

Second, it is to examine the thought of those few leadership scholars who have suggested unconventional and nonhegemonic approaches to the study of leadership. These are approaches which, not coincidentally, assume the communication problematics that must ultimately inform the study of leadership.

Any theory of communication, or of leadership, is also, necessarily, a theory of human nature. Every proposition about the *direction* of human consequences, which implies both leadership and communication, is an answer to the question: what are people for?

So a theory of leadership will not stand without a theory of followership, and neither without a better theory or a more appropriate understanding of human communication. These are the issues that are next examined.

In the seventh section, we will stand on the preceding to conclude how leaders and followers *and* their relationships are created and maintained *in* communication, and what we *should* be saying about the relationship between communication and leadership.

In the short last section of the chapter, I set forth the reasons why we could most fruitfully see the leader as a compelling story teller—a modest but hopefully compelling proposal.

So, where begin?

Perhaps with the likelihood that most of our current thinking about leadership (and communication, of course) is ethnocentric—that it tells us more about ourselves than it does about leadership *or* communication. What Peter tells us about Paul, Spinoza suggested, tells us more about Peter than it does about Paul.

In the same way, it is likely, our contemporary fascination with the idea of leadership tells us more about the changing nature of the culture we share than it does about leadership. But this has ever been a condition of human inquiry.

It is a condition that would seem to be inescapable. Those who profess immunity by reason of being "scientific" are for all that no less susceptible to this condition of being human. It was Heisenberg himself who saw that the object of research in science was no longer that of revealing nature, but of investigating man's investigation of nature. And he cites his great colleague Eddington as follows (Heisenberg, 1958, p. 24):

> We have found that where science has progressed the farthest, the mind has but regained from nature that which mind has put into nature. We have found a strange foot print on the shores of the unknown. We have devised profound theories, one after another, to account for its origin. At last, we have succeeded in reconstructing the creature that made the footprint. And lo! It is our own.[1]

The definitive survey is Bass's 1981 edition of Stogdill's *Handbook of Leadership*. There are approximately *4,700* studies and related documents cited in this compendium. Another central figure in the field (McCall, 1977) tells us that there are more than 170 *research* studies alone published on leadership every year.

---

[1] Which, of course, is Kantian: the so-called "laws of nature" are *put into* nature by the mind. They do not exist *there*, nor as something independent of the mind.

So what does this increasing mass tell us about ourselves and the nature of the culture in which we live?

And what composite picture does it paint of the idea of leadership?

And what, if anything, is left to be said about what leadership has to do with communication, and what communication has to do with leadership?

I

What is most revealing about the sheer bulk and the frenetic pace of inquiry is that the Western mind has inadvertently sentenced itself to an unrelieved restiveness. Perhaps this was what Pascal was foreseeing when he wrote (in 1657),

> I have discovered that all human evil comes from this, man's being unable to sit still in a room,

an observation that has been echoed by Lewis Thomas (1979) and by T. S. Eliot (1930) ("Teach us to sit still").

It is that we have construed ourselves and the purpose of life in such a way that we must forever be pursuing the "Truth," but never be satisfied with whatever we catch. Laurence Sterne seems to have captured a presentiment of this predicament of the condition of modern intellectual life when he wrote, in *The Life and Opinions of Tristam Shandy, Gentleman* (about 1760):

> Tell me, ye learned, shall we for ever be adding so much to the bulk — so little to the stock?
>
> Shall we for ever make new books, as apothecaries make new mixtures, by pouring only out of one vessel into another?
>
> Are we for ever to be twisting, and untwisting, the same rope? for ever in the same track — for ever at the same pace?
>
> Shall we be destined to the days of eternity . . . to be shewing the relics of learning, as monks do the relics of their saints — without working one — one single miracle with them?

What is revealed in the sheer bulk and the frenetic pace of the pursuit of our fascination with the idea of leadership in the twentieth century is indeed something peculiar to the modern mind. That is our (usually unstated) conviction that there is a past which is explainable and, if rightly explained, would thereby enable us either to predict or to control the future.

We are fascinated with the idea of leadership because it is our understanding that present conditions are a result of past happenings; that future conditions will be a result of present happenings; and that, without visible leadership, we are adrift in the seas of time. The claim of the modern intellect is that there is a tangible future for humankind on this earth, and that those who are enfranchised in any way to speak authoritatively about that future have therein a special responsibility. For the intellectual and the academic observer, that responsibility seems to have devolved upon a way of explaining what has happened in such a way that the future can be insured: that what will happen is what *ought* to happen.

Leadership is one such explanation.

It was a concept largely unknown to the American Indian. For, as Ruth Beebe Hill

(1979) has pointed out to us, "His was the spirit not seeking truth but holding on to truth." His concern was individual: how to achieve his maximum spiritual potential. That was all he needed to know. And to know that, he needed neither to lead nor to be led. He understood that whatever he needed to know, nature sooner or later would reveal to him.

Leadership is universal (Lewis, 1974; Cohen & Middleton, 1967; Werner, 1984; Dumont, 1970; Barth, 1965; Ford, 1938; Kracke, 1978). How it functions in a given society, and what its legitimate sources and ends may be, are given in understood social arrangements. But to *conceive* of leadership, as we have in the West, is to endow "it" with the life of a tool. In becoming conscious of such a thing as leadership, we have become uniquely burdened by it. We do not see leadership as the means by which we bring the present into alignment with the past, but by which we make the future out of the present. In this, we differ from every civilization that has preceded us. In our belief that how we understand the world and what we do about it bears upon our future, we have come more and more to *have* that future which has been continuously created in those ways we have understood the world and how we have acted upon those understandings.

Our way of understanding leadership is based in the belief that we can, and perhaps must, guide the course of human affairs. Or, at the very least, that the nature of leadership is that it does, whatever the details of its workings, change the course of human affairs, small or large. The idea of leadership fascinates us not because of the way it is, but because of the way we are.

There has to be a certain angst in that odd mix of motives that has produced more than 5000 studies of leadership thus far in this century, yet precludes any sense of having grasped its final quarry, of having arrived at its destination. But it is a nemesis of our own making, a bugbear of modernism itself. For if our way of seeing the world requires us to understand as self-evident that the direction of things is toward an ever-unfolding future — that what happens today is determined by what happened yesterday, and that the seeds we plant today may bear fruit only in the future — then so must our explanations of things today be forever unfinished, tentative, vaguely incomplete, equivocal, and not quite satisfying, as a means to some end yet to come.

It is this linearity of our own thought, of our own peculiar way of coming at the world, that poises us ceaselessly between a past we feel compelled to explain and a future we are condemned to anticipate. What that ever-proliferating bulk of studies reveals of our culture is not that we have missed some facts, but that we have and will continue to use our facts to build whatever bridge to the future may strike our fancy.

A future yet to happen is a truth yet to be gained. Fifty thousand studies will not succeed where 5,000 have failed. An ultimate truth would stop history. And it is not to truth, but to history, that we belong.

II

So we will go on making studies of leadership, and we will not "arrive."

Even at the outset, however, there are other impediments. They inhere, not in the object of our fascination, not in the thing itself, but in certain peculiar convolutions of the Western mind (as is always the case).

There is one bit of wisdom which is sometimes (probably wrongly) attributed to Herodotus: "Any event, once it has occurred, can be made to appear inevitable by a competent historian" (Dickson, 1978). A variation on this skepticism as to the explainability of events is Ben Franklin's (in *Poor Richard's Almanack*): "Historians relate not so much what is done as what they would have believed." Still another is von Schlegel's (1798) that "An historian is a prophet in reverse."

The theme of Carlyle's seminal treatise on "leadership," *On Heroes and Hero Worship,* is simply that "The history of the world is but the biography of great men"—what we know today as the resurgently influential "great man theory" of history. Lee Iacocca's recent book (Iacocca, 1984) belongs to this genre—which hinges upon the belief that events are consequences (or effects) which have causes, and that the cause is some "great man," in the past a hero, today a "leader."

There is, of course, no way of determining how valid our accounts of the world may be—whether we are scientists or historians. What we do know is that the "paradigms" or basic assumptions we employ to make sense of the world color our accounts in ultimately indecipherable ways. Is the "leader" merely an instrument of the workings-out of events, or does he *make* those events happen? To address this dilemma, Sidney Hook (1955) proposed that there are two kinds of leaders, or heroes: the "eventful" man, who just happens to be at the right place at the time of a turning or a change; and the "event-making" man, who causes events to take a different (*his*) course. Hook's is the middle ground between Carlyle's position and that of the Spencerians and the Marxists and the radical evolutionists, who argue that individuals are irrelevant to the working out of history: It wouldn't have made any difference who would have been in what position, or what he had or had not done; history would have turned out the same way.

These are remarkably different beliefs, and remarkably different ways of explaining why things happen the way they do. Each side can muster evidence which is convincing at least to those who begin with that particular belief, which is as much the case here as it is in science and folklore. A "theory" of something may work, but that does not preclude the possibility that another "theory" of the same thing might not work equally well. Wave theories and particle theories of light, for example, seem to work equally well in some instances.

Do certain individuals, then, having certain characteristics and doing certain things, *make* events happen, or do they merely "midwife" those happenings? It could hardly go unnoticed that even our purported leaders typically want to have it both ways. If a particular company is failing, for example, or if our nation's economy is not performing as promised or predicted, the explanation is frequently that "events" have somehow conspired and that there is "nothing that can be done about what is happening." On the other hand, if a particular company is succeeding, in spite of adversity, or if the nation's economy is doing well in spite of contrary predictions, there always seems to be someone in some high office ready and willing to take credit for this turn of events—ready to be acclaimed the indispensable leader, the one responsible for making those things happen.

It is the same paradox that enmeshed the Marxist ideology: the Revolution was historically inevitable—so get out there, disciples, and make sure it happens.

In one sense, it is easy to understand that even the best and most powerful amongst us is ever poised to argue the case either way. For there is no critical test of the truth of one position over the other. The rub is that all historical events are unique, and that history is cumulative and irreversible. Did Lee Iaccoca "lead" Chrysler to success, or would Chrysler's fate have turned around under the circumstances regardless of who had been chairman? We can never know. No one else *was* chairman of Chrysler during that period of time, and there is no way to test any one else *as* chairman under those same circumstances, since they have come and gone. The same predicament holds for Churchill, Gandhi, Hitler, De Gaulle, Martin Luther King, Jr.—for any of history's supposed leaders. We can take the position that they were, as individuals, indispensable to how things turned out. Or we can take the position that there was a set of circumstances brewing such that any number of individuals, having any number of personal characteristics, could have provided the necessary "leadership"—i.e., the movement from one state of affairs to another.

This is not to take anything away from such leaders—past, present, or future. It is merely to acknowledge the rather profound dilemma that the nature of the beast is such that we could never really know for sure.

Although it is occasionally revived, either for sentimental reasons (as was likely the case with John F. Kennedy), or by some graduate student (whose tools are likely to dictate his thoughts), this is what dealt the death blow to the long-standing "trait" theory of leadership inspired by Carlyle (cf. Jennings, 1960; Wildavsky, 1984; Bass, 1981, esp. Part 2).

Still, there is something about *us,* about the way particularly we Americans are constructed in our minds, that makes it difficult to give up wanting it to be the case that there are certain individuals having certain characteristics who make history. Would someone else have "discovered" America if Columbus hadn't? Would someone else have made a "tin Lizzie," or a motor car for the folk, if Henry Ford and Adolf Hitler hadn't? We know that the *idea* of evolution was percolating before and all around Darwin. Would we have been without the crucial influence on our thought and way of life that has been produced by the idea of evolution if it hadn't been for Darwin, the man? Would we have had the "New Deal" if someone other than Franklin D. Roosevelt had been elected President at that time? Would we have been without "modern" music if Stravinsky hadn't lived?

We can say no, or we can say yes. And we can do so confident that the one is no more, or less, speculative and faith-fired than the other.

III

There is another impediment to the *way* we would like to understand the phenomena of leadership, and which inheres in another unique bias of the Western mind—of our assumptive way of "coming at" the world. We would do well to consider it before moving on to ask what our interpretations of the nature of leadership tell us to this point and what, if any, useful alternatives there may yet be.

It is, indeed, a problem having ancient roots. It was once known as the fallacy of post hoc, ergo propter hoc—essentially our inclination to look for the cause of something in some other thing that preceded it, and to reason backward: since this happened, this must have "caused" it.

The problem in practice is a bit more complex. It is that, having posited a preceding cause of a subsequent effect, we could now, by placing the cause in place, produce the effect. The difficulty for our penchant for wanting to do something *with* our understanding of leadership is obvious: having posited, for example, that a certain leadership "style" is the critical factor, we set about trying to inculcate in people that certain "style" so that they too can "lead."

This way of thinking is so deeply ingrained in the Western mind, both popular and scientific, that textbooks are written (and consumed) purporting to "teach" people how to be leaders—by developing this or that trait, by pursuing this or that "style," by manipulating the situation or the environment in this or that way, by practicing this or that skill of "relating to" people, and so on. To the making of prescriptions for leadership based upon such reasoning, there would seem to be no limits. While, it would seem, some panacea-promising twist on a currently fashionable bit of conventional wisdom about how-to-do-it is the key to the management best-seller (e.g., *The One-Minute Manager, The Search for Excellence,* etc., *etc.*), most management and management-related books (and, more recently, most books about politics) offer explicit or implicit recipes for leadership. That this is "asking for trouble" (Levitt, 1970) seems not to have stayed the flood.

After a while, this puts us in the peculiar position of having more experts *on* leadership than we have leaders, if we are to give credence to "Our Critical Shortage of Leadership" (Reichley, 1971). Or of acknowledging, with some consternation, that while we were busy generating thousands of studies *about* leadership in the U.S., there were others all over the globe *assuming* leadership in one or more industrial, intellectual, or technological pursuits.

What it comes down to, of course, is that there is no apparent relationship between what we presume to be our cumulative knowledge about leadership, as evidenced by the growing bulk of studies, tracts, and treatises on that subject, and our apparent ability to create, produce, or enable the kind of leadership we desire in our organizations and institutions. Our so-called "crisis of leadership" (Peters, 1979; Jaworski, 1982) has occurred in the midst of our rapidly-expanding "understanding" of "it."

Is it possible that our highly scientized, rational, linear, cause → effect world-view actually prevents us from seeing what we might otherwise be able to see, from knowing what we really want to know about leadership? Is it possible that that way of seeing and explaining the world which has been so fruitful for us in our mastery and exploitation of the material world is just not an appropriate way of looking at and understanding leadership?

To understand something in the human world does not mean that one can thereby control it or reproduce it. We may understand in some sense *how* Michelangelo went about his sculpting. But is there anything we could know about how he did so that would permit us to create another Michelangelo? Or is his importance to us in part that there has been only one?

Those who followed Matisse may have learned something by studying his way of going about things that influenced *their* ways of creating images on canvas. But don't we value his work because it was unique, and their work because *it* was unique?

And Bach could only have happened once. After that, he would not have captured attention, because he had already happened.

If one replicated in one's own life every event that occurred in Roosevelt's life, would one therefore *be* Roosevelt? Would one therefore even be recognized as a "leader"? If how Iaccoca "did it" is all that readily understandable and transferable, why doesn't someone at Ford simply learn how he "did it" and beat him at his own game?

Is the logic of all such matters such that the "right" leader will emerge in all cases? Is there some "secret hand," some intelligence at work which makes things turn out the way they *should*? Why do they seem so in retrospect? Would Jesus Christ even get a hearing today? Where? And how? Or is a leader a kind of "superman," able to muster whatever resources and strategies and powers over people and things that, in retrospect, turn out to have been just what was necessary?

We are burdened with a mentality which has given us to seek interpretations that better fit what we would believe than what might be going on. In a high school physics lab, we can safely make three assumptions: one, that the best way to understand something is to break it down into its parts; two, that all of the parts of the same category—carbon atoms, for example—are interchangeable; and three, that one can reconstitute a whole if one puts the right set of parts together in the correct fashion. In permitting our ways of thinking to become scientized, we've imported those kinds of assumptions everywhere—certainly, to a large extent, in the study of leadership (and in the social and behavioral "sciences" generally).

But:

1. The social whole, in which what we want to understand as leadership occurs, is never merely the sum of its parts. Indeed, what is most important about that social whole is lost when one begins to focus on its supposed parts. A social whole—a group, a movement, a community, a civilization—has vital characteristics of its own, which are not to be found in any of its parts.

2. The parts of any social whole—any social enterprise, any institution—are ultimately people, and ultimately that which makes them human: their ideas, their hopes their fears, their beliefs, their understandings, their feelings, their ways of being and doing and knowing and having and saying in the world—*and* the relationships that obtain between and among them. Lives are cumulative and irreversible. The parts of social wholes are not interchangeable, even with themselves at another time, or in another place, or as otherwise related. And those relationships—each and all—are inescapably systemic: a change in one part alters the whole, just as it necessitates readjustment of the other parts.

3. Social wholes are not constituted of interchangeable building blocks. A different set of people at the constitutional Congress, saying different things and reacting differently—thinking differently, believing differently—would surely have launched this nation differently, if at all. Presumably, Winston Churchill was still Winston Churchill at the end of World War II. But he was not elected again to high office. He was not interchangeable, even with himself.

Nor are these flaws in our overly-scientized Western mind-set negated by a shift of focus away from leadership "traits" and "styles" to "the situation," or the locus of cause to "contingencies." (These variations are surveyed in detail in Bass, 1981, esp. Parts 4, 5, and 6; since there are excellent and extensive reviews of the various "theories" of leadership available, as, e.g., in Chemers, 1984, and J. Hunt, 1984, we need not repeat those efforts here.) They are all, more or less, colored by this same flawed set of predispositions.

What we need, apparently, is a different kind of paradigm—one that does not assume that the characteristics of a leadership situation are separable from that situation, *nor* that the characteristics of leaders and followers are separable from those persons in that place and at that time. The *un*likelihood of this occurring in the foreseeable future is given in Hosking, Hunt, Schriesheim, & Stewart (1984). But the balance of this paper will be given over to an attempt to provide some additional impetus for that shift.

IV

There have been a number of observers who have proposed alternative ways of approaching leadership that seem to be grounded in, or pointing toward, a different kind of paradigm: S. Hunt, 1984; Gibb, 1969; Beer, 1972; Nafe, 1930; Bennis, 1982; Tucker, 1981; Nisbet, 1950; McGregor, 1966; Bailey, 1969; Mitroff, 1983; Almond, 1973; Geertz, 1977; Prentice, 1961; Grob, 1984; Needleman, 1982; and the several papers in McCall & Lombardo, 1978—e.g., Pondy, Weick, Vaill, Pfeffer. Since there seems to be growing consensus on at least one aspect of the study of leadership, that "Conceptually and methodologically, leadership research has bogged down" (McCall & Lombardo, 1978, p. 152), we can look to these and like voices—including some older ones—for ideas on which to ground a concept of leadership that might generate more relevant and productive inquiry, and perhaps inform a more humane practice.

Nafe, for example, was saying as early as 1930 that the attributes of leadership exist only in the minds of the led. This is a posture that seems to me to be unavoidable, and indispensable to any grounded way of seeing leadership; but it has nonetheless been largely lost on those who have for years pursued the "traits" of leaders, or who have more recently been championing the cause of "styles" of leadership. It may be (indeed, must certainly have been for traditional or "primitive" peoples) that those followers have in common an image or a set of criteria for attributing leadership, and this would make it appear that there is something ("charisma"?) emanating from the designated leader. But the leader cannot *have* what his or her followers can not or will not attribute to him or her. What this should suggest to us is that leadership is not only subjective, but intersubjective: a designated leader who does not perform in a manner consistent with his or her followers' expectations is a leader without followers, which is to say, not a leader. That a leader have certain characteristics observable to an outsider is neither a necessary nor a sufficient condition of leadership. What is, is that those who enfranchise a leader (his or her followers or constituency) see or believe him or her to *be*, to *know*, to *have,* to be *doing*, or to be *saying* that for which they *would* enfranchise him or her.

Gibb (1969) makes a very similar point when he suggests that it is not per se the personalities of leaders and/or followers, or even the characteristics of situations, that enter into the leadership relation, "but rather the perception of the leader by himself and by others, the leader's perception of those others, and the shared perception by leader and others of the group and the situation" (p. 268). What is consequential in any situation, he is saying, is, as we would say today, "the definition of the situation" by the followers, and by the leader, a vital concept derived from W. I. Thomas (Thomas & Znaniecki, 1918).

Nisbet writes: "It is not possible to regard problems in social relations in the same perspective in which the physicist or chemist regards his problems" — for the several reasons I have previously set forth. And he continues, crucially, I believe: "To draw organization out of the raw materials of life is as much the objective of the leader as it is of the artist. *Structure or organization is the primary concern of the leader, as form is the concern of the artist.* Leadership is no more comprehensible than any other imaginative creation" (Nisbet, 1950, pp. 708–709). The perhaps culturally imbedded thrust of much of what has been written about leadership is to see the leader somewhat as an "engineer" — as one who forges social or historical events with certain tools and technics. And the task of the observer is to determine what those tools and technics are, so that they might be characterized, categorized, and handed on to other, aspiring leaders (or observers). Thus learning (or learning about) leadership is very much like learning how to "engineer" something (or how things are "engineered"). What Nisbet is saying, however, is that leaders are much more like *bricoleurs* (Lévi-Strauss's useful term) than like engineers. A *bricoleur* is a person who makes things work by ingeniously using whatever is at hand, being unconcerned about the "proper" tools or resources. The net effect is that neither the leader nor the situation nor the particular "hows" are reproducible; each instance is unique, since it is created out of whatever is available (as seen by the leader and the followers) at the moment — including beliefs and resources. The leader's function is therefore *bricolage* (fixing things on the spot through a creative vision of what is available and what might be done with it — people, ideas, resources) — and not *method*.

By way of contrast, it is interesting that Burns (1978), in the 460-odd pages of his Pulitzer Prize and American Book Award-winning *Leadership,* seemingly considered by most to be the definitive study to date, never once mentions *entrepreneurship*. While granting the myopia that facilitates political "scientists' " assumption that it is politics that makes the world go 'round, economists that it is the economy, psychologists that it is the psyche, there is something more basic at work here: *how* we understand leadership, and how we — how our own minds work — are reflected in that understanding. And what the human consequences may be of one vs. another understanding. What better example of leadership do we have than in successful entrepreneurial activity? Couldn't Martin Luther King, Jr. (who operated from what Tucker, 1981, refers to as an "unconstituted" leadership position) be seen — fruitfully — as an entrepreneur?

Prentice's (1961) contribution was that he encouraged us, not to focus upon issues such as popularity, power, showmanship, or even wisdom in long-range planning — but upon "the accomplishment of a goal through the direction of human assistants." He wanted to return people (not method or technique) to the center of things: "When the leader succeeds, it will be because he has learned two basic lessons: men are complex, and men are different." And to remind us that leaders cannot make happen what their followers cannot make happen, he says, "Toscanini could not get great music from a high-school band." Further, about the making of leaders: "no one can become a Toscanini by imitating his mannerisms." Why? In part, because those who interpreted and acted upon his mannerisms on the podium were themselves accomplished musicians, and had voluntarily and wholeheartedly deferred to his direction, which accumulated in those mannerisms, *as interpreted*.

McGregor's influence is well-known. In addition to his commitment to the humanizing of our organizations and institutions (in opposition to "scientific" management), McGregor also stood outside of the hegemonic mind-set of the day by stressing not factors, but *relationship:* "leadership consists of a relationship between the leader, his followers, the organization, and the social milieu (McGregor, 1966), a view that might have been furthered by the current "contingency" theories of leadership, had it not been for the fact that contingency theorists typically reduce the whole to its parts, thereby mutilating the very phenomenon we want to understand and, I believe, as McGregor wanted it to be understood. McGregor also pointed to our captivation by the scope and the celebrity-status of "mass" leaders, and felt strongly that we need to "find ways to reward (people) that will persuade them that we consider outstanding leadership at any level to be a precious thing." We don't, of course, and this is one reason why we turn to those visible "leaders" in government — particularly federal government — to solve our problems *for* us. But, as we will see, local scale problems not only do not have their solution at this lofty level, but are actually exacerbated there. The need to see leadership as a necessary function at all levels of social life, and in all arenas of life, from politics and work to everyday community life, is a key point also for Nisbet (1950) and Tucker (1981).

While his whole approach to the strategy or the "politics" of leadership is provocative, the focalizing issues we might take from Bailey (1969) are (a) that leadership is an enterprise, and (b) that duties performed by followers (out of a sense of righteousness) "impose upon the leader the obligation not merely to serve the cause, but also to shine forth as an exemplar of its ideals" (p. 37). It is a point which helps to make clearer the *nature* of the relationship between leader and follower — that it is no wise unidirectional, that it is not limited by the leader's "powers" of influence, and that followers influence leaders altogether as much as leaders influence followers, but in different ways.

In his "Centers, Kings, and Charisma: Reflections on the Symbolics of Power," Geertz (1977), following Edward Shils' interpretation of Weber's concept of "charisma," asks us to remember that charisma is (a) symbolic — and not psychological, i.e., not a matter of traits; and (b) not a matter of popular appeal but of being at the heart of things (and their inherent — to those involved — sacredness). A leader's influence, if that is what we must call it, is never "merely" rhetorical, as some reductionists would have us believe, and cannot be had from a bag of tricks, no matter how astute or well-researched. The scientizers miss, because they would ignore as "not scientific," the very conditions that undergird leadership. We should look, Geertz says, for "the vast universality of the will of kings" (and of presidents, generals, party secretaries, and those at the forefront of any social "movement," one would suppose) "in the same place we look for that of gods: in the rites and images through which it is exerted" (p. 124). And there it is "numinous" — not amenable to the secular, literal, "objective" orientation of the scientific mind. There is, in every form of leadership, both governance *and* a set of symbolic forms "expressing the fact that it is in truth governing," a point we will return to below.

Almond (1973) emphasizes the creative aspects of leadership when he suggests that the "innovative leader [all leaders of any import?]" is the one who offers new options, or combines resources in creative ways, thereby suggesting that the patron thinker for the study of leadership should have been Bergson, perhaps, and not Comte; Nietzsche, perhaps, and not Newton. Or perhaps Needleman (1982), who writes: "Life has a meaning when a new question appears, and when the external circumstances of life arrange themselves as material for the investigation of that question" (p. 121). The leader's proposition is the question, and what he makes possible is the followers' investigation of that question. Van Gogh, like Gandhi, posed a question; all who "followed" (in spirit) the one or the other sought some special meaning of life in the pursuit of that question.

Mitroff (1983), like Beer (1972), focuses upon relationship. Beer, especially, although he does not specifically address "leadership," seems to be suggesting that what we are looking for is to be found in the *relationship* as such, and not in the components of that (or any) relationship. What leadership offers is not so much the relationship with the leader as an alternative relationship with oneself. What leaders create, with the help of their followers, are what George Steiner (1975) refers to as "alternities" — "The world can be other" (than it is). Every instance of leadership is an instance of an alternity, an alternative sense of being in the world which brings leader and follower into a very special relationship in a unique enterprise. Not only do those who "follow" and appreciate Picasso relate to him (his symbolic works, their interpretations of "him") in a unique way, but this changed relationship with or within oneself leads one (the follower) to "see" the world and the work of other painters differently from that point on. It is leadership that enables those changes within oneself that change the world (in the sense that one's relationships with certain aspects of the world are altered). Every leader–follower relationship hinges upon a mutually imagined alternity.

Many of the papers gathered in McCall & Lombardo's *Leadership: Where Else Can We Go?* (1978) are thought-provoking, but in different ways. For the most part, as the title would indicate, they raise questions about the conventional wisdoms of leadership, both lay and academic. Vaill, for example suggests that leadership is not at all a science, but a "performing art," and needs to be approached as such. Weick's is an attempt, through a sophisticated mechanical metaphor, to propose that there is a sort of logic to the leader-follower "connection," but that it is not at all as simplistic and as unconvoluted as present models would have us assume. Pfeffer would remind us that our belief in, and attribution of "leadership" to, our leaders is a way of legitimating our own belief in the effectiveness of individual control. We want to believe that we as individuals have a range of control over our own lives and what happens, and subscribe to certain leaders (indeed, keep alive the very *idea* of leadership) in order to reinforce that belief. For Pondy, all instances of leadership are novel. Leadership is thus a matter of "improvisations that work" (recalling Almond). Pondy suggests that Wittgenstein's ideas on language games are relevant, first, because they suggest "that we begin to think of leadership, like language, as a collection of games with *some* similarities, but no single characteristic common to all of them." Second, to do so "begins to map out the philosophical underpinnings of the role of language and meaning in leadership and behavior," underpinnings which the majority of observers and researchers have been able to do without but which, in this perspective, seem crucial to our understanding.

In *Theaetetus,* Socrates plays one of Wittgenstein's language games by recreating leadership through the metaphor of midwife. Grob (1984) examines the Socratic "model," concluding that "the midwife-leader . . . is the epitome of the leader as one who, having acknowledged his or her own need to examine the course of life (p. 279)," enables others to do the same — providing what Burns (1978) refers to and gives preference to as "transformative" leadership. It is an idea which is nicely played by Nietzsche, who saw the leader as providing the injunction to "overcome" one's present self, and as the *Übermensch* — as the "bridge" to transcendence, not as goal.

It may be, as Weber suggested, that the increasing routinization and disenchantment of the world has increased our need to believe in heroes and great figures, just as the probability of their appearance becomes less likely. Leadership then becomes a kind of "personification of social causality," as Pfeffer called it. Nonetheless, what we ought not be able to overlook in our approach to leadership is that reality is socially constructed (S. Hunt, 1984, after Cooley, 1909; Lippmann, 1922; Cassirer, 1944; Schutz, 1940–1953; Berger & Luckmann, 1966; Holzner, 1968; Polanyi & Prosch, 1975; Brown & Lyman, 1978; etc.), and that, whatever else a leader may be said to do, it is his or her indispensable function — with the complicity of his or her followers — to be a creator of social reality.

For Bennis (1982), this comes down to "the capacity to create and communicate a compelling vision of a desired state of affairs" in the first instance, and "the capacity to communicate (that) vision in order to gain the support of . . . multiple constituencies" in the second. The social reality thus created (though he does not use the term) provides the necessary space for empowerment, and for transformation.

It may be, as Lombardo and McCall (McCall & Lombardo, 1978) say, that "leadership in its present sense is a myth designed to simplify events and their causation." If so, the clear challenge is to create a concept of, an approach to, leadership which better describes ubiquitous social phenomenon on which so much of our present and future lives depends.

V

From the vantage points provided by such paradigmatic alternatives as these, we can better consider the implications of three of the most thoughtful and thought-provoking documents on leadership available to us today; Niccolò Machiavelli's *The Prince* (1903); Aaron Wildavsky's *The Nursing Father: Moses as a Political Leader* (1984); and Antoine de Saint-Exupéry's *The Wisdom of the Sands* (1948).

In the case of Machiavelli, it will be a matter of *re*consideration. Machiavelli is one of those authors who, like Freud, is more often referred to than read, and whose interpretation is therefore a matter of popular opinion. "Machiavellianism" is a neologism of modern popular opinion; it was not invented by Machiavelli. Throwing Machiavelli out because he seems to be saying some things we don't currently want to hear would be a bit like throwing the baby out with the bath water.

Machiavelli's basic premise was a very simple one. It was that the Prince's primary responsibility was to enact his office in such a way that the state would be preserved and nurtured for the benefit of the people. Where those of us of the more liberal Western political suasion differ is not on this point, but on *how* it is to be accomplished. Machiavelli lived and wrote in a time when every educated and responsible person, whether in church or government or academy, *knew* that what was good for the people, and therefore for the state, was not and could not be decided *by* the people (we forget that this is a *very* modern idea), but had to be decided by those who, by one rationale or another, held positions of legitimate responsibility. What some might refer to as our present radical democratism or radical egalitarianism is based in the belief that the more people involved in governance, of a state or a corporation or even a family, the better, somehow, the decisions that are taken are going to be—both for the group or the polity, and for the individuals who comprise it. Although we could hardly disagree with the proposition that having those in power decide for us does not always lead to better human or social circumstances, we would at the same time have to admit that there is no incontrovertible evidence that simply administering *public* opinion invariably leads to better human or social circumstances. So we should hear out what Machiavelli had to say, recognizing that he was immersed in a world-view very different from our own—or better, perhaps, that our potential misreading of him may come from the fact that we are immersed in a world-view very different from his.

So what did he have to say that might still have at least the value of thoughtful provocation for us?

For one, Machiavelli saw it as "an infallible rule that a prince who is not wise himself cannot be well advised" (p. 95). He would not agree that any ambitious person off the street who wanted to go into a bookstore and purchase a how-to-do-it book on leadership could thereby in any way become a great (or even a good) leader. The reason? You can't be a leader unless you are well advised, and you can't be well advised unless you are yourself wise. The Murphy's-law-like variant on this is that "If you know the difference between good advice and bad advice, you don't need advice." That this seems paradoxical cannot be taken to mean that it does not give us some kind of vital glimpse into the nature of leadership. For Machiavelli, the indispensable element in leadership is wisdom. For many moderns, it is seen to be method, or tactics. One wonders: which of these is the more "Machiavellian"?

Here is another misreading. Consider this passage carefully, for what it says (or implies) about how a leader must "lead":

> A prudent prince must . . . (choose) in his state wise men, and (give) these alone full liberty to speak the truth to him, but only of those things that he asks and of nothing else; but he must ask them about everything and hear their opinion, and afterwards deliberate by himself in his own way, and in these councils and with each of these men comport himself so that every one may see that the more freely he speaks, the more he will be acceptable (p. 94).

How modern this sounds. "Prudent" is a key word for Machiavelli. The "prudent" prince: by this, he means "being able to know the nature" of what is going on, of problems or difficulties, or the consequences of one path vs. another. It is the leader's wisdom that gives him this capacity to "know" the nature of things, not his office or his power. In this, Machiavelli was far less "Machiavellian" than the authors of many of our current best-sellers. What is also suggested in this particular passage is that the leader must not abdicate his ultimate responsibility for setting the agenda for those matters to which he and his (wise) ministers will give their attention and energies. Nor ought he, in the guise of any "ism," vaguely diffuse his ultimate responsibility for making judgments. Machiavelli would never have permitted his ideal prince to say, "*We* made that decision, and it appears to have been a wrong one." What he believed was that people had a different sense of *moral* responsibility for decisions that affected the lives of other people depending upon whether they were individually responsible for those decisions, or some group was. Machiavelli was more skeptical of bureaucratic machinations, and of the "bureaucratic mind," than even Weber.

Machiavelli saw the "good" leader's will as being essentially spiritual in its operation, or "numinous," as Geertz suggested. To those who looked up to him, he was not so much a man as a symbol—embodying all that they imagined in the possibilities of his governance. So he believed that the leader must always "show himself a lover of merit"—a point we hear repeated over and over in the current spate of books on "excellence"—but more, that he should always "honour those who excel in every art." And what he would be demonstrating here is not arrogance, but the value to each of his followers of that capacity to *discern* the excellent from the merely gaudy or noisy or fashionable, or even the normative, since mediocrity can be made normative. The problem with promoting excellence at work is not that people resist it, but that they can't discriminate it. And this incapacity, from Machiavelli's view, must be laid to their leaders.

Another of Machiavelli's provocations which may deserve our mulling over is his understanding that hatred is gained as much by good works as by evil. It is perhaps this kind of candor that offends us in Machiavelli. But again it may be our belief (which may be anchored in our belief in evolution and progress, etc.) that good will out, and that, if we enable universal suffrage, then we will have achieved the best of all possible ways of governance—that things will then turn out for us in the best possible way. What Machiavelli is suggesting, of course, is what the Romans knew: that you cannot confer a benefit on an unwilling person. People do not always do what is in their own best interests—overeating, undermoving, poor diets, smoking, drinking, unmeaningful jobs, militant ignorance or pedantry, believing oneself deserving of love but unable to give it: there are dozens upon dozens of examples. In a pluralistic society such as our own, it is becoming difficult to imagine that there is any legislative decision that can be made that would not anger *some* group somewhere, even if it were understood by those who devised it as being particularly for the benefit of the members of that group. So what is a leader to do? What Machiavelli would say to would-be leaders is that a decision which people like is not necessarily one that is good for them, and that a decision which is hated is not necessarily one that is bad for them. It isn't, he said, that easy. Is it the elected official's responsibility to "please" his constituency—to which Edmund Burke so eloquently replied "No!"—or to do what is "right"—for them and for the state? Is it the manager's job to "please" his employees (even if the business fails), or the parson's job to "please" his flock (even though a religious ideal fails), or the parent's job to "please" the children (even though *they* may fail as a result)? If there is a certain fashionableness to this view, does that make it right?

One of the most controversial passages in Machiavelli addresses this complex and sensitive issue. Inevitably, he said, there

> arises the question whether it is better to be loved more than feared, or feared more than loved. The reply is, that one ought to be both feared and loved, but as it is difficult for the two to go together, it is much safer to be feared than loved, if one of the two has to be wanting. For it may be said of men in general that they are ungrateful, voluble dissemblers, anxious to avoid danger, and covetous of gain; as long as you benefit them, they are entirely yours; they offer you their blood, their goods, their life and their children . . . when the necessity is remote; but when it approaches, they revolt. And the prince who has

relied solely on their words, without making other preparations, is ruined, *for the friend-ship which is gained by purchase and not through grandeur and nobility of spirit is mer-ited but not secured* . . . And men have less scruple in offending one who makes himself loved than one who makes himself feared; for love is held by a chain of obligation which, men being selfish, is broken whenever it serves their purpose; but fear is maintained by a dread of punishment which never fails . . . men love at their own free will, but fear at the will of the prince, and a wise prince must rely on what is in his power and not on what is in the power of others" (pp. 66, 68; emphasis added)

This is a truly remarkable passage. Machiavelli is not saying that there is an abstract moral or religious principle that can be taken to justify such behavior. He is saying that, *given* the way people *are* (not the way we imagine them to be, or the way they *should* be), there are certain strategies of conduct that must be employed, especially if one is to benefit those people despite themselves. The bitterest and costliest strike in General Electric's history — one which might well have disemployed everyone involved — followed from an at-tempt made by a well-intentioned contract negotiator to cut out all of the expensive and bad-tempered banterings connected with lengthy negotiations. He reasoned that, since it would all come down pretty close to X-position eventually anyway, why not be frank and open and simply "communicate" that and get it over with? The union negotiator, hearing the rationale, along with the company's "bottom-line" position, said, in effect, "Fine, let's start there."

If people were not as they are, leaders wouldn't have to adopt certain ways of seeing things, and certain ways of doing things — certain strategic postures; they could just do the "right thing." Given the direction that things took, who was the "leader" in the Garden of Eden: God, or the Devil?

This sounds very much like contemporary "contingency" theories of leadership. The difference is that Machiavelli is saying that a leader can be no better than he is wise; the con-temporary "contingency" theorists are saying that a leader is no better than his ability to change stripes, to take on the cloak of a different "style," some "tricks" that can be picked up at the corner bookstore. We would have modern leaders "purchase" their friendships, or the loyalty of their followers, and thereby to have them merited (in Machiavelli's view), but not secured. And leader-follower relations not secured is a present and future not secured.

About the leader's role in change, which seems to be a catchword of our modern world (cf. Kanter, 1983), Machiavelli offered this caveat: "there is nothing more difficult to carry out, nor more doubtful of success, nor more dangerous to handle, than to initiate a new or-der of things. For the reformer has enemies in all those who profit by the old order, and only lukewarm defenders in all those who would profit by the new order" (p. 22). Was there ever a politician, or a Mozart, who did not meet this in one form or another?

Machiavelli also spoke to the mutual dependence that leader and follower come to have on the other. "It is the nature of men," he wrote, "to be as much bound by the benefits that they confer as by those they receive" (p. 43). The nature of the bonds that fall upon the leader as a consequence of conferring benefits would seem to be much better understood by leaders in cultures other than our own. In Japan, for example, the obligations that the leader accumulates as he accepts increasing responsibilities are far more important to daily corporate life than are his privileges (DeMente, 1981). So only those who seek and can handle increased obligation are likely to become leaders. In America, those who seek lead-ership are often in pursuit of privilege and status, not obligation. This issue is dealt with also in a most stimulating way by Hyde (1983) and Doi (1973). Whatever the specific under-standings that enfranchise the leader–follower relationship, it is the viability of that relationship, and not a leader or followers as such, that is in all places and all times the sine qua non.

Machiavelli would have been as dismayed by our sense of expediency as we are by what we impute to him as his "Machiavellianism." He saw it necessary that the "prudent man should always follow in the path trodden by great men and imitate those who are most excellent, so that if he does not attain to their greatness, at any rate he will get some tinge of it" (p. 20). Is a leader to lead by "following"? Do people in small or large numbers "take the path trodden" by the greatest or most excellent? Is leadership merely a matter of identifying and aiding others to achieve their wants or to fulfill their appetites? The problem with the notion of "democratic" leadership is analogically set forth by Saint-Exupéry, who writes: "For man is so built that his appetite is the outcome of the food he eats and thus, if a part of you is always undernourished and half asleep for lack of a certain kind of food or exercise, you never think to ask for that food or exercise" (p. 200). Machiavelli, like Saint-Exupéry, believed that it was a part of every leader's responsibility to "awaken" his followers to that "food" or "exercise" they didn't know they needed. Can one determine what this is by asking them?

Almost 500 years later, at another time and another place, we have the voice of Wildavsky, whose anchorage point is that the highest stage of leadership is to teach one's followers how to do without help by helping them learn how to lead themselves. And how does he do this? By being himself ever a learner. Wildavsky suggests, in fact, that to learn about leadership is mainly and primarily to learn about learning. It is what a leader knows about learning that informs his ability to lead; it is what a leader is able to learn from his failures that stands as the measure of his greatness.

Wildavsky took Moses as the epitome of the learning, the "nursing," father. "What else is a leader if not a 'nursing father'? . . . The more power leaders seem to have, the more people depend on them" (p. 58). And how does one become a "nursing" father rather than merely a "father"? By transforming the "collective consciousness of a people so that they can live on without him" (p. 180). The indispensable executive, or parent, or teacher, or minister, or even friend, is not a leader but merely a parasite, one who is addicted to others' dependency.

The question of who is to be empowered to "awaken" whom and to what (of who is to be empowered to influence whom, and to what ends, or of who is to be empowered to lead whom, and where) is, of course, *the* political problematic — of every human society, past, present, and future. Human "ambivalence about leadership — yearning to be led while fearing to be oppressed" — is not peculiar to our own time and our own place, though we may have an exaggerated distaste for the apparent "elitism" involved in the inequality of influence. "For followers," Wildavsky continues, "the classical dilemma of leadership is that a regime or leader strong enough to get them through enormous difficulties may prove too great a threat to their future liberties" (p. 171). Churchill, who was not popularly chosen either before or after World War II, may be an example. Similarly, wanting the comforts and the mama-magic of home, but wanting to be "out from under" parental authority and "on one's own," is a dilemma for many young people in our Western world at a certain age. Wildavsky poses the problem for leaders in these terms:

> Just as people need rulers and yet fear them, just as leaders need followers and yet fear them, so Moses needed God and feared Him. Moses' experiences are suffused with ambivalence; he cannot be slave and free. How to marry the opposing qualities required for leadership — passion with patience, acceptance with reunication, authority with sharing power — is Moses' perpetual problem (pp. 39–40).

The need and the fear are both mutual. Our inclination, it would seem, is to oversimplify, or to mystify. We want to believe that if the would-be leader will follow certain rules or recipes, all will be well. But followers have always within their power that of disenfranchising a particular leader (President Nixon's resignation was not entirely his own idea, nor Eva Peron's hers), symbolically if not literally (as Chinese thought was purged of Confucianism, and Russian of Stalinism). Indeed, the leader "needs" his followers as much as they "need" him. And, to the extent the conditions of the fulfillment of these needs could be denied or withdrawn at any time, there is always risk in being either leader or follower.

A common complaint amongst novice administrators and would-be leaders is that they have insufficient "authority" to fulfill their "responsibilities." But this is precisely where leadership comes in, says Wildavsky: "Authority has got to be less than responsibility or the task would be completed before it was begun. Closing that gap is what leadership is about" (p. 60).

Given our peculiar cultural predispositions, we are increasingly enchanted with the notion that the obligation of those in power is to share it, and thereby to harness the dedication of subordinates. And Moses "teaches Joshua one lesson—leaders ought not to fear sharing authority. In the revolts that follow, Moses also teaches Joshua another—don't give away the store; you can't share what you haven't got" (p. 143). Our attempt to literalize equality leads us (and isn't this leadership as well?) to believe that we can (share what we haven't got); we not only believe in the absolute right of each to speak his piece, we'd like to fix things so that each utterance is treated as of equal import. We want "leadership," but we insist upon equality. This won't work. "Ordinary leadership is anathema because it is a prima facie instance of inequality" (p. 198). The crisis of leadership in the modern world may well be a crisis of belief: our belief that leadership can be had without inequality. And "the greater the gap between demand (for leadership) and support (for leadership), the larger the leadership problem" (p. 201).

Our impetus is to resolve such difficulties. There is a certain, to us, self-evident logic in that. But is that necessarily the path either to leadership or to our understanding of leadership? "The Mosaic books teach us (as Moses himself first had to learn) to recognize, without necessarily reconciling, difficulties," says Wildavsky. "If we observe Moses with all his flaws and comprehend his rule as an obstacle to as well as an opportunity for the people, if we recognize him as a source of harm as well as help, then we already have begun to learn about leadership" (p. 211).

And, finally, "Even as Moses was forced to accept his human limits, the failure to reach the Promised Land, we have to accept failure in our attempts to formulate a direct, didactic theory of leadership good for all regimes under every condition" (p. 211). Leadership is a creative achievement. Understanding leadership is, as well, a creative achievement. Whether we succeed or not is not the issue; whether or not those who put themselves into our hands are more capable of leading themselves as a result of having done so is.

Falling between the two in time, but beholden to neither, is the remarkable work of Antoine de Saint-Exupéry. Originally entitled *Citadelle,* in French, it is the story of the education of a great chieftain (caïd), who is being taught by his father, and who is trying to learn from his own experiences as the people's leader how to discern which moral and behavioral factors elevate, and which degrade, the people, which strengthen the empire, and which may cause it to decay. *Citadelle* is, literally, "man's estate." The aim of the great chieftain's life is to build a citadel in men's hearts. Everything revolves upon the twists and turns of the great chieftain's ruminations—as he works through his absolute commitment to learning how best to create the good state, which he knows can only be accomplished by creating and invoking those social conditions that compel virtue in his people.

He has learned, as did Joshua, that you can't share what you haven't got. So he recognizes that the true good of the individual and the pragmatic good of the state coincide (cf. Jonas, 1984). But he foresees that the pragmatic good of the state can only be assured through personal excellence. And the key factor, he comes to believe, is duty: "The imposition of duty on a man, and his acceptance of duties to be performed, are defined as the only means by which a citadel may be constructed. The central moral lesson is expressed in a metaphor: 'But the trees that I have seen shoot up the straightest were not those that grew in freedom' " (p. x).

He speaks with a voice very much unlike our modern one. Still, we seek a better understanding of leadership in spite of our modern predilections.

For Saint-Exupéry, the matter came down ultimately to communication. He understood his book to be an extended answer to the one central question: "What can one, what *must* one, say to men?" And the paradoxical truth, observed Andre Gide, is that man's happiness lies not in freedom but in his acceptance of duty. The leader's responsibility is above all else, therefore, "to nurture a fellowship of men in which each *must* do his duty by all, and all do theirs by each, at the behest of love" (p. xvii). So the leader is "a ferryman to whom God has entrusted a generation and who bears them safe from shore to shore . . . I have enfolded my people in love" (p. 14). "My work," the great chieftain says, "is to found men" (p. 10), "so I resolved to enrich them with their love, despite their unwillingness" (p. 16).

What is different here is the notion that loving or caring for one's followers or dependents does not mean indulging or coddling or pandering to them, but refusing to let them default themselves — which is always necessarily defaulting others, and indirectly the state, the pragmatic good of which is indispensable to the future. The great chieftain saw that hierarchy is vital to the "house" within which all men dwell: "Where men are becoming clotted together in a morass of uniformity I re-establish hierarchies . . . I renew directives where men have settled tamely down, each in his pothole, calling stagnation happiness" (p. 18) . . . "I rearm man so he may *be*" (p. 19).

Otherwise, he believed, men will destroy "their best possession, the meaning of things." He knew that "the meaning of things lies not in the things themselves but in our attitude toward them," so his obligation was to be the architect of man's dwelling-place (his meanings). "I build my civilization . . . as poets build their poems" (p. 21), for "those tribes degenerate who no logner write their poems but read them" (p. 30).

He believed that true happiness "comes from the joy of deeds well done, the zest of creating things new" (p. 37), and that "the quality of my empire's civilization rests not on its material benefits but on men's obligations and the zeal they bring to their tasks" (p. 30).

Why should I, he says elsewhere, take sides with that which *is*, against that which *should* be or *might* be? To be just, he believed, we have to choose. To judge another, we have to judge in virtue of that other's trust. The question is of what was he, or of what should he have been, a trustee? Justice means regarding oneself or another as a vehicle or a pathway — to what true good or virtue?

The great chieftain also came to understand that virtue (we would say today "excellence") arises from the quality or the import of that to which we give our concern. So it was incumbent upon the leader to give his concern only to those things which would enable the construction of the good. And "Nothing I see worthy of my concern but the fertile collaboration of one man through another" (p. 40). "For a civilization is built on what is required of men, not on that which is provided for them. True it is that, after the long day's work, this wheat supplies their food. But this is not the side of things that means most for a man:

what nourishes his heart is not what he gets from the wheat, but what he gives to the wheat" (p. 43).

The great chieftain understood that the value of the leader lay not in what he did or did not do, but in how he perceived things, not in themselves, but always compared to how they ought to be — for the good of the people. He also understood that the ultimate measure of the greatness of a leader was to be found in the greatness that he induced and nurtured (or made necessary) in his people, those to whom he was obligated. And the key to this was always *meaning,* the creation or the architectonics of the higher meaning of things:

> Wherefore it is our bounden duty to quicken whatever is great in man, and to exalt his faith in his own greatness.
> For the nourishment of which he stands in greatest need is drawn not from things themselves but from the knot that holds things together . . . not from a tract of sand but from a certain relation between it and the tribesman." (p. 55)

For any leader, the issue of power is always problematic. How is one to lead, truly, not because of one's power, but in spite of it? The great chieftain's answer to this dilemma is that "power does not justify itself by severity, but wholly by the simplicity of the language it sponsors . . . I can enforce my will when I *simplify,* when I constrain each man to become different, clearer visioned, more generous and feverent — in a word, at one with himself and his aspirations" (p. 60) (cf. Janda, 1960; Zaleznik & deVries, 1975). He saw also that power corrupts, and that the great leader first establishes himself as incorruptible even in the seat of absolute power. Then he is fit to lead others.

The leader's contribution is always and everywhere a special way of *seeing* — of somehow being immune to the pitfalls of words and the handicaps of conventional wisdom. On this point, the great chieftain's father says to him, "Learn, my son, to listen, not to the sounds of words that weave the wind, nor to reasonings that throw dust in your eyes. Learn to look farther" (p. 67). And by this he understood that one's looking is enabled and constrained by what one is looking *for,* by one's convictions about what the nature of things *should be.* So it is gaining a keener and keener sense of how things should be that one comes to have this special perception that is indispensable to the leader's judgment and to his sense of justice.

What the great chieftain saw was that the course of events is given in men's actions, in what they do, or don't do. And that right action is a function of right thought, which is in turn a function of the *necessity* of the situation. So it was the leader's duty to construct those necessities in the situation. "What you do, you stablish; and that is all . . . We do not deceive the tree; it grows as we train it to grow — and all else is words that weave the wind" (p. 70).

The question of whether the leader is one who more clearly sees and forecasts the future has long been with us. The great chieftain says, "I would be wrong were I to say I had been able to forecast, when what I did was to create . . . . The future is what we build." And he returns to the idea of our construction of reality in our poetic expression of it, as he continues,

> giving much thought to the future is vain. Only one task is worthy of doing and that is to *express* the Here and Now. And to express means building, out of the infinite diversity of the Here and Now, a visage dominating it. (p. 84)

The leader is thus one who alters or guides the manner in which his followers "mind" the world by giving it a compelling "face." A leader at work is one who gives others a different sense of the *meaning* of that which they do by recreating it in a different form, a different "face," in the same way that a pivotal painter or sculptor or poet gives those who follow him (or her) a different way of "seeing"—and therefore saying and doing and knowing in—the world. A leader does not tell it "as it is"; he tells it as it *might be*, giving what "is" thereby a different "face."

What we know as the deadening vacuousness of life in the more bureaucratic of our organizations and institutions stems from a certain logic: the logic of rationality. For the great chieftain, logic is the death of life. Where we may strive for the perfect efficiency through the logic of rules or "operations," the great chieftain moved contrarily. "Build not an empire where everything is perfect," he says. "Nay, rather build an empire where all is zeal" (p. 45). The rational organization and the rational manager are antithetical to leadership, as it is understood here.

And we are witness to how large organizations are often anathema to creativity, to innovation. On this, the great chieftain says, "we must not subject him who creates to the desires of the multitude. It is, rather, his creation that must become the multitude's desire" (p. 92). It is the leader's task to create the "system" (as we would say today) wherein this is not only possible, but necessary. "Salvation lies, my father said, in necessity" (p. 97).

For the follower as much as for the leader, life's work is ever to greaten oneself. For "such is man that he rejoices only in what he himself builds up, and, to enjoy the poem, he needs must underto the toil of its ascent" (p. 119) . . . "for a man owes himself to that which he creates" (p. 126). The leader is the "architect" of all of those everyday necessities which make the follower the architect of *his* own destiny. The leader does not give life. He gives his followers the tools with which to make life, *and* the necessity to do so. It is thus that each compels the other to grow greater. It is a process of leading them higher on *their* mountain.

The great chieftain well understood the reciprocal nature of the leader-follower relationship: "I who reign am more subject to my people than any of my 'subjects' is to me" (p. 138). But that does not mean, for him (as it does for many contemporaries), that one leads others by following them. It means, rather, than one is more obligated to one's followers than they to him. And the nature of that obligation is wisely to construct and express things so that there will always be an ineluctable necessity for the follower to greaten himself in his duties to himself, his fellows, and the polity (or the social environment, which the ancient Chinese referred to as "The Great Mother"). The one thing that matters is the performance of one's task, the effort. "It [the task] continues, whereas the end to be attained is but an illusion of the climber" (p. 141). "It is the going-towards that matters, not the destination" (p. 150). "As for the future, your task is not to foresee, but to enable it" (p. 155).

And always the great chieftain comes back to the centrality of the *meaning* of things: "For your life goes to the rhythm of an empire built not of things but of the meaning of things" (p. 240). The leader's task is the creation and the re-creation of the meaning, not of things-in-themselves, but of the relations between things. He would know, too, that people give birth to that on which they fix their minds, and that his (or her) task is therefore to "fix their minds" on that which will greaten them, and give them endless zeal for that which they do, and are. In all of this, he would fix their minds upon their duty, to themselves and to others. For "when a man complains that the world has failed him, it means that he has failed to do his duty by the world" (p. 304). To greaten oneself is little by little to realize and take joy in being the instrument of one's own destiny, and thus of the world's. It is the leader's responsibility to enable his people to be the architects of their own greatness, out of the conditions of mind and spirit which he has orchestrated for them.

These are weighty matters. Very little of what one reads in that amassing body of literature about leadership reflects such considerations as these. We seem to be in pursuit of a quicker "fix."

The great chieftain would have been appalled by the very possibility that anyone could believe that he or she could become a great (or even a good) leader for $15.95 and the minute or so it takes to "read" the book for managers by that name. But perhaps he would merely have been dismayed for having spent his whole life trying to orchestrate things in such a way that people were bound to greaten themselves, and each other, not realizing how cheaply it could be done.

So we need to ask: through what kind of understanding of leadership have we enabled that future that is now *our* present?

VI

For all who would practice the art of leadership, each of the foregoing is an idea worth "chewing on." What they call into question is not the world, but one's understanding of the world; not the way things are, but the way we see them. And they are useful, each and all, for just that reason. One who would lead others must first lead oneself. A leader's special way of "seeing" begins with seeing into himself, with bringing into question the very way he (or she) sees the world.

Such ideas as those just explored may seem, to the practical man, a bit "philosophical." But every leader *is* a philosopher — perhaps not in the traditional or pejorative sense. And perhaps not even in the sense of being a "reflective practitioner" (Schön, 1983). But always and inescapably in this sense: that any way of comporting oneself in the human world, whatever the consequences, implies a philosophy. "What you do, you stablish," said the great chieftain, "and that is all" (Saint-Exupéry, 1948, p. 72). The way one *is* in the world is inescapably a philosophy of man.

So it is likewise inescapable that every way of understanding or approaching leadership also rests on a set of assumptions about the nature of man himself — that is, about what people are *for*. Those assumptions about what people are for may be implicit and may, in fact, for the individuals involved, be inarticulate. But they are no less consequential for that.

So the real differences among "theories" of leadership, or approaches to the study of leadership, are not merely differences of opinion or of method or of implementation. They are differences at the most fundamental level: at the level of assumptions about what people are for. Our contemporary "theories" and models of leadership are not different because they are more sophisticated, or because they are based upon more, or better, data. Or because they are based upon "research" or upon "scientific method." They are different because scientific and academic discourse about leadership has implicit in it a concept of man — of the nature of man, of what people are *for* — which moves in the direction of control, of efficiency, of effectiveness (cf. Loye, 1977), of engineering, of administration, of getting things done *through* people, and not *for* people.

So the understanding of leadership which Saint-Exupéry gives to his great chieftain, for example, is not comparable to a contemporary "contingency" theory of leadership. The two are not simply variations on the same pursuit; they are fundamentally different pursuits.

There is this same fundamental difference between understandings of the same term, given different assumptions about the nature of man — about what people are *for*. For example, it is fashionable these days to see an organization's "culture" as that which the leader must capture and manipulate in order to make the organization more "effective" (e.g., Deal & Kennedy, 1982). How they conceive of "culture" is different from the way Saint-Exupéry conceived of "culture": "To bestow culture, my father said, is to bestow thirst; then all the rest comes naturally" (1948, p. 291). Their respective conceptions of the same term are different, not because they lived in different epochs, but because they hold fundamentally different assumptions about the nature of man, about what people are *for*.

For there are no neutral descriptions of any human behavior — leadership included. Whether that description is implicit in a leader's actions, or explicit in an academic philosopher's words, it says something about how the maker of that description sees the nature of man.

It is this underlying bias or inclination that brings writer and reader together (we probably select whatever we read about leadership on the basis of how well it seems to conform with our implicit assumptions about what people are for), and follower and leader. And it is this inescapable *moral* aspect of leadership/followership that may lead us (an intriguing form of leadership) to question Hitler's "leadership," or to other such concerns as expressed by Burns (1978).

That leaders and followers may "connect" in some cases out of a sense of affinity for a particular view of man also makes possible what we would identify as "pathological" instances of leadership/followership. Our current concern about cults, cult leaders, and cult followers would be an example (Mosatche, 1983; Halperin, 1983; Appel, 1983). It was such social "movements" as might arise from some "pathological" (our current Western point of view) condition of the follower or the leader (or both) that Eric Hoffer focused upon in his *The True Believer* (1951). It is worth our attention here, not as an analysis of social perversions, but because it is *some* view of what people are for that animates both follower and leader. Our short-range, amoral approach to leadership in business may well one day be seen as "pathological." What we know is that we cannot escape the consequences of the particular view of man that is implicit in every act of leadership/followership. Where are we, today, being "led" by that view of man which is implicit in our favored modes of seeing and practicing leadership? Leadership/followership are no "better," no more moral, than the assumptions about what people are for that bring leader and follower together.

What Hoffer saw as the basis of the "true believer's" life was, first of all, a vague disenchantment with the way things are and, second, a vague hope that they could (or should) be "better." That vague disenchantment with the way things are is a gnawing dissatisfaction with oneself; "There is apparently some connection between dissatisfaction with oneself and a proneness to credulity." The burden of the "true believer" (which, of course, is all of us to a greater or lesser degree) is that of self-sufficiency. "The freedom the masses crave is not freedom of self-expression and self-realization, but freedom from the intolerable burden of an autonomous existence" (p. 140). There is, he writes, "perhaps no more reliable indicator of . . . ripeness for a mass movement than . . . unrelieved boredom. . . . When people are bored, it is primarily with their own selves that they are bored. The consciousness of a barren, meaningless existence is the main fountainhead of boredom" (p. 50, 51). And boredom arises where people are not badly off, but are yet without the abilities or the opportunities for creative work or useful action. It is small wonder that unionization has perhaps been easiest in those organizations or industries where neither the abilities nor the opportunities for creative work or useful action were in place. If the great industrialists of past years had been the kind of leader described by Saint-Exupéry, it seems unlikely that we would have seen the emergence of that divisive doctrine that lives on with us today in the form of the adversarial relationship assumed between "labor" and "management." And all because of a somewhat less than humanizing view of what people are for.

And what failures of leadership past have brought us close to that state of affairs, which Nietzsche envisioned, in which each would be humane nurse to the other? The founding fathers saw responsibility and not privilege or "right" as being the building blocks of the American enterprise. This was based, perhaps, as Hoffer puts it, on the fact that "A man is likely to mind his own business when it is worth minding. When it is not, he takes his mind off his own meaningless affairs by minding other people's business" (p. 14). What sort of leadership would bring us to that state of affairs where there are more tax-dependents in the U.S. than there are tax-payers? Did our shortsightedness, our inclination to see people merely as means to an end, to see leadership as merely one more tool for increasing productivity, have anything to do with the kinds of problems we are faced with today? As "philosophical" as he may sound to us today, Saint-Exupéry's great chieftain offered practical advice: Create those conditions wherein each is bound (and enabled) to greaten himself — where excellence is self-excellence. Otherwise, as Hoffer suggests, "The less justified a man is in claiming excellence for his own self, the more ready he is to claim all excellence for his nation, his religion, his race, or his holy cause" (p. 14). Or, we might add, to look to those collectives, or to some peddler of this or that form of utopianism, as the solution to *his* limitations as, even, a rationale for his shortcomings. For, if one's self is ineffectual, of what avail is freedom to choose? Since "Freedom of choice places the whole blame of failure on the shoulders of the individual . . . [it] aggravates at least as much as it alleviates frustration. . . . We join a mass movement to *escape* individual responsibility" (p. 30).

One of Hoffer's messages to the modern leader is similar to that of Saint-Exupéry's great chieftain: You must see through the buzzwords of the day. Example: "Those who see their lives as spoiled and wasted crave equality and fraternity more than they do freedom . . . The passion for equality is partly a passion for *anonymity*: to be one thread of the many which makes up a tunic; one thread not distinguishable from the others" (Hoffer, 1951, pp. 31–32). How is a leader to know, when there is a clamor for "equality," or for "participation," that it is in fact an attempt to be rid of one's self-responsibility, to lose oneself in the anonymity of "group-think?" How is the leader to immunize himself to the conventional wisdoms of the day, to do what is in the best interests of people, even if against their will or contrary to the "public" opinion of the day?

The more freedom people have, the more uncertain they may be (in the absence of strong leadership), and the more susceptible to another's fanatical convictions. If we are free, we are free to choose those whom we will follow. Has the public will always been that intelligent that it has chosen always in its own best, long-term interests? A key difference between what we might call immoral (or amoral) leadership and moral leadership is that the moral leader makes himself dispensable. His task, as Wildavsky said, is to enable his followers to further their own best self interests, their own humanity, without him. The "pathological" leader/follower system is one in which the follower is made to be more, not less, dependent (cf. Memmi, 1984; Tuan, 1984); one in which the leader is given the prerogative to think *for* the follower; one in which the follower's own best interests are abrogated in the name of a doctrine — whether that be a religious one, an industrial one, a political one, a social one, or a scientific one.

Ever to "greaten" oneself is a task that can be carried on only if it is *necessary* and *possible* for one to do so. Whether in a parent, a teacher, a friend, an administrator, a celebrity, or an executive or foreman, the kind of leadership that is good for people is the kind of leadership that continuously rekindles these two conditions.

VII

So what, if anything, can we say we have learned?

And what, if anything, is left to be said?

There is an old Spanish proverb: *No es lo mismo hablar de toros, que estar en el redondel,* which translates, "It is not the same thing to talk of bulls as to be in the bullring." So it is with us here. It is not the same thing to talk of leadership as to be in a leadership situation; to *talk of* leadership, as we do here, is not the same thing *as* leadership.

We also know that the practical or the "theoretical" or the human value of any utterance is not to be found in the utterance, but in the auditor's interpretation of it. "A word to the wise," Thurber said, "is not sufficient if it doesn't make any sense." And if it is *wisdom* that previous leaders and observers of leadership would pass on to us, we might want to recall Siddhartha's caveat (in Herman Hesse's novel of the same name) that "Wisdom is not communicable."

So we cannot reduce all that has been said and thought about leadership to a recipe. Or even to a set of "truths." What we know is that the leader is much more like an artist or a poet than like an engineer. The leader is not so much the bridge-builder as he (or she) is the bridge itself. To describe leadership is therefore as uniquely creative as any other work of art. What one learns is not how to *be* a leader, or even how to think about leadership. What one learns is what one is capable of learning about all such matters.

What we know is that every leader—whether in the arts or the sciences or in business or politics, or in everyday life—is a learner (Roskill, 19654; Wildavsky, 1984). It is not so much what one learns that counts, as being always in a "learning mode" (cf. Needleman, 1982). It is not so much that the leader is more of a "seer" than others; it is that he or she becomes more and more judicious in asking questions. His or her special wisdom lies in how his or her questioning takes him or her beyond the obvious. The special wisdom that leaders seem to possess lies not in their achievement of a superior verbal knowledge of things, but in their willingness to remain forever in pursuit of understandings that lie beyond language as such. As Saint-Exupéry's great chieftain says, "wisdom is not a matter of finding answers to problems, but a cure for the vagaries and imperfections of language" (1948, p. 130). The leader is not so much a problem-solver as a creative problem re-namer. The engineer, the administrator, the head, the bureaucrat—is a mere problem-solver. The art of leadership lies in redefining the problem, of creating other possibilities for seeing, of creating possible "alternities," of creating different meanings for things.

In a very critical way, which seems in retrospect always to have been inevitable, the leader is a sense-*giver*. The leader always *embodies* the possibilities of escape from what might otherwise appear to us to be incomprehensible, or from what might otherwise appear to us to be a chaotic, indifferent, or incorrigible world—one over which we have no ultimate control. This is a point raised by Hoffer (1951), of course, but also by such writers as Edelman (1967): "Because it is apparently intolerable for men to admit the key role of accident, of ignorance, and of unplanned processes in their affairs, the leader serves a vital function by personifying and reifying (those) processes" (p. 78). The leader symbolizes for us the possibility that *everything* depends upon us, that we are, after all, in control. The modern leader, at least, embodies that critical human belief that we are, or could be, the masters of our own destiny. Every idea that asserts this in some way has been, for the modern world, a "leading" idea. The leader is a leader because he gives meaning to our lives in this sense. What we need, said Baldelli (1971) is some "justification of our existence," some clear sense that *something* depends upon our existence. Every idea, and every leader, that that we have given ourselves over to in modern life has been one that offered us this sense of importance to our lives.

An idea of that sort is very special. And a leader of that sort is very special. Such ideas, and such leaders, are for us followers "numinous" (Geertz, 1977) — sacred, mysterious, miraculous. We want to be led, but we want to be led by superhuman ideas or people. "Authority," writes Sennett (1980), "is founded on the illusions of miracle and mystery, and they are necessary illusions" (p. 195). As Wheelis puts it in *The Illusionless Man,* those who lose or who attempt to escape those necessary illusions become psychologically inadequate. We are led, ultimately, by our understandings. A leader is one who provides or reaffirms understandings that restore our psychological adequacy. The "false" or "pathological" leader is one who feeds upon our psychological inadequacies by exploiting or pandering to them (cf. Wilson, 1959; Burns, 1978).

We know, too, that leadership/followership always occurs in relationship, and that to try to reduce that relationship to factors that are independent is always misleading.[2] The leader and the follower define one another: the leader is not a leader without followers, and followers are not followers without a leader. The leadership/followership relation is therefore always "systemic," both in its character and its functioning — in the sense that a change in one part brings about changes in the others, and therefore in the whole.[3] Since these are in some sense "roles" that must be more or less successfully assumed and carried off, the patterns and rationales for leadership/followership are both enabled and constrained by cultural imperatives. Thus the orientations of what Highwater (1981) refers to as the "primal mind," as exemplified by the American Indians (Farb, 1978), were quite different from our own. In those cultures, which were cyclical, the leader's role was much more circumscribed, and he led, not because he was "superior," but because that was his role. In our own culture, as Janeway (1981) suggests, leadership may be provided mainly by "followers": consumers may "lead" producers more than producers lead consumers. Our belief in "progress," in the linearity or the "making" of our history, is critical to our understanding of the leadership/followership roles. A good example is the far-reaching implications for the exercise of leadership that lie in the assumption of *collective* responsibility for decisions and the quality of performance in organizations held by the Japanese mind (Smith, 1983), a cultural difference that has made the importation of Japanese ways of "leadership" (e.g.,

---

[2] Notice that, just as we can be "led," we can be "misled." Since the latter is typically thought to involve a "misleading" idea, it is interesting to speculate on why it does not seem to us that we are more often "led" by ideas than by persons. Cf. Burns (1978, p. 454):

The most lasting and pervasive leadership of all is intangible and noninstitutional. It is the leadership of influence fostered by ideas imbedded in social or religious or artisitic movements, in great seminal documents, in the memory of great lives greatly lived.

Are there "misleading" people?

[3] On wholes and parts in the leader/follower relation, see Wildavsky (1964).

"quality control circles") very problematic. They simply see the leadership/followership relation differently than we do.

So the issue is not what leadership "means," but what we "mean" by it, in our, or another, culture or universe of discourse: leadership is not understood by journalists or generals in the same way as it is by physicists or politicians. If one, as a function of his or her being a member of some particular culture or subculture understands leadership differently, is "it" in fact different? We often confuse leadership with "headship," for example, or with authority or power or control, or even influence. And we may confuse followership with dependence or with responsibility. We may entertain such confusions because ours is a "command-and-control" mentality. Unlike the Japanese, who see dependence as a "natural" and even positive aspect of social relations, we understand it pejoratively. But we may have more problems of dependence ("welfarism," for example) than do the Japanese. Everything hinges not upon what something "is," but upon how we, in our culture, have come to understand it. The consequences of our practice of leadership follows not from what "it" is, but from how we understand it.

We know also that leadership is not a function only of heroes and celebrities (what Klapp [1964] calls "symbolic leaders"). Leadership functions at all levels of life, and in all walks of life (cf. Hook, 1955; Wildavsky, 1964). Our own cultural biases may "lead" us to look to heroes and celebrities to make things right *for* us. But this gives us a certain myopia: we miss seeing everyday leadership—that provided by friends and parents, classmates and organizational peers, physicians and clerks and bureaucrats of all sorts. Everyone, in fact, is involved in leadership. For all things social move in *some* direction, and one is either guilty of complicity in that, or in effecting some alternity.

Plato believed that, if the leader be wise, then the State will be wise. But the burdens of leadership fall to people often without regard to their wisdom. Our "leaders," for example, are not always elected—either to the Presidency or to the top corporate rung or to parenthood or to high scientific prestige—*because* they are wise. In describing the qualities of Pericles (who did for Athens 2400 years ago what Churchill did for Britain in the early 1940s), Plutarch wrote: "Moral good has a power to attract towards itself." This may be. But so does evil have an attraction for some—although those we come to see as the most evil typically understand their doctrine as being for the good of everyone. So what we can know is that leadership itself is neither moral nor immoral. What counts is the image of man which is implicit in the motives of the followers who select certain people or ideas as their leaders. All consequences flow from those images of what people are *for*.

What is *not* centrally reflected in that great and growing body of literature on leadership is that leadership and followership, insofar as they have any meaning for us whatsoever, are things of the mind. What we look at them *with* is our concept of the one or the other, or of the relationship between the one and the other (Blumer, 1969). This is what Eddington had in mind when he wrote that what we see in nature is that which mind has attributed to nature. And this is what Cooley (1902) had in mind when he wrote:

> the imaginations which people have of one another are the *solid facts* of society . . . I do not mean merely that society must be studied *by* the imagination—that is true of all investigations in their higher reaches—but that the *object* of study is primarily an imaginative idea or group of ideas in the mind, that we have to imagine imaginations. The intimate grasp of any social fact will be found to require that we divine what men think of one another. (p. 7)

To *be* a leader, therefore, is to be *seen as* a leader (and not as something else) by those who see themselves as his or her followers. That relationship is a property of how they—leader and follower—*understand* the relationship between leader and follower. As the old geometrician says to the great chieftain: "for indeed the only relations between things are those which you create in your mind" (Saint-Exupéry, 1948, p. 321). And the things of the mind must necessarily be created and maintained *in* communication.

So the most remarkable thing about the bulk of these studies on leadership is that they do not begin and end in communication. Why? Because the world we know, the only world we *can* know, is given in *how* we know it—and this, human reality, is created and maintained in communication. The mind itself is a social product. And the things of the mind—what *is* in the world, what is valued in the world, how things are related in the world, what follows from what, and what *ought* to be—are all products of communication. The fact that we think, and the way we think, is a function of *how* we communicate. Every aspect of every culture, and every social arrangement in every human society, are both products of and producers of ways of communication.

As we spoke of a human world, we created one. Once in place, it creates us (to paraphrase a famous Churchill aphorism), and constrains how we *may* speak of it.

The difficulty is that communication is not a subset of the study of leadership. Rather, leadership is a subset of the study of communication. It is perhaps not unexpected that political "scientists" (politologists?), for example, would reveal their disciplinary myopia by simply mystifying the process: to say that leaders "interact" with their followers, or that leaders "persuade" their followers is pure mystification. The notion that either truth or clever rhetoric will necessarily move people into one's camp is wishing away what is necessary to be explained: how one person is "effective" and another is not, or even how one is "effective" on one occasion and not another. Churchill was surely as "persuasive" and as clever, rhetorically, after the war as he was before; yet he was denied office by those who previously were "followers."

The details of how we came to ignore that which most needs explaining go beyond the scope of this essay. It may be sufficient here to raise the difficulty by putting the key question: How *do* people conduct their everyday affairs—political, economic, whatever—except in and through some form of communication? Leaders emerge in communication. All leadership, Cooley (1902) said, can only occur in the communication of ideas. And some will "buy into" those ideas, and some won't. Some will understand them one way, some another. Some will "hear" them, some won't. A would-be leader may be given a "voice," or he or she may not. But it is precisely the communication aspects of leadership that must ultimately inform our understanding of that process. There isn't any way for leaders to be leaders, and followers to be followers, except in and through some form of communication.

So it is remarkable that the word "communication" does not even appear in the index to Burns' (1978) award-winning book on "leadership." But it is more remarkable still that most of those who presume to be writing about the communication aspects of leadership nonetheless seem to end up writing about the psychological or the sociological or the political or the "management" aspects of leadeship—as certain ways of talking about those aspects become more or less academically fashionable.

There are, so far as I know, but two books which, by title, at least, are *about* "leadership" and "communication": de Mare's *Communicating for Leadership: A Guide for Executives* (1968), and Stech's *Leadership Communication* (1983). Both lead from certain concepts of managerial psychology that were in vogue at the time of their writing. And both trivialize the role of communication in leadership by reducing it to some expedient tactics or skills. For example, to say that a leader should be a good listener is not saying much: to *what* should a leader listen, and to *whom*, and *how*? A leader is not a listener; he or she is a discerner. The difference is profound: the one is but a trick, rather easily performed by anyone who wants to make the effort. Discernment implies wisdom. The word appears in neither index.

The nature of the beast being what it is, one could hardly fault such authors for not being serious about either leadership *or* communication. They are writing books for those who are wanting recipes, not wisdom. We are living in a culture which demands of its thinkers and researchers: How can *this* be done? Not how must an individual *be* in order to be good for the world. The one requires dedicated, disciplined artists; the other, merely social plumbers.

Much the same can be said for the increasing numbers of shorter studies which are beginning to be reported in such indexes as *Organizational Communication* (Sage, 1976 –), and for the general orientation of texts and other books in "organizational" and "managerial" communication. Some of the exceptions have already been noted. In his chapters on "Shaping Communications" and "Orchestrating Ceremonies," Siu (1984) is one of the few authors who addresses some of the minor strategies of communication in more than trivial ways (cf. Cribbin, 1981). But he writes, ostensibly, neither about leadership *or* communication, although he recognizes that "to be a great leader is to be a shaman. You must be seasoned in the art of using images to instill an unshaken belief among your followers that you will always succeed in whatever you undertake" (Siu, 1984, p. 157). Yet "instill" may smack of mystification. *How,* instill? Is there any way except *in* communication?

So what *should* we be saying about the relationship between communication and leadership?

We should begin, perhaps, with a thoroughgoing realization that human reality is socially constructed, and that the human context is comprised not of things, but of the socially constituted *meanings* of things. It is this world—the world of the socially constructed and socially constituted meanings of things—that leader and follower alike dwell in, and it is this world within which whatever is going to happen must happen. For "you enter into communication not with things," Saint-Exupéry's great chieftain said, "but with the knots binding them together" (1948, p. 198). The "knots" binding them together are what comprise the minds of leader and follower alike.

These are "knots" that are created and maintained *in* communication. *How* we talk of things implies the "knots" that "bind" those things together. The world we know is created in our explanations of things—in our explanations of why this or that happened, of why this or that might happen, or will happen, or should happen. We practice by explaining things to ourselves; one need only have heard a toddler in the process of falling asleep to know what we mean here by "practice." The "knots" are what obtain in our explanations of things: our futures are given in our present explanations, and our present in our past explanations. A social structure establishes who has the prerogative to explain things to other people, whose explanations are incumbent upon others (a parent's explanations are incumbent upon the child; a journeyman mechanic's upon the apprentice; a boss's upon the subordinate[4]; a President's upon the most ranking general, etc.). An amoral leader is one

---

[4] A humorous example of the prerogative to explain to others which is "built into" social arrangements is given in the following, now apocryphal, story:

To the first job applicant: "There is a simple test we would like to give you to determine your suitability for the job, okay? How much is two plus two?" First applicant: "Four." To the second applicant: "How much is two plus two?" Second applicant: "Whatever the boss says it is." The second applicant got the job.

who exploits a compelling explanation. A moral leader is one who enables others to explain things as *they* "ought." None of this can be undertaken or carried on except in communication.

Language itself "leads" us. Not words as such, but the meanings we have come to attribute to them, the concepts they embody, the mental artifacts they invoke or conjure. We do not lead, can not follow, those with whom we do not share a way of talking about (of "minding") things. How we may lead, or how follow, is given *in* those ways of talking about (of "minding") things. A leader is one who either legitimates and "enforces" the entelechies implicit in certain ways of talking about things, or else alters a people's way of talking about (of "minding") things. He or she can do neither except *in* communication.

Leadership has thus the function of social poiesis: of social governance and/or redirection. Since the world we know must be daily made anew, it must be done in communication—in, essentially, our daily comprehensions and expressions of things—in conversation, in our takings-into-account and our tellings. To make an alternity is to alter others' customary ways of recreating the world, to enable them to make of the world something other than it seems to be. The leader is one who tinkers with social governance—as that has its source in the meanings of things, in the "knots"that bind things together.

A leader is a meaning-maker. His or her concerns are not the things of the world, but the way people *mind* the things of the world, the "knots" that bind the things of the world together.

This is, minimally, what communication has to do with leadership.

VIII

Perhaps, then, I might be permitted a modest proposal:

Everything is always in the process of becoming what it is. This is as much the case for people as it is for the things of the world, as much the case for things of the mind as for things of nature.

We are *led*, in our minding of the world, in our social affairs as in our individual lives, by whatever is weightiest in us. We are led not by what *is*, but by who we *are*. And we are, no more and no less, that set of possibilities that is given in how we are able to comprehend, and how express, the world. Who we *are*, and the world we *know*, are two aspects of the same thing.

All consequences flow, not from things, but from our interpretations of things. Things are the way they appear to us to be because of the interpretations we have made in the past. Things will be as we will come to see them because of the interpretations we make today. The "knots" that bind the things of the world we know together are continuously recreated in our interpretations and explanations of things, whether they be revealed to us or not.

A culture's or a subculture's way of interpreting things is epitomized in the stories people tell each other and themselves. Our stories are always about four things: about what is going on, about what will happen as a result of what is going on, about what *should* be going on or what *should* happen as a result of what should be going on, and about what to do about the one or the other.

Our ways of knowing and predicating the world carry their own entelechies—that which urges everything in the direction in which it is constructed. We are, individually and socially, governed by the entelechies implicit in our ways of knowing the world, in the stories we tell about it.

Leadership is thus the self-fulfilling governance of these entelechies in our individual and social lives.

A *leader* is one who creates human/social alternities by telling a compelling story about what is, about what will be, about what should be or about what should (or could) be done about one or the other.

A leader is a person who enchants him or herself ("bewitches" himself or herself) with the story he or she tells. That story may be a theory, a painting, an idea, a political or social doctrine, a belief, an organizational "philosophy," or a creative description. In its telling, others may become enchanted with it. The more people who become enchanted with it, the more "truthful" and "right" it appears to be, both to the leader and to his or her "followers." It may then become institutionalized, and become a part of the way the world "is," the way the world is known, for future generations. We are first "led" by the ways the world might be, and then by the way the world "is." A leader revitalizes or changes our ways of "minding" the world.

In his *The Meaning of the Twentieth Century,* Kenneth Boulding (1964) says, in effect, that leaders "must create a drama" whose social function is that of giving its auditors "a role in the drama it portrays." The leader is the meaning-giver, the myth-giver. He is the compelling story-teller.

It is the leader's stories that *mediate*, for all those who would follow, an alternative way of being, doing, knowing, having, or saying in the world.

It is the leader who, in the stories he or she tells, and in his or her unique way of telling them, kindles human and social alternity.

REFERENCES

Almond, G. (1973). Approaches to developmental causation. In G. A. Almond, S. C. Flanagan, and R. J. Mundt (Eds.), *Crisis, choice, and change.* Boston, MA: Little, Brown.

Appel, W. (1983). *Cults in America.* New York: Holt, Rinehart and Winston.

Bailey, F. G. (1969). *Strategems and spoils: A social anthropology of politics.* New York: Schocken.

Baldelli, G. (1971). *Social Anarchism.* Chicago, IL: Aldine, Atherton.

Barnard, C. (1948). *The functions of the executive.* Cambridge, MA: Harvard University Press.

Barth, F. (1965). *Political leadership among swat pathans.* New York: Humanities Press.

Bass, B. M. (1981). *Stogdill's handbook of leadership: A survey of theory and research* (rev. ed.). New York: Free Press.

Beer, S. (1972). Preface. In H. R. Maturana & F. J. Varela (Eds.), *Autopoiesis and Cognition.* Dordrecht, Holland: Reidel, 1980.

Bennis, W. (1976). *The unconscious conspiracy: Why leaders can't lead.* New York: Amacom.

Bennis, W. (1982). Leadership transforms vision into action. *Industry Week,* May 31, pp. 54–56.

Bennis, W., & Nanus, B. (1985). *Leaders: The strategies of taking charge.* New York: Harper & Row.

Berger, P. L., & Luckmann, T. (1966). *The social construction of reality.* Garden City, NY: Doubleday.

Blumer, H. (1969). *Symbolic interactionism.* Englewood Cliffs, NJ: Prentice-Hall.

Boulding, K. E. (1964). *The meaning of the twentieth century.* New York: Harper & Row.

Brown, R. H., & Lyman, S. M. (Eds.). (1978). *Structure, consciousness, and history.* Cambridge, England: Cambridge University Press.

Burns, J. M. (1978). *Leadership.* New York: Harper & Row.

Carlyle, T. (1908). *On heroes and hero worship.* London: Dent. (Originally published in 1840.)

Cartwright, D. (Ed.). (1959). *Studies in social power.* Ann Arbor, MI: Institute for Social Research, University of Michigan.

Cassirer, E. (1953). *An essay on man.* Garden City, NY: Doubleday. (Originally published in 1944.)

Chemers, M. M. (1984). The social, organizational, and cultural context of effective leadership. In B. Kellerman (Ed.), *Leadership: Multidisciplinary perspectives.* Englewood Cliffs, NJ: Prentice-Hall.

Cohen, R., & Middleton, J. (Eds.). (1967). *Comparative political systems.* Garden City, NY: Natural History Press.

Cooley, C.H. (1902). *Human nature and social order.* New York: Scribner's.

Cooley, C. H. (1962). *Social organization.* New York: Schocken, (Originally published in 1909.)

Cribbin, J. J. (1981). *Leadership: Strategies for organizational effectiveness.* New York: Amacom.

Deal, T. E., & Kennedy, A. A. (1982). *Corporate cultures: The rites and rituals of corporate life.* Reading, MA: Addison-Wesley.

de Mare, G. (1968). *Communicating for leadership: A guide for executives.* New York: Ronald.

DeMente, B. (1981). *The Japanese way of doing business: The psychology of management in Japan.* Englewood Cliffs, NJ: Prentice-Hall.

Dickson, P. (1978). *The official rules.* New York: Delacorte.

Doi, T. (1973). *The anatomy of dependence,* J. Bester, trans. Tokyo: Kodansha International

Drucker, P. F. (1967). *The effective executive.* New York: Harper & Row.

Dumont, L. (1970). *Homo hierarchicus.* M. Saintsbury, trans. Chicago, IL: University of Chicago Press.

Edelman, M. (1967). *The symbolic uses of politics.* Urbana, IL: University of Illinois Press.

Eliot, T. S. (1930). *Ash-Wednesday: I.* In *Collected Poems 1909–1962.* New York: Harcourt, Brace & World.

Erikson, E. H. (1958). *Young man Luther.* New York: Norton.

Erikson, E. H. (1969). *Gandhi's truth.* New York: Norton.

Farb, P. (1978). *Man's rise to civilization: The cultural ascent of the Indians of North America* (2nd ed.). New York: Dutton.

Ford, C. S. (1938). The role of the Fijian chief. *American Sociological Review, 3,* 541–550.

Geertz, C. (1977). Centers, kings, and charisma: Reflections on the symbolics of power. In *Local knowledge: Further essays in interpretive anthropology.* New York: Basic Books.

Gibb, C. (1969). Leadership. In G. Lindzey & E. Aronson (Eds.), *Handbook of social psychology* (Vol. 4, 2nd ed.). Reading, MA: Addison-Wesley.

Gibb, C. (Ed.). (1969). *Leadership.* Baltimore, MD: Penguin.

Gouldner, A. W. (Ed.). (1950). *Studies in leadership.* New York: Harper.

Grob, L. (1984). Leadership: The Socratic Model. In B. Kellerman (Ed.), *Leadership: Multidisciplinary perspectives.* Englewood Cliffs, NJ: Prentice-Hall.

Halperin, D. A. (Ed.). (1983). *Religion, sect, and cult.* Boston, MA: Wright-PSG.

Heisenberg, W. (1958). *The physicist's conception of nature.* A. J. Pomerans, trans. New York: Harcourt, Brace.

Heller, T. (1982). *Women and men as leaders: In business, educational, and social service organizations.* New York: Praeger.

Highwater, J. (1981). *The primal mind: Vision and reality in Indian America.* New York: Harper & Row.

Hill, R. B. (1979). *Hanta yo.* New York: Doubleday.

Hoffer, E. (1951). *The true believer: Thoughts on the nature of mass movements.* New York: Harper.

Holzner, B. (1968). *Reality construction in society.* Cambridge, MA: Schenkman.

Hook, S. (1955). *The hero in history.* Boston: Beacon Press.

Hosking, D. M., Hunt, J. G., Schriesheim, C. A., & Stewart, R. (1984). Conclusions: On paradigm shifts in studying leadership. In J. G. Hunt, et al. (Eds.), *Leaders and managers.* New York: Pergamon.

Hunt, J. G. (1984). Organization leadership: The contingency paradigm and its challenges. In B. Kellerman (Ed.), *Leadership: Multidisciplinary perspectives.* Englewood Cliffs, NJ: Prentice-Hall.

Hunt, S. M. (1984). The role of leadership in the construction of reality. In B. Kellerman (Ed.), *Leadership: multidisciplinary perspectives*. Englewood Cliffs, NJ: Prentice-Hall.

Hyde, L. (1983). *The gift*. New York: Vintage.

Iaccoca, L., with W. Novak (1984). *Iaccoca*. New York: Bantam.

Janda, K. F. (1960). Towards the explication of the concept of leadership in terms of power. *Human Relations, 13,* 345–363.

Janeway, E. (1981). *Powers of the weak*. New York: Morrow.

Jaworski, J. (1982). The attitude and capacities required of the successful leader. *Vital Speeches,* November 15.

Jay, A. (1967). *Management and Machiavelli: An inquiry into the politics of corporate life*. New York: Holt, Rinehart & Winston.

Jennings, E. E. (1960). *An anatomy of leadership: Princes, heroes, and supermen*. New York: Harper.

Jonas, H. (1984). *The imperative of responsibility: In search of an ethics for the technological age*. Chicago, IL: University of Chicago Press.

Kanter, R. M. (1983). *The change masters: Innovation for productivity in the American corporation*. New York: Simon & Schuster.

Klapp, O. E. (1964). *Symbolic leaders: Public dramas and public men*. Chicago, IL: Aldine.

Kracke, W. H. (1978). *Force and persuasion: Leadership in an Amazonian society*. Chicago, IL: University of Chicago Press.

Levitt, T. (1970). The living legacy of Peter Drucker. In T. H. Bonaparte & J. E. Flaherty. (Eds.), *Peter Drucker: Contributions to business enterprise*. New York: New York University Press.

Lewis, H. S. (1974). *Leaders and followers: Some anthropological perspectives*. Reading, MA: Addison-Wesley.

Lippmann, W. (1922). *Public opinion*. New York: Penguin, 1946.

Loye, D. (1977). *The leadership passion: A psychology of ideology*. San Francisco, CA: Jossey-Bass.

Maccoby, M. (1981). *The leader: A new face for American management*. New York: Simon & Schuster.

Machiavelli, N. (1903). *The prince*. L. Ricci, trans. London: Oxford University Press. (Originally published 1513.)

March, J. G. (Ed.). (1965). *Handbook of organizations*. Chicago, IL: Rand McNally.

McCall, M. W. (1977). *Leaders and leadership: Of substance and shadow*. Technical Report #2. Center for Creative Leadership.

McCall, M. W., & Lombardo, M. M. (Eds.). (1978). *Leadership: Where else can we go?* Durham, NC: Duke University Press.

McClelland, D. C. (1975). *Power: The inner experience*. New York: Irvington.

McGregor, D. (1966). In W. Bennis & E. H. Schein, (Eds.), *Leadership and motivation*. Cambridge, MA: MIT Press.

Memmi, A. (1984). *Dependence*. P. A. Facey, trans. Boston, MA: Beacon.

Mitroff, I. I. (1983). *Stakeholders of the organizational mind*. San Francisco, CA: Jossey-Bass.

Mosatche, H. S. (1983). *Searching: Practices and beliefs of the religious cults and human potential groups*. New York: Stravon.

Nafe, R. W. (1930). A psychological description of leadership. *Journal of Social Psychology, 1,* 248–266.

Needleman, J. (1982). *The heart of philosophy*. New York: Bantam.

Neustadt, R. (1960). *Presidential power*. New York: Wiley.

Nisbet, R. A. (1950). Leadership and social crisis. In A. W. Gouldner (Ed.), *Studies in leadership*. New York: Harper.

Peters, T. J. (1979). Leadership: Sad facts and silver linings. *Harvard Business Review,* Nov-Dec.

Polanyi, M., & Prosch, H. (1975). *Meaning*. Chicago, IL: University of Chicago Press.

Prentice, W. C. H. (1961). Understanding leadership. *Harvard Business Review,* Sept–Oct.

Reichley, A. J. (1971). Our critical shortage of leadership. *Fortune,* September.

Roskill, S. W. (1964). *The art of leadership.* London: Collins.

Rustow, D. A. (Ed.). (1970). *Philosophers and kings: Studies in leadership.* New York: Braziller.

Saint-Exupéry, A. (1948). *The wisdom of the sands (Citadelle).* S. Gilberg, trans. New York: Harcourt, Brace.

Schön, D. A. (1983). *The reflective practitioner: How professionals think in action.* New York: Basic Books.

Schutz, A. (1940–1953). *Collected papers I: The problem of social reality.* The Hague, Netherlands: Nijhoff.

Selznick, P. (1957). *Leadership in administration.* New York: Harper & Row.

Sennett, R. (1980). *Authority.* New York: Vintage.

Siu, R. G. H. (1984). *The craft of power.* New York: Quill.

Smith, R. J. (1983). *Japanese society: Tradition, self, and the social order.* N.Y.: Cambridge University Press.

Stech, E. L. (1983). *Leadership communication.* Chicago: Nelson-Hall.

Steiner, G. (1975). *After Babel.* Oxford, England: Oxford University Press.

Thomas, L. (1979). *The medusa and the snail.* New York: Viking.

Thomas, W. I., & Znaniecki, F. (1918). *The Polish Peasant in Europe and America.* Boston: Badger.

Tuan, Y. F. (1984). *Dominance and affection.* New Haven, CT: Yale University Press.

Tucker, R. C. (1981). *Politics as leadership.* Columbia, MO: University of Missouri Press.

Verba, S. (1961). *Small groups and political behavior: A study of leadership.* Princeton, NJ: Princeton University Press.

von Schlegel, F. (1798). *Athenaeum.*

Vroom, V. H., & Yetton, P. W. (1973). *Leadership and decision making.* Pittsburgh, PA: University of Pittsburgh Press.

Werner, D. (1984). *Amazon journey: An anthropologist's year among Brazil's Mekronoti Indians.* New York: Simon & Schuster.

Wheelis, A. (1966). *The Illusionless Man.* New York: Norton.

Whyte, W. F. (1955). *Street corner society* (rev. ed.). Chicago, IL: University of Chicago Press.

Wildavsky, A. (1964). *Leadership in a small town.* Totowa, NJ: Bedminster.

Wildavsky, A. (1984). *The nursing father: Moses as a political leader.* University, AL: University of Alabama Press.

Williamson, P. B. (1979). *Patton's principles.* New York: Touchstone.

Wilson, C. (1959). *The stature of man.* New York: Greenwood.

Zaleznik, A. (1977). Managers and leaders: Are they different? *Harvard Business Review,* May–June, pp. 67–78.

Zaleznik, A. & de Vries, M. F. R. K. (1975). *Power and the corporate mind.* Boston: Houghton-Mifflin.

Chapter 12

Communication As Process: The Manager's View

Roger D'Aprix

Principal
Towers, Perrin, Forster, & Crosby, Inc.

ABSTRACT

D'Aprix considers lack of trust the major employee relations problem facing corporate managements at the end of the twentieth century. International competition, deregulation, corporate downsizing, and a work force that is more involved and better educated require management to manage and communicate much more effectively than they have to date.

Employees are no longer merely a cost of doing business. In today's economy, they are the very means *of doing business. That circumstance requires that employee communication must become a management system with a strategy, management accountability, and the training to make it all work. The alternative, argues D'Aprix, is communication anarchy.*

Consultant Stanley Peterfreund observed in a 1982 speech to the American Society for Personnel Administration that the principal barrier to effective employee communication is lack of trust.

From that charge, he detailed an interesting bill of particulars:

- We fail to expect the best of people. We guard information closely.
- Our leadership styles are built around sophisticated control systems.
- We have a fetish for measuring everything.
- We decide what employees "need to know."
- We shoot the messenger of bad news.
- We structure jobs so as to restrict initiative.
- We centralize decision making at the top.
- Our actions often belie our sermons as we talk responsibility and withhold authority.
- We police employees constantly with security guards, time clocks, inspectors, and the like.
- We communicate promises and pledges, and then fail to deliver.
- And our various employee publications paint a world so different from people's experience that they barely recognize it.

In brief, we are in his words, "trust busters."

After 30 years as a corporate communication manager and consultant, I agree with Peterfreund's analysis. That *is* the way it is.

And yet, there are hopeful signs on the horizon. Because of international competition in many of our most basic industries, because of deregulation of many others (which are now forced to be competitive for the first time), and because of a new breed of worker with greater financial independence, more education, and a penchant for self-fulfillment, the world of work is changing.

The most dramatic change is that employees are no longer merely a cost of doing business. They are now the engine that drives the business in our service-oriented, knowledge-worker oriented society.

Those major developments—international competition, deregulation, and workers who are harder to intimidate—have turned the employee communication task upside down. In times past, management could communicate pretty much according to its whims and timetable. Predictably, such communication was a reaction to events.

Something happened, and you reported it—if and when you got around to it. Never mind that you simply were corroborating what the grapevine had been saying for days or weeks. You told them what *you* thought *they* needed to know—when *you* were ready.

In times past, you told them almost exclusively in print, in publications with the anachronistic name of "house organs." Or maybe you wrote a bulletin board notice. But you did it when and how *you* felt best.

A lot of that still goes on in the twilight of the twentieth century. But things are changing.

Senior managements in most of our institutional organizations are beginning to understand the need to do things differently. And that applies—to varying degrees—whether we're talking about a corporation, a hospital, a university, or a governmental agency.

What is beginning to be clear is that employee communication must become a much higher management priority than it has been heretofore. Two interesting recent studies are straws in the wind. When chief personnel officers were asked by Spencer Stuart & Associates to rank their 13 key concerns, employee communication came up as number nine. Only 3 years earlier, it had ranked at the bottom of their list.

In still another survey of the "pressure points" facing senior personnel officers, employee communication was ranked second on a list of 24 concerns. Regardless of where it's being ranked, employee communication unquestionably is getting more attention than ever before.

The difficult question is how to respond to employee needs. That question is particularly troubling because the state-of-the-art—if it could be referred to in those terms—has been primitive.

Traditionally, employee communication has been perceived as the right combination of print and audiovisual programs. The line manager in most cases was regarded as a bystander who was simply one more member of the employee audience.

Our more enlightened organizations are changing such views. They are beginning to see communication as a process, a management system that must be managed in much the same way as all the other management systems in the organization.

As part of that changing vision, the supervisor or manager is now seen as the organization's primary communicator. Whatever we call this person—group leader, department head, boss, or manager—it is to him or her all of us look for encouragement, counsel, job information and our most persuasive view of the organizational climate.

The irony is that so little has been done to prepare such people for their role, or even to understand its importance. Their communication responsibility has been regarded as extracurricular and incidental.

By definition, that means that a fairly massive effort will need to be mounted in any organization to develop managers who can and will take on this responsibility.

To understand what's involved, consider the very real problem of trying to bring order to the chaos and neglect that have been fairly typical of employee communication even in well-managed companies.

The most urgent need is for a logical, well ordered management system to remove employee communication from the organizational limbo to which it has long been relegated. That limbo has been its status as a nice-to-do-if-the-spirit-ever-moves-you management activity.

No management in its right mind would treat any other management system so casually. Planning? Budgeting? Building and marketing a new product? Distribution? None of these are left to chance, good intentions, or the personal whims of company managers.

Instead, each system is carefully supported with a planned strategy, with monitoring and checking procedures to ensure managerial accountability, and with either formal or on-the-job training.

So it must come to be with an employee communication system. It must be guided by a carefully thought-out plan. It must have provision for holding people accountable. And it must provide for training as a precondition of that accountability.

The manager's communication role must also be institutionalized within the overall communication strategy. He or she must be regarded as the most influential spokesperson any employee deals with. The key question is how to communicate the nature of this responsibility convincingly to the manager. Perhaps the best way is to see it as a primary means to achieve broader organizational goals.

A real-life case example may help. In a small division of a large manufacturing company, a formal Quality of Work Life Program (QWL) had been operating with mixed results for over 2 years. Management was perplexed at the polarization the program had created.

At one end, QWL participants praised the program as the first time ever that they could affect company policy and results directly. At the other end, supervisors groused at the fact that "the company was pampering lazy hourlies" who had joined what they mockingly call the "Quit Work and Loaf Program."

Salaried people were put off because they felt that the "gains" made by the hourlies in their influence somehow were at their expense. The final result was that QWL was shaping up as a failure in its primary objective of tapping employee ingenuity and productivity.

When the problem was analyzed in a company research study, it became clear that the managers and supervisors were actually being obstructive. No one had prepared them for the change in their roles that employee participation would inevitably bring.

To address the problem, management decided to launch a massive training program for supervisors and managers. In turn, that program was to be reinforced by a company communication policy and an anonymous feedback system in which employees could comment on the boss's communication behavior and style. Their reactions were tabulated and given to the manager, who was then required to discuss corrective actions with the work group, things that the group could do together to improve the quality and quantity of communication and cooperation.

The result was an almost palpable improvement in the work climate as well as much broader support for Quality of Work Life as a legitimate—and even vital—company effort. But the question remains—how do you *describe* the requisite communication role to managers? In my experience, the best answer is to look at the issue from the perspective of the person who depends on that manager. What are his or her basic communication needs?

The most obvious is the need to understand the basic demands of the job. What do you expect me to do around here to earn my keep? What job standards can I expect you to hold me to? When you assign a specific job task to me, will you give me enough information so I know essentially what you want done and why? Will I have the opportunity to add value to the task by using my imagination and creativity?

In a simple question: *What is my job?*

When I have a decent understanding of the general dimensions of the job, are you prepared to give me continuing feedback on my performance? Not just its shortcomings, but also those things I do well, those times when I give you more than you asked for? Do you know how to say "thank you"? Are you willing to see that "thank you" as a means of establishing a sense of teamwork between us?

Again, in a simple question: *How am I doing?*

Once I have some sense of that, are you willing to move with me to the next higher level of my job needs? Do you have the courage to tell me I count for something in this total effort? Will you occasionally tell me of my value to the organization? Or will you be cowed by the usual fears that such expressions will lead to unreasonable demands and expectations on my part?

In short, *can you and will you make it clear that you, at least, value me and my work.*

The failure of that process ultimately leads to the disastrous conclusion that "nobody cares" and all the apathy that goes with that conclusion.

All three of these questions: What's my job? How am I doing? Does anyone care about me? are obviously focused on self and personal needs, the starting point for anyone's commitment to an organization. When those "I questions" are dealt with—if they ever are—then the individual is ready to cross the important line to "the world of we."

That crossover can actually be heard when people start speaking first of their organizational work unit as "we" and then, ultimately, in such phrases as "we own that business" or "we are going to market such and such a product." At that point, the individual is beginning, for better or worse, to merge his or her identity with the institution.

At that point, I as employee want to know *our* work unit objectives and plan. What are we trying to accomplish? Why is it important. How are we doing as a work group? Are we meeting your expectations as the manager of this effort? How could we work better together?

In short, *what are we up to and how are we doing?*

My next "we question" is a matter of closure. Where do we as a work group fit in the total organization? What is our role vis-a-vis other work groups? How do we support them? What do they do for us? How does this whole enterprise fit together?

When I finally have some reasonable answers to all of those questions, then—and really only then—am I prepared to ask with conviction the most important question any employee can ever ask in a work organization.

That question is: *How can I help?*

That clearly is the *beginning* of human commitment, imaginative human productivity, and even of job satisfaction. And the intriguing fact is that the only person who can draw it out as the loving gift it is is the manager.

People don't work for abstractions, or even necessarily for tangible rewards. The normal, healthy personality is more likely to seek the approval of someone whose good opinion he or she respects and cares about. Ergo the importance of the manager as communicator.

The traditional manager who believes that results can best be obtained through raw power and intimidation is troubled by the suggestion that managers should behave differently. He or she sees this sort of change as an abdication of power and as unnecessarily "permissive." The dichotomy for such a manager can be expressed by the simplistic notion that "you can be tough and get results, or you can be soft and get taken advantage of."

That set of attitudes is still held by perhaps the majority of our institutional managers. Whether the external realities of today's world demanding greater efficiencies, more competitiveness, and different management styles will defeat this entrenched and largely negative view of people and their motives remains to be seen.

It may turn out that we cherish our biases so deeply that we will stick with them regardless. If we do, communication with the work force will remain reactive, fragmented, and dominated by our mutual desires to be adversaries rather than teams of problem solvers, pursuing commonly understood goals.

Under such circumstances, mistrust will predominate in our work organizations. That will be more than an unfortunate circumstance. In today's organizational world, it could turn out to be a death wish.

The importance of trust to management effectiveness can be demonstrated by the experience of one major company I know first hand. In that company, employees have the opportunity to rate their manager's style in a paper and pencil questionnaire. At the end of the questionnaire are three direct bottom-line questions:

- How would you rate your manager's overall effectiveness?
- Would you see your manager as a role model for other managers?
- Given the chance, would you work for your manager again?

There is one item in the survey that gets at the issue of trust and the work climate that the manager promotes. Company experience shows clearly that the correlation between the evaluation of the manager's effectiveness and that one item of trust is almost 100 percent. High trust equals a perception of high effectiveness. Low trust equals a perception of low effectiveness.

The implication for any company that wishes people to respect and follow management direction should be obvious. In the same organization, a continuing attitude survey has demonstrated for years that the communication questions are predictors of the bottom-line survey results any management team can expect. Good communication means positive attitudes, and vice versa.

But perhaps the most interesting correlation seen in this company is that those organizations with positive attitudes also have the best business results. The trust busters — as Peterfreund has labelled them — are not merely polluting the work climate. They are undermining the organization's success!

Under such circumstances, how does management begin to change an organization riddled with distrust? How do they begin to construct a true communication system which they can manage as a system?

Not easy questions by any means.

The trust issue clearly is a matter of performance. People tend to wait and see when we pronounce ourselves cured of nasty habits. A good analogy may be the abused child who raises more than a skeptical eyebrow when he or she is told the beatings are over and that "things will be different."

In time, and with parental behavior that matches the promise, he or she may become a believer. But any sign of back-sliding will renew his or her former apprehension almost instantly.

An axiom of organizational distrust is that the most distant sources from the employee tend to engender the greatest suspicion. Hence the belief that top management is uncaring and even diabolical.

Recent books like *Megatrends* (Naisbitt, 198) and *In Search of Excellence* (Peters & Waterman, 1983) suggest that our work organizations will become "flatter" and more entrepreneurial as time goes on. In that case, senior management will certainly have to pay greater attention to the creation of a management system to monitor and control the organization's communication activities.

In a sense, they will need to reinvent the ways we communicate with the people who staff these new organizations. Some of this has already been started, but it is mostly very rudimentary.

And, predictably, a lot of the early effort has been focused on technology and the desire for quick fixes. Here is one area where the quick solution will not be forthcoming. Instead, because we are dealing with human complexity, the communication system will have to be designed to accommodate humans. Computers and others electronic technology may be useful tools for the system, but they can't be a substitute for human presence.

Irrespective of technology, managers must play a personal and visible role in this reinvented communication system. In fact, that system will have three key elements.

The first is a well thought out communication strategy. What are the major survival issues of the organization? How can these be forcefully and clearly formulated, and then communicated repetitively so that everyone understands his or her role?

What are the necessary tools and media that must be used to communicate these issues? How will managers be kept informed so that they can play their proper role as spokespersons for the organization and for the people they manage? What employee audiences have special communication needs and preferences to attend to? All of these questions must be addressed in constructing the organization's communication strategy.

The second key element is accountability. No management system ever works without some sense by managers that they are being held accountable for its success. Unfortunately, we have tended to see accountability as a punitive thing. It doesn't have to be.

We won't be able to measure with any exactitude the strength or weakness of a manager's communication effort. But we can evaluate those efforts through the sort of survey efforts alluded to earlier. That kind of feedback from one's co-workers can do much more to give us a sobering look at how we're perceived and to begin to change our behavior.

Finally, the third key element is training. If we're going to hold people accountable, we must train them in these new behaviors.

John Naisbitt says that one of the major tasks facing us in the remaining years of the twentieth century is the retraining of managers for the reinvented corporation. Some managers won't be able to adapt. We must decide if they can remain in their managerial roles or if they should be reassigned to nonpeople responsibilities — out of harm's way.

These three elements taken together — strategy, accountability, and training — will be the essential elements of the organizational communication system with the line manager as the primary catalyst in the process.

To make all of that work, however, the leadership of the organization must develop and commit to a new vision of managing people. That new vision will see people as the organization's key asset — not in the typical lip-service sense that such phrases have meant in the past, but in the real sense that they are the *means* of producing the organization's service or product.

Without such a shared leadership vision, the communication system we need will simply not be forthcoming. And if, by some accident, it should be created in a given organization where the leadership has not developed and endorsed its shared vision, the system will eventually wither from lack of senior management commitment.

If the bill of particulars in Stanley Peterfreund's indictment is not resolved—if the "trust busters" continue their bad habits, there is little hope for this vision to succeed.

Fortunately, survival is a strong inducement to organizational change. The need to survive is our best hope for understanding and dealing with communication as a management system.

SECTION 2

METHODOLOGICAL APPROACHES

It is unfortunate that people tend to think about communication research methodologies only as the techniques employed by scholars studying communication, in general and organizations, in specific, from a positivist perspective. The epistemological approaches that are labelled "methods" are designed for the most part to allow the researcher to make quantitative statements about the nature of the relations between variables. This would include statistics, mathematical modelling and the operational procedures which are used to gather quantitative data through surveys and experiments. Further, there is a tendency to pejoratively suggest that these methodologies are used without either the guidance of theory or for the purpose of evaluating and constructing theory as the ultimate end. Inherent in this evaluation is the notion that the qualitative approach to the study of communication is embedded to a greater degree in theory and, therefore, in some sense, of greater worth. Of course, both claims are nonsense.

Still the organization of this volume (and indeed, some of the chapters in Section 1) might reinforce these stereotypes about "methods". All the chapters in this section tend to take a positivist and quantitative approach to communication research. Certain chapters could have been moved from the theoretical perspectives section to the methods section without any loss of integrity. For example, the conversation by Hawes, Pacanowsky and Faules (Chapter 3) is very methodological. The discussants talked about qualitative methods such as, ethnography. Let it suffice to say that the categories "theory" and "methods" are not mutually exclusive and that the organization of this volume is somewhat arbitrary.

The first chapter in Section 2, "Organizational Communication Evaluation: An Overview 1950–1981" by Howard Greenbaum, Susan Hellweg and Raymond Falcione, could have been included in Section 1 for it deals with conceptual advances in evaluation research. It has been included here to make explicit the notion that research methodologies do not exist apart from theoretical concepts. The authors integrate thirty years of research on communication evaluations in natural settings. From this analysis, a taxonomy is developed which contains three categories—interpersonal, group and organization-wide communication. Each of these was further categorized into more specific subject areas (information flow, message content, communication climate, individual testing and organizational development). Finally, and perhaps the ultimate reason that this chapter is in the methodological approaches section, the authors review three standardized audit procedures.

One of the most widely used audit procedures is network analysis (Goldhaber & Barnett, in press). Network analysis is a set of research methods for identifying structures in social systems based on the relations among the components. In communication research, this relationship is the exchange of information among the parts (generally individuals) of organizations. Network analysis may be used to describe an organization's communication structure based upon the patterns of interaction or the flow of information among organizational members and task groups. These procedures are discussed in detail by Rolf Wigand in "The Generation and Description of Patterns in Social Relationships".

David Johnson develops a new technique for examining communication structures in organizations which he labels "communication gradients". Communication gradients essentially involve the representation of differing types of communication intensity in a physically bounded plane. This chapter uses data to illustrate the method. Sample gradient plots with four communication intensity measures are generated: frequency of contacts, average frequency of individual contacts, response satisfaction and importance. The results reveal the rich potential of this technique for analyzing organizational communication structure.

The final chapter in Section 2, "Organizational Infographics and Automated Auditing" is by James Danowski. The chapter reviews the traditional biases in organizational communication theory and research. It then presents a model for research including level in the heirarchy, cognitive schemata, messages, media and networks. Integrated within the model are variables that deal with: level of analysis, types of organizational media, communication management functions, and representations of organizational communication. The infographic model of organizations forms the basis of automated auditing of textual, traffic, voice and visual forms of organizational communication and for describing aspects of these methods. Examples of automated auditing are presented.

Many of the ideas presented by Danowski foretell the changes taking place in organizational communication and the readings in section three. Automated monitoring of communication processes within the context of organizational activities is made possible only through the advent of recent technological innovations based around the microprocessor. These technologies and their impact upon organizational communication will be discussed in Section 3.

REFERENCES

Goldhaber, G. M., & Barnett, G. A. (in progress). *Organizational communication auditing in the information age.* Norwood, N.J.: Ablex Publishing Corporation.

Chapter 13

Organizational Communication Evaluation: An Overview, 1950–1981

Howard H. Greenbaum

Hofstra University

Susan A. Hellweg

San Diego State University

Raymond L. Falcione

University of Maryland

ABSTRACT

Significant steps have been taken over the last 30 years in developing and implementing organizational communication evaluation procedures. To date, there have been limited efforts to integrate the available literature relative to the numerous unpublished case studies of organizational communication in natural settings. The purpose of this chapter was to classify and examine the rationale of such studies, noting communication problems, findings and conclusions. From this analysis, a taxonomy of writings was developed within the three broad areas of interpersonal, group, and organization-wide communication, each of which was further categorized into the more specific subject areas of information flow studies, message content studies, communication climate studies, and individual training and organizational development studies. The chapter is concluded with a review of three standardized instruments for the evaluation of organizational communication.

INTRODUCTION

Writings on the subject of organizational communication evaluation first entered the social science literature in the early 1950s (Davis, 1953; Nilsen, 1953; Odiorne, 1954). Since then, the literature concentrating on the evaluation process in this context has grown significantly with the availability of many doctoral dissertations, scholarly convention papers, and published articles and textbooks. There has been an outpouring of works relating to the construction and utilization of individual data-collection instruments, the formulation of full audit approaches, case studies that employ single-instrument and multi-instrument approaches, the construction of norms based on data secured through case studies, the development of criteria and standards applicable to the process of appraising organizational communication, and critiques of the most publicized appraisal process, the ICA Communication Audit.

Presently, the information as to the evaluation of organizational communication is dispersed, and is not conveniently available for review, nor is the specific location of such literature known to more than a handful of researchers. Some fine general summaries have appeared (e.g., Goldhaber, 1983; Goldhaber & Rogers, 1979; Goldhaber, Dennis, Richetto, & Wiio, 1979), but, for the most part, summaries by others have concentrated on only one of the several appraisal processes (Goldhaber, 1976a; Rudolph, 1972), or on one aspect of the appraisal process, such as criteria and standards (Farace, Taylor, & Stewart, 1978). Our search of the literature relative to the evaluation of organizational communication processes has uncovered a large number of published and unpublished writings. It is our view that the interested scholar and practitioner should have better access to these works.

Purpose

For many, the term "communication audit" is synonymous with the ICA Communication Audit, as a result of the considerable visibility surrounding this audit program. The purpose of this chapter was to review the entire literature on the subject of organization communication evaluation (OCE), including the ICA Communication Audit as one stage in the development of evaluation concepts and procedures. Our objective was to classify the literature in this area into meaningful categories, and to analyze the state of the art in each category, noting progress, problems, and opportunities for investigation.

The research questions relevant to the above problem follow:

1. What is the rationale for evaluating organizational communication?
2. What evaluation concepts have been developed?
3. What overall audits or specific behavioral communication studies have been completed?

Scope of Chapter

Sincoff and Goyer (1977) have noted that the evaluation of organizational communication systems may be considered from the viewpoints of (a) the organization and (b) the research community, and that organizational communication evaluation (OCE) cannot proceed unless it has benefits to the organization. It is to this last point that this chapter addresses itself, in the main. If OCE is to be a useful and durable procedure for organizations, it is important that both the researcher and management personnel understand the goals and objectives of the process, as well as being cognizant of the different available approaches, criteria employed, and impacts which may be potentially realized.

In taking the organizational point of view primarily, we consider OCE to be applied research involving the examination of the organizational systems in a manner similar to medical diagnosis, as a tool to uncover potential communication problems and formulate recommendations for remediation. The writings we selected for this overview include conceptual studies and analyses of specific measurement instruments, as well as comprehensive case studies of organizations, and subunits thereof. There are writings discussed that concentrate only on one specific area of communication, e.g., downward communication, top-level executive oral communication, workgroup meetings, written communication, and information flow. In general, the writings selected can be termed "descriptive," but no one research category appears to be applicable, as consideration is given to field studies, prescriptive-descriptive essays, and theoretical-conceptual works. Generally, laboratory studies have been excluded. In some of the publications, as is true of most doctoral dissertations, a formal set of hypotheses is established, which involve independent and dependent variables, but this is not true of most of the references herein. The basic test for selection of a written work was if it was informative on the subject of organization communication evaluation, and if it could help in the task of finding answers to one or more of the three research questions noted above.

For the purpose of outlining the development of ideas and procedures in the area of organizational communication evaluation, the literature which follows focuses upon those works that have been preponderantly or entirely concerned with internal communication of organizations rather than those writings devoted entirely or significantly to external communication, i.e., organization to environment communication. The references utilized herein are mainly from studies in the time period 1950–1981.

Plan of Chapter

To accomplish the purposes noted above, the following discussion of organizational communication evaluation includes major sections about: (a) rationale for the evaluation of organizational communication processes; (b) the history of internal OCE concepts and procedures, specifically in terms of interpersonal communication evaluation studies in organizations, group communication evaluation studies in organizations, and organization-wide communication evaluation studies; and (c) the development of standardized audit instrument and data banks.

RATIONALE FOR THE EVALUATION OF ORGANIZATIONAL COMMUNICATION PROCESSES

The arguments in favor of the evaluation of organizational communication evaluation processes can be classified into four broad and overlapping categories:

1. OCE develops benchmarks: i.e., it gathers information so management is aware of the status of communication systems.
2. OCE improves the internal communication system: i.e., the kinds of information furnished by the evaluation process improve the factors influencing the communication system, as well as variables affected by that system.
3. OCE aids the management process of planning and control: i.e., the improvement of the communication system enables management to do a better job of planning and control of operations, resulting in better outcomes in the form of employee satisfaction, adaptiveness, and performance.
4. OCE bridges many existing organizational communication gaps: i.e., (a) the lag in communication system adaptation to the needs of the organization, (b) inadequate at-

tention to interpersonal and group communication processes within and between organizations, and (c) the inability of the individual organization to compare status of its own communication system to that of comparable organizations.

Develops Benchmarks

In their survey of major corporations as to communication policies and practices, Hellweg and Phillips (1983) reported that 45% of the reporting *Fortune* 500 companies had undergone an organizational communication audit, and 40% recognized the need to evaluate their communication systems regularly; when asked why, the rationale given by the respondents was that the evaluative process offered a *benchmark* for the progress and future of corporate programs. Goldhaber (1983, p. 374) pointed to the benchmark concept when he stated that audit data may be used to measure the status of the communication system at two or more points in time, so as to judge the impact of organizational innovations such as: (a) restructuring; (b) addition of a computer; or (c) a new organizational development program. Krivonos (1975a) noted that measured communication variables in a communication audit could be considered as "benchmarks" to be examined for strengths and weaknesses, to be diagnosed so as to determine if actual or perceived communication practices corresponded to those considered best for effective organizations.

Improves the Internal Communication System and Related Variables

Goldhaber and Rogers (1979, p. 2) noted the opinions of management theorists and practitioners about the strikingly important role of communication in the operation of organizations in the area of motivation, innovation, decision making, and coordination, and then stated that, because the communication system is so important, managers must have information about the operation of that system to solve communication problems, to keep the system operating efficiently, and to improve the system by creating more efficient and effective ways of communicating. This information can be furnished by periodic communication audits.

In their review of the ICA Communication Audit and perceived communication effectiveness changes in 16 audited organizations, Brooks, Callicoat, and Siegerdt (1979) concluded that most organizations tended to adopt changes as a result of the audit, especially changes in structure (e.g., work units, job specification, committee memberships), communication methods (e.g., feedback spans, group planning sessions, meetings with employees), and training (e.g., workshops on communication, orientation training, reorientation training), and that 85% of the organizations responding indicated that the audit resulted in perceived favorable changes in communication effectiveness.

Goldhaber (1983, p. 375) noted the kind of information that a communication appraisal can furnish, considering these factors to be (a) influences on the communication system, or (b) subject to the influence of the communication system: structural elements, impact of stress and fear, mechanization effects, employee isolation, media effectiveness, communication preferences, relationships between organizational levels, effect of timing of communication on morale and productivity, effect of changing values, and environmental influences.

Aids Management Planning and Control

Greenbaum and White (1976) maintained that, prima facie, the communication process is vital to organizations, and should be managed by planning, organizing, and controlling communication networks, policies, and activities, noting that control implies the presence of standards and the knowledge of what is actually happening in the organization, and that the periodic communication audit could provide the necessary feedback. There is an assumption that a periodic audit can provide an organization with a sensoring system necessary for adaptiveness and for detecting negative communication situations in their formative stages, before flexible conditions become solidified and develop into serious "people problems." Organizational communication reviews can provide the monitoring which allows the organization to take a preventive stance regarding communication problems rather than a corrective stance.

Rogers and Goldhaber (1978, pp. 55-69) have noted that the appraisal of communication processes represents an important step in effecting change. The audit generates information permitting the recognition of problems, suggestions for changes, and identification of opportunities, and furnishes the diagnosis required for starting the process of improving morale, diminishing grievances, and increasing productivity and performance.

Goldhaber (1983, pp. 373-374) has compared the communication audit to checkups by accountants to prevent financial crises, and examinations by physicians to prevent health breakdowns, noting that, in these situations and in the communication audit, the client can receive sufficient advance notice of impending ailments so as to avoid or mitigate undesirable consequences. The communication audit provides an organization with advance information to prevent a major breakdown that would limit overall effectiveness, replaces guesswork with accurate data so that problems can be forecast, identifies key communication groupings as an aid to restructuring and successful reorganization, and aids in the development of new communication training programs geared to solve real organizational problems identified by the audit.

Sincoff, Williams, and Rohm (1976) have noted two objectives for a communication audit that distinctly characterize the evaluation process as a management tool related to planning and control: (a) mapping the communication flaws within an organization, and (b) ascertaining if the appropriate communication elements are present within the existing organization structure.

Bridges Organizational Communication Gaps

In respect to the lag in communication system adaptation to the needs of the organization, Greenbaum (1974) has noted that variables causing changes in marketing, production, and finance also require changes in organizational communication. Although changes in communication processes do constantly occur, planned and otherwise, there tends to be a lag in such adaptation, and a continuous program of appraisal provides necessary feedback leading to changes.

In respect to the inadequate attention given to interpersonal and small group communication processes, Hickson, Greenbaum, Falcione, and Goldhaber (1975) reported that the basic communication activities of larger organizations receive varying degrees of technical communication management, with most attention being given to organization-wide activities (e.g., newsletters, bulletin boards) and least to small group and interpersonal activities. Moreover, this survey indicated an absence of evaluation for 47% of organization-wide activities, 67% of interpersonal activities, and 66% of small group activities. The audit of communication processes can bridge this gap between the employee communication manager concerned with organization-wide information dissemination, and public relations management concerned mainly with stockholders, investors, and the government.

In respect to the organizational communication gap that has existed because of the inability of the individual organization to compare the status of its own communication system to that of comparable organizations, Goldhaber, Porter, and Yates (1977) have reported that the ICA Communication Audit has begun to formulate conclusions about organizational communication behavior across different types of organizations. With the publication of their paper, containing norms developed from 13 ICA audits, the dream of comparative analyses is becoming a reality. They caution against too much enthusiasm at this time, however, by noting that the norms are based on a small sample, so that such norms are highly tentative, and that analyses indicate the need for considering the contingencies operating for particular organizations. While this organizational communication gap may not be closed at present, and, while the road ahead indicates much work necessary, it is clear that OCE can help in the process of obtaining comparative organizational communication data.

HISTORY OF INTERNAL OCE CONCEPTS AND PROCEDURES

This section has the purpose of outlining the development of OCE ideas and approaches as noted in various studies in natural settings related to *internal* organizational communication evaluation. Most of the writings report field study investigations, but a small percentage represents conceptual works generalizing on communication evaluation in natural settings.

Previous compilations of organizational communication literature by Guetzkow (1965), Redding (1966), Tompkins (1967), Carter (1972), Redding (1972), Porter and Roberts (1976), Goldhaber (1978), and Daly and Korinek (1982) have had other purposes; none has limited its review to communication evaluation in natural organization settings. Only Redding (1972) has given full consideration to unpublished doctoral dissertations, while a most recent state-of-the-art work by Jablin and Sussman (1983) concentrating on organizational group communication includes laboratory studies, due to the scarcity of writings reporting research in natural settings in that particular subtopic area.

The following discussion of internal OCE literature classifies writings as to (a) Interpersonal Organizational Communications; (b) Group Organizational Communication; and (c) Organization-Wide Communication. For each of these major categories, there is a further division into the four subclasses of (a) Information Flow Studies—i.e., channels, initiators, feedback, network participants, etc.; (b) Message Content Studies—i.e., meaning, purpose, qualities, accuracy, redundancy, distortion, etc.; (c) Communication Climate Studies—i.e., attitudes and feelings about the communication process in terms of member satisfaction with sources, media, adequacy, participation, etc.; and (d) Individual Training and Organization Development Studies—i.e., needs assessments for communication development of individuals and organizations. Therefore, for each of the interface-based categories of interpersonal, group, and organization-wide, there are the four analytical subcategories of communication flow, message content, feelings, and development, thus providing 12 possible classifications in which to categorize a writing. In many cases, the writing was of such a nature that it required treatment under more than one category—e.g., Odiorne (1954) concentrated on message content and communication climate, and Ross (1954) and Sanborn (1961) both produced case studies that involved information flow, message content, and communication climate factors. Also, most studies touch on communication climate, no matter what the particular emphasis, so it is important to recognize that the classification of writings is subject to considerable shortcomings, and the reader should note that the classification assigned to a writing was considered to be a major emphasis in that particular study, and that same writing might well be concerned with other classes to a lesser extent.

In total, 65 writings were incorporated in this survey of *internal* organizational communication evaluation: 18 in the Interpersonal Communication Class, 13 in the Group Communication Class, and 34 in the Organization-Wide Communication Class. Each of these major classes of writings concerned with OCE is discussed below.

Evaluation of Interpersonal Communication in Organizations

Table 1 presents a chronological listing of selected writings in evaluation of interpersonal organizational communication. There are references to ten dissertations, two articles and six unpublished papers. The frequency of specific subclasses representing the communication area emphasis of these studies follows:

Communication Area Emphasis	Frequency
Information Flow Studies	8
Message Content Studies	6
Communication Climate Studies	6
Training & Development Studies	5

The total writings per subclass does not agree with the total writings per Table 1 for the reason that many writings were judged to have more than one area of emphasis.

The chronological listing in Table 1 presents details about each writing, furnishing the year of presentation, the name of the author, the nature of publication format, abbreviated title, notation as to whether each is a field study (F/S) or a conceptual work (T/C), the communication area of emphasis, and the measurement instruments employed.

Whereas Table 1 presents interpersonal OCE writings in chronological order, providing the several details noted immediately above, Table 1-A, derived from the same writings noted in Table 1, presents an analysis of the variables studied under each of the major communication constructs of information flow, message content, communication climate, and individual and organizational development. The discussion that follows relates directly to Table 1-A, furnishing a guide to the variables studied in the selected works:

1. Information Flow Studies: included consideration for channels, feedback, communication direction and efficiency, communication initiation, and communication reception activities:

Channels: Dahle (1954) concluded that the best communication results were obtained if information was presented orally and, at the same time, printed materials concerning the same information were distributed; *Brisley* (1957) reported that 80% of all executive communication was oral speech communication; *Level* (1959) did not fully accept the hypothesis that the principal channels of communication are those determined by the organization structure; and *Madden* (1967) found that one-to-one oral speech activity was the predominant type of interaction for top-level executives, while noting differences for middle-management executives and top-level executives in smaller companies.

Feedback: Nilsen (1953) reported that there was insufficient checking up to see whether

Table 1. Selected Writings in Evaluation of Interpersonal Organizational Communication 1950–1981

| Year | Author | P.F. | Title (Abbreviated) | R.T. | Emphasis of Study | | | | |
					IF	MC	CC	T&D	MI
1953	Nilsen, T.	D	The Communication Survey	F/S	X		X		I,O
1953	Angrist, A.	D	Communication Problem & Practices of Executives	F/S		X		X	Q
1954	Dahle, T.	A	An Objective & Comparative Study of Five Methods of Transmitting Information	F/S	X				O
1954	Ross, R.	D	Communication Breakdowns in The General Telephone Co. of Indiana	F/S	X	X	X		Q,I
1957	Brisley, C.	D	Oral Communication in Executive Behavior	F/S	X				I,O
1959	Level, D.	D	A Case Study of Human Communication in an Urban Bank	F/S	X		X		Q,O,I
1967	Madden, F.	D	Oral Communication Patterns Used by Top Level Execs.	F/S	X			X	O
1969	Cole, W.	D	The Characteristics of Written Communications	F/S				X	I,O
1969	Minter, R.	D	A Comparative Analysis of Managerial Communication	F/S			X		I,Q
1972	Brenner, M. & Sigband, N.	P	Organizational Comm.: An Analysis Based on Empirical Data	F/S	X				I,Q
1972	Goldhaber, C. & Horan, H.	P	A Communication Systems Analysis of KOB-TV	F/S			X		I
1975	Krivonos, P.	D	Subordinate-Superior Comm. as Related to Intrinsic & Extrinisic Motivation	F/S		X			O,Q
1978	Level, D. & Johnson, L.	A	Accuracy of Information Flows Within the Superior-Subordinate Relationship	F/S		X			Q,I
1978	Downs, C. & Conrad, C.	P	A Critical Incident Study of Superior–Subordinate Communication	F/S	X	X			Q
1980	Klauss, R. & Bass, B.	P	Communication & Leader Behavior	F/S			X		Q
1980	Jenkins, K.	P	The Impact of Supervisor Communication Effectiveness	F/S		X			O,Q
1981	Wohlgamuth, W.	D	Evolution of Structured Interpersonal Communication	F/S				X	Q
1981	Prado Garza, M.	P	Health Communication Program Evaluation	F/S				X	Q

Codes:
P.F. – Publication Format: Book (B); Dissertation (D); Published Article (A); (Q).
R.T. – Research Type: Field Study (F/S); Theoretical Conceptual (T/C).
I.F. – Information Flow.
M.C. – Message Contents and Skills.
C.C. – Communication Climate (feelings and attitudes).
T&D – Individual Training and Organization Development, including Communication Audits.
M.I. – Measurement Instruments: Interview (I); Observation (O); Questionnaire (Q).

Table 1-A. Interpersonal Communication in Organizations
A Taxonomical Analysis of Evaluation Studies in Natural Settings, Years 1950–1981

Taxonomic Level				
1		*Organization Communication Evaluation (OCE)*		
2		*Interpersonal Communication in Organizations*		
3	*Information-Flow Studies*	*Message Content Studies*	*Communication Climate Studies*	*Individual Training and Organization Development Studies*
4	*Channels*	*General Message Qualities*	*Communication Structure*	*Individual Training*
5	Dahle (1954)	Ross (1954)	Nilsen (1953)	Angrist (1953)
	Brisley (1957)	Angrist (1953)	Level (1959)	Madden (1967)
	Level (1959)	Downs & Conrad	Minter (1969)	Cole (1969)
	Madden (1967)	(1978)	Goldhaber & Horan (1972)	Wohlgamuth (1981)
4	*Feedback*	*Accuracy and Distortion*		*Organization Development*
5	Nilsen (1953)	Krivonos (1975)		Prado Garza (1981)
	Brenner & Sigband (1972)	Level & Johnson (1978)		
	Downs & Conrad (1978)	Jenkins (1980)		
4	*Communication Direction and Efficiency*		*Participation & Change*	
5	Nilsen (1953)		Nilsen (1953)	
	Ross (1954)		Level (1959)	
	Brenner & Sigband (1972)			
4	*Communication Initiation*		*Media*	
5	Nilsen (1953)		Ross (1954)	
	Downs & Conrad (1978)			
4	*Communication Reception*		*Sources & Receivers*	
5	Level (1959)		Level (1959)	
	Downs & Conrad (1978)		Minter (1969)	
			Role Clarity	
			Level (1959)	
4			*Communication Importance*	
5			Nilsen (1953)	
			Level (1959)	
4			*Leadership Behavior*	
5			Minter (1969)	
			Klauss & Bass (1980)	

283

information had been received or understood; *Brenner and Sigband* (1972) indicated that subordinates keep their superior better informed when the former know what will be done with their ideas; and *Downs and Conrad* (1978) reported that effective subordinacy was marked by timely provisions of feedback, and (b) the check on perceptions through paraphrasing.

Communication Direction and Efficiency: Nilsen (1953) noted that poor communication existed between the payroll supervisor and the chief fiscal officer, and between the chief fiscal officer and the timekeeping supervisor; *Ross* (1954) suggested a theory based on the frequency of the media used by the supervisor, and the primary directional orientation (up, down, horizontal) of the superior's communication; and *Brenner and Sigband* (1972) reported that communications were more effective if the individual received such communications from his or her immediate superior.

Communication Initiation: Nilsen (1953) reported a failure to talk about production problems until a critical situation had developed, and that supervisors did not elicit suggestions from employees, nor stimulate an interchange of ideas; and *Downs and Conrad* (1978) noted the following message-related elements as important for effective subordinancy: communicates in a timely manner, asks questions, anticipates superior's needs, and volunteers input.

Communication Reception: Level (1959) found support for the hypothesis that effective supervisors must be good listeners when dealing with subordinates, and rejected the hypothesis that all personnel possess a satisfactory understanding of company policies and practices; and *Downs and Conrad* (1978) indicated communication attributes important for effective subordinacy to include (a) listens well, and (b) follows instructions.

2. Message Content Studies: yielded conclusions that can be classed in terms of (a) General Message Qualities and (b) Accuracy and Distortion:

General Message Qualities: Ross (1954) provided a message-content analysis of the readability and human interest of six company publications; *Angrist* (1953) concluded that some communication practices in business and industry were not in accord with accepted principles; and *Downs and Conrad* (1978) reported the following message-related elements as most important for effective subordinacy: encodes clear messages, speaks briefly and concisely, and reports are factual and thorough.

Accuracy and Distortion: Krivonos (1975b) found support for the hypothesis that intrinsically motivated employees will perceive downward communication directed to themselves as being more accurate than will extrinsics; found minimal support for the hypothesis that, when communicating upward, intrinsically motivated subordinates will distort messages less than will extrinsically motivated subordinates; and found mixed support for the hypothesis that supervisors will perceive messages from subordinates they perceive to be intrinsically motivated as being less distorted than messages from subordinates they perceive as extrinsically motivated; *Level and Johnson* (1978) concluded that, in upward communication, the subordinate's tendency to distort information concerning responsibility was decreased when the superior's consideration leadership style increased; in downward communication, flows are more accurate on more objective, measurable topics; and there is a highly significant relation between the subordinate's distortion of information and the accuracy of supervisory controlled information; and *Jenkins* (1980) concluded that worker performance was positively related to effective communication on job content, and to supervisor communication effectiveness.

3. Communication Climate Studies: included consideration for feelings and attitudes as to structure of communication, participation and change, media, sources and receivers, role clarity, the general importance of communication, and leadership communication behavior:

Communication Structure: Nilsen (1953) reported a lack of free exchange of ideas between management and personnel, that civilian staff found it difficult to communicate to Navy officers in the Navy Purchasing Office, but were able to communicate with civilian supervisors, and that there was a need for structured opportunities for employees to express grievances and feelings to someone in authority; *Level* (1959) found that employees felt that the company atmosphere permitted face-to-face communications, but that employees did not feel free to make suggestions and complaints; *Minter* (1969) examined the attitudes and perceptions of managers to selected communication factors including upward permissiveness, influence of organizational level on "semantic distance," and the influence of contrasting innovative and technical climates on the attitudes and perceptions of supervisory personnel; and *Goldhaber and Horan* (1972) reported adverse feelings as to communication practices with a television station involving lack of dissemination of general information, and poor distribution of specific information concerning actions by managers.

Participation and Change: Nilsen (1953) noted that employees resented the introduction of new procedures with little or no discussion prior to implementation; and *Level* (1959) indicated that his examination of a bank's communication processes found no support for the hypothesis that employees received advance notice of changes which affected them.

Media: Ross (1954) provided an analysis of supervisor reactions toward three of the company's written media, and an analysis of supervisor attitudes toward the day-to-day oral communication in respect to direction and particular media employed.

Sources and Receivers: Level (1959) found support for the hypothesis that employees feel they get messages from appropriate sources, that supervisors are good listeners when dealing with subordinates, and that supervisors are competent in basic speech skills; and *Minter* (1969) examined the attitudes of managers toward the subjects of frankness and openness within the organization, and general communication satisfaction.

Role Clarity: Level (1959) reported that employees in his bank case study believed that they knew what was expected of them.

General Importance of Communication in Organizations: Nilsen (1953) reported that management in the industrial organizations he studied did not consider communication to be related to high levels of labor turnover; and *Level* (1959) concluded that the bank management reviewed did not feel that communication was an important function.

Leadership Behavior: Minter (1969) examined the attitudes of managers relative to the credibility of management and the sensitivity of bosses toward feelings of employees; and *Klauss and Bass* (1980) identified the type of leader behavior that resulted in maximum communication satisfaction on the part of subordinates, concluding that considerate leader behavior (consultative, participative, and delegative) more strongly relates to satisfactory communications than directive or negotiative leader behavior.

4. Individual Training and Organization Development Studies: related to the communication development of individuals, and the communication development of the organization:

> *Communication Development of Individuals in Organizations: Angrist* (1953) found that some communication events are not viewed similarly by (a) organization executives, and (b) recognized communication texts, recommending that individual communication training would be helpful in the development of executives; *Madden* (1967) recommended that speech education should give attention to the important business skills of interviewing, listening, questioning, keeping to the point, group interaction, public speaking, reading quickly, and writing effectively; *Cole* (1969) concluded that business educators should motivate students in business writing classes by emphasizing the fact that success and advancement in industry depends upon the ability to communicate; and *Wohlgamuth* (1981) concluded that structured interpersonal communications, in the form of three-person groups arriving at a composite product, served to increase student achievement of business-writing principles.
>
> *Communication Development of the Organization: Prado Garza* (1981) reported that the communication evaluation program used in hospital settings in Mexico had the following purposes: (a) that participants get to know themselves and understand their behaviors, (b) that the participants know the impact that their behaviors cause to other persons, and (c) that the participants learn to develop personal abilities to work in a group effectively, and enhance the effectiveness of the organization.

5. Summary of Internal OCE Concepts and Interpersonal Communication Studies: In summary, in respect to interpersonal communication, the review of 65 studies of internal organizational communication in natural settings yielded eight studies of information flow, six studies of message content, six studies of communication climate, and five studies classed as individual and organization development.

The information flow studies concentrated on the basic variables of channels, feedback, direction, initiation, and reception, with the greatest attention being given to channels, feedback, and direction, and little replication being evidenced other than in the area of the dominance of oral-speech channels, and the importance of listening.

Message content studies were divided as to variables termed general message qualities (readability, clarity, brevity, factual, etc.) and accuracy and distortion; and only in the category of accuracy and distortion was there evidence of the same variable being studied in a natural setting by more than one investigator.

The communication climate studies, concerned with feelings and attitudes toward communication variables, were divided as to communication structure, participation and change, media, sources and receivers, role clarity, communication importance, and leadership behavior, with some replication being evidenced in the areas of structure, change, and the general importance of communication in organizations.

Finally, the individual training and organization development studies included a wide diversity of investigations emphasizing the need for training individuals in communication principles to enhance opportunities for organizational success; and the need for individuals to realize their impact on fellow workers and to develop personal abilities to work in groups. In the five studies reviewed in this area, repetitive findings were present only in one area of recommending that speech education be given to develop skills of interviewing, listening, questioning, reading, and writing.

Evaluation of Group Communication in Organizations

Table 2 presents a chronological listing of selected writings in evaluation of group communication in organizations. There are six dissertations and books, three articles, and five unpublished papers noted. The frequency of specific subclasses representing the communication area emphasis of these studies follows:

Communication Area Emphasis	Frequency
Information Flow Studies	6
Message Content Studies	2
Communication Climate Studies	6
Training & Development Studies	4

The chronological listing in Table 2 presents details about each writing, furnishing the year of presentation, the name of the author, the nature of format, abbreviated title, notation as to whether each is a field study (F/S) or a conceptual work (T/C), the communication area of emphasis, and the measurement instruments employed.

Whereas Table 2 presents organization group communication writings in chronological order, providing the several details noted immediately above, Table 2-A, derived from the same writings noted in Table 2, presents an analysis of the variables studied under each of the major communication constructs of information flow, message content, communication climate, and individual and organizational development. The discussion that follows relates directly to Table 2-A, furnishing a guide to the variables studied in the selected works:

1. **Information Flow Studies:** included consideration for channels, communication initiation, group leadership, and problem solving:

Channels: Nilsen (1953) examined questions of how often groups meet, and when group meetings are held, concluding with a postulate that, where regular or occasional meetings among different levels of supervision are not held, areas of misunderstanding among such levels of supervision can be assumed to exist; *Healey* (1958) found that, in the absence of policy manuals, group conferences and oral presentations were the principle methods used for the communication of policies to immediate subordinates, concluding that almost half of the executives participating in the survey employed conferences to keep their subordinates alert to the objectives of the firm; *Ahmed's* (1965) study of the comparative effectiveness of formal and informal channels of communication in projects of curriculum development requiring coordination of administrative and teaching personnel concluded that face-to-face communication in group meetings was the most effective means of communication, and functionally formalized channels were more convenient and efficient than either the formal channels of the organization chart, or completely informal channels. The functionally formalized channels recommended by Ahmed appear to be equivalent to task force committees, or formal groups of individuals with the know-how to accomplish a specified objective.

Communication Initiation: Nilsen (1953) examined the question of whether all members of the group feel free to voice opinions and bring up problems, and the related question of how opinions, suggestions, and problems are received when voiced at group meetings. Among his postulates relating to group communication was one stating that,

Table 2. Selected Writings in Evaluation of Group Organizational Communication, 1950–1981

Year	Author	P.F.	Title (Abbreviated)	R.T.	IF	MC	CC	T&D	MI
						Emphasis of Study			
1953	Nilsen, T.	D	The Communication Survey	F/S	X		X	X	I,O
1958	Healy, J.	B	Executive Coordination and Control	F/S	X				Q
1959	Level, D.	D	Human Communication in an Urban Bank	F/S			X		
1965	Ahmed, Z.	D	A Study of Administrative Communication in a Selected School System	F/S	X				I
1967	Maier, N.	A	Assets & Liabilities in Group Problem Solving	T/C				X	
1972	Jain, H.	P	Employee Knowledge of Hospital Compensation Policies	F/S	X				Q
1972	Nelson, M.	D	Intragroup Communication Effectiveness of Small Workgroup Supervisors	F/S			X		Q,O
1977	Huseman, R.	A	The Role of the Nominal Group in Small Group Communication	T/C	X				
1979	Krohn, V.	D	Vertical Communication as Perceived by Administrators & Teachers	F/S			X		Q
1980	Jain, H., Kanungo, R., & Goldhaber, G.	A	Attitudes Toward Communication System: A Comparison of Anglophone & Francophone Employees	F/S			X		Q
1980	Conger, D.	P	Using Team Building to Increase Communication Effectiveness	F/S				X	Q,I
1980	Greenbaum, H.	P	Appraisal of Workgroup Meeting	F/S				X	Q,O
1983	Spataro, L., & Holden, E.	A	Effectiveness						
1981	Kelly, L. & Gleason, M.	A	Ranking Member Effectiveness in Problem-Solving Groups	F/S	X	X	X		Q
1981	Bednar, D. & Glauser, M.	P	Interaction Analysis of Collective Bargaining	F/S		X			O

NOTE 1: Subject matter of writings indicated in this table include (a) intragroup communication studies, and (b) group-to-group communication within an organization.

Codes:

P.F.— Publication Format: Book (B); Dissertation (D); Published Article (A); Convention Paper (P).

R.T.— Research Type: Field Study (F/S); Theoretical Conceptual (T/C).

I.F.— Information Flow and Media.

M.C.— Message Contents and Skills.

C.C.— Communication Climate (feelings and attitudes).

T&D— Individual Training and Organization Development, including Communication Audits.

M.I.— Measurement Instruments: Interviews (I); Observation (O); Questionnaire (Q).

where group meetings are called only when a pressing problem or a critical situation has arisen, the effectiveness of such meetings is reduced, members tend to be on the defensive, and a permissive atmosphere is difficult if not impossible to achieve.

Group Leadership: Jain (1972) tested the assumptions found in much of the management literature that the first-line supervisor is a key communicator of organizational policies to employees, concluding that no significant relationship was found between supervisory performance scores and employee knowledge of compensation policies; and *Kelly and Gleason* (1981) rated performance of group meeting participants on the basis of service, contribution, and leadership, with the leadership component being de-

Table 2-A. Group Communication in Organizations
A Taxonomical Analysis of Evaluation Studies in Natural Settings, Years 1950–1981

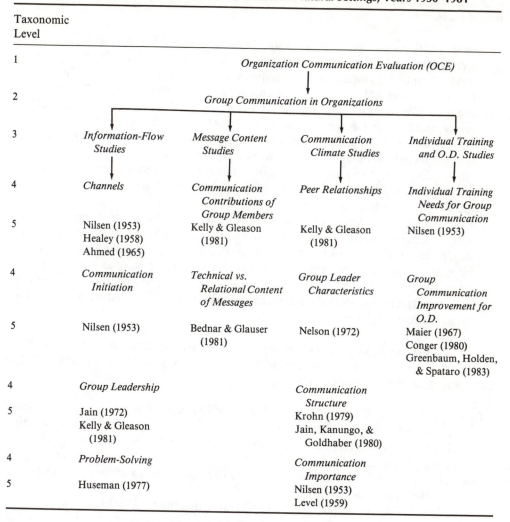

Taxonomic Level				
1		*Organization Communication Evaluation (OCE)*		
2		*Group Communication in Organizations*		
3	*Information-Flow Studies*	*Message Content Studies*	*Communication Climate Studies*	*Individual Training and O.D. Studies*
4	*Channels*	*Communication Contributions of Group Members*	*Peer Relationships*	*Individual Training Needs for Group Communication*
5	Nilsen (1953) Healey (1958) Ahmed (1965)	Kelly & Gleason (1981)	Kelly & Gleason (1981)	Nilsen (1953)
4	*Communication Initiation*	*Technical vs. Relational Content of Messages*	*Group Leader Characteristics*	*Group Communication Improvement for O.D.*
5	Nilsen (1953)	Bednar & Glauser (1981)	Nelson (1972)	Maier (1967) Conger (1980) Greenbaum, Holden, & Spataro (1983)
4	*Group Leadership*		*Communication Structure*	
5	Jain (1972) Kelly & Gleason (1981)		Krohn (1979) Jain, Kanungo, & Goldhaber (1980)	
4	*Problem-Solving*		*Communication Importance*	
5	Huseman (1977)		Nilsen (1953) Level (1959)	

fined as offering new and creative ideas, maintaining member attention to the task, exerting pressure to meet deadlines, and providing levity and good will when needed.

Problem Solving: Huseman (1977) examined the advantages and disadvantages of conventional group problem solving, proposing that nominal group techniques (no verbal interaction) at certain points in the process are advantageous and can be supportive of the interacting group procedures. His evaluation concluded that the nominal group procedure appeared to be superior in problem identification, and generation of possible solutions, while the interacting group procedure was superior for information evaluation and group consensus obtention.

2. Message Content Studies: yielded conclusions that can be classed in terms of (a) communication contributions of group members, and (b) technical versus relational content of messages:

Communication Contributions of Group Members: Kelly and Gleason (1981) were concerned with the evaluation of communication performance of individuals in group activities, employing the criteria of contribution, service, and leadership. Contribution was defined to include provision of factual information, willingness to permit others to ask questions, offering opinions without combat, questioning and criticizing others gently, maintaining the agenda, and extending courtesy and good will.

Technical versus Relational Content of Messages: Bednar and Glauser (1981) tracked both the technical content and the relational aspects of messages, in an attempt to obtain a more complete understanding of communicating behavior in collective bargaining groups. Messages from seven bargaining sessions were coded both as to technical content (substantive, strategic, persuasive, task, affective, procedural), and relational (control, deference, equivalence) behavior, and compared over time, i.e., early sessions versus later sessions, concluding that (a) communicative behavior in bargaining has an excessive focus on task; (b) the primary pattern of interaction is competitive, as distinguished from decision-making groups where equivalent (cooperative) symmetry is found; and (c) there were distinct phases of group bargaining meetings, with the structure of technical content statements remaining stable, but relational messages changing over time.

3. Communication Climate Studies: included consideration for feelings and attitudes about peer relationships, group leader characteristics, structure of communication, and the general importance of communication:

Peer Relationships: Kelly and Gleason (1981) ranked individual performance in small, task-oriented groups, based on the criteria of contribution, service and leadership, noting elements that related to the communication climate in which the group operated, e.g., maintaining courtesy and good will, criticizing others gently, offering opinions without combat, willingness to perform necessary tasks, and providing levity and good will when needed.

Group Leader Characteristics: Nelson (1972) identified the significant characteristics of supervisors who appeared to be more effective intragroup communicators, employing among other instruments measures of employee attitudes and morale, and concluding that leadership characteristics correlating with supervisory interpersonal and leadership success included small-sized groups, older and experienced supervisors, interpersonal sensitivity to group attitudes, and higher scores on human relations abilities.

Structure of Communication: Krohn (1979) found that (a) administrators in the school system were more satisfied than teachers with the quantity of downward communication, but that there was no significant difference between teachers and administrators in their satisfaction with the quantity of upward communication; and (b) administrators perceived the quality of communication between themselves and the teachers to be significantly higher than the quality of this communication as perceived by the teachers, both for downward and upward communication; and *Jain, Kanungo, and Goldhaber* (1980), in their study of French and English Canadians in a large general hospital, concluded that Anglophone employees consistently showed lower levels of satisfaction than Francophone employees with the various aspects of the communication system.

General Importance of Group Communication: Nilsen (1953) included, in his long list of research questions, the following: (a) What are employee, foreman, and superintendent attitudes toward group meetings?, and (b) Does group discussion have any importance in the eyes of foremen or superintendents? His conclusion was that communication in general was not considered to be an important element in determining performance, the same conclusion of which was later drawn by *Level* (1959).

4. Individual Training and Organization Development Studies: related to individual training needs for group communication, and organizational group communication development for the improved effectiveness of the organization,

Individual Training Needs for Group Communication: Nilsen (1953) concluded his study with a number of postulates, including that (1) effective discussion is not automatic when a group of people are brought together for discussion purposes, and (b) effective discussion is the result of carefully evaluated experience and deliberate training. In addition, he noted that managerial personnel in his study were not aware of their lack of skill in leading discussion, and being unaware took no steps to develop such skill, and the lack of such skill reduced the value of the meetings significantly.

Group Communication Improvement for Organization Development: Maier (1967) furnished a most comprehensive assessment of problem-solving group advantages and disadvantages, including an emphasis on the group leadership function, and the analysis has served as a valuable foundation on which to base training for more effective groups; *Conger* (1980) examined the dynamics of improving communication in work relationships through a team-building intervention, noting that the basic reason for improving communication was to increase performance. He indicated that, prior to beginning a team-building workshop with a group, one must assess the state of the intrapersonal dimension and the interpersonal dimension of group members, so as to determine whether additional training is needed by the group members. The intrapersonal dimension included being aware of one's own competence, knowing one's own inadequacies and values, and being comfortable with one's self. The interpersonal dimension consisted of listening skills, and giving and receiving feedback constructively. He also noted that the success of the team improvement project is often based on the leader's ability to accept criticism openly and deal with it nondefensively; this called for special training of group leaders to be open to other positions, avoid win–lose strategies, seeking consensus rather than compromise, being suspect of easy agreement, and building on the ideas of others; and *Greenbaum, Holden, and Spataro* (1983) examined the influence of a change in organizational structure on the functional communication processes of an organization. The change in organizational structure related to the introduction of structured workgroup meetings throughout an industrial company; and the functional communication processes were defined in terms of four communication subsystems, the regulative-task network, the adaptive-innovative network, the integrative-maintenance network, and the informative-instructive network. It was concluded that the introduction of the organization-group program significantly improved each of the four communication subsystems.

5. Summary of Internal OCE Concepts of Organizational Group Studies: In summary, in respect to organizational group communication, the review of 65 studies of internal organizational communication in natural settings yielded six studies of information flow, two studies of message content, six studies of communication climate, and four studies of individual and organizational communication needs.

The information flow studies concentrated on the basic variables of channels, communication initiation, group leadership, and problem solving, with supportive findings between investigations being present only in the instance of verifying the importance of group communication in organizations.

Message content studies involving organizational groups constituted only one natural setting study in each of the two categories: (a) contributions of group members, and (b) technical versus relational content of messages, and so did not allow for any confirmation of findings between investigations.

The communication climate studies, concerned with feelings and attitudes toward communication variables, were subdivided into peer relationships, group leader characteristics, communication structure, and the importance of communication, with the only similar conclusions being drawn by two studies about the fact that, in the middle 1950s, group communication was not considered to be important in the eyes of management as reported by different investigators.

Finally, the individual training and organization development studies consisted of four investigations, involving diverse variables, all related to organizational groups, and to some extent generally overlapping, but no two of which could be viewed as replicative of the other.

Evaluation of Oragnization-Wide Communication

Table 3 presents a chronological listing of selected writings relative to the evaluation of organization-wide communication. There are listed 14 dissertation/books, 8 articles, and 12 unpublished papers. The frequency of subclasses representing the communication area emphasis of these studies follows:

Communication Area Emphasis	Frequency
Information Flow Studies	19
Message Content Studies	6
Communication Climate Studies	7
Training & Development Studies	10

The chronological listing in Table 3 presents details about each writing, the furnishing year of presentation, the name of the author, the nature of the format, abbreviated title, notation as to whether each is a field study (F/S) or a conceptual work (T/C), the communication area of emphasis, and the measurement instruments employed.

Whereas Table 3 presents organization-wide writings in chronological order, providing the several details noted immediately above, Table 3-A, derived from the same writings noted in Table 3, presents an analysis of the variables studied under each of the major communication constructs of information flow, message content, communication climate, and individual and organizational development. The discussion that follows relates directly to Table 3-A, furnishing a guide to the variables studied in the selected works:

Table 3. Selected Writings in Evaluation of Organization-Wide Communication 1950–1981

Year	Author	P.F.	Title (Abbreviated)	R.T.	Emphasis of Study				
					IF	MC	CC	T&D	MI
1950	Peters, R.	B	Evaluating Communication Media (Ch. 10 in *Communication Within Industry*)	T/C	X				
1953	Davis, K.	A	Management Communication and the Grapevine	F/S	X				Q
1953	Funk, H., & Becker, R.	A	Measuring the Effectiveness of Industrial Communication	F/S		X			Q
1954	Odiorne, G.	A	An Application of the Communication Audit	F/S		X	X		Q,I
1954	Lull, P., Funk, F., & Piersol, D.	A	What Communication Means to the Company President	F/S				X	Q
1955	Perry, D. & Mahoney T.	A	In-Plant Communications	F/S			X		Q
1956	Management Review	A	Does Your Communications Program Measure Up?	F/S	X				Q
1960	Ross, G.	D	A Study of Informal Communication Patterns in Two Elementary Schools	F/S	X				Q
1961	Simons, H.	D	A Comparison of Communication Attributes & Rated Job Performance of Supervisors	F/S	X	X			Q,I
1961	Sanborn, G.	D	An Analytical Study of Oral Communication Practices	F/S	X		X		Q,I,O
1962	Tompkins, P.	D	An Analysis of Communication Between Headquarters & Selected Units of a National Labor Union	F/S	X	X			Q,I,O
1966	Todd, J.	D	A Study of Communication & Coordination in Marketing Organizations	F/S	X				Q,I
1967	Moran, W.	D	Intra-Organizational Control and Communication	F/S	X				I
1968	Schwartz, D.	D	Liaison Communication Roles in a Formal Organization	F/S	X				Q
1970	Boyd, J.	P	An Analysis of the Internal Communication in the Boulder Community Hospital	F/S	X		X		I,Q
1972	Steber, J.	D	Communication Within an Organization	F/S				X	O,I
1972	Timpano, D.	D	A Study of Communication Network Characteristics in Schools by ECCO Analysis	F/S	X				Q
1972	Veninga, R.	D	A Case Study in Organization Development: The Role of Communication	F/S				X	I,Q
1972	Farace, R. & Russell, H.	P	Message Diffusion as a Communication Audit Tool	F/S	X				Q
1974	Greenbaum, H.	A	The Audit of Organizational Communication	T/C				X	

(Continued)

Table 3. *(Continued)*

Year	Author	P.F.	Title (Abbreviated)	R.T.	IF	MC	CC	T&D	MI
					Emphasis of Study				
1974	Sadler, W.	D	Communication in Organizations	F/S	X				Q,I
1974	Pacilio, P. Jr.	P	An Internal Communication Audit of Kent State University	F/S	X				I
1974	Dennis, H.	D	Managerial Communication Climate in Complex Organizations	F/S			X		
1974	DiSalvo, V., Larsen, D. & Seiler, W.	P	Communication Audit by Organizational Position	F/S	X				Q
1975	Mazza, J.	D	A General Systems Analysis of an Organizational Communication Climate	F/S			X		I,Q
1976	Sincoff, M., Williams, D. & Rohm, C.	P	Steps in Performing a Communication Audit	T/C				X	
1977	Tompkins, P.	A	Management Qua Communication in Rocket Research and Development	F/S	X	X	X	X	I,O
1978	Harris, L.	P	A Roles Based Model for the Analysis & Evaluation of Organizational Communication	F/S				X	Q
1978	Breen, M.	P	Technology in Organizational Communication: A Plan for Study	T/C	X				
1979	Lewis, P.	P	Communication Evaluation in Organizations: A Model for Training Directors	T/C				X	
1979	Driver, R.	P	The Relative Efficacy of Different Methods for Communicating Benefits	F/S	X				Q
1980	Smith, R.	P	Analysis of Organizational Audit Consulting Techniques: The Educational Organization	T/C				X	
1980	Downs, C.	P	Communication Audits of Medical Organizations	F/S				X	I,Q
1980	Eadie, W., Goyer, R., Liebowitz, E., Spiker, B., & Gossett, J.	P	A Communication Audit of a State Mental Health Institution	F/S	X				I,Q

Codes:
P.F. — Publication Format: Book (B); Dissertation (D); Published Article (A); Convention Paper (P).
R.T. — Research Type: Field Study (F/S); Theoretical Conceptual Writing (T/C).
I.F. — Information Flow and Media.
M.C. — Message Contents and Skills.
C.C. — Communication Climate (feelings and attitudes).
T&D — Individual Training and Organization Development, including Communication Audits.
M.I. — Measurement Instruments: Interview (I); Observation (O); Questionnaire (Q).

Table 3-A. Organization-Wide Communication in Organizations
A Taxonomical Analysis of Evaluation Studies in Natural Settings, Years 1950–1981

Taxonomic Level	Information-Flow Studies	Message Content Studies	Communication Climate Studies	Individual Training and O.D. Studies
1	*Organization Communication Evaluation (OCE)*			
2	*Organization-Wide Communication*			
3	*Information-Flow Studies*	*Message Content Studies*	*Communication Climate Studies*	*Individual Training and O.D. Studies*
4	*Channels*	*Accuracy and Distortion*	*Adequacy of Information*	*Individual Training Needs*
5	Davis (1953); Ross (1960); Sanborn (1961); Todd (1966); Boyd (1970); Pacilio (1974); DiSalvo, Larsen & Seiler (1974); Sadler (1974); Tompkins (1977)	Odiorne (1954); Simons (1961)	Odiorne (1954)	Lull, Funk, & Piersol (1954)
4	*Communication Patterns & Networks*	*Readability & Comprehension*	*Morale and Communication Satisfaction*	*Organization-Wide Communication Development*
5	Davis (1953); Todd (1966); Moran (1967); Schwartz (1968); Farace & Russell (1972); Timpano (1972)	Peters (1950); Funk & Becker (1953); Tompkins (1962); Tompkins (1977)	Perry & Mahoney (1955); Sanborn (1961)	Steber (1972); Veninga (1972); Greenbaum (1974); Sincoff, Williams, & Rohm (1976); Tompkins (1977); Harris & Cronen (1978); Lewis (1979); Smith (1980); Downs (1980)
4	*Communication Direction*		*Communication Importance*	
5	Davis (1953); Tompkins (1962); Boyd (1970); DiSalvo, Larsen & Seiler (1974); Tompkins (1977); Eadie, et al. (1980)		Boyd (1970)	
4	*Feedback*		*Dimensions of Communication Climate*	
5	Management Review (1956)		Dennis (1974)	
4	*Technology*		*Leadership Behavior*	
5	Tompkins (1977); Breen (1978); Driver (1979)		Mazza (1975)	
4	*Communicator Attributes*		*Openness & Trust*	
5	Simons (1961)		Tompkins (1977)	

1. Information Flow Studies: included consideration for channels, communication patterns and networks, direction of communication, feedback, technology, and communicator attributes:

Channels: Davis (1953) provided a description of informal communication operations, and the relationship of the informal channels to the formal communication system. *Ross* (1960) examined the informal communication patterns in two elementary schools for the purpose of revealing the interrelationships of the formal and informal channels, concluding that (a) administrators should provide time and places for personnel to get together informally so as to facilitate the development of interpersonal associations which can enforce the normal operations; and (b) holders of general administrative positions should recognize the importance of social interaction to their positions, as findings indicate that administrators who are active informally tend to be central figures in the informal communication patterns of the schools studied; and *Sanborn* (1961) concluded that the typical executive spends most of his time in purposeful verbal communication, that communication practices were not uniformly carried out, and that typical messages within the organization did not reach their intended destination through appropriate channels and timing.

Todd (1966) indicated that informal communication channels in marketing organizations assumed a central position both in the development and the implementation of specific marketing decisions; *Boyd* (1970) applied a channel analysis to the internal communication systems of a hospital organization, looking at the most frequently used channels, preferred channels, most effective channels and directions of the channels. He noted that the easiest means of communication were generally employed—i.e., oral-verbal communication, though this oral dependency resulted in the ineffectiveness of overall communication; and *Pacilio* (1974) utilized an interview approach to conclude as to the use of oral-verbal and written-verbal channels employed by faculty and students of Kent State University, noting frequency of the use of these channels by senders in respect to specified receiver groups.

DiSalvo, Larsen, and Seiler (1974) concluded that oral-verbal information was the most important source of organizational communication, followed by written sources, then by quantitative, and behavioral (observation-based) sources of information. Listening received the highest rating, followed by routine information exchange, advising, persuading, small group problem solving, giving orders, and interviewing. It was noted that personnel-oriented positions placed a greater emphasis on verbal sources of information than did finance-oriented positions. However, both position types rated listening as the most important activity, with routine information exchange and advising rated second and third in importance. *Sadler* (1974) indicated that (a) communication did not follow the patterns of organization charts, (b) formal communications in the vertical authority structure were less frequent than formal horizontal interactions, (c) formal communications were most closely associated with external messages, and informal messages were most frequently associated with fellow workers, (d) formal and informal quantities of communication changed together at the departmental and individual levels, not compensating for the lack of the other but increasing as does the other, and (e) informal communication provides verbal stroking—the more workers use communication in the task, the more the workers appear to rely upon communication for personal needs; and *Tompkins* (1977), in his participant-observer study of the Marshall Space Center, included, as a communication problem, the point that, as the organization grew larger, managers were upset due to their inability to "walk across the hall" to speak to the boss.

Communication Patterns and Networks: Davis (1953) studied the flow of information via informal channels employing the technique of "ECCO Analysis" to develop patterns of communication networks. He noted the characteristics of grapevine communication in respect to speed, message selectivity, locale of grapevine membership, and relationship to the formal communication system, indicating that a cluster type chain was the dominant pattern of informal communication, and pointing to the need to compensate for the isolation of certain individuals or groups geographically separated due to job demands, finding that, the lower the organizational level, the greater the tendency to be isolated; and *Todd* (1966) examined the patterns of information flow through the informal structure of a marketing department, and factors relating to the establishment of communication centers, concluding that (a) there is typically one individual serving as a communication center for a specific marketing decision area, (b) the communication-center position is occupied by different people at different stages of a marketing project, and (c) the individual charged with the responsibility for a particular function tends to act as the communication center for information relating to that function.

Moran (1967) compared 11 universities in respect to the influence of size and decentralization as it impacted on intraorganizational communication patterns; and *Schwartz* (1968) examined all of the faculty and administrators whose offices were located within a single, multifloor building of a large university, with the purpose of studying liaison versus nonliaison persons regarding communication roles, communication behavior, and interpersonal and organizational influence potential. He concluded that (a) liaison role persons, those having interlinking communication contacts with two or more separate sociometric workgroups or cliques in the organization, were more likely to serve as the initial source of organization-related information for their contacts than would nonliaisons for their contacts, (b) liaisons were perceived by their nonliaison contacts to have more important secondary contacts, (c) liaisons were perceived to have more influence over members of the power structure than did the nonliaisons, (d) liaisons devoted almost twice as much time to committee work than did the non-liaisons, (e) administrators were more strongly represented in the liaison group, and (f) the male–female distribution was almost exactly equal between liaison and nonliaison groups.

Farace and Russell (1972) applied the message diffusion technique to trace specific messages through the organization, considering that technique to be more advantageous than other methods for determining communication patterns in organizations when the criteria included (a) cost, and (b) applicability for the measurement of factors as structure, load, message flow rates, message distortion, redundancy, pathway efficiency, and message function; and *Timpano* (1972) employed ECCO Analysis to study communication networks in an elementary school and a secondary school, being interested in communication data about diffusion, accuracy, liaison, isolation, speed, direction, and media. Conclusions noted that (a) communication networks can be studied by employing a simple questionnaire, providing built-in checks, and assuring anonymity to respondents, and (b) studies can be designed to examine school-community communications, and effectiveness of public relations, and to explore communication's relationships with variables as morale, leadership, organizational climate, and personal motivation.

Direction of Communication: Davis (1953) concluded that management can improve communication by telling people what affects them as soon as possible, and management should give special attention to the need for horizontal communication structures; *Tompkins'* (1962) examination of downward and upward communication in a labor union concluded that (a) rank and file members were not well informed, (b) upward directed communication was poor and there was a need for horizontal communication within the brotherhood, and (c) members preferred to get more of their information through greater face-to-face communication; *Boyd* (1970) indicated that the hospital he investigated had major problems with downward and horizontal communication; and *DiSalvo, Larsen, and Seiler* (1974) found that, when the context of the communication is to those above the work unit or within the work unit, listening is the most important activity, followed by routine information exchange and advising; when the context is to those below the respondent's position, listening is the most important, with instructing and routine information exchange tied for second and third; and, when the context is outside the work unit, the order of importance is listening, routine information exchange, advising, and persuading.

Tompkins (1977) reported that management at the Marshall Space Flight Center viewed communication as being necessary in the up, down, and lateral directions. There was an awareness of the critical importance of the credibility of the source, and this was implemented through innovative systems. One of these systems was called the "Monday Notes" system, whereby each department head supplied top management with a brief statement of the previous week's progress and problems, and, after editing by top management, the edited notes of all departments were supplied to each department. This communication program was judged to be a successful technique, for the reason that it performed both an upward communication function and a horizontal or lateral function. Each department head knew each week what all other departments had experienced in the way of progress and problems, and sometimes were in a position to help out. Further, it kept the channels open during a period of decreased face-to-face communication, and in turn fostered a system on the part of department heads of consulting their own employees weekly so as to obtain the information to pass upward and outward.

Eadie, Goyer, Liebowitz, Spiker, and Gossett (1980), in regard to the direction of communication at a mental health center, concluded that (a) for downward communication, the grapevine was heavily employed due to the insufficiencies of written communication, difficulties with bulletin board operations, poor leadership of group meetings, and the tendency for downward message flow to be interrupted by the hoarding of information; and (b) upward communication flow tended to be blocked and inefficient, due to the inclination of certain units to consider themselves as "islands" with no need to report to supervisors, the tendency to bypass levels of authority unnecessarily, the lack of commonly perceived goals by all levels of the organization, and the tendency for information flowing upward to go up only one level, to an employee's immediate supervisor.

Feedback: The editors of the *Management Review* ("Does Your," 1956) described a system employed by Standard Oil Company of New Jersey for obtaining feedback on organization-wide communication, including (a) individual members of management, (b) union management and union members, (c) local top management and corporate office management and (d) the "return flow" of reactions, ideas, and suggestions from nonsupervisory personnel to local top management.

Technology: Among the problems recognized by *Tompkins* (1977) in his NASA Marshall Space Center experience was that of the "formalism-impersonality syndrome," whereby important managerial personnel denounced the formalism and impersonality of many of the management tools used (e.g., computers, control centers, reviews, and PERT) on the basis that "things" rather than people were in control. *Breen* (1978) has criticized recent writers in the field of organizational communication for not emphasizing the increasing role of technology in organizational communication, e.g., the improvements represented by satellite communications, computer hardware and software, teleconferencing, high-speed work processing, intraorganizational film-making, voice recognition, automated telephone answering, and photocopying. Breen proposed that organizational communication be studied through the interaction effects of the communication medium, the type of communication, and the structure of the organization; and *Driver* (1979) hypothesized that subjects receiving employee benefit communication via a projector-slide presentation and discussion session would have significantly greater benefits knowledge than those subjects receiving information via booklets, brochures, and benefit manuals. Findings supported the conclusion that the two-way flow of communication in the slide and discussion presentation was far superior in terms of knowledge imparted than the traditional techniques of benefit communication in the form of booklets and brochures.

Communicator Attributes: Simons (1961) provided a comparison of communication attributes and rated job performance of supervisors, concluding that more high-rated than low-rated supervisors consulted with employees before rescheduling, discussed suggestions proposed by employees irrespective of merit, asked or persuaded rather than told or demanded in assigning unpleasant work, and took care to reprimand employees in private rather than in front of others.

2. Message Content Studies: included consideration for accuracy and distortion, and readability and comprehension:

Accuracy and Distortion: Odiorne (1954) investigated the question of whether certain general information relative to the company had reached all employees without distortion, and recommended research into the effect of organizational levels upon the speed and accuracy of communication; and *Simons* (1961) concluded that more high-rated supervisors than low-rated supervisors said that new employees should be told both good and bad about the organization, rather than good only.

Readability and Comprehension: Peters (1950) as Head, Employee Relations Department, Esso Standard Oil Company, employed the Flesch Formula and the Gunning Formula tests for readability in order to improve employee publications through evaluation techniques, claiming that the attainment of higher readership indicated that expenditures for such improvements were justified; *Funk and Becker* (1952) concluded that employees and their supervisors in the organizations reviewed were not fully informed concerning the policies and practices previously communicated via oral and written media in manuals, memoranda, and conferences; *Tompkins* (1962), in his study of a national labor union, concluded that rank and file members were not well informed about their union, and there was a large communication gap (i.e., semantic distance) between union officers and members; and *Tompkins* (1977), in his diagnostic study of the Marshall Space Flight Center as a communication system, recognized a large number of problems including that of the "science-technology barrier," manifested by the fact that some scientists felt left out and neglected, while certain engineers envied the fact that the scientists served as principal investigators which permitted them to maintain a communication loop with NASA headquarters not available to the engineers. Further, the different technical languages made it difficult for the two parties to understand one another even in face-to-face communication.

3. Communication Climate Studies: included consideration for the following subcategories: (a) Adequacy of information, (b) Morale and communication satisfaction, (c) General importance of communication, (d) Dimensions of communication climate, (e) Leadership communication behavior, and (f) Openness and trust:

Adequacy of Information: Odiorne's (1954) communication audit determined the feelings of lower level personnel (engineers) about the effectiveness of communication channels, finding the management rated adequacy of information more favorably than did the engineers, and most of the engineers felt they had inadequate opportunities to express their feelings to management.

Morale and Communication Satisfaction: Perry and Mahoney (1955) found support for the hypothesis that morale is related to the amount of information *given* to employees, rather than to the amount *retained* by them; and that this relationship is less applicable to within-workgroup situations, where all employees receive about the same amount of information, than to the among-workgroups situation, and particularly among different firms, where differences in level of information reflect differences in the amount of information received; and *Sanborn* (1961), in his study of a national retailing organization, was not only concerned with communication procedures and media, but also sought to determine the attitude of personnel at different levels toward these communication practices, and the relationship between communication satisfaction and morale. Sanborn concluded that communication satisfaction of personnel was positively related to the degree with which desirable communication practices were present in the organization.

General Importance of Communication: Boyd's (1970) study of a hospital communication system concluded that there were major problems with downward and horizontal communication, and a general ineffectiveness of overall communication, with the staff not highly concerned with communication effectiveness.

Dimensions of Communication Climate: Dennis (1974) examined communication climate in terms of the eight dimensions of supportiveness, individual autonomy, trust, openness, high performance goals, structure, reward orientation, and consideration; and he identified five factors of communication climate:

1. Superior–subordinate communication, particulary the supportiveness from a superior;
2. Perceived quality and accuracy of downward communication;
3. Perceptions of communication relationships, especially the affective aspects as perceived openness and empathy;
4. Perceptions of upward communication opportunities and of degree of upward-directed influence; and
5. Perceptions of reliability of information.

Leadership Communication Behavior: Mazza's (1975) study of one industrial communication climate inquired into the attitudes and perceptions of communication at three organizational levels, concluding that:

1. Employees desired increased personal and group communication in contrast to the limited interaction permitted by the present emphasis on production and production schedules;
2. Variances in the communication satisfaction levels between employee divisions were caused by differences in supervisory feedback receptiveness and responsiveness;
3. Employee communication satisfaction levels ranged from "often satisfied" to "neutral," and these could be changed to higher satisfaction levels by opening the communication system and by increasing feedback reception and response; and
4. The machine shop and shipping divisions of the organization needed a complete change in supervision to improve their communication satisfaction levels.

Openness and Trust: Tompkins (1977) indicated several problems in communication climate at the Marshall Space Center, including:

1. A lack of lateral openness, a condition in which competitiveness between departments had reached the point where a lack of trust and secrecy dominated their lateral communication, not telling others what they needed to know unless asked;
2. Animosity between the older members of the organization and newer management employees, based on the belief that the founding (older) members were a strong cohesive informal group;
3. A morale problem on the part of civil service workers below the level of lab director, evidenced by rapid growth of union membership, and fostered by a feeling that the contractor employee working beside the civil service employee was being paid more for the "same" work; and
4. The uncertainty as to the future of the organization abetted by rumors of possible reduction in force, and the absence of any official word coming down the line.

4. Individual Training and Organizational Development Studies: included the two major categories of individual training needs, and organization-wide communication development:

Individual Training Needs for Organization-wide Communication: Lull, Funk, and Piersol (1954) concluded that:

1. Ability in oral communication is an important factor in managerial effectiveness;
2. There is a definite relationship between communication and productivity;
3. Major causes of breakdowns in industrial communication come from lack of communication ability in management, inadequate use of communication media, and inadequate communication training programs;
4. Communication ability is a combination of natural talent and skill that may be developed by training and experience; and
5. All levels of management should receive training in methods of communication.

Organization-wide Communication Development: Steber (1972) investigated the ways in which goal attainment by the Reading, Pennsylvania Model Cities Program was affected by communication, concluding that poor communication practices severely limited resident participation and goal attainment. *Veninga* (1972) examined the role of communication in the organizational development program of a hospital, specifically in respect to a 1-week training program including the following four concepts relative to communication:

1. The natural result of the communication process is partial misunderstanding;
2. The asking of pertinent questions may produce conflict in the organization;
3. Communication abhors a vacuum, therefore it is natural to expect the emergence of informal groups within the organization; and
4. The number of communication misunderstandings is not related to the effectiveness of the organization, the difference between an effective and ineffective organization being related to the way misunderstandings are handled.

Veninga provided several general conclusions relative to O.D. and organizational communication, including:

1. Any O.D. program dealing with the improvement of interpersonal communication through laboratory education should provide necessary resources so that participants can receive assistance on a one-to-one basis;
2. The primary responsibility for the success of an O.D. effort should be with the members of the organization and not the consultant; and
3. The primary role of the consultant should be in helping the organization diagnose itself and to decide on particular programs to correct problems, and implement the programs.

Greenbaum (1974) suggested that the organizational communication system could be considered as the sum of a group of subsystems or functional communication networks, each of which is related to one or more organizational goals. He identified the networks as (a) regulative-task, (b) adaptive-innovative, (c) integrative-maintenance, and (d) informative-instructive, noting that each network consisted of specific communication policies implemented through individual communication activities, and that a continuous program of communication appraisal was recommended in order to provide control of the communication system.

Sincoff et al. (1976) developed a step-by-step process for the conduct of a communication audit intended to determine the communication effectiveness of an organization, and to aid researchers involved with natural setting audits of communication. Audit steps were noted to include the following:

1. Choose a potential client;
2. Determine approach methodology to contact such client;
3. Arrange an interview with client in which there is a clear statement of audit objectives, audit process, and client interests;
4. Decide whether to continue or not;
5. Select data collection instruments and discuss with client;
6. Apply the selected techniques;
7. Analyze the data;
8. Evaluate the effectiveness of communication by comparing present state of communication processes to optimal state of effectiveness;
9. Make recommendations to improve communication in the organization.

Tompkins (1977) reported several communication problems at the Marshall Space Center relating to needs for communication development of that organization:

1. A communication bottleneck at the Office of Research and Development Operations, where the Director had 12 organizational units reporting to his office;
2. A lack of adequate coordination of the staff offices, due in large part to the fact that the Deputy Director of Administration, who was responsible for such coordination, was spending an increasing amount of time as an interface with NASA headquarters; and
3. A condition involving an excessive number of external interfaces (point of contact between two organizational units) due to the complexity of the work. The external interfaces involved the Marshall Space Center relationships with NASA headquarters, NASA field centers, university scientists, prime contractors, and support contractors. Moreover, the bonds between the organizations were of poor quality and reliability, especially when the quality of technical personnel of other organizations was not up to the level required.

Harris and Cronen (1978) developed a rules-based model for the analysis and evaluation of organizational communication, applying the theory to the social science department of a private college. The model suggests that an organization is analogous to a culture and that it can be analyzed by identifying its collectively defined master contract, defined in terms of constitutive rules (i.e., rules developed by individuals to bring about outcomes, proceeding from the particular beliefs and goals of the organization).

Harris and Cronen postulate that the organization processes can be evaluated in terms of the competence with which members coorient themselves to the master contract and coordinate their activities within the rules established by the organization. Data secured from the study of the social science department supported the position that organizations can be understood in light of (a) the creation and maintenance of their own self-image, and (b) the ability of their members to accurately perceive and to agree upon that image, which is associated with the individual members' communication competence.

Lewis (1979) suggested an approach to evaluating communication performance that was aimed at a training director audience, noting that a major cause of communication ineffectiveness was the lack of an effective evaluation system to ferret out problems leading to change proposals both as to policies and specific activities. He recommended a Communication Performance Audit involving more a preventive stance than a remedial action by calling for the analysis of activities in terms of (a) policy (where and whom do we impact?), (b) strategy (how do we best impact what?), and (c) tactics (what are the specific things one must do to make people more efficient in communication?).

Lewis notes that the Communication Performance Audit allows the analyst to discriminate between deficiencies which can be best corrected through training, and those which require changes in the particular environment. Moreover, and most important, he points out that this approach suggests a shift in the distribution of training manpower from a heavy emphasis on development to at least an equal distribution between development and evaluation.

Smith (1980) analyzed communication audit consulting techniques in higher educational organizations, noting that the communication evaluator (researcher and change agent) must be aware of the unique differences between educational and industrial/governmental/service organizations, particularly at three points in the relationship with the client: (a) entering, (b) data collecting, and (c) change strategizing.

Smith indicates that the perspective used (i.e., choice of model) by the consultant in approaching the research problem controls the outcome, noting that the customary method is to select a traditional management model with tightly managed corporate structures as a foundation.

Smith comments that the traditional management model is inappropriate for educational institutions, which are closer to a participative leadership model in which there is deliberate ambiguity characterizing the top echelon, where the central management core is generally more in a caretaker role, and the system tends to be deliberately reactive, and only rarely proactive.

Further, Smith notes that the ICA Communication Audit uses a set of instruments developed from management models appropriate for tightly managed corporate structures; and the Audit presumes from its parent models a particular type of leadership structure, and that neither of these characteristics is an appropriate point of departure for colleges and universities. He concludes by stating that consultation in educational institutions requires differently shaped tools, in that one must respect the unique features of the organization.

Downs (1980) reviewed three independent communication audits of medical facilities wherein the researchers had employed the ICA Audit, noting the following data collection problems:

1. There was suspicion about completion of the network analysis questionnaire and many would not fill out the survey, due to the fear that the network information might be used against certain groups;
2. The Communication Diary instrument encountered resistance, because people refused to take the time to fill it out;
3. Physicians were not cooperative, and either did not participate or balked at filling out the questionnaire, and few could be interviewed; and
4. Due to the existence of high levels of turnover in hospital departments, it was not possible to do a meaningful longitudinal study.

Downs concluded that conducting an audit of a hospital may be little different from examining any other organization in the respect that (a) entry has the same pitfalls; (b) collection of data encounters the same problems, only more so, with the unwillingness of doctors to participate being unique, and network, diary, and critical incidents not being generally acceptable; (c) analysis of data can be standardized; and (d) the feeding back of data may encounter enthusiasm or reluctance, and it is necessary to plan feedback processes on the specific circumstances of the host organization.

5. Summary of Internal OCE Concepts and Organization-wide Communication Studies: In summary, in respect to organization-wide communication, the review of 65 studies in natural settings yielded 19 studies of information flow, six studies of message content, seven studies of communication climate, and 10 studies of individual and organizational development.

The 19 information flow studies of organization-wide communication represented the highest concentration of studies in any single classification, whether interpersonal, group, or organization-wide, comprised almost 50% of all organization-wide studies, and almost double that of the next largest class, that of training and development studies. The information flow studies were concerned with the basic variables of channels, patterns and networks, direction, feedback, technology, and communicator attributes.

In the channels class, the variable of informal communication channels was the subject of four studies providing a description of the process, and concluding with the importance of the process in obtaining high levels of effectiveness; and the variable of formal communication channels was treated by five studies emphasizing the importance of oral-verbal and written-verbal communication. The studies of communication patterns and networks mostly involved the informal communication network, in respect to the nature and utility of message diffusion techniques as ECCO analysis and similar techniques for determining informal communication patterns, and factors relating to the formation of informal communication centers within the functional units of an organization. Communication direction studies concentrated on upward, downward, and lateral communication, with conclusions being diverse in light of the particular objectives of the study. Finally, the individual categories of feedback, technology, and communicator attributes included individual works of importance, but no generalizations are possible due to the lack of additional studies in the area.

The message content studies were divided into two categories of variables, two writings concerned with accuracy and distortion, and four writings concerned with readability and comprehension, with several of the works being concerned with the amount of information conveyed to employees and retained by employees, while many other conclusions were unique to particular studies.

The communication climate studies, concerned with feelings and attitudes toward various communication variables, were divided in emphasis among the topics of adequacy of information, morale and communication satisfaction, communication importance, dimensions of communication climate, leadership behavior, and openness and trust.

Finally, the ten individual training and organization development studies included seven writings relative to communication audit concepts and procedures, with research objectives differing substantially so that each writing represented a different segment of the field, rather than an examination in depth of the same subject.

DEVELOPMENT OF STANDARDIZED INSTRUMENTS AND DATA BANKS, 1971–1979

In the early 1970s, both Osmo Wiio and associates in Finland and Gerald Goldhaber and associates in the United States *independently* set out to develop standardized instruments for the evaluation of organizational communication, and by 1974 both groups had implemented evaluation programs capable of producing information for data banks that were intended to provide norms for individual organizations. The audit instruments developed by each of these groups were dissimilar in many respects, so the two areas of development tended to complement each other, rather than compete. The communication audit programs developed have been identified as (a) The LTT Audit System, (b) The OCD Audit System, and (c) the International Communication Association (ICA) Audit System.

The LTT Audit System

The LTT instrument was named after the Finnish research institute supporting the work of Osmo A. Wiio and Martti Helsila, developers of the technique. The instrument was developed as a result of several requests to the Institute for help from industry. The LTT instrument was based on several previous studies and a pilot study by Martti Helsila (1971), and was designed to be extremely simple and adaptable for data analysis, all the data in each questionnaire being punched on one standard card with 80 columns (Goldhaber, 1983, p. 398).

The LTT was developed mainly as a study of organizational communication climate (Wiio, 1978a, p. 86). The communication climate of an organization was construed to be the perceived atmosphere of opinions and attitudes relative to house magazines, frequency of discussion of work, bulletins, supervision, company policies, working conditions partic-ipation, and information received as to the organization from superiors and other sources. In addition, communication climate was construed to include satisfaction with information about own work from superiors and other sources, satisfaction with information about work, overall organization, and organization changes, areas in which the employee would like to see improved communication, relationships with superiors and peers, degree to which employee could influence matters concerning own work, and general attitudes as to company communications (Wiio, 1978a, pp. 141–146).

The idea of a standard audit package was accepted from the very beginning in 1971, as the need for communication auditing was much larger than the existing research resources, and, by using a standard procedure, it would be possible to minimize the use of time and money. The need for communication auditing arose as a result of special conditions ex-isting in Finland, where so-called "Information Committees," provided in the 1971 Infor-mation Agreement between Finnish management and labor and considered to be internal joint action committees within an organization, could order the application of an organizational communication audit. In such cases, the committee supervised the actual auditing, using LTT standard procedures and materials. The questionnaires, after applica-tion, were sealed by the committee and returned to the Institute for processing and prepara-tion of reports. At that time, the early 1970s, the costs for the organizations were between $500 and $2,000, depending on the size of the sample and the number of organizational units (Wiio, 1974, p. 8).

Apart from being a relatively inexpensive communication appraisal, the presence of a high degree of standardization, both in questionnaire format and data analysis, made it posssible to use the same computer program in each case, resulting in a fast through-put time (an average processing period of 6 weeks from beginning to end of the audit process, including a formal report) (Wiiio, 1974, p. 3).

But the advantages of a standard package were seen to go beyond the question of time and money. Wiio (1974, p. 3) pointed out that it also meant having a yardstick for compari-son, i.e., the more firms audited, the more information about attitudes about communica-tion and job satisfaction in different types of firms. Standardized measuring instruments could make it possible to compare different organizations at one point in time, and the same organization at different points in time (Wiio, 1978b, p. 2).

In summary, the LTT Audit System is a low-cost standardized instrument consisting of 75 questions, developed to measure the communication climate in organizations. The in-strument has some flexibility to take organizational differences into account and, within a period of 6 weeks, an audit team can complete an investigation, utilizing a computer pro-gram to process the raw data, and report the results. This audit system, first operational in 1973, has been employed entirely in the European area, and by late 1977, 23 organizations had been audited, with a total sample of 5,578 persons from a population of 30,000 persons (Wiio, 1978b).

The OCD Audit System

A second standardized audit system was developed by Wiio in 1976–1977 based on the analysis of the results and experiences of the LTT Audit. This new system is titled "The

Organizational Communication Development Procedure," or OCD. By 1980, the OCD Audit System had been implemented in six Finnish organizations, with a total sample of 1,500 persons (Wiio, Goldhaber, & Yates, 1980).

The OCD is an improved LTT audit system as a result of experience with that latter system in the period 1972–1978. It is an audit system designed to help the organization find out what is wrong with the communication system, as a first step to developing methods of improvement (Wiio, 1977a, p. 12).

OCD offers a standardized procedure so that results from one organization can be compared with results from other organizations. It is a participatory development system, wherein members of the organization are expected to take an active role in the process, and feedback is an integral part of the process (Wiio, 1977a, pp. 14–15).

Management generally initiates the OCD Audit, but the recommendation that there is a need for communication evaluation may come not only from management but also from general personnel, joint committees of management and labor, labor unions, outside consultants, and others. The evidences of need for organizational communication analysis via OCD is given by Wiio as (a) difficulties in operational communication (inappropriate performance, delays, misunderstandings), (b) human relations problems (low job satisfaction, difficult labor relations, mistrust, complaints about insufficient information), and (c) organizational changes (mergers, expansion, moving, new technology, etc.) (Wiio, 1977a, p. 13).

While the decision to initiate the audit is a management decision, involved personnel should be consulted because results are entirely dependent upon their cooperation (Wiio, 1977a, p. 14). The existence of a joint committee (management and labor) has been found to be very useful in the planning, implementation, and controlling of the OCD Audit System, being an extension of the procedures in the original LTT Audit studies, wherein the auditing was always conducted in cooperation with a joint committee.

Other than initiating an OCD Audit due to one of these evidences of need, Wiio pointed out that management might employ a preventive approach, sponsoring periodic OCD Audits, so as to know about the state of the organization, even if a crisis is not present. The analysis of comparative data, available through the OCD procedure, may well disclose the existence of problems that could be given attention much before the crisis point is reached.

The 1977 IHC report by Osmo Wiio is clearly a "how to do it" book, which is based on the author's experience in many communication audits. It is precise, clear, and concise, with illustrations of both the instrument and the data processing following therefrom. From the viewpoint of an organization manager, a staff specialist with suitable background would well use this as a guidebook for the application of the OCD Audit System. The in-house communication audit is very feasible employing the guidelines presented by Wiio. In this respect, the OCD System is most attractive—a single instrument approach that can be administered inexpensively by qualified staff in-house.

The International Communication Association Audit System

Whereas the European programs of communication evaluation had their origin in a "call for help" from industry, and were initially developed to fulfill that pragmatic need, the development of internal OCE in the United States in the 1970s was initiated as a result of a dissatisfaction with the research design aspects of the then existing evidences of OCE. However, in both the European and the United States development of internal OCE, there were considerations for both the practical and the theoretical areas. In the United States, the rationalization for developing the ICA Communication Audit was that such a program would improve organizational communication theory first, and potentially this would benefit industry. In Finland, the beginnings were quite the reverse, but the works of Wiio et al. demonstrated both the practical and theoretical utility of LTT and OCD findings.

In the Finnish experience, the fulfillment of the practical needs of industry permitted the accumulation of information for a database that provided norms for reference, not only for industry, but also for communication scholars. In the United States, in striving to build a basis for theoretical research, scholars found that the individual audits provided practical utility to the host organizations that received a complete report of the investigation with recommendations.

Goldhaber and Krivonos (1977) and Goldhaber and Rogers (1979) pointed out that earlier U.S. studies, back to Odiorne (1954), suffered from methodological weaknesses that limited their utility. The major problems included:

1. *Single-instrument approach*: reliance upon only one instrument to gather data, thus limiting the representativeness of findings.
2. *Situationalism*: collection of data in a single organization, thus limiting the generalizability of findings.
3. *Small, unrepresentative samples*: utilization of very small samples, usually composed of managers and other professionals, again limiting the representativeness of findings.
4. *Lack of standardization and norms*: employment of nonstandardized procedures and instruments, so that norms could not be established describing communication behavior, thus preventing comparative analysis and limiting external validity.
5. *Limited measurement of actual behaviors*: assessment of attitudes and perceptions with limited measurement of actual behaviors, thus limiting conclusions in respect to feeling, thinking, and performance.
6. *Measurements not done over time*: with a few exceptions (Burns, 1954; Kelly, 1964; Sutton & Porter, 1968), measurement at one point in time and not over time, thus producing "snapshots" instead of "movies" of organizational communication performance.

The labors that achieved the ICA Communication Audit were started in the period 1971–1973 in response to recognizing the above shortcomings of previous communication evaluation studies for the needs of theorists interested in generalizations that had predictive validity. As Krivonos (1975a) noted, previous audits had been valuable but each offered only a case study of one or two organizations, and did not satisfy the requirements for construction of a broader-based communication theory.

1. General Nature of the ICA Audit

The ICA Communication Audit is a measurement system of instruments and procedures for studying organizational communication; it is a process of information gathering, analysis, and evaluation, administered by a team of qualified professionals, and focuses on the internal communication system of an organization at a point in time (Goldhaber & Rogers, 1979). It is unique as a measurement approach, because it is a standardized system of five instruments using both computerized analysis and feedback procedures and a normed data bank to enable comparisons between the communication systems of various organizations (Goldhaber, 1983).

The ICA Communication Audit was designed to provide organizations with reliable, factual data about their internal communication, and to do so in a way that permitted comparability with similar organizations. It measures information flow, message content, communicator attitudes, and perceptions; provides attitudinal, perceptual, and behavioral data; uses a variety of measurement techniques; allows for measurement of communication over time; uses standardized procedure for data collection and analysis of data; allows for limited organizational input to customize the instruments and administration procedures without disrupting the standardization needed for organizational comparisons; uses trained and credentialed ICA communication auditors; uses specially prepared computer programs for data analysis; and allows organizational comparisons on specified communication behaviors, perceptions and attitudes by norming audit data (Goldhaber & Rogers, 1979). The ICA Audit System is different from the LTT and OCD Systems, wherein only the communication climate variable is examined, one questionnaire instrument is employed, and the organization's own personnel administer the audit.

2. Purposes and Products of the ICA Audit

The long-range goals of the ICA Communication Audit have been frequently summarized as follows (Goldhaber & Krivonos, 1977; Goldhaber, Lesniak, Porter & Yates, 1978; Goldhaber, 1983):

1. To establish a normed data bank to enable comparisons to be made between the communication systems of various organizations.
2. To establish, through these comparative studies, a general external validation of many organizational communication theories and propositions.
3. To provide research outlets for faculty, professionals, and graduate students.
4. To establish the ICA as a visible center for organizational communication measurement.

These long-range goals include objectives of high utility both to researchers and practitioners. A researcher reviewing the objectives could easily construe all four to be research-oriented, while a management practitioner invested with the responsibility for implementing communication audits would be greatly interested in goals 1 and 2, and perhaps could feel that assistance could be obtained from ICA when problems were encountered in processing and interpreting the information collected (goals 3 and 4).

The interests of the ICA Audit System leaders in the practical utility of the ICA Audit for organization managers is brought out clearly by the following statements on the part of Goldhaber and Rogers (1979, p. 8):

> The overall objective of the ICA Communication Audit System is to evaluate the organization's communication system, providing information and recommendations which should help an organization improve both its communication practices and its overall effectiveness as an organization. Specific objectives during the audit relate to (1) information underload and overload; (2) quality of information from various sources; (3) extent of interpersonal trust and overall job satisfaction; (4) operational communication networks, both formal and informal; (5) potential bottlenecks and gatekeepers of information; (6) identifying commonly occurring positive and negative communication experiences; (7) describing patterns of actual communication behaviors related to sources, channels, topics, length and quality of interactions; and (8) providing general recommen-

dations which call for changes or improvements in attitudes, behaviors, practices, and skills.

Goldhaber and Krivonos (1977) noted the following *products* that the organization would have upon completion of such an audit:

1. An organizational profile of perceptions of communication events, practices, and relationships, analyzed according to demographics such as age, sex, education, supervisory status, division, and department.
2. A map of the operational communication network for rumors, and for social and job-related messages.
3. Summaries of successful and unsuccessful communication experiences related to communication problems and strengths.
4. A profile of actual communication behaviors, allowing comparisons between actual and perceived communication behaviors relative to message sources, receiver topics, channels, length, and quality.
5. A set of recommendations indicating which attitudes, behaviors, and practices, should be continued, added, changed, or eliminated.
6. Familiarization by personnel *in the organization* with the ICA audit instruments and procedures, thereby helping the organization to take the major initiative in conducting future audits themselves.
7. Future access to the ICA data bank, allowing the organization to compare the results of present and future audits with those of similar organizations.

In addition to this imposing list of products available to the organization, Goldhaber and Rogers (1979) added the important point that, through the communication audit, organization managers are furnished with *benchmarks* on communication behaviors and perceptions that can be used for pre-/post-measurement comparisons to diagnose organizational change and development events.

3. The Development and Demise of the ICA Audit

The development of the ICA Communication Audit involved three phases: (a) development of a conceptual framework and data collection instruments, (b) pilot-testing, and (c) implementation.

Initial discussions of communication auditing techniques took place at the 1971 and 1972 conventions of the International Communication Association, with theoretical and applied presentations by Greenbaum (1971, 1972), and Goldhaber and Horan (1972), among others. From this point in time, a group of communication researchers including Gerald Goldhaber, Gary Richetto, Harry Dennis, Raymond Falcione, and Donald Rogers worked together as a team through 1974 to develop the multi-instrument approach that became known as the ICA Communication Audit, consisting of five audit instruments (interview, questionnaire, critical incident, diary, and network analysis).

The next 2 years, 1974–1976, were utilized for pilot-testing the instruments, developing original computer programs to analyze audit data, and revising the instruments and procedures. The original auditing program was applied for the first time to the internal communication activities of an Arizona public utility company during the period October 1974–January 1975 (Wood, Perrill, & Buley, 1975). This was followed by four audits in 1975, five audits in 1976, and eight audits in 1977, for a total of 18 audits to July 1977

(Goldhaber & Krivonos, 1977). By 1979, the ICA Communication Audit had been implemented in 19 organizations in the United States and Canada, with a sample of some 5,000 persons (Goldhaber & Rogers, 1979). The organizations subjected to the communication audit included educational institutions (e.g., Richetto & Dennis, 1976; Goldhaber, 1976b), federal government offices (e.g., Falcione, 1976; Werner, Falcione, & Temkiewicz, 1978), hospitals (e.g., Jain, 1977; Jain, Kanungo, & Goldhaber, 1980), a public utility company (i.e., Wood, Perrill, & Buley, 1975), as well as manufacturing companies, banks, and a municipal government housing project. Writings relative to norms derived from the ICA audit findings were provided at various points in time, including Yates, Porter, Goldhaber, Dennis, and Richetto, 1976; Goldhaber, Porter, and Yates, 1977; Porter, 1979; and Goldhaber & Rogers, 1979.

In 1978, as reported by Falcione, Goldhaber, Porter, and Rogers (1979), the ICA Board of Directors decided that the audit project, as a research and development project of that professional association, had achieved its goals, and that it was in the best interests of the International Communication Association to end its sponsorship of the audit program. The resolution eliminated the authority of any group to employ the ICA organization name in reference to auditing communication, and the audit programs became public property. In the future, communication audits would not be done by "ICA auditors," but by independent professionals in the field of communication.

Today, the main elements of organization relative to this audit program and attached data banks will be found at the Department of Communication, SUNY at Buffalo, under the leadership of Gerald Goldhaber. It is noteworthy that the ICA Communication Audit Questionnaire has been obtaining a growing acceptance from independent researchers in the field, as attested by research reported in Volume 6 (Greenbaum & Falcione, 1981) and Volume 8 (Greenbaum, Falcione, & Hellweg, 1983) of the *Organizational Communication Abstracts* series.

SUMMARY AND CONCLUSION

In summary, this chapter has reviewed the major empirical and conceptual writings in the years 1950–1981 relative to field studies in organizational communication evaluation. The rationale for conducting communication evaluations in organizations was emphasized as an important control process serving to alert the organization to needed change and development efforts, while developing benchmarks and improving the internal communication system, which, in turn, facilitates all managerial processes.

Sixty-five writings were classified first under the three broad categories of interpersonal, group, and organization-wide communication. Then these major categories were further divided into the four subclasses of information flow studies, message content studies, communication climate studies, and individual training and organizational development studies. This provided a 12-category system for analysis of this literature.

Additionally, three standardized organizational communication evaluation methods and instruments were reviewed. They were the LTT, OCD, and the ICA audit systems. The general nature, purpose, and products derived from each system were presented for the years 1971–1979, a time period coincidental with the development and demise of the ICA audit.

The intent of this chapter was not to present a critical, interpretive review of organizational communication evaluation, but to provide the reader with some sense of the historical nature of this intriguing area of research. It is our hope that, as researchers and practitioners continue to conduct organizational communication evaluations, they also continue in the development of predictive models based upon a systemic perspective of organizations.

REFERENCES

Ahmed, Z. (1965). *A study of administrative communication in a selected school system.* Unpublished doctoral dissertation, Indiana University.

Angrist, A. W. (1953). *A study of the communication problems and practices of executives in business and industry.* Unpublished doctoral dissertation, Ohio State University.

Bednar, D. A., & Glauser, M. (1981, August). *Interaction analysis of collective bargaining: The Barrington Oil Company case.* Paper presented at the Academy of Management Convention, San Diego, CA.

Boyd, J. A. (1970, May). *An analysis of the internal communication in the Boulder Community Hospital.* Paper presented at the International Communication Association Convention, Minneapolis, MN.

Breen, M. P. (1978, June). *Technology in organizational communication: A plan for study.* Paper presented at the Communication Association of the Pacific Convention, Tokyo, Japan.

Brenner, M. H., & Sigband, N. B. (1972, April). *Organizational communication: An analysis based on empirical data.* Paper presented at the International Communication Association Convention, Atlanta, GA.

Brisley, C. L. (1957). *Oral communication in executive behavior in a medium sized industrial firm in Detroit, Michigan.* Unpublished doctoral dissertation, Wayne State University.

Brooks, K., Callicoat, J., & Siegerdt, G. (1979). The ICA communication audit and perceived communication effectiveness changes in 16 audited organizations. *Human Communication Research, 5,* 130–137.

Burns, T. (1954). The directions of activity and communication in a department executive group. *Human Relations, 7,* 73–97.

Carter, R. M. (1972). *Communication in organizations: An annotated bibliography and sourcebook.* Detroit, MI: Gale Research Company.

Cole, W. H. (1969). *The characteristics of written communications and attitudes toward communication in a selected corporation with implications for improvement in business writing instruction.* Unpublished doctoral dissertation, Oklahoma State University.

Conger, D. S. (1980, May). *Using team building to increase communication effectiveness in a changing environment.* Paper presented at the International Communication Association Convention, Acapulco, Mexico.

Dahle, T. L. (1954). An objective and comparative study of five methods of transmitting information to business and industrial employees. *Speech Monographs, 21,* 21–28.

Daly, J. A., & Korinek, J. T. (1982). Organizational communication: A review via operationalizations. In H. H. Greenbaum & R. L. Falcione, *Organizational communication: Abstracts, analysis, and overview* (pp. 11–46). Beverly Hills, CA: Sage Publications.

Davis, K. (1953). A method of studying communication patterns in organizations. *Personnel Psychology, 6,* 301–312.

Dennis, H. S. (1974). *A theoretical and empirical study of managerial communication climate in complex organizations.* Unpublished doctoral dissertation, Purdue University.

DiSalvo, V., Larsen, D. C., & Seiler, W. J. (1974, April). *Communication audit by organizational position.* Paper presented at the International Communication Association Convention, New Orleans, LA.

Does your communication program measure up? (1956). *Management Review, 45,* 400–405.

Downs, C. W. (1980, May). *Communication audits of medical organizations.* Paper presented at the

International Communication Association Convention, Acapulco, Mexico.

Downs, C. W., & Conrad, C. (1978, August). *A critical incident study of superior-subordinate communication.* Paper presented at the Academy of Management Convention, San Francisco, CA.

Driver, R. W. (1979, August). *The relative efficacy of different methods for communicating benefits: A quasi-experiment in a field setting.* Paper presented at the Academy of Management Convention, Atlanta, GA.

Eadie, W. F., Goyer, R. S., Liebowitz, E., Spiker, B., & Gossett, J. (1980, May). *A communication audit of a state mental health institution.* Paper presented at the International Communication Association Convention, Acapulco, Mexico.

Falcione, R. L. (1976, August). *Communication audit of a U.S. senator's office.* Paper presented at the Academy of Management Convention, Kansas City, MO.

Falcione, R. L., Goldhaber, G. M., Porter, T. D., & Rogers, D. P. (1979, May). *The future of the ICA communication audit.* Paper presented at the International Communication Association Convention, Philadelphia, PA.

Farace, R. V., & Russell, H. M. (1972, April). *Beyond bureaucracy—message diffusion as a communication audit tool.* Paper presented at the International Communication Association Convention, Atlanta, GA.

Farace, R. V., Taylor, J. A., & Stewart, J. P. (1978). Criteria for evaluation of organizational communication effectiveness: Review and synthesis. In B. D. Ruben (Ed.), *Communication Yearbook 2* (pp. 271-292). New Brunswick, NJ: International Communication Association.

Funk, H. B., & Becker, R. G. (1952). Measuring the effectiveness of industrial communication. *Personnel, 24,* 237-240.

Goldhaber, G. M. (1976a, August). *The ICA communication audit: Rationale and development.* Paper presented at the Academy of Management Convention, Kansas City, MO.

Goldhaber, G. M. (1976b). *A communication audit of a division university relations.* A Report to the Vice President of University Relations, State University of New York at Buffalo.

Goldhaber, G. M. (1978). Evaluating internal communication: The ICA communication audit. In G. M. Goldhaber (Ed.), *Improving institutional communication* (pp. 37-54). San Francisco, CA: Jossey-Bass.

Goldhaber, G. M. (1983). *Organizational communication.* Dubuque, IA: Wm. C. Brown Company.

Goldhaber, G. M., Dennis, H. S. III, Richetto, G. M., Wiio, O. A. (1979). *Information strategies: New pathways to corporate power.* Englewood Cliffs, NJ: Prentice Hall.

Goldhaber, G. M., & Horan, H. (1972, April). *A communication systems analysis of KOB-TV.* Paper presented at the International Communication Association Convention, Atlanta, GA.

Goldhaber, G. M., & Krivonos, P. D. (1977). The ICA communication audit: Process, status, critique. *Journal of Business Communication, 15*(1), 41-55.

Goldhaber, G. M., Lesniak, R. D., Porter, T., & Yates, M. P. (1978). Organizational communication: 1978. *Human Communication Research, 5,* 76-96.

Goldhaber, G. M., Porter, D. T., & Yates, M. P. (1977, June). *ICA communication audit survey instrument: 1977 organizational norms.* Paper presented at the International Communication Association Convention, Berlin, Germany.

Goldhaber, G. M., & Rogers, D. P. (1979). *Auditing organizational communication systems: The ICA communication audit.* Dubuque, IA: Kendall/Hunt Publishing Company.

Greenbaum, H. H. (1971, April). *Organizational communication systems: Identification and appraisal.* Paper presented at the International Communication Association Convention, Phoenix, AZ.

Greenbaum, H. H. (1972, April). *The appraisal of organizational communication systems.* Paper presented at the International Communication Association Convention, Atlanta, GA.

Greenbaum, H. H. (1974). The audit of organizational communication. *Academy of Management Journal, 17,* 739-754.

Greenbaum, H. H., & Falcione, R. L. (1981). *Organizational communication: Abstracts, analysis, and overview.* Beverly Hills, CA: Sage Publications.

Greenbaum, H. H., Falcione, R. L., & Hellweg, S. A. (1983). *Organizational communication: Abstracts, analysis, and overview.* Beverly Hills, CA: Sage Publications.

Greenbaum, H. H., Holden, E. J., & Spataro, L. P. (1983). Organizational structure and communication processes: A study of change. *Group and Organization Studies, 8,* 61–82.

Greenbaum, H. H., Spataro, L. P., & Holden, E. J. (1980, May). *Communication in organizations: Appraisal of workgroup meeting effectiveness.* Paper presented at the International Communication Association Convention, Acapulco, Mexico.

Greenbaum, H. H., & White, N. D. (1976). Biofeedback at the organizational level: The communication audit. *The Journal of Business Communication, 13*(4), 3–15.

Guetzkow, H. (1965). Communication in organizations: In J. March (Ed.), *Handbook of organizations* (pp. 534–573). Chicago, IL: Rand McNally.

Harris, L., & Cronen, V. E. (1978, April). *A rules-based model for the analysis and evaluation of organizational communication.* Paper presented at the International Communication Association Convention, Chicago, IL.

Healey, J. H. (1958). *Executive coordination and control* (Monograph No. 78). Ohio State University, Bureau of Business Research.

Hellweg, S. A., & Phillips, S. L. (1983, March). *Communication policies and practices in American corporations.* Paper presented at the Western Regional Meeting, American Business Communication Association, Marina del Rey, CA.

Helsila, M. (1971). *Viestinta oeollisessa organisaatiossa.* Unpublished master's thesis, Helsinki School of Economics.

Hickson, M. III, Greenbaum, H. H., Falcione, R. L., & Goldhaber, G. M. (1975). Symposium on organization communication, 1975. *Journal of Applied Communications Research, 3,* 103–116.

Huseman, R. C. (1977). The role of the nominal group in small group communication. In R. C. Huseman, C. M. Logue, & D. L. Freshley (Eds.), *Readings in interpersonal and organizational communication* (pp. 493–502). Boston, MA: Holbrook Press.

Jablin, F. M., & Sussman, L. (1983). Organizational group communication: A review of the literature and model of the process. In H. H. Greenbaum, R. L. Falcione, & S. A. Hellweg (Eds.), *Organizational communication: Abstracts, analysis, and overview* (pp. 11–50). Beverly Hills, CA: Sage Publications.

Jain, H. C. (1972, April). *Employee knowledge of hospital compensation policies and supervisory effectiveness.* Paper presented at the International Communication Association Convention, Atlanta, GA.

Jain, H. C. (1977). Organizational communication: A case study of a large urban hospital. *Industrial Relations Industrielles, 31,* 588–608.

Jain, H. C., Kanungo, R. N., & Goldhaber, G. M. (1980). Attitudes toward communication system: A comparison of anglophone and francophone hospital employees. *Human Communication Research, 6,* 178–184.

Jenkins, K. M. (1980, August). *The quality dimension of worker performance: An empirical investigation of the impact of supervisor communicative effectiveness.* Paper presented at the Academy of Management Convention, Detroit, MI.

Kelly, J. (1964). The study of executive behavior by activity sampling. *Human Relations, 17,* 277–287.

Kelly, L, & Gleason, M. E. (1981, May). *Ranking member effectiveness in problem-solving groups.* Paper presented at the International Communication Association Convention, Minneapolis, MN.

Klauss, R., & Bass, B. (1980, August). *Communication and leader behavior.* Paper presented at the Academy of Management Convention, Detroit, MI.

Krivonos, P. D. (1975a, November). *A brief background of the ICA audit.* Paper presented at the Western Speech Communication Association Convention, Seattle, WA.

Krivonos, P. D. (1975b). *Subordinate-superior communication as related to intrinsic and extrinsic motivation: An experimental field study.* Unpublished doctoral dissertation, Purdue University.

Krohn, V. (1979). *Vertical communication as perceived by administrators and teachers in a Nassau*

County school district. Unpublished doctoral dissertation, Hofstra University.

Level, D. A., Jr. (1959). *A case study of human communications in an urban bank.* Unpublished doctoral dissertation, Purdue University.

Level, D. A., Jr., & Johnson, L. (1978). Accuracy of information flows within the superior/subordinate relationship. *Journal of Business Communication, 15*(2), 12–22.

Lewis, P. V. (1979, August). *Communication evaluation in organizations: A model for training directors.* Paper presented at the Academy of Management Convention, Atlanta, GA.

Lull, P. E., Funk, F. E., & Piersol, D. T. (1954). What communications mean to the corporation president. *Advanced Management, 20,* 17–20.

Madden, F. T. (1967). *Oral communication patterns utilized by top-level executives in two manufacturing companies.* Unpublished doctoral dissertation, Wayne State University.

Maier, N. R. F. (1967). Assets and liabilities in group problem solving: The need for an integrative function. *Psychological Review, 74,* 239–249.

Mazza, J. M. (1975). *A general systems analysis of an organizational communication climate.* Unpublished doctoral dissertation, University of Missouri, Columbia.

Minter, R. L. (1969). *a comparative analysis of managerial communication in two divisions of a large manufacturing company.* Unpublished doctoral dissertation, Purdue University.

Moran, W. E. (1967). *A comparative study of intra-organizational control and communication.* Unpublished doctoral dissertation, The University of Michigan.

Nelson, M. J. (1972). *An analysis of factors contributing to the intra-group communication effectiveness of small work group supervisors in selected Oklahoma business, manufacturing and government service situations.* Unpublished doctoral dissertation, University of Oklahoma.

Nilsen, T. R. (1953). *The communication survey: A study of communication problems in three office and factory units.* Unpublished doctoral dissertation, Northwestern University.

Odiorne, G. (1954). An application of the communication audit. *Personnel Psychology, 1,* 235–243.

Pacilio, J., Jr. (1974). An internal communication audit of Kent State University: A report of a pilot study. In S. J. Bruno (Ed.), *Proceedings, Southwest ABCA Spring Conference* (pp. 45–78). Canyon, TX: Center for Business and Economic Research, West Texas State University.

Perry, D., & Mahoney, T. A. (1955). In-plant communications and employee morale. *Personnel Psychology, 8,* 339–346.

Peters, R. W. (1950). Evaluating communication media. In R. W. Peters (Ed.), *Communication within industry* (pp. 140–155). New York: Harper & Row.

Porter, D. T. (1979, May). *The ICA Communication audit: 1979 norms and instrument documentation for seventeen audits using the survey (1974–1979).* Paper presented at the International Communication Association Convention, Philadelphia, PA.

Porter, L., & Roberts, K. (1976). Communication in organizations. In M. D. Dunnette (Ed.), *Handbook of industrial and organizational psychology* (pp. 1553–1589). Chicago, IL: Rand McNally.

Prado Garza, M. de la Luz (1981, May). *Program of development at the San Jose hospital: Evaluation of interpersonal relations workshops taken by physicians, administrative personnel and nurses of the hospital, Monterrey, N. L., November 27, 1980.* Paper presented at the International Communication Association Convention, Minneapolis, MN.

Redding, W. C. (1966). The empirical study of human communication in business and industry. In P. E. Ried (Ed.), *Frontiers in experimental speech communication research* (pp. 47–81). Syracuse, NY: Syracuse University Press.

Redding, W. C. (1972). *Communication within the organization.* New York: Industrial Communication Council.

Richetto, G. M., & Dennis, H. S. III (1976, August). *Communication audit of a public school system.* Paper presented at the Academy of Management Convention, Kansas City, MO.

Rogers, D. P., & Goldhaber, G. M. (1978). Conducting one's own communication audit. In G. M. Goldhaber (Ed.), *Improving institutional communication* (pp. 55–69). San Francisco, CA: Jossey-Bass.

Ross, G. E. (1960). *A study of informal communication patterns in two elementary schools.* Unpublished doctoral dissertation, The University of Illinois.

Ross, R. S. (1954). *A case study of communication breakdowns in the general telephone company of Indiana, Inc.* Unpublished doctoral dissertation, Purdue University.

Rudolph, E. E. (1972, April). *An evaluation of ECCO analysis as a communication audit methodology.* Paper presented at the International Communication Association Convention, Atlanta, GA.

Sadler, W. J. (1974). *Communication in organizations: An exploratory study.* Unpublished doctoral dissertation, The University of Wisconsin.

Sanborn, G. A. (1961). *An analytic study of oral communication practices in a nationwide retail sales organization.* Unpublished doctoral dissertation, Purdue University.

Schwartz, D. F. (1968). *Liaison communication roles in a formal organization* (Communimetrics Report No. 1). North Dakota State University, Department of Communication.

Simons, H. (1961). *A comparison of communication attributes and rated job performance of supervisors in a large commercial enterprise.* Unpublished doctoral dissertation, Purdue University.

Sincoff, M. Z., & Goyer, R. S. (1977). Communication audit critique: The researcher's perspective. *Journal of Business Communication, 15*(1), 57–63.

Sincoff, M. Z., Williams, D. A., & Rohm, C. E. T., Jr. (1976, April). *Steps in performing a communication audit.* Paper presented at the International Communication Association Convention, Portland, OR.

Smith, R. M. (1980, May). *Analysis of organizational communication audit consulting techniques: The educational organization.* Paper presented at the International Communication Association Convention, Acapulco, Mexico.

Steber, J. M. (1972). *Communication within an organization: A case study of the Reading, Pennsylvania model cities program.* Unpublished doctoral dissertation, Pennsylvania State University.

Sutton, H., & Porter, L. (1968). A study of the grapevine in a governmental organization. *Personnnel Psychology, 21,* 223–230.

Timpano, D. M. (1972). *A study of communication network characteristics in schools by means of ECCO analysis.* Unpublished doctoral dissertation, Hofstra University.

Todd, J. M. (1966). *A study of communication and coordination in marketing organizations.* Unpublished doctoral dissertation, The University of Texas.

Tompkins, P. K. (1962). *An analysis of communication between headquarters and selected units of a national labor union.* Unpublished doctoral dissertation, Purdue University.

Tompkins, P. K. (1967). Organizational communication: A state-of-the-art review. In G. Richetto (Ed.), *Conference on organizational communication.* Huntsville, AL: NASA, George C. Marshall Space Flight Center.

Tompkins, P. K. (1977). Management qua communication in rocket research and development. *Communication Monographs, 44,* 1–26.

Veninga, R. L. (1972). *A case study in organization development: The role of communication.* Unpublished doctoral dissertation, University of Minnesota.

Werner, E. K., Falcione, R. L., & Temkiewicz, J. M. R. (1978, April). *A communication audit of a federal agency at two points in time.* Paper presented at the International Communication Association Convention, Chicago, IL.

Wiio, O. A. (1974, April). *Auditing communication in organizations: A standard survey – the LTT communication audit.* Paper presented at the International Communication Association Convention, New Orleans, LA.

Wiio, O. A. (1977a). *Organizational communication and its development* (Research Report No. 2A771220). Institute for Human Communication, Helsinki, Finland.

Wiio, O. A. (1978a). *Contingencies of organizational communication: Studies in organization and organizational communication* (Research Report No. 1A771218). Institute for Human Communication, Helsinki, Finland.

Wiio, O. A. (1978b, April). *Organizational communication studies: The LTT and OCD procedures.* Paper presented at the International Communication Association Convention, Chicago, IL.

Wiio, O. A., Goldhaber, G. M., & Yates, M. P. (1980). Organizational communication research: Time for reflection? In D. Nimmo (Ed.), *Communication Yearbook 4* (pp. 83–97). New Brunswick, NJ: Transaction Books.

Wohlgamuth, W. L. (1981). *Evaluation of structured interpersonal communication in the achievement of business-writing principles.* Unpublished doctoral dissertation, The Louisiana State University.

Wood, R. N., Perrill, N. K., & Buley, J. (1975, April). *Pilot testing the communication audit questionnaire: First field test for the ICA, Division 4, communication audit project.* Paper presented at the International Communication Association Convention, Chicago, IL.

Yates, M. P., Porter, D. T., Goldhaber, G. M., Dennis, H. S. III, & Richetto, G. M. (1976, April). *The ICA communication audit system: Results of six studies.* Paper presented at the International Communication Association Convention, Portland, OR.

Chapter 14

Communication Network Analysis: History and Overview

Rolf T. Wigand

ABSTRACT

Communication networks consist of the regular pattern of communication contacts which develop among people within a social system as they use various forms of communication (face-to-face conversations, memoranda, telephone calls, etc.) to accomplish certain organizational tasks. Information regarding the proper functioning of the various types of human communication networks is important, since it can be used to understand the organization's flow of information and to assess its effectiveness and efficiency. The goals of network analysis are (a) to detect and (b) to describe any structure at the dyadic, group, and organizational level of the network. Various networks characteristics of individuals and groups can be identified such as connectedness, integrativeness, etc.

This presentation describes procedures and methods for analyzing communication networks in large organizations. These include (a) the identification and evaluation of networks, (b) the assessment of the organizational hierarchy vis-a-vis the findings from the network analysis, (c) the appraisal of various network components, and (d) evaluating the individual and group communication behavior.

Various approaches are possible to analyze the communication behavior in organizations. Among them are the standard questionnaire survey, which allows us to address a vast number of communication issues; one can conduct face-to-face interviews in order to crystallize problems; one may ask respondents to share their communication experiences, i.e. critical episodes, to create a picture of the communication climate; one may ask employees to keep communication diaries for specified communication activities; and lastly, one may involve employees in communication network analysis. Network analysis is a process in which respondents indicate the extent to which they typically communicate with each individual in their unit or organization about certain topics. It is this latter approach that has, in recent years, gained particular attention in the United States, and has been demonstrated to be a very fruitful approach as an organizational tool to analyze the communication behavior and patterns within an organization.

INTRODUCTION

This chapter is an attempt to trace and demonstrate various methodological approaches to recognize patterns in social relationships. In addition, it describes some characteristics of these patterns once they have been recognized. Generally, the focus is with the field of communication rather than with related social science areas, and the emphasis is on communication networks rather than on kinship, power, and other networks.

Various definitions are presented that are considered as necessary, first, in order to provide a joint vocabulary, and, secondly, to arrive accurately and logically at the discussions in the following sections.

Several key cluster-seeking techniques for relational data are reviewed. Two indices, one for integrativeness and another for flexibility, are presented. The purpose of the chapter is to take a uniform approach in synthesizing the various techniques and methods, and to demonstrate their relative contribution toward the joint goal of generating some groups, clusters, or cliques, and other characteristics among interrelated members of an organization.

There has been a long-standing interest in network analysis among many scholars in various fields of the social sciences, e.g., small group researchers, sociometricians, and anthropologists. These studies are far too numerous to reference here. Feger, Hummel, Pappi, Sodeur, and Ziegler published, in 1981, a bibliography of social network studies listing, worldwide, more than 3,250 entries. Also, Feger et al. (1978), Freeman (1976), Klovdahl (1979), Pitts (1979), and Wellman and Whitaker (1974) have provided lengthy bibliographies. Nehnevajsa (1955, 1967) has written an early history of the field — more specifically early sociometry, the book by Rogers and Kincaid (1981), *Communication Networks: Toward a New Paradigm for Research*, belongs into the reference library of every network analyst, and Wellman (1981), as well as Rice and Richards (1985) provide an excellent overview of network analysis methods and computer programs.

Communication *per se* is a relatively complex social process with many dimensions. Essential functions in any social system are accomplished through processes of communication.* These essential functions have been divided into three basic categories by Barnard (1938): (a) production, (b) maintenance, and (c) innovation. Although other scholars developed different schemes into which the functions of social systems can be categorized, members of all social systems engage in activities that resemble Barnard's thinking. These functions, however, can only be carried out through various forms of communication. If the researcher studies the forms of communication in which the three functions of production, maintenance, and innovation are inherent, it can then be said — within limitations — that the social system has been analyzed with regard to communication. Each time the researcher focuses on one of these three activities, he specifies a particular communication network. If one would superimpose all existing communication networks within a system, this overall network could be considered to reflect the communication behavior of a social system.

One area, systems theory, provides insights into methods for describing large, complex systems. Buckley (1967), for example, considers the notions of wholes, parts, structure, interdependence, etc. of primary importance. Similar emphasis can be found with von Bertalanffy (1940), Rapaport (1970), and many others. Since a specification of how to find parts or units of the *formative process* has not been adequately established, this constitutes one of the major issues in systems theory today (Krippendorff, 1971). Communication net-

---

* *Communication* is defined as that process by which messages are transmitted via certain channels from a source to a receiver. This causes the receiver to change or at least minimally modify an existing behavior pattern. The effects of the message on the receiver are assumed to be observable by the source through a response to the original message.

work analysis attempts to overcome some of these inadequacies, and takes into account some of the notions that are central to systems theory.

This chapter focuses on the techniques and methods underlying the generation and analysis of communication networks in large, complex social systems. *Communication networks consists of the detected patterns of communication contacts among individuals within a social system.* These contacts can be "arrested" for analysis purposes by assessing the attributes of face-to-face communication, communication by memoranda, by telephone, by letters, etc. Pool (1973) has described networks as the *thread* that holds social systems together. The analysis of networks can thus provide descriptions and characterizations of the system's structure. It should be noted that the applications of the network analysis technique are appropriate to many forms of social systems, such as organizations, villages, classrooms, entire industries, interorganizational analysis, and others (cf., e.g., Farace & Wigand, 1979a&b; Wigand 1976a,b, 1977a,b,c,d; Wigand & Larkin, 1975).

A DEFINITION OF RELATIONSHIP

The basic unit of analysis in all social networks is a relationship between two individuals. Typically, in the analysis of relational data one finds the network, sociogram, sociomatrix, probability-theoretical models, matrix manipulations, graph theory, factor and cluster analysis (cf. Mayntz, Holm, & Huebner, 1971). Data sets analyzed by all these methods represent symbolically structures in the sense of individual and group characteristics.

These methods do not, unfortunately, describe structures or relationships that allow for causal interpretations. In the context of causal-analytical procedures, these methods represent scaling techniques that can be differentiated mainly with respect to their level of measurement. Network configurations such as the dyad, triad, or the chain measures certain relationships at the nominal level; whereas indices such as the index of social integration or social distance and similar measures have metric characteristics. The values of such indices are aggregate data and thus allow themselves for inferential statistical treatment.

Before one can be concerned with the various methods of analysis of social-relational network data, i.e., methods that process and allow the researcher to recognize order or patterns with relational data, a definition of relationship ought to be presented.

Bain (1943) attempts to present a general conceptualization of relationship, specifically a sociometric relationship, by stating that sociometry will remain a generic term to describe *all* measurement of societal and interpersonal data. In an attempt to delineate this type of data, Bjerstedt (1956) identifies 13 different definitions of sociometry which he had submitted to a panel of 269 experts for rating. The 131 returns suggested that the modal response was that sociometry is the quantitative treatment of "preferential interhuman relations."

Sociometrically similar data, however, are collected by several areas within the social sciences. It seems that,over the last 20 years, sociometrically similar techniques and methods have been used in several areas of the behavior sciences. This suggests also that Bjerstedt's definition is no longer adequate. There are several areas, as in communication, geography, economics, and others, where the relational interhuman data are by no means preferential. For the purposes of this chapter, wherever appropriate, the term sociometric is largely substituted by the term *network analytic* still emphasizing the applicability to interhuman relations, omitting the adjective "preferential."

The basic unit of analysis in relational analyses is, most obviously, a relationship itself. Such a relationship may be recognizable between two individuals within the same social system. Generally, in network analysis one is interested in functional relationships, i.e., active interactions between related individuals. Conceptually, the existence of a relationship between two individuals is constituted by the recognition of some *constraint* which restricts the behavior of one or both of the individuals. Such a constraint suggests one other characteristic of a relationship, namely, some *interdependence* between the individuals.

Social scientists frequently have urged the need for relational analysis by emphasizing the importance to turn away from monadic and aggregate data (cf., e.g., Coleman, 1972; Krippendorff, 1970; Rogers & Bhowmik, 1971; Rosenberg, 1972). The proponents of this approach to view "reality" argue that the researcher not only manages to arrest data of two elements, A and B, as in the monadic analysis, but that additional information is added to the recognition of constraints or, generally, a relationship between A and B. We can view such a relationship, R, as a unit or element of system S. A relationship R_s is said to structure the system S. Such relationships may be classified according to various qualities or properties they possess within the relational system S. Eight major properties, in part analogous to Torgerson (1958, pp. 25–26), of such relational constraints are discussed and identified: elements, attributes, magnitudes, quantity, directionality, symmetry, specificity, and transitivity. For the purpose of this paper, a relationship is conceptually defined as:

> the mode or process in which members of a social system are connected or associated interdependently among or between each other; i.e. a partial unification of members which when considered irrespective of such a relation, would be incapable of being conceived together. (Wigand, 1979b, p. 182)

Any graph — or, here, relationship — may, in fact, be used to realize a *discrete source of information* according to the abstract definition by Shannon and Weaver (1949, p. 9). Analogous to Torgerson (1958, pp. 25, 26), four major properties of a relationship are here identified. These are elements, attributes, magnitudes, and quantities. Furthermore, the issue of directionality of a relationship is of importance.

Elements

An element for the present purpose is — thus somewhat different from its conventional usage — understood as an elemental part of a system such as in a relationship, R, between A and B, ARB. R *constitutes the element of that system ARB*. Torgerson (1958, p. 25) refers to these elements as objects or the "thing" which carries or possesses properties. Other terms are entities, items, atoms, etc. Elements are primitive in the sense that they have no further structure, but can only be distinguished from one another and may enter into interrelationships with each other. Any relationship may, in fact, be used to realize a *discrete source of information* according to the abstract definition by Shannon and Weaver (1949, p. 9). In this sense, relational elements are thought of as basic units that cannot be further broken down into subcomponents without losing some of their characteristics.

Attributes

Attributes will refer to measurable properties of a relationship. Attributes as properties are capable of gradations per definitione. In the case of network analysis, attributes may be such concepts as attraction, friendship, etc.

Magnitudes

Magnitudes, to use Torgerson's term, are essentially anything capable of being greater than or less than something else. A magnitude may then be understood as a particular amount of an attribute. Figure 1 makes this distinction clearer. One may represent an attribute of a relationship analogous to a continuum of points. A particular point on that continuum, here point K, represents the location and magnitude of point K as compared to all other points, L and M, on that continuum.

Figure 1. The magnitude of an attribute represented in a continuum of points.

Quantity

Quantity of a relationship is defined as a particular instance of magnitude. For example, after a measurement scale has been developed, one may ascertain that the quantity of a magnitude is 5. Russell (1938, p. 167) states that "two quantities which result from particularizing the same magnitude are said to be equal."

For example, in terms of attraction, the above specified four terms are understood as follows: an *element* will be identified by the relationship R as in ARB between the nodes of actors A and B and specified through the concept "attraction." It should be noted that this relationship between A and B may have many other properties besides "attraction." *Attribute* refers to the conceptual continuum of the concept of attraction. The term *magnitude* would be constituted by the point in the continuum corresponding to the attribute "attraction" of the relationship ARB as compared to other points on that continuum. Magnitude could be operationalized as the strength, intensity, influence, or perceived importance of the attribute "attraction" between A and B in ARB. The term *quantity* would refer to the measured magnitude or amount of attraction of R in ARB.

Directionality

A relationship R can be furthermore specified with regard to its *directionality*. Specifically, is R constituted and recognized by its direction from A to B, B to A, A to B as well as B to A, or is R *extended* to another element R', as in A to B, then B to C? As suggested in this question, a relationship R between two nodes may be expressed in two directions. Either A precedes B, or B precedes A.

Symmetry

A relationship R is said to be symmetrical among the actors A and B within a social system S, if, whenever one observes AR_SB, this implies that one can consequently also observe BR_SA. Worded differently, whenver A is in a relation with B, then B is also in a relation with A, for all A, B in S, or, shortly, R_S is symmetric if $AR_SB \rightarrow BR_SA$ (all A, B $\in$ S). This relationship is asymmetrical if AR_SB does not imply BR_SA. Since it is usually assumed that communicative acts are a two-way process, communication would be a symmetrical relationship between two people by definition. An asymmetrical relationship would merely indicate a one-way flow of information, influence, etc.

Specificity

The specificity of a relationship expresses the extent to which the relationship is not able to be replaced by another relationship that would allow for the occurrence of the same behavior of the relational system as before. In relational expressions, if the R_S in AR_SB cannot be replaced by some other R_S, e.g., AR_SC, the original R_S is defined as being specific to A and B. In terms of social systems settings, it is easy to conceive of situations in which there is only one person that has specific information and where this person could not be replaced by another person in order to achieve the same, initially intended goal.

Transitivity

Transitivity of a relationship R_S, the last property to be presented for the purposes of this chapter, is then existent when AR_SB and BR_SC together imply AR_SC. Consequently, R_S is said to be intransitive if the first two relationships do not imply the third relationship. In short, R_S is transitive, if AR_SB and $BR_SC \rightarrow AR_SC$ (all A,B,C $\in$ S). In terms of a communication situation, a transitive communication relationship suggests that A influences B and B influences C, and that, at least in part, the behavior of C is influenced by A via B. Transitivity is one of the key features of most balance-theoretic conceptualizations of social relationships (cf. Bales, 1950; Harary, Norman, & Cartwright, 1965; Heider, 1958; Newcomb, 1953).

With regard to network analytic purposes, a system is viewed as a set of relationships imbedded in a network of relationships. So far, the units of analysis, i.e., relationships, have been described and specified. Next, the collection of relationships constituting a network must be analyzed such that certain regularities or patterns can be recognized. In order to specify such patterns or groups a definition of *group* is presented.

A Definition of Group

Analysts of networks have always been interested in detecting groups and specifying group structure. Groups, typically, have been defined as ensembles of individuals that are somehow connected by stronger or weaker links, or being in some fashion or another closer to or more distant from each other. Naturally, during the development of network analytic techniques, a considerable effort went into methods of how network data can be partitioned into such groups.

In the sociometric area, a group or clique was being defined as a set of individuals of which each prefers the presence of at least one other member of the group in a specified activity more than any other individual outside of this group. Festinger, Schachter, and Back (1950) defined a group as a subsystem of three or more elements in mutual interaction with each other. A graph-theoretical notion of group was formulated by Luce and Perry (1949): a maximal complete subgraph, i.e., a set of completely linked points not contained in a larger completely linked set. Luce (1950) expanded and generalized this definition of a group to the *n-clique*. The n-clique is a group in which individuals with n links of each other are treated as directly connected and groups were then extracted from this n-graph.

Most reviewed group definitions and criteria for such definitions attempt to allow for definite partitioning, i.e., to assigning individuals to groups such that each individual is a member of one and only one group. A group of researchers — originally at Michigan State

University during the 1970s—in network analysis uses such a definition in the context of communication activities of individuals. Specifically, a group is defined by a percentage criterion: for example, if 50.1% or more of the communication linkages exist among the same set of individuals.

Two terms deserve special attention in the attempts to present a more formal definition of group: *system* and *structure*. A group is here understood as a system. In this context, a system is defined as the number of nodes (system parts) and relations (reflective of interactions and interdependencies) observable between these nodes. The structure is represented by the number of relations between these nodes. A group then is formally defined as:

at least two nodes i and j of a finite number N that forms a pair through the relation R_{ij}
$N \times N$

The nodes within a group are individuals, and the relations are the representations of actions by those individuals as, for example, in the case of a sociometric choice. Typically, the first node in the above representational form of a relationship is the sender, the second node is the receiver of that action.

This definition, admittedly, represents a compromise, since some researchers do not recognize the existence of a group unless there are three or more individuals in the group. Considering several pattern-recognition algorithms to be presented later on, this definition of a minimal N of 2 appears to be most suitable in this elementary form.

The connection of nodes (relationships) have the character of informational couplings. These couplings can be represented in a structural matrix. Since most fields in the behavioral sciences disregard reflexive couplings, i.e., couplings of nodes with themselves, such a matrix looks as follows:

$$S = \begin{bmatrix} 0 & c_{12} & c_{13} & c_{14} & \cdot & \cdot & \cdot & c_{1N} \\ c_{21} & 0 & c_{23} & c_{24} & \cdot & \cdot & \cdot & c_{2N} \\ c_{31} & c_{32} & 0 & c_{34} & \cdot & \cdot & \cdot & c_{3N} \\ & \cdot & & \cdot & & & & \cdot \\ & \cdot & & \cdot & & & & \cdot \\ & \cdot & & \cdot & & & & \cdot \\ c_{N1} & c_{N2} & c_{N3} & c_{N4} & \cdot & \cdot & \cdot & 0 \end{bmatrix}$$

where S = structural matrix,
C_{ij} = couplings between node i and node j,
i = the sender (row index), i = 1, 2, . . . , N
j = the receiver (column index), j = 1, 2, . . . , N
N = the number of nodes in the group.

The structural matrix is nothing more than an ordered scheme for all possible relations of the product $N \times N$. Typically, each matrix cell receives the binary symbol 1 or 0, but higher or lower numbers, both positive and negative, can be used. The symbol 1 indicates that the coupling C_{ij} exists; 0 indicates that it does not exist. Shephard (1972) and Coombs (1964) provide further detailed discussions about the properties of data matrixes.

How the information contained in such a structural matrix can be used to recognize patterns, clusters, and groups is discussed in the following sections of this chapter.

THE REPRESENTATION OF A STRUCTURAL MATRIX IN A CARTESIAN COORDINATE SYSTEM

One way to express quantitative characteristics about individuals of a system represented in the form of a structural matrix is through the sums of each row and column (cf. the matrix above). These sums represent aggregate information about each individual. Each individual can receive a number pair consisting of the sum of the choices made by the individual and the sum of the received choices. The choices can be graphically represented in a coordinate system.

Such a coordinate system presents the following advantages:

(1)   the aggregate network data allow for graphic representation;
(2)   various measures, such as indices, can be derived that can later be related to the processed data.

In this representational form, network indices can be interpreted geometrically; the problem of their theoretical interpretation, however, remains unsolved. Therefore, one ought to consider such indices merely as indicators of operational definitions of theoretical characteristics or classes thereof. It appears that this problem is characteristic for the field of network analysis, since most of the analysis methods and techniques developed were of a strongly heuristic nature. Basically, network analysts have searched for structure and regulatory processes. In this attempt, it was avoided, to start with certain underlying assumptions, explicit hypotheses, or theories that later on could be tested empirically (cf. Sherif & Sherif, 1969; Lindzey & Byrne, 1968; Shelly, 1960; Moreno, 1954).

Specifically, a rectangular, two-dimensional coordinate system in a Euclidian space is assumed. The space created by this coordinate system can be understood as a two-dimensional vector space whose bases are represented by the x-axis and the y-axis. The created space is metric, since it consists of a number (N) of points (x, y, z, . . .). These points are specified as follows: with any two points x N and y N, there exists a nonnegative, real number D (x,y) (= distance) with the following characteristics:

(1) $D (x,x) = 0$,
(2) $D (x,y) = D (y,x)$ (0 for x = y),
(3) $D (x,y) = D (x,z) + D (x,y)$.

Next, it becomes imperative to look in some detail at the meaning and interpretation of the coordinate system in sociometric context. Each member in a sociometric situation expresses a choice, preference, or simply a relation to another member of a system. Such a sociometric datum expresses, therefore, a two-digit, empirical relation. Both digits are characterized in the sense that the analyst can distinguish between an active or a directly made choice vs. a passive or received choice. The relationship between the active (AR) and passive relation (PR) sums; i.e., the sum of row cells vs. the sum of column cells of an individual in a structural matrix, is represented for each matrix member through a vector. Figure 2 demonstrates the representation of the relationship between individuals A and B in such a coordinate system. The relationship is expressed through the coordinate locations A (2,4) and B (3,2).

The vector representation suggests an analogy to the term *force* from physics. Active and passive relations that are recognized within the activities of members of the same system are understood similarly to these physical forces, and thus express a two-dimensional dependency that provides for each system member a resultant force with regard to that system.

Figure 2 is divided into four quadrants. Quadrant 1 (Q_1), $0° < \alpha < 90°$ (α = angle of the vectors), indicates the positive membership or belongingness based on the positively active and positively passive relationships to other members of the system. When $\alpha < 45°$, then the passive relations exceed the active ones. In this area, one will locate those members—depending on the nature and characteristic of the relationship or choice—that are sought out more, or are more active or central, than other members of that system located in a different quadrant. With an angle of $\alpha > 45°$, the positive belongingness to the system is based on a prevailing active relationship. Individuals located in this space are identified by the fact that they prevail rather in attributing a particular characteristic to themselves than that this characteristic is attributed to them by other members (those not located in this space) of their system.

If one would allow the relationships of a system to be expressed in positive as well as negative numbers (as can be conceived of in liking, preference, etc. scales), quadrants 2,3, and 4 can be interpreted. Q_2, $90° < \alpha < 180°$, represents an asymmetrical belongingness to that system, since the active relations are positive but the passive relations are negative. Q_3, $180° < \alpha < 270°$, completes the negative belongingness sectors of the coordinate system. Here, the active as well as passive belongingness are negative. Q^4, $270° < \alpha < 360°$, shows an asymmetrical belongingness to the system, whereas the passive belongingness is positive, but the active belongingness is negative.

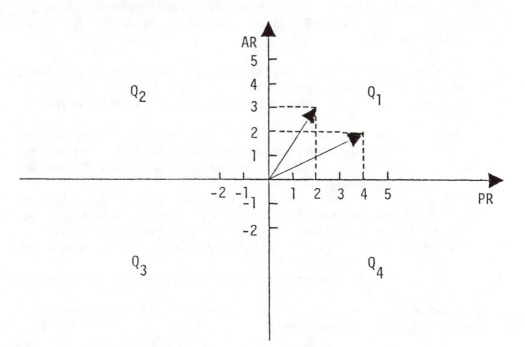

Figure 2. A vector space for the representation of network data (a hypothetical example). (Note: AR = Active Relation sums; PR = Passive Relation sums).

A REVIEW OF CLUSTER-SEEKING TECHNIQUES FOR RELATIONAL DATA

The essential characteristic of the techniques and methods described in this section is sorting and identifying the set of data patterns into subsets, such that each subset contains data points that are as much "alike" as possible according to present criteria. Obviously, methods that arrive at these subsets differ considerably. In the following pages, attempts are made to describe the known techniques briefly: to identify some underlying dimensions, as well as ways in which they are significantly different.

Sociometric and network analytic research has been reviewed by Farace, Richards, Monge, and Jacobson (1973), Lindzey and Byrne (1968), Nehnevajsa (1967, 1955), Rice and Richards (1985), Richards (1975), Wigand (1973, 1979b), and others. Roistacher (1974) and Guimaraes (1968) have reviewed mathematical techniques of network analysis, as have Glanzer and Glaser (1959). The following section describes a number of techniques that make network analysis possible.

Sociometric Analysis

The most commonly known method to partition networks into groups is the use of *sociograms* (Moreno, 1934) as an extension of graph theory (Harary, Norman, & Cartwright, 1965; König, 1936). A sociogram consists of various points or nodes that may or may not be connected by lines. Typically, each point represents an individual whose relationship to another chosen individual is expressed by a connecting line. Directionality of this line may be expressed through the addition of an arrow. All nodes and lines within a sociogram represent the structure of a network in terms of the recognized relationships. There are a number of rather severe limitations to the use of sociograms for a rigorous social scientist (Wigand, 1974b):

(1) The data input for sociograms does not allow for a multidimensional representation of the relationships among system members.
(2) The strength of a relationship is difficult to express and as N becomes larger, nearly impossible.
(3) Sociograms may be of some use for the representation of the system that is relatively small. As N becomes 50 or larger, there are severe spatial limitations to represent the system two-dimensionally. Consequently, it becomes increasingly difficult to produce and interpret a large sociogram.
(4) Few criteria, if any, exist that specify the length of a link or relationship; i.e., it is to be decided by the researcher whether the length of a link is to express the amount, frequency, or duration of communication, or a combination thereof.
(5) It is unclear how the analyst can specify the angles constituted by the incoming and outgoing links at a given focal node.
(6) With the availability of computers, the sociometric representation is being tedious, cumbersome, and inefficient.
(7) There is no a priori reason for the usefulness of representing a group's structure in a given two-dimensional Euclidian space.

There is no doubt that the sociogram as a representational tool of network structure has proven itself as being useful. As indicated above, problems exist when using a sociogram to detect the initial group structure. In order to overcome partially some of the problems associated with sociograms, Northway (1940) suggested the *target sociogram* in which through the use of concentric circles a particular choice status can be expressed. Borgatta (1951) suggested to draw sociograms such that a minimal number of crossed lines appear. Rapoport and Horvath (1961), Foster, Rapoport, and Orwant (1963), and Foster and Horvath (1971) studied large sociometric networks with probabilistic and statistical methods.

Kadushin and Tichy (1972) present output of a network analysis program in sociogram form in which the sociogram is drawn through a computerized plot routine resulting in densely drawn parts of the sociogram, and are very difficult to read and interpret. Therefore, Kadushin and Tichy (1972) present the analyst with an enlargement or "blow up" of this plot. It appears that, even with additional enlargements, it would be rather difficult to precisely delineate lines and nodes.

A Sociometric Representation of Relational Systems. Sociometry is a procedure for detecting interpersonal relationships (e.g., preferences, attractions, repulsions, indifferences) that exist among the members of a system. These relationships are represented in the form of a sociogram: the individuals or nodes are pictorially indicated by circles and their relationships (or, e.g., preferences when applied) by arrows pointing from one individual to another (cf. Figure 3). In drawing these relationships, each system member is asked to choose one or more system members with whom he or she would like to study, work, or share some other relevant activity.

Moreno (1934) originally developed sociometry, and all lines and nodes within a sociogram represent the structure of that system in terms of the detected relationships. The sociometric representation of relationships has been discussed by numerous authors (e.g., Bastin, 1967; Bjerstedt, 1956; Höhn & Schick, 1964; Moreno, 1946, 1954; Spilerman, 1966).

Graph-theoretical Analyses

Another technique that still enjoys attention are various *graph theoretic models*. Graph theory may be understood as a branch of mathematics, although it is today widely used in applied studies of such fields as marketing, geography, logistics, operation research, etc., as well as social psychology. As a discipline, graph theory was first formally established by

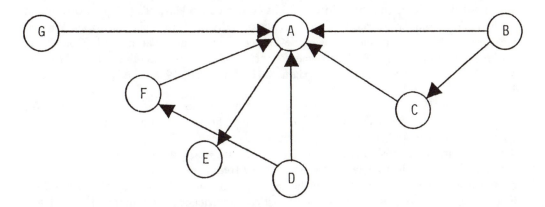

Figure 3. A sociogram representing the relationships among system members A, B, C, D, E, F and G.

König (1936) and has since been developed with considerable detail in numerous fields. For the purpose of this chapter, Harary, Norman, and Cartwright's (1965) definition of a graph is presented which is largely synonymous with the definitions of Harary (1969), Ziegler (1968), Flament (1963), Berge (1967), and Ore (1962). A directed graph is defined by Harary et al. (1965) in terms of four primitives and four axioms:

The primitives defining a graph are:

P1: A set V of elements called "points."
P2: A set of X elements called "lines."
P3: A function f whose domain is X and whose range is contained in V.
P4: A function s whose domain is X and whose range is contained in V.

The axioms defining a graph are:

A1: The set V is finite and not empty.
A2: The set X is finite.
A3: No two distinct lines are parallel.
A4: There are no loops.

In this context, a graph may look like a sociogram. Obviously, the underlying assumptions differ considerably.

Bavelas (1948, 1950) first applied graph theory to the analysis of the communication structure in small groups. Luce and Perry (1949) suggested a graph-theoretic definition of clique: a maximal complete subgraph which is a set of points completely connected to each other and not part of a larger, completely connected set of points. Luce (1950) introduced the term "n-clique," which is a clique in which each node is connected to every other node by a path of n or fewer lines. Alba (1972) added to this definition the criterion that the longest path must be of length n, since, otherwise, nodes of an n-clique could be connected through nodes who are not clique members.

Considerable effort has been placed on the extension of Heider's (1946) concept of balance theory and structural balance. In this scheme, the various directed lines in a graph can be indicants of positive or negative relations — as in "likes" and "dislikes" dimensions — typically expressed through the values " + " and " − ". Harary (1954) defined a graph as being balanced when all cycles are positive. Flament (1963) extended Haray's definition to triads and demonstrated that his definition was equivalent to Harary's (1954). Lorrain and White (1971) discuss the structural equivalence of individuals in social networks. Various measures of the degree of balance were developed, since balance can be understood as an extreme condition of a graph (Norman & Roberts, 1972; Davis & Leinhart, 1972; Holland & Leinhart, 1970; Peay, 1970; Cartwright & Harary, 1956, 1968; Davis, 1967; Harary, 1954).

Gleason (1971) developed DIP, a directed graph processing program that allows for the manipulation of graphs in matrix form. DIP in addition to standard matrix operations, computes distances and connectivity matrices for graphs.

Leinhart (1971) designed SOCPAC-I, a program whose algorithm decomposes a directed graph into existing triads. It then tests the frequency of various types of triads in comparison to a random graph with the same amount of null, asymmetric, and mutual links. This test provides measures of statistical significance by utilizing Holland and Leinhart's (1970) distribution theorem.

Other network analysts who have worked with graph theory and its applications are

Atkin (1974), Alba (1973), Alba and Gutman (1974), Alt and Schofield (1975), Burton (1970), Cartwright and Harary (1956), Doreian (1981), Farace and Mabee (1980), Felling and van der Weegen (1976), Freeman (1980), Gengerelli (1963), Gleason (1971), Gould (1980), Harary and Ross (1957), Harary et al. (1965), Luce (1950), Luce and Perry (1949), Mokken (1979), Purdy (1973), Seidman (1981), Seidman and Foster (1978), and others.

Graph theory, in general, has little internal unity and cannot provide much information about interrelations between relations. This approach to the analyses of relational data deals basically with isolated graphs. Furthermore, graph theory does not provide criteria for the reduction and comparison of graphs.

Graph Theoretical Representation of Relational Systems. One way of representing relationships and networks is through the use of graph theory (König, 1936; Hararay, Norman, & Cartwright, 1965). Let R_S be a relation within system S. According to graph theory, one can represent objects in S by points in the plane of the paper and specify that $(A, B) \in R_S$ by designating a directed line (or graph or edge) from A to B. The constructed graph is a pictorial representation of the relational system S. The following example in Figure 4 demonstrates the use of graph theory. Note that all nodes are labeled by the numbers they represent. The system S is composed of the nodes 1, 2, and 3, namely $S = \{1, 2, 3\}$. R_S is composed of the following sets of relationships:

$R_S = \{(1,2), (2,3), (3,1), (1,3)\}$.

Matrix Analysis

Almost all group structure work since Forsyth and Katz (1946) uses in some fashion or another the *matrix representation* of network data. The various features and assumptions of a sociomatrix have been discussed already. Forsyth and Katz (1946) developed a technique that allowed for the rearrangement of rows and columns in the matrix such that mutual choices were brought closer to each other with respect to specific matrix cell locations. Furthermore, it was attempted to maximize this proximity by trying to locate these individuals along the diagonal of the matrix. This technique and various aspects thereof were refined by Katz (1947), Festinger (1949), Chabot (1950), Luce (1950), Jacobson and Seashore (1951), Weiss and Jacobson (1955), and Weiss (1956). Through this development, it was possible to represent relationships in networks such that groups or cliques and other features could be detected. Beum and Brundage (1950) wrote an algorithm that allows for this clustering effect along the main diagonal; Borgatta and Stolz (1963) computerized this algorithm. Spilerman (1966) developed a matrix permutation technique in which a priori definitions for groups were not necessary, and allowed the analyst to make unbiased a

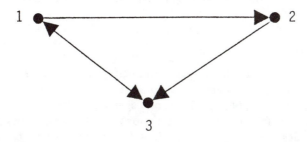

Figure 4. A graph theoretic representation of the relational system S.

posteriori partitions into groups based on the information provided by the rearranged matrix. Rattinger (1973) describes an iterative, computerized procedure by using a matrix manipulation algorithm for group detection. Richards (1971) presented an algorithm that also has been computerized, and allows for the detection of groups and other features without using the actual matrix representation but utilizing in essence the same information that is typically found in a sociomatrix. Richards' algorithm has the advantage that it does not operate on the basis that all the information provided in a n × n matrix has to be considered at all points in time during the calculation process. It is well known that the utility of analyzing networks through matrix methods is high as long as the total N is small. Even the use of computerized techniques becomes prohibitively expensive when N becomes larger, if not impossible. For example, when N equals 100, each of the 100 individuals could communicate with 99 other individuals. Consequently, 9,900 possible connections could exist. If N would be 5,000, nearly 25,000,000 possible links exist. Richards' (1971) algorithm is discussed in some more detail in a presentation of computerized techniques later on.

A Matrix Representation of Relational Systems. The connection of nodes (relationships) have the character of informational couplings. These couplings can be represented in a structural matrix. The use of matrices — sometimes also called sociomatrices — is described in detail by Harray et al. (1965), Bishir and Drewes (1970), Luce and Perry (1949), and others.

Generally, a matrix is a rectangular array of numbers arranged in rows and columns. A matrix element or entry is labeled as a_{ij} if it is at the intersection of row i and column j. Let R_S be a relational system. If we label the objects in S with integers 1, 2, . . . , n, we then define

$$a_{ij} = \begin{cases} 1 \text{ if object i has a relation R to object j} \\ 0 \text{ if not} \end{cases}$$

The generic notion for an arbitrary matrix A is:

$M_A = (a_{ij})$
Where M_A = Structural Matrix,
a_{ij} = Couplings between node i and node j,
i = The sender (row index), i = 1,2, ... ,m
j = The receiver (column index), j = 1,2, ... ,n

The row index i has a domain {1, 2,. . . ., m} ; the column index j has a domain {1,2,. . . , n}; where matrix M_A has m rows and n columns. The above described arbitrary matrix M_A has an order as follows:

$M_A^{m \times n}$

The structural matrix is nothing more than an ordered scheme for all possible relations of the product m × n. Typically, each matrix cell receives the binary symbol 1 or 0, but higher or lower numbers, both positive and negative, can be used. Shephard (1972) and Coombs (1964) provide further detailed discussions about the properties of data matrices.

The example depicted in Figure 5 describes the use of a matrix representation. Let the relations be such that one has graph A in Figure 5:

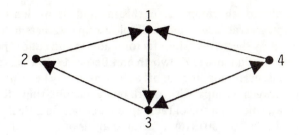

Figure 5. Graph A depicting relationships among four nodes.

Then the adjacency matrix for graph A is given by:

$$M_A = \begin{Bmatrix} 0 & 0 & 1 & 0 \\ 1 & 0 & 0 & 0 \\ 0 & 1 & 0 & 1 \\ 1 & 0 & 1 & 0 \end{Bmatrix}$$

Katz (1947), Festinger (1949), Chabot (1950), Luce (1950), Jacobson and Seashore (1951), Weiss and Jacobson (1955), and Weiss (1956) have utilized matrices to represent relationships in networks in which various techniques allow for the detection of groups or cliques as well as certain characteristics thereof. The analysis of networks through matrix methods are of utility as long as N remains small. Even the use of computerized techniques becomes prohibitively expensive when N becomes larger, if not impossible, when N equals, e.g., 100. With an N of 100, each of the 100 could communicate with 99 others. Consequently, 9,900 possible connections would exist. If N is 5,000, nearly 25,000,000 possible links exist.

Factor Analysis

The first study using *factor analysis* for relational data was by Bock and Husain (1950). These authors transformed the choice matrix into a correlation matrix upon which a centroid factor analysis was performed. Roistacher (1974) and others argue that the rationale behind the use of factor analysis is that a group can be seen as a set of individuals that tend to make similar choices, or, conversely, that a group is a set of individuals who tend to be chosen by individuals who are similar to them.

The factor-analytic technique treats each group as a factor, and the resulting dimensionality of the space is equal to the number of groups. Group membership may then be expressed in terms of a set of factor loadings which define the strength of an individual's association with each group.

MacRae (1960) introduced a varimax factor analysis, as did Wright and Evitts (1961). Beaton (1966) developed MacRae's technique by considering the chooser and chosen structures as two batteries of variables, and analyzed these data by an interbattery factor analysis. Factor analytic results were compared with several matrix multiplication techniques by Nosanchuk (1963). He reported that factor analysis allows for better reconstruction of a preconstructed neetwork. Bonacich's (1972) scheme is based on various factoring and weighting approaches that, among other features, allows for the identification of groups. See also the work by Freeman (1968), Holzinger and Harman (1941), as well as Tryon and Bailey (1970).

There are a number of shortcomings in this method. Individuals within a network may, of course, load on several factors and multiple group membership and group size depend on decisions made by the analyst, i.e., factor loadings and cut off points. These decisions are largely subjective in nature. Killworth and Bernard (1974) state that, because of high overall correlations, even a loading cut off as high as .6 may be insufficient to differentiate appropriately between groups with overlapping membership. Rice and Richards (1985, p. 116) note that, whereas a sociogram represented within a Euclidian space may be insufficient to depict a subclique structure, factor analysis of relational data may produce the precise opposite of this dilemma, i.e., provide too much structure. Bock and Husain (1950) had to stop their analysis at 11 factors while explaining merely 67% of the variance in a network of directed links.

Blockmodelling Techniques

The term *block* is here conceived as a set of network nodes with similar, i.e., structurally equivalent, relations to nodes in other blocks. At the same time those nodes are identified within a particular area of the overall matrix of relations. Blockmodelling as a method is either similarity-based or linkage-based. Arabie, Boorman, and Levitt (1978) and Arabie and Boorman (1982) provide excellent introductions and overviews of this method. The conceptual and mathematical origins of this technique date as far back as 1899.

Farace and Mabee (1980) state that trait and activity data are more appropriate to be analyzed using blockmodelling than when trying to analyze sociometric data. More specifically, blockmodelling is an ideal technique when trying to analyze data with regard to network roles or role types. Breiger and Pattison (1978) argue that block structures maintain their stability over time, even though network membership may change, as roles, hierarchical structures, and other relational patterns tend to remain relatively stable over time in society.

Other researchers who have studied blockmodelling and used this technique in network analysis include: Arabie et al. (1978), Breiger (1976a, b), Breiger, Boorman, and Arabie (1975), Carrington and Heil (1981), Heil and White (1976), Sailer (1978), White (1974a, b), White and Breiger (1975), White and Sailer (1979).

The reader should note that there are a number of other network techniques and computer programs available that may deviate slightly from the above-discussed techniques. These are not discussed here, as many may be too specific and at times esoteric to be discussed for the purposes and overview provided in this chapter.

Multidimensional Scaling (MDS) Techniques

Nonmetric as well as *metric scaling techniques* have been applied to the analysis of relational data. One of the underlying assumptions of metric MDS is high measurement reliability. Nonmetric MDS requires that the data support Euclidian distances. If the researcher uses nonmetric MDS techniques on non-Euclidian data, such data may be transformed into approximate metric values, but this should only be done if the data are highly reliable. But even if the researcher has highly reliable data and uses nonmetric MDS, this results in the introduction of some error in the results (cf. Woelfel & Danes, 1980). Carroll and Arabie (1980) discuss the types of data acceptable for numerous MDS programs.

Both nonmetric and metric multidimensional scaling techniques require as input a matrix of proximities or distances—typically, a correlation matrix. Roistacher (1974) states that, in nonmetric scaling, only the row-wise rank orders of the values in the matrix are used for the analysis. Rank orders of proximity are generated after an iterative trial-and-error procedure. The results obtained from this procedure are configurations of a set of points in a space of unknown metric and dimension. This set of points is then given an analog set of points in a Euclidian space of given dimensionality. Once this space has been generated, several clustering techniques may be utilized. A detailed description of the entire procedure can be found with Green and Rao (1972), Shephard, Romney and Nerlove (1972), as well as Green and Carmone (1970).

Newcomb's (1961) preference data were converted into a geometric representation by Gleason (1969) via a nonmetric scaling program. The resulting points were then analyzed by a hierarchical clustering technique which generated groups.

The metric MDS computer program GALILEO deserves to be emphasized here, as it has been used by many communication researchers. GALILEO's theoretical foundations are described by Woelfel and Danes (1980). In accordance with metric MDS criteria, GALILEO assumes that sociometric data represent non-Euclidian distances or relationships. GALILEO works with Reimann spaces (cf. Barnett & Rice, 1985) to describe network structure, and the program can analyze up to 45 nodes. Users of GALILEO state that this computer program preserves and analyzes more information contained in the data than many other MDS programs. Three-way dimensional analysis is possible, and, in some, research time intervals were used as the third dimension, making this program a useful analytical tool for longitudinal (up to 25 time periods have been analyzed) non-Euclidian network studies (cf., e.g., Barnett & Palmer, 1983; Barnett & Rice, 1985; Rice & Barnett, 1985). Rice (1981) provides a detailed review and lengthy bibliography of longitudinal network analyses.

Goldstein, Blackman, and Collins (1966) look at sociometric measures as indicators of distance among group members. The study compares multidimensional scaling methods with sociometric measures, and, while there is some overlap, multidimensional scaling appears to offer a promising approach to the relationship among group members.

Other researchers who have used multidimensional scaling in network analysis include Bloombaum (1970), Carroll (1973), Carroll and Arabie (1980), Gillham and Woelfel (1977), Goldstein et al. (1966), Green and Rao (1972), Guttman (1968), Kruskal (1964a and b, 1969), Kruskal and Wish (1978), Lingoes (1973), Norton (1980), Shephard (1972), Woelfel and Danes (1980), and others. The interested reader may especially look at the work by Carroll and Arabie (1980), Green and Rao (1972) and Kruskal and Wish (1978) for comprehensive reviews and critiques of this technique. It appears that the currently most popular nonmetric MDS computer program is MAPCLUS, developed by Arabie and Carroll (1980, 1983). GALILEO—the metric MDS computer program—developed by Woelfel, Barnett, and others initially at Michigan State University, has enjoyed considerable attention by network researchers in the field of communication.

Cluster Analysis

Various clustering techniques appear to be amenable for the analysis of relational data. Cluster analysis is based on the concept of similarities, and, in this particular application, analyzes the similarities among network members. The "distances" measured here are then really (dis)similarities, closeness, etc. The group definition criterion here is then dependent on a function of the procedures used to generate the distance matrix and the cut off point utilized (Arabie, 1977; Arabie & Carroll, 1983; Arabie et al., 1978; Carrington & Heil,

1981; Davies & Bouldin, 1979; McPhee & Poole, 1979). Clustering techniques can be characterized by the sorting of patterns by use of multiple cluster points. The initial recognized patterns are tentatively accepted as clusters, but are improved until the means of the clusters adequately describe the data. Cluster analysis basically differs in the techniques that are used to find the *best* description for the data. Bailey (1974) published an excellent discussion of cluster analysis methods. Other detailed discussions on this topic can be found with Ball (1965), Blashfield (1976), Cormack (1971), Hartigan (1975), Jardine and Sibson (1968), Krippendorff (1980), Kuiper and Fisher (1975), McPhee and Poole (1979), and Williams (1971). Additional applications and specific methodological discussion the reader may want to review can be found with Arabie and Shephard (1973), Baker (1974), Breiger et al. (1975), Davis (1967, 1970), Delattre and Hansen (1980), Farace and Mabee (1980), Kuiper and Fisher (1975), and Salzinger (1982).

Tryon (1976) predicted group differences by cluster analysis procedures through his BC TRY computer system. He found three basic dimensions—conservatism, territoriality and exclusiveness—that allow for the prediction of demographic and attitudinal characteristics of neighborhoods of a metropolitan area.

Coleman (1970) describes a model and an associated computer program that cluster elements in a space of a predetermined number of dimensions. His model may also be used for multidimensional scaling analyses and for the construction of sociograms. The program takes as input data a set of "affinities" between elements, the inverse of which is considered as the psychological or sociological distance. The elements are then *jiggled* in a Euclidian n-space toward the point where the geometric distance is equal to the given psychological or sociological distance, as if a set of attracting and repulsing forces were acting upon each element from other elements. A method that is somewhat comparable to Coleman's scheme was developed by Gengerelli (1963).

Alba (1972) and Alba and Gutmann (1971) computerized a network analysis technique, SOCK, which consists of a set of routines for subsetting and clustering sociomatrices. This particular program reads in data in the form of relationships, and assigns each individual a unique identification number. SOCK allows for the decomposition of disconnected groups, which can then be analyzed individually. It also features routines for assessing measures of proximity and pairwise association. Typically, the user then applies Johnson's (1967) hierarchical clustering algorithm for linkage analyses. If proximity matrices have been generated within SOCK, Kruskal's (1964a, b) MDSCAL is incorporated into SOCK to analyze the distances.

Alba's (n.d.) COMPTL program can be used to analyze network data or to cluster a symmetric matrix of similarities. COMPTL uses Bierstone's algorithm that was computerized by Auguston and Minker (1970). Roistacher (1974) emphasizes that Mulligan and Corneil (1972) showed that Auguston and Minker's (1970) algorithm was incorrect, and that Purdy (1973) developed an algorithm for finding the groups of a graph that is twice as fast and also presented a formal proof that his algorithm is correct. Both programs, SOCK and COMPTL, show severe limitations with respect to the viual interpretability of the two-dimensional sociometric output as suggested earlier. These programs provide several indicators of proximity, goodness-of-fit solutions, and various statistical measures of network structure. Arabie and Carroll (1980, 1983) developed MAPCLUS, a computer program that allows overlapping clusters and yields a measure of goodness-of-fit, i.e., variance explained, of the solution. The user can specify the number of resultant subsets, but a size limitation for a 30 × 30 input matrix must be considered by the user.

An Application and Example of Network Analysis Using NEGOPY

It was indicated earlier that Richards (1972) developed an algorithm that bypasses the analysis of relational data by using a matrix format. This, obviously, has the advantage that the size of a matrix is no longer a constraint for the analyst. Richard's (1975) NEGOPY program is particularly useful for the analysis of large networks. It has been used extensively in the field by many communication scholars, and NEGOPY is widely available at many universities in North America and Western Europe. Although details of the algorithm are not discussed here, what will follow is a brief discussion of some of the key features inherent in this particular computerized program, and how one can utilize this technique in order to analyze communication relationships within an organization. Furthermore, the example will demonstrate how network analysis results can be superimposed onto the organization chart in order to make recommendations for structural changes within the organization under study.

The unique characteristic of NEGOPY is the method by which groups are formed. The method first considers the entire pattern of relationships among individuals before a decision is made about what constitutes a group (clique or cluster). This implies that if persons in the network leave, or if studies of the same network are conducted over several points in time, different groups are likely to be detected. The network analysis technique, then, divides the system into parts only after descriptive data are obtained such that this method of analysis can be regarded as reflecting more adequately emergent properties of a system than methods which merely impose a structure before the analysis begins. A priori decisions with regard to the partitioning of a system are inappropriate. It becomes quickly apparent that, in the case of communication, for example, all communication relationships to be analyzed in the system must be considered before a division into parts can be taken into account that is appropriate to that system. All individuals that interact in a system must be considered in order to describe — and definitely not to prescribe — the communication structure which is present.

The above suggested procedure has been translated into the form of a computerized algorithm (Richards, 1971) using many concepts drawn from matrix analysis (Jacobson & Seashore, 1951; Weiss, 1956), and graph theory (Festinger, 1949; Harary et al., 1965; Flament, 1963). The present program entitled NEGOPY is capable of the efficient analysis of the relationships within systems of up to 4,096 members and up to 80,000 links, due to its linked-list data structures rather than full-matrix representations of the data. Lesniak, Yates, Goldhaber, and Richards (1977) developed various plotter routines in conjunction with NEGOPY allowing for the graphical depiction of network analytical results.

Measurement and Data Representation

Network analysis allows the researcher to identify the communication structure of a social system (e.g., company, school, classroom, village, "invisible colleges"). The analysis is started by building the existing structure with the smallest units of analysis that constitute the input data. The smallest units of analysis are relationships or interactions or links. It is essential that these relationships within a social system are found and recorded. These relationships can take on various forms of interaction, such as in face-to-face communication, telephone calls, communication via memoranda, letters, etc. The more interaction exists between two members of a social system, the stronger is the communication link.* The overall communication structure of the system is determined by the recognized patterns of these communication links and their relative strengths.

The detected properties of each network provide certain insights into the way in which communication flows within a social system. In order to find the communication links from these properties, a network analysis data gathering instrument is administered to all or a representative (cf. Coleman, 1972) set of members of the social system to be analyzed. This instrument is used to determine, among other areas of interest to the researcher, the existence and strength of links (and, consequently, the lack thereof) between members of a social system. Each instrument minimally anticipates five basic requirements:

(1) a definition of the social system.
(2) a definition of the network type to be investigated,
(3) the identification of the respondent,
(4) the identification of the respondent's contact(s) or contactee(s),
(5) determining the frequency and strength of the link between the respondent and his or her contact(s).

A sample data-gathering instrument is attached in the appendix, from which all information can be transferred onto computer records. Generally, the data are sequenced as follows: respondent identification (ID) number, the ID number of the respondent's first contact, the value for the frequency of that communication link, the value for the communication strength of that link, the ID number of the respondent's second contact, etc., continuing until all of the respondent's contacts have been recorded. Typically, the following format is used:

Columns:

1-2	Project identification code
3-5	Respondent's ID number
6-8	First contact ID number
9	Link value (frequency) for first network
10	Link value (importance) for first network
11	Link value (frequency) for second network (if needed)
12	Link value (importance) for second network (if needed)
.	
.	
n_1-n_3	Second contact ID number
n_4	Link value (frequency) for first network
n_5	Link value (importance) for first network
.	
.	
etc.	etc.

---

* It should be noted, however, that the informal strength of dyadic communication relationships is inversely related to the degree of homophily and the strength of the attraction between the source and the receiver. This phenomenon has been described as "the strength of weak ties" (Granovetter, 1973; Liu & Duff, 1972).

There are a few considerations that need to be kept in mind when considering data that become input for network analysis. First, it should be noted that a link is not necessarily to be understood like a relationship with all its characteristics. A link is merely an indicator of the existence of a relationship, obtained through the process of measurement.

Secondly, the properties of the type of relationship under consideration should be mirrored in the data; the data themselves do not constitute the properties or relationships.

Thirdly, the data can only be isomorphic to the real world to the extent to which the measurement process is precise, accurate, and representative.

NEGOPY has two primary goals: (a) to produce the typological description of the network under investigation (more specifically, a list of the groups within the system and a description of the roles of all the individual members within the system), and (b) to calculate a number of statistics descriptive of several parts of the system at various levels of analysis.

With regard to the desired structural aspects to be detected from the system, the following set of definitions and criteria emerged:

I. *Nonparticipant nodes* are either not connected to the rest of the network or are only minimally connected. They include:
   1. *Isolates type one*, nodes that have no links and are truly isolated within the network.
   2. *Isolates type two*, nodes which have merely one link.
   3. *Isolated dyads*, nodes with a single link between themselves.
   4. *Treenodes*, nodes that have a single link to a participant and have some number of other isolate attached to themselves.
II. *Participants* are nodes that have two or more links to other participant nodes. Usually, this type of node makes up for the majority of network elements and thus allows for the development of communication structure. They include:
   1. *Group members*, nodes with more than some percentage of their linkage with other members of the same group. This percentage is hereafter referred to as α-criterion.
   2. *Liaison nodes* fail to meet the α-criterion with members of any group within the network, and they have the majority of interactions with members of groups, but not with members of any single group.
   3. *Type other*, nodes which fail to meet the α-criterion as well as the classification of the liaison and group member role.
III. For the *recognition of a group*, the following five criteria must be met:
   1. There must be at least three members.
   2. Each must meet the α-criterion with the other members of this group.
   3. There must be some path lying entirely within the group, from each member to each other member (connectiveness criterion).
   4. There may be no single node (or arbitrarily small set of nodes) which, when removed from the group, causes the rest of the group to fail to meet any of the above criteria (the critical node criterion).
   5. There must be no single link (or subset of links) which, if cut, causes the group to fail to meet any of the above criteria (the critical link criterion).

The classification of the members of the system in terms of these specifications is achieved through two major steps. First, an approximate solution is generated through the use of a pattern-recognition algorithm to the results of an iterative operation. This operation treats each link or relationship existing between two nodes similar to a vector. Vectors have two basic attributes: direction and magnitude. The *direction* of each vector is understood as a nominal variable specifying to whom the link goes. The *magnitude* is a particular amount of an attribute (e.g., attraction) i.e., the extent to which the behavior of the two nodes is influenced due to this relationship. Other measures of *magnitude* can be operationalized as the amounts of such attributes as importance, intensity, etc. The tentative solution that is generated through the above described algorithm is only an approximate description of the system's structure.

An exact solution is generated after the above specified criteria are applied to the approximate solution. Similar to the process described in the first stage, several heuristic devices are applied such that the efficiency of the algorithm can be maximized.

Once communication networks have been analyzed according to the above described criteria (cf. Figure 6), it is then possible to represent this network with a focal emphasis on groups (cf. Figure 7), on liaisons (cf. Figure 8), and other network roles. In addition, these detected network roles can be utilized in the form of an overlay onto the formally designed, hierarchical structure of a system, e.g., a company (cf. Figure 6 with Figure 9). This comparison between the actual communication structure and the designed hierarchical structure may then be utilized as a rather powerful and heuristic method in redesigning a social system — in this case, a company (cf. Monge & Lindzey, 1974; also Wigand, 1974a, 1976b; Farace & Wigand, 1975). This method, generally, relies on more precise data than most other known techniques in the many and highly popular, but frequently dubious, forms of organization development. Many of these popular techniques have not been tested for their

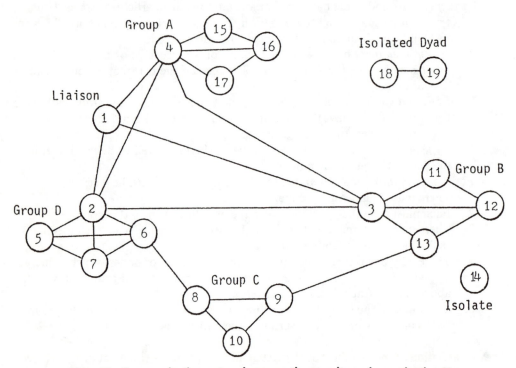

Figure 6. Communication network among the members of organization X.

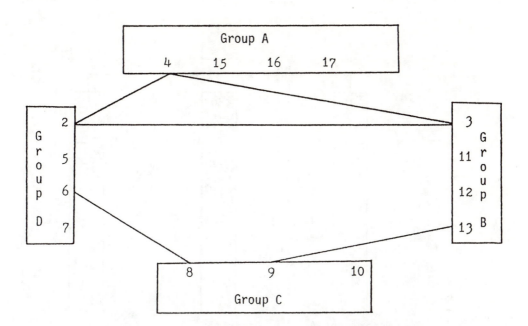

Figure 7. Communication links among the four communication groups in the network of organization X.

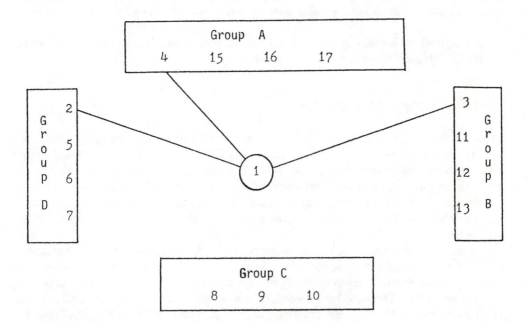

Figure 8. Liaison linkages among the four communication groups in the network of organization X.

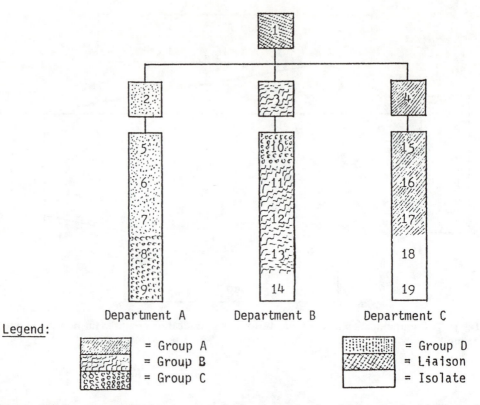

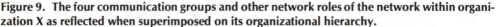

Figure 9. The four communication groups and other network roles of the network within organization X as reflected when superimposed on its organizational hierarchy.

effectiveness; there is a lack of longitudinal studies, and some of them do not take into account the multidimensionality of social behavior.

THE DERIVATION OF INDICES

With any processing of data, one realizes an irreversible loss of information. As described earlier, the generation of active and passive relations sums from the structural matrix means also that the information of who initiates a contact (relationship) with whom, and who is the recipient of a contact from whom, is lost. If positive and negative relations are interpreted algebraically, one obviously will find that each negative relation equalizes a positive relation. If one forms indices about these relationships, one will realize a further information loss.

It is, therefore, each time the researcher's judgment that justifies the usage or derivation of a particular index in the context and the nature of his or her data set and analysis goal. Many indices have been developed over the last 40 years in the network literature (cf., e.g., Barnes, 1969a; Davis, 1977; Edwards & Monge, 1977; Eisenberg et al., 1985; Felling, 1975; Freeman, 1978, 1979; Horan, 1975; Hubert & Baker, 1978; Jablin, 1980; Katz & Powell, 1960; Lin, 1976; Luce, 1950; Moch, Feather, & Fitzgibbons, 1980; Mouton, Blake, & Fruchter, 1960; Phillips & Conviser, 1972; Rogers & Kincaid, 1981; Tichy, Tushman, & Fombran, 1979).

Considerable overlap and different operationalizations exist many times of the very same construct or concept expressed in the form of an index. Freeman (1979), Freeman, Roeder and Mulholland (1980), Friedkin (1981), and others have made comparisons of the results of the *same* measure or index, and have investigated the measure's validity across indices.

Available space here does not permit to review the numerous indices discussed in the literature in detail. Such measures and indices can be grouped into categories, and are described in partial accordance with Rice and Richards (1985, pp. 113–115) below:

1. Proximity Measures. These measures have transformed the description of relationships into matrices of similarities or distances. Researchers have used correlations, scaling techniques, and structural equivalence to get at proximity measures.

2. Measures of Connectivity (Density) and Connectedness. This measure is typically expressed in the form of a ratio, specifically a comparison of the degree to which members of a network or clique are actually connected (observed measure) among each other, with the total number of maximally possible connections within the network or clique.

3. Measures of Integrativeness. The integrativeness of an individual measures the degree to which people linked with that individual are connected among each other. Similarly, group intergrativeness—sometimes called openness—measures the degree to which group members are linked with outside groups (e.g., Freeman, 1980).

4. Measures of Structure. Numerous researchers have defined structure as organization or deviation from randomness or deviation from some criterion, and, accordingly, some have developed precise measures to determine the degree to which networks or groups deviate from a given random model. Based upon expected dyad- or triad-type frequencies, group and system entropy, shared linkages, and similar measures, the results of structural measures indicate that the larger the deviation, the more highly structured, differentiated, ordered, or organized is the network under study (e.g., Holland & Leinhardt, 1973; Killworth, 1974; Richards, 1974).

5. Group Connectedness. A measure that indicates the number of connections or density among the members of a group is labeled *connectedness*. If a group has a large number of within-group links, it is said to be highly connected; if it has only a few within-group links, it is said to be loosely connected. If every node within a group were connected with each other, then the group connectedness would be 100%. Obviously, this measure is dependent on the group size, since members of large groups have to communicate an unusually high amount in order to communicate with everyone else. One must, therefore, use this measure with care, so that it does not lose its meaningfulness. As already suggested, this measure can be expressed as a percentage; it is also possible to derive a ratio measure through the use of graph-theoretic applications:

$$C_g = \frac{2 \sum_{i=1}^{N} L_i}{\sum_{i=1}^{N} Nd_i \left(\sum_{i=1}^{N} Nd_i - 1 \right)}$$

Where C_g stands for connectedness of Group G,
L stands for an actual within-group link
Nd stands for a node in the group

The magnitude of C_g may range from 0.0 to 1.0.

6. Integrativeness Index. The term *integration* or *integrativeness* has been operationalized in various forms (cf. Richards, 1975; Guimaraes, 1972; Hofstätter, 1963; Nehnevajsa, 1955; Criswell, 1947; and others). In the context of this chapter, an index of integrativeness is developed that is analogous to the earlier-introduced geometrical representation of relationships in a Euclidian space. Individual integration, I, of a member A into his or her relevant system or group is equal to the region, R, below the vector of individual A, as measured and compared to the maximally possible area (cf. with Figure 2). The size of the maximal area is dependent upon the size of the system, N, and is dependent upon the number of possible choices or relations.

The individual integrativeness for person A is

$$I_A = \frac{\left(\sum_{j=1}^{N} a_{Aj}\right) \times \left(\sum_{i=1}^{N} a_{iA}\right)}{(N-1)^2}$$

This expression can be rewritten in simpler form as:

$$I_A = \frac{PR_A \times AR_A}{(N-1)^2} \, ,$$

where PR_A (= the sum of all passive relations of individual A) replaces $\sum_{j=1}^{N} a_{Aj}$, and where

AR_A (= the sum of all active relations of individual A) substitutes $\sum_{i=1}^{N} a_{iA}$.

A system integrativeness index SI is defined as the arithmetic mean of the integrativeness scores of all system members:

$$SI = \frac{\sum_{i=1}^{N} I_i}{N}$$

Individual as well as system integrativeness are comparable measures, and range from -1 to $+1$, or $-1 \leq I \leq +1$. This index of integrativeness is based on the theoretical assumption that a system or group is maximally integrated when all possible symmetrical relations appear with the same positive number for both the active and passive dimensions. One may then state that the system is, with regard to the notion of integrativeness, in balance.

7. Index of Flexibility. In terms of flexibility*, when considering the relationships expressed in a structural matrix, one easily will conceive that the most restrictive network structure is the cyclic network. Consequently, it follows that the highly decentralized network is the least restrictive structure with respect to flexibility. These two extremes can be designated as either 1-flexible, for the decentralized network, or 0-flexible, for the cyclical network.

A network with N nodes $\sum_{i=1}^{N} nd_i$ is defined as having a minimum of links (L_{min}) when $L_{min} = nd$, where $nd = 1$. A maximum of links (L_{max}) exists when

$$L_{max} = \frac{\sum_{i=1}^{N} nd_i \left(\sum_{i=1}^{N} nd_i - 1 \right)}{2}, \text{ where } nd_i > 1.$$

Obviously, by definition, access must be provided to each node and each node must be accessible to any other node within the network. The following index allows for the assessment of the degree of flexibility (f) of networks with N nodes (nd) and with N links (L) from nd_i to nd_j:

$$f\text{-flexibility} = \frac{\sum_{k=1}^{N} L_k - \sum_{k=1}^{N} nd_k}{\sum_{k=1}^{N} nd_k \left(\sum_{k=1}^{N} nd_k - 2 \right)},$$

where $\sum_{k=1}^{N} L_k$ represents the sum of all links** (bi-directionality counts as two links),

---

* Note here the distinction from *accessibility* (Wigand, 1974a). A network is defined as being *a*-accessible where *a* indicates the minimum number of referrals necessary to enable complete accessibility, i.e., every node has access to every other node. Generally, accessibility is determined by raising a structural matrix to a given power, i.e., the power to which a matrix is raised allows for the precise identification of the number of steps necessary to reach any individual in that matrix equal to the raised power. Specifically, accessibility is defined by the matrix entry $(m_{ij})^N$ which gives the number of choices for access involving individual node, nd_i:

$$a\text{-accessible} = \sum_{j=1}^{N} (m_{ij})^N, \quad \text{where } (m_{ij})^N \text{ specifies the number of cycles of referrals in a matrix from } nd_i \text{ to } n_j \text{ via n-many steps or sequences.}$$

For example, the value $(m_{A31})^2 = 2$ indicates that in matrix $(M_A)^2$ — derived from graph A in Figure 5 — there are 2 sequences of length 2 in graph A from node 3 to node 1, namely, node 3, node 2, node 1 and node 3, node 4, node 1.

** The term link (L) is here defined as being merely unidirectional; thus; only existing in the direction of nd_1 to nd_2, or, nd_2 to nd_1, but not both or constituting a reciprocal relationship. If a recirpocal relationship exists between two nodes, the value for L then equals 2.

and where $\sum\limits_{k=1}^{N} nd_k$ represents the sum of all nodes in the network.

The above formula for flexibility meets the initial considerations of determining the cyclic network as 0-flexible, and determining the decentralized network as 1-flexible. Figure 10 shall explicate the flexibility index.

It follows that the flexibility index is calculated:

$$f = \frac{9 - 5}{5\,(5 - 2)}$$

$$= \frac{4}{15}$$

$$= .267\text{-flexible with five nodes}$$

Other Measures. Various other measures with regard to distance, dominance, centrality, etc. are available, but are not presented here due to space limitations.

A set of dispersion metrics has been developed that demonstrates the extent to which units vary in the degree to which they show some property: the variance in the number of links each node has, the variance in the entries of a given row or column of a distance matrix for a subset of the network, etc. Among the dispersion metrics also included are information-theoretic measures, since they refer to the extent to which relative frequencies of occurrence vary from event to event within the set of all possible events (e.g., uncertainty measures, etc.).

Much of the above-discussed measures can be readily represented by the analyst in "communicator's profiles" for each individual network member. Typically, such a "communicator's profile" gives information about the individual's network type, his or her network role, membership in a specific group, information about his or her links (e.g., total number, within-group, to- or from-group bridges and liaisons, reciprocated and unreciprocated), the percentage of individual connectedness, his or her percentage contribution to group liaison linkage, as well as his or her percentage contribution to between-group linkage, and others.

The calculation of any index in network analyses deserves, obviously, to be modified when certain conditions exist (e.g., the meaningfulness of a connectedness score when the N of a group is excessively large, etc.). Furthermore, it is important to relate the interpretation of an index to concrete network questions that typically describe an individual or group characteristic in a given situation.

$$M_G = \begin{Bmatrix} 0 & 0 & 1 & 1 & 0 \\ 1 & 0 & 1 & 0 & 1 \\ 0 & 1 & 0 & 0 & 1 \\ 1 & 0 & 0 & 0 & 1 \\ 0 & 0 & 0 & 0 & 0 \end{Bmatrix}$$

Network G   Adjacency matrix M_G of network G

Figure 10. A network with its adjacency matrix.

SOME ISSUES OF VALIDITY AND RELIABILITY

A number of studies concerned with the practice of measurement in the light of validity and reliability have been reported (Petersen, Komorita, & Quay, 1964; Davis & Warnath, 1957; Mouton, Blake, & Fruchter, 1955a, b; Byrd, 1951; and others). There are few studies that address themselves to test-theoretical problems. The few authors who concern themselves with this topic (e.g., Lindzey & Borgatta, 1954; Criswell, 1949; Harmon, 1949; Pepinsky, 1949) show a rather skeptical outlook toward the value of a testable theory for networks. They doubt that a scheme for testing this theory, which initially was developed by psychometrists, is readily amenable for network issues. Some even go as far as considering such tests as unnecessary and superfluous.

Specifically, Lindzey and Borgatta (1954) argue, with regard to reliability, that the user of network measures has to be content with possible constant changes among his variables. They point out that this is due to a peculiar artifact of network analyses, the relations between individuals, and their relative instability.

Criswell (1949) doubts that it would be correct to compare network techniques to tests in the common sense. He argues that network analysis is an elemental research technique and there would be no need for reliability and validity. Criswell (1949, p. 140) emphasizes that, with every network and sociometric choice made by a subject, the interpersonal relationship as well as the group activity enter as factors in the particular choice made by the subject. It has been demonstrated that a sociometric choice has social consequences. Moreno (1954) recognizes such consequences during the measurement process, describes them as essential parts of any sociometric procedure, and justifies them by stating that they only insure the seriousness of the choice and also insure the validity of the procedure. It should be noted that in not all network-analytic procedures the respondent is to make a social *choice*, i.e., there are not necessarily social consequences at stake.

Harmon (1949) argues somewhat differently. Test-theoretical issues become important and necessary when, through the use of sampling data, generalizations about a population need to be made. In such situations, justifications and parameters for the generalizations must be shown. Harmon believes that, in contrast to psychometry, network or sociometric tests do not need these requirements for generalizations, since, in network analysis, a sample is typically already identical to the population to be generalized. Consequently, possible sources of error that may affect the reliability are much more likely to be found with administrative and mechanical errors than those sources related to sampling.

A number of scholars developed highly particular mathematical tests that allow for the statistical comparison in specific situations. Each test is, to some extent, dependent upon which network choice procedure was used, whether or not the number of possible choices was limited, whether ranking procedures were used, and other considerations. Katz and Powell (1953) suggest their index of concordance to test the similarity between two matrices through a ϕ-coefficient. Using this test, one observers the corresponding cell entries of matrices A and B, which, for example, may contain the values 0 or 1. One then counts the numbers of pairs which contain 2 zeroes and 2 ones, the number of pairs with a 1 in A and a 0 in B and those with a 0 in A and a 1 in B. The results can be represented in a scheme as follows (cf. Table 1):

Katz and Powell (1960) calculate the ϕ-coefficient as follows:

$$\phi = \frac{n_{11} \times n_{00} - n_{10} \times n_{01}}{\sqrt{n_{.0} \times n_{.1} \times n_{0.} \times n_{1.}}} \, .$$

Table 1

		B		sum
		0	1	
A	0	n_{00}	n_{01}	$n_{0.}$
	1	n_{10}	n_{11}	$n_{1.}$
sum		$n_{.0}$	$n_{.1}$	$n(n-1)$

Under the assumption that both matrices are independent from each other, a χ^2-test can be utilized to ascertain the degree of difference.

If the assumption of independence between matrices is warranted and when several matrices are to be compared among each other, one then can utilize procedures to determine the internal consistency. One can create a total test value by simply adding the matrices (weighted and unweighted) that are to be compared. The various matrices are then analogous to items in psychometric tests (Lindzey & Borgatta, 1954).

Mouton, Blake, and Fruchter (1955a, b) present results of their investigations with regard to reliability and validity of sociometric tests. For a more detailed overview, the reader is referred to Lindzey and Byrne (1968), Bernard, Killworth and Sailer (1980), Killworth and Bernard (1979), Killworth and Bernard (1976), as well as Bernard and Killworth (1977).

By far the majority of investigations are concerned with the issue of stability within network structures. Of these particular studies, the majority are concerned with sociometric status; only a few compare the entire sociomatrix (cf. Lindzey & Byrne, 1968, p. 478; Scandrette, 1951; Horrocks & Thompson, 1946; Northway, 1943).

SUMMARY AND CONCLUSION

This chapter attempted to trace and demonstrate various methodological approaches to recognize patterns in social relationships. Several definitions are presented for key terms such as relationship and group. Leading cluster-seeking techniques for relational data are reviewed, and their key features are described and compared. Indices for integrativeness and flexibility are presented. An effort is made to take a uniform approach in synthesizing the various techniques and methods, and to demonstrate their relative contribution toward the joint goal of generating some sort of group, cluster, or clique among relational data.

A number of problem areas remain unresolved by researchers in the field of network analysis. It seems that there are those researchers making the assumption that almost any kind of arithmetic treatment may be undertaken with network data; then there are those researchers who will not allow further assumptions than those acceptable by a weak order relation on the data.

Lastly, it appears to be very fruitful if social scientists from various areas would use the same vocabulary with respect to networks. Frequently, researchers in sociology, psychology, computer science, geography, anthropology, economics, communication, and mathematics seem to be concerned with the same, or at least highly similar, issues (cf. e.g., Cummings, Manly, & Weinand, 1973) of network analysis, and considerably more cooperation in terms of the exchange of knowledge, developments, etc. could occur.

REFERENCES

Alba, R. D. (1972). A graph-theoretic definition of a sociometric clique. *Journal of Mathematical Sociology, 3,* 113–126.

Alba, R. D. (1973). A graph-theoretic definition of a sociometric clique. *Journal of Mathematical Sociology, 3,* 113–126.

Alba, R. D. (n.d.) *COMPTL: A program for analyzing sociometric data and clustering similarity matrices* (mimeo). New York: Columbia University, Bureau of Applied Social Research.

Alba, R. D., & Gutman, M P. (1971). *SOCK: A sociometric analysis system* (mimeo). New York: Columbia University, Bureau of Applied Social Research.

Alba, R. D., & Gutman, M. P. (1974). *SOCK: A sociometric analysis system.* New York: Columbia University, Bureau of Applied Research.

Alt, J. E., & Schofield, N. (1975). CLIQUE: A suite of programs for extracting cliques from a symmetric graph. *Behavioral Science, 20,* 134–135.

Arabie, P. (1977). Clustering representations of group overlap. *Journal of Mathematical Sociology, 5,* 113–128.

Arabie, P., & Boorman, S. A. (1982). Blockmodels: Developments and prospects. In H. Hudson (Ed.), *Classifying social data* (pp. 177–198). San Francisco, CA: Jossey-Bass.

Arabie, P., Boorman, S. A., & Levitt, P. R. (1978). Constructing blockmodels: How and why. *Journal of Mathematical Psychology, 17,* 21–63.

Arabie, P., & Carroll, J. D. (1980). MAPCLUS: A mathematical programming approach to fitting the ADCLUS model. *Psychometrika, 45,* 211–235.

Arabie, P., & Carroll, J. D. (1983). Conceptions of overlap in social structure. In L. Freeman, A. K. Romney, & D. R. White (Eds.), *Methods of social network analysis.* Berkeley, CA: University of California Press.

Arabie, P., & Shephard, R. N. (1973). Representation of similarities as additive combinations of discrete, overlapping properties. Paper presented to the Mathematical Psychology Meetings, Montreal (month unknown).

Atkin, R. H. (1974). *Mathematical structure in human affairs.* New York: Crane, Rusak.

Augustson, J. G., & Minker, J. (1970). *An analysis of some graph-theoretical cluster techniques.* College Park, MD: University of Maryland, Computer Science Center, TR-70-106.

Bailey, K. D. (1974). Cluster analysis. In D. R. Heise (Ed.), *Sociological methodology 1975.* San Francisco, CA: Jossey-Bass, 59–128.

Bain, R. (1943). Sociometry and social measurement. *Sociometry, 6,* 206–213.

Baker, F. B. (1974). Stability of two hierarchical grouping techniques, case I: Sensitivity to data errors. *Journal of the American Statistical Association, 69,* 440–445.

Bales, B. F. (1950). *Interaction process analysis: A method for the study of small groups.* Reading, MA: Addison-Wesley.

Ball, G. H. (1965). Data analysis in the social sciences: what about the details? In *American Federation of Information Processing Societies conference proceedings, fall joint computer conference, Part 1, 27,* (pp. 533–559).

Barnard, C. I. (1938). *The functions of the executive.* Cambridge, MA: Harvard University Press.

Barnes, J. A. (1969a). Graph theory and social networks: A technical comment on connectedness and connectivity. *Sociology, 3,* 215–232.

Barnes, J. A. (1969b). Networks and political process. In J. C. Mitchell (Ed.), *Social networks in urban situations.* Manchester, England: Manchester University Press.

Barnett, G. A., & Palmer, M. T. (1983). Longitudinal network analysis using multidimensional scaling. Paper presented to the International Communication Association, Dallas, TX.

Barnett, G. A., & Rice, R. E. (1985). Longitudinal non-Euclidian networks: Applying Galileo. *Social Networks, 7,* 287–322.

Bastin, G. (1967). *Die soziometrischen Methoden.* Bern, Switzerland/Stuttgart, Germany: Huber.

Bavelas, A. (1948). A mathematical model for group structures. *Applied Anthropology, 7,* 16–30.

Bavelas, A. (1950). Communication patterns in task-oriented groups. *Journal of the Acoustical Society of America, 57,* 271–282.

Beaton, A. E. (1966). An interbattery factor analytic approach to clique analysis. *Sociometry, 29,* 135–145.

Berge, C. (1967). *Théorie des graphes et ses applications.* Paris: Dunod.

Bernard, H. R., & Killworth, P. D. (1977). Informant accuracy in social network data II. *Human Communication Research 4*(1), pp. 3–18.

Bernard, H. R., Killworth, P. D., & Sailer, L. (1980). Informant accuracy in social network data IV: a comparison of clique-level structure in behavioral and cognitive network data. *Social Networks, 2*(3), 191–218.

Bertalanffy, L. von. (1940). Der Organismus als physikalisches System betrachtet. *Die Naturwissenschaften, 28,* 521–531.

Beum, C., Jr., & Brundage, E. (1950). A method for analyzing the sociomatrix. *Sociometry, 13,* 141–145.

Bishir, J. W., & Drewes, D. W. (1970). *Mathematics in the behavioral and social sciences.* New York: Harcourt, Brace & World.

Bjerstedt, A. (1956). *Interpretations of sociometric choice status.* Copenhagen, Denmark: Munksgaard.

Blashfield, R. K. (1976). Mixture model tests of cluster analysis: Accuracy of four agglomerative hierarchical methods. *Psychological Bulletin, 83,* 377–388.

Bloombaum, M. (1970). Doing smallest space analysis. *Journal of Conflict Resolution, 14,* 409–416.

Bock, R. D., & Husain, S. Z. (1950). An adaptation of Holzinger's B-coefficients for the analysis of sociometric data. *Sociometry, 13,* 146–153.

Bonacich, P. (1972). Factoring and weighting approaches to status scores and clique identification. *Journal of Mathematical Sociology, 2,* 113–120.

Borgatta, E. F. (1951). A Diagnostic note on the construction of sociograms and action diagrams. *Group Psychotherapy, 3,* 300–308.

Borgatta, E. F., & Stolz, W. (1963). A note on a computer program for rearrangement of matrices. *Sociometry, 26,* 391–392.

Breiger, R. L. (1976a). Community at the village level: A case of sparse networks. Unpublished paper, Harvard University, Department of Sociology.

Breiger, R. L. (1976b). Career attributes and network structure: A blockmodel study of a biomedical research specialty. *American Sociological Review, 41,* 117–135.

Breiger, R. L., Boorman, S. A., & Arabie, P. (1975). An algorithm for clustering relational data with applications to social network analysis and comparison with metric dimensional scaling. *Journal of Mathematical Psychology, 12,* 328–383.

Breiger, R. L., & Pattison, P. E. (1978). The joint role structure of two communities' elites. *Sociological Methods and Research, 7,* 213–226.

Buckley, W. (1967). *Sociology and modern systems theory.* Englewood Cliffs, NJ: Prentice-Hall.

Burton, R. (1970). KLICOR: A CDC 6400 program for finding subgraphs of sociometric nets. *Behavioral Science, 15,* 536.

Byrd, E. (1951). A study of validity and constancy of choices in a sociometric test. *Sociometry, 14,* 175–181.

Carrington, P. J., & Heil, G. H. (1981). COBLOC: A hierarchical method for blocking network data. *Journal of Mathematical Sociology, 8,* 103–132.

Carroll, J. D. (1973). Models and algorithms for multidimensional scaling, conjoint measurement and related techniques. In P. E. Green and Y. Wind (Eds.). *Attribute decisions in marketing.* Appendix B. New York: Holt, Rinehart, & Winston.

Carroll, J. D., & Arabie, P. (1980). Multidimensional scaling. *Annual Review of Psychology, 31,* 607–649.

Cartwright, D. P., & Harary, F. (1956). Structural balance: A generalization of Heider's theory. *Psychological Review, 63,* 277–292.

Cartwright, D. P., & Harary, F. (1968). On the coloring of signed graphs. *Elemente der Mathematik, 23,* 85–89.

Chabot, J. (1950). A simplified example of the use of matrix multiplication for the analysis of sociometric data. *Sociometry, 13,* 131–140.

Coleman, J. S. (1970). Clustering in dimensions by use of a system of forces. *Journal of Mathematical Sociology, 1,* 1–47.

Coleman, J. S. (1972). Relational analysis: A study of social organization with survey methods. In P. F. Lazarsfeld, A. K. Pasanella, & M. Rosenberg (Eds.), *Continuities in the language of social research* (pp. 258–286). New York: Free Press.

Coombs, C. H. (1964). *A theory of data.* New York: Wiley.

Cormack, R. M. (1971). A review of classification. *Journal of the Royal Statistical Society (A), 134,* 321–367.

Criswell, J. H. (1947). The measurement of group integration. *Sociometry, 10,* 259–267.

Criswell, J. H. (1949). Sociometric concepts in personnel administration. *Sociometry, 12,* 287–300.

Cummings, L. P., Manly, B. J., & Weinand, H. C. (1973). Das Messen von Assoziationen in Netzproblemen. *Geoforum, 13,* 43–51.

Davies, D. L, Bouldin, D. W. (1979). A cluster-separation technique. *IEEE Transactions on Pattern Analysis and Machine Intelligence PAMI-I, 1*(2) 224–227.

Davis, J. A. (1967). Clustering and structural balance in graphs. *Human Relations, 20,* 181–187.

Davis, J. A. (1970). Clustering and hierarchy in interpersonal relations: testing two graph theoretical models on 742 sociomatrices. *American Sociological Review, 35,* 841–851.

Davis, J. A. (1977). Sociometric triads as multi-variate systems. *Journal of Mathematical Sociology, 5,* 61–60.

Davis, J. A., and Leinhardt, S. (1972). The structure of positive interpersonal relations in small groups. In J. Berger, M. Zelditch, Jr., & B. Anderson (Eds.), *Sociological Theories in Progress* Vol. II. Boston: Houghton Mifflin, pp. 218–251.

Davis, J. A., & Warnath, C. F. (1957). Reliability, validity and stability of a sociometric rating scale. *Journal of Social Psychology, 45,* 111–121.

Delattre, M., & Hansen, P. (1980). Bicriterion cluster analysis. *IEEE Transactions on Pattern Analysis and Machine Intelligence PAMI-2,* pp. 277–291.

Doreian, P. (1981). Polyhedral dynamics and conflict mobilization in social networks. *Social Networks, 3,* 107–116.

Edwards, J. A., & Monge, P. R. (1977). The validation of mathematical indices of communication structure. *Communication Yearbook, 1,* 183–194.

Eisenberg, E. M., Farace, R. V., Monge, P. R., Bettinghaus, E. P., Kurchner-Hawkins, R., Miller, K. I., & Rothman, L. (1985). Communication linkages in interorganizational systems: Review and synthesis. *Progress in Communication Sciences, 6,* 236–261.

Farace, R. V., & Mabee, T. (1980). Communication network analysis methods. In P. R. Monge & J. N. Cappella (Eds.), *Multivariate techniques for human communication research* (pp. 365–392). New York: Academic Press.

Farace, R. V., Richards, W. D., Monge, P. R., & Jacobson, E. (1973). Analysis of human communication networks in large social systems. Unpublished paper. East Lansing, MI: Michigan State University.

Farace, R. V., & Wigand, R. T. (1975, April). *The communication industry in economic integration: The case of West Germany.* Paper presented to the International Communication Association convention (top four papers), Chicago, Illinois.

Feger, H., Hummel, H. J., Pappi, F. U., Sodeur, W., & Ziegler, R. (1978). *Bibliographie zum Projekt Analyse sozialer Netzwerke* (Report). Hamburg, Germany: Universität Hamburg.

Feger, H., Hummel, H. J., Pappi, F. U., Sodeur, W., & Ziegler, R. (1981). *Bibliographie: Forschungsprojekt Analyse Sozialer Netzwerke* (Report). Hamburg, Germany: Universität Hamburg.

Felling, A. J. A. (1975). A graph-theoretical approach to the structure of local elites. *Zeitschrift für*

Soziologie, 4, 221–233.

Felling, A. J. A., & van der Weegen, T. (1976). *Programmer's notes for main program NCLIQUE.* Nijmegen, The Netherlands: Mathematical Sociology and Research Technical Department, University of Nijmegen.

Festinger, L. (1949). The analysis of sociograms using matrix algebra. *Human Relations, 2,* 153–158.

Festinger, L, Schachter, S., & Back, K. (1950). *Social pressures in informal groups: A study of human factors in housing.* Palo Alto, CA: Stanford University Press.

Flament, C. (1963). *Applications of graph theory to group structure.* Englewood Cliffs, NJ: Prentice-Hall.

Forsyth, E., & Katz, L. (1946). A matrix approach to the analysis of sociometric data. *Sociometry, 9,* 340–347.

Foster, C. C., & Horvath, W. J. (1971). A study of a large sociogram III: Reciprocal choice probabilities as a measure of social distance. *Behavioral Science, 16,* 429–435.

Foster, C. C., Rapoport, A., & Orwant, C. J. (1963). A study of a large sociogram II: Elimination of free parameters. *Behavioral Science, 8,* 56–65.

Freeman, L. C. (1968). *Patterns of local community leadership.* Indianapolis, IN: Bobbs-Merrill.

Freeman, L. C. (1976). *A bibliography of social networks.* Monticello, IL: Council of Planning Librarians, Exchange Bibliography.

Freeman, L. C. (1978). On measuring systematic integration. *Connections, 2* (1), 13–14.

Freeman, L. C. (1979). Centrality in social networks: Conceptual clarification. *Social Networks, 1,* 215–239.

Freeman, L. C. (1980). Q-Analysis and the structure of friendship networks. *International Journal of Man-Machine Studies, 12,* 367–378.

Freeman, L. C., Roeder, D., & Mulholland, R. R. (1980). Centrality in social networks: II: experimental results. *Social Networks, 2,*(2) 119–141.

Friedkin, N. E. (1981). The development of structure in random networks: an analysis on the effects of increasing network density of five measures of structure. *Social Networks, 3,* 41–52.

Gengerelli, J. A. (1963). A method for detecting subgraphs in a population and specifying their membership. *Journal of Psychology, 55,* 457–468.

Gillham, J., & Woelfel, J. (1977). The Gallileo system of measurement: preliminary evidence for precision stability, and equivalence to traditional measures. *Human Communication Research 3*(3), 222–234.

Glanzer, M., & Glaser, R. (1959). Techniques for study of group structure and behavior: I. Analysis of structure. *Psychological Bulletin, 56,* 317–332.

Glanzer, M., & Glaser, R. (1961). Techniques for the study of group structure and behavior: II. Empirical studies of the effects of structure in small groups. *Psychological Bulletin, 58,* 1–27.

Gleason, T. C. (1969). *Multidimensional scaling of sociometric data.* Unpublished paper. Ann Arbor, MI: University of Michigan, Institute for Social Research.

Gleason, T. C. (1971). *DIP: A directed graph processor.* Ann Arbor, MI: University of Michigan, Institute for Social Research.

Goldstein, K. M., Blackman, S., & Collins, D. J. (1966). Relationship between sociometric and multidimensional scaling measures. *Perceptual and Motor Skills, 23,* 639–643.

Gould, P. (1980). Q-Analysis, or a language of structure: An introduction for social scientists, geographers and planners. *International Journal of Man-Machine Studies, 13,* 169–199.

Green, P. E., & Carmone, F. J. (1970). *Multidimensional scaling and related techniques in marketing analysis.* Boston, MA: Allyn & Bacon.

Green, P. E., & Rao, V. R. (1972). *Applied multidimensional scaling: A comparison of approaches and algorithms.* Hinsdale, IL: Dryden Press. *American federation of information processing societies conference proceedings, 43,* p. 71.

Guimaraes, L. (1968). *Matrix multiplication in the study of interpersonal communication.* Unpublished M.A. thesis. East Lansing, MI: Michigan State University, Department of Communication.

Guimaraes, L. (1972). *Communication integration in modern and traditional social systems: A comparative analysis across twenty communities of Minas Gerais, Brazil.* Unpublished doctoral dissertation. East Lansing, MI: Michigan State University, Department of Communication.

Guttman, L. (1968). A general nonmetric technique for finding the smallest coordinate space for a configuration of points. *Psychometrika, 33,* 469–508.

Harary, F. (1954). On the notion of balance of a signed graph. *Michigan Mathematical Journal, 2,* 143–146.

Harary, F. (1969). *Graph theory.* Reading, MA: Addison-Wesley.

Harary, F., Norman, R. Z., & Cartwright, D. (1965). *Structural models: An introduction to the theory of directed graphs.* New York, NY:Wiley.

Harary, F., & Ross, I. (1957). A procedure for clique detection using the group matrix. *Sociometry, 20,* 205–215.

Harmon, L. R. (1949). A note on Pepinsky's analysis of "validity" and "reliability" of sociometric data. *Educational Psychological Measurement, 9,* 747.

Hartigan, J. A. (1975). *Clustering techniques.* New York: Wiley.

Heider, F. (1946). Attitudes and cognitive organization. *Journal of Psychology, 21,* 107–112.

Heider, F. (1958). *The psychology of interpersonal relations.* New York: Wiley.

Heil, G. H., & White, H. C. (1976). An algorithm for finding simultaneous homomorphic correspondences between graphs and their image graphs. *Behavioral Science, 21,* 26–35.

Hofstätter, P.R. (1963). *Einführung in die Sozialpsychologie.* Stuttgart, Germany: Kroner.

Höhn, E., & Schick, C. P. (1964). *Das Soziogramm.* Göttingen, Germany: Hogrefe.

Holland, P. W., & Leinhart, S. (1970). A method for detecting structure in sociometric data. *American Journal of Sociology, 76,* 492–513.

Holland, P. W., & Leinhart, S. (1973). The structural implications of measurement error in sociometry. *Journal of Mathematical Sociology, 3,* 85–111.

Holzinger, K. J., & Harman, H. H. (1941). *Factor analysis.* Chicago, IL: University of Chicago Press.

Horan, P. M. (1975). Information-theoretic measures and the analysis of social structures. *Sociological Methods & Research, 3,*(3), 321–340.

Horrocks, H. E., & Thompson, G. C. (1946). A study of the friendship fluctuations of rural boys and girls. *Journal of Genetic Psychology, 69,* 189–198.

Hubert, L. J., & Baker, F. B. (1978). Evaluating the conformity of sociometric measurements. *Psychometrika, 43,* 31–41.

Jablin, F. M. (1980). Organization communication theory and research: An overview of communication climate and network research. In D. Nimmo (Ed.), *Communication Yearbook 4* (pp. 327–347). Beverly Hills, CA: Sage.

Jacobson, E. W., & Seashore, S. E. (1951). Communication practices in complex organizations. *Journal of Social Issues, 7,* 28–40.

Jardine, N., & Sibson, R. (1968). The construction of hierarchic and non-hierarchic classifications. *Computer Journal, 11,* 177–184.

Johnson, S. C. (1967). Hierarchical clustering schemes. *Psychometrika, 32,* 241–254.

Kadushin, C., & Tichy, N. (1972). Network analysis group. Unpublished manuscript. New York: Columbia University, Teachers College.

Katz, L. (1947). On the matrix analysis of sociometric data. *Sociometry, 10,* 233–241.

Katz, L., & Powell, J. H. (1953). A proposed index of the conformity of one sociometric measurement to another. *Psychometrika, 18,* 249–256.

Katz, L., & Powell, J. H. (1960). A proposed index of the conformity of one sociometric measurement to another. In J. L. Moreno (Ed.), *The sociometric reader* (pp. 298–306). Glencoe, IL: Free Press.

Killworth, P. D. (1974). Intransitivity in the structure of small closed groups. *Social Science Research, 3,* 1–23.

Killworth, P. D. & Bernard, H. R. (1974). CATIJ: A new sociometric and its application to a prison living unit. *Human Organization 33,* 335–350.

Killworth, P. D. & Bernard, H. R. (1976). Information accuracy in social network data. *Human Organization 35*(3), 269–286.

Killworth, P. D., & Bernard, H. R. (1979). Informant accuracy in social network data III: a comparison of triadic structure in behavioral and cognitive data. *Social Networks 2*(1), 19–46.

Klovdahl, A. S. (1979). *Social networks: Selected references for course design and research planning.* Monticello, IL: Vance Bibliographies.

König, D. (1936). *Theorie der endlichen und unendlichen Graphen (Kombinatorische Topologie der Streckenkomplexe).* Leipzig, Germany: Akademische Verlagsgesellschaft m. b. H.

Krippendorff, K. (1970). On generating data in communication research. *Journal of Communication, 20,* 241–269.

Krippendorff, K. (1971). *The "systems" approach to communication.* Paper presented to the American Association for the Advancement in Science, Philadelphia, PA.

Krippendorff, K. (1980). Clustering. In P. R. Monge & J. N. Cappella (Eds.), *Multivariate techniques for human communication research* (pp. 259–308). New York: Academic Press.

Kruskal, J. B. (1964a). Multidimensional scaling by optimizing goodness to fit to a nonmetric hypothesis. *Psychometrika, 29,* 1–27.

Kruskal, J. B. (1964b). Nonmetric multidimensional scaling: A numerical method. *Psychometrika, 29,* 115–130.

Kruskal, J. B. (1969). Nonmetric multidimensional scaling: A numerical method. *Psychometrika, 29,* 115–159.

Kruskal, J. B., & Wish, M. (1978). *Multidimensional scaling.* Beverly Hills, CA: Sage.

Kuiper, F. K., & Fisher, L. (1975). A Monte Carlo comparison of six clustering processes. *Biometrics, 31,* 777–783.

Leinhart, S. (1971). SOCPAC I: A FORTRAN IV program for structural analysis of sociometric data. *Behavioral Science, 16,* 515–516.

Lesniak, R., Yates, M. P., Goldhaber, G. M., & Richards, W. D., Jr. (1977). *NETPLOT: An original computer program for interpreting NEGOPY.* Paper presented to the International Communication Association, Berlin, Germany.

Lin, N. (1976). *Foundations of social research.* New York: McGraw-Hill.

Lindzey, G., & Borgatta, E. F. (1954). Sociometric measurement. In G. Lindzey (Ed.), *Handbook of social psychology,* (Vol. 1, pp. 405–448). Reading, MA: Addison-Wesley.

Lingoes, J. (1973). *The Guttman-Lingoes nonmetric program series.* Ann Arbor, MI: Mathesis Press.

Lorrain, F., & White, H. C. (1971). Structural equivalence of individuals in social networks. *Journal of Mathematical Sociology, 1,* 49–80.

Luce, R. D. (1950). Connectivity and generalized cliques in sociometric group structure. *Psychometrika, 15,* 169–1190.

Luce, R. D., & Perry, A. (1949). A method of matrix analysis of group structure. *Psychometrika, 14,* 94–116.

MacRae, D., Jr. (1960). Direct factor analysis for sociometric data. *Sociometry, 23,* 360–371.

Mayntz, R., Holm, K., & Huebner, P. (1971). *Einführung in die Methoden der empirischen Soziologie.* Köln/Opladen, Germany: Westdeutscher Verlag.

McPhee, R. D., & Poole, M. S. (1979). *Workshop on developmental methodology.* Urbana, IL: University of Illinois-Urbana.

Moch, M., Feather, J. N., & Fitzgibbons, D. (1980). Conceptualizing and measuring the relational structure in organizations. In S. E. Seashore (Ed.), *Assessing organizations: A guide to practice.* New York: Wiley Interscience.

Mokken, R. J. (1979). Cliques, clubs and clans. *Quality and Quantity, 13,* 161–173.

Monge, P. R., & Lindzey, G. N. (1974, April). *The study of communication networks and communication structure in large organizations.* Paper presented to the International Communication Association convention, New Orleans, Louisiana.

Moreno, J. L. (1934). *Who shall survive?* (Monograph No. 58). Washington, DC: Nervous and Mental Disease.

Moreno, J. L. (1946). Sociogram and sociomatrix. *Sociometry, 9,* 348–349.

Moreno, J. L. (1954). *Die Grundlagen der Soziometrie.* Köln/Opladen, Germany: Westdeutcher Verlag.

Mouton, J. S., Blake, R. R., & Fruchter, B. (1955a). The reliability of sociometric measures. *Sociometry, 18*(1), 7–48.

Mouton J. S., Blake, R. R., & Fruchter, B. (1955b). The validity of sociometric responses. *Sociometry, 18*(3), 181–214.

Mouton, J. S., Blake, R. R., & Fruchter, B. (1960). The reliability of sociometric measures. In J. L. Moreno (Ed.), *The sociometric reader* (pp. 320–361). Glencoe, IL: Free Press.

Mulligan, G. D., & Corneil, D. G. (1972). Corrections to Bierstone's algorithm for generating cliques. *Journal of the Association of Computing Machinery, 19,* 244–247.

Nehnevajsa, J. (1955). Soziometrische Analyse von Guppen. *Kölner Zeitschrift für Sozialpsychologie, 7,* 119–157 & 187–302.

Nehnevajsa, J. (1967). Soziometrie. In R. König (Ed.), *Handbuch der empirischen Sozialforschung* (Vol. 1, pp. 226–239). Stuttgart, Germany: Enke.

Newcomb, T. N. (1953). An approach to the study of communicative acts. *Psychological Review, 60,* 393–404.

Newcomb, T. N. (1961). *The acquaintance process.* New York, NY: Holt.

Norman, R. Z., & Roberts, F. S. (1972). A derivation of a measure of relative balance for social structures and a characterization of extensive ratio systems. *Journal of Mathematical Psychology, 9,* 66–91.

Northway, M. L. (1940). A method for depicting social relationships obtained by sociometric testing. *Sociometry, 3,* 144–150.

Northway, M. L. (1943). Social relations among preschool children. *Sociometry, 3.*

Norton, R. W. (1980). Nonmetric multidimensional scaling in communication research: Smallest space analysis. In P. R. Monge and J. N. Cappella (Eds.), *Multivariate techniques for human communication research.* New York: Academic Press, pp. 308–331.

Nosanchuk, T. A. (1963). A comparison of several sociometric partitioning techniques. *Sociometry, 26,* 112–124.

Ore, O. (1962). *Theory of graphs.* Providence, RI: American Mathematical Society.

Peay, E. R., Jr. (1970). *Extensions of clusterability to quantitative data with an application to the cognition of political attitudes.* Unpublished doctoral dissertation. Ann Arbor, MI: University of Michigan.

Pepinsky, P. N. (1949). The meaning of "validity" and "reliability" as applied to sociometric test. *Educational and Psychological Measurement, 9,* 39–49.

Peterson, R. J., Komorita, S. A., & Quay, H. C. (1964). Determinants of sociometric choices. *Journal of Social Psychology, 62,* 65–75.

Phillips, D. P., & Conviser, R. H. (1972). Measuring the structure and boundary properties of groups: Some uses of information theory. *Sociometry, 35,* 235–254.

Pitts, F. (1979, May) *A bibliography of social networks.* Paper presented to the Seminar on Communication Network Analysis. East-West Communication Center, Honolulu.

Pool, I. de Sola. (1973). Communication systems. In I. de Sola Pool, F. W. Frey, W. Schramm, N. Maccoby, & E. B. Parker (Eds.), *Handbook of communication.* Chicago, IL: Rand-McNally.

Purdy, G. (1973). *Finding the cliques of a graph* (Technical Memorandum). University of Illinois Center for Advanced Computation.

Rapaport, A. (1970). Modern systems theory — An outlook for coping with change. *General Systems, 15,* 15–26.

Rapaport, A., & Horvath, W. J. (1961). A study of a large sociogram. *Behavioral Science, 6,* 279–291.

Rattinger, H. (1973). Eine einfache Methode und ein FORTRAN-Program zur Ermittlung von Cliquen. *Zeitschrift für Sozialpsychologie, 4*(1), 5–14.

Rice, R. E. (1981). Resources for longitudinal network analysis. *Connections, 4* (2), 10–22.

Rice, R. E., & Barnett, G. A. (1985). Group communication networking in an information environment. In M. McLaughlin (Ed.), *Communication Yearbook, 9*. Beverly Hills, CA: Sage.

Rice, R. E., & Richards, W. D., Jr. (1985). An overview of network analysis methods and programs. In B. Dervin & M. J. Voigt (Eds.), *Progress in Communication Sciences, Vol. VI*. Norwood, NJ: Ablex, pp. 105–165.

Richards, W. D., Jr. (1971, April). *An improved conceptually-based method for analysis of communication network structures of large complex organizations*. Paper presented to the International Communication Association convention, Phoenix, AZ.

Richards, W. D., Jr. (1974, April). *Network analysis in large complex systems: Techniques and method-tools*. Paper presented at the International Communication Association convention, New Orleans, Louisiana.

Richards, W. D., Jr. (1975, May). *Social network analysis: An overview of recent developments*. Paper presented at the annual conference of the American Society for Cybernetics, Philadelphia, PA.

Rogers, E. M., & Bhowmik, D. K. (1971). Homophily-heterophily: Relational concepts for communication research. *Public Opinion Quarterly, 34*, 523–538.

Rogers, E. M., & Kincaid, D. L. (1981). *Communication networks: Toward a new paradigm for research*. New York: Free Press.

Roistacher, R. C. (1974). A review of mathematical methods in sociometry. *Sociological Methods & Research, 3*(2), 123–171.

Rosenberg, M. (1972). Conditional relationships. In P. F. Lazarsfeld, A. K. Pasanella, & M. Rosenberg (Eds.), *Continuities in the language of social research* (pp. 133–147). New York: Free Press.

Russell, B. (1938). *Principles of mathematics*. New York: Norton.

Sailer, L. D. (1978). Structural equivalence: Meaning and definition, computation and application. *Social Networks, 1*, 73–90.

Salzinger, L. L. (1982). The ties that bind: The effects of clustering on dyadic relationships. *Social Networks, 4*, 117–145.

Scandrette, O. C. (1951). Friendship in junior high 7th graders. *Clearing-House, 25*, 364–366.

Seidman, S. B. (1981). Structures induced by collections of subsets: A hypergraph approach. *Mathematical Social Sciences, 1*, 381–396.

Seidman, S. B., & Foster, B. L. (1978). A graph-theoretic generalization of the clique concept. *Journal of Mathematical Sociology, 6*, 139–154.

Shannon, C., & Weaver, W. (1949). *The mathematical theory of communication*. Urbana, IL: University of Illinois Press.

Shelley, H. P. (1960). Focused leadership and cohesiveness in small groups. *Sociometry, 23*, 209–216.

Shephard, R. N. (1972). A taxonomy of some principle types of data and of multidimensional methods for their analysis. In R. N. Shepard, A. K. Romney, & M. B. Nerlove (Eds.), *Multidimensional scaling: Theory and applications in the behavioral sciences* (Vol. 1). New York: Seminar Press.

Shephard, R. N., Romney, A. K., & Nerlove, M. B. (Eds.) (1972). *Multidimensional Scaling: Theory and Applications in the Behavioral Sciences* (Vol. 1). New York: Seminar Press.

Sherif, M., & Sherif, C. W. (1969). *Social psychology*. New York: Harper & Row.

Slepian, P. (1968). *Mathematical foundations of network analysis*. New York: Springer Verlag.

Spilerman, S. (1966). Structural analysis and the generation of sociograms. *Behavioral Science, 2*, 312–318.

Tichy, N. M., Tushman, M. L., & Fombrun, C. (1979). Social network analysis for organizations. *Academy of Management Review, 4*, 507–520.

Torgerson, W. S. (1958). *Theories and methods of scaling*. Reading, MA: Addison-Wesley.

Tryon, R. C. (1967). Predicting group differences in cluster analysis: The social area problem. *Multivariate Behavioral Research, 2*(4), 453–475.

Tryon, R. C., & Bailey, D. E. (1970). *Cluster analysis*. New York: McGraw-Hill.

Weiss, R. S. (1956). *Processes of organization*. Ann Arbor, MI: University of Michigan, Institute for Social Research.

Weiss, R. S., & Jacobson, E. W. (1955). A method for the analysis of complex organizations. *American Sociological Review, 22,* 661–668.

Wellman, B., & Whitaker, M. (Eds.) (1974). *Community network communication: An annotated bibliography.* Toronto, Ontario: University of Toronto, Centre for Urban and Community Studies. (Report #4.)

Wellman, B., (1979, September). What is Network Analysis? Notes on its Development, Explanatory Goals and Some Key Formulations. Research Paper No. 1. Toronto, Canada: Structural Analysis Programme, Department of Sociology, University of Toronto.

White, H. C. (1974a). Models for interrelated roles from multiple networks in small populations. In P. J. Knopp & G. H. Meyer (Eds.), *Proceedings of the Conference on the Application of Undergraduate Mathematics in the Engineering, Life, Managerial and Social Sciences.* Atlanta, GA: Georgia Institute of Technology.

White, H. C. (1974b). *Multiple networks in small populations, II: Compound relations and equations.* Unpublished paper, Harvard University, Department of Sociology.

White, H. C., & Breiger, R. L. (1975). Patterns across networks. *Society, 12,* 68–73.

Wigand, R. T. (1973). *Some contributing aspects toward a theory of communication networks.* Unpublished paper. Michigan State University, Department of Communication, East Lansing, MI.

Wigand, R. T. (1974a, November). *Análisis de redes de comunicación: Un enfoque computactional hacía la ingeniería de sistemas y organización* [Communication network analysis: A computerized approach toward the engineering of systems and organizations]. Paper presented to the II Interamerican Conference on Systems and Informatics, Mexico City, Mexico.

Wigand, R. T. (1974b, April). Communication, integration and satisfaction in a complex organization. Paper presented to the International Communication Association convention, New Orleans, Louisiana.

Wigand, R. T. (1976a, May) *Communication and interorganizational relationships among complex organizations in social service settings.* Paper presented to the International Communication Association, Portland, Oregon.

Wigand, R. T. (1976b). La comunicación vs. la jerarquía. *Nonotza—Revista de Difusión Cientifica, Tecnología y Cultura, 2*(5), 22–23.

Wigand, R. T. (1977a). Communication network analysis in urban development. In W. E. Arnold & J. Buley (Eds.), *Urban communication—Survival in the city* (pp. 137–170). Cambridge, MA: Winthrop.

Wigand, R. T. (1977b) A dynamic model of interactions among complex organizations within an organization-set. In R. Trappl, F. de P. Hanika, & F. R. Pichler, Washington, DC: Hemisphere Publishing, pp. 32–37.

Wigand, R. T. (1977c) A model of interorganizational communication among complex organizations. In K. Krippendorff (Ed.), *Communication and control in society.* New York: Gordon & Breach, pp. 367–387.

Wigand, R. T. (1977d, May-June). *A path-analytic evaluation of communication among social service organizations.* Paper presented to the International Communication Association convention, Berlin, Federal Republic of Germany.

Wigand, R. T. (1979a). A model of interorganizational communication among complex organizations. In Klaus Krippendorff (Ed.): *Communication and Control in Society.* New York: Gordon & Breach, pp. 367–387.

Wigand, R. T. (1979b). Some recent developments in organizational communication: Network analysis—A systemic representation of communication relationships. *Communications: International Journal of Communication Research, 2,* 181–200.

Wigand, R. T. (1982). The communication industry in economic integration: The case of West Germany. *Social Networks, 4,* 47–79.

Wigand, R. T., & Larkin, R. J. (1975, April). *Interorganizational communication, information flow and service delivery among social service organizations.* Paper presented to the International Communication Association convention, Chicago, Illinois.

Williams, W. T. (1971). Principles of clustering. *Annual Review of Ecology and Systematics, 2,* 303–326.

Woelfel, J., & Danes, J. (1980). Multidimensional scaling methods for communication research. In P. R. Monge & J. N. Cappella (Eds.), *Multivariate techniques in human communication research* (pp. 333–364). New York: Academic Press.

Wright, D., & Evitts, M. S. (1961). Direct factor analysis in sociometry. *Sociometry, 24,* 82–98.

Ziegler, R., (1968). *Kommunikationsstruktur und Leistung sozialer Systeme.* Meisenheim am Glan, Federal Republic of Germany: Verlag Anton Hain.

APPENDIX
NETWORK ANALYSIS SAMPLE DATA GATHERING INSTRUMENT

Your ID Number _____

Below are the names of persons in this organization. First, please circle your *own* name and then record the number next to your name in the blank space provided for *"Your ID Number"* at the top of this page. Using the Communication Frequency Scale below, indicate how often you communicate with each person *about production activities*. Then, evaluate this communication with regard to the importance of that communication frequency by using the Communication Importance Scale below. Lastly, repeat this procedure for communication *about maintenance* and *innovation activities*. Then continue with the next person, etc.

Communication Frequency Scale:

6 - Several times a day or more
5 - Once or twice a day
4 - Several times a week
3 - Once a week
2 - Several times a month
1 - Once a month

Communication Importance Scale:

```
  +          +          +
  1          5          10
low                    high
        IMPORTANCE
```

How often do you communicate with these persons? How important do you judge this communication?

	....ABOUT PRODUCTION ACTIVITIES		....ABOUT MAINTENANCE ACTIVITIES		....ABOUT INNOVATION ACTIVITIES	
	Frequency	Importance	Frequency	Importance	Frequency	Importance
001 Don Adams						
002 Jackie Black						
003 Bob Calder						
004 Fred Dawsey						
005 Phil Erickson						
006 Sid Fulton						
. . .						
etc. etc. etc.						

Chapter 15

On the Use of Communication Gradients*

J. David Johnson

Department of Communication
State University of New York at Buffalo

Abstract

The key to conceptual advances in any discipline lies in the development of new techniques for thinking about and analyzing its central phenomena. This chapter develops a new technique for examining communication structure in organizations, one that embodies rich visual imagery. Communication gradients essentially involve the representation of differing types of communication intensity in a physically bounded plane. This chapter uses illustrative data to generate sample gradient plots with four communication intensity measures: frequency of contact, average frequency of individual contacts, response satisfaction, and importance. These variables are linked to respondent's work stations and rest stations, and are also analyzed over three points in time in a large retail store. The results reveal the rich heuristic potential of this technique for analyzing organizational communication structure.

One of the essential factors associated with the growth of any discipline is the availability of a number of techniques by which the researcher or theorist can conceptualize and/or analyze the phenomenon of interest. The need for those new methodologies in organizational research has generated much interest and concern in the last several years (e.g., Hackman, 1982). Communication gradients will be examined here to determine their utility as a new methodology for investigating the communication structures associated with the physical setting of an organization.

For the last 20 years, most investigations into large scale organizational information systems have been primarily governed by two world views, human relations and network analysis, with both having their own associated methodologies (e.g., self-report questionnaires coupled with MANOVA for human relations approaches) (Jablin, 1980). Regrettably, these world views and associated methods must be strained to address critical research

* The author wishes to acknowledge the support of the Arizona State University Faculty Grant-in-Aid program in the furtherance of this research. He would also like to thank Cathy Savage, for her assistance in generating computer related graphics, and Dr. Ed Greenberg and the other consultants at the Academic Computing Services of Arizona State University.

questions related to the impact of technologies, especially task design, and of physical lay-out on communication in bounded spaces.

It would appear that the use of gradients to represent communication patterns would offer a better watch of research technique to these and other problems. Gradients essen-tially detail the rate of increase or decrease of a variable in magnitude through topological or graphical representations. For communication research, gradients represent communi-cation levels and/or flows of varying intensity within some physically bounded plane, such as the floor of an assembly plant. Gradients have long been used to describe phenomenon in other disciplines such as geology and meteorology (Monkhouse & Wilkonson, 1971).[1] As a result, there are a number of computer programs available to investigate the utility of this analytic technique in communication research. The advances in computer graphics are par-ticularly important, since they provide the link between raw information and the visual im-ages necessary to perceive it.

Figures 1 and 2 contain more concrete representations of the application of gradients to communication problems. Figure 1 contains a map of a typical office arrangement, with the boxes representing enclosed offices of various sizes. The numbers represent levels of communication activity. For example, they could represent frequency, levels of communi-cation satisfaction, importance, etc. In this particular representation, the numbers are asso-ciated with individuals who are located in the same spaces where the numbers are present. There are, of course, other ways of representing communication activity. Instead of tying them to locations of individuals, the office could be delineated by a grid and the levels of ac-tivity, regardless of individuals within the grid, could be recorded (see Monge & Kirste, 1980). Now, just looking at the numbers themselves might be quite instructive. For exam-ple, there appears to be trend for higher levels of activity in the larger corner offices and in the spaces, which are not bounded by walls, off hallways.

Figure 2 transfers this representation to one of the available gradient programs, CON-TRA (Academic Computing Center, 1977). This graphic representation provides us with a much more dramatic topological presentation of the communication relationships, re-vealing, through contours, the dramatic hills and valleys of communication activities in this particular office. Further, this representation reveals, through the surrounding white space, how isolated most communication activity in the office is, with only four clusters of individuals being grouped within one set of contours.

Gradients can serve as a very useful complement to the other major means of examin-ing communication structure in organizations, especially network analysis. Communica-tion structure refers to "the arrangement of the differentiated elements that can be recog-nized in the patterned communication flows in a system" (Rogers & Kincaid, 1981, p. 346). Gradients are particularly useful in revealing the antecedent conditions, such as the physical structure, associated with the emergence of particular communication structures, since they directly link communication behaviors to manifest organizational elements. However, in-vestigations of communication structure have been somewhat constrained in recent years because of the primacy of network analysis. In fact, network analysis has become essen-tially synonymous with the concept of communication structure in the minds of some (see Monge, Edwards, & Kirste, 1978).

---

[1] Typically, these fields have done this with choropleth maps, which are used to portray rates and ratios in clear, delimited areas, or isoline maps, where points having identical values are joined together by continuous flowing lines (Schmid & Schmid, 1979).

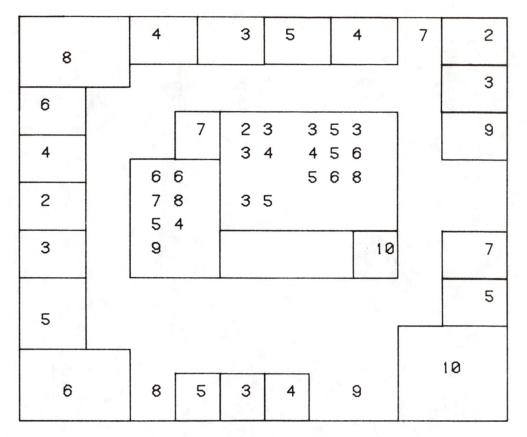

Figure 1. Organizational map.

Many of the specific aspects of network analysis which have been criticized in recent years (see Jablin, 1980; Bernard & Killworth, 1977; Stohl & Kakarigi, 1985) can be ameliorated through the use of gradients (see Johnson, 1986, for a more complete discussion). First, gradient software is not as limited in the size of the networks which can be examined. Second, by design or in practice most network analysis can be conducted only with primitive scaling, usually binary data (Johnson, 1984), really complete (polythetic) descriptions of linkages are difficult to accomplish. In contrast, gradients almost demand the use of precise scaling, and there is the possibility, with overlays of color coding, for very rich descriptions of comunication linkages. Third, gradients are more robust in the face of problems with missing data or nonresponse. Fourth, gradients are typically generated by computer software, which has received considerable testing and refinement. Fifth, gradients produce more compelling visual images. Finally, since gradients are intimately tied to such organizational factors as physical structure and technologies they offer more heuristic potential for generating precise theoretical statements. For example, gradients could be used to discover precisely the linkage between physically bound technologies, such as assembly lines, and communication behaviors. These points should become clear in the remaining sections of this chapter, which describe the illustrative data to be used here, discuss the sample gradient plots generated using this data, and detail the implications of potential applications of this technique to problems related to communication structure.

Figure 2. Contour map.

METHOD

 Although some research involving communication in physically bounded spaces has been conducted recently in organizations (e.g., Monge & Kirste, 1980; Sundstrom, Burt, & Kamp, 1980), the data-gathering techniques used need to be modified to fit the requirements of the more sophisticated analytic options provided by gradient computer programs. The primary problems which new instruments need to address is the efficacy of various alternative means of locating communication activity with precision within physically bounded spaces.

        On the other hand, data related to communication intensity can be gathered using a variety of well-established techniques. For example, self-report systems such as CATIJ (Killworth & Bernard, 1974), systematic observation (Sykes, 1983), or diaries (Conrath, 1973) all might be appropriate. The foregoing suggests a wealth of potential alternative data-gathering procedures. However, for demonstration purposes we will focus on intensity data gathered by means of conventional network analysis techniques, and self-reports of respondents of their location within a retail store.

The pilot study was conducted on a census of organizational personnel in a retail outlet of a large national chain in a major midwestern metropolitan area (initial n of 207). The study was conducted over three points in time from December to March, separated by roughly 6 week intervals, which provides us with an opportunity to investigate also the evolutionary nature of communication within physically bounded spaces. Since the physical layout of the store was limited to one floor, with a minimum of physical barriers between store personnel, it is uniquely suited for examination of this research problem.

Intensity Indicants

The intensity indicants examined here were all generated from a network analysis instrument derived from the format used in the International Communication Association communication audit (see Goldhaber, Yates, Porter, & Lesniak, 1978). The questionnaire used a structured approach which provided a roster of the entire population under study. In a modified version of this instrument, respondents were asked to report on three variables for each work related link: importance, response satisfaction, and frequency. The general instructions for the questionnaire follow:

> As you complete this form, it is important for you to think about the people you communicated with today (or the last time you worked) on work related matters. This includes face-to-face and telephone conversations.
> You will notice that only WORK RELATED communication is being requested. WORK RELATED communication is defined as any conversation where the primary topic deals with information concerning your job.

Two frequency measures will be examined here. One, EECNT, is based solely on the number of contacts an individual reported. The other, AVFREQ, was determined by averaging the number of work related contacts an individual reported for specific others in the network in any oral modality on a daily basis. A daily time frame was used to ameliorate problems relating to memory and bias often found in these instruments.

> *Frequency.* The column FREQUENCY asks you to indicate how many times you talked with a person on *work related* matters today. If you talked with a person 8 times and 5 of those times were primarily about work related matters, you should place a 5 in the space provided.

The instructions for response satisfaction were read out loud to the respondents and its average score across all links were used as an indicant of intensity (AVSAT).

> RESPONSE SATISFACTION asks you to think about how *satisfied* you *feel with the way in which a person responds to you during* a conversation. Does the person appear interested, helpful or responsive to your questions? These behaviors would suggest positive RESPONSE SATISFACTION (VERY SATISFIED). Does the person appear disinterested, not very helpful or unresponsive to your questions? These behaviors would suggest dissatisfaction with the response (VERY DISSATISFIED). Place an X in the box which most accurately reflects your feelings about how satisfied you were with the response.

The variable importance (AVIMP) was calculating by its score averaging across all reported links. The instructions, which were again read out loud, follow:

> We want to rate on a scale from 1 to 9 how critical the information you receive is to the completion of your job. A "1" indicates the information you received has *minimal* importance to the completion of your job. A "6" indicates the information is *somewhat* important and a "9" indicates the information is *critical* in completing your job. Place the appropriate rating in the space provided under the column *IMPORTANCE*.

For each of the network analysis indicants, respondents were directed to look at an example provided for them on the bottom of the questionnaire.

Location Measures

While it would appear to be a relatively straightforward procedure to measure elements of physical structure, a number of conceptual difficulties and measurement problems need to be considered (see Korzenny, 1978; Monge & Kirste, 1980). This research uses an illustrative example with data generated from only one of a number of different possible techniques.

Respondents were provided with a map of the store (Figure 3) which blocked out and

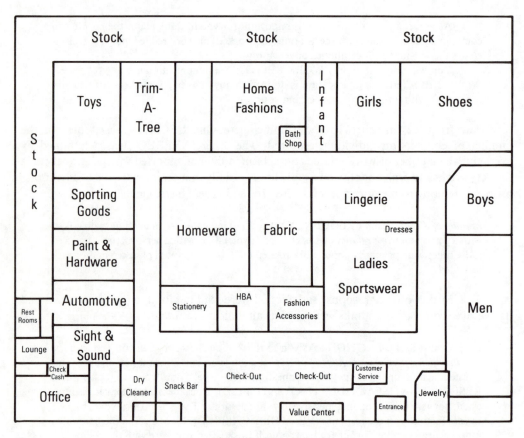

Figure 3. Store map.

identified the major sections into which the store was divided (e.g., main office, lounge, sporting goods, etc.). They were then asked: "Please place a small *x* as close as possible to where you *spend most of your working time* on the map *on the following page.*" These instructions were repeated verbally by an experimenter, who was there to assist the respondents if necessary. They were also asked to "Please place a small *o* on the map where you most often *spend non-work time,* for example, take breaks or have lunch, etc." These procedures have been redefined in pretests.

The placement of the x and o were then used to derive the location of the respondents on a grid of the store. Each grid represented a 8' × 8' square, or 64 square feet of space, in the store. The store was divided into 41 horizontal and 31 vertical units, with the coordinates for every individual located in the grid depending on where the respondents marked their locations on the map provided them.

ANALYSIS

In this section, various plots of the illustrative data will be compared to demonstrate the utility of gradients for examining communication structure. SAS/GRAPH, which is a component of the more general Statistical Analysis System (SAS) (SAS Institute, 1982), will be used to represent communication intensity within a plane of coordinates; GCONTOUR, a contour plotting program; G3D, which produces three dimensional grids of data points; and, G3GRID, which interpolates data into a regular grid given particular functions (SAS Institute, 1981).

Figures 4 through 13 contain the sample graphs which will be used to examine the utility and heuristic value implicit in the gradient approach for analyzing communication structure. All these graphs were generated by the G3D procedure of the SAS/GRAPH package, since it best fits the characteristics of this illustrative data set. Figure 4 will be used to describe some of the conventions common to all of these graphs. First, these graphs provide us with representations of communication intensity within the bounded plane represented by the map of the store found in Figure 3. The grid which forms the plane plots out the locations within the store with the horizontal coordinates (HCORDW1) for work stations arrayed along the bottom, and the vertical work coordinates (VCORDW1) arrayed along the right side of the figure.[2] These coordinates, then, represent locations in the plane of the store, with dimensions drawn to scale of 41 horizontal units and 31 vertical units.

The z axis always contains the intensity indicant, in this case frequency of contacts (EECNT1). The values of the frequency of contacts measure at each coordinate in the grid were represented by the heights of the gradients found rising from the floor of the plane. In this instance coordinate 6,2 (the horizontal coordinate will always be listed first, followed by the vertical coordinate) represented the highest level of communication activity and coordinate 32,6 was among the lowest.

Comparing these figures with the map presented in Figure 3 is instructive. We find that these levels of activity make sense, especially in the case of 6,2, which was the closest work station to the entrance of the store, and thus a location where a lot of incidental contacts could occur. The other clusters of high activity were associated with the manager's of-

---

[2] The program automatically scales all three axis of the graph. It does, however, allow the user some freedom in tilting of the representation. The EECNT graphs are all titled at the default value of 70 degrees, while all of the remaining graphs have a tilt of 25 degrees.

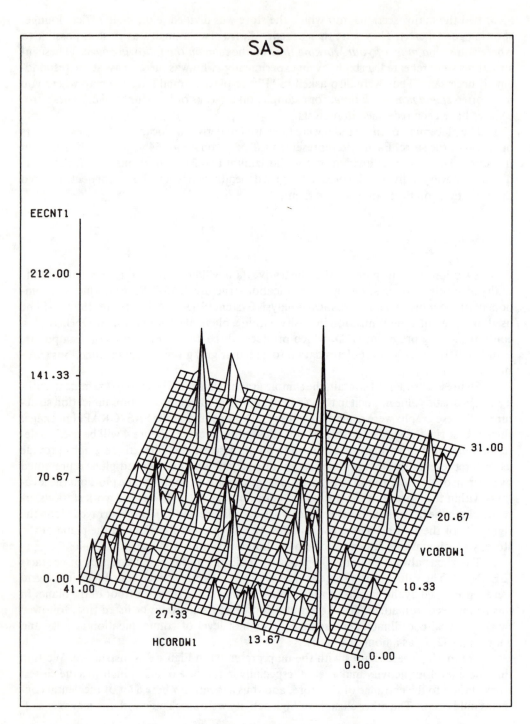

Figure 4. Number of contacts at work stations.

fice, sporting goods, automotive, ladies sportswear, and the candy sections of the store, as well as toys and trim-a-tree, all areas of high volume traffic during the Christmas season. In addition, the communication activity in the store was arrayed along the front and right side aisle-ways, again places of high visibility where incidental contacts could occur.

Figure 5 contains the gradients for the average frequency variable (AVFREQ1). Since an individual's location in the grid will be the same for all of these variables, naturally there are a lot of similarities in these figures; what the gradients represent, however, are interesting differences in intensity across the various communication indicators. A comparison of this figure with Figure 4 reveals the often complementary nature of the frequency variables. First of all, as we might expect, because of the averaging process, there are less dramatic hills and valleys in this figure. Most interestingly, however, there was a tendency for the high frequency of contact locations (e.g., 6,2) to become low AVFREQ locations, and the low EECNT positions (e.g., infants in the rear of the store) to have much higher relative values. However, people with moderate values in the center of the store for EECNT1 also tended to have moderate values for the AVFREQ measure.

Figure 6 plots the intensity measure of average importance (AVIMP1). There was a fairly clear trend for those who were relatively low in AVFREQ to also have low values for AVIMP (e.g., 4,18). Curiously, however, management did not have a dramatic increase in value, which could be partly a function of their less central location in the store. On the other hand, the more central locations and those locations associated with the Christmas season tended to be relatively high importance.

Figure 7 contains the final work station intensity measure, average satisfaction (AVSAT1). First, because respondent's average satisfaction ranged from 5 to 9, there were more peaks in this representation than for AVIMP1, where responses encompassed much more of the range in the scale of this variable. Thus, in general, those who were relatively high in AVIMP1 tended to have dramatically higher AVSAT1 values. This points to the necessity for discrimination within intensity measures for precise interpretations of this sort of data.

Figures 8 through 11 demonstrate another application of this technique. Coordinates were generated for both a respondent's work station, and also for the place where they normally took breaks. This is somewhat akin to separating both production and maintenance contacts in network analysis, and it permits us to focus specifically on particular types of communicative functions associated with specific spatial locations. As all four figures reveal, the rest areas in this store center around two locations, the snack bar (28,3) and the lounge (39,5). The pattern of the intensity measures around the lounge were very similar, especially when the general elevation of the satisfaction indicant is considered. However, while AVIMP and AVSAT were very similar in the snack bar, there does appear to be diminished frequency-related activity around its periphery, which might indicate this was a space in which workers could isolate themselves from work related contacts.

Figures 4, 12, and 13 present the results for the frequency of contact (EECNT1, EECNT2, and EECNT3) variables over the three points in time. They reveal some very interesting differences in retail activities over the various time points examined. First, there was a general decline in activity for the right hand side of the store, particularly at the jewelry station. Curiously, the office area had a curvilinear set of contacts, with a peak at time 2 which coincided with a series of management interventions which resulted in substantial layoffs in the store immediately before this time period. The cashiers generally had an increase in frequency over these three points in time.

Perhaps most interesting were patterns involved in the shifts in contacts which appear

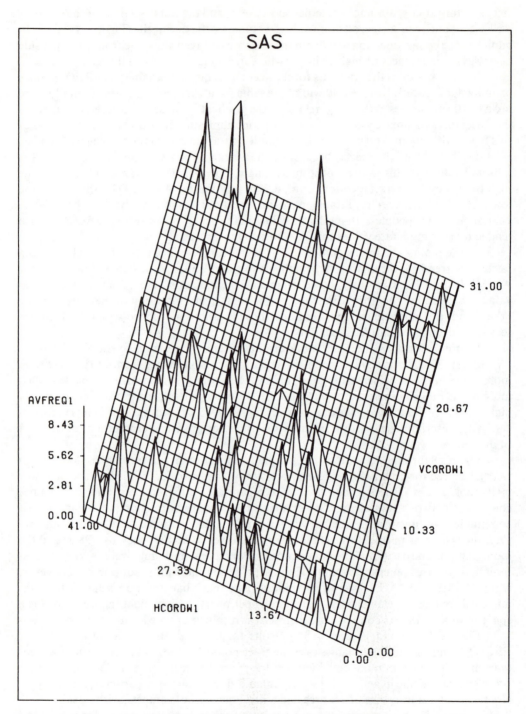

Figure 5. Average frequency at work stations.

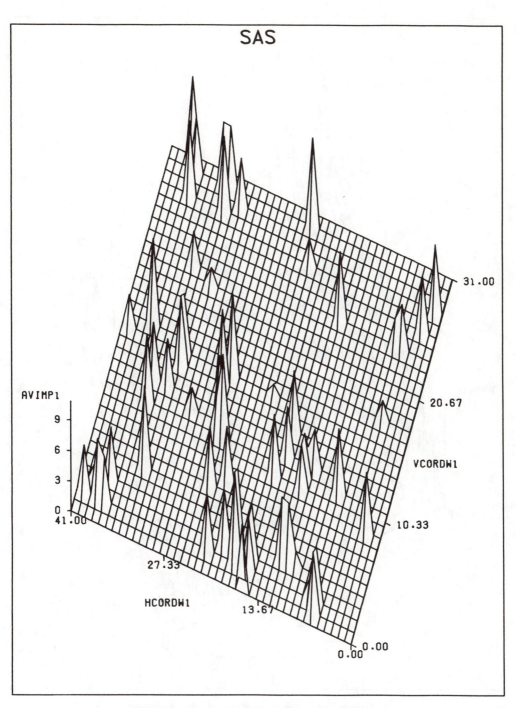

Figure 6. Average importance at work stations.

SAS

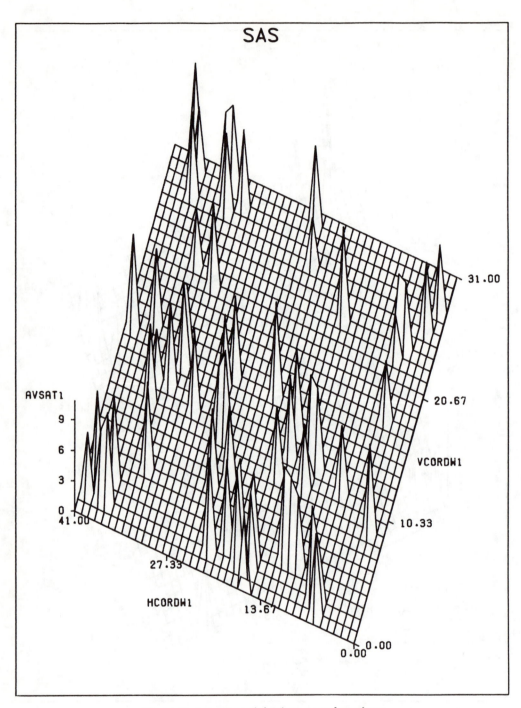

Figure 7. Average satisfaction at work stations.

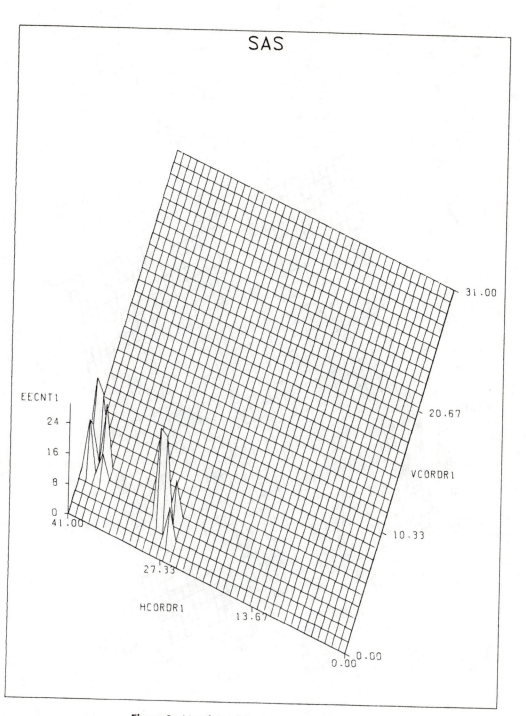

Figure 8. Number of contacts at rest stations.

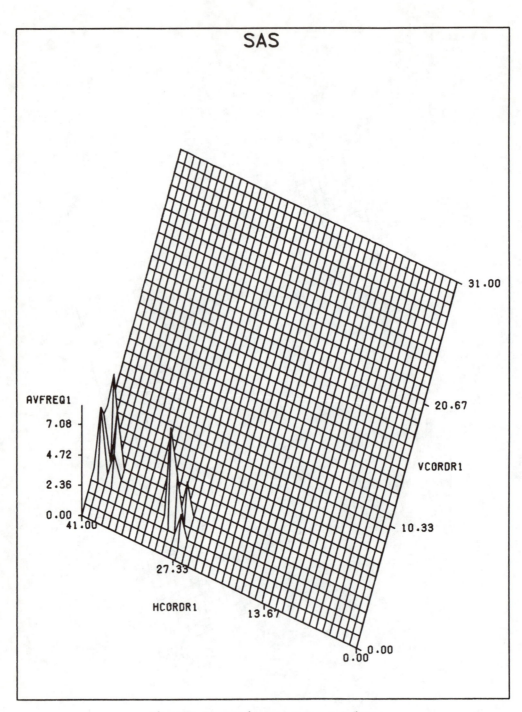

Figure 9. Average frequency at rest stations.

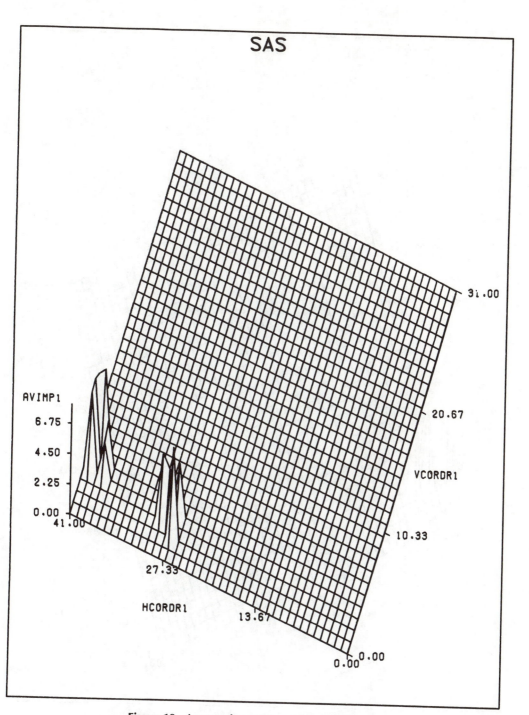

Figure 10. Average importance at rest stations.

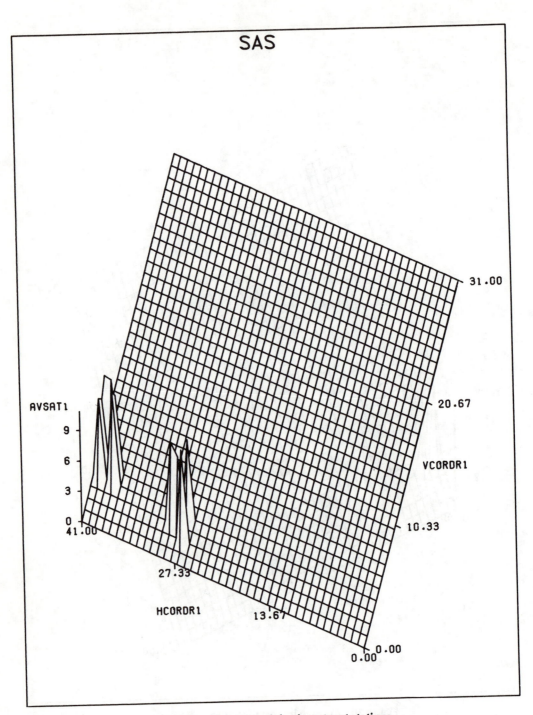

Figure 11. Average satisfaction at rest stations.

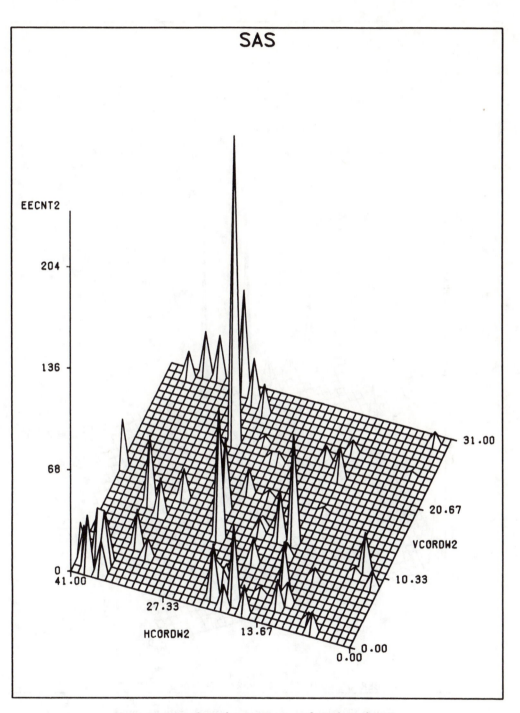

Figure 12. Number of contacts at work stations time 2.

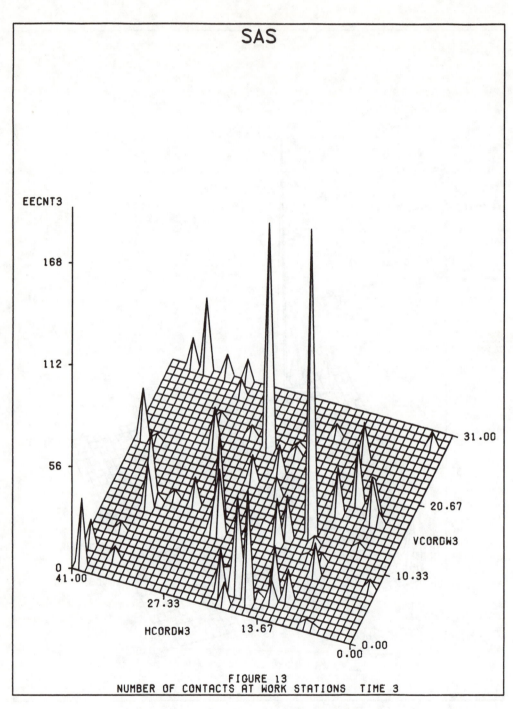

Figure 13. Number of contacts at work stations time 3.

to reflect seasonal variations in retail activity. At time 1, the peak activity areas were centered around toys, trim-a-tree, and jewelry; at time 2, which was in mid-February, house wear and fabrics became more important, perhaps reflecting the bitter winters in this area; and finally, at time 3, in March, just before Easter, there was a cluster of activity around ladies wear. In general, there also appeared to be an overall trend to greater peaks in contacts over time.

Even at this early stage of the development of this technique, several problem areas are evident. According to Monkhouse and Wilkonson (1971), four main factors determine the manner in which gradients can be generated. First, the selected value intervals, which can lead to data acquisition errors (Stott, 1977). For example, the EECNT variable had an extreme range of values, which made the generation of contours problematic, and the AVSAT variable had a restricted range of values, clustered at the high end of its scale, which produced elevated peaks in the G3D representations. In the current study, tying the intensity measures to individual locations also produced more dramatic contrasts, then identifying every location in an organization, and then recording all contacts within them regardless of the individuals involved (see Monge & Kirste, 1980). This procedure would probably produce smoother, more fine-grained contours.[3]

Second, the shapes and sizes of units for which statistics are available; and, third, the situation of plotting points (more of less central to peaks and/or key features). In particular, the size of the coordinates and how meaningful they are ultimately determine the precision of the mapping. Fourth, the method of interpolation, or smoothing, between points, which especially for contours is one of the primary sources of errors (Stott, 1977). The SAS/GRAPH programs have a difficult time dealing with missing data, because of interpolation problems. Because, in the current application, there were a large number of store locations in which no individual was located, this factor made the G3D program preferable to GCONTOUR, since it is much more sensitive to missing information.

One cannot overlook the fact that these tools have been developed for other disciplines and for other problems. However, examining their applicability to our own discipline could lead to the development of more precise tools of our own. For example, several key modifications to this technique would be helpful in making it an even more valuable addition to our set of tools for analyzing communication structures in large information systems. First, it would be more heuristically valuable to have the actual map, instead of the grid, drawn on the plane of coordinates. Second, the acquisition of data for all communication in specific, fine grained locations would reveal even more information about the relation of communication to physical structures, and a better picture of the flow of information in a work space. Third, techniques for picturing communication in organizations which have more than one floor or which are physically separated are needed, since the current representations are limited to one contiguous, flat plane. Finally, the comparative advantages of different graphical representations need to be assessed. For example, Figure 2 presents a contour plot which appears to have more potential for overlaying maps and drawing in other information, such as network ties between individuals. On the other hand, this representation does not graphically have the dramatic visual image of intensity, which the G3D grid format offer us.

---

[3] Because G3D needs values for every coordinate in the grid, a procedure was written which specified a zero for every location where no individual was present. In the instances where more than one individual was present, the mean score of all respondents in this location was used. For work stations there were 48 individuals with overlapping work stations at t1, 19 at t2, and 23 at t3. This problem was much more severe for the rest area plots, which had 99 overlapping individuals.

IMPLICATIONS

Since the growth of organizational communication is intimately interrelated with the growth of techniques for examining its unique problems, this approach offers a wealth of potential payoffs. The most direct one is to provide researchers with an alternative means of investigating communication structure. Currently, there is really only one technique available for systematically examining structural communication relationships: network analysis. Visual imagery has always been one of the most important ingredients of network studies, but, unfortunately, the nature of these images has not advanced very far in the last 40 years (Klovdahl, 1981; Wigand, 1977). In the last several years, network analysis has come under increasing criticism on other grounds as well (see Bernard & Killworth, 1977; Jablin, 1980; Stohl & Kakarigi, 1985); however, no alternative to it has yet emerged.

Communication gradients appear to offer such an alternative, one that has the considerable advantage of more directly and precisely examining major sources of constraint (and hence the explanatory foundations of structure) in communication systems, such as physical barriers and technological factors. The continuous-motion features of some graphic systems also permits the analysis of communication processes over time, such as diffusion processes. This technique also has the advantage of having a direct link to mathematical expressions, especially in relation to topological representations of planes, as well as statistical analysis, as demonstrated by SAS/GRAPH's linkage to a sophisticated statistical analysis systems.

Development of gradient-related techniques can lead to conceptual advances, since it provides researchers with new means of thinking about and analyzing the relationship between organizational communication and the physical environment. One of the primary ways that it does this is through its inherent visual representation. These visual representations have the potential for becoming metaphors of powerful heuristic value.

> The highest art, both in itself and in graphical display, is finding the unexpected. Done properly pictures . . . offer us the greatest hope of doing just this. (Tukey, 1980, p. 492)

These visual images may be used pragmatically by consultants to describe more concretely complex communication relationships in a manner which makes them more comprehensible and which can stimulate analytical thinking and investigation (Schmid & Schmid, 1979).

In fact cartographers have increasingly come to see their maps as a communication instrument (Taylor, 1983). They delineate three uses for maps, which nicely parallel the range of potential applications of communication gradients.

> A *communicative* use for the storage and dissemination of spatial information; an *operative* use involving the direction solution on maps . . . of various practical problems . . . and a *cognitive* use, for spatial and even spatial-temporal investigations of natural and social phenomenon, and the acquisition of new knowledge about them. (Salichtchev, 1983, pp. 12–13)

In general, it has been argued that some of the most useful discoveries in the history of science have been associated with visual imagery and visual representations (Klovdahl, 1981). Today's advances in computer graphics offers us a host of opportunities for the development of new tools for examining communication structure. SAS/GRAPH itself has a range of potential graphics which could be applied to these problems, giving us many different perspectives. Architects, industrial designers, and geologists have also developed computer software which can be potentially applied to the sort of communication problems identified here.

Communication gradients also can aid in the pursuit of specific conceptual questions in the area of organizational communication, such as the relationships between communication intensity and productivity, satisfaction, privacy, and social density. Much like network analysis, they can reveal cliques and isolates in organizational settings. For example, very much in the manner described by Rogers and Kincaid (1981), the physical structure of a social system often serves as an antecedent to the development of network groupings. In fact, gradients and networks can offer complementary views of a phenomena which could be helpful in achieving method triangulation.

Gradients can also provide an alternative means for examining a classic organizational dilemma: the difference between what is supposed to be happening "officially" and what is actually happening. Industrial design has traditionally focused on the most efficient means of accomplishing organizational tasks through maximizing the utility of physical layout. However, very little research has been conducted to determine the discrepancies between these ideal states of physical layout, which assume values of efficiency and productivity, and the human needs expressed in actual communication relationships. By using such computer programs as CRAFT (Buffa, Armour, & Vollman, 1964), the current research can also assess the discrepancies between managerially prescribed industrial layouts and actual communication relationships, and the impact of such discrepancies on communicative satisfaction and organizational productivity.

Since gradients represent a markedly different approach, they offer us the potential to explore new areas or to reexamine old ones in a different light. Proximity provides us with but one example of a promising area of inquiry which has been stalled because of a lack of appropriate methodologies. A number of studies have found that proximity is positively related to communication (Barnlund & Harland, 1963; Caplow, 1947; Festinger, Schacter, & Back, 1950; Gullahorn, 1952; Merton, 1948). The early interest in this area dissipated partly because of the dearth of techniques available for precisely investigating the relation of physical environments to communication, techniques which were rich in their heuristic implications. More recent studies have focused on the impacts of office landscaping, which requires even more precise techniques for linking communication to physical factors, with findings that open office environments increase communication (Allen & Gerstberger, 1973) and decrease feelings of privacy and satisfaction (Oldham & Brass, 1979; Sundstrom, Burt, & Kamp, 1980). To date, most of these studies have been hampered by rather primitive measurement and analytic techniques (except perhaps for Monge & Kirste's 1980 study). Gradients offer a set of tools for much more sophisticated analysis of the impacts of physical structure on communication.

In sum, this chapter examined the utility of a new method for investigating communication structure in large information systems. Development of this technique can lead to theoretical advances, since it provides researchers with new means of thinking about, describing, and analyzing organizational communication in physically bounded spaces.

REFERENCES

Academic Computing Center (1977). *CONTR and CONTRA contour graphic subroutines.* Madison, WI: Academic Computing Center.

Allen, T. J., & Gerstberger, P. G. (1973). A field experiment to improve communications in a product engineering department: The non territorial office. *Human Factors, 15,* 487–498.

Barnlund, D. C., & Harland, C. (1963). Propinquity and prestige as determinants of communication networks. *Sociometry, 26,* 467–479.

Bernard, H. R., & Killworth, P. D. (1977). Informant accuracy in social network data: II. *Human Communication Research, 4,* 3–18.

Buffa, E. S., Armour, G. C., & Vollman, T. E. (1964). Allocating facilities with CRAFT. *Harvard Business Review, 42,* 136–158.

Caplow, T. (1947). Rumors in war. *Social Forces, 25,* 298–302.

Conrath, D. W. (1973). Communication environment and its relationship to organizational structure. *Management Science, 20,* 586–603.

Festinger, L., Schacter, S., & Back, K. (1950). *Social pressures in informal groups: A study of a housing project.* New York: Harper.

Goldhaber, G. M., Yates, M. P., Porter, T. D., & Lesniak, R. (1978). Organizational communication: 1978. *Human Communication Research, 5,* 76–96.

Gullahorn, J. T. (1952). Distance and friendship as factors in the gross interaction matrix. *Sociometry, 15,* 123–134.

Hackman, J. R. (1982). Preface. In J. E. McGrath, J. Martin, & R. A. Kulka, (Eds.), *Judgment calls in research* (pp. 7–9). Beverly Hills, CA: Sage.

Jablin, F. M. (1980). Organizational communication theory and research: An overview of communication climate and network research. In D. Nimmo (Ed.), *Communication Yearbook 4* (pp. 327–347). New Brunswick, NJ: Transaction Books.

Johnson, J. D. (1984, February). *Multivariate communication networks.* Paper presented to the Fourth Annual Social Networks Conference. Phoenix.

Johnson, J. D. (1986). *A comparison of communication gradients and of network analysis: Two alternative approaches for analyzing communication structure.* Proceedings of the Eastern Academy of Management Twenty Third Annual Meeting, 244–249.

Killworth, P. D., & Bernard, H. R. (1974). Catij: A new sociometric and its application to a prison living unit. *Human Organization, 33,* 335–350.

Klovdahl, A. S. (1981). A note on images of networks. *Social Networks, 3,* 197–214.

Korzenny, F. (1978). A theory of electronic propinquity: Mediated communication in organizations. *Communication Research, 5,* 3–24.

Merton, R. K. (1948). Social psychology of housing. In W. Dennis (Ed.), *Current trends in social psychology* (pp. 163–217). Pittsburgh, PA: University of Pittsburgh Press.

Monge, P. R., Edwards, J. A., & Kirste, K. K. (1978). The determinants of communication and communication structure in large organizations: A review of research. In B. D. Rubin (Ed.), *Communication Yearbook 2* (pp. 311–331). New Brunswick, NJ: Transaction Books.

Monge, P. R., & Kirste, K. K. (1980). Measuring proximity in human organizations. *Social Psychology Quarterly, 43,* 110–115.

Monkhouse, F. J., & Wilkonson, H. R. (1971). *Maps and diagrams: Their compilation and construction.* London: Methuen.

Oldham, G. R., & Brass, D. J. (1979). Employee reaction to an open office: A naturally occurring quasi-experiment. *Administrative Science Quarterly, 24,* 267–284.

Rogers, E. M., & Kincaid, D. L. (1981). *Communication networks: Toward a new paradigm for research.* New York: Free Press.

Salichtchev, K. A. (1983). Cartographic communication: A theoretical survey. In D. R. F. Taylor (Ed.), *Graphic communication and design in contemporary cartography* (Vol. II, pp. 11–35). New York: John Wiley.

SAS Institute. (1981). *SAS/GRAPH user's guide.* Cary, NC: SAS Institute.

SAS Institute. (1982). *SAS user's guide: Basics.* Cary, NC: SAS Institute.

Schmid, C. F., & Schmid, S. E. (1979). *Handbook on graphic presentation* (2nd ed.). New York: John Wiley.

Stohl, C., & Kakarigi, D. (1985, November). *The NEGOPY network analysis program: A critical appraisal.* Paper presented to the Speech Communication Association Annual Convention, Denver.

Stott, J. P. (1977). Review of surface modeling. In Institution of Civil Engineers (Eds.), *Surface modeling by computer*. London: Institute of Civil Engineers.

Sundstrom, E., Burt, R. E., & Kamp, D. (1980). Privacy at work: Architectural correlates of job satisfaction and job performance. *Academy of Management Journal, 23,* 110–117.

Sykes, R. E. (1983). Initial interaction between strangers and acquaintances: A multivariate analysis of factors affecting choice of communication partners. *Human Communication Research, 10,* 27–53.

Taylor, D. R. F. (1983). Graphic communication and design in contemporary cartography: An introduction. In D. R. F. Taylor (Ed.), *Graphic communication and design in contemporary cartography* (Vol. II, pp. 1–10). New York: John Wiley.

Tukey, J. W. (1980). Methodological comments focused on opportunities. In Cappella, J. N., & Monge, P. R. (Eds.), *Multivariate techniques in human communication research* (pp. 489–528). New York: Academic Press.

Wigand, R. T. (1977). Some recent development in organizational communication: Network analysis — A systematic representation of communication relationships. *Communications, 3,* 181–200.

Chapter 16

Organizational Infographics and Automated Auditing: Using Computers to Unobtrusively Gather As Well As Analyze Communication

James A. Danowski

University of Illinois at Chicago

ABSTRACT

This chapter reviews traditional biases in organizational communication theory and re-search. It then presents an improved model including level in the hierarchy, cognitive schemata, messages, media, and networks. Integrated within the model are variables dealing with: levels of analysis, types of organizational media, communication manage-ment functions, and different representations of organizational communication knowl-edge. The infographic model of organizations forms the conceptual basis for automated auditing of textual, traffic, voice, and visual forms of organizational communication, and for profiling the features of these methods. Ten examples of automated auditing are presented.

Overview and Objectives

We take a dangerous approach in this chapter. We look at organizational communication through a methodological window. Many researchers recommend looking first through a theoretical one (Miller & Nicholson, 1976). Then, methods should be examined only as they follow from the constructs in view. Yet we are framing our perspective in this chapter around methods, in particular those that can be programmed to automatically capture and analyze organizational communication data. Our term to refer to this process is "auto-mated auditing" of organizational communication.

Before we discuss this issue of methodological danger, let's define what we mean by "automated auditing." Unlike typical communication research, in which computers are used only to analyze data, automated research also uses computers to *capture* the data. To the extent that this system learns rules and meta-rules about organizational communica-tion, it is an "automated intelligence" system for communication management.

Because of the rich features of these automated auditing systems, the dangers of method-centered views of organizations are not as pronounced as they appear at first blush.

Although a risk, Kaplan's (1964) "little boy with hammer" syndrome, in which the method-driven social scientist pounds on every problem in sight with his tool, is not likely. As this chapter will outline, automated auditing can be sufficiently comprehensive, contextual, and culturally sensitive that the methods do not limit theoretical perspectives. Rather, they can enhance them.

Accordingly, before treating the methods directly, we will overview the theoretical conceptualizations of organizational communication that provide a context for automated auditing. Note that, throughout this chapter, our intent is to illustrate by example some basic types of automated auditing. Other treatments of the topic with more extensive literature reviews can be found in Rice and Borgman (1983), and empirical examples seen in Rice (1982), Barnett and Rice (1985), and Rice and Barnett (1986), among others.

Also note that, by "automated auditing," we are not refering to the use of traditional communication research methods that do not capture data via computers to investigate communication technology-based systems. For example, work such as Barnett and Segal's (1985), which evaluates uses of the online database system LEXIS, is valuable in its own right. It is, however, outside the primary scope of this chapter, because it used paper-and-pencil instruments to gather data from users. So did Steinfield's (1985) study of electronic mail users.

Infographics

You have seen that the title of this chapter includes the term "organizational infographics." This concept refers to the segmentation of systems according to their communication and information processing behaviors rather than by demographic or psychographic variables (Danowski, 1976a, 1976b, 1984b). Segmentation can be applied to loosely coupled systems like media audiences and consumer marketing targets, and to highly organized systems like large complex organizations.

Demographic segmentation of an organization partitions it according to formal structural locater variables, such as member position, tenure, tasks, departments, etc. Then the analyst examines some other variable, such as communication satisfaction, according to these partitions.

Psychographic segmentation partitions according to attitudinal or work-style orientations. For example, the analyst may use segmentation variables like upward-mobility orientation (Sypher & Zorn, 1986), or job burnout, or identification with particular professional cultures like accounting or marketing. Then variations in some other variable, like preference for face-to-face communication over telephone or electronic mail, might be examined according to these partitions.

Infographic segmentation partitions the organization according to communication or information processing variables, then examines other variables within or across infographic segments. For example, such segmentation might be performed by cognitive schemata (Barlett, 1932; Delia, O'Keefe, & O'Keefe, 1982; Smith, 1982; Sypher & Applegate, 1984; Graber, 1984). It could be performed by messages (Danowski, 1982), or channel preference (Hughey, 1985), or channel use (Danowski, 1983b; Rice, 1984), or relational communication style (Rogers & Farace, 1974; Farace, Monge, & Russell, 1977), or communication network structures (Danowski, 1980; Rice, 1982; Albrecht, 1984; Barnett & Rice, 1985; Rice & Barnett, 1986; Love & Rice, 1986; Danowski, 1986a, 1986b).

Exemplifying the latter approach, Danowski (1980) defined organizational units of analysis according to groups identified through a communication network analysis of who talked with whom in an organization (n = 963), then tested hypotheses about how internally connected groups (n = 51) were in relation to their attitudinal uniformity. Albrecht (1984) segmented by linker and nonlinker network roles, and tested hypotheses about cognitive structures and content. Rice and Love (1986) segmented by participant and peripheral roles in the network and analyzed socio-emotional content.

For theoretical purposes, of the three approaches — demographic, psychographic, and infographic segmentation — infographics offers the most promise for communication theory building. It puts communication variables at the center. Also, for practical purposes infographic segmentation is increasingly useful as managers view their organizations as information processing systems. In fact, this latter trend of the "information society" (Bell, 1973; Porat, 1977; Dizard, 1982) offers potential for substantial integration of theoretical and practical issues and methods in the organizational communication field. Automated auditing tools are compatible with this thrust. Examining traditional biases in organizational communication provides further insights into the potential values of automated auditing for rectifying them.

Traditional Conceptualizations

Historically, organizational communication research has included several biases: face-to-face medium bias, intraorganization bias, and atomistic bias.We discuss each of these in turn.

Face-to-Face Bias. Traditionally, scholarly treatment of organizational communication (Redding, 1972; Farace, Monge, & Russell, 1977; Rogers & Agarwala-Rogers, 1976; Farace, Taylor, & Stewart, 1978) has included two major limitations. First, face-to-face modes of communication have been of primary interest, while interactions via technologies such as telephone and computers have been ignored. Even print-based interpersonal communication through memos, letters, and reports has seen little scientific treatment. As well, most research on employee publications like magazines and internal newsletters has not examined them much from an hypothesis-testing perspective. Medium of communication was virtually transparent to the analyst.

Growing exceptions to treating media as "transparent" are the industry-driven and academically-connected research on communication technology uses and effects in organizations (Rice & Bair, 1984; Johansen, 1984; Kling, 1980). Such studies reflect a paradigm inversion and synthesis, a kind of network dialectic. The old engineering thesis was that "networks" were made of technology units as nodes, with people as transparent. In antithesis, organizational communication researchers treated communication "networks" as with people as nodes, and technology for linking them as transparent. Now the synthesis view is of a people-as-node network interacting with a technology-as-node network. This paradigm reflects a network revolution and evolution.

Intraorganization Bias. The second main circumscription of traditional organizational communication has been nearly exclusive treatment of intraorganizational communication. Although, in the last decade or so, we have seen a movement toward conceptualization of interorganizational information exchanges (Wigand, 1979; Eisenberg et al., 1985), again the focus has been mainly on interpersonal communication in face-to-face modes. For the most part, public relations activities, using media directed toward external audiences or gathering information from them, have been overlooked. This is despite the fact that, in most large organizations, external public relations activities constitute the bulk of managed information flow across organizational boundaries (Grunig & Hunt, 1984).

An exception to the lack of investigation of public relations from an organizational communication perspective is the work of Grunig (1982), Salmon (1986), and McMillan (1986). Also, Danowski, Barnett, and Friedland (1986) conceptualized interorganizational relations in terms of a network defined by sharing of public relations firms by client organizations. They tested hypotheses linking network centrality, diversification, media coverage, and effects on stock prices.

Atomistic Bias and Interpretive Approach

Traditional organizational communication research also had an atomistic bias. In other words, it treated organizational elements as detached individual units, each of equal import. Exemplifying such an approach, the "climate" school of organizational communication would study individual attitudes toward information, and compute averages on a series of unidimensional questionnaire items. (For reviews of climate research, see Redding, 1972; Jablin, 1980; Falcione & Kaplan, 1984; Hellriegel & Slocum, 1974; James & Jones, 1974; Barnett, Hamlin & Danowski, 1982.) Perhaps in part as a reaction to the bias of climate views of organizational communication, which used simple quantitative methods, the "interpretive school" (Putnam & Pacanowsky, 1983; Dandridge, Mitroff, & Joyce, 1980; Louis, 1980; Martin, 1982; McLaughlin, 1984; Weick, 1985; Smith & McLaughlin, 1986) has sought to identify the symbols, myths, rituals, stories, and meanings that members have, and has gravitated toward traditional qualitative methods.

Nevertheless, what used to be polar opposites of methods, qualitative and quantitative, are converging into hybrids which have more of the advantages of each. Linkage-type methods such as network analysis (Rogers & Kincaid, 1981)—whether of who sends messages to whom, or of words as nodes within message content, or of cognitions as nodes in cognitive schemata—are what we might call "qualiquant" methods. So are distance model techniques like factoring, multidimensional scaling (Kruskal & Wish, 1978; Woelfel & Fink, 1981), and cluster analysis (Krippendorff, 1980a). Both linkage and distance-based methods for relational analysis identify patterns, a qualitative feature, but do so in a systematic way with large volumes of a data, a quantitative feature. The outcome is qualitative information yielded by quantitative procedures. These are performed on data which are in relational form (focusing on linkages among elements), rather than in atomistic form (focusing only on attributes or traits of elements).

Automated auditing methods described in this chapter are largely qualiquant. These methods illustrate that distinctions between qualitative and quantitative methods have decreasing meaning in the era of convergence. Key distinctions increasingly involve theoretical variables and relationships, rather than methods for gathering and processing data.

Fortunately, convergence is occurring in the contemporary study of organizational communication. We are seeing more multichannel perspectives on conceptualizing the processes (Huber, 1984). We are also seeing them as involving a number of relatively distinct functions: personnel, telecommunications management, library services, internal public relations or employee publications, and external public relations including media relations, community relations, investor relations, lobbying, consumer relations, etc. (Danowski, 1976a). This chapter attempts to capture the spirit, although certainly not the full substance, of this emerging convergence in its look at automated methods for gathering data about various forms of organizational communication. To further set the conceptual context of automated auditing, we turn next to overviewing a model for organizational communication.

Descriptive Model of Organizational Communication

The focus of this model is not on explaining the full range of diversity in organizational communication via an axiomatic theory. Rather, the concern is with providing a simple descriptive framework to order the main kinds of variables in communication processes. Such a model can stimulate subsequent theory construction, as well as help organize managers' understanding of their organizational communication experiences. (The model benefitted from interaction with Kothari, personal communication, May, 1986). The key dimensions of the model are: communicator level in the hierarchy, information processing orientation, and locus of communication variables.

Level of the communicator in the organizational hierarchy is grouped in three broad categories: top executives, middle managers, and operatives. Information processing orientation is examined in the three categories of: generating information, interpreting information and applying information. Communication variable loci are: cognitive schemata, messages, and channel of distribution.

Table 1 shows these dimensions of the model. It indicates that the primary orientation of top executives is to generate information they hope structures the culture and the lower levels of the organization. Middle managers' orientations are primarily to interpret information. One main kind is that which top executives generate for structuring lower-level communication and behaviors. Another is what information middle managers obtain from

Table 1. Descriptive Model of Broad Features of Organizational Communication

	GENERATE INFORMATION Focus: Cognitive Schemata	INTERPRET INFORMATION Focus: Messages	APPLY INFORMATION Focus: Networks
TOP EXECS	Select and project values, beliefs, goals, and visions. Create meta-rules for middle management.	Communicate meta-rules to middle management. Evaluate strategic feedback from middle management.	
MIDDLE MANAGERS		Shape messages for distribution based on top execs generative info. Formulate rules for operatives. Gather operations feedback for top execs. and interpret.	
OPERATIVES		Provide mid. mgmt. feedback on "rule fit" to operation situations.	Follow rules for who-to-whom comm. about what and how via communication technology.

lower levels, and from outside the organization, as feedback to top executives on the functioning of systems. Operatives' primary orientation is to applying information, as they follow the systems of communication shaped and implemented by middle management as it interprets top management's goals. Operatives also provide feedback upward about how well the implemented systems are working.

It is useful to apply a rules perspective (Cronen, Pearce, & Harris, 1982). From this view, we can suggest that top management seeks to create the meta-rules — rules about rules — for communication and behavior in the organization. Middle management establishes the rules, based on the premises and assumptions generated by top mangement's meta-rules. Operatives follow the rules. (And they create their own rules for working inside or outside the top-down rules, or their own rules for communication not constrained by the top-down rules.)

Top management, in terms of basic orientation to communication variables, is centrally concerned with its own cognitive schemata for the organization. It is interested in individual executives' views about values, norms, beliefs, goals — its projection of the organization's culture. Accordingly, while top executives often balk at providing traditional audit data on their own communication networks and messages, they are more willing to provide data on their cognitive schemata for values, beliefs, assumptions, goals, etc.

Middle managers, because they focus on the interpretation of information flowing back and forth between executives and operatives, are most concerned with message content, its form of packaging, and the contextual factors providing opportunities and problems for message management. Accordingly, middle managers are most likely to wish to provide audit data on message content, form, information load, and problems in coupling top executive levels with operative levels, particularly in implementing new or revised communication systems.

Operatives, being mainly oriented to applying information and rules from middle management, are focused most on the communication networks in which they are imbedded. They are centered on issues of who is actually communicating with whom in the operations processes as contrasted with who middle managements and themselves think should be communicating with whom.

In addition to the interpersonal information flow networks in production processes, operatives are also concerned with networks defined in terms of technologies for communication. Operatives are likely to focus on who does and should have access to production control systems, and on systems for communicating upward with middle management about production, via such technologies as electronic mail, voice-mail, etc. In short, operatives are network oriented, both interpersonally and technologically, in terms of applying the rules, information and systems implemented by middle management. Operatives are most likely to conceptualize and provide audit data on communication networks. One such type of data is on what individuals or work units exchange information with others. Another type of data is on evaluation of communication technology networks which they are supposed to use.

Overall, as we will demonstrate in the examples in this chapter, rather than asking people to provide communication data (Goldhaber & Rogers, 1976; Wiio, 1976), automated auditing obtains it automatically via computer-based capture. Automated auditing is, therefore, best at obtaining information on operative-level processes and to some extent on middle management-level processes. Top executives' cognitive schemata are largely outside the domain of automated auditing.

An exception is analysis of causal belief structures from documentary evidence such as memos (Axelrod, 1976). While these causal belief methods have been applied to the thinking of foreign policy analysts, they could just as well be applied to intraorganizational analysis of cognitive structures of executives. Their memos and letters could be optically scanned, converted to computer text files, and subject to content analysis. Electronic mail, which could be similarly analyzed, is not widely used by top executives (Rice & Bair, 1984).

Functional Responsibilities for Organizational Communication

In the descriptive model, most information management functions occur at the middle management, rather than top executive, levels. Depending on the organization, some information management is the responsibility of staff who report to top executives. Functionally, these staff are more similar to middle managers than to top executives. Some information management responsibility is also centered among actual middle managers who are in the authority network (Guetzkow, 1965) in the organization. In short, there is diversity across organizations over whether particular information management functions are staff or line, and to which level in the hierarchy these functions report. But, in industrial organizations, the basic processes are of a middle management character. In contrast, in some service organizations, these functions may be at the operative level. Again, the service information operatives have much of the character of middle management positions in the manufacturing and resource extraction or processing sectors.

Table 2 summarizes major functional responsibilities over communication in large industrial organizations. While there is a great deal of diversity in how communication management functions are organized in particular settings and what these functions are actually called, most large organizations will have some version of the following functions and objectives.

Features of Automated Auditing

The techniques we overview in this chapter for auditing organizational communication across the various functions and objectives treated in Table 2 have a common link. This is

Table 2. Main Units Involved in Managing Organizational Communication

Functional Unit	Objectives
Personnel/Human Resource Management	Improve communication skills of employees, analyze and recommend changes in formal and informal communication processes primarily of an interpersonal nature.
Public Relations, or Corporate Communication	Manage external communication, and "mass" internal employee media such as publications, bulletin boards, video news, audio-video teleconferences.
Telecommunications Management	Implement and manage telephone services (normal and "voice mail") and networks (internal and external interfaces), and sometimes data communication and electronic mail.
Data Processing, or Management Information Systems, or Decision Support Systems	Develop and operate computer hardware and software tools for management.
Library/Information Services	Archive, reference, search, and retrieve information on demand, either manually or via computer databases maintained internally or provided by vendors.

using computer-based methods, not only for analyzing data, as most modern communication and social science methods do, but for initially capturing the data. Table 3 details some of the key features of automated auditing. It is efficient, complete, unobtrusive, natural, translation reducing, relational, and time-frame flexible. These attributes provide methodological value for organizational communication research. As well, the methods have theoretical payoffs. They elaborate our view of different conceptualizations of organizational communication processes. Theoretical questions may follow as to correspondence rules which may link these different representations and account for their degree of fit, extent of synchrony, etc.

Representations of Communication

Automated auditing brings into perspective a number of different representations of organizational communication processes. In contrast, traditional approaches have centered almost exclusively on representations as perceived and reported by participants. Sometimes observers are used (Bernard, Killworth, & Sailer, 1980). But there is evidence that observers cannot reliably represent participant perceptions. Beyond participant and observer forms of representing these communication processes, other forms of representation had not been often conceptualized.

Automated auditing methods include the first and second of the representations listed in Table 4: objective and analyzed. They put into perspective the remaining ones: socially-synthetic, observer-perceived, user-perceived, recalled, projected, and desired.

Within the eight main types of representations of organizational communication described in Table 4 is a host of different variables that can be conceptualized. The next section outlines a framework for organizing variables.

Table 3. Features of Automated Auditing of Organizational Communication

Feature	Description
Efficient	Automated procedures often require little human intervention once they are turned on and they can capture information over time without interruption.
Complete	All interactions can be obtained, avoiding problems of user recall, misrepresentation, or alternative cognitive framing of the communication process or event.
Unobtrusive	Records are captured without visible evidence to the users. Although some may be aware of monitoring, they may not behave reactively because of the transparency of monitoring and its constancy over time.
Natural	Rather than constructing artificial units in laboratories or observing partial units in the field, automated auditing enables studying units such as individuals, groups organizations, etc. as they actually occur.
Translation Reducing	The number of measurement translations between the behaviors and data analyzed are reduced compared to traditional research. This reduces one form of measurement error.
Relational	The methods enable more full implementations of relational methods such as network analysis and multidimensional scaling, thus staying closer to the original character of the behaviors studied.
Time-Frame Flexible	Analysts can aggregate data into a range of time intervals, depending on needs.

Table 4. Different Representations of Organizational Communication

Representation	Definition
1) Objective:	Recorded by an automated device, such as a computer program that monitors audio, video or text communication.
2) Analyzed:	Results from the analyst's filtering of the objective communication record through parameters and variable thresholds.
3) Socially-synthetic:	Constructed by non-scientific observers such as journalists, or public relations practitioners.
4) Observer-Perceived:	Observed and reported by non-participants in the communication activities.
5) User-Perceived:	Cognized by the participants as the communication takes place, and typically recorded by them in a log.
6) Recalled:	Remembered by participants after communication has taken place.
7) Projected:	What a participant thinks is occurring among other communicators.
8) Desired:	Currently not occurring, but wished for by organizational members, managers, or observers.

Frameworks for Conceptualizing Communication Variables

Cutting across these different representations of communication, and therefore applying to automated methods as well as others, are the kinds of variables that can be measured. Four dimensions can organize their diversity: participant level of analysis, cognitive schemata, message content, and channel.

Participant Level of Analysis. This is the level of observation and/or analysis, ranging from individual through dyad, small group, larger network, organization, inter-organization, sector, societal, international, (perhaps eventually "intergalactic" and "interintelligence"), and so on. Note that this distinction about levels is different from that described earlier in the descriptive model of organizational communication. There, the descriptive treatment of participant level was in terms of position in the organizational hierarchy. Here, from a methodological view, we are concerned with level of *analysis*: individual, dyad, group, etc. These levels cut across the hierarchy. For example, one could study individual operatives, middle managers, or top executives. Or one could study groups at the various hierarchy levels, and so on.

In terms of the realities of scientific research, however, levels are chosen based on the nature of the theoretical problem to be investigated about organizational communication. On the other hand, in applied communication problem-solving research, top executives often want researchers to adopt the individual level when dealing with top executives, the group level when dealing with middle managers, and the larger macro-network level or department level when dealing with operatives. This is because in practice, level of analysis tends to be inverse to locus of power. The more powerful the layer of the hierarchy, the more micro the level of analysis desired for it by top management.

This basic notion was often violated by communication researchers, particularly those of the "climate" school. They have done individual-level research on operatives' attitudes toward the information from top and middle management. Climate researchers may have sometimes inadvertently given too much power to the lower levels of the organization from the points of view of top executives.

Message Content. This is the manifest information communicated in terms of substance, themes, etc. (Krippendorf, 1980b), as well as the interpretations of its meanings for the participants (Adler, 1986), and the intentions of the actors.

Message Form. This is the manner in which the message is organized or packaged. Rather than dealing with the semantics of communication, as does content, form deals with the syntactics, structure, or "grammar" of communication. It is not what is "said," but how it is said via message organization, paralinguistics, visual form, multi-media mix, etc.

Channels. These are the modes of message distribution. Unlike traditional thinking about organizational communication, we can conceptualize quite a diverse range of channel types (Gumpert & Cathcart, 1986; Danowski, 1986a). Table 5 summarizes these with detailed examples of each type. Three broad categories include "individual-organizational," "interpersonal," and "mass organizational."

"Mass organizational" channels include those that have the features of mass media, but limited to the organizational system. For the most part, these channels involve centralized distribution of the same messages to a large audience at the same time, like corporate video news delivered via a closed-circuit network. In contrast, "interpersonal channels" involve interaction between two people or within groups, either face-to-face or mediated. "Individual-organizational" channels, in contrast to mass organizational ones, involve the individual as the source of the communication which is not directed to a specific individual or group on a one-shot or single-event basis. An example is creation of database records. Individual-organizational media are mostly one-way forms of communication, like mass organizational, but with the individual in the source role rather than the receiver role.

Variables

A wide range of communication variables can be operationalized through automated auditing. Participant levels of analysis provide a convenient way to group these variables. In Table 6, some examples of variables are noted. This table is not exhaustive, but illustrative of the attributes that may be useful to characterizing behaviors of communication systems.

Table 5. Different Types of Organizational Communication Channels

INDIVIDUAL-ORGANIZATIONAL	
Self-Expressive:	furnishings, clothing, buttons, stickers, etc.
Computer:	text "broadcasting," databases, expert systems and artificial intelligence.
INTERPERSONAL	
Face-to-Face:	conversions and speaking in dyads, small groups, and large groups.
Electronic Interpersonal:	telephone, audio and video teleconferencing, electronic mail, computer conferencing.
Print Interpersonal:	letters, notes, memos.
"MASS" ORGANIZATIONAL	
Display:	signs, posters, banners, bulletin boards, exhibits, electronic sign.
Pictoral:	photographic or graphic representations of real objects or persons.
Video:	linear video such as broadcast, CCTV, or tape, or interactive video tape or disk used for training, organizational news, etc.
Audio:	radio, public address, telephone announcement systems.
Print:	employee publications, reports, manuals, newsletters, brochures, messages printed checks or customer bills, press releases, etc.

Table 6. Selected Examples of Organizational Communication Variables

Variable	Definition
A. Individual	
Schemata Complexity:	discrimination, differentiation, and integration of cognitive structure in a particular domain.
Load:	amount and complexity of information processed.
Radiality:	degree of centrality in the person-centered network.
B. Dyad	
Frequency:	how often two individuals communicate.
Duration:	amount of time two people communicate.
Control:	extent to which message flow deviates from symmetry (two-way) and which node initiates.
C. Group	
Connectivity:	density of links in the group relative to to total possible $((n(n-1))/2$, where n = # of nodes.
Radiality:	degree of centrality in of a group in its network of groups.
D. Organization	
Differentiation:	number of groups relative to organizational size.
Integration:	extent of intergroup linkage.
Centralization:	degree of inequality in distribution of intergroup linkage.
Media Load:	amount of media coverage relative to organizational size.
Media Radiality:	degree of centrality of an organization among organizations comentioned in news stories about the organization.
Media Image:	word-networks occurring across news stories about the organization
Controlled Media Richness:	number and distribution of controlled media used by the organization for internal and external communication.

Other chapters in this book provide conceptual definitions of variables that may also be operationalized with automated auditing techniques.

Hardware and Software Configurations

Capturing communication data in different media requires different hardware and software configurations. Some of the basic features by medium are overviewed in Table 7. The

Table 7. Basic Hardware and Software Configurations by Channel

CHANNEL	HARDWARE-SOFTWARE	FUNCTIONS
Face-to-Face	speaker identification and speech recognition; voice-text converters	determines who is talking with whom, and what they are saying
	body sensors	determine who is proximate to whom over time.
Print	optical character reader	converts typed text into computer files.
Video	image processor	distinguishes objects, people, motions, scene complexity.
Computer-based Text	word analysis software	measures readability, grammatical features, word occurrences, word cooccurrence networks.
Electronic Interpersonal Traffic	traffic monitor and network analyzer	maps who-to-whom network of message exchange via telephone, electronic mail, and group computer conferencing.

table is organized by: type of channel monitored, necessary hardware and software, and function performed. Hardware and software configurations, of course, evolve, and are at different stages of development. Most of the necessary tools can be purchased off-the-shelf, and integrated with the organization's existing information systems. For some applications, custom configurations would be desirable.

EXAMPLES OF AUTOMATED AUDITING

In this section of the chapter, we turn to examples of automated auditing applications. The examples are organized in three broad categories, based on analysis of: (a) interpersonal networks, (b) tasks, and (c) messages, both internal and external.

Messages are the most central components of the communication process, and closest to the center of the communication discipline (Miller, 1966). But the treatment of categories here starts with networks, then moves through messages. This reflects the historical trends in the organizational communication research that has taken a relational view. It began first with who-to-whom network analysis, then moved to task, climate, and environmental influences on networks, and more recently to testing hypotheses about message structures flowing through who-to-whom networks.

In this chapter, network-oriented examples include: (a) intra-organizational telephone network analysis and (b) electronic mail traffic network analysis. A task-oriented example is of change overtime in the pattern of software usage in an organization. Internal message-oriented analysis examples include: (a) group teleconference network and content analysis, (b) computer conferencing network and content analysis, and (c) electronic mail content analysis. External message-oriented analysis examples include: (a) content analysis of interorganizational networks represented in news stories, and of advertisements; and (b) content analysis of focus groups' discussions.

Each example is described in terms of: purpose, organization, application, methods, results, and other theoretical and practical applications. The objectives are to show some of the diversity of possibilities. Each example could merit its own paper, but, given the current objectives, the reporting will be telescoped.

Who-To-Whom Network Examples

Example 1: Intra-Organizational Telephone Traffic Network

Purpose

Research on boundary-spanning (Tushman, 1977) has operationalized "key" internal communicators as those in the top 20% of the internal communication volume distribution. Tushman, however, did not empirically test this assumption. Such a test was the main purpose of our own analysis of the organization's internal telephone traffic patterns.

Another, more methodological, research objective was to explore whether automated call records could be effectively used to map the network of internal telephone traffic among employees. This would enable unobtrusive network analysis for hypothesis-testing research.

Organization

The organization investigated was a small, service-oriented one with approximately 231 employees in San Diego, California. As is typical, it had a private branch exchange (PBX) telephone switch to handle internal station-to-station calls as well as external calls. Each month, long-distance telephone records were analyzed for cost-control purposes.

Most organizations monitor their long-distance telephone traffic for cost control purposes using a standard device attached to their local telephone switch (PBX). Although the devices can capture both internal and long-distance call records of what phone numbers call what other numbers for what duration, the internal call records are typically discarded.

Methods

In this study, we simply arranged for a telephone accounting service firm that had the focal organization as a client to save both internal and external call records for a 2-week period in 1979. We then subjected the internal traffic data to network analysis. We used the network analysis program NEGOPY (Rice & Richards, 1981), version 6.0 for IBM mainframes (Richards, 1982). Parameter settings were at default levels for the algorithmic and group detection procedures. In addition to identifying functional communication groups and intergroup linker nodes, the program also computes the centrality of each node in the node-centric network. In other words, the program determines the extent to which the nodes to which a particular node is linked are also linked with one another. This variable is a type of node integration (Richards, 1974).

We correlated the node integration measure with a dummy variable representing whether or not the node was in the top 20% of the internal call distribution (Danowski, 1984a). This provided a test of the Tushman assumption used in "boundary-spanning" research.

Results

The simple correlation between node integration and being in the top 20% of the internal call volume distribution was an insignificant − .08 (see Table 8). These results, showing essentially no relationship between being central in a network and communicating in the high

Table 8. Correlations Between Internal Telephone Traffic Network Integration Volume of Calling: A Test of the Tushman Assumption

	NODE INTERGRATION*
TOP 20% OF TOTAL CALL DURATION (Dummy coded: 1 = top 20%, 0 = not)	− .09
TOP 20% OF TOTAL NODES CALLED (Dummy coded: 1 = top 20%, 0 = not)	− .08
TOTAL CALL DURATION (Continuous variable)	− .05
TOTAL NODES CALLED (Continuous variable)	− .02
TOP 20% OF TOTAL CALL DURATION PARTIALLING NUMBER OF TOTAL NODES CALLED	− .10

end of the distribution, provided no support for the validity of the "key communicator" operationalization underlying the boundary-spanning research. The application shows that telephone traffic data can provide useful bases for testing hypotheses.

Other Theoretical and Practical Uses

Theoretical questions that can be addressed with these methods include ones about relationships between intraorganizational communication structure and boundary-spanning (Allen, 1977), causal sequencing between these variables, relationships between network structures with different communication channels, and other questions which conceptualize variables in a network view.

At a practical level, although we had a rather narrowly focused research purpose — evaluating construct validity for the "key communicator" variables others had used — there are many diverse applications of automated auditing of organizational telephone traffic networks. Some of these include:

- describing the basic structure of internal telephone communication, identifying functional groups, intergroup linkers, and the various structural properties of the network.

This information can be used as a surrogate for traditional auditing of internal networks which relies on self-reports of who talks with whom. The advantages include those profiled in Table 3. To the extent that internal telephone traffic is representative of the overall communication networks regardless of medium, automated auditing of telephone traffic is a useful way to map internal communication structures.

Studies have yet to be done, however, which measure the degree of correspondence between telephone communication between pairs of individuals and their communciation via face-to-face and other modes. Such research would be useful. We would hypothesize based on anecdotal experiences that such networks would be quite correspondent except among those sharing the same local office spaces. Although not measuring networks directly, some evidence suggests that electronic mail substitutes for telephone communication, regular ("snail") mail, and group meetings (Dormois, Fioux, & Gensollen, 1978; Picot, Klingensberg, & Kranzle, 1982; Danowski, 1983a).

- overlaying long-distance call patterns onto the internal network.

Theoretical objectives about the relationships between intra- and inter-organizational communication (Danowski, 1974b; Wigand, 1979) can be achieved through linking internal and external telephone call patterns. External call patterns can be correlated with nodes' positions within the internal station-to-station network, enabling hypothesis testing. Records of communication traffic across organizational boundaries as well as internal traffic provide advantages over questionnaire data.

Practical applications can also be constructed. For example, a telecommunications manager may want to develop custom long-distance call control policies for different nodes that are based not merely on formal organizational status or departmental affiliation, but on functional position in the internal organizational network. Perhaps nodes in more central positions should have more access to long distance calling to improve organizational efficiency.

Example 2: Electronic Mail Traffic Network Analysis

Purpose

We had been conducting evaluation research to help improve implementation and use of an electronic mail system in an organization. In addition to surveying users, we captured all electronic mail text over a 1-year period. Serendipitously, a crisis occurred which enabled us (Danowski & Edison-Swift, 1985) to test hypotheses about crisis effects on communication (Schramm, 1971; Coleman, 1957; Rogers & Sood, 1981; Perry & Mushkatel, 1984), particularly on network structures.

Organization

The organization investigated in this study was a state-wide extension organization in a Midwestern state. As do most such organizations, this one had offices in each county of the state and central offices on a large public university campus. The organization maintained an electronic mail system for use by all personnel. It contained both private messaging and "broadcast" or mass mailing software. These communication services were part of the more extensive computer system developed mainly to provide county offices with software to aid decision making by residents. Numerous programs for agricultural management and consumer services were maintained.

In October 1981, it was announced that the organization would merge with another one and would have funding and operational changes. A freeze was placed on all hiring and spending. Employees engaged in a letter-writing campaign to protest legislators' budget cuts. Observers noted that the organization was experiencing a significant crisis.

Methods

The researchers captured full content of all messages exchanged from May 1981 to April 1982 (except for January, for which data were lost). Only private messages, numbering 2592, were analyzed. We implemented procedures to protect user privacy by not allowing researchers to examine individual messages. They looked only at the results of processed messages.

For each month, a network analysis of who sent messages to whom was performed using the NEGOPY (Rice & Richards, 1981) computer program, version 6.0 for IBM mainframes (Richards, 1982, 1986). Parameter settings were at default levels for all group detection and other algorithmic functions. The following variables were extracted from the network analysis results and plotted on a monthly basis: number of users, number of links, degree of interlocking among each user's contacts, percentage of reciprocation among pairs of nodes, and the number of group members identified.

Message content analysis was performed at the word level of analysis. Messages for each month were input to software that counted the number of times each unique word occurred. Word frequencies were made relative by computing the number of occurrences per 1000 words.

Results

The full results are reported in Danowski and Edison-Swift (1985). In summary, as hypothesized: amount of communication increased, number of communicators increased, messages became shorter, individual-level networks became less interlocking, one large user group formed, and communication structures largely returned to baseline levels without oscillation. Content analysis of messages revealed statistically significant increases in words associated with the organizational changes. This evidence helped rule out rival explanations for the communication changes observed. Figure 1 and Table 9 exemplify the information available in the larger report.

Other Theoretical and Practical Uses

An important issue in theory building is defining units of analysis that fit the conceptual structure of the theory. For example, if groups are the unit theorized about, then actual groups should be analyzed in the organization. Organizational researchers, however, have faced difficulties in measuring actual groups. Much of our knowledge of group processes is based on laboratory studies using newly constructed groups of strangers drawn from un-

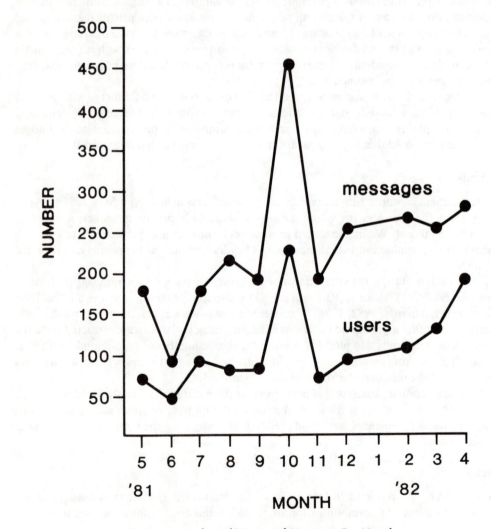

Figure 1. Number of Users and Messages Per Month

Table 9. Word Cooccurrence Change for October

	SEPT.	OCT.	NOV.
INCREASING WORDS	occurrences per 1000 words		
authorize	.4	3.2	.91
because	1.9	6.1	2.7
consequence	.7	2.5	.5
cooperative	.7	33.6	.5
cost	6.0	15.2	9.6
decision	3.4	11.6	1.4
detail	.4	5.8	1.4
different	1.1	4.0	11.4
directly	.4	3.3	.9
eliminate	.7	3.3	.5
explanation	.4	4.3	1.8
extension	7.1	45.1	15.1
federal	2.2	40.0	1.4
finance	.7	6.9	.5
forced	.4	7.6	.0
function	1.5	11.9	.5
funds	2.2	48.0	1.8
further	1.5	5.4	2.3
give	2.6	10.1	10.5
increase	1.1	23.1	0.0
joint	.4	7.6	2.7
legislature	.7	8.7	.5
never	.7	2.5	.5
potential	.4	4.7	.5
purpose	1.9	4.7	1.8
recommendation	1.9	10.8	.9
relevant	.7	15.2	.0
salary	1.5	7.6	.5
separate	1.5	3.6	1.8
statement	.4	4.7	3.2
strong	2.6	6.1	.0
support	.7	7.2	4.1
these	5.6	17.3	12.3
today	2.2	9.0	2.3
various	.7	5.8	.5
where	2.2	6.9	.9
DECREASING WORDS			
agenda	7.4	1.8	3.2
concern	10.4	4.3	6.4
content	4.1	.4	1.8
description	3.4	22.7	3.2
determine	6.7	1.4	1.8
file	9.3	2.9	14.2
person	13.8	1.8	6.4

*Words selected are those that show a statistically significant increase or decrease from September to October.

dergraduate university classes. But as some research has exemplified (Danowski, 1980) network analysis can be used to identify naturally occurring groups in organizations and test hypotheses about group communication structure and other variables. With automated network analysis of communication traffic, the group identification process can be made easier than occurs when asking for self-reports of communication behaviors. To the extent that electronic mail groups represent more broadly defined communication groups in the organization, the advantages noted for such data in Table 3 come into play.

Another consideration is that theories in which change over time is important, such as diffusion, can be tested with a sensitive representation of communication network structures. These have been found important in mediating the diffusion process through social systems (Rogers, 1983). Sometimes there are practical advantages to doing over-time analysis. These involve managing the course of innovations. For example, to evaluate electronic mail communication being introduced for managers nationwide, in a telecommunications company, the author conducted a monthly network analysis of electronic mail traffic.

The research goal was to see if, based on the first 6 months of implementation, adjustments were needed in the diffusion management process. Table 10 shows a plot of the number of groups each month. Because the trend line fit the "start-up" and "take-off" portions of the classic S-shaped curve for diffusion of innovations, the author concluded that no management interventions were necessary; the diffusion process was naturally occurring on course. Indeed, subsequently the system became successfully integrated and usage continued to complete the full S-shaped diffusion curve up to 2 years later.

Automated auditing of electronic mail traffic also enables creation of sensitive field experiments. One can do a baseline network analysis to define groups or other network roles. These can then be assigned to treatment and control groups. Experimental treatment messages can then be disseminated via the electronic mail system or other media, and effects variables measured in either an automated or nonautomated fashion.

Task-Oriented Example

Example 3: Software Usage Patterns-Multidimensional Scaling

Purpose

Computer software is a set of meta-messages. Programmers encode information on how to process other information and display it to users. It is akin to other such specifications of communication rules, like management handbooks, or operations manuals, but adds the variable of interactivity. Users give some information to the meta-message before it yields output. As such, software usage patterns become interesting communication variables to theorize about and investigate.

Our purpose was to explore a means of profiling a program use space across a set of users. Once such a method were workable, one could test hypotheses about the structure of the space and its change over time as a function of other variables, such as the communication network structure of the organization. Our first task was to see if a form of cooccurrence analysis could work as a way to profile software usage spaces.

Our premise was that we could define relationships between pairs of software programs according to how often individuals used them together in a time period. Then the set of pair-wise data could be subjected to multidimensional scaling or network analysis. The result is a space or network using software as objects (nodes) which reflects aggregate pro-

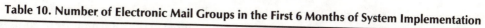

Table 10. Number of Electronic Mail Groups in the First 6 Months of System Implementation

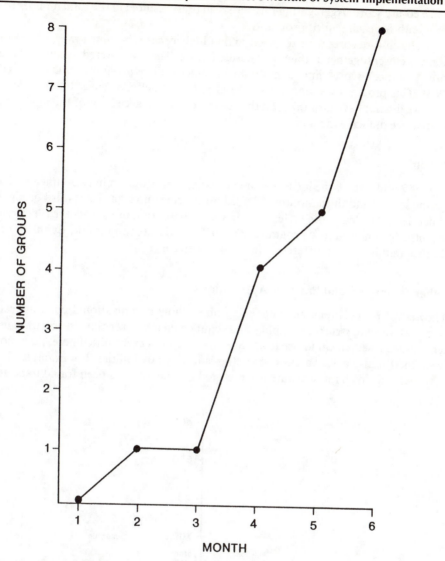

gram co-use patterns across users. On a theoretical level, one could test hypotheses about communication messages that may reconfigure software use behaviors. On a management level, results of such analysis could help manage the introduction of new software into the organizational user community.

Organization

The extension organization described earlier provided data for this research.

Methods

For each of 3 consecutive months, we obtained results of automated software use accounting programs. These indicated for each user how many times he or she had used each of 22 software packages in a month. We looked at all possible pairs of such programs and generated a co-use score. Aggregating this across all users resulted in the total number of co-uses per month for each pair of programs.

The co-use scores were reversed so that higher scores became lower, indicating that a pair was closer together as they were co-used more. Then we entered a matrix of these pairwise "distance" scores into a multidimensional scaling program, MDSCAL (Kruskal, 1964). This program was chosen over GALILEO (Woelfel & Fink, 1980) because, at the time, we did not have it running on the computer we had access to for the research project, whereas we did have the nonmetric MDSCAL available.

Results

Figures 2 and 3 show the locations of each computer program in two-dimension solutions for the second and third months. The scaling revealed no significant third or higher-order dimensions. One can note differences in relative program use across the time-series. Note the introduction of a new program, "OTHER" in the second month. By the third month, the program is located differently in the usage space.

Other Theoretical and Practical Applications

Theoretical propositions are interesting about how organizational communication networks of varying structure amplify and dampen change over time in software usage patterns. Such research could use techniques like the ones exemplified here. At a more micro level, there is also a wide array of hypothesis-testing possibilities. For example, differences in the way in which the software is structured for the user has been found to be associated

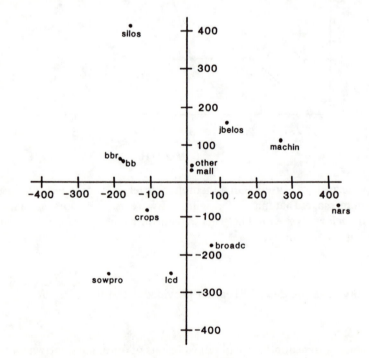

Figure 2. Cooccurrence of Computer Programs by Users: February

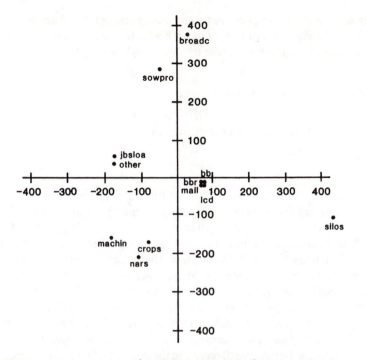

Figure 3. Cooccurrence of Computer Programs by Users: March

with variations in users' cognitive styles (Lewis, 1986). Perhaps cognitive styles are associated with a pattern of using clusters of software that vary in interaction style. The current method can profile users according to software patterns, so that hypothesis about software attributes and information-processing styles can be readily tested.

Practically, managers of information systems could use techniques such as those exemplified here to describe their users' software use patterns. The relational approach of MDS provides an easy to communicate graphic representation, as the figures show. Maps of software usage patterns can help in "navigation" for the information system.

Beyond description, managers could develop strategies for introducing new software. The analysis of results from the early introduction period could show which programs are most often co-used by the earlier adopters. Then, other users of these programs could be given specific messages informing them about the features of the new software and encouraging them to use it. In this way, management of subsequent diffusion is most likely to enhance naturally occurring usage patterns. At the same time, message efficiency would be high. Such controlled field experiments are relatively easy to construct and implement.

Location and site analysis could also be performed with these techniques. For example, let's say that managers of a bank's automatic teller machines (ATMs) were interested in mapping which ATMs were related through co-use. Then clusters of ATMS could be managed similarly. For each ATM user, co-use of different machines could be indexed and scaled. It may be that the geographic map of ATM locations and the functional usage map could look quite different. The latter would reflect the behavioral space of users rather than only the physical space of ATM placement.

Similar applications could be used in mapping product purchases, if the sales data showed which products were bought by the same consumer. One could scale the product spaces using the results of supermarket optical-scan checkout data. Similarly, in the videotex area different types of content that users accessed could be co-use scaled and the results used for management or testing hypotheses. In fact, any sort of database use could be looked at in terms of the coselection of entries by users.

Internal Message-Oriented Examples

Example 4: Content Diversity in a Computer Conference

Purpose

One of the major questions framed in the communication sciences and related ones like sociology is how message content is associated with interpersonal communication network structure. Granovetter's (1973) "strength of weak ties" notion suggests, at the dyadic level, that individuals who are more similar have stronger emotional bonds, and that, as this affective strength increases, informational strength decreases. This is because, as individuals are more similar, they have less unique information they can share. Moving from the dyadic case to the network case, individuals with diverse contacts with others will have weaker emotional ties to them and stronger information, or instrumental ties.

In this research, we focused on the latter aspect, the informational one. We tested the hypothesis that individuals more central in a network, and individuals with a greater volume of links, would have more diversity in the content of their messages. The communication activities occurred via a computer conferencing system.

Organization

The organizational context for the study was the International Communication Association. A computer conference about ways to increase uses of communication technology for member communication was sponsored by the Human Communication Technology Interest Group. The author organized the conference and held it on the University of Wisconsin-Madison's mainframe computer in 1982. Users accessed the conference via the TELENET network. The conference ran for 2 weeks.

Methods

Two coders analyzed the transcript of all messages, and created a list of elemental content. The lists were synthesized and then used to code each message for which of the content elements were included in each. Coder reliability exceeded .90. A third coder resolved disagreements.

Messages were then grouped by sender and each was given a score for content diversity. This was the information theoretic measure of H: $- \Sigma\ pi\ (\log_2 pi)$, where pi is the proportion of messages in the "ith" content category (Shannon & Weaver, 1949; Danowski, 1974c). The index then reflects both the number of categories invoked by a user's messages and the rectangularity of frequencies across these categories. Increases in either add to content diversity.

Network analysis was performed on the messages as well, for purposes of mapping who sent messages to whom. If an individual explicitly mentioned another user's name in the message header or text, this was coded as a link between these users. Additionally, if the message did not mention a specific other user, but made reference to a topic that a prior user had initiated, then a link was coded between the two users.

Network analysis results enabled computing the centrality of each node as well as the number of links to different other users. These two variables were correlated with content diversity.

Results

Figure 4 shows both the network structure and the results of the Pearson correlations. Both number of links and centrality were positively related to content diversity, but number of links had a stronger relationship. The hypothesis was supported, with the implication that when considering relationships to content diversity, total number of links to different people in a computer conference is more important than being centrally positioned among users. The relatively lesser potency of centrality may be due the nature of the medium's effects on communication. Being central in a network in which all participants see the messages of all others may wash away some of the information power that a central individual may have in a setting in which there is less than full access of all to the messages exchanged. This occurs in private electronic mail, or in traditional organizational communication settings, using a variety of media.

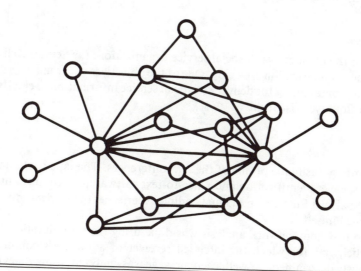

	NUMBER OF CATEGORIES	CONTENT DIVERSITY
NODE CONNECTEDNESS (Number of Links)	.62*	.45*
NODE INTEGRATION	.22	.31
n = 16		

* $p < .05$.

Figure 4. Individual Node Integration, Connectedness, and Content Diversity in a Computer Conference

Other Theoretical and Practical Applications

An area for further research is to examine effects of individual centrality and number of links on the natural language patterns of messages. Word-network structures, rather than category distributions, would give a finer-grained picture of message diversity. As well, causal sequencing could be examined. What effect does using language in a particular way have in the longer term on ones positioning in a network? Or is the causal flow in the other direction only?

Example 5: Teleconferencing Participation

Purpose

As part of a course at the University of Wisconsin-Madison about the evaluation of communication programs, the author formed a student research team to desgin and conduct evaluation research for a client. Because the client representatives and the researchers were located in distant geographic locations, we used audio teleconferencing to conduct some of the initial project planning meetings. As a side interest, research team members wanted to analyze the transcripts of the teleconference to gain additional research experience. This interest led to the present example.

Organization

The client for the research was a social service organization, the Service Delivery Project, funded by the Administration on Aging. One of the objectives of the unit was to develop cable television programming for delivery of social service information to elderly residents of Trempeleau County, Wisconsin.

Methods

A tape recording was made of one of the teleconferences. The tape could have been analyzed using speaker identification and voice-to-text software, hence fully automating that part of the analysis. But to gain manual coding experience, the student investigator processed the tape himself.

A who-to-whom network analysis was done using the total duration of interaction among participants for which the intended receiver of a speaker's comments could be unambiguously determined. As well, each message was analyzed, using Bales (1950) coding scheme for assessing content.

Results

Figure 5 shows the results of the teleconference analysis. The substantive features are not of direct relevance to this example and are left undiscussed.

Other Theoretical and Practical Uses

Theoretically, hypotheses can be tested about how qualitative features of media such as "social presense" (Short, Williams, & Christie, 1976) mediate relationships found in tradi-

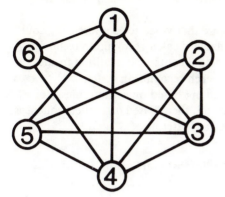

Bales Category KEY:

1. Shows solidarity
2. Shows tension release
3. Agrees
4. Gives suggestion
5. Gives opinion
6. Gives orientation
7. Asks for orientation
8. Asks for opinion

Categories 9-12 did not occur in this teleconference: Asks for suggestion, Disagrees, Shows tension, Shows antagonism.

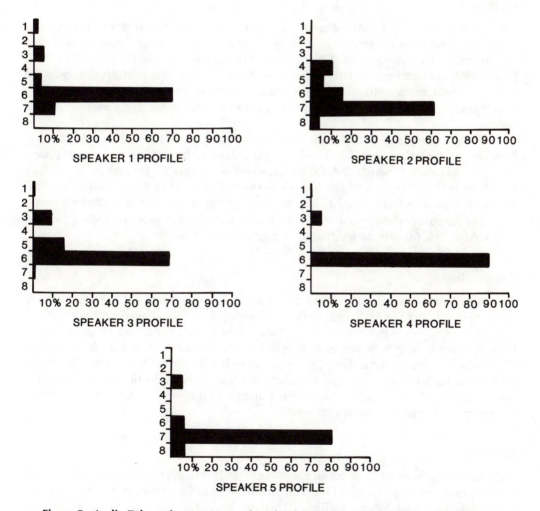

Figure 5. Audio Teleconference Network and Bales Interaction Profiles of Participants

tional small group research about communication (Shaw, 1964) conducted in face-to-face mode.

More practical methodological considerations are that video teleconferencing could also be analyzed using similar techniques. With available speaker recognition technology, the analysis could be fully automated. Much of the actual content, in addition to speaker identification, could be analyzed with voice-to-text speech recognition systems.

Purposes could be for managing speaker turn-taking based on certain rules. For example, if it were desired that participation be more equal, then, based on earlier sequences of interaction, speaker priority could be programmed to foster it.

Example 6: Computer Bulletin Board Content-Multidimensional Scaling

Purpose

We were interested in developing methods for automated content analysis of computer-based text. Two methods seemed promising for this, one being multidimensional scaling and the other network analysis. One particular type of MDS, "GALILEO" (Woelfel & Fink, 1980), appeared particularly well suited to our needs in that it offers the option of finding optimal messages to subsequently change discourse within a language community. This feature is desirable for hypothesis testing, as well as for managing a communication system.

Unfortunately, GALILEO is limited to analyzing 40 concepts. Not bound in this way, however, is network analysis. The NEGOPY procedures to be highlighted in a subsequent example, can handle upwards of 4,000 nodes, which in our case are concepts or words. But a problem is that network analysis has not developed procedures for generating optimal messages, a good feature of GALILEO. So, at this point, each method has its own uses.

The purpose of this particular analysis was to develop means for using MDS, particularly GALILEO, for content analysis of computer-based messages.

Organization

Computer bulletin board systems, which include a form of group conferencing, dyadic electronic mail, and file exchange, are now widespread in communities and in organizations, with estimates of more than 3,000 systems in operation. In the mid-1970s, computer bulletin board systems were just beginning to operate. One of the first boards on the East Coast was operated by the Boston Computer Club. It used the software from "Ward and Randy's" bulletin board in Chicago (Christensen & Suess, 1978), the first popular board to operate in the U.S.A. We captured the first 6 months of messages (constituting a sort of a computer conference) on the Boston board.

Methods

Methods were described in detail in Danowski (1982). Here we provide a summary. In 1978, we first recorded all content from the first 6 months of operation of the Boston Computer Bulletin Board System (CBBS). Then we extracted message pairs—meaning a message posted and a response to it. All concepts in these messages were inventoried, and the top 25 most frequently occurring were selected.

Taking each concept pair one at a time, we gave a cooccurrence score of 1 to each pair of concepts that appeared across each message pair. This procedure was repeated for each pair, and the matrix of cooccurrences was aggregated. Then the cooccurrence scores were reversed, so that lower scores meant that concepts were "closer" in cooccurrence. Finally, these values were scaled using the GALILEO multidimensional scaling program.

Results

Table 11 and Figure 6 show the results of the scaling in coordinate and graphic terms. The optimal message generation procedures were also tested. One of the distant concepts, "user group," was selected as the concept to move closer to the center of the space. The vector optimization procedures yielded the concepts of "free," "games," and "source code." This means that, if one wanted to move the concept of "user group" closer to the center of discussion, the best strategy would be to say that the group offers for free the source code software of computer games.

Other Theoretical and Practical Applications

Theoretically, such methods can be used to test hypotheses about diffusion of information and its effects on message structures. Diffusion research has largely ignored the message content constructed by potential adopters about the innovation. Rather, diffusion research has focused on the innovation itself, on media exposure, and on characteristics of adopters (Rogers, 1983). Detailed time-series views of how the potential and actual adopters' seman-

Table 11. Coordinates of CBBS Message Concepts on Three Dimensions

Concept		Dimension 1	Dimension 2	Dimension 3
1	CBBS procedures	125.5	6.6	− 137.5
2	Modems	77.0	198.4	− 52.3
3	Request help/info.	− 79.2	− 140.9	5.7
4	Give help/info.	− 37.7	− 56.4	87.0
5	Offer information	380.0	− 77.5	− 9.6
6	Salutation	157.5	− 99.9	− 109.7
7	Give address/phone no.	− 226.1	233.3	119.7
8	Software	− 3.0	282.1	137.4
9	User group	− 251.2	− 59.1	213.4
10	Offer something free	− 159.1	− 298.6	12.7
11	Computer games	− 282.5	− 62.6	258.4
12	Request leave message	− 306.7	13.1	− 46.5
13	Refer to earlier message	146.0	− 127.7	355.0
14	Computer for blind	− 59.4	188.0	− 89.2
15	Express interest	7.7	393.3	− 162.4
16	Source listing	− 238.2	− 29.7	201.5
17	Other computer system	260.9	− 147.8	63.4
18	Hard copy	407.4	− 121.8	107.9
19	Thank you	260.2	− 59.4	120.3
20	Acknowledge message receipt	335.0	165.5	− 31.8
21	Discuss own computer problems	− 120.7	137.9	− 69.0
22	Request message deletion	− 264.7	− 170.3	− 184.4
23	Fantasy	− 95.0	− 290.9	− 324.4
24	Ask for participation	− 31.4	− 189.9	− 334.7
25	Will send info. by other means	− 2.2	314.4	− 130.9

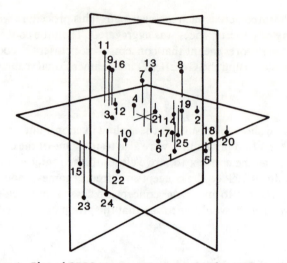

Figure 6. Plot of CBBS Message Concepts in Three Dimensions

tic structures associated with the innovation are shaped can stimulate theoretical work in this area. Additionally, Kaplowitz and Fink's (1982) theoretical propositions about message diffusion and effects, using physics principles about wave dynamics like "fixed-mass spring models," can be tested in highly-controlled ways. Researchers can capture the full text of subjects' communication. These data could be joined with additional data obtained directly from subjects.

Another area for theoretical work is on the concept of "message warp." Earlier, Woelfel and Fink (1980) explicated the concept of "cognitive warp," referring to the occurrence of imaginary dimensions in a spatial solution for cognitive data. Cognitive warp appears to index the abstractness of the cognitive system. A parallel concept could be conceived for messages. "Message warp" is a function of imaginary dimensionality in a space based on concept cooccurrences. More warped messages are likely more abstract. Such a message construct would enable testing hypotheses that individuals with more warped cognitive systems generate more warped messages. Also testable would be hypotheses about how individuals with more "Euclidean" (less warped) cognitive systems process warped messages, with what effects.

Considering more practical uses, the techniques outlined could be applied to ongoing management of organizational communication via computer-based communication. If management wanted certain concepts to become more central to employee discussions, for example "safety," then optimal messages using existing concepts from the employee linguistic community could be generated. These messages could then be sent to individuals. Similarly, concepts that management did not wish as often talked about could be analyzed to see which messages would optimally move the concepts away from the center of discussion. Then these optimal messages could be disseminated to subsequently move the undesired concepts further out in the conversational space.

Example 7: Network Analysis of Computer-Based Messages

Purpose

Given the results described in the second example, in which the automated methods detected a crisis that had impacted organizational communication behaviors, we were interested in looking more closely at the content of interactions. Recall that, in the earlier study, we used word frequency counting to automatically determine which words were significantly more and less likely to be talked about during the apparent crisis month. This kind of content analysis, while revealing, treated words atomistically (Stone, 1966; Bales & Cohen, 1979). No information was available on the patterns of relationships in word usage, only on their frequencies of occurrence.

So, in this study, we wanted to take a more relational approach. Because there were so many words, however, we did not want to limit our analysis to the top 40 words, as would be required by GALILEO. Therefore, we needed to explore network analysis. This study sought to develop the software for parsing text into words, and automatically generating word cooccurrence scores. Then words could be treated as nodes in a network and their strength of linkage based on the number of cooccurrences in messages.

Organization

The organization providing data for this research was the same extension organization as described in Example 2.

Methods

We wrote software (Danowski & Andrews, 1985) to scan text by sliding a window along the words and giving cooccurrence scores to pairs of words that appeared within the window. In this case, we used a window 5 words wide on each side of a word. This yielded a functional window size of 10 words, 5 on each side of a word. As the window passed over each word, the cooccurrence scores were updated.

Once the cooccurrence scanning was finished, we then input the data to the NEGOPY network analysis program. These data indicated, for each word, which other words it cooccurred with and the number of times this happened across the entire set of messages.

Results

NEGOPY identified three groups of words. Figure 7 shows one of these groups. The words appear to concern the operation of, and access to, the computer system itself. It is a sort of meta-communication, that is, communication about the communication medium. The other results, and their implications for the particular research objectives, are described in the more complete paper. Here, we simply present the graphic representation of one of the word-network groups for illustrative purposes.

Extending the work network analysis to the time-series case (Danowski, 1986b), the author tested hypotheses about who-to-whom network structures and word-network structures. Based on the "strength of weak ties" principle (Granovetter, 1973), one would expect that, as the interpersonal network becomes more interlocked, word-networks become more interlocked. In other words, stronger network ties yield less information, indicated by more interlocking of words. We also expected, based on the study of crisis effects on who-to-whom network structures (Danowski & Edison-Swift, 1985), that word-network structures would destabilize after the crisis.

Results were that crisis destabilized content networks; the crisis nearly quadrupled the amplitude of oscillation over the subsequent 6 months in size of the largest word group (see Figure 8). Also, as node integration in the interpersonal network increased, node integration in the word network increased; but node integration in the interpersonal network was

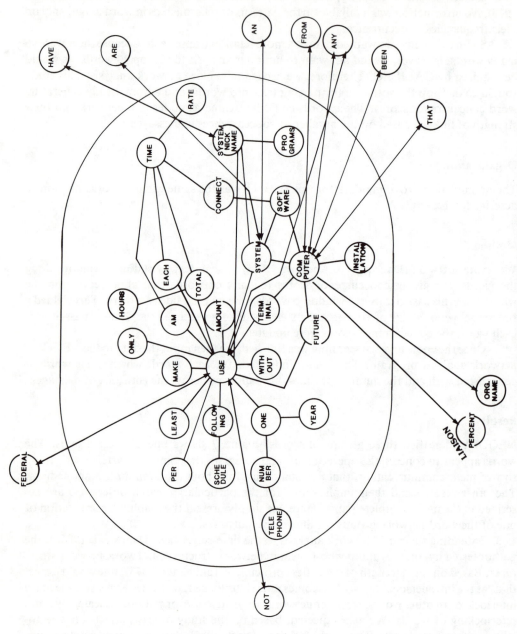

Figure 7. Electronic Mail Word-Network Group: "Systems Talk"

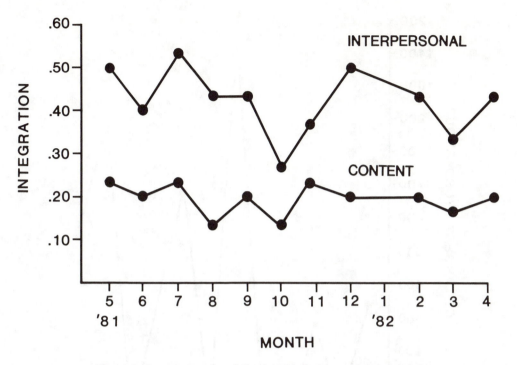

Figure 8. Interpersonal and Content Node Integration by Month

2.5 times more elastic over time than node integration in the word network (see Figure 9).

As word-node integration decreased, the number of word groups declined, as one of the word groups became very large. Overall, the size of the largest word group was positively correlated with the number of group members, indicating that the volume of shared content increased. Finally, there was an apparent 1-month lagged relationship between the number of messages (and users) and the number of word groups, with changes in the number of messages occurring prior to word group changes. This suggests that the infusion of diverse information in a month results in differentiation of word groups in the subsequent month.

Other Theoretical and Practical Uses

For theory-building purposes, these methods can be used to test hypotheses about network structure and language patterns. In the example, message content was treated only structurally in terms of node integration, rather than substantively in terms of the semantic features of the word network (Pollack & Waltz, 1986). Further research could examine the specific words identified in the content network. For example, hypotheses could be tested that individuals in more radial positions in the who-to-whom network use more power and autonomy words and more abstract words (Danowski, 1986b). Additionally, Granovetter's (1973) "strength of weak ties" notion suggests hypotheses that more radial networks are associated with more instrumental word patterns, while more interlocking networks are associated with more socio-emotional expressive word patterns.

For other kinds of theoretical problems, it is useful to test for whether two networks are significantly different from one another in structure. Is the network at time 1 different

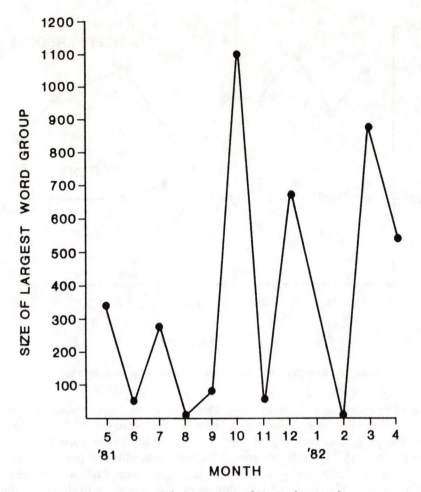

Figure 9. Size of the Largest Word Group by Month

from the network at time 2? In the example here, we used structural indicators of the network. But, in other research, a node/link level of comparison may be more appropriate. Baker and Hubert (1981) discuss ways to do this.

Another theoretical application is for organizational story analysis. One could scan electronic mail and conferencing texts (Kerr and Hiltz, 1982) for certain prologue structures (McLaughlin, 1984) to stories. Then, the selected texts could be analyzed with automated word-network techniques to identify story content and structure. These variables could in turn be linked with other variables about organizational structure and processes hypothesized to relate to story variables.

Another application is to identify the key features of organizational cultures, so that these can be used in testing hypotheses about how organizational structures and processes predict various cultural attributes. We can define organizational culture (Danowski & Andrews, 1985; Danowski, 1986c) as activations of associations among concepts. In turn, concepts are activations of word networks. In other words, word-cooccurrence networks define organizational concepts, and at a higher order, cooccurrence of concepts over time define organizational cultures.

More practically, this kind of word-network analysis maps the culture of the organization (Weick, 1985) in a sensitive, comprehensive, and systematic way (Danowski, 1986b). The techniques avoid problems of some "interpretive" research which tries to map the semantic features of a culture with qualitative techniques only. Here, we can deal with the fine-grained relationships among words that culture members use, but do so in an objective quantitative way.

One could use these techniques to describe the culture of an organization or subunit. Other applications could include more specific purposes. Let's say that managers wanted to make a concept more central in discussions, and to change its meaning. First, all electronic mail (or other messages that originated in other medial) would be word-network analyzed to identify the meanings of the focal word for the particular organizational culture. Then, for example, if the managers wanted to re-configure the cultural content of "quality" concepts, a second stage analysis using GALILEO and optimal message generation could be implemented. Subsequently, messages could be disseminated to optimally redefine the organizational meanings for the concept of "quality."

External Message-Oriented Examples

Example 8: Content Analysis of Individual News Stories

Purpose

We wished to apply automated content analysis techniques to the message domain of the mass media. From a broad perspective, it is useful to develop compatible automated techniques, not only to analyze the internal communication of organizations as exemplified earlier. It is also useful to apply the same techniques to external communication. Application of similar methods can reduce error in hypothesis-testing research. As well, they can add to coordinated public relations management. Accordingly, we selected a stream of news stories and performed an exploratory analysis. One of the research team members was interested in relationships between interorganizational communication and adherence to federal standards for database security.

Organization

Large organizations typically have public relations personnel responsible for managing the flow of information across organizational boundaries via the mass media and other channels. In this particular example, there was no actual organization as client for the study. However, the research to be described could have been conducted for the public affairs unit of any of the organizations noted in the results.

Methods

We obtained all stories appearing in the *New York Times Index* about these topics for the first 6 months of 1981. We were interested in identifying which organizations were the key actors. So, in each story we gave cooccurrence scores to pairs of organizations that were comentioned in the story. These scores were aggregated across all stories in the set. Then we performed network analysis on the data using the same procedures and NEGOPY.

To obtain data on adherence to federal standards for database security, we asked two experts, faculty member specializing in security in the Computer Science Department at the

University of Wisconsin-Madison, to indicate which organizations they thought adhered to the standards. They were given a randomized list of organizations. Only those organizations about which the two experts agreed were coded as the darkened circles in Figure 10.

Results

The figure reflects a second stage of analysis after network analysis. As you can see, there is an apparent relationship with the group structures found through the network analysis. Of the two largest groups, the one with the more radial internal structure had the highest perceived adherence, 90%. The more connected group, which contains more government agencies as nodes, had the lowest perceived adherence, 13%. For smaller network units like the triad and the dyads, at least 50% of the nodes were perceived to adhere to the federal security standards. Both isolated nodes were so perceived.

The findings about the two large groups are compatible with the relationships found between network centrality and power, autonomy, and control (Danowski, 1984b). Having secure computer databases seems associated with maintaining such a profile. As well, radial network structures are more innovative (Danowski, 1976; Rogers & Kincaid, 1981), and the federal security standards were an innovation at the time the data were obtained.

Other Theoretical and Practical Uses

Theoretical value can be obtained from such methods. Danowski, Barnett, and Friedland (1986) found evidence for hypotheses that position in interorganizational networks is associated with amount of media coverage and stock prices. They also illustrated how automated content analysis could be used to move beyond media coverage volume to measuring qualitative features of the content linking with cognitive schemata of audiences. In turn, these may predict stock price changes and other behaviors, such as activation of interpersonal networks that may penetrate the interorganizational domain. Figures 11 and 12 show an example of network analyses of cognitive structures. As a pilot study, a sample of stock brokers (n = 6) was asked the open ended question, "When you think of ITT Corporation, what comes to mind?" Then cooccurrences scores of words and phrases within individuals' response sets were computed. These were then network analyzed. Open-end data such as these can be automatically captured by asking questions of individuals who are on computer communication systems, like electronic mail and conferencing. For questions answered orally, one could perform voice-text conversion, then conduct the word-network analysis.

Among other applications, one could test hypotheses about how media message content is processed by and affects individuals with different cognitive schemata. Such research could be done with mass media or organizational media messages.

Other theoretical questions testable with the broader set of methods illustrated in the Danowski et al. (1986) study include how variations in inter- and intraorganizational structures are associated with variations in the press release content that organizations project to the mass media. In turn, researchers can study how these organizational variables and media institutional variables may predict the degree of acceptance of press release content by journalists, and the degree of modification of such messages, as well as the ratio of reporter-initiated to source-initiated content that is presented in the mass media.

More practically, public relations (public affairs or public information) managers could use similar techniques to aid in managing their functions. Not only the names of organizations could be the focal point. Issues could be analyzed, as well as words used to de-

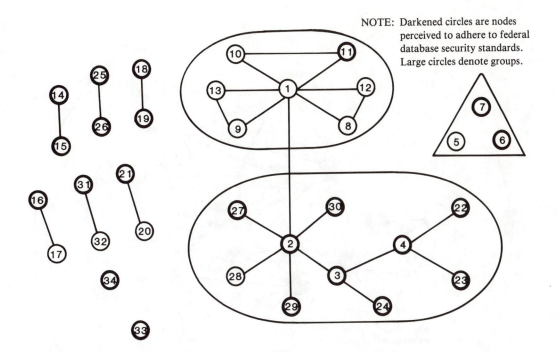

NOTE: Darkened circles are nodes perceived to adhere to federal database security standards. Large circles denote groups.

NODE NUMBER	ORGANIZATION	NODE NUMBER	ORGANIZATION
1	United States Justice Department	18	U.S. Army
2	IBM	19	Norden Systems Inc.
3	Bernay, Smith, Upham, Inc.	20	Safeway Food Stores
4	Sperry Univac Inc.	21	MSI Data Corp.
5	Brazilian Government	22	Mitsubishi Heavy Industries
6	Honeywell Information System	23	Mega-Data Corp.
7	Inspec	24	NCR
8	OPM Leasing Services	25	Dow Jones and Company
9	N.Y. Institute of Technology	26	Tandy Corp.
10	Government Services Adminis- tration (GSA)	27	European Economic Community (EEC)
11	Computer Sciences Corp.	28	Greyhound Computer Corp.
12	Cali Trading International, Inc.	29	Matsuishita, Inc.
13	Balmon Inc.	30	Morgan Stanley Company
14	Quotron Systems Inc.	31	Control Data Corporation
15	Beehive International	32	University of Brock
16	Data Products Corp.	33	Burroughs
17	American Airlines	34	Northern Telecom

Figure 10. Perceived Adoption of Database Security Standards by Organizations Represented in New York Times About Databases

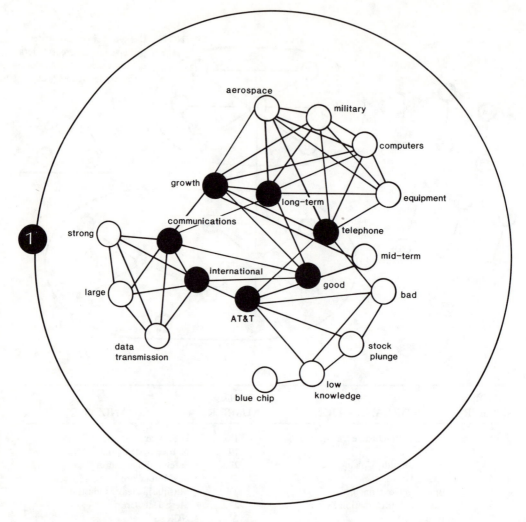

Figure 11. Cognitive Network about ITT Corp. Held by Stockbrokers

scribe them and the organization or individuals. Such an approach would yield an "image map"of press coverage.

The uses of such research could include:

- describing the images communicated in the press,
- comparing press release information to news story content to determine which information is most likely discarded, and
- finding which image components to include in releases introducing new concepts so that acceptance is increased.

Advertising could also be analyzed with similar techniques. Sinno (1982) found, through experiments, that subjects would pay more money for automobiles which had more factual advertising content and less evaluative content in classified newspaper ads. So, in a follow-up test of hypotheses about price and advertising content networks, Jin-Lin Liang and I selected automobile advertisements appearing in the top 10 consumer maga-

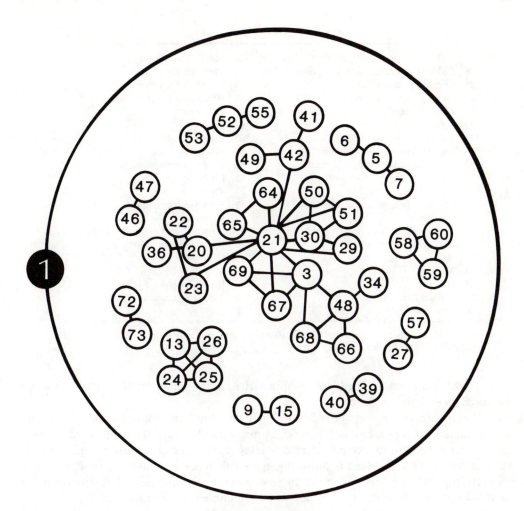

KEY TO FIGURE 12

1	ITT	*19	Chernow Communications
* 2	Qume	20	Malaysia
3	U.S. Army	21	GTE
* 4	United Telecommunications	22	NEC
5	Nigeria	23	Fujitsu
6	International Monetary Fund	24	LM Ericsson
7	Mobil Oil	25	Seimens AG
* 8	Medscience	26	Central Intelligence Agency
9	U.S. Air Force	27	U.S. Government
*10	Spain Telephone	*28	California Public Utilities Comm.
*11	Chase Manhattan Bank	29	Pacific Telesis
*12	British Telecom	30	MCI
13	Turkey	*31	Spain
*14	Teletas	*32	IBM
15	Texas Instruments	*33	Coins Group
*16	EDS	34	Britain
*17	Times Mirror Corp.	*35	Standard Oil of Ohio
*18	Times Mirror Microwave	36	Treego Bina PTY, Ltd.

Figure 12. Organizations Cooccurring in News Stories about ITT in the Wall Street Journal in 1984

KEY TO FIGURE 12 (*continued*)

*37	Bell Telephone Manufacturing	57	Soviet Government
*38	Federal Communications Commission	58	Christian Rovsing As
39	Laxard Freres and Co.	59	Denmark PKA Pension Fund
40	Golman Sachs and Co.	60	Handelsbank Copenhagen
41	General Electric	*61	Fortune
42	AT&T	*62	Forbes
*43	Federal Trade Commission	*63	Screenplay, Inc.
*44	On-Line Software International	64	Bellsouth
*45	Securities and Exchange Commission	65	Allnet Communications
46	West Germany	66	Plessy Co. pic
47	Hungary	67	Thomas sa
48	Standard Telephone and Cables pic	68	Rockwell International
49	Virginia	69	Raytheon
50	Southern Tel	*70	Nippon Telephone and Telegraph
51	TDX Systems	*71	New American Library
52	Ralston Purina	72	Compushop, Inc.
53	Moody's	73	MBank of Dallas
54	U.S. Navy	*74	New York Stock Exchange
55	Standard and Poors	*75	Sonat Exploration Co.
56	Deutsche Bank		

NOTE: Organizations noted with an asterisk co-appeared only with ITT and, to facilitate readability, do not appear in Figure 12.

zines in 1985. Copy was entered into computer files, and we then ran network analysis on the words cooccurring in the copy.

The copy for cars prices above $16,000, compared to those below $9,000 (controlling for the amount of copy), had nearly twice as many word groups (11, contrasted with 6). This indicates that, for higher-priced automobiles, copy writers use more recurrent word-patterns across the ads. There is more aggregate coherence or consensus in what is said about the top-end vehicles. Content of these word groups more often dealt with technical features of the automobiles. The results were compatible with the earlier study.

Organizational "mass" media, such as employee publications, could also be treated with the word-network analysis techniques. Letters from consumers could be automatically analyzed too.

Back to news research considerations, single news stories can be analyzed as well as series of stories as illustrated already. The author worked with Shult (1984) in developing similar techniques to analyze the structure of a news story about covert military operations among some southern African countries. Figure 13 shows the two-dimensional multidimensional scaling of the concepts. The story was an actual one, but the names were changed to reduce bias in the experimental design Shult was using. She was testing hypotheses about cognitive structure and learning from message structures, and wished to minimize the effects of prior foreign affairs knowledge of the particular events treated in the news story.

Example 10: Word-Network Analysis of Focus Group Discussions

Purpose

Voice-to-text converters that take audio tape or real-time human voices and create text files of the raw natural language enable a wide array of automated auditing of messages,

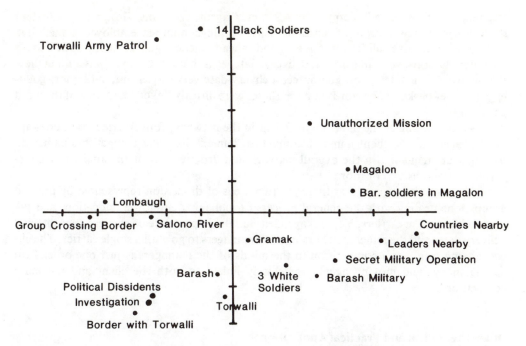

Figure 13. News Story Analysis: Cooccurrence Content Analysis Plot of First Two Dimensions

both internal and external to the organization. To test the automated word-network analysis procedures for content analyzing vocally generated language, we obtained three focus groups who discussed the same topic. Our purpose was simply to pilot test the techniques to see if they would work, anticipating more widespread dissemination of the voice-to-text converters that have been developed by major computer organizations.

Organization

Focus groups were conducted by an advertising agency for a moving van client interested in managers' of corporate employee relocation views of the moving company's services and those of competitors. Corporate traffic managers of household goods movement participated in focus groups in New York, Chicago, and Los Angeles.

Methods

Transcripts of each focus group were combined into a single computer file and input to the word-network analysis software described earlier. A window size of three words, resulting in a functional window size of seven words, was used. Since the first analyses when larger windows were used, the author has found, through extensive testing, that the seven-word functional window yields virtually the same results as the larger ones and yet is much more economical of computer resources. The resulting word-cooccurrence scores were network analyzed with NEGOPY, using default settings for the algorithm and group detection.

Results

Network analysis identified two groups. Group 1 (n = 60) had the following nouns in order of centrality: people, moves, carriers, year, time, companies, dollars, household, service, money, "client name," "competitor A's name," agent, problems. Group 2 (n = 36) had the following nouns in order of centrality: carrier, things, number, employee, somebody.

There were five full liaison nodes: good, ahead, agency, guaranteed, down; and six secondary liaisons: very, important, delivery, date, eggs, basket. Connections among these liaison words include: good-guaranteed-delivery-date-very-important, and (not)-good-eggs-(in-one)-basket. (The words in parentheses were directly linked but in one of the word groups.)

When looking at the name of the client in the network, four interlocking nodes appeared: agentXuseX"client name"X"competitor name." Six other competitors names do not cooccur frequently in the overall network and dropped out of the analysis at cooccurrence strengths of 3 or more.

These results suggest that there are two areas of discussion represented by the two groups, one dealing with the general process of managing employee relocation, and the other with specific carriers. Key linkage ideas are the importance of carriers guaranteeing delivery dates and the reluctance of relocation managers to go with a single carrier. The client moving company's competition in the minds of the managers is just one other firm among many, and moving agents are closely linked to both the client and the main competitor.

Other Theoretical and Practical Applications

Theories about group communication structure and discourse can be tested with these methods. Most content analysis of conversation requires extensive and time-consuming human coding. In contrast, the word-network analysis takes only seconds to perform and minutes to interpret. Because of the coding difficulties, conversational analysis has been limited to somewhat atomistic rather than pattern-oriented constructs, and focuses on rather small samples of conversants. The automated techniques are highly relational in approach to content, being network- and pattern-oriented, and can quickly process large volumes of text from different communicators.

Practical applications to focus groups are possible, but presently limited by current practices. The qualitative research industry relies most of the time on the focus group moderator writing the report without even examining a transcript of the interaction. This kind of report is sold to clients without difficulty. So demand for alternative means of analyzing focus groups is low. Yet the automated techniques provide an objective means for generating reports, rather than relying on the subjective impressions of the moderator, a participant observer with intentional or unintentional biases. Many moderators and supplies informally comment that their role is to tell the client what they want to hear. Clients may not want such self-serving treatment, and may wish a more objective report under some conditions. Another value to the automated techniques is as a quality control check on different moderators who may be in varying stages of expertise. The automated methods provide a consistent gauge of how reports may vary from the objective record.

Other applications are for analysis of open-ended survey responses. Up to this time, research suppliers have been reluctant to ask open-ended questions because of the difficulties of quickly coding them with low-skilled researcher workers. Automated word-network techniques eliminate these barriers. The methods are particularly suited to computer-assisted telephone interviewing (CAT1) configurations that are increasingly used for survey research.

OTHER AUTOMATED AUDITING APPLICATIONS

Bibliometrics

Automated auditing can also be readily performed on information contained in databases. In addition to content such as news stories or abstracts retrievable from database searches, there is bibliographic information. For example, analysis has been done on the patterns of citation or cocitation among journal articles retrieved from databases (Small & Griffith, 1974; Garfield, 1979; Brittain, 1985; Barnett, Fink, & Eckert, 1986). Citation network analysis can be linked with other automated analysis, such as of keyword cooccurrences describing database entries, or their full text, as well as data on authors' communication via other means (Danowski & Martin, 1979; Lievrouw, Rogers, Lowe, & Nadel, 1986). Theoretical value from such approaches is considerable. Practical application can also be made to organizations which have research and development functions in which their members publish in the engineering and science literature (Allen, 1977).

In addition to the examples presented using traffic, text, and voice analysis, it is easy to conceptualize other applications of technology for automated communication auditing quite different from those described. These other methods involve image processing, the analysis of visual information.

Image processing methods have seen their most full development through techniques for robotic vision, and originally for processing satellite intelligence data about what is on the ground. Interestingly, many of the methods are based on network analysis approaches. For example, the image is divided into a grid of pixels. Each pixel is analyzed for light intensity (gray scale), and scored. Then, pixels above a threshold intensity are treated as a node. The pattern of node placement defines a network structure. Then a reference dictionary is formed, including the network structures and the objects they are known to represent. Subsequently, when new pictures are analyzed, they are converted to network form, and then the particular network structure is checked against the dictionary with pattern matching algorithms. If a pattern matches, it has been identified.

At present, many of these procedures are computer intensive and require large numbers of processors connected in parallel. The hardware is too expensive for practical application for many organizations. Yet artificial intelligence development is proceeding in the direction of large scale integration of circuits to do this kind of distributed processing with computer chips that integrate many microprocessors. With these developments, image processing can be conducted quite inexpensively. A more promising approach appears to be neural network computers. These are optical, analogic computers, rather than digital ones. They function as biological brains' synaptic networks do (Grossberg, 1987).

With cost-effective image processing technology available, it is possible to automatically analyze photographic or video data on human communication activity. This will enable handling of nonverbal as well as verbal communication (which can already be automatically analyzed quite well). Body images can be coded and stored in reference files, and pattern matching can occur to determine who is talking with whom and in what nonverbal manner as new visual information is fed to the pattern-matching software.

Another approach to nonverbal analysis along with the verbal is to use sound data instead of using visual information. Similar to sonar applications used in undersea monitoring, "soma" or body prints of individuals can be taken and stored in a reference dictionary. Then, as spaces are subsequently monitored, new sound data can be pattern matched for person identification. In addition to monitoring person-to-person interaction in organizational spaces, body-scanning could be used to evaluate viewership of organizational news videos and other such media.

IMPLEMENTATION

There are several types of issues associated with implementing the procedures described in this chapter. Some of these issues concern the ethics of automated auditing. Other issues concern security, while yet others concern organizational "politics."

Privacy

The concept of "privacy," like most abstract concepts, has a range of societal referents (Burgoon, 1982). Paralleling the old adage is the notion that one person's "privacy" is another person's "paranoia." Yet we do not wish to make light of privacy issues. These issues remain and periodically rise on mass media issue agendas despite the apparent trend of increasing long-term acceptance by members of "information societies" of computer-assisted monitoring of individual behavior. Telephone traffic (numbers called, not content), banking, shopping, cable television viewing, VCR tape rentals, automatic teller machine use, mainframe computer use, credit purchases, and an expanding array of other behaviors are computer monitored with little protest by those observed.

The locus of the most pitched privacy problems, if they are to occur, is likely to be in the work setting. There, people perceive a more direct impact of monitoring on their job security, remuneration, status, and promotion than from the more diffuse monitoring that occurs for services offered to the general public. There is also more ego involvement and power-oriented activity at work that intertwines with privacy issues. Privacy and power are polar concepts in inter-ego dialectics. "Privacy" is often a shield for defense against power offenses. These seek to control others. On the other hand, used as an offensive, "privacy" is an issue linked to autonomy desires.

For reasons such as these, privacy has heightened salience in the workplace. Yet, as organizational cultures vary (Frost, Moore, Louis, Lundberg, & Martin, 1985), so too do policies and ethics regarding employee monitoring. For optimal implementation of automated auditing, managers must tailor their procedures, their uses, and their communication about auditing to the particular organizational culture. Yet beyond this level of orgo-ethical relativity, individuals may have personal ethical thresholds which they use to judge the acceptability of various monitoring activities. These personal ethics interact with organizational culture ethics and further complicate discussion of the issue.

Underlying all of this is the concept of "trust." To the extent that people trust those managing monitoring and its uses, privacy issues are unlikely to peak. The notion sometimes expressed about domestic societal surveillance—"only those doing something wrong have anything to fear about being monitored"—is grounded on the belief that those in charge will make the proper judgments about what is right and wrong behavior, and use surveillance data properly. In the organizational setting, the management of this belief among employees is central to successful automated auditing.

The less trust there is in the organization, the more that some or all of the following steps may damp privacy problems:

- analyzing and presenting data at the aggregate, not individual, level,
- blinding human interfaces to monitoring data to the exact identities of individuals,
- prohibiting individuals from examining the raw stream of monitored data, allowing them to see only processed summaries generated by software,

- hiring only those employees who do not object to extensive monitoring, and
- using the employee communication vehicles of speeches, video news, publications, etc. to show the benefits of monitoring.

Security

Closely related to the privacy issues are security issues, maintaining the integrity of data and controlling access to it. Besides ethical aspects, however, are other motives, concerning data quality, subversion, and competitive intelligence. We will treat each of these in turn.

Data quality can be compromised to the extent that those being monitored change their behaviors because of monitoring. They become self-reflexive. This, however, is a problem only to the extent that the monitored data is used for objective representation and description of organizational communication processes. On the other hand, if monitoring is used as a regulatory device, such as the reporting to individuals of their monthly long-distance telephone expenses as part of a program to control such costs, then self-reflexive behavior is a positive feature of monitoring applications. So the data quality issue hinges on the purposes for monitoring.

A more basic data quality issue, however, concerns the error in monitoring itself, not the adjustments in behavior by those aware of monitoring. Care should be taken to do regular multiple checks on data accuracy. Traditional "number cruncher" researchers know how deceptively error-free some statistical information can appear. Only diligent double checking, particularly of the more transparent layers of numerical transformations, can reduce the delusions of dirty data.

Subversion is another problem to contend with in organizational communication auditing. Employees can covertly intervene in monitoring processes, analysis, and applications and disrupt with malicious intent. The "computer hacker-invader" type of person publicized and characterized today in the mass media as pubescent punks getting sublimated sexual kicks by inserting their "Trojan horse" software into others' computers, may represent the personality profile of one kind of organizational saboteur. Others may have more strategic destabilization purposes for surreptitiously trespassing into computer files. Computer-based terrorism potentials call for well-conceived security procedures for automated auditing, with no relaxation on checking and enforcement.

Competitive intelligence gathering may also be a problem to contend with with respect to automated auditing. As industrial espionage increases in apparent frequency and sophistication, more security precautions are needed. The more rich in detail and comprehensive in capturing communication behaviors auditing is, the higher the payoff for competitors to intercept these data, either for their own use or for sale to others. In implementing automated auditing, a view toward these possible threats should guide the setup of security procedures. In the least, the same procedures which experts recommend for securing organization's other computer facilities and systems should be implemented for hardware, software, and data files used for automated auditing of organizational communication.

Political Problems

The by now almost trite phrase "information is power" (Goldhaber, Dennis, Richetto, & Wiio, 1979) has some interesting harmonics in the context of auditing communication behaviors. Auditing information is a meta-information process. This creates an exponential information power function. In the contemporary management environment, when notions about normal information power are widely held, the meta level is quickly recognized as a potent domain for power dynamics among those jockeying for dominance.

The struggle over who should control automated auditing is unlikely to be smoothly resolved in many organizations. At a minimum is the barrier of normal resistance to change (Rogers, 1983) that most people have entrenched individually and organizationally. As well, different departments typically have control over different technologies and communication functions, as summarized in Table 2. Centralized management of automated auditing is probably desirable, but whether this is politically feasible in some organizations is problematic.

Cost-Effectiveness

One key management problem to highlight is cost-effectiveness. Is the cost of automated auditing worth the benefits? On the one hand, small scale, localized applications, such as some of those exemplified in this chapter, are low-cost yet may have high utility. On the other hand, full-scale integrated systems for automated auditing, particularly across the range of media possible, may not be worth their expense, at least given current system costs. Yet such judgments are relative to the organizational culture and its goals and objectives.

SUMMARY

 This chapter has presented a conceptual architecture for viewing organizational communication. We described different methods for automatically gathering, as well as analyzing, organizational communication data. Cognitive schemata, messages, tasks, and communication networks can in various ways be automatically audited, using computer hardware and software configurations that capture and process text, traffic, visual, and voice data. These methods have theoretical value in increasing the effectiveness and efficiency of hyopthesis testing. As well, the methods form an automated intelligence system for managing organizational communication. Some of the sociopolitical and administrative issues in implementing automated auditing were highlighted.

REFERENCES

Adler, I. (1986). *Uses and effects of mass media in a large bureaucracy: A case study in Mexico.* Unpublished doctoral dissertation, University of Wisconsin-Madison.

Albrecht, T. L. (1984). Managerial communication and work perception. In R. Bostrom (Ed.), *Communication yearbook 8.* Beverly Hills, CA: Sage.

Allen, T. J. (1977). *Managing the flow of technology: Technological transfer and the dissemination of technological information within the R & D organization.* Cambridge, MA: M.I.T. Press.

Axelrod, R. (1976). *Structure of decision: The cognitive maps of political elites.* Princeton, NJ: Princeton University Press.

Baker, F. B., & Hubert, L. J. (1981). The analysis of social interaction data: A non-parametric technique. *Sociological Methods and Research, 9,* 339–361.

Bales, R. F. (1950). *Interaction process analysis: A method for the study of small groups.* Cambridge, MA: Addison-Wesley.

Bales, R. F., & Cohen, S. P. (1979). *SYMLOG: System for the multiple level observation of groups.* New York: Free Press.

Barlett, F. C. (1932). *Remembering: A study in experimental and social psychology.* London: Cambridge University Press.

Barnett, G. A., Fink, E. L., & Eckert, M. B. (1986). *The diffusion of academic information: A mathematical model of citations in the sciences, social sciences and arts and humanities.* Paper presented to the International Communication Association.

Barnett, G. A., Hamlin, D., & Danowski, J. A. (1982). Use of fractionation scales for communication audits. In M. Burgoon (ed.), *Communication yearbook, 5,* 455–471. New Brunswick, NJ: Transaction Books.

Barnett, G. A., & Rice, R. E. (1985). Longitudinal non-Euclidean networks: applying Galileo. *Social Networks, 7*(4), 287–322.

Barnett, G. A., & Segal, G. (1985). *The diffusion of computer-assisted legal research systems.* Paper presented to the International Communication Association.

Bell, D. (1973). *The coming of post-industrial society: A venture in social forecasting.* New York: Basic Books.

Bernard, H. R., Killworth, P., & Sailer, L. (1980). Informant accuracy in social network data IV. *Social Networks, 2,* 191–218.

Brittain, J. M. (1985). National limits of information flow. *Society, 22,* 3–9.

Burgoon, J. K. (1982). Privacy and communication. In M. Burgoon (Ed.), *Communication yearbook 6* (206–249). Beverly Hills, CA: Sage.

Christensen, W., & Suess, R. (1978, November). Hobbyist computerized bulletin board. *Byte,* pp. 150–157.

Coleman, J. S. (1957). *Community conflict.* New York: Free Press.

Cronen, V. E., Pearce, W. B., & Harris, L. M. (1982). The coordinated management of meaning. In F. X. Dance (Ed.), *Human communication theory* (pp. 61–89). New York: Harper and Row.

Dandridge, T. C., Mitroff, I., & Joyce, W. F. (1980). Organizational symbolism: A topic to expand organizational analysis. *Academy of Management Review, 5,* 77–82.

Danowski, J. A., (1974a, May). *An uncertainty model: Friendship communication networks and media-related behaviors.* Paper presented to the International Communication Association.

Danowski, J. A. (1974b, May). *An information processing model of organizations: A focus on environmental uncertainty and communication network structuring."* Paper presented to the International Communication Association.

Danwoski, J. A. (1974c, August) *Alternative information theoretic measures of television messages: An empirical test."* Paper presented to the Association for Education in Journalism.

Danowski, J. A. (1976a) Communication specialists in the aging organization. In H. J. Oyer & E. J. Oyer (Eds.), *Communication and aging.* Baltimore, MD: University Park Press.

Danowski, J. A. (1976b). An inforgraphic model of media access for elderly advocate organizations. In P. A. Kerschner (Ed.), *Advocacy and age.* Los Angeles, CA: University of Southern California Press.

Danowski, J. A. (1980). Group attitude-belief uniformity and connectivity of organizational communication networks for production, innovation, and maintenance content. *Human Communication Research, 6,* 299–308.

Danowski, J. A. (1982). Computer-mediated communication: a network-based content analysis using a CBBS conference. In M. Burgoon (Ed.), *Communication Yearbook 6* (pp. 905–924). Beverly Hills, CA: Sage.

Danowski, J. A. (1983a, May). *Perceived effects of computer-communication media on other organizational communication modes.* Paper presented to the International Communication Association.

Danowski, J. A. (1983b, May). *Organizational communication and communication technology.* Paper presented to the International Communication Association.

Danowski, J. A. (1984a, May). *Automated network analysis: A survey of different approaches to the analysis of human communication relationships.* Paper presented to the International Communication Association.

Danowski, J. A. (1984b, *May). Personal network structure, exposure to mass and non-mass media, attitudes, and psychological orientation.* Paper presented to the International Communication Association.

Danowski, J. A. (1986a, May). *Automated word-network analysis: An illustration with electronic mail over a one-year time series.* Paper presented to the International Communication Association.

Danowski, J. A. (1986b). Interpersonal network structure and media use: a focus on radiality and non-mass media use. In G. Gumpert & R. Cathcart (Eds.), *Intermedia* (3rd ed.). New York: Oxford University Press.

Danowski, J. A. (1986c, August). *Automated analysis of organizational cultures.* Paper presented to the Academy of Management.

Danowski, J. A., & Andrews, J. R. (1985, February). *A network analysis method for representing social concepts: an illustration with words cooccurring across electronic mail messages.* Paper presented to the Sunbelt Social Networks Conference.

Danowski, J. A., Barnett, G. A., & Friedland, M. H. (1986). Interorganizational networks via shared public relations firms: Centrality, diversification, media coverage, and publics images. In M. McLaughlin (Ed.), *Communication yearbook 10.* Beverly Hills, CA: Sage.

Danowski, J. A., & Edison-Swift, P. (1985). Crisis effects on intra-organizational computer-based communication. *Communication Research, 12,* 251–270.

Danowski, J. A., & Martin, T. H. (1979). Evaluating the health of information science: Research community and user contexts. *Final report to the National Science Foundation,* no. 1ST78-21130.

Delia, J. G., O'Keefe, B. J., & O'Keefe, D. J. (1982). The constructivist approach to communication. In F. X. Dance (Ed.), *Human communication theory.* New York: Harper and Row.

Dizard, W. P. (1982). *The coming information age: An overview of technology, economics, and politics.* New York: Longman.

Dormois, M., Fioux, F., & Gensollen, M. (1978). Evaluation of the potential market for various future communication modes. In M. Elton, W. Lucas, & D. Conrath (Eds.), *Evaluating new telecommunication services* (pp. 367–384). New York: Plenum.

Eisenberg, E. M., Farace, R. V., Monge, P. R., Bettinghaus, E. P., Kurchner-Hawkins, R., Miller, K. I., & Rothman, L. (1985). Communication linkages in inter-organizational systems: review and synthesis. In B. Dervin (Ed.), *Advances in communication science* (pp. 231–261). Norwood, NJ: Ablex.

Falcione, R. L., & Kaplan, E. A. (1984). Organizational climate, communication, and culture. In R. Bostrom (Ed.), *Communication yearbook 8* (pp. 285–309). Beverly Hills, CA: Sage.

Farace, R. V., Monge, P. R., & Russell, H. (1977). *Communicating and organizing.* Reading, MA: Addison-Wesley.

Farace, R. V., Taylor, J. A., & Stewart, J. (1978). Criteria for evaluation of organizational communication effectiveness: Review and synthesis. In B. Ruben (Ed.), *Communication yearbook 2.* New Brunswick, NJ: Transaction.

Frost, P. J., Moore, L. F., Louis, M.R., Lundberg, C. C., & Martin, J. (1985). *Organizational culture.* Beverly Hills, CA: Sage.

Garfield, E. (1979). *Citation indexing: Its theory and application in science, technology, and humanities.* New York: Wiley, 1979.

Goldhaber, G. M., Dennis, H. S., Richetto, G., & Wiio, O. (1979). *Information strategies: New pathways to corporate power.* Englewood Cliffs, NJ: Prentice-Hall.

Goldhaber, G. M., & Rogers, D. P. (1978). *Auditing organizational communication systems: The ICA communication audit.* Dubuque, IA: Kendall-Hunt.

Graber, D. A. (1984). *Processing the news: How people tame the information tide.* New York: Longman.

Granovetter, M. S. (1973). The strength of weak ties. *American Journal of Sociology, 73,* 1361–1380.

Grossberg, S. (1987). *The adaptive brain, I & II.* Amsterdam: North-Holland.

Grunig, J. E. (1982). The message-attitude-behavior relationship: Communication behaviors of organizations. *Communication Research, 9,* 163–200.

Grunig, J. E., & Hunt, T. (1984). *Managing public relations.* New York: CBS College Publishing.

Guetzkow, H. (1965). Communication in organizations. In J. G. March (Ed.), *Handbook of organizations* (pp. 354–413). Chicago, IL: Rand McNally.

Gumpert, G., & Cathcart, R. (1986). Mediated interpersonal communication: Toward a new typology. *Quarterly Journal of Speech, 69,* 267–277.

Hellriegel, D., & Slocum, J. W. (1974). Organizational climate: Measures, research, and contingencies. *Academy of Management Journal, 17,* 255–280.

Huber, G. (1984). The nature and design of post-industrial organizations. *Management Science, 30*(8), 928–951.

Hughey, J. D. (1985, May). *Media preference and empathy.* Paper presented to the International Communication Association.

Jablin, F. M. (1980). Organizational communication theory and research: An overview of communication climate and network research. In D. Nimmo (Ed.), *Communication yearbook 4.* New Brunswick, NJ: Transaction.

James. L. R., & Jones, A. P. (1974). Organizational climate: A review of theory and research. *Psychological Bulletin, 81,* 1096–1112.

Johansen, R. (1984). *Teleconferencing and beyond: Communications in the office of the future.* New York: McGraw-Hill.

Kaplan, A. (1964). *The conduct of inquiry: Methodology for behavioral science.* San Francisco: Chandler Pub. Co.

Kaplowitz, S. A., & Fink, E. L. (1982). Attitude change and attitudinal trajectories: A dynamic multidimensional theory. In M. Burgoon (Ed.), *Communication yearbook 6* (pp. 364–394). Beverly Hills, CA: Sage.

Kerr, E. B., & Hiltz, S. R. (1982). *Computer-mediated communication systems: Status and evaluation.* New York: Academic Press.

Kling, R. (1980). Social analyses of computing: Theoretical perspectives in recent empirical research. *Computing Surveys, 12,* 61–110.

Krippendorff, K. (1980a). Clustering. In P. R. Monge & J. N. Cappella (Eds.), *Multivariate techniques in human communication research.* New York: Academic Press.

Krippendorff, K. (1980b). *Content analysis: An introduction to its methodology.* Beverly Hills, CA: Sage.

Kruskal, J. B. (1964). Nonmetric multidimensional scaling: A numerical method. *Psychometrika, 29,* 115–129.

Kruskal, J. B., & Wish, M. (1978). *Multidimensional scaling.* Beverly Hills, CA: Sage.

Lewis, E. (1986, May). *A typology of cognitive strategy behavior for performance and learning while using an interactive information system.* Paper presented to the International Communication Association.

Lievrouw, L. A., Rogers, E. M., Lowe, C. U., & Nadel, E. (1986, May). *Communication networks among biomedical scientists: Triangulation as a research methodology.* Paper presented to the International Communication Association.

Louis, R. R. (1980). Surprise and sensemaking: What newcomers experience in entering unfamiliar organizational settings. *Administrative Science Quarterly, 25,* 226–251.

Love, G., & Rice, R. (1985). *Electronic emotion: Socio-emotional content in a computer-mediated communication network.* Paper presented to the International Communication Association.

Martin, J. (1982). Stories and scripts in organizational settings. In A. H. Hastork & A. M. Isen (Eds.), *Cognitive social psychology* (pp. 255–305). New York: Elsever/North-Holland.

McLaughlin, M. L. (1984). *Conservation: How talk is organized.* Beverly Hills, CA: Sage.

McMillan, S. J. (1986, May). *Public relations in trade and professional associations: Location, model, structure, environment, and values.* Paper presented to the International Communication Association.

Miller, G. R. (1966). *Speech communication: A behavioral approach.* New York: Bobbs-Merrill.

Miller, G. R., & Nicholson, J. H. (1976). *Communication inquiry.* Reading, MA: Addison-Wesley.

Perry, R. W., & Mushkatel, E. H. (1984). *Disaster management: Warning response in community relocation.* Westport, CT: Quorum Books.

Picot, A., Klingensberg, H., & Kranzle, H. P. (1982). Office technology: A report on attitudes and channel selection from field studies in Germany. In M. Burgoon (Ed.), *Communication year-*

book 6 (pp. 674–692). Beverly Hills, CA: Sage.

Pollack, J., & Waltz, D. L. (1986). Interpretation of natural language. *Byte,* (1986), *11*(2) 189–200.

Porat, M. U. (1977). *The information economy.* Washington, DC: U.S. Department of Commerce (OT Special Publication 77-12(1)).

Putnam, L. L., & Pacanowsky, M. E. (1983). *Communication and organizations: An interpretive approach.* Beverly Hills, CA: Sage.

Redding, C. A. (1972). *Communication within the organization: An interpretive review of theory and research.* New York: Industrial Communication Council.

Rice, R. E. (1982). Communication networking in computer-conferencing systems: A longitudinal study of group roles and system structure. In M. Burgoon (Ed.), *Communication Yearbook 6* (pp. 925–944). Beverly Hills, CA: Sage Publications.

Rice, R. E. (1984). Media style and organizational use of computer-based communication systems. In R. E. Rice (Ed.), *The new media: Users and impacts.* Beverly Hills, CA: Sage Publications.

Rice, R. E., & Bair, J. (1984). New organizational media and productivity. In R. E. Rice (Ed.), *The new media: Communication, research, and technology* (pp. 185–215). Beverly Hills, CA: Sage.

Rice, R. E., & Barnett, G. (1986). Group communication networking in an information environment: Applying metric multidimensional scaling. In M. McLaughlin (Ed.), *Communication yearbook 9* (pp. 315–326). Beverly Hills, CA: Sage.

Rice, R., & Borgman, C. (1983). The use of computer-monitored data in information science and communication research. *Journal of the American Society for Information Science, 34,* 247–256.

Rice, R., & Richards, W. D., Jr. (1981). NEGOPY network analysis program. *Social Networks, 3,* 215–223.

Rice, R. E., & Torobin, J. (1986, May). *Expectations about the impacts of electronic messaging: The role of media usage, task complexity, network lines, and organizational status.* Paper presented to the International Communication Association.

Richards, W. D., Jr. (1982). *The NEGOPY network analysis program: Version 6.0.* Computer program, Simon Frazier University, Burnaby, Canada.

Richards, W. D., Jr. (1984, May). *Network analysis in large complex systems: Metrics.* Paper presented to the International Communication Association.

Richards, W. D., Jr. (1986). *The NEGOPY Network Analysis Program.* Monograph, Simon Frazier University, Burnaby, B.C., Canada.

Rogers, E. M. (1983). *Diffusion of innovations.* New York: Free Press.

Rogers, E. M., & Agarwala-Rogers, R. (1976). *Communication in organizations.* New York: Free Press.

Rogers, E. M., & Kincaid, D. L. (1981). *Communication networks: Toward a new paradigm for research.* New York: Free Press.

Rogers, E. M., & Sood, R. (1981). *Mass media operations in a quick-onset, natural disaster: Hurricane David in Dominca.* Working paper #41. Boulder, CO: Natural Hazard Center, University of Colorado.

Rogers, L. E., & Farace, R. V. (1974). Relational communication analysis: New measurement procedures. *Human Communication Research, 1,* 222–239.

Salmon, C. T. (1986, May). *The agency—client relationship: Implications for the management of public relations firms.* Paper presented to the International Communication Association.

Schramm, W. (1971). Communication in crisis. In W. Schramm & D. F. Roberts (Eds.), *The process and effects of mass communication* (pp. 525–553). Urbana, IL: University of Illinois Press.

Shannon, C., & Weaver, W. (1949). *The mathematical theory of communication.* Urbana, IL: University of Illinois Press.

Shaw, M. E. (1964). Communication networks. In L. Berkowitz (Ed.), *Advances in experimental social psychology* (Vol 1, pp. 111–147). New York: Academic Press.

Short, J., Williams, E., & Christie, B. (1976). *The social psychology of telecommunications.* New York: Wiley.

Shult, L. (1984). *The match between cognitive complexity and message complexity.* Masters thesis, School of Journalism and Mass Communication, University of Wisconsin-Madison.

Sinno, A. R. (1982). *Determinants of advertising content.* Unpublished doctoral dissertation, University of Wisconsin-Madison.

Small, H., & Griffith, B. C. (1974). The structure of scientific literatures 1: Identifying and graphing specialties. *Science Studies, 4,* 17–40.

Smith, M. J. (1982). Cognitive schemata and persuasive communication: Toward a contingency rules theory. In M. Burgoon (Ed.), *Communication yearbook 6* (pp. 330–363). Beverly Hills, CA: Sage.

Smith, S. W., & McLaughlin, M. L. (1986, May). *Thematic dimensions of organizational storytelling.* Paper presented to the International Communication Association.

Steinfield, C. W. (1985, May). *Explaining task-related and socio-emotional uses of computer-mediated communication in an organizational setting.* Paper presented to the International Communication Association.

Stone, P. J. (1966). *The General Inquirer: A computer approach to content analysis.* Cambridge, MA: M.I.T. Press.

Sypher, B. D., & Zorn, T. E. (1986). Communication-related abilities and upward mobility: A longitudinal investigation. *Human Communication Research, 12*(3), 420–431.

Sypher, H. E., & Applegate, J. L. (1984). Organizing communication behavior: The role of schemas and constructs. In R. Bostrom (Ed.), *Communication yearbook 8* (pp. 310–329). Beverly Hills, CA: Sage.

Tushman, M. (1977). Communication across organizational boundaries: Special boundary-spanning roles in the innovation process. *Administrative Science Quarterly, 22,* 587–605.

Weick, K. E. (1979). *The social psychology of organizing* (2nd ed.). Reading, MA: Addison-Wesley.

Weick, K. E. (1985). The significance of corporate culture. In P. J. Frost, L. F. Moore, M. R. Louis, C. C. Lundberg, & J. Martin (Eds.), *Organizational culture* (pp. 381–389). Beverly Hills, CA: Sage.

Wigand, R. T. (1979). A model of interorganizational communication among complex organizations. In K. Krippendorff (Ed.), *Communication and control in society* (pp. 367–387). New York: Gordon and Breach Science Publishers.

Wiio, O. (1976, May). *Organizational communication: Interfacing systems in different contingencies: Results of three years of auditing in Finnish organizations.* Paper presented to the International Communication Association.

Woelfel, J., & Fink, E. L. (1980). *The Galileo System: A theory of social measurement and its application.* New York: Academic Press.

Section 3

INTRODUCTION – ORGANIZATIONAL COMMUNICATION IN THE INFORMATION AGE

Osmo Wiio suggested in Section 1 that the best predictor of organizational communication is a contingency model, and that one factor in this model is the culture of the society in which the organization is embedded. The culture of a society may be characterized by the productive activities of its members. Currently, the North American, Western European, and Japanese societies are in transition from economics based upon industrial production to ones which revolve around communication and information processing (Bell, 1973; Naisbitt, 1982; Toffler, 1980). Thus, it comes as no surprise that communication scholars feel compelled to discuss the impact of these technologies as the entire fabric of society changes. Indeed, the influence of this contingency can be found on our group of organizational communication scholars as represented by this volume. In Section 1, Cushman, King, and Smith discussed the communication rules at IBM, the papacy of those caught up in the fevor of the information age. Barnett describes case studies of organizations also involved in the computer industry. The techniques for the analysis of organizational culture and all the research methodologies in Section 2 – communication audit procedures, network analysis, the method of communication gradients, and inforgraphics require the technologies which characterize post-industrial society. The chapters in this final section focus explicitly on the impact of information technologies on organizational communication.

The first chapter in this section is by Everett Rogers. Its purpose is to trace the historical development of the new information technologies, and to show how these innovations may be changing the nature of communication in organizations. Today and into the future, organizational communication will be centered about interactive computerized communication systems. Rogers demonstrates how academic research has shifted in recent years from a focus on organizational innovativeness to the innovation process in organizations. The shift has improved our understanding of innovation behavior in organizations.

Larry Browning and Bonnie Johnson examine action bias as a dimension of organizational culture. This bias impacts on the development of technology. They differentiate two different types of organizational culture. One is characterized by mediation and planning. Organizations of this type slowly come to a decision. The other type of organization is quick-paced, and strives for action, rapid feedback and corrective action. To examine the utility of this typology, they examined 60 organizations who have implemented word processing over the last 6 years. The results indicate that word processing can increase action bias in an organization's culture.

The final chapter in the volume is by Sandra O'Connell. She argues that organizational communication is changing rapidly as technological innovations become widely adopted. These changes require an increase in understanding of the interaction between communication mediated by technology and human communication. These two processes are contrasted using four variables: how meaning is established, accuracy, speed and access, and the degree of structure. While high technology communication is accurate, fast, low in context, and highly structured, human communication is inexact, rich, subtle, and highly complex, because it is embedded in the context of human experience. Two points emerge from this examination. There will be changes in information processing and decision making, and changes in interpersonal relationships. Although abundant information will be available, it is not clear that it will improve decision making. Managers will need to learn new decision making skills as the new technologies are adopted. The content, format, and opportunities for contact will be altered as channel effects impact upon interpersonal relationships in the automated workplace. The chapter ends with six hypotheses that deal with the role of technology in the organization.

REFERENCES

Bell, D. (1973). *The coming of post-industrial society: A venture in social forecasting*. New York: Basic Books.

Toffler, A. (1980). *The third wave*. New York: William Morrow.

Naisbitt, J. (1982). *Megatrends: Ten new directions transforming our lives*. New York: J. Wiley and Sons.

Chapter 17

Information Technologies:
How Organizations are Changing[1]

Everett M. Rogers

Annenberg School of Communications
University of Southern California

ABSTRACT

The purpose of this chapter is to trace the historical development of the new information technologies (especially the microcomputer), and to show how these innovations are changing the nature of communication in organizations. We show how scholarly research has shifted in recent years from a focus on organizational innovativeness, to the innovation process in organizations, thus improving our understanding of innovation behavior in organizational structures. A theme of this chapter is to show the beginnings of a new era of communication technology, one centering on the interactivity of computerized communication systems.

Probably the most important single change in organizations in the past century is now well under way: The impacts of new communication technologies. These innovations involve applications of microelectronics, including telecommunications and the computer, to problems of organizational communication.

Information technologies are founded on advances in semiconductor chips, particularly the microprocessor, which puts the control functions of a computer on a silicon chip. Invention of the microprocessor in 1971 by Ted Hoff, then at Intel Corporation in Santa Clara, California, facilitated the miniaturization of computer power, sharply reduced the price of computing, and caused a rapid diffusion of computers among the public (Rogers & Larsen, 1984). The micropprocessor, along with the prior invention of the transistor in 1948 at Bell Labs, must rank among the most important technologies of the twentieth century. Both are today involved in the new information technologies that are affecting organizations. The spread of microcomputers and other microelectronics technologies constitutes an information revolution, through which the United States, Japan, and most Western European nations are rapidly becoming information societies.

---

[1] This chapter includes material adapted from Rogers (1984), Rogers and Larsen (1984), Rogers and Rafaeli (1985), and Rogers and Kim (1985).

Microcomputers are affecting homes, schools, factories, entertainment, and, especially, the office. Because computers are information tools, they are being utilized wherever information is input, processed, or output. Organizations are basically communication bodies (with the special characteristic of a rather high degree of formal structure, such as that imposed by authority and hierarchy), so they are natural sites for the application of the new communication technologies. Considering this natural fit, it is rather surprising that office automation has not had an even greater impact to date. But although at least 20% of U.S. businesses have adopted some kind of office automation, the rate of adoption has slowed down in recent years (Uttal, 1982). Three general factors account for this trend.

1. Although office automation promises to increase productivity, such improved performance, if it does occur, is difficult to measure. Organization leaders have to adopt these expensive technologies largely on faith. The advantages of office automation have often not been great enough to convince organizations to make the sizable initial investment that they require. A respondent in one survey of users of office technologies (Johnson & Rice, 1983, p. 197) described the difficulties of measuring their benefits: "Measurement of work activity gets to be a little strange sometimes. You can take one and half hours to write a glossary that will do the job; another person will take three hours each time to do it manually. It doesn't make any difference to the administration because it only sees the number of pages and the number of lines. No account is made of time required or time saved."

2. Serious transition problems have often occurred in organizations that introduced the new information technologies. The basic requirements for proper implementation (employee training, for example), the extensive changeover that the new systems demand, and the seriousness of their negative consequences (such as possible unemployment of office workers) all argue against facile adoption. Implementation is one of the main problems of organizations that have tried to adopt office automation.

3. Finally, computer-based office automation technologies have many shortcomings: User unfriendliness, relatively high cost, and rapid technological change (which means that an organization must constantly purchase new machines to keep up to date).

Despite these hindrances, however, office information technologies have the potential for major impacts on organizations, the first signs of which are already evident. Office automation today seems to be having important desirable, direct, and anticipated effects, but I expect that it may also lead to an expanding set of undesirable, indirect, and unanticipated consequences (Rogers, 1983).

Our viewpoint in this chapter is one of *technological determinism,* the belief that certain social changes result from technological innovations. The fundamental technology driving the current changes in human communication is the computer (Rogers, 1986). Computer technology has both a hardware (that is, the physical equipment) and a software component (consisting of the social organization, values and beliefs, and information that accompany computers).

COMPUTERS AND COMMUNICATION

Computers have in recent years become a means of human communication, even though the original function of this technology was quite different. The transformation of computers into a tool of communication occurred because (a) of a line of technological developments through which computers became much smaller in size and cheaper in cost, and hence much more widely accessible; and (b) of an accompanying realization of the potential of computers for communication networking functions. Computers add the quality of interactivity to communication systems, and thus are forcing a very basic change in the previously one-way nature of mass media communication. Thus, one hallmark of the emerging information society will be its basis in highly interactive communication systems. In order to study and understand this new form of human communication, scholars must shift from linear to convergence models of human communication, and move away from their rather singular focus upon communication effects, an emphasis that has characterized most past research (Rogers & Kincaid, 1981).

The Beginnings of Computer Technology

One cannot adequately understand the present-day impacts of interactive communication technologies in organizations without knowing something of the history of computer development.

The electronic era began in 1912 in Palo Alto, California, with the invention of the amplifying qualities of the vacuum tube. Lee de Forest and two colleagues from the Federal Telegraph Company, an early radio engineering firm on the West Coast, leaned across a table and watched a housefly walk across a sheet of paper. They heard the fly's footsteps amplified 120 times, so that the steps sounded like marching boots. This event marked the birth of the electronics era (at least one of the several births that are variously claimed). Electronic amplification opened the way for the later invention of radio broadcasting, television, and computers.

The problem with vacuum tubes in electronic communication systems was that the tubes burned out, generated a lot of heat, and used considerable electronical power. These shortcomings of vacuum tubes were illustrated by the first mainframe computer, ENIAC, at the University of Pennsylvania. It filled an entire room and used so much electricity that the lights of Philadelphia dimmed when the computer was turned on. In order for computers to become cheaper, smaller, and more widely-utilized, an alternative to vacuum tubes would have to be found.

Beginnings of the Semiconductor Industry

Bell Labs carries out the largest basic research program in electronics in the world. For over 50 years, Bell Labs has spawned a flood of technological innovations; currently, it holds 10,000 patents and produces about one per day. Bell Labs' most significant discovery was the transistor, which some call the major invention of the century. The transistor (short for "tranfer resistance") was important because it allowed the magnification of electronic messages, as did vacuum tubes, but transistors required only a little current, they did not generate much heat, and they were much smaller in size.

At the time of the transistor's invention in 1947, it was obvious that many useful applications would be made. But it proved difficult to manufacture reliable transistors, and the first commercial use did not appear until 1952, 5 years later, when transistors were used in hearing aids. Gradually, the commercialization of transistor technology advanced, and, by the time that William Shockley and his two co-inventors received the Nobel Prize in 1956, 20 companies were manufacturing transistors. One of these was Shockley Semiconductor Laboratory in Palo Alto, California, Shockley's hometown.

Shockley started the first semiconductor company in Silicon Valley in order to exploit commercially the technology which he had invented at Bell Labs. His stated goal was to make a million dollars, through starting-up a new company to capitalize on technological innovation. His firm was short-lived and unsuccessful, but Shockley astutely had recruited eight bright young men who became the cadre for the semiconductor industry that was to sprout in Silicon Valley. The entrepreneurial spirit they learned from Shockley has since characterized the microelectronics industry in Santa Clara County, California. Within a year of their employment at Shockley Semiconductor Laboratory, the eight defected to start semiconductor manufacturing companies of their own.

The beginning of the semiconductor industry in Silicon Valley is illustrated by the photograph of a dozen men toasting Shockley in 1956 on the occasion of his winning the Nobel Prize. Noteworthy about the photo is the youth of the men surrounding Shockley. Robert Noyce looks like a boyish college sophomore. Actually, he was 31 at the time of the photo in 1956; in a year or two, he was to become the chief at Fairchild Semiconductor, the company that he began with others of the Shockley Eight. Today, Noyce is the most admired entrepreneur-engineer of Silicon Valley, and a multimillionaire.

Noyce is noteworthy as a Silicon Valley entrepreneur for having founded two of the most successful semiconductor firms in the world. Launching the second was relatively easy. All it took was a couple of million dollars, some very talented people, and a certain degree of technical genius. The millions came mainly from Arthur Rock, an early venture capitalist in Silicon Valley. Rock had been impressed by Noyce since the 1950s, when Rock helped arrange the financing for Fairchild Semiconductor. So, says Noyce, "It was a very natural thing to go to Art and say, 'Incidentally Art, do you have an extra $2.5 million you would like to put on the crap table?' " Noyce and cofounders of Intel invested about $250,000 each of their own money, amassed from their original investments in Fairchild. Rock got on the phone, and in 30 minutes he lined up the $2.5 million to start Intel.

Invention of the Microprocessor

Other than the invention of the transistor at Bell Labs, the most significant innovation in the microelectronics industry is the microprocessor, invented in 1971 by Marcian E. (Ted) Hoff, Jr. While Intel's main emphasis was originally upon semiconductor memory chips, it welcomed customers like Busicom, a now-defunct Japanese manufacturer who wanted Intel to design special chips for its proposed family of desk-top calculators. Hoff told a visiting Japanese engineering team their design was too complex for Intel to handle.

Near Hoff's desk was a PDP-8 minicomputer, which he used in his research. Once, he had thought about the possibility of designing something like a microcomputer. The idea of a computer-on-a-chip was still on Hoff's mind: "I looked at the PDP-8, I looked at the Busicom plans, and I wondered why the calculator should be so much more complex." Then Hoff worked out the design for a microprocessor. A *microprocessor* is a semiconductor chip that serves as the central processing unit (CPU) controlling a computer. In other words, a microprocessor is the computer's brains. In defining the world's first microprocessor, Hoff had the inspiration to pack all the CPU functions on a single chip. He attached two memory chips to his microprocessor: one to hold data, and another to contain the program to drive the CPU. "Hoff now had in hand a rudimentary general-purpose computer that not only could run a complex calculator (like Busicom's), but also could control an elevator or a set of traffic lights, and perform many other tasks, depending on its program" (Rogers & Larsen, 1984, p. 105).

Gordon E. Moore, President of Intel, described the elegance and power of Hoff's microprocessor: "Now we can make a single microprocessor chip and sell it for several thousand different applications." That was the beauty of the microprocessor: it could serve as a component in any electronic product where one wanted miniaturized computing power. This flexibility of application, of course, had tremendous commercial implications. In short, Ted Hoff had invented a means for Intel to get rich quick.

As Hoff explains: "The cost of a chip is a function, a strong function, of its size. The smaller a chip the more of them you can get on a wafer, so the price is correspondingly cheaper." The direction of progress in the semiconductor industry for the past decade or so has been to put more and more memory capacity on the same-sized semiconductor chips. This tendency has greatly reduced the cost per bit of computer memory. The most widely sold memory chip (RAM, or random access memory) in the semiconductor industry has moved from the 1K (one thousand bits of information) to the 4K to the 64K; the cost per bit of computer memory has decreased correspondingly about 28% per year. This lowered cost translated directly into more and more ubiquitous computers in society. Most of the millions of computers sold in the past decade are microcomputers, built around the microprocessor that Ted Hoff invented at Intel in 1971.

THE RISE OF COMPUTERIZED COMMUNICATION

The word "computer," with overtones of counting and calculation, correctly describes the machine's past uses, but misrepresents their present and potential use as a means of communication.

Communicating via computers has its roots in the fact that mainframe computer power was (until very recent years) rather expensive. Until the mid-1970s, with the introduction of microcomputers, computers were owned and operated by The Establishment: Government, big corporations, universities, and other large institutions. These mainframe computers were mainly used for data-crunching tasks: accounting, record-keeping, research and data-analysis, and routine transactions like airline ticketing. Large organizations established management information systems that utilized computers to amass and analyze data for the organization's managers (Keen & Scott-Morton, 1978). Single users could not afford to own a mainframe computer of their own. Various solutions evolved in response to the high cost of using mainframe computers. One solution was shared usage of the expensive capacity of the mainframe. Numerous users took part in a time-sharing system in which a single mainframe computer was wired so that it would perform more than one task simultaneously, thus "sharing" its time across several users. The technology of time-sharing allowed users to communicate with large computers using either "dedicated" or public telephone lines. The user enjoyed the convenience of spatial independence from the central computer.

A series of networks emerged in which users and computers were linked. These networks were established mainly to provide an environment of pooled computer power. But they also become a kind of "public commons," an arena in which users could not only share mainframe power, but could also communicate among themselves and share a common collection of information like a database. Computer communication technology began to provide users with the opportunity to converse with each other over temporal and spatial distance, and to share in the creation and utilization of databases.

Enter the factors of miniaturization, decreased cost, and the widespread diffusion of microcomputers (discussed previously), and a tremendous explosion in computer networking occurred. Computers had now become a special medium of communication. Networks that were previously the exclusive domain of computer users in industry and academia were now accessible for a rapidly-growing user public. Microcomputers are particularly well suited for replacing mainframe computers in networking functions. By 1986, an estimated 18% of U.S. households owned a home computer, with a very rapid rate of adoption in recent years. Microcomputers are widely adopted in work organizations, where various types of electronic messaging systems and other networking uses are very common.

At present, the main uses of home computers are for playing video games and for word-processing (that is, computer-assisted typing and editing) (Rogers, Daley, & Wu, 1982). Electronic games can also be played in arcades, in the home on video game equipment that attaches to a television set, or on a home computer. At present, only about one-fourth of home computer owners have a modem (a computer peripheral that allows one to connect a microcomputer via the telephone system to an information bank like The Source or CompuServe, or to a mainframe computer or a minicomputer at a place of work, or to a network of other microcomputer users). While most computer users are of a communication nature (for example, word-processing), the recent trend toward an increasing use of microcomputers as networking devices demonstrates the potential of computers for *interactive* communication.

Such computer networking illustrates a type of "machine-assisted communication" (Dominick, 1983), which differs from either (a) interpersonal communication, in which face-to-face information exchange occurs (without any type of equipment involved); or (b) mass media communication, in which some mass media like print, radio, television, or film allows one or several individuals to disseminate messages to a large, geographically-dispersed audience. Machine-assisted communication via the telephone, telegraph, or computer networks has certain of the characteristics of both interpersonal communication (like its interactive nature) and of mass media communication (such as that some type of electronic communication equipment is involved).

Due to microcomputer technology, the number of active networks has multiplied in the past several years. Hundreds of thousands of new computer owners have been searching, and finding, communication outlets for their newly acquired computing power. Such outlets include electronic bulletin boards; online information utilities; dial-in news, banking, and shopping services; as well as access to computer teleconferencing and time-sharing (services that were established prior to the recent microcomputer boom).

Several thousand microcomputer-hosted bulletin boards (the most primitive, but very popular, version of computer networks) are presently operating in the United States. These bulletin boards compete with more-established commercial utilities, each of whose subscribers may number in the tens of thousands. While the commercially operated utilities are profit oriented, many of the publicly accessible electronic bulletin boards are run by individuals for other than economic motives. In northern California, for example, there are currently a dozen bulletin boards devoted to political issues, none of which charges its users. Other bulletin boards are established to exchange information of a sexual, economic, or other nature (the anonymity of such bulletin boards facilitates the exchange of sensitive information). Many bulletin boards exist in work organizations so as to provide an electronic messaging system for the organization's members. A relatively small but increasing portion of Americans are "telecommuters" who work at home on a computer linked to their co-workers.

INTERACTIVE COMMUNICATION VIA COMPUTERS

The communication environment created by the computer as a medium is very different from that inherent in earlier modes of communication. The nature of communication has always been, at least in part, a product of the technology of the medium. This technology-dependency of the communication process is particularly apparent today, with computers assuming an increasing role. Changes in information technology have begun to redefine the process of human communication itself.

The communciation process among participants in computer networks is typified by several unique characteristics. This process is interactive, asynchronous,[2] and it is relatively rapid (Rogers, 1986). Communication via computers is not a linear, one-way process. Computerized communication is different from mass-mediated communication in the past, in that the audience is "de-massified"[3] in nature (although it is potentially as large as ever).

Interactivity is a salient feature of computerized communication systems. "Participants" in computerized communication systems (the combined set of what previously were called "sources" and "receivers") have a very high degree of control over their communication process. Those individuals who use the system determine its content. Computerized communication is, at least potentially, a very democratic process.

Computerized communication is nonlinear, because the traditional unidirectional model of the communication process is demonstrably no longer applicable. During the era of print communication (from the days of Gutenberg until the present), a linear model of the communication process that postulated sender, message, channel, and receiver was formulated and widely used by communication scholars, based on the Shannon and Weaver (1949) model of communication. This linear model persisted through the era of film, radio, and television (from approximately the 1920s until the present). The mass audience was the receiving end of a linear process of communication. Such a linear model is not appropriate to computer communication. For instance, the distinction between sender and receiver is blurred, and one must speak of participants in a computerized communication system. Further, no single message is at the center of the communication process. It is impossible to distinguish a "message" from "feedback."

THE RESTRUCTURING OF ORGANIZATIONAL COMMUNICATION

The new information technologies allow the restructuring and/or destructuring of organizational communication. "The Office of the Future concept is not just the automated office or the electronic office; rather, it is one in which new technologies give senior management the opportunity to consider entirely new approaches as to how best to organize, manage, and control the enterprise" (Strassmann, 1980, p. 55). This kind of impact is very grand, and at present exists only in a rather hazy vision. We cannot now point to an organi-

---

[2] The asynchronous nature of communicating via a computer permits the retention and accessibility of messages over extended periods of time. For example, a participant in an electronic messaging system may receive a message from another participant whenever he or she logs on to the computer. Thus, the time of receiving a message can be managed or controlled. The discourse is enriched by the ability to reach back into the automatically compiled minutes of past communication events. The possibility of asynchronous communication fosters interaction among people or groups who are not on coordinated schedules.

[3] The *de-massification* of the audience inherent in computerized communication is an extended and enlarged version of the market segmentation processes witnessed by the electronic and print media in past decades. In a similar but much more pronounced way, computerized communication focuses on topical information of a specialized kind. De-massification means that information is now available in a much wider variety than previously. The target audience for each individual type of communication content is shrinking in size, down to a single individual in certain cases. Both the audience and the medium are thus being de-massified, although the aggregate effect need not necessarily be a smaller audience on the whole.

zation that has utilized the computer-based technologies to create really new alternatives in organizational form, communication, and structure. But the potential exists. Here are some examples.

- In a recent evaluation of an electronic messaging system in one large organization, we found that much bypassing of layers in the hierarchy occurred, especially when the new communication system was first installed. Workers sent many copies of a message, in part perhaps because it was so easy to do so — "Just push the 'send' button." Such electronic networking systems decrease the influence of organizational hierarchy on communication patterns; they are usually highly decentralized systems in which messages flow with few constraints (Rogers, 1986).
- Two managers, one sitting beside a pool in Los Altos Hills, California, and the other in Austin, Texas, write a joint memo about plans for collaboration between their divisions. At one point they ask another individual at company headquarters (in Sunnyvale, California) to produce a set of color charts and insert them in their memo. All their communication is via computer terminals. In fact, the two managers have not met since they were introduced at a company beer-blast 5 years ago. Yet they talk with each other, by computer network, at least once a week (Rogers & Larsen, 1984).
- A large German bank provides full services to about 40,000 customers by means of the *Bildschirmtext* system, a videotext service begun in the 1980s. All banking is done via computer terminals, telephone lines, and home television sets. No bank buildings, no vaults, no tellers. The electronic bank has only 39 employees — a president, a secretary, 37 computer programmers, and of course, one big computer (Rogers and Picot, 1985). Because of its lower overhead costs, the bank can pay 1 per cent higher interest on deposits than other German banks. Needless to say, the bank is growing rapidly.

These examples show how the new information technologies can overcome the usual limitations that time, spatial distance, and organizational hierarchy impose on communication patterns. The new information technologies will help us change our conception of what the work organization is, and can be. They will free us from conventional thinking about our relationships with work associates, and lead us to question how essential it is to be with them in the same place at the same time. Out of the present groping explorations of information technology applications may come a new type of organization that is particularly suited to the emerging information society.

RESEARCH ON INNOVATION IN ORGANIZATIONS

In recent years, an important advance has occurred in research on the innovation process in organizations. The scope of this newer type of scholarly research can be expressed as a question: How are innovations adopted and implemented in organizations, and to what effects?

Historical Background

In the late 1960s and early 1970s, the classical model of the diffusion of innovation was applied to the study of innovation in organizations (Rogers, 1983). This early research looked at the determinants of *organizational innovativeness,* defined as the degree to which an organization is relatively earlier in adopting new ideas than other, similar organizations. This research approach consisted of a correlational analysis of cross-sectional survey data of innovativeness in a sample of several hundred organizations. This rather stereotypic methodological approach provided insight into the characteristics of innovative organizations, but very little understanding about intraorganizational innovative behavior was generated.

Although the organization was the unit of analysis, the unit of observation (that is, of data gathering) was usually still the individual, typically the chief executive of the organization (such as a school superintendent, a public health officer, a hospital administrator, or a factory manager). These individuals were treated just as the farmers had been in the Ryan and Gross study of hybrid corn diffusion (1943). The individual-oriented classical diffusion model was too directly applied to the study of organizational innovativeness.

The study of innovativeness in local public health departments by Mohr (1969) is a good example of the many organizational innovativeness studies that were completed. He investigated 93 county-level health departments in Illinois, Michigan, New York, Ohio, and Ontario. The data were gathered primarily by interviews with each health department chief to identify the determinants of innovativeness in organizations. The innovativeness of the health departments, the dependent variable, was measured by the number of health innovations that each health department had adopted. Mohr examined independent variables at the individual, organizational, and community level: Attitudes of the health officials toward innovation, organizational obstacles to innovations, the size of the health department, resources available to the health department, community obstacles to innovation, and community size. Mohr performed a correlational analysis of these variables with innovativeness and concluded that innovativeness was a function of motivation, obstacles, and resources.

The Paradigm Shift to Studying the Innovation Process

Empirical studies of the innovation process in organizations have recently shifted (a) from a "variance" approach to a "process" approach,[4] and (b) from the "organization" or the "innovation" to an "innovation-application" or an "organization-in-relation-to-an-innovation" as the unit of analysis (Downs & Mohr, 1976).

The new research uses theoretical and methodological approaches more appropriate to the new context of innovation in organizational settings. This change represents a shift from the classical diffusion model in several ways. For example, the "bottom line" for the innovation process in organizations is *implementation* (including institutionalization of the new idea), not just the adoption decision per se. Also important is the realization that the "adopter" can play an active, creative role in the innovation process, in matching the innovation with a perceived organizational problem, and possibly in re-inventing the innovation. An innovation should not be conceived as a fixed, invariant, and static element in the innovation process, but as a flexible and adaptable idea that is consecutively defined and redefined as the innovation process gradually unfolds.

Finally, instead of an overdependence on surveys and cross-sectional data analysis of the correlates of innovativeness, researchers began to engage in more in-depth case studies

---

[4] Mohr (1982, p. 3) defined a "variance" approach as centering on determining the covariance among a set of variables without determining their time-order. In contrast, a "process" approach seeks to determine the time-ordered sequence of a set of events.

of the innovation process in organizations. The turn away from the highly structured, quantitative methods of investigating organizational innovativeness led to more qualitative, hypothesis-generating case studies of the innovation process in organizations.

Certainly, innovation is a *process*, a sequence of decisions, events, and behavior changes over time. Past research designs did not adequately allow analysis of the temporal aspects of innovation necessary to explore its process nature. Very little past research included data at more than one observation point, and almost none at more than two such points. Therefore, almost all past research was unable to trace the change in a variable over "real" time; these past investigations dealt only with the present tense of innovation behavior. Organizational innovation thus became, in the actuality of research operations, an artificially halted snapshot.

THE INNOVATION PROCESS IN ORGANIZATIONS

A Model of the Innovation Process

Most recent investigations of the innovation process in organizations follow a relatively unstructured, open-ended, case-study approach to data-gathering. Essentially, they consist of "tracer studies" of the innovation-decision process for single innovation in an organization. These investigations are guided by a model of the innovation process in organizations.

An *innovation* is defined as an idea, practice, or object that is perceived as new by an individual or other unit of adoption (Rogers, 1983). The innovation process is conceptualized as consisting of five stages, each characterized by a particular type of information-seeking and decision-making behavior. Later stages in the innovation process usually cannot be undertaken until earlier stages have been settled. Thus, there is a logical sequence to the five stages in the innovation process, although there are exceptions. The five stages are organized under two broad subprocesses, initiation and implementation, divided by the point at which the decision to adopt is made (Figure 1).

Initiation

The first two stages of the innovation process are together known as the initiation phase or subprocess. *Initiation* is all of the information gathering, conceptualizating, and planning for the adoption of an innovation, leading to the decision to adopt.

Stage #1: *Agenda-Setting.* The first step in the initiation of an innovation occurs when an organization's leaders define a general organizational problem, which may create a perceived need for an innovation and set off a search of the organization's environment for innovations that may help solve the organization's problem. Agenda-setting is a continuous process in organizations that occurs when (a) administrators look within the organization to identity problems and to create solutions, and (b) leaders seek answers outside of the institution's boundaries. To a certain degree, innovations can create their own demand.

Stage #2: *Matching.* Administrators match the innovation with their organization's problem to determine whether it fits their needs. Typical of such an assessment is creation of a mental scenario in which the innovation is vicariously adopted and administrators estimate its impacts. At this point, a decision is made whether to adopt, perhaps on a trial basis, or to reject.

STAGE IN THE INNOVATION PROCESS	MAJOR ACTIVITIES AT EACH STATE IN THE INNOVATION PROCESS
I. *Initiation:*	All of the information-gathering, conceptualizing, and planning for the adoption of an innovation, leading up to the decision to adopt.
1. AGENDA-SETTING	General organizational problems, which may create a perceived need for an innovation, are defined; the environment is searched for innovations of potential value to the organization.
2. MATCHING	A problem from the organization's agenda is considered together with an innovation, and the fit between them is planned and designed.
--- The Decision to Adopt ---	
II. *Implementation:*	All of the events, actions, and decisions involved in putting an innovation into use.
3. REDEFINING/ RESTRUCTURING	(1) The innovation is modified and re-invented to fit the situation of the particular organization and its perceived problem, and (2) organizational structures directly relevant to the innovation are altered to accommodate the innovation.
4. CLARIFYING	The relationship between the innovation and the organization is defined more clearly as the innovation is put into full and regular use.
5. ROUTINIZING	The innovation eventually loses its separate identity and becomes an element in the organization's ongoing activities.

Source: Rogers (1983).

Figure 1. Stages in the Innovation Process in Organizations

Implementation

Following the decision to adopt are three stages in the innovation process which together constitute the implementation subprocess. *Implementation* is all of the events, actions, and decisions involved in putting an innovation to use.

Stage #3: *Redefining/Restructuring*. The application of a new idea often differs from the uses planned before adoption. Thus, an adjustment must begin. If the fit between the problem and the innovation is good, then alternations are minimized. In many cases, however, at least some degree of modification occurs. This modification is called *"re-invention,"* the degree of change in an innovation as it is assimilated by an adopter (Rogers, 1983). The innovation usually causes modifications—which are sometimes profound—in the structure of the organization.

Stage #4: *Clarifying*. As the innovation becomes integrated into the day-to-day operations of the organization, its meaning gradually becomes clear to the members of the organization. The innovation eventually loses its newness and becomes embedded in established protocols.

Stage #5: *Routinizing*. Now, the innovation has been well defined and becomes part of the infrastructure of the organization. Eventually, the innovation loses its newness and is no longer recognized as a separate entity in the organization. It has just become part of the ongoing procedures.

We draw on the results of our investigation of the adoption of microcomputers in nine California high schools (Rogers, McManus, Peters, & Kim, 1985) in order to illustrate the nature of the innovation process. Figure 2 shows the five-step innovation process for microcomputers at Milpitas High School, a California school system that enrolled 1,700 students, 42% of whom are minority members (principally Hispanic and black). The main events in the innovation process seem to generally fit fairly well into the first four of the five stages in the model (routinizing had not yet occurred at the time of our data gathering).

However, in the larger sample of nine California high schools of study, several deviations from our model were found. In four of the nine schools, there was either a false start in adapting computers to the classroom, or there was little planning of how to integrate microcomputers into the curriculum (the machines arrived before educators could define their use). In such cases, a computer corporation typically gifted equipment to the school, or else parents and/or students demanded micros before educators were prepared to offer instruction with the computer. Thus, pressures from *outside* of the school often initiated the innovation process. In five schools, the agenda-setting and matching stages occurred before the adoption decision (these schools had a more successful experience with computers and were farther along in applying them to instructional tasks).

	Stages in the Innovation Process				
	— Initiation — →		(Decision) —	→ Implementation — →	
Time	1. Agenda-Setting	2. Matching	3. Redefining/Restructuring	4. Clarifying	5. Routinizing
1979	(1) Assistant Principal sees microcomputers as administrative aid; and (2) a means of upgrading classes for expanding college-prep curriculum.				
1980		(1) Assistant Principal hires computer teacher; (2) Visits computer centers at other high schools; and (3) Concludes that computers excite students about learning.			
1981			(1) Money raised to purchase first computer equipment.		
1982			(2) Teacher training begins; (3) Teachers begin to change courses to accommodate microcomputers.		
1983				(1) 19% of faculty are using micros; (2) Classroom uses expand;	
1984				(3) Microcomputer applications revised/improved.	
					No routine yet established.

Figure 2. Classifying the Adoption of Microcomputers at Milpitas High School by Stages in the Innovation Process

In sum, about half of the nine schools fit the innovation process model at the initiation phase; the other half represent an after-the-fact reaction to the physical presence of computers brought into the school by gifts, by school parents, or by the determination of a single teacher acting independently.

Important Roles in the Innovation Process

Innovation is a keenly social process in which certain key roles govern whether adoption takes place, and, when it does, the speed and adequacy of implementation. Here, we illustrate these roles with examples and findings from our study of the adoption of computers in nine California high schools.

1. **The *Innovation Champion:*** Typically this role was played by a teacher of mathematics, business, or science, who saw the usefulness of computers in instruction before others in the high school. This individual—and it is usually *one* person at the start of the innovation process—finds a way to begin the series of events and decisions leading to obtaining computers. Called a "computer buff" by Sheingold, Kane, and Endreweig (1983), the innovation champion often does not remain at one high school, or at least does not stay in his or her previous full-time teaching capacity. In two of our nine schools studied, the computer champions were tapped by the school district for administrative work in diffusing computers throughout the school system. In one school, the champion left for a university teaching position. In other cases, the champion began writing instructional computer software in what became a transition out of the classroom and into being a self-employed entrepreneur.

Typically only a small core of two to five teachers and administrators (out of a total faculty of 70 to 100) were involved in the innovation process for computers in each of the nine high schools of study. Thus, adoption of microcomputers in the schools of study is fragile in that (a) only a few teachers have much knowledge about computers, and (b) the regular school budget was usually not involved in obtaining them.

While corporate computer gift programs increase a high school's use of microcomputers, such a donation is often a "Trojan horse" in that the cost and time required for setting up a computer center, obtaining courseware, training teachers, and maintaining the system requires considerable continuing budgetary support, estimated to be four or five times the hardware costs (Levin, 1984). With individual responsibilities assigned, continuing costs, and, eventually, a line item in the school budget, launching a computer center in a high school represents an important change in the school's organizational structure.

2. **Organizational Administrator.** A second key actor in the innovation process is the organization's top executive (the principal in our schools of study). If the computer champion were the principal or were allied with the principal, the spread of microcomputers for instruction in a high school occurred faster than when the champion was a teacher without support of the top of the organization. By no means, however, does the innovation decision simply consist of the executive deciding and then giving orders for implementation.

A variety of other influences in a school's environment affect the innovation process for microcomputers: parents, the computer industry, and various sources of funding for school computers.

SOCIAL IMPACTS OF COMPUTERS IN ORGANIZATIONS

There are many ways to classify the consequences of a technological innovation; Rogers (1983, pp. 380–391) suggests a threefold typology.

Desirable consequences are the functional effects of an innovation on an individual or a social system. *Undesirable consequences* are its dysfunctional effects.

Direct consequences are the changes in an individual or social system that occur in immediate response to an innovation. *Indirect consequences* are the changes that result from the direct consequences of an innovation.

Anticipated consequences are changes caused by an innovation that are recognized and intended by the members of a social system. *Unanticipated consequences* are changes that are neither intended nor recognized.

A usual investigative approach is to gather data about the impacts of a technological innovation by comparing a system on certain variables before and after the introduction of the new technology (this is a pre-post evaluation). There are many difficulties with social science research on the consequences of innovations. Basically, our research methods are not very successful in studying a process that extends into the future. Most social research methods work best as rear-view mirrors; only under special conditions can we adapt them to predict phenomena. One means of studying the impacts of new information technologies is to investigate advanced organizations in which these innovations have been used, and then to extrapolate from them to other organizations. In fact, this is the basic design for most consequences studies of office automation.

The impacts of office automation cannot be fully understood without also considering the current home computer revolution. One of their uses (in addition to playing video games) is word-processing, often in connection with work (Rogers, Daley, & Wu, 1982). In some cases, this use amounts to teleworking, with an employee working at home on a microcomputer or terminal for at least several days a week. Trips to the office for conferences and other personal discussions still seem to be important socio-emotionally for most employees. In most current cases, however, an organizational member simply works at home for a few hours a night and/or on weekends. In this situation, the addictive power of computing becomes a problem. The typical workaholic can now easily spend more hours of work per day by working at home. This desegregation of work and home poses difficulties for many people, who have yet to find effective means of managing these dilemmas.

Figure 3 shows the numerous other impacts of new information technologies on organizations. Computers can be used to supervise employees very closely. For example, in some organizations a supervisor monitors the number of keystrokes per hour made by each employee in a word-processing pool; an automatic warning message is printed on the screen of an employee whose performance is not up to standard. In contrast, computers can be utilized as tools for employee independence and responsibility, allowing an individual to work with great autonomy. The choice between such antithetical uses of the technologies depends on how an organization decides to implement its new tools.

An interesting experiment in office automation is occurring at Apple Computer, Inc., of Cupertino, California. A few years ago, the top officials at Apple did away with secretaries and typewriters. Each employee has an Apple computer on his or her desk, and another one at home; all are expected to prepare their own documents. Every 15 or 20 employees have one "area assistant," who provides certain administrative-secretarial services, such as taking telephone messages, arranging meetings, and so on. Essentially, Apple has used computer technology to create a rather high degree of autonomy among its professional

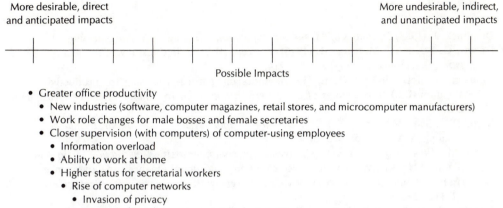

Source: Rogers (1984, p. 172).

Figure 3. Possible Organizational Impacts of the New Information Technologies

employees. It has also eliminated most of the usual tasks of secretaries. One of several motivations for banning typewriters and secretaries was to foster greater occupational equality among Apple employees. But that consequence is part of a much larger potential impact of the new information technologies — they may "disorganize" organizations in certain important ways.

One significant consequence of office automation is changes in social status. Often managers and executives gain status by using computers, and certainly clerical staff do. Some high-level officials, however, perceive computer use as typing, which they consider a low-status job. When a high-status individual in an organization shows that he or she supports the new technology, much of the resistance to office automation is likely to melt. For instance, when an electronic messaging system was introduced at Stanford University a few years ago, a photograph of the University president using the system was published in the university newspaper.

FUTURE IMPACTS ON RESEARCH

What are the implications of the new information technologies for research? The new communication technologies in organizations allow us to gather new kinds of data and to analyze them in novel ways. One example is computer-recorded data about how extensively a computer-based office technology is used by individuals or by organizational units. The computer component in the new communication systems provides their interactivity, their humanlike ability to conduct a "conversation" with the user. Although there are obvious ethical and analytical ramifications of using such data, they represent an improved approach to investigating the social impacts of the new technologies on organizations (Rice & Rogers, 1984).

Finally, we are beginning to realize that the computer-based technologies can provide freedom from the constraints of time and place on person-to-person communication. How can this asynchronous and space-freeing quality best be utilized in new work arrangements? That, indeed, is the meta-issue for the future of the new information technologies.

REFERENCES

Dominick, J. (1983) *Dynamics of Mass Communication,* Reading, MA: Addison-Wesley.

Downs, G. W., Jr., & Mohr, L. B. (1976). Conceptual issues in the study of innovation. *Administrative Science Quarterly, 21,* 700–714.

Johnson, B. McD., & Rice, R. E. (1983). Redesigning word-processing for productivity. In R. Vondran (Ed.), *Proceedings of the American Society of Information Science,* Washington, DC.

Keen, P. & Scott-Morton, M. (1978). *Decision support systems: An organizational perspective.* Reading, MA: Addison-Wesley.

Levin, M. (1984). *Costs and cost-effectiveness of computer-assisted instruction.* Palo Alto, CA: Stanford University, Institute for Research on Educational Finance and Governence.

Mohr, L. B. (1969). Determinants of innovation in organizations. *American Political Science Review, 63,* 111–126.

Mohr, L. B. (1982). *Explaining organizational behavior: The limits and possibilities of theory and research.* San Francisco, CA: Jossey-Bass.

Rice, R. E., & Rogers, E. M. (1984). New methods and new data for the study of new media. In R. E. Rice & Associates (Eds.), *The new media: Uses and impacts,* Beverly Hills, CA: Sage.

Rogers, E. M. (1983). *Diffusion of innovations* (3rd ed.). New York: Free Press.

Rogers, E. M. (1984). A sociological research perspective. In F. W. McFarlan (Ed.), *The information systems research challenge: Proceedings.* Boston, MA: Harvard Business School Press.

Rogers, E. M. (1986). *Communication technology: The new media in society.* New York: Free Press.

Rogers, E. M., & Kincaid, L. D. (1981). *Communication networks: Toward a new paradigm for research.* New York: Free Press.

Rogers, E. M., & Kim, J. I. (1985). Diffusion of innovations in public organizations. In L. Merritt & A. J. Merrit (Eds.), *Innovation in the public sector.* Beverly Hills, CA: Sage.

Rogers, E. M., & Larsen, J. K. (1984). *Silicon Valley fever: Growth of high-technology culture.* New York: Basic Books.

Rogers, E. M., & Rafaeli, S. (1985). Computers and communication. In B. R. Ruben (Ed.), *Information and behavior* (Vol. 1, pp. 95–112), New Brunswick, NJ: Transaction.

Rogers, E. M., Daley, H., & Wu, T. (1982). *The diffusion of home computers* (Report). Palo Alto, CA: Stanford University, Institute for Communication Research.

Rogers, E. M., McManus, J. H., & Kim, J. I., (1985). *Microcomputers in the School: A Case of Decentralized Diffusion* (Research Report). Palo Alto, CA.

Ryan, B., & Gross, N. C. (1943). Diffusion of hybrid seed corn in two Iowa communities. *Rural Sociology, 8,* 15–24.

Shannon, C. E., & Weaver, W. (1949). *The mathematical theory of communication.* Urbana, IL: University of Illinois Press.

Sheingold, K., Kane, J., & Endreweig, M. E. (1983). Microcomputer use in schools: Developing a research agenda. *Harvard Educational Review, 53,* 4.

Strassman, P. (1980). The office of the future: Information management for the new age. *Technology Review, 82,* 55–56.

Uttal, B. (1982, May 3). What's detaining the office of the future? *Fortune,* p. 176.

Chapter 18

Technology and Culture: Action Bias Effects in the Implementation of Word Processing

Larry D. Browning

The University of Texas at Austin

Bonnie McD. Johnson

Aetna Life Insurance

ABSTRACT

This paper examines action bias as a dimension of organizational culture with decided impacts on the development of technology. Is the culture a mediated, planning culture that slowly comes to a decision, or is it a quick-paced, quick-feedback setting that thrives on action and corrective action? The implementation of word processing is a technological advancement that provides a research focus for this question. Since word processing provides quick turnaround and quick transmission, does it affect the structure of a culture? This question is developed in a qualitative study of 60 organizations which have implemented word processing over the last 6 years. The results show that word processing can increase the action bias in cultures. The action bias is analyzed for its wider effects on organizational culture.

INTRODUCTION

Our society bears little resemblance to that theorized by the founders of social science — Marx, Weber, and Durkheim . . . The generation and dissemination of information so pervades our institutions and practices that traditional conceptual strategies are either out moded or in need of basic revision. With few exceptions, the work of the social sciences has failed to register, much less confront this possibility. (Posner, 1982, p. 994)

We take this statement of doubt about available constructs for understanding modern organizations, and use ethnographic research to complete team analyses of 60 organizations' efforts at implementing word processing to handle written communication. Following the suggestions by Mohr (1982) and Van de Ven (1984) that innovations must be studied in context to understand their complex processes, this report builds a theoretical case for the impact of technology on cultures and, reflexively, the impact of cultures on technology. To keep these concepts from fading into each other and losing distinction, the specific techology studied, *word processing,* is treated as an innovation or object of study, and *culture* is limited to a single dimension—the speed of feedback (Deal & Kennedy, 1982).

Since word processing allows for a quicker movement from idea to distribution of document, the technology—at least in principle—can alter the value of information, and ultimately, perhaps, culture. One could speculate that quick feedback via word processing (a widespread phenomenon today, with personal computers growing like rabbits among professional personnel in most corporations) could change cultures into action organizations, or, alternatively, that it bogs down action by generating messages that confuse attention.

The study presented here does not address the relationship of communications via word processing per se on culture. Rather, this study examines the history of implementation of word processing in a critical time—1978 to 1983. In 1978, video display technology, combined with reasonably inexpensive terminals (down to about $15,000 from over $30,000), made word processing an attractive technology for secretarial personnel. Computer power to support clerical work had previously been limited to mainframe transaction processing like order entry. Word processing offered a capability to manipulate words once available only to expert systems users. A whole new world of possibilities was opening up. Today we are realizing these possibilities through innovations like desktop publishing and text-oriented databases.

The focus of the word processing study (data collected and analyzed from 1982 to 1985) was what factors (from cognitions to actions) account for the observation that some individuals and organizations "reinvented" word processing in imaginative and productive ways much more than others. Today, the accomplishments of word processing in those early days may seem trivial. Consider, however, how much our concepts of what can be done have changed. In those early days, justifying expensive equipment for "typing" jobs was not an easy task. After the equipment was acquired, the tough work of how to manage its effective use began. Examining the implementation of word processing provides insights into some core areas of culture and action. Implementers faced the challenge of bringing in an artifact with little cultural understanding of what it was (what its potential might be) or how to manage it (what were the useful roles, procedures, cultural practices). As one respondent told us, "Word processing was a baby."

In this report, we present one slice of a larger study—the action bias of implementers and cultures where word processing became an artifact in a context of creativity. Other factors are discussed elsewhere (Johnson, 1985; Johnson and Rice, 1987).

AN APPROACH TO CULTURE

The language approach to culture emphasizes symbolic actions of leaders who, through intuition and vision, make correct business or policy decisions and "give off" (Goffman, 1959) dramatic renditions of these practices (Deal & Kennedy, 1982). These actions are the grist for stories, myths, and metaphors (Brown, 1981) that contain simple morals or rules intense enough to have wholesale distribution and persistent effects. Both the language research, which offers proof that stories are remembered more than statistical data (Martin & Powers, 1983) and that stories in later stages of socialization contain more moral fiber than earlier ones (Brown, 1981), and the managerial books using case data written for popular audiences suggest that symbolic cultures with rich languages, lead to intense activity and commitment (Deal & Kennedy; 1982, Peters & Waterman, 1982).

The approach to culture and technological implementation presented here is contextual and draws on Sowell's concepts in *Knowledge and Decisions* (1980): knowledge itself is the central resource and commodity in the economy. In his review of Sowell's book, White (1982) argues that this often-ignored fact has led us to a "physical fallacy," where we convince ourselves there is intrinsic value to an object, when in fact its value depends on its relationship to other objects in society at a given time.

There are two classification schemes that address these qualities of culture: the group-grid model of Mary Douglas (Douglas, 1982; Douglas & Wildavsky, 1982), and the cultural diagnosis model of Deal and Kennedy (1982). In Douglas's view, the central element of a decision is the risk involved in action and the calculation necessary to reduce risk. Douglas builds on risk by connecting it to blame. Blame may be foreign to organizational communication theory, but its flip side, approval, is a central link for a host of social science concepts from social reinforcement to cohesion. Douglas believes cultural practices rise from the explicitness or structure members put on their environment (high structure to low structure) in relation to the institutional values the membership holds towards risk taking (group risk or individual risk). The typology generated by Douglas shows several distinctive types of social organization. One is a society of competitive individualism (individual risk-low structured problems) that produces a system of *stars*. A second is a hierarchical, compartmentalized organization (group risk-high structured problems) which produces a system of *teams*. A third is an egalitarian voluntary society (group risk-low structured problems) which produce a *sect* (Douglas, 1982). Douglas's view is important because it questions the ability to change culture by manipulating its symbolic form. She questions the ability to change culture by simply altering the symbols like one adds salt to the stew.

The emphasis of Deal and Kennedy (1982) is more transparent and applied than Douglas's. They identify (a) a "world of individualists who regularly take high risks and get quick feedback on whether their actions were right or wrong," *tough guy cultures* (p. 107); (b) "cultures with big stakes decisions (high risk) where years pass (slow feedback) before employees know whether decisions have paid off, *"bet your company cultures* (p. 108); (c) "a world of little or no feedback where employees find it hard to measure what they do; instead they concentrate on how it is done," *process cultures* (p. 108); (d) "fun and action is the rule here, and employees take few risks, all with quick feedback" *work hard–play hard cultures* (p. 108).

The Douglas and Deal and Kennedy models overlap on the relationship between individuality and risk. If individuals under real conditions of risk take more actions than a group (Latane & Darley, 1970), then individuality and risk taking are indirect slices of the same idea and make integration of the two models for analysis of word processing possible.

The ties between these models and word processing technology are the individual actions of those who directed implementation of the technology; in some cases, we see executives who literally changed the context of action to bring about acceptance of the technology and thus promote the conditions for creativity in its use.

ACTION BIAS

The most popular presentation of action bias is in Peters and Waterman's *In Search of Excellence* (1982). Action bias is presented through examples from interviews, rather than a tight logical definition with explicit ties to theory. A definition drawn from a review of the book's examples shows action bias to be single actions by an individual that are completed quickly: "a string of practical tasks done right" (p. 126). The lead examples presented by Peters and Waterman focus on: (a) quick reorganization to meet a problem; (b) short-term studies completed by organization members who have enough authority to treat their plans as solutions rather than recommendations; (c) problem definitions that break things up to keep organizations fluid; and (d) informal communication and unrehearsed presentations without massive reports.

While action bias as formulated by Peters and Waterman is intended to influence the behavior of managers, a line of thinking by Weick on cognition and action, reported by Malcolm (1983), supports their formulation and shows how action bias creates information for decision makers.

Weick develops a differentiated notion of action through use of the verbs *focuses, replaces, degrades,* and *improves.*

1. **Action focuses cognition.** Any old plan will do. Maps motivate people — get them moving. The motion, not the plan, should be the locus. Even a wrong map is a plausible map. A map allows the holder to anticipate a certain kind of order which is sufficient to lure one into the situation, to start acting and imposing an order predicted or anticipated on the basis of the map.

2. **Action replaces cognition.** Action in the situation gives perceptual data that will make cognition unnecessary. As people are more active in situations, they cut down the necessity to think about the situation at all. Restriction of mobility (inaction) increases the need for elaborate cognitive processes; mobility allows for multiple perspectives and reduces the need for cognitive processing; visual illusions are destroyed. When individuals in organizations are overloaded, they use cognition badly; they cannot do the equivalent of walking around their problems; they are forced back into inferences; the quality of cognition they do is poor; therefore, the inferences they make are more flawed.

3. **Action degrades cognition.** Action rationality is different from decision rationality, and the two may run in counter directions. When one wants to consolidate and energize action to sustain some course of forceful action, things that lead to a bias in commitment make enormous sense because they lead into situations where they generate forceful action. For action rationality: (a) analyze few alternatives (focus motivation on a few alternatives); (b) think only of the positive features of this alternative (increase commitment to the alternative); (c) do not formulate objectives and then decide what will get you there. Ask: "What's most likely to happen?" then take that consequence and say, "That's what we want to do." Such reasoning smooths out and streamlines the action taken in the situation.

4. **Action improves cognition.** Situations where rationality works best are those where the environment changes slowly. With slow change in the environment, more deliberation, more plans, and more objectives are possible. Rationality works best when the situation is well controlled, by people with some centralized activity, or there are some stable means and preferences.

It is possible those people who are strong, confident actors in the situation are the most able to use rational decision making. Their action hammers the environment into shape so they can direct rational processes. This is important because those who follow action rationality, those who leap before they look, may slow down the rate at which the environment is changing. A limited set of beliefs, continually imposed in the situation, creates a sheer redundancy of beliefs that insert a regularity, a smoothness, a sameness, a pattern which was not there before. The situation becomes more predictable and stable, and rational processes can be used to get something done.

The thread that extends through Weick's idea is that motion is as important as goals; action gives definition. In word processing implementation, typically, goals were nonsensical — without experience, implementers could not set goals. Initially, there was no definition of "management of word processing," for there were no cultural antecedents — those who used typewriter or data center models missed the point of word processing entirely. Hence, only those who acted succeeded in defining.

FIVE CASES IN ACTION BIAS

These case examples are drawn from a nationwide study of word processing implementation that began with structured telephone interviews. From a pool of 200 telephone interviews, a sample of 60 organizations was selected for on-site interviews and observations. From a review of the case manuscripts, 13 were selected because of the amount of emphasis in the case text on action bias. Five cases were selected from a pool of 13 for presentation in detail, because of their representativeness or uniqueness (Davis, 1971).

Each case invites comparison and distinction. The Federal Law Agency, for example, had similar implementation dynamics to other federal agencies. It acted like a traditional bureaucracy, despite the clear effects of legal tradition on the culture. The Audit Office-AO, which one would expect to be the home of a process-bureaucratic culture, had a vitality and innovativeness different from any other government agency. Space Systems, Inc. is used because the director is a classic example of technological implementation in the hands of a culture leader. Bell and Will, the private law firm, shows how a traditional organization bends to adapt to modern technology. Bay Research Hospital Procurement is used because of its recent change of fortune as a result of technological competence.

The cases have been edited from one half to one third of the original length of the field notes. The next section contains the five edited cases, with an interpretation following each case presentation.

The Federal Law Agency

Bob Laten, the interviewee, heads Civil Service personnel in the office. He directs employees in all three divisions — civil, criminal, and claim/judgments. Under him is Jane Bell, with whom we did the telephone interview, and secretaries for the criminal division and the collections division.

"My job is to see that this office operates as efficiently as possible. The measures of this would be low turnaround time, reduce the secretarial turnover rates, and get a higher quality of work. Main decisions to achieve this are made in this office. We have a review group in Washington and we try to develop a range of rapport between them and us."

The head attorney is a political appointment and tends to be changed every 4 years; at least that has been the pattern with the last several elections — new administration, new attorney, new attorney-staff. But the support personnel tend to remain in place. "We are therefore concerned with the quality of life of the secretary, the paralegal assistant. Their jobs are to provide flexibility for the principal (the attorney). Vis-a-vis the competition—i.e., the private sector, the government side is badly outgunned."

Each federal attorney has some autonomy from Washington. They may focus the emphasis of the office on the kind of cases he will handle; he has some latitude in allocating resources.

The distribution of the system is strictly for the purposes of the "one federal attorney." He refers to the Hell's Angels case and the Juan Corona case, to show the competitive nature of their work. "Like a fighter pilot has one hundred and thirty support personnel on the ground to keep a plane in the air, a federal lawyer leverages one group of people to give him local control and flexibility." In view of this, Laten's goal is to optimize the "principal," which includes three secretaries, one paralegal, and three "getting" secretaries: "Suzie Q" can go down the hall (and do this and this and this); otherwise the one attorney will be "hamstrung" and "badly outgunned."

"The biggest problem here is justification. We have only half of what we need in the way of equipment, supplies, and support personnel."

Word processing was introduced on a pilot basis. There has been a great work overload on secretarial personnel, a lack of standardization, excessive reproduction of briefs, and generally poor quality work.

This is a poor market for competing with the private sector. Legal firms tend to pay much more for private secretaries. The office tends to get people at low classifications whom they have to train.

Equipment procurement went from getting bids from 40 vendors, down to six vendors, to three for final specifications. They went with NBI because they had a state-of-the-art machine for the legal profession, especially designed for legal applications. "We considered it a step up from a typewriter with memory rather than a step down from a computer."

The office has a weak administrative centralized background. "There are 45 cowboys/cowgirls here all doing their own thing." Word processing was organized along the administrative lines already in place, rather than trying to reorganize the administrative system to conform to the automation process. The chief secretaries for each division are trying to reorganize the administrative system to conform to the automation process. They make the decisions for that division, and they tend to be backed up by the heads of those divisions. Laten sees his job as one of coordinating all these disparate interests, and trying to satisfy them as best as can be done under the circumstances.

The reason for the distributed system is that the office has a weak administration, with little centralized control over attorneys. Given that, they went with the present norm rather than require standardization and control. They went with present organization lines instead of change, which allows the myth of local control to be maintained: "I gave it to my secretary."

The biggest problem is that, if you put in a center and say the people are operators of word processing machines, you have to hire grade-4 people (GS4). They get around this by saying that, because the system is distributed, the operators are not predominantly word processing operators, but are legal secretaries, hired at the GS6 level. Word processing becomes a skill, or a technical ability that allows the secretary to be more responsive to the needs of the attorneys.

They tell civil service that there is no typing pool (when in fact many of the secretaries—although not the word processing operators—do work in a kind of typing pool arrangement within the building). All of the operators must know legal terminology, legal forms, legal processes, etc. So, in the strictest sense, they are not just word processing operators, nor are they just typist-clerks. Even so, they have difficulties in getting and holding onto highly skilled and competent people. "If you need a high quality product, you must have highly skilled people working for you."

When first introduced, there was a great deal of record keeping, primarily for justification of more equipment and personnel. Washington (the federal government) has a whole anthology of horror stories on computerization. Seven systems have been proposed; seven systems have bombed out. Each system has had to be compatible with 14 different interfaces, each doing different types of things. It is difficult to meld all these different things into one computerized operation. Therefore, each office has tended to select its own options. "Now we have a system designed in Washington, and what works in Washington most often doesn't work locally."

"Washington has said that we should not go too far down this line (of implementation) because they have a computer they are going to foist onto us. It is a system that will also handle much of the legal case load. Process information management systems— PROMIS. What a bad pun. It is still just a promise and from what we hear it will always be just a promise. It was due here last October and we still have nothing to show."

They are not enthused about PROMIS. "We can get everything they can on the computer, and we are compatible with our own typing system."

"But when the PROMIS system comes in, it will be networked into 17 other of the largest US attorney's offices in the country."

"The future, it's incredible. Most dynamic applications of word processing are in law offices. Attorneys are wordsmiths. Best utilization of word processing is in files management, making changes, adding, deleting, handling cases, indexing references, etc."

"The impact of word processing has been phenomenal. Speed of changes has freed the attorney to handle more cases. Up by 10%. Quality is dependent on the attorney. I've insisted on quality anyway."

"The flexibility at late times allows for procrastination. It makes the attorney more willing to make changes; often we talk the first draft."

Direction in 3 years, good case load, an inventory of all cases so the supervisor can see the "burden" level. Now his secretary enters cases and closes down cases. Case inventory allows for more informed decisions. Before, when a big case came in, he had to talk to each attorney about case load. Time consuming. They are putting a module on word processing to track docketing dates and status conference dates. Now getting schedules is like pulling teeth. This is all about the PROMIS system which has been so slow to come to this office that they call it the "broken promise" system. But they love it in San Diego.

The PROMIS system will allow the branch chief to make more informed decisions; can seek additional positions for documentation. It has an activity code that revises a big–small, active–inactive dimension on legal cases that is easy to code and over which there is much reported agreement. The way it was organized before, there was no way to determine the activity levels and time constraints. Thus, work load was an independent attorney decision before.

Bell and Will Private Sector Law Firm

Pat, the department manager's background: 3 years' previous experience with another company in the maritime business. She claims her background is "technical," but that means she was an operator. Her first position was starting a word processing department (in a shipping company). She had taken word processing classes.

Production is 55,000 pages a day, with turnaround of 3 hours. Pat approves rush jobs. The place seems to be busy, but not frantic. They have 300 disks of stored material (this seems like a lot compared to other law offices). Three years ago, there were eight operators and one telecommunications person. Now, six operators, two proofers, and one telecommunications specialist do the work; everyone is trained to do all jobs. The legal staff has grown from 39 lawyers to 60. Used to have secretary one to one; now two or three to one. For word processing alone $250,000 a month is billed to a major client.

When she has trouble with someone (lawyers) not following procedures about submitting work, she "sits them down next to an operator and lets them see they're not miracle machines." She communicates with them to explain how they are slowing others' work.

When Pat took over the center, there was no supervisor. Lawyers came down and pushed their own work. Filing system was a mess. Established logs and work requests with information about who was using the equipment. It was a marketing device (she uses the term "marketing" a lot).

She has learned to document their work, to justify new equipment and to project peaks and valleys of work so that she can plan people. She hires temps.

She reviews all documents; if she sees the same basic text coming in from different authors, she suggests a form.

She is an externally oriented supervisor. For example, when she took over, she conducted three seminars of 2 hours each with lawyers. She had slides made of unclear handwriting to "show them what it does to an operator." She outlined her long range objectives for the center. She sets priorities by case. She reminds lawyers of things like tables of contents.

Pat is aware of interpersonal and organizational conflicts that can impact on the center, and how it is viewed by others. She observes that secretaries don't like to hear their boss say that *word processing* produced a wonderful document. Those who work in the center have to be sensitive to others' perceptions of them. Secretaries are the hardest sells. They are included in orientation. If a secretary is not doing input correctly, Pat calls her in to see her document being scanned. (Pat again emphasizes the importance of first-hand experience.) Lots of times, secretaries cannot be bothered.

She took a survey of lawyers to determine if they wanted a user's manual. They overwhelmingly preferred personal instruction.

Pat is explicit about her boundary-management strategies: "I run defense between user and word processors. Users just see the finished form. Sometimes I hear that so and so upstairs is badmouthing the dept. I make an appointment to see that person to find out what the problem is. It is easy to criticize word processing because they have so little contact with us."

Operators reported how Pat had improved operations with examples such as getting a cable so that material does not need to be rekeyed to be communicated. She had to "juggle money" to buy.

Driving force there is to "make the lawyers look good!"

Though the word processing manager has strict rules (like the 3-day work week can't be worked in straight days), proofers find her flexible. Pat lets Jeff leave early if there is no backlog. (One proofer works 7–7; one 12–12.)

There are two deadline cases here (Webb & Weick, 1983). At the U.S. Attorney's office, things were slow and didn't work. There were signs of urgency in every corner of the agency, but they were sluggish and unable to respond to problems. In contrast, the private firm's responses to urgency had come to rest in a central person. The implementation step at Bell and Will was centralized after an early disaster which probably affected the amount of control they were willing to give an information technician to form a center. Other cases of centers had their own sets of problems, such as low morale and being over-proceduralized, but this rarely happened unless the word processing department became too large. At Bell and Will, the private firm, anything that slowed things down or caused errors was reason enough to make a change to correct it. The list of action responses by Pat at Bell and Will is among the highest of the 60 organizations from which case data is collected. At the slightest discontent from lawyers, the word processing department quickly hired two editors — one with an M.A. in English — to read all reports for typos and grammatical errors.

The government office law agency described the environment as formidable when they compared themselves with the highly paid private-sector law firm adversaries they face in court. Part of the action bias is tied to slack resources. For even if they were those adversaries' professional equals, the efficiency of the word processing department in the private sector outdid them as they negotiated the different meetings that led up to a settlement or trial. The pay scale available to good word processors, and the regulation of positions to fill them, meant that the federal law agency had resource and regulation limits that kept them from being as crisp and active as the private firm.

The government law agency knew the importance of quickness for their word processing department, but their response was piecemeal rather than strategic. The strategy of having a word processing department that could respond to last-minute rush jobs to meet court deadlines was common knowledge, but an early decision that tied them to local attorney/managers left them in poor shape for competition with private law firms. The decision to implement the technology by reflecting then-current cultural norms set the direction on how word processing would be handled. The opening "cowboy" description of the competitiveness and individuality of attorneys at the government law office captures the culture. The dispersal of equipment to the control of these stars meant the critical force needed to demonstrate the full capacity of the technology could not be gathered.

Bay Research Hospital Procurement

Ray, the supervisor, began at Bay Research Hospital Procurement (BRHP) about 2½ years ago. He came from U.S. Leasing, where he had gotten a job as a "temp." He came to San Francisco from Denver, where he had taught word processing and business courses.

At that time, BRHP had gone from mag cards to the Wang 30, a dedicated typewriter mode. There were three operators, a 2- to 3-week backlog/turnaround, a high rate of errors, and many complaints from the buyers. Word processing operators were tending to use their typewriters more than the word processing equipment, and were not aware of many of the features of the system — especially automated features. Many complained that it took such a long time to train an operator to process a purchase order. Much of the work was in a batch mode, with seven copies of purchase orders required. There was constant keyboarding, many skipped forms, and stacks of unused purchase orders piled around "for future use" via typewriters, etc.

Most of the work now is still purchase orders for buyers, also requests for quotations — anything over $5000 must solicit bids from vendors, and these tend now to be standardized boilerplates of paragraphs, terms, and conditions, etc. These paragraphs also must appear on the purchase orders once bids are let, so they must be duplicated. These are ideal kinds of materials to be put on word processing equipment for storage and recall.

The operation is now so automated that there is never more than 1-day turnaround time, usually less than 1 hour. There are still only three operators full-time, plus the supervisor. He does mostly systems analysis work, automating various functions, putting new operations on the glossaries of the Wang, and getting other things onto the Honeywell system they have purchased. Some operators complain that they have too little to do, and spend much time sitting and waiting for work to come from the buyers. Also, they are doing many different kinds of things than they used to do, especially in automating other jobs for the buyers that were formerly done by hand — i.e., anything that requires duplication of effort, repetition of materials, compilation of quotations, etc.

Ray wrote the main glossaries originally. Now he has trained the supervisor to write additional glossaries.

An Interview with an Operator.

This office is the food buyer for the main campus and hospitals in the area. There is a lot of patient feeding, totaling over $1 million on food. Some contracts are let on a monthly basis, some weekly, depending upon the kind of article and how great the fluctuation in that particular market, seasonality, etc. Most of her work is highly repetitive. Ray has created for her a master draft sheet that combines a number of what were formerly separate operations. Saves her time by greatly reducing her paper work, combining operations, and simplifying her procedures. Finds she has much more time available than she used to.

Requests for proposals go to vendors; these consist mostly of standardized clauses in which she fills in the blanks with standardized information, or specialized information as is required. The sentences may remain the same, but she may have to alter a number here, an item name there, a quantity number somewhere else. Before going on system, she had to photocopy each draft. Now she has typed her specifications into boilerplate paragraphs in the machine. Each time she needs to assemble a bid proposal, she selects the needed paragraphs, indicates the changes to be made for that particular bid, and has the machine do it all at once, producing all the needed copies of the final document. She usually needs eight sets, four pages each on 40 items.

This used to take her 2 days to complete each week. Now she does the entire operation in 15–20 minutes.

The former supervisor of the center, before Ray, compartmentalized all the jobs, defined them in such a way that nobody could do anybody else's job, and there were, of course, only jobs that the supervisor was capable of doing. This created chaos — when one person was out, nobody could do her job, and work backed up. When another was out, the same occurred. Also led to great lack of confidence on the part of the operators.

Now everybody can do everybody else's job. This led to a radical change in the way the center functioned. Greater confidence among staff, two promoted to non-word processing jobs — administrative assistant levels at another research facility. Two new operators have been integrated immediately into the system. Less absenteeism among staff.

Ray developed a glossary that would take information by categories of date, purchase order, store on master disk, and generate requisition specs, buyer lists, status of orders, bids, etc.

What was the impact of the quicker turnaround time? Attitude of everybody in the office changed from very negative to highly positive. Every order had been marked "rush"; now, "rush" orders are rare. Before, rush orders would be from 1 to 2 weeks; now, "rush" means "need within the hour." Complaints from users are now almost nonexistent. Ray and center have been commended in the university newsletters.

Much of the work is being shifted to the Honeywell computer system, because (a) it can communicate with six or eight people in other locations; (b) it can do more file generation and file merge activities, with automatic calculations of bids, etc., than the Wang system. On the Honeywell, one operator could do all the purchase orders. They would retain one operator on the Wang as they own the machine, and there would be no reason to junk it while it is still operable.

An Interview With a User.

"We enter orders as they are received and we keep tabs. You can give a status report of who talked to who. It also allows for lemon lists, which gives data on buyers success. It is a way of checking on users. There was once an attempt to do it manually but it was virtually impossible."

Still, she sees the system as having a long way to go. Vendors, categories of vendors, and all sorts of aggregation are possible for her use. When asked about the lemon lists, she says, "I'm checking over mine now; I've been asked to speak to the manager. She sees it as a good reminder to users, it creates an awareness of work load and creates immediate attention. Purchasing has so many variables: dollar amount, uniqueness of item, and the number of items of research necessary to fill the order that it is only a rough estimate of the real work."

Ray has recently been promoted to systems analyst, and is enthusiastic about that. Had been bored because the system was working too well, not enough for him to do; he had written most of the major glossaries and had automated to the point where any more or any quicker would have led to problems with staff buyers (can only do so much so quickly with people; they have to get used to change). He had seriously considered going back to teaching. He had begun to pick up a little data processing background by taking some programming courses. He finally applied for job when they asked him why he hadn't done so. He was the only data processing person on the site, had experience there, and could serve a sort of double function because he would still "oversee" the word processing operations and advance the automation there too. His salary has doubled in 2 years.

Ray says operators here are getting a little concerned, as they see more and more of their jobs automated and they have less and less to do in the day. "However, I believe they have confidence that I am being protective of their jobs, and of them. I always show them what I've done, what I am doing. I try to say 'this will make your job easier;' but that doesn't work any more because they come back at me that 'it's too easy already.' "

This is an action bias recovery case. Everything was in shambles, and a single person with technical competence reorganized, cross-trained, and simplified the work until the technology was being used correctly. The image presented of the past by the operators and manager suggests this culture was changed from a dreary, ragged office with piles of paper everywhere to a clean setting where work was done efficiently. The demands were switched from being oppressive *on them* to being exported *to others*.

One version of creating resources is doing constant work with fewer people. There was already a payoff, because two people had been promoted up and out of the word processing division. The success was offset by the operators' fear that they might lose their jobs and that they had no way to protect them. Even the kind words of an effective supervisor could not satisfy them.

The creation of "lemon lists" had a direct impact on the buyers. Previously, their handling of documents was made invisible by the chaos in the word processing department, but the new procedure meant that, in addition to catching up, the word processing department produced a list indicating buyer purchasing errors. The buyers report their lives are much better because of the stress and overload relieved by the turnaround in the word processing department; the lemon lists are respected and taken seriously by the buyers. The value of this case is the restructuring it reflects as a result of implementing technology. People progressed in status; people became inconsolably fearful at the same time they were successful. The restructuring shows movement in positions on a chart and the shifting of power (a) from one subgroup to the next; (b) out of the organization, to create a cross-boundary tie; and (c) toward a reticent supervisor who mainly wants to do interesting work.

Space Systems Incorporated

"We didn't set out to do word processing. We set out to find out how we could get our work done."

"We wanted to get intelligent terminals to use when the big computer was down. We knew there were people who didn't known how to use Xentec computers. We got them. We had a lot of software people." The general manager of Space Systems has regular meetings on issues of interest. "After we got them and used them for a while, we made a presentation on the potential of micros. We described the things we'd done with our scrounged micros (4 of them). There are a lot of people around here who are afraid of micros because they don't understand them or understand what they can do with them. The morning after the presentation I took the general manager a request for 20 more micros. I got fifteen. I put them to work in 1982. I requested and got 12 more — a dozen Osbornes (35 in all). There were 3 or 4 entrepreneurs among the job group interested in adapting software to our work. They appeared randomly."

"Our former method of developing work was to write it out by hand. We couldn't send it to word processing because they couldn't read it. So we had typists do it. Then we would edit and cut and paste a version to send to word processing. About three weeks after we started we would be semi-finished. Our objective was to capture what the individual was doing. Even if a user would hunt and peck, he could do it better than writing it out. The computer is the most powerful eraser in the world."

Production: "We cut our work turnaround from three weeks to three days. Secretaries like it. We could merge pieces of a larger report."

"If a guy has five people working for him, he could keep up with the work each is doing without interfering."

"When we got the original four machines, I used them rather visibly. It was obvious to everyone that I was interested in them. This is the most important part of putting in a system. If the person in charge is interested enough to use it himself, then everyone else will give it a try."

"If I had to justify, I never could have gotten it. You probably never can justify before you have one. How many people could justify a TV the first time they bought one? I got it to learn. I wanted to know if an old codger like me could keep up with the kids."

"You have to have one where you can use it in private. Have you ever thought about how tough it would be to practice piano in public? Another thing you have to learn to do is your own programming."

"We had 21 terminals for our big computer. That was not enough."

"We also do a lot of proposals. I said to myself, 'What would I do if I had a lot of home computers and wanted to do a proposal?' I worked out a concept. I shared the idea with other people. They had an idea of where we could get the computers."

"The major motivation for managers and supervisors to use their equipment is that they will understand how they can have their people use it. They must want to keep up with the kids."

"We do not have an acceptable communications mode here. DEC made a presentation a few weeks ago. They presented a requirements analysis. It was an excellent tutorial on the structure of micros. But the user interface was too complex. Networking should be totally invisible to the user."

"Systems must be installed gradually. Unless you get some hands-on work and try it, it won't work. Tribal customs in any organization prevent acceptance. There is a division of work that leads people to ask, 'Should I have anything to do with writing a program?' These systems blur organizational lines."

"There is also an issue of what level of privacy a person should have. I need a certain amount of privacy in how I do a job. Tribal rituals set what those are and change slowly. People must develop an understanding of what is happening. In our system, when I oversaw work done on the system, I didn't penalize, but I did compliment. We publicized when people developed something new. We didn't track problems. All mistakes are positive steps in learning."

"The system evolved. A manager in software (who didn't ever work for me) turned out to be one of the most active users. Formal assignment of people to work with the equipment would have hindered our progress. A secretary was a prime user. We configured an installation around her. We could leave disks with her to format. She helped people; she's still there."

"I have a strong desire to tinker. Had it since I was a boy. It has nothing to do with being an engineer though. It never lets up. I am the area's leading expert on re-inking ribbons. I make presentations on the topic. First you spray with WD-40; after that, use NCR 575 ink."

"In any organization you have bear trappers and bear skinners. You need bear trappers to sell the program and bear skinners to do it. I'm a skinner."

Productivity; overhead. "Look at the trade-off. Microcomputers can increase productivity. I felt I could deliver a man year of work for every computer put in. But in this company, and any other that does federal contracting, it is not that easy. I have to look at both direct costs and overhead costs. If I can do all my work with one person who has a computer, I am not necessarily making money. Computers are charged to overhead."

"Computers have their limits. If I get information from a computer, I don't know how to judge its credibility. If I look a person in the eye, I know better what to trust."

This action bias case is set apart by the string of successes the manager had to get word processing implemented. This occurred in cases where individuals promoting the implementation have long-term tenure and reputations for knowing and doing the core activity of their organization. This director described himself as a "bear skinner," and made it believable. This person's combined tenure and job knowledge caused his requests for support to receive attention. His presentation of folksy examples on such topics as practicing in private (like a piano) and getting something you are unsure of how you will finally use (like a television) showed a depth of his cultural knowledge. He consciously modeled actions he wanted others to take, and committed considerable energy to arranging details others might consider trivial. At the same time, he was unstructured about global issues of accomplishment. He was flexible with rules until he found a good match with the requirements of the work.

Auditing Office

This interview focuses on the auditor, who may have 50 projects going at any given time.

Auditing projects: they can be as small as 100 to 500 staff days or as large as 1,000 or 5,000 staff days. They accumulate enough information to fill 5–10 boxes, letters, regulations, etc.

In an AO report, each word is checked for documentation. They check references, they check on data (which requires double checks). The auditor must show logic indicated and the source data preserved to leave an audit trail.

There is no middle-man between an auditor and his work. Therefore, they get professionals involved in basics. They consider this leading-edge stuff to provide technical assistance to get the professional involved in word processing.

What must be overcome is a barrier between data processor and user that is technical and political. With their old mission, there was antagonism. Auditor lost control and didn't understand language.

They use several steps to move to a new mission of having the auditor more directly on the machine. They discount the past. "As long as you are doing this you are limiting yourself from doing bigger and better things." Yes, they are giving up something but it is being replaced with something better.

They also use team building with technical assistance group for 3 months on issues, interpersonal concerns, directions, and organization.

Jones was selected for this work because of his work in technical assistance groups in the '60s and '70s, his auditing background, his work in automation, and his electric workstation experience. He is invested in the managing of word processing, because he sees it as a way to affect change and because this is where things are going. "You rarely see in a person's lifetime the kinds of changes I've seen in the last few years." Jones got this position because he proposed the idea of using word processors — microcomputers. His original suggestion was rejected by headquarters, but when the assistant to the commissioner was in San Francisco on an audit, Jones proposed the idea to him. This person suggested it in Washington and it received experimental status.

One issue they have to fight is that scarce resources — in this case, word processing machines — are claimed at a higher level in the organization for a broader purpose. In this region, "we had to fight off management from using it for administrative purposes." In this office, the regional director wanted to put an inventory of office equipment on the machine. Jones (and this is a classic example of a person using negotiation to further a professional purpose) suggested to him, "We can do that, but the records could be kept just as well in a loose leaf folder." This comment was accepted by the higher level administrator, and the equipment was protected from trivial uses.

As a beginning tactic to introduce word processing for professional use, they sent out a memo. Who can use the typewriter? They asked them to estimate the number of days a month they could justify a typewriter. They prioritized the requests and put their name on the machine to emphasize the ownership.

This was a big move in this agency, because of the history of professional roles in the agency over the past 20 years. In 1961 and 1962, and in that period in general, there were two career lines in AO: there were auditors who worked with a pen, and there were detectives who, in Mickey Spillane fashion, banged out their reports on a typewriter. The detectives were looked upon as second class, if not suspect citizens, so identifying anything with them was avoided. If an auditor used a machine or expressed an interest in the use of a machine, it was quickly poo-pooed. "You aren't a typist, you are an auditor. Professionals don't type; secretaries type."

One other attempt at spreading the innovation was to put together a tape to show people the use of word processing: how to use the machine rather than paper and pencil. The training cadre became regional trainers on work paper rescheduling, addition, subtraction, division and multiplying, moving data, merging files and text editing.

Interview with Auditor One.

Three years ago, their documentation was cut-and-paste; they rarely typed their work themselves. They did data analysis, schedules, and findings that were all tied to detailed work. The word processing allows them to be more creative in their writing; it allows them to create a project on the screen. "When you write on a piece of paper it is difficult to see what you've done. The information is there in your mind."

"The machine allows for easier documentation. It allows you to schedule out database, decide what you want to show, and put your feelings on the machine. In the past the product was geared toward acceptability; you wrote to it. But you put off preciseness of conclusions. Now you can make more assumptions and test them."

Interview with Auditor Two.

He has been here for two decades. First he went to the Air Force, then college and here. He describes himself as a traditional rabble rouser. "The Air Force could compare directly. Their boss gave me hell, got mad at me." He has a machine-carpenter background, which makes word processing make sense. "I just think and it comes out. You don't have to scribble around. There is more focus on the job, and less bureaucracy." As in the previous example, someone once said to him: "You aren't paid for typing." His reply: "I'm not typing, I'm writing . . . ." "When you work on a machine the priority #1 stuff gets done, because it's done by you."

The machine allows him to write his report "like he thinks. In rushes." Knowing what the machine can do allows him to "get it down, and move it around later." The tradition is the "first draft is the toughest. Using word processing there is immediate satisfaction. It keeps the train of thought going over and over, rather than breaking concentration; do a part, and wait; do a part, and wait." He reports high concentration on word processing: "When someone comes along and says hello, I jump through the ceiling."

There is some tug of war among those who want the equipment. The technical assistance groups want it for themselves, because they do not have adequate technology for their own work.

The competitive theme around here is with Atlanta. San Francisco imagines itself as having more drive and intensity than elsewhere in AO. Atlanta is good, but "more conservative." There is "friendly competition."

Jones has stories to tell of traditional auditors who were adamant in the resistance to technology. One particularly outspoken, hard-headed guy had a job that required following medical records. They taught him how to use the equipment. Now he doesn't want to do an audit without it.

The question of technical and cultural interdependence is addressed by this case. By most standards, the audit and accounting group of the federal government would be the classic example of an overly proceduralized bureaucracy, but the General Accounting Office in San Francisco matched the activity level and the results of any private sector company in the 200-organization sample. It is a textbook case of being sensitive to the past culture when planning implementation, cutting across organizational lines to get support for an idea, using participative methods to spread the use of the innovation, and using negotiation to protect the integrity of the innovation from trivial interests.

The explanation for this case is as an isolated example of a bureaucracy that works well. The reputation of the AO is as the Cadillac of the federal agencies, and their direct contact with the offices of congressional leaders keeps them sensitive to an immediate customer. Their reputation, combined with the rewards of doing original work, created a vitality that clearly existed before word processing was implemented in the agency. At the same time, their success at implementation allowed them to maintain their position as a quality agency under conditions of technological change. While this is one case in 200, it is an example of an organization acting out of character as a cultural type. It does not show an agency changing culturally as a result of technology, but it does show maintenance of a position when most other government agencies are falling farther behind their private sector competitors as a result of poor implementation.

TYPES OF ACTION BIAS REPORTED IN THIS DATA

The action bias of successful implementers can be seen in the focus and language with which they create organizational contexts. Four kinds of focus live in the language of the innovators portrayed in these cases.

Orientation Toward the Future

Their language is rich in metaphors and concern for the future. They explicitly link technology and the future, portraying technology as the path to action. Technology is a way of beating the competition in the future; technology is a way of moving their organization beyond current constraints.

They constantly experiment with new tools. While they are committed to tools, they never settle on one, but, like Tony, who was moving her word processing center to a "communications" center, they are always growing into the next technology — learning by doing.

They stretch tools beyond known limits. None were using word processing equipment merely as text editors. All were trying to build databases (even spreadsheets, far before Lotus 1–2–3 hit the technology scene). They were learning about the future by inventing it through tricking whatever technology they could get.

They put commitment behind their implicit faith in technology by actions such as adding tools instead of people when the volume of work increased, and by assuring that their support and training resources were adequate to do the job they envisioned.

Finally, they worked largely out of their "cuff link budget" — often hiding whatever expenses they believed would not be understood by others. If financial justification was necessary for more equipment they needed, and they could not produce that justification, they found another way around the problem. Even getting the equipment in the first place often skirted official rules of equipment justification in an action-oriented fashion. The major distinction here is between bureaucracies and markets (Lindbloom, 1977). Bureaucracies require more detailed justification, and more approval by more units, which slows down the speed of equipment acquisition. Markets have simpler equipment acquisition criteria.

Action-oriented people took a "market approach" to their organization. Whenever possible, they got the equipment quickly and let its use determine the fate of the technology. In most cases, the ability to operate in this fashion was protected with high-level support during an incubation period, to allow the word processing department to stabilize.

Focus on Results

They directed their attention to critical applications within their organizations which established grounds to show the tools' usefulness. They were all careful to distinguish "play" from the "real work" done with the tool. In the Audit Office, word processing machines were not "word processing machines," but rather analysis machines used by professional auditors. One of the 60 cases was an international pharmaceutical research firm whose research and development laboratories were in competition with other companies to meet a filing deadline with the Food and Drug Administration for a similar type of product. The ability to transmit 400-page revisions between laboratories in the United States and Great Britain in an hour, via their Wang word processors, allowed them to beat their competition by 6 months.

"Speed to act" was the primary motive of those with an action bias. In the Federal Law Agency, they could not move quickly enough to develop a system which would give them speed in dealing with private law firms. In the Space case, the manager's focus was the ability of the tool to move the thoughts of the writer onto paper and out to be useful. Word processing, as an ally of those with an action bias, moves thoughts to action. On the other hand, in rigid and out-of-touch word processing centers, "word processing" became synonymous with action bog.

Implementers insisted that people use the tools. Unlike the process-oriented locations (Deal & Kennedy, 1982) where equipment often was left to sit unused, in the sites directed by action orientation, people were given support in learning and using word processing, and were required to use it. One manager observed that only two things are really necessary:

"You need Mary Kraft (the support person) and knowing *when* to use the hammer." He was certainly not "all talk" about his commitment to change.

Finally, an action bias, because it uses action to focus, replace, and improve cognition, emphasizes evaluation of results. By concentrating on the outcomes of action, one learns the meaning of action. All the action sites had definite ways, though not always numerical measurements, to evaluate their results.

Appreciation of Ownership

No one can do everything at once. The action-oriented sites were characterized by boundaries within which the action took place. Hence, most of the creative sites we found were in word processing centers where the boundaries of invention and attention were easily recognized. In places where word processing terminals were placed around offices, the technology often remained without a boundary of protection, and, thus, without a clearing in which innovation could be nurtured.

The action-oriented individuals, however, were neither missionaries nor imperialists. "Let others learn by the example of what we do here" was a frequent refrain from action-oriented managers. They moved by *doing* and *showing* rather than about *talking about*.

Emphasis on People

As people who act, the innovative managers of word processing understood that only people act. Thus, unlike their analytic counterparts who concentrated on procedures and abstract concepts, they acted through concentrating on people. For example, they described what they did to win over what we might call the "culture carriers" — the senior secretaries, the senior auditors, the senior engineers. These respected cultural members then carried the efforts forward.

They symbolized a new way of working *constantly* through their own actions. They used the system, in some cases putting their terminals *outside* their offices so that others could see them on the system.

They talked in the language of the listener, understanding that action takes place in listening, not in talking. They were articulate about how they needed to describe their activities to be understood by their bosses, as well as the people within their unit.

CONCLUSION

Technology has the potential to change the basic dimensions of substantive culture laid out by Deal and Kennedy (1982) and Douglas and Wildavsky (1982). It can promote increasing speed of reaction, changing culture by making action easier, more inviting, and more imaginable. The relationship of technology to cultural change, however, was not one of simple technological determinism (Davis & Taylor, 1979). Rather, we found that individuals with an action bias exploited the capability of word processing to enable action. In approximately one third of the cases examined, a single leader's ability accounts for the action bias. Word processing, with its promise of "a new way of working," was a lever for a single person to create change. On the other hand, word processing, with its invitation to "word smith" and create ever longer documents, can enable larger patterns of action congestion.

REFERENCES

Brown, M. H. (1981). *That reminds me of a story: A study of the effects of stories on socialization.* Unpublished doctoral dissertation, The University of Texas at Austin.

Davis, L., & Taylor, J. (1979). *Design of jobs* (2nd ed.). Santa Monica, CA: Goodyear.

Davis, M. (1971). That's interesting: Toward a phenomenology of sociology and a sociology of phenomenology. *Philosophy of Science, 1,* 309–344.

Deal, T., & Kennedy, A. (1982). *Corporate cultures: The rites and rituals of corporate life.* Reading, MA: Addison Wesley.

Douglas, M. (1982). *An institutional ecology of values.* Paper presented at the meeting of the Tocqueville Society, Chicago, IL.

Douglas, M., & Wildavsky, A. (1982). *Risk and culture.* Berkeley, CA: University of California Press.

Goffman, E. (1959). *The presentation of self in everyday life.* New York: Doubleday, Anchor.

Johnson, B., & Rice, R. E. (1987). *Managing organizational innovation: From word processing to office systems.* Columbia University Press.

Johnson, B. McD. (1985). *Innovation in office systems implementation.* (Report No. 8110791). Norman, OK: National Science Foundation.

Latane, B., & Darley, J. M. (1970). *The unresponsive bystander: Why doesn't he help?* New York: Appleton Century Crofts.

Lindbloom, C. E. (1977). *Politics and markets: The world's political and economic systems.* New York: Basic Books.

Malcom, R. (1983, Autumn). Unpublished notes from a Karl Weick lecture on action, the Graduate School of Business, The University of Texas at Austin.

Martin, J., & Powers, M. E. (1983). Truth or corporate propaganda: The value of a good war story. In L. R. Pondy, P. J. Frost, G. Morgan, & T. C. Dandridge (Eds.). *Organizational symbolism.* Greenwich, CT: JAI Press, 93–108.

Mohr, L. (1982). *Explaining organizational behavior.* San Francisco, CA: Jossey-Bass.

Peters, T., & Waterman, R. (1982). *In search of excellence: Lessons from America's best run companies.* New York: Harper and Row.

Posner, L. (1982). Review of *The Myths of Information: Technology and Post Industrial Culture. American Journal of Sociology, 87,* 993–994.

Sowell, T. (1980). *Knowledge and decisions.* New York: Basic Books.

Van de Ven, A. (1984). The Minnesota innovation research program (Discussion paper no. 10, Strategic Management Research Center. Minneapolis, MN).

Webb, E., & Weick, K. (1983). Unobtrusive measures in organizational theory: A reminder. In J. Van Maanen (Ed.), *Qualitative Methodology* (pp. 209–224). Beverly Hills, CA: Sage.

White, M. J. (1982). A review of Sowell's "Knowledge and Decisions." *American Journal of Sociology, 87,* 1003–4.

Chapter 19

Human Communication in the High Tech Office

Sandra E. O'Connell

ABSTRACT

Organizational communication processes are changing dramatically as technological innovation becomes widely adopted. The proliferation of desktop computers, inexpensive 20-megabyte hard disks, sophisticated software, local area networks, as well as increased capacities for sharing data, record storage, and retrieval are responsible for the integrated office. We need to understand the interaction between high tech communication and human communication. In this chapter, the two processes are contrasted using four variables: how meaning is established, accuracy, speed and access, and degree of structure.

High tech communication is accurate, high speed, low context, and highly structured, while humans communicate with the inexactness, richness, subtlety, and complexity which comes from human experience.

Two themes emerge from this examination: changes in information processing and decision making, and changes in relationships. Although abundant information will be available, it is not clear that it will necessarily lead to improved decision making. New decision-making skills will be needed as managers learn to use the technology. The content, format, and opportunities for contact will be altered as channel effects impact relationships in the automated workplace.

The chapter ends with six hypotheses that deal with the role of technology in the organization. Some caution is in order, as we learn to deal with the new dimensions of organizational communication.

The long heralded promises of technology are at last being realized. Powerful processors, miniaturization, telecommunications, integrated software, networks, multi-user systems, and plummeting costs are all part of the technology of the 1980s. The proliferation of desktop computers, inexpensive 20-megabyte hard disks, sophisticated software, local area networks, as well as increased capacities for sharing data, record storage, and retrieval means that the work of the entire organization — executive, managerial, professional, technical, and administrative — can take advantage of the technology.

Automation is no longer simply replacing a routine task or number crunching with computing power. Rather, it represents a significant change in communication technologies. Cherry (1978, p. 31) observed that "societies can develop and advance only as far and fast as they can acquire, use and maintain systems of communication: systems of acquiring, recording, assimilating and disseminating information." These very processes are being drastically altered by the technology. As the changes go on around us, we need to think more clearly about the impact of the technology on organizational communication processes. The purpose of this chapter is to define some of the issues of human communication in the automated workplace, and to identify areas for needed research.

HUMAN COMMUNICATION AND HIGH TECHNOLOGY COMMUNICATION

One way to begin to understand the interaction of humans and the technology is to contrast the principles of human communication with the communication principles for the technology. Four critical variables are selected for discussion: how meaning is established, accuracy, speed and access, and the degree of structure. The list is not exhaustive.

How Meaning is Established

Human communication relies on our ability to select information from a large field, and interpret it in many different ways; randomly, in familiar patterns, or in new combinations not experienced before. Our ability to use context to establish new meaning makes human communication quite variable. Meaning shifts depending on the perception and interpretation of the events in the particular situation. In fact, this ability to recognize differences in apparently similar situations is a critical factor in growth and maturity. Perception, interpretation, and naming of our experience are the basis of meaning. Non-verbal feedback plays a vital role in establishing meaning. The cues from voice, body, and facial expression supply a significant portion of our interpretation of any given communication event. Our ability to share meaning is conditioned by experience — our own and that of the person with whom we wish to communicate. Meaning, then, as we all come to learn, is not wholly predictable.

In sharp contrast, meaning in the operation of technology is highly predictable. Meaning must be precisely defined in order for computers to work at all. The core of meaning lies in the binary code of the off–on switch which is at the center of computing technology. ASCII, the machine language of most computers is the basis for programming languages. ASCII does not allow for variation in meaning, perception, or interpretation. The world of computer coding is quite literal. The binary code 01110011 stands for the character "s" or decimal code 115. It doesn't mean "s" sometimes, and "p" at other times. Computer code can be strung together in ways to generate new meaning, but each bit and byte have the same ASCII meaning.

Whether text or symbols on the screen, electronic communication is one-dimensional, providing limited sources for humans to derive total meaning. "The most significant difference between computer-mediated and face-to-face communication, [according to researchers at Carnegie Mellon] is the lack of nonverbal feedback." (Ruby, 1984, p. 127) One effect of missing non-verbal cues is a lack of communication coordination — the words alone have to convey the entire message.

In summary, meaning for the computer is established through precisely defined code. Humans, with rich experience and nonverbal cues to draw upon, establish meaning through context and interpretation. One can predict with great accuracy how the computer will react in response to a command, while human reaction is much less predictable. Computers are currently restricted to much narrower confines of meaning than are humans.

Accuracy

Much to our irritation and sometimes dismay, human communication seldom results in fully accurate sharing of information. Indeed, as Goldhaber, Dennis, Richetto, and Wiio (1979, p. vii) point out, "unsuccessful communication seems to be the rule and not the exception." Managers who operate on the assumption that communication efficiency is 100%, or anything close to it, are headed for difficulty. Effective managers realize that communication needs reinforcement, use of several media, follow-up, and feedback. The notorious inaccuracy of human communication in organizations is due to a number of complex factors—size, serial transmission effects, role, formal structure, and channels among them. Yet humans often assume that communication should be accurate. The desire to achieve a high degree of reliability in message transfer in organizations is a major issue for communication practitioners. Many of the organization's communication processes and programs are compensation for the inherent lack of accuracy in human communication.

One of the virtues of computer technology is its accuracy and, therefore, predictability of meaning. The ability to respond to the same command in exactly the same way each and every time is the norm in the world of computers. Anyone who searches a database with tens of thousands of records and reaches the right file each and every time, or uses wordprocessing to be freed from multiple proofreading, values the computer's predictability. The copy you have already proofread will appear the same way in succeeding versions. What you tell the computer to do, it will do (given the right programming). We have come to expect perfection and, when we don't get it, we know a human was involved. Our yearned for accuracy in communication has been achieved by the computer.

Inaccuracies in human communication are compensated for by interpretation and feedback. The secretary who asks if you meant to exclude your boss from the memo distribution, the analyst who corrects the formula for the budget before running the numbers, the researcher who pursues an unfamiliar citation, each is interpreting from past experience. We rely on these daily interpretations and corrections to function. The computer will not make these adjustments unless a program has instructed it to do so. Although much of the business software is sophisticated enough to ask questions such as "Do you really want to erase this file?" not all of our errors and inaccuracies as humans will be caught by the computer. Nor can it add the richness which comes from our experience.

Speed and Access

The human brain is capable of complex information processing, taking in information from many sources. The message "Come into my office" is comprised of many "inputs," such as the person's posture, dress, facial expression, rate of speech, inflection, and other cues. Our ability to interpret events as they occur in both similar and dissimilar circumstances relies on quite complex neuron programming in the brain and by and large speedy transmission of messages. Indeed, the brain is "unsurpassed at making shrewd guesses and at grasping the total meaning presented to it" (Campbell, 1982, p. 190).

Yet the brain is no match for the computer at swift computation. The supercomputer of 1985, the Cray-1, does 1.2 billion mathematical calculations per second—making it 4,000 times faster than the IBM PC. This reduces the PC to a mere 300,000 calculations per second ("News Trends," 1985). Microcomputer chips capable of even faster processing are currently on the market. The speed of microcomputers, and of today's electronic data transmission, are startling to anyone not used to working in an electronic environment. It is easy to be awed when you see hundreds of columns of numbers in a spreadsheet change faster than your eye can follow on the screen, or to receive data "downloaded" from a mainframe computer half way around the world. Perhaps the most impressive dimension of the technology is the computer's ability to search and find. The mere storage of data is not necessarily an advantage. It is the speedy finding of precisely the right name or zip code in a file of thousands is that makes the computer a highly practical tool. Our own brains are wonderful for storage, but quite a muddle when it comes to locating needed information.

An increased tempo for work is apparent in nearly every organization. The widespread expectation of immediate turn-around has been brought about in large part by the personal computer and telecommunications. We have come to think it is normal to redo what was 2 weeks' worth of work in a half an hour. Law briefs are edited and reprinted, the budget is recalculated with different assumptions, graphs are redrawn, the project plan with several hundred tasks is completely rescheduled, the new plans are transmitted to an office across the country. The communications technologies have altered the distribution of information while increasing the speed of communication. Humans too are expected to provide fast turnaround on everything from memos to major projects.

Degree of Structure

The degree of structure in human communication is highly variable. Some people follow a strict sequence in presenting their information and ideas. Others seem to be speaking in random order. Some of us experience the world quite differently, seeing wholes rather than subsets or even a divergent pattern of organization. What is logical to one is capracious to another. However one wishes to label these differences—right-brain vs. left brain, creative vs. technical, intuitive vs. analytical, visual vs. linear—the inescapable fact is that homo sapiens organizes data in an intriguing variety of ways. Divergent thinking is responsible for much of our creativity. Whether due to differences in personality, neuron structure in the brain, or experience, humans represent a range of behavior in how they organize information and experience.

Computers, on the other hand, are relentlessly linear and structured. In fact, they simply will not work at all unless programmed with strict sequencing. The linear nature of programming demands discipline and structure. Many managers are ineffective in automation efforts because they don't realize the degree of structure required for a computer to be useful. When the tasks and work flow are not well organized, automation brings not relief, but chaos. New computer users are often deeply frustrated to find that simply misplacing a space in a command will result in either an error or, more likely, nothing at all. A computer will do exactly what you tell it to—no more, no less. And if it doesn't understand the command, it will do nothing at all or give you an error message. The computer imposes strict logic and structure on those who want access to its power. For some, the trade-off will be difficult.

Summary

The basic principles of the communication process are quite different for humans and computers. Although there are many similarities, there are significant differences between how the brain functions and how the computer functions (Campbell, 1982). As integrated information processing becomes widespread, we face the interaction of human and techno-logical communication processes. Our expectations of technological communication may gradually transfer to our expectations of human communication. That is, after experiencing a day of accurate, high speed, low context, highly structured information, we may begin to expect the same of fellow workers. Or, perhaps, some will become so desper-ate for human experience that relationships will take on new value and meaning.

COMMUNICATION ISSUES IN THE WORKPLACE

Scenario One: A public utility brings in microcomputers for financial analysts who are able to provide quick, detailed data in response to "what-if" questions. The controller be-gins to go directly to the analysts for speedy turn-around of budget and market projections. Upset by the changes, and cut out of the normal communication channels, the division manager grows increasingly withdrawn and erratic as his primary responsibility of assimilating and distributing information is performed by the computer.

Scenario Two: A bank installs a calendar function as part of its network. This allows secretaries to check calendars electronically when scheduling meetings, thus eliminating the time consuming process of playing "telephone tag" for several days. The system is easy to use and highly efficient. The electronic network eliminates direct phone contact among ex-ecutive secretaries; they share less information spontaneously, and have fewer opportuni-ties to develop their own informal network.

Scenario Three: An engineering firm which has been using teleconferencing success-fully for several years expands the operation to include meetings where conflicts on a major project have to be resolved. Three of the West Coast staff, and two of the East coast staff, are new to the project. The two hour meeting goes without a technical hitch, with docu-ments exchanged and full screen video. The misunderstandings and lack of commitment to deadlines only begin to surface several months into the project.

In each of these situations, too much attention was paid to the technology and not enough to its effect on the staff and their communication patterns. As a result, the organi-zations aren't getting a good return on their investment or the hoped-for gains from auto-mation. Instead, there are new and difficult problems to solve: The staff is frustrated and demoralized, the informal network is weakened reducing the amount of useful business in-formation, misunderstandings occur which interfere with work results, and expectations aren't met. Two themes emerge which should influence the investigation of communication in organizations: changes in information processing and decision making, and changes in relationships.

CHANGES IN INFORMATION PROCESSING AND DECISION MAKING

Nearly 20 years ago, Drucker (1970, p. 3) commented, "The one thing we do know is that the abundance of information changes the communication problem and makes it both more urgent and less tractable." Today's technology provides an "abundance of informa-tion" to all levels of employees. By 1990, 65% of all professional, managerial, technical, and administrative workers will use personal computers. "The advent of desk-top comput-ers and other information tools, linked together by advanced telecommunications networks that provide access to widely diverse sources of data, heralds a huge surge in productivity"

(*Business Week,* 1983, p. 68). It may also herald an increase in problems of information overload. The technology provides managers with more data than they can use in a given situation. Human information processing skills may need to be improved if we are to achieve the predicted gains in productivity.

Microcomputers are alerting the structure of organizations as data bases, electronic mail, and networks provide fast, direct access to information. No longer does the controller need to go through two layers of management for an update on cash flow. Instead, the information is in the system, available instantly, and can be reformatted to answer different questions. As information is easier to assemble and manipulate, it is likely that the number of middle managers and corporate staff will be reduced. Computers are faster, less expensive, and more accurate than managers doing the same work. As early as 1983, *Business Week* discussed "The Shrinking of Middle Management," citing example after example of cutbacks in corporate staff and middle management related to automation. "Companies will be leaner, more fluid, with fewer levels of management and more direct lines of communication between the top and bottom" (p. 54). The new patterns of information flow tend to alter formal communication channels as well as formal relationships within the organization.

Early research suggests that electronic communication increases the amount of contact individuals have with each other, and reduces the time needed for decision making (Uhlig, 1977, p. 122). Electronic communication provides the words, not the subtle overlay of meaning which comes from non-verbal language. The loss of nuances of speech can result in "monumental misunderstandings." (Uhlig, p. 123) Yet, the reduction of status cues from the communication process tends to encourage broader participation in discussions (Ruby, 1984, p. 129). A great deal more research needs to be done to determine how these changes in communication will impact organizational decision making.

With middle management ranks thinned due to an automation, some business decisions will be made at lower levels in the corporate structure. The danger, of course, is that those in lower-level jobs may not have the experience or maturity to exercise good business judgment, although they will have access to a great deal of information. The computer is especially helpful on decisions that are routine and repetitive, where most of the variables are known. Decisions which are unique and unstructured are more difficult for the computer to support (Christie, 1985, p. 171). As expert systems are developed, more routine and repetitive decisions will be identified and supported by software. Nevertheless, many critical decisions will remain in the category of unique and unstructured.

The challenge is to manage the "abundance of information" and to build effective decision-making processes which use the computer. According to a study by Booz, Allen, and Hamilton, enhanced decision making is a key benefit that managers seek from new systems (Christie, 1985, p. 288). Lower level or inexperienced employees may not know enough corporate context to be able to interpret data. Managers need to know how to use the personal computer as a decision-making tool that helps to store, organize, maintain, and analyze information (Fersko-Weiss, 1986).

Studies of the effects of automation in industrial operations documented the skill shift from motor coordination and craft skills to mental, perceptual, and decision-making skills (Davis & Taylor, 1975). As we now move into the automation of professional and managerial work, another skill shift may be required. These skills may include selecting the appropriate computer tools, assimilation of information, selection of essentials, interpretation of organizational context, drawing inferences, organization of conclusions, and weighing of multiple alternatives.

Ironically, it is possible that the quality of decision making could be reduced. The sheer volume of data, along with endless ways of arranging it, is tempting for decision makers. If we rely only on digitalized data, the net result could be a loss of insight and wisdom. The human ability to grasp idea holistically, to derive meaning from context, to select from a vast information field, to draw new inferences, should not be overwhelmed by the computer's ability to spew out numbers. The popularity of graphics software lies in its capacity to present volumes of data in coherent and meaningful form. The search for meaning in human endeavors need not be obscured by abundant data.

CHANGING RELATIONSHIPS

Technology is not only changing the way organizations conduct business, it is altering relationships and communication among employees. These changes are primarily the result of "channel effects." As defined by Godwin Chu (1978), channel effects are the changed patterns of communication made possible by the mere availability of new communication technology.

For example, a manager communicates with his or her CEO infrequently, using formal memos in response to requests made through his or her manager. With electronic mail, the CEO fires off short queries to anyone, bypassing organizational channels. The norm for this new media is to respond informally, briefly, speedily. The frequency and format of the interaction has changed as a consequence of the technology. The very existence of electronic mail has made possible a new pattern of communication.

In the normal flow of business, most people exchange much social or ritualized information, discussing sporting events and family along with conversations about work. Personal contact helps to establish the context needed for human communication. This small talk is a background ingredient in the development of shared experience — a key factor in establishing common understanding and perceptions. As technology reduces the number of face-to-face contacts and abbreviates messages, new means may be needed to develop trust. Often it is the phone call, the casual encounter over a cup of coffee, or the chat after a meeting that produces an extra piece of information or insight that would not be picked up in a highly-structured electronic work environment — where notes are left in a coworker's computer files.

Not surprisingly, there is a high level of personal, informal communication at excellent companies (Peters & Waterman, 1982). The ICA audits (Goldhaber & Rogers, 1979) and my own studies corroborate the importance of informal, face-to-face communications for getting the job done. So far, the technology does not lend itself to this vital kind of human interaction. In addition to a decrease in face-to-face, work-related communications, office automation may reduce social interaction even further by changing the social structure. Large numbers of people facing a machine most of the day may become the norm in many companies.

In *The Third Wave*, Alvin Toffler (1980) predicts a widescale move to telecommuting. In this new form of work, people have offices in their homes that are linked electronically to their employers through terminals or computers. Toffler's prediction, however, overlooks the nature of humans as social beings. "No matter how attractive the home environment, perhaps humans will periodically want to meet up in large social groups to fulfill some instinctive gregarious need" (Evans, 1979, p. 272). Although some 30,000 people now telecommute (*Washington Post,* July 7, 1985, pp. B1–2), most of us would be unhappy if we worked at home full time. What the majority would like is the discretion to choose to work at home, as the task and personal circumstances dictate.

With current views of control and productivity, managers hardly seem ready to cope with this option. In dealing with employees who telecommute, managers must become more effective communicators. Because telecommuting employees are not in the office every day, managers must learn to effectively convey information and feedback without being face-to-face with their workers. Managers also must define the telecommuting employee's expected work results and goals, and then trust them to accomplish the job in a timely manner. The employee who telecommutes needs to realize that he or she is not in the office for the spontaneous face-to-face interaction which helps to build relationships. Those relationships, in turn, are what help to get the work done. Humans are social animals who need others for identity, reinforcement, stimulation, and role models. Interaction at the office helps fulfill this need.

Summary

The range of channel effects, and their impact on relationships, is evolving as the technology is installed and integrated into the processes of organizational communication. We cannot generalize about the technology, because each form produces its own effects. For example, working on a computer for most of the day tends to reduce interaction, while electronic mail may increase opportunity for a different form of interaction. Teleconferencing provides more opportunities for groups to meet and for message dissemination, while not being appropriate for conflict negotiation (O'Connell, 1982). Most of us will experience these effects long before they are understood. Channel effects are not easy to predict—they are the result of the interaction between technology and humans. Yet, historically, social structure and relationships have been altered by technology.

SOME HYPOTHESES

Although the fully automated office is still not widespread, many of the technologies have been in use for several years. The speed with which integrated information resource management is progressing means that we have a great deal to learn in a very short amount of time. Some of the ways in which organizational communication might change are presented as hypotheses. Each could serve as the basis for needed research.

1. Opportunities for face-to-face contact will be diminished, information from non verbal cues will be reduced. Consequently opportunities for random, spontaneous information sharing will be reduced. Managers will need to structure work and relationships to provide more opportunities for face-to-face contact to occur. Meaning will be derived increasingly from text and symbols.
2. More informal messages and "short-circuiting" of the hierarchy will occur as new formats are accepted due to the remote nature of an electronic network. Organization structure and formal information flow will be redefined.
3. Channel effects will mean that messages of affect and values will decrease. Digitized data, with less context and interpretation, will be the norm. Consequently, decision making may be impaired rather than enhanced. Ambiguity in interpreting information will increase, and the quality of decisions could decrease with the lack of organizational values and context. Organizations will need to work harder at com-

municating their values and corporate history. Managers will have to seek new ways of communicating the affective component of messages. New and improved decision-making skills will be needed.

4. Trust will play a changed role in communication. Trust develops with shared experience, values, give and take, the result of human communication. Satellites, electronic mail, and networks could reduce the dimensions of trust to which we are accustomed. New ones may spring up in their place.

5. The computer imposes a discipline of linear thinking. Data is processed at speeds which increase with each new version of the chip. Consequently, people may develop less patience and tolerance for individual styles of communicating. Organizations may find themselves less tolerant of people who do not think or perceive in a strict linear mode. They will need to find ways to encourage and protect nonlinear thinking and communicating.

6. Expectations of work performance may be machine driven. As we become accustomed to the speed and accuracy of the computer, we may expect employees to have the same qualities and produce in a similar manner. Employees in some organizations will perceive this as dehumanizing and cohersive. Unions will take up the human environment as an issues. New ways of defining and using performance standards will be needed.

SUMMARY

These hypotheses, and many others, need to be tested as we hurtle towards the integrated automated office environment. Research is needed to assist decision makers in making the automated workplace both productive and satisfying to human beings. If the majority of office workers, 10 years from now, are little more than data entry clerks who work by rote, then we will have gained little from technology. Decisions about the implementation of the technology have most often been made by the engineers and systems technicians. When managers are intimidated by information processing technology, the system design and installation are relegated to the specialists (Pava, 1983). Workplace decisions involve, not just the hardware/software and computer communications, but the social/psychological assumptions about people in the organization. The decisions that executives and managers make will influence how the majority of us will function at work. There are choices to be made; we do not have to be in the grip of technological determinism in which the technology relentlessly dictates our behavior.

REFERENCES

Campbell, J. (1982). *Grammatical man: Information, entropy, language, and life.* New York: Simon and Schuster.

Cherry, C. (1978). *World communications: Threat or promise? A socio technical approach.* Chichester/New York: John Wiley and Sons Ltd.

Christie, B. (Ed.). (1985). *Human factors of information technology in the office.* Chichester: John Wiley and Sons.

Chu, G. C. (1978, September). Communication technology and social organization: A systemic perspective of effects. In G. C. Chu, S. A. Rabim, & D. L. Kincaid (Eds.), *Communication Monographs,* #4.

Davis, L. E., & Taylor, J. C. (1975). Technology effects on job, work, and organizational structure: a contingency view. In L. Davis & A. Cherns (and Associates), *The Quality of Working Life* (Vol. 1). New York: The Free Press.

Drucker, P. (1970). *Technology, management, and society.* New York: Harper & Row.

Evans, C. (1979). *The micromillenium.* New York: Washington Square Press.

Fersko-Weiss, H. (1986). Managing Your Employees to Level 3. *Personal Computing,* June, pp. 95–101.

Goldhaber, G. M., Dennis, H. S., Richetto, G. M., & Wiio, O. (1979). *Information strategies: new pathways to corporate power.* Englewood Cliffs, NJ: Prentice-Hall.

Goldhaber, G. M., & Rogers, D. P. (1979). *Auditing organizational communication systems: The ICA communication audit.* Dubuque, IA: Kendall/Hunt Publishing.

How Computers Remake the Manager's Job. (1983). *Business Week,* April 15, pp. 68–70.

News Trends. (1985). *Fortune,* July 8, p. 9.

O'Connell, S. (1982). New survey supports technology. *Communication World,* August, pp. 1 & 3. International Association of Business Communicators.

Pava, C. (1983). *Managing new office technology.* New York: The Free Press.

Peters, T. J., & Waterman, R. H. (1982). *In search of excellence: Lessons from America's best run companies.* New York: Harper & Row.

Ruby, D. (1984). Terminal Behavior. *PC Week,* November 13, pp. 127–129.

The Shrinking of Middle Management. (1983). *Business Week*, April 25, pp. 54–61.

Toffler, A. (1980). *The third wave.* New York: William Morrow.

Uhlig, R. P. (1977). Human factors in computer message systems. *Datamation,* May, pp. 120–126.

AUTHOR INDEX

SUBJECT INDEX